LEIBNIZ: BODY, SUBSTAr

MW00830204

Daniel Garber presents an illuminating study of Leibniz's conception of the physical world. Leibniz's commentators usually begin with monads, mind-like simple substances, the ultimate building-blocks of the *Monadology*. But Leibniz's apparently idealist metaphysics is very puzzling: how can any sensible person think that the world is made up of tiny minds? In this book, Garber tries to make Leibniz's thought intelligible by focusing instead on his notion of body. Beginning with Leibniz's earliest writings, he shows how Leibniz starts as a Hobbesian with a robust sense of the physical world, and how, step by step, he advances to the monadological metaphysics of his later years. Much of the book's focus is on Leibniz's middle years, where the fundamental constituents of the world are corporeal substances, unities of matter and form understood on the model of animals. For Garber monads only enter fairly late in Leibniz's career, and when they enter, he argues, they do not displace bodies but complement them. In the end, though, Garber argues that Leibniz never works out the relation between the world of monads and the world of bodies to his own satisfaction: at the time of his death, his philosophy is still a work in progress.

Daniel Garber is Stewart Professor of Philosophy at Princeton University.

LEIBNIZ: BODY, SUBSTANCE, MONAD

Daniel Garber

OXFORD
UNIVERSITY PRESS

OXFORD
UNIVERSITY PRESS

Great Clarendon Street, Oxford OX2 6DP

Oxford University Press is a department of the University of Oxford.
It furthers the University's objective of excellence in research, scholarship,
and education by publishing worldwide in

Oxford New York

Auckland Cape Town Dar es Salaam Hong Kong Karachi
Kuala Lumpur Madrid Melbourne Mexico City Nairobi
New Delhi Shanghai Taipei Toronto

With offices in

Argentina Austria Brazil Chile Czech Republic France Greece
Guatemala Hungary Italy Japan Poland Portugal Singapore
South Korea Switzerland Thailand Turkey Ukraine Vietnam

Oxford is a registered trade mark of Oxford University Press
in the UK and in certain other countries

Published in the United States
by Oxford University Press Inc., New York

British Library Cataloguing in Publication Data

Data available

Library of Congress Cataloging in Publication Data

Data available

Typeset by Laserwords Private Limited, Chennai, India
Printed in Great Britain
on acid-free paper by
MPG Biddles Ltd., King's Lynn, Norfolk

ISBN 978-0-19-956664-8 (Hbk.)
ISBN 978-0-19-969309-2 (Pbk.)

10 9 8 7 6 5 4 3 2 1

Preface

Aristotle tells us that philosophy begins in wonder. And so does the history of philosophy, for me at least. When I began reading Leibniz, I wondered how someone as smart as he was supposed to be could believe in something so strange as monads. I tried to find and follow the arguments, but I found them incomplete and not altogether satisfactory. And so I turned to history—the history of Leibniz's development and the larger intellectual context of his thought.

This book started some years ago. In fact, it might be said to have started as early as the beginning of the 1980s when I published my first papers on Leibniz, in particular the essay "Leibniz and the Foundations of Physics: the Middle Years," my youthful folly.[1] In that essay, I argued that in what I called the middle years, from the early 1680s to 1700 or so, Leibniz adopted a metaphysics grounded not in monads but in corporeal substance. It was originally given at a conference on Leibniz at the University of Toronto in the fall of 1982. Ted McGuire was in the audience. (Please, stop me—or skip over the passage—if you have heard this one before: many have.) After my talk, he raised his hand to ask the first question. He began: "This is so wrong I don't know where to begin." My heart sank, my knees began to buckle. I was afraid that I had stuck my young neck out too far. But after he began to talk, I regained my composure and realized that I could answer his objections, to my satisfaction if not to his. The story is true, really. Sent into the world, my idea took root and gained some defenders, even though many remained skeptical. At best. But to my great pleasure, many discussed it and took it seriously.

---

[1] Garber (1985). While working out the main thesis of this essay, I found that a view very similar to the one that I was developing had been advanced some years earlier by C. D. Broad, in a series of lectures at Cambridge given in the late 1940s and published in 1975. See Broad (1975), 87–90. Much more recently, while working on this book I found a brief exposition of something very much like what I had originally had in mind in a paper published in the proceedings of the 1972 Leibniz Congress; see Scarrow (1973). So much for originality, even in the study of the history of philosophy. While in my essay and in this book I develop the view in much more detail than Broad or Scarrow did, using texts to which they did not have access at the time, I am very impressed by their insight into Leibniz and by their courage to go against the grain of standard interpretations of the day.

Meanwhile the evidence slowly gathered as the volumes of the Vorausedition to series 6 of the Akademie Edition came out, one by one every year. The texts were published together in A6.4 in 1999, arranged by topic in chronological order, philosophical writings from 1677 to 1690. I became more and more convinced that I had been on to something, and that the monadology was simply the wrong framework in which to understand Leibniz's philosophy in this period, though I came eventually to wince at the crudeness of some of my earlier formulations of the thesis and claims. I tried to update my view several times, with mixed success. I finally came to the decision that I should try to pull my views together in the form of a monograph. I thought that it was a pretty straightforward project that I should be able to get off my desk in a year or so. I was wrong.

The project began in earnest with an NEH Summer Seminar on Leibniz and His Contemporaries that I did with Roger Ariew at Virginia Tech in the summer of 2003. There I had an excellent audience, a group of very serious Leibniz scholars, a number of whom were not altogether sympathetic to my point of view. It was a wonderful challenge. They were the best audience I could have had at that moment, knowledgeable, skeptical, and deeply interested in Leibniz's thought. As I was struggling to organize my thoughts and outline a series of chapters that would be coherent and capture my vision, I was invited to give the Isaiah Berlin Lectures at the University of Oxford in Michaelmas Term 2004. This forced me to put together six lectures in fairly quick order. I am deeply grateful to the audience for these lectures who kindly indulged my obsession with the minutiae of Leibniz's thought over the course of a number of long weeks. In a book, you can skip over the dull and obsessive passages; in a lecture, you can only grin and bear it, or leave. But it was one of the happiest times of my professional life. The lectures were given on Tuesday afternoons. I had planned out what I wanted to do in outline before I came to Oxford, but I left the actual drafting of the lectures to be done after I arrived. The week before each lecture, days and evenings were taken up with reading and thinking and sketching things out, culminating in the lecture itself. Then, the morning after, the lecture was polished and posted to the web, and I would start immediately on the next. All this was punctuated with lunches and dinners at Corpus Christi College, and with friends and colleagues at Oxford. (I would especially like to thank the President of Corpus Christi College, Sir Tim Lancester, for his gracious hospitality.)

But I don't think that I have worked so intensely on a single project for years. These lectures provided the skeleton for this book; I have spent these last few years filling them out.

What started as a simple update of Garber (1985) has turned out to be a massive rethinking of the thesis there. That rethinking started somewhat before the summer seminar and the Oxford lectures, in a long series of articles that has continued up until now. Unfortunately, the articles are not altogether consistent with one another; the desire to get feedback on my thinking, together with the pressure to publish coming from various directions, has caused me to leave a succession of half-baked ideas in the wake of this book.[2] I have borrowed liberally from my earlier writings in constructing this book. By this stage, however, it is difficult to say what of those earlier texts remains. In most cases, I have revised them quite significantly in the course of the composition of the book so that they are barely recognizable. In other cases, I suspect that there may be whole undigested paragraphs from other writings that have found their way into these chapters. In any case, I hope that I have attained a kind of closure on these issues and that I won't be bothering people with them any more.

Many, many people have helped me formulate and refine the ideas in this book. I am deeply grateful for the sometimes heated discussions I have had with colleagues in the field about the issues in this book. Robert Adams and Robert Sleigh have been especially important to me, both through their work and through more personal interchanges. We will continue to disagree, I'm sure, but in the most productive ways. Michel Fichant has been important to me as well. Distance has prevented frequent contact, but his work stands as a model for my own, always clear, deep, historically sophisticated and philosophically astute. Roger Ariew has been my closest philosophical colleague for almost thirty years now. He and I have collaborated on much, including the NEH Summer Seminar that started this book rolling. I continue to depend on him for advice. I first met Don Rutherford and Christia Mercer when they were students. I value both as senior colleagues from whose work I have learned a lot, especially when it disagrees with my own. I have also learned a great deal from two of my own students who wrote dissertations on Leibniz with me, Brandon Look

---

[2] Paul Lodge has chronicled some of these vacillations and hesitations in Lodge (2005a). While I'm very flattered that he thought it interesting enough to try to sort things out, I am somewhat embarrassed that my view has wobbled so much that it was necessary to do so.

and, more recently, Lea Schweitz, both of whom commented on various aspects of the book while it was in progress. Brandon and Don Rutherford also helped me out enormously by sharing their translation and edition of the Leibniz/Des Bosses correspondence with me before it was published. Paul Lodge shared his soon-to-be-published edition and translation of the de Volder letters, which was also crucial to the project. I also owe a great debt to Paul for conversation over the years and during the time I was giving the Isaiah Berlin Lectures in Oxford, and especially for his detailed comments on an earlier draft of the ms. as the reader for Oxford University Press. He pressed me to make some changes that I initially resisted, but that I now see as essential. I would also like to thank an anonymous second reader for the Press, whose somewhat briefer comments were also very helpful. Others who read the whole ms. were Graeme Hunter and Ursula Goldenbaum, whom I thank for their generous comments. Ursula was in Princeton as a member of the Institute for Advanced Study during this last year, while I was doing final revisions. Her constant conversation and advice was very important to making the book as good as I could make it. Though I didn't see them as much, Catherine Wilson, Ric Arthur, and Sam Levey were also generous with their work and their conversation over the years. I have learned from them all. Maria Rosa Antognazza shared with me the proofs of her wonderful new biography of Leibniz and made it possible for me to take it into account in my own book. Mogens Laerke also shared with me the proofs of his new book on Leibniz and Spinoza, as well as helping me out in a number of ways on the subtle points of the relation between the two. Philip Beeley helped me greatly with points relating to Leibniz's early years. He was especially helpful at getting scans and copies of Leibniz manuscripts when I needed to check something, as well as editions in progress at Münster of texts about which I was curious. Various audiences saw pieces of the ms. while it was in progress. The penultimate version of the ms. was the text for a seminar I gave at Princeton in fall 2007. I would like to thank the whole seminar, but especially Des Hogan, Ohad Nachtomy, and Christian Leduc for their extensive comments. I also gave chapters at Yale, Harvard, the Montreal Interuniversity Workshop in the History of Philosophy, Marta Fattori's seminar at the University of Rome "La Sapienza," Giulia Belgioioso's working group at the University of Lecce, and Massimo Mugnai's group at the Scuola Normale in Pisa. The discussion was fantastic at all of these venues, but I would like especially to thank Jeff McDonough, Katherine Dunlap, Michael Della Rocca, Larry Jorgensen, Justin Smith, François Duchesneau, Massimo Mugnai, Vincenzo De Risi, and Stephano DiBella. There have been many, many more to whom I owe a great deal, and my sincerest apologies to any whom I have omitted by mistake.

And finally, I would like to dedicate this book to my wife Susan Paul and to our children, Elisabeth and Aaron Garber-Paul, who have consistently corrected any misapprehensions I may have had about being a dominant monad.

Daniel Garber
Princeton, New Jersey

Contents

Preface   v

Abbreviations and Conventions   xii

Introduction   xv

1. First Thoughts   1

2. Reforming Mechanism: Unity   55

3. Reforming Mechanism: Body and Force, Matter and Form (I)   99

4. Reforming Mechanism: Body and Force, Matter and Form (II)   127

5. Complete Individual Concepts, Non-Communication, and Causal Connection   181

6. Divine Wisdom and Final Causes   225

7. Leibnizian Phenomenalisms   267

8. Enchanting the World: "After Many Corrections and Forward Steps in my Thinking..."   303

9. Monads, Bodies, and Corporeal Substances: the Endgame   351

Epilogue   389

Bibliography   393

Index   413

Abbreviations and Conventions

The following abbreviations are used in the notes:

A   Leibniz, Gottfried Wilhelm (1923–). *Sämtliche Schriften und Briefe.* Deutsche Akademie der Wissenschaften zu Berlin (eds.) (Berlin: Akademie-Verlag). References include series, volume, and page. So 'A6.4.1394' is series 6, volume 4, p. 1394. Note that 'A2.1².123' refers to p. 123 of the second edition of series 2, volume 1.

[handwritten: Academy Editions]

AG   Leibniz, Gottfried Wilhelm (1989). *Philosophical Essays.* Roger Ariew and Daniel Garber (eds. and trans.) (Indianapolis: Hackett).

AT   Descartes, René (1996). *Oeuvres de Descartes*, Charles Adam and Paul Tannery (eds.). 11 vols. (Paris: J. Vrin). References include volume and page. So 'AT VII 80' is volume 7, p. 80.

CP   Leibniz, Gottfried Wilhelm (2005). *Confessio philosophi: Papers Concerning the Problem of Evil, 1671–1678*, R. C. Sleigh, Brandon Look, and James H. Stam (eds. and trans.) (New Haven: Yale University Press).

E   Spinoza, *Ethica*, in Spinoza (1925), vol. 2. The individual sections of the *Ethica* are abbreviated in the standard way, where the numeral following 'E' designates the part of the *Ethics*, 'p' designates 'proposition,' 's' designates a scholium, 'app' designates an appendix, etc. So 'E1p33s1' refers to *Ethica*, part 1, proposition 33, scholium 1.

G   Leibniz, Gottfried Wilhelm (1875–90). *Die philosophischen Schriften*, C. I. Gerhardt (ed.) 7 vols. (Berlin: Weidmann). References include volume and page. So 'G VII 80' is volume 7, p. 80.

GM   Leibniz, Gottfried Wilhelm (1849–63). *Leibnizens mathematische Schriften*, C. I. Gerhardt (ed.). 7 vols. (Berlin: A. Asher). References include volume and page. So 'GM VII 80' is volume 7, p. 80.

HPN   Leibniz, Gottfried Wilhelm, *Hypothesis physica nova*, A6.2.219–57.

[handwritten: The Loemker] L   Leibniz, Gottfried Wilhelm (1976). *Philosophical Papers and Letters*, Leroy E. Loemker (ed. and trans.) 2nd edn. (Dordrecht: Reidel).

LDB   Leibniz, Gottfried Wilhelm, and Bartholomeus Des Bosses (2007).
            The Leibniz–Des Bosses Correspondence, Brandon Look and Donald
            Rutherford (eds. and trans.) (New Haven: Yale University Press).

LH   This refers to Leibniz's manuscripts, as catalogued in Bodemann
            (1895). The first digit after 'LH' always refers to the chapter
            divisions as set out in the 'Inhalt' of Bodemann's catalogue.
            The other digits refer to successive divisions in Bodemann's
            organization of the manuscripts. The last digit always refers to a
            folio, followed by 'r' (recto) or 'v' (verso) when appropriate.

Nouv. Ess.   Leibniz, Gottfried Wilhelm, *Nouveaux essais sur l'entendement*, in
            A6.6.

RA   Leibniz, Gottfried Wilhelm (2001). *The Labyrinth of the Con-
            tinuum: Writings on the Continuum Problem, 1672–1686*, Richard
            Arthur (ed. and trans.) (New Haven: Yale University Press).

SR   Leibniz, Gottfried Wilhelm (1992). *De summa rerum: Metaphysical
            Papers, 1675–1676*, G. H. R. Parkinson (ed. and trans.) (New
            Haven: Yale University Press).

TMA   Leibniz, Gottfried Wilhelm, *Theoria motus abstracti*, A6.2.258–76.

WF   Leibniz, Gottfried Wilhelm (1997). *Leibniz's 'New system' and
            Associated Contemporary Texts*, R. S. Woolhouse and Richard
            Francks (eds. and trans.) (Oxford: Oxford University Press).

In referring to Leibniz's texts, the original-language citation is given first, followed by the English translation in parentheses, when available.

The titles of Leibniz's works are given in the original language of the text cited. Books are given in italics, and shorter pieces (essays, notes, etc.) are given in roman. Leibniz's own titles are given in double quotes, and editors' titles in single quotes. Thus, "Specimen dynamicum" (Leibniz's title) but 'Discours de métaphysique' (an editor's title).

The metaphysical theory of Leibniz's later years that centers on the view that monads are the ultimate elements of things is referred to as the 'monadology' or 'monadological metaphysics,' but the essay from 1714 that presents a canonical statement of that view is referred to as the 'Monadologie.'

The *De summa rerum* refers to the collection of papers Leibniz wrote in Paris just before leaving, while "De summa rerum" refers to the individual piece to which Leibniz gave that title.

Introduction

In his Éloge in memory of Leibniz, Bernard Le Bouvier de Fontenelle, the "Secretaire Perpetuel" of the Académie Royale des Sciences in Paris, presented a vivid picture of his subject. Fontenelle emphasized the vast range of Leibniz's intellectual interests. He remarks:

In a way like the ancients who had the skill to drive up to eight horses harnessed abreast, he drove all of the sciences abreast.[1]

This, in turn, shapes Fontenelle's Éloge:

Thus, we are obligated to divide him up here, and, to speak philosophically, to decompose him. While antiquity made one Hercules out of many, we make many savants out of one M. Leibniz.[2]

In the Éloge that follows, Fontenelle goes through the long list of the different domains in which Leibniz worked and in which he excelled. After extensively praising Leibniz's poetry, Latin, French, and even German, Fontenelle discusses his work as a historian, a physicist, a mathematician, a metaphysician, and a theologian, among other things.

When beginning to write (or read) a book on Leibniz it is important to keep these things in mind. In this book, we shall concentrate on one very small part of Leibniz's thought, the part that deals with body and substance, force and individuality, and related domains as they are necessary to make out the main themes of interest to me. I want to give a close account of Leibniz's developing thought on the make-up of the physical world and its metaphysical grounding. This is an important theme, but we also must remember that it is only one theme among many in Leibniz's philosophical thought. This book is not intended as a general introduction to Leibniz's philosophy or even an advanced handbook on his thought; I shall not be giving much attention to Leibniz's views on necessity and contingency, possible worlds, logic, relations and language, freedom and theodicy, not to mention the vast domains outside of what we now generally consider

Contra idealist interp.

[1] Fontenelle (1740), 425.
[2] Ibid., 425–6.

philosophy. I do not want to mistake my rather narrow focus on this aspect of Leibniz's thought for the whole thinker.

But, at the same time, we are in a position to investigate my chosen theme in far greater depth than Fontenelle and almost any of his contemporaries. When Leibniz died, little was known about the range of his philosophical thought. A Leibniz was constructed from the available materials, a Leibniz that has proved to be very durable and difficult to go beyond. But in the last few decades, the Akademie edition first started at the end of the nineteenth century has made available an enormous trove of previously unpublished materials. Supplemented by recent volumes of the *Yale Leibniz*, we now have materials that enable us to get at the real flesh-and-blood Leibniz. I want to help set aside the doctrinaire philosopher who had a few hobby-horses—monads, Principle of Sufficient Reason, continuity, contingency, logic—and who rode them mercilessly, and replace him with a deep, subtle, and wide-ranging intellect, constantly thinking and rethinking his position, constantly engaged, who develops and grows, even if, in the end, he never arrives at a position with which he is fully satisfied.

In this context it is important to keep in mind another theme that runs through Fontenelle's text: his comments on Leibniz's work habits and intellectual temperament. Fontenelle noted that Leibniz didn't write anything in the way of a grand treatise on his mathematics, something that also characterizes his style of working in a number of other domains. Instead he published many rather shorter articles, and communicated many of his views only in letters. About this Fontenelle makes the following comment:

> He didn't publish any body of mathematical works, but only a quantity of detached pieces, of which he could have made books, if he had wanted. . . . He said that he liked to see the plants for which he had furnished the seeds growing in other people's gardens. These seeds are often more important than the plants themselves. . . .[3]

This conception shapes Fontenelle's view of Leibniz more generally. What emerges from Fontenelle's Éloge is the picture of a polymath, a universal genius who was interested in virtually every area of intellectual inquiry. He was a great mathematician, but he also had something interesting to

---

[3] Ibid., 448–9.

say about almost everything else. And he could write elegant poetry too! Along with this went the personality of a kind of charming eccentric, too absorbed in his intellectual life to marry, or even to go to bed most nights. But, at the same time, this picture suggests a kind of dissipated activity. In working on everything at once, Leibniz seemed to threaten a lack of intellectual focus, his immense energy disbursed in every direction at once, works started but not finished, ideas thrown out in embryonic form, seeds tossed out on fertile fields for others to cultivate, but threatening to lie fallow. Fontenelle notes that "le savant Monsieur Eckard,"[4] Leibniz's assistant and, in a sense, his literary executor, was planning to collect some of Leibniz's published articles together. Fontenelle remarks: "that would be, so to speak, a resurrection of a body whose limbs had been widely disbursed, and the whole would gain a new life through this reunification."[5] This, in a sense, would put back together the one Leibniz that Fontenelle himself had dissected into a multitude of parts. But clearly it was a problem for these early readers: how to put the parts together to get a sense of the disconnected, or, at the very least, very complicated whole.

And it remains a problem for the modern reader as well. Leibniz's thought comes in a wide variety of forms, ranging from published essays and books, through essays apparently written for publication but, for various reasons never published, to letters sent, unsent, and their drafts, down to personal notes and fragments. But there is no document, published or unpublished, book or essay that can be put forward as a canonical statement of Leibniz's thought, nothing corresponding to Descartes's *Meditations* or Locke's *Essay concerning Human Understanding*. And, as I shall argue in some detail, there is very good reason to believe that Leibniz was always thinking and rethinking his positions on important matters; while there are some elements that remain relatively constant throughout his career, there are also a lot of doctrines on which his views change and evolve over time. One needs a good bit of judgment to sort all of this out and figure out what Leibniz thought at any given time, and how his view changes over time. In establishing that Leibniz believed something, it is not enough to point to a text in his hand: some texts do, indeed, represent considered beliefs, but others may be things he held for only a short time. Some

---

[4] Ibid., 476.
[5] Ibid., 480.

[handwritten margin note:] Could be why he didn't write a Magnus Opum

may even be philosophical experiments, attempts to state and work out a position just to see if it could be done; Leibniz may not have believed such propositions even at the moment that he was writing them! One needs a certain kind of judgment to use these texts that we now have at our disposal, and different scholars may make different judgments about how to take different texts. Putting it all together is, in a way, more an art than a science, somewhat like reasoning with infinitesimals in his day. Sometimes they are to be ignored, and sometimes they make all the difference. It is the skill and eye of the user that determines which. It is similar with respect to Leibniz's texts.

For these reasons it may seem foolhardy to attempt a book summarizing Leibniz's complicated views on body, substance, and even theology, something that Leibniz himself never really attempted to do. And surely he knew a lot more about the subject than I do. But that, in a way, is just what I am attempting here. I should warn the reader that the story is not simple and clear-cut. Unlike many books on Leibniz written by philosophers, this one does not offer a reconstruction, rational or otherwise, of Leibniz's view. My account is largely developmental: I want to make Leibniz's views intelligible by showing how he came to them. I shall, insofar as I can, try to put my finger on the *reasons* why Leibniz came to adopt the positions that he did, and in that respect the book is intended to be argumentative and philosophical. But my methodology is historical: I am primarily interested in what Leibniz thought and why he thought it. To the best of my ability I shall try to capture the ins and outs of Leibniz's development, where his doctrines come from, the hesitations and changes as well as the doctrines that remain firm, once established. My account in this book is not quite as contextual as I had originally thought it would be, or as some of my work on earlier seventeenth-century thought was.[6] But using the documents that we have, many of which have only recently been edited and published, I shall try to capture the complex development of Leibniz's complex thought.

I shall begin with an account of Leibniz's early thought about body and substance in Chapter 1, and end in Chapters 8 and 9 with his last thought, the monadological metaphysics of his last years. But much of the focus

---

[6] Apologies to Ursula Goldenbaum, who pointed this out and pressed me to be more historical. The full contextual history of Leibniz's thought is yet to be written, and, I'm genuinely sorry to say, it probably won't be written by me.

of this book in Chapters 2–7 is on what I earlier called the middle years that go from roughly the late 1670s to the mid- or late 1690s. One of my main theses is that in the middle years, Leibniz had not yet come upon the monadological metaphysics that will characterize his later years, the doctrine that everyone knows best from such texts as the 'Monadologie', which, for many readers, is emblematic of Leibniz's thought. Instead, what one finds there is a metaphysics grounded in corporeal substance, extended unities of matter and form. This thesis, which I first defended some years ago in Garber (1985), has raised a lot of opposition; there are many who still hold the traditional view that it's all monads all the time from the late 1670s (or even earlier) on to the end of Leibniz's life. There has even been some debate about whether or not we should isolate the middle years as a separate period in Leibniz's intellectual history. I think that it is a genuine period, distinct from what precedes and what follows, and I take the argument of this book to make that case.

But this is a rather subtle argument to make. It just seems to me that when one reads the texts of this period in a careful and historical way, looking at them from the point of view of their historical and intellectual contexts, and reading them in the most natural way, one sees corporeal substances and nothing more: there is simply no reason to suppose that Leibniz is presenting a monadological metaphysics, either explicitly or beneath the surface. If Leibniz hadn't explicitly adopted the familiar metaphysics of the 'Monadologie' in his later years, I think that we would have almost no substantive reason to believe that he held any such view in these earlier texts. I don't doubt that one can impose a monadological reading on the texts, but I find it puzzling why anyone would want to do that. In general, given that he is not at all explicit in accepting monads at that moment, and given that the most natural reading of the texts takes us in quite a different direction, it seems to me that the burden of proof is strongly on those who want to maintain that Leibniz's metaphysics is monadological at this stage in his career. It is not enough to show that the texts of this period *can* be read as being consistent with the monadology: one must show why they *should* be read in this way. Now, much of the commentary on Leibniz has been written under the assumption that Leibniz did adopt something like the monadology fairly early in his career; I take my positive argument to be an answer to those readings. But more recently, in the last ten or fifteen years, a number of commentators have responded to the challenge and attempted an explicit defense of the traditional view.[7] It would not be appropriate to attempt a systematic response to all of the different arguments of this kind that have been presented in the literature. But while I have concentrated on making the positive case for my reading of Leibniz's thought, I have also tried to answer the most influential of the arguments against the position that I develop here.

One reason for focusing on the middle years is connected with my thesis about Leibniz's intellectual development with respect to the monadology. But there are other reasons as well. For one, this period has been relatively little studied as an independent period of Leibniz's thought. In my view, the charms of this period in Leibniz's thought deserve such a study. I hope to reveal the beautiful and largely unknown and unappreciated world that Leibniz occupied on the way to the better-known monadological metaphysics, about which there is already a very extensive literature. Secondly, because of the recent work of the editors of the Akademie edition, we now have virtually all of the philosophical texts written before 1690 (though not all the letters), which finally gives us the ability to trace out Leibniz's views in this period in great detail. And finally, if I am right, the middle years provide the link between Leibniz's early and somewhat idiosyncratic Hobbesian view of the world, and his later monadology. In this way, by understanding the philosophical views he held in the middle years, their strengths and their weaknesses, we can understand how he passed from the one to the other.

Looking at Leibniz's career from this point of view changes the focus in an interesting way. I want to begin—and end—firmly anchored to the world of bodies in which we live. This is where Leibniz began in his first studies of the physical world in the late 1660s and early 1670s, and he never lost his interest in understanding the material world. On my story, Leibniz only later adds a metaphysical sub-basement of non-extended monads as part of an attempt to make larger sense of the created world. However, in doing so, he doesn't necessarily lose his grip on the material world. His last

---

[7] For some attempts to argue explicitly for a monadological metaphysics in the 1680s, in part in response to Garber (1985), see particularly Sleigh (1990), 110ff; Adams (1994), part III *passim*; Rutherford (1995), ch. 6; Baxter (1995). More recently, Fichant (2003) and Fichant (2005) have presented a systematic view of Leibniz's development that shares elements with the view that I am defending here, though it differs in crucial ways as well. In addition, Stuart Brown (1999) argues for what he calls a "proto-monadology" in the mid-1670s. Mercer (2001), chs. 7–10 argues for a version of the monadology in Leibniz's thought as early as 1671; see esp. Mercer (2001), 256 and 298.

problem, as I see it, is how to put these two together, how to understand the relations between the bodies that we experience and the monads that are, in some sense, their metaphysical foundation. And, as I shall argue, this is a problem that Leibniz never solves to his complete satisfaction. Beginning the story with a focus on the monadology, as commentators usually do, introduces a certain bias into the investigation. If we begin with the idea that monads are all there really are in Leibniz's world, then it is difficult to see how we can ever get from there to the world of bodies in a fully satisfying way. There are, of course, moments in his later writings when bodies seem to dissolve into the mist. But these should be understood in the context the larger project of Leibniz's later years, which is to outline a rich conception of the world that takes full account of stones and clocks, fish ponds and human beings, as well as the foundation he later gave them all in a world of monads.

1

First Thoughts

Leibniz's conception of his own intellectual development and temperament is nicely summarized in the following letter, which he wrote to Nicolas Remond, counselor to the Duc d'Orléans in Paris, on 10 January 1714:

Besides always taking care to direct my study toward edification, I have tried to uncover and unite the truth buried and scattered under the opinions of all the different philosophical sects, and I believe I have added something of my own which takes a few steps forward. The circumstances under which my studies proceeded from my earliest youth have given me some facility in this. I discovered Aristotle as a lad, and even the scholastics did not repel me; even now I do not regret this. After having finished the trivial schools, I fell upon the moderns, and I recall walking in a grove on the outskirts of Leipzig called the Rosental, at the age of fifteen, and deliberating whether to preserve substantial forms or not. Mechanism finally prevailed and led me to apply myself to mathematics. It is true I did not penetrate into its depths until after some conversations with Mr. Huygens in Paris. But when I looked for the ultimate reasons for mechanism, and even for the laws of motion, I was greatly surprised to see that they could not be found in mathematics but that I should have to return to metaphysics. This led me back to entelechies, and from the material to the formal, and at last brought me to understand after many corrections and forward steps in my thinking, that monads or simple substances are the only true substances and that material things are only phenomena, though well founded and well connected. I have found that most of the sects are right in a good part of what they propose, but not so much in what they deny. . . . I flatter myself to have penetrated into the harmony of these different realms and to have seen that both sides are right provided that they do not clash with each other; that everything in nature happens mechanically and at the same time metaphysically but that the source of mechanics is in metaphysics. It was not easy to uncover this mystery because there are few men who take the pains to combine both types of study.[1]

This is a late letter, from the very end of his long life, and one would not be surprised to find inaccuracies, exaggerations, and, as often happened with Leibniz's autobiographical reminiscences, rhetorical elements that owe more to the position for which he is arguing than to any serious attempt to remember the past. (Later in the book we shall return to Remond and examine the context in which this letter was written.) It also gives us a rather narrow view of Leibniz's intellectual activities: there is little mention of mathematics, and no mention at all of his work in logic, linguistics, history, theology, law, or jurisprudence, not to mention his wide activities as a practical diplomat and engineer. But still, this gives us a pretty good idea of what Leibniz thought was important in one aspect of his complex intellectual personality. It is especially noteworthy here that his account of how he came to the monadology seems to go squarely through his natural philosophy, a point to which I shall return a number of times below.

Leibniz's openness to different philosophical positions is quite noteworthy. He presents himself as having tried a bit of everything, and as seeing the value in all. He begins by reminding his reader that he started by studying the schoolmen; indeed, he is even somewhat proud of his acquaintance with these texts. But he has also studied the moderns, which he also appreciates. In fact, he purports to see something of value in all the main opposing schools of thought. To this extent we might see Leibniz as an eclectic, building a philosophy out of elements taken from different places and times, a kind post-modernist architect *avant la lettre*. But that isn't entirely fair. Though he obviously had an irenist streak, Leibniz also had a very definite program which he advanced and explained by telling Remond exactly how he came to adopt it. The implicit message is that he, Leibniz, over the course of his long career, had considered carefully the claims of all the opposing schools, and had not rejected them precipitously, but proceeding carefully, taking what each had to offer, had been led

---

[1] G III 606 (L 654–5). There is a briefer but similar account of his walk in the woods and conversion to mechanism in the letter to Thomas Burnett, 8/18 May 1697, A.1.14.224. For some remarks on the historical aspects of the recollection, at least as regards Leibniz's early years, see Antognazza (2008), 53ff. As Leibniz uses the term in this particular context, 'entelechy' is roughly equivalent to the notion of substantial form. On this term and its history, both in Leibniz and before, see Latour (2002).

step by step to his own rather surprising and original view. Leibniz here tells Remond the story about his youthful studies in traditional school philosophy, his conversion to the mechanical philosophy, perhaps at the age of fifteen, while walking in the woods, perhaps in the years following. (Mechanism *finally* prevailed, but maybe not immediately.) And then he tells us about the slow path, "after many corrections and forward steps," from mathematics and matter, through metaphysics and forms, arriving eventually at the monads that we all know and love. This is the path that I want to trace in the course of this book. My hope is that we can make these later metaphysical views more intelligible if we can start with a view that appears at least somewhat sensible to us, such as the mechanical philosophy, and show how, step by step, Leibniz arrived at his mature views.

In this chapter we shall begin with Leibniz's early views, examining his first thoughts about the physical world, deeply inspired by the physics of Thomas Hobbes, and how they fit into his early concerns about the nature of mind. I shall argue, in fact, that the young Leibniz should be understood as a heretical Hobbesian. Also important, though, are Leibniz's early views on certain questions in theology. It is important to understand these early views in order to appreciate the nature of the change that took place in the late 1670s, which marks the start of the period in Leibniz's thought that we will be examining in successive chapters.

Some Background

To understand Leibniz's earliest thought, we must understand something of its starting place in the debates over Aristotelian natural philosophy that began earlier in the century.

The seventeenth century was a period of rapid development in the sciences, the period in which the Aristotelian science that dominated the Middle Ages and the Renaissance schools was replaced with what was soon to become classical physics. At the beginning of the century, every student learned physics from Aristotle; only one hundred years later, Aristotelianism was definitely on the defensive, if not in eclipse.

While Aristotelian physics was a matter of some complexity, the fundamental principles under debate were relatively straightforward. For

Aristotelian physics, the basic explanatory principles were matter and form. Together, matter and form were taken to compose body. Matter is what remained constant in change, while form is what changed when a body changed its properties; accidental form explained changes in accidents (from brown to yellow hair, from hot to cold), while substantial form explained changes in substance, from air to water, or from prince to frog. And so, for the Aristotelian physicist, the characteristic properties of bodies were explained in terms of these forms, thought of as innate tendencies bodies have to behave in one way or another; stones were thus thought to fall, and fire to rise, fire to heat and water to cool by virtue of the forms that the bodies in question have.[2]

While Aristotelian natural philosophy was controversial from its first reintroduction into Western Europe in the late twelfth and early thirteenth centuries, by the beginning of the seventeenth century it had become the orthodoxy in the schools.[3] But early in the century it came under a new kind of attack. Central in this regard was the new mechanical philosophy. According to this, the only explanatory principles in physics were size, shape, and motion. And so, it was held, the properties bodies have are to be explained not in terms of form, accidental or substantial, but in terms of the broadly geometrical properties of the tiny particles that make up larger bodies, in terms of the motion of tiny corpuscles of different sizes and shapes, whose motion changed through collision alone. And so, heat and cold are to be explained in terms not of form, but of the shape of the particles that make up a body or the speed at which they move, and heaviness is to be

---

[2] For representative developments of the foundations of Aristotelian natural philosophy, see, e.g., St. Thomas Aquinas' "De principiis naturae," translated in Thomas Aquinas (1965); part III of Eustachius a Sancto Paulo's *Summa Philosophae Quadripartita* [Eustachius (1609)], a popular textbook originally published in 1609, but often reprinted later; and Scipion Dupleix, *La physique*, originally published in 1603, also reprinted later, and now available in an edition edited by Roger Ariew, based on the 1640 edition [Dupleix (1990)]. For recent accounts, see, e.g., Grant (1971) and Lindberg (1978).

[3] On the transmission of Aristotelian texts in the twelfth and thirteenth centuries, see, e.g., Dod (1982) and Lohr (1982). For the thirteenth-century condemnations, see also see Dod and Lohr, as well as Grant (1979). Attacks in the thirteenth century mostly came from conservative theologians whose more traditional ideas were in danger of being displaced by the new Aristotelian fashions. By the fifteenth and sixteenth centuries, Aristotelianism is the established philosophy, and the attacks come now from the innovators, from Humanists, sceptics, advocates of some variety of Platonism, Hermeticism, etc. See, e.g., Ingenio (1988) and Menn (1998). Despite the later attacks, the Aristotelian philosophy, including the Aristotelian natural philosophy, was central to the colleges and universities well into the seventeenth century. See Schmitt (1983).

explained not in terms of innate tendencies to fall, but, perhaps, in terms of the collisions between a falling stone and the particles in the atmosphere that push it downward. This new billiard-ball world was the work of many in the century, including Galileo, Descartes, Hobbes, Huygens, Gassendi, Boyle, and others. For some it was linked to the doctrines of the ancient atomists, with their unsplittable atoms swimming in a void, while others saw infinitely divisible material substance constituting a substantial plenum; for some it was linked with the framing of precise mathematical laws, while others were content with more general and less precise descriptions of the *Fullness* behavior of bodies; for some it was experimental, while for others it was largely a priori. There was also profound disagreement about just how new this new mechanical philosophy really was. While some adherents represent it as quite revolutionary, many, including Leibniz in some parts of his career, represent it as quite continuous with the old Aristotelian thought, consistent with either medieval Aristotelianism, or with what Aristotle himself originally intended, however much Aristotle's thought may have been distorted by later thinkers.[4] It is against this background that we must view Leibniz's thought about the physical world.

→ Arist. physics for L

First Approaches: Mechanism, Motion, and God

Leibniz's earliest reading and education were certainly in the scholastic tradition, and the first physics that he learned was almost certainly fundamentally Aristotelian, though probably intermixed with other strains of thought.[5] But very early on, if his own later testimony is to be trusted, Leibniz turned toward the moderns. Nothing survives from this very earliest mechanist period, which would have commenced in 1661, if we

---

[4] For a survey of the mechanical philosophy, see Westfall (1971a); Shapin (1996); Dear (1995); and Dear (2001). For seventeenth-century attempts to reconcile Aristotle and the new mechanical philosophy, with special reference to Leibniz, see especially Mercer (1990). It should be noted that the mechanical philosophy was by no means the only alternative to Aristotelian natural philosophy in the running in the seventeenth century; in addition there were various kinds of magical, occult, and alchemical philosophies which had their partisans. However, from Leibniz's point of view, the mechanical philosophy was the main challenger to Aristotelianism. For an account of the period that emphasizes some of these other trends, see Newman (2006).

[5] For Leibniz's earliest education, see Ariew (1995) and Antognazza (2008), ch. 1.

are to believe what he wrote to Remond. But by the mid- and late 1660s, there is ample evidence of Leibniz's interest in the new mechanical philosophy. The earliest evidence is in a letter he wrote to his mentor, Jakob Thomasius, on 16/26 February 1666, where Leibniz discussed a question raised by Thomasius as to why Anaxagoras spoke of the possibility of black snow, and showed some acquaintance with mechanist doctrines of perception.[6] In *De arte combinatoria* of 1666, published when Leibniz was only twenty years old, there are a number of references to Hobbes's materialistic tract *De corpore*, and a brief discussion of atomistic explanations, with reference to the atomistic tracts of Gassendi and J. C. Magnenus.[7] In the theses for public disputation that Leibniz added to the work, he also included a claim that the four Aristotelian primary qualities, hot, cold, dry, and moist, could be reduced to density and rarity, in the style of the earlier seventeenth-century philosopher, Sir Kenelm Digby.[8]

Important in these very early years are two letters that Leibniz wrote to his mentor, Jacob Thomasius, in 1668 and 1669, in which he discusses the new mechanists.[9] Leibniz considered the letter of 20/30 April 1669 important enough as a statement of his views that a year later he reprinted it largely unchanged in the preface to an edition of Marius Nizolius's *De veris principiis et vera ratione philosophandi libri IV* that he published in 1670.[10] In the second of these letters, Leibniz declares: "I maintain the rule which is common to all of these renovators of philosophy, that only magnitude, figure, and motion are to be used in explaining corporeal properties."[11] Like many of the new mechanists, Leibniz saw the nature of body as consisting of its broadly geometrical properties, extension and antitypy (impenetrability).[12] But at the same time, he makes it quite clear that, as a mechanist, he is not a follower of Descartes. After giving a long

---

[6] A2.1².7–8. Hannequin (1908), 30–1 relates this discussion to Gassendi. Hannequin (1908) remains one of the best studies of Leibniz's early thought, despite the fact that he wrote before the publication of A6.1 and A6.2, which give many texts from the period that he did not know. A more recent study, also excellent, that focuses on Leibniz's early views on the physical world and takes account of this more recently available material is Beeley (1996a).

[7] See A6.1.178, 183, 194, 216. Leibniz's earliest acquaintance with Hobbes and Gassendi probably goes back to as early as 1663. See Antognazza (2008), 52.

[8] See A6.1.229, and Digby (1644), bk I chs. III–IV.

[9] A2.1² nos. 9 and 11. On Thomasius, see Wundt (1939), 142ff; Mercer (2001), 33–8; Richard Bodéüs's notes in Leibniz and Thomasius (1993).

[10] A6.2.433–44.   [11] A2.1².25 (L 94).   [12] See A2.1².36 (L 101).

list of Cartesians and other renovators in philosophy (including Clauberg, Raey, Spinoza,[13] Clerselier, Heerbord, Andreae, Regius, Bacon, Gassendi, Hobbes, Digby, and van Hoghelande), Leibniz writes:

As to myself I confess that I am anything but a Cartesian. I maintain the rule which is common to all these renovators of philosophy, that only magnitude, figure, and motion are to be used in explaining corporeal properties. Descartes himself, I hold, merely proposed this rule of method, for when it came to actual issues, he completely abandoned his strict method and jumped abruptly into certain amazing hypotheses. . . . Hence I do not hesitate to say that I approve of more things in Aristotle's books than in the meditations of Descartes; so far am I from being a Cartesian! In fact, I venture to add that the whole of Aristotle's eight books [of the *Physics*] can be accepted without injury to the reformed philosophy. This by itself meets your arguments about the irreconcilability of Aristotle and the moderns.[14]

In this way Leibniz declares his independence both from Descartes and from his teacher.[15]

Leibniz's mechanism in these letters is not exactly the standard version that his later recollections in the letter to Remond might lead one to expect. Much of the Thomasius letter is concerned with showing in detail how the new mechanistic philosophy is consistent with the philosophy of Aristotle.[16] Leibniz begins by distinguishing between Aristotle and the scholastic philosophy, a distinction made by many of Leibniz's contemporaries.[17] He writes:

First about Aristotle. The scholastics have strangely perverted his meaning; no one knows this better than you, distinguished Sir, who were the first to bring many errors of this kind to light.[18]

---

[13] This would have to have been the Spinoza of the *Renati Des Cartes Principiorum Philosophiae Pars I & II more geometrico demonstratae* (Spinoza (1663)), the only work of Spinoza's that Leibniz could have known at this moment. Though Spinoza of the *Tractatus theologico-politicus* and the *Ethica* will become very important to Leibniz later in the next decade, at this moment Leibniz is thinking of him as a Cartesian commentator.

[14] A2.1².25 (L 94).

[15] It is interesting to note here that even though Leibniz emphasizes his independence from Descartes, he admits a few years later that at this stage of his career, he hadn't really read Descartes, at least not directly, nor had he probably read very many of the figures that he so prominently cites. See Leibniz to Foucher, 1675, A2.1².388–9 (AG 2–3).

[16] Interestingly enough, the kind of mechanist Aristotelianism of the letter to Thomasius is rather different from the kind of Aristotelianism that is found in the theological manuscripts of the period, as we shall see later in this chapter.

[17] On this theme, see Mercer (1990); Mercer (1993); and Bodéüs (1991).   [18] A2.1².26 (L 95).

It is thus the *real* Aristotle, and not the Aristotle of the scholastics, that Leibniz will reconcile with the mechanical philosophy. Leibniz then announces how he will show the consistency of the two:

I cannot better show the possibility of reconciling the two [i.e., the philosophy of Aristotle and the mechanical philosophy] than by asking for any principle of Aristotle which cannot be explained by magnitude, figure, and motion.[19]

The reconciliation, then, will proceed by showing that, properly understood, Aristotle could be read as a mechanist as well!

The first two questions that Leibniz takes up are matter and form. About matter, Leibniz writes:

Primary matter is mass itself, in which there is nothing but extension and antitypy or impenetrability. It has extension from the space which it fills. The very nature of matter consists in its being something solid and impenetrable and therefore mobile when something else strikes it, and it must give way to the other. Now this continuous mass, which fills the world while all its parts are at rest, is primary matter, from which all things are produced by motion and into which they are reduced through rest.[20]

Primary ουσια is extended substance

Thus, Leibniz argues, Aristotle's primary matter is just the extended substance of the mechanical philosophy. Form is just as easily accommodated:

Let us pass from matter to form in good order. Here too everything agrees remarkably if we assume that form is nothing but figure. For since figure is the boundary of a body, a boundary is needed to introduce figure into bodies. . . . If mass were created discontinuous or separated by emptiness in the beginning, there would at once be certain concrete forms of matter. But, if it is continuous in the beginning, forms must necessarily arise through motion . . . . For division comes from motion, the bounding of parts comes from division, their figures come from this bounding, and forms from figures; therefore, forms come from motion.[21]

In this way, the mysterious forms of the Aristotelians are resolved into shapes.[22] Leibniz goes on to give similar accounts of Aristotelian notions like

 *forms = shape, from motion*

---

[19] A2.1².26 (L 95).   [20] A2.1².26 (L 95).   [21] A2.1².27 (L 95–6).

[22] Interestingly enough, this account of Aristotelian form is very different from the account he gives of the notion in the almost-contemporaneous essay, "De transsubstantione," discussed below in this chapter, where he explicitly adopts the notion of substantial form in a much more orthodox Aristotelian fashion, in accordance with which the "concurrent mind" that makes a body into a genuine substance

change, quality, and generation. All of these arguments show that Aristotle's philosophy *can* be interpreted in terms of the mechanical philosophy of the moderns. But, in addition, Leibniz wants to show that it *should* be so interpreted. For this conclusion, Leibniz argues as follows:

> For what does Aristotle discuss, in the eight books of the *Physics*, besides figure, magnitude, motion, place, and time? If the nature of body in general can be explained in terms of these, then the nature of a particular body must be explained in terms of a particular figure, a particular magnitude, etc. In fact, he himself says in the *Physics*, Book iii, Section 24 [202b 30], that all natural science concerns magnitude (with which figure is, of course, associated), motion, and time. He also says, repeatedly [e.g., 201a 12], that the subject of physics is movable bodies and that natural science deals with matter and motion.[23]

In this way, Leibniz claimed, Aristotle is actually the father of the new mechanical philosophy, generally unacknowledged simply because he has been so badly misread for so long.

Leibniz realized full well that he was not the only of his contemporaries to interpret Aristotle in this way, and attempted to reconcile his philosophy with the new mechanism. In his letter to Thomasius, Leibniz mentions a number, including Jean Baptiste du Hamel, Johannes de Raey, J. C. Scaliger, Kenelm Digby, Thomas White, Abdias Trew, and Erhard Weigel. Indeed, the reconciliation of Aristotle and the moderns in roughly this way was a genuine cottage industry among philosophers in the seventeenth century.[24] In wanting to stand both among the ancients and among the moderns in 1669, Leibniz was occupying well-trod ground. As his physics grew and matured, and as he gave up the naive mechanism of his youth, Leibniz gave up this naive reconciliation between Aristotle and the moderns, replacing it with a much more complex and sophisticated view of their relations.

These letters read as a kind of declaration of independence from his earlier self, an announcement that Leibniz had attained intellectual maturity, and was now thinking for himself. But perhaps more important, and of more enduring interest for Leibniz's later intellectual development, is another

---

counts as such a form. Understood in that way, a form cannot be the figure of a body. This, perhaps, should make us wonder whether Leibniz is being entirely serious here with Thomasius.

[23] A2.1².30 (L 98).

[24] For discussions of the seventeenth-century movement to reconcile the old and the new philosophies, and Leibniz's place in it, see Mercer (1993) and Lennon (1993), 52–62.

context in which the new mechanical philosophy arises in his thought. The letters to Thomasius show little interest in the role that God might play in the physical world. But theological questions were very much on Leibniz's mind at that moment.

In early 1668 Leibniz entered the service of the Elector of Mainz, in good part through the patronage of Baron Johann Christian von Boineburg.[25] In Mainz, the young Leibniz entered into Boineburg's circle of Catholic intellectuals, where the young Protestant from Leipzig was thrust into a very different environment than anything he had experienced earlier in his life.[26] It is not without justification that Ursula Goldenbaum has characterized Leibniz's reaction to Mainz as "culture shock."[27] This experience led Leibniz to one of the most important intellectual projects of his young life, the "Demonstrationes catholicae," a project that absorbed him from 1668 until Boineburg's death in 1672.[28] This project involved, among other things, articulating a philosophical view that would undergird a theology consistent with his commitment to the mechanical philosophy around which both Catholics and Protestants could unite.[29]

It is not surprising that theology would intersect with the mechanical philosophy in the writings of this period. There was a certain tension between these two domains, to both of which Leibniz was committed. The mechanical philosophy was deeply suspect in certain circles as leading to atheism and materialism. Gassendi the atomist was suspected of being a materialist, with good reason; Hobbes was certainly a materialist, and was suspected of being an atheist, with good reason. Descartes, a founding father of the mechanical philosophy, claimed to be a dualist and a pious Catholic, but people had their doubts. How, then, could one be both a mechanical philosopher and pious at the same time?

---

[25] On Boineburg and his early acquaintance with Leibniz, see Antognazza (2008), 85f.

[26] On the strongly intolerant Lutheran context of Leibniz's early upbringing in Leipzig, see Antognazza (2008), 24–30.

[27] Goldenbaum (1999a), 88. More generally, on the importance of Mainz and Boineburg for Leibniz's intellectual development in these years, see Antognazza (2008), 85ff and Goldenbaum (1999a), 87ff. Goldenbaum paints a vivid and convincing picture of the centrality of theology in this period. On this, see also Goldenbaum (2002).

[28] See Antognazza (2008), 90ff and 118ff. The project was revived again in 1679, when Leibniz was in Hanover under the Duke Johann Friedrich. See Antognazza (2008), 234ff.

[29] On Leibniz's theological projects as they relate to his mechanical philosophy, see Beeley (1996a), ch. 4; Fouke (1992); Goldenbaum (1999a).

This question is addressed in a short essay Leibniz wrote in 1668 or 1669, the "Confessio naturae contra atheistas."[30] Part I of the essay is entitled "That corporeal phenomena cannot be explained without an incorporeal principle, that is, God."[31] There Leibniz argues directly that not only is the mechanical philosophy consistent with theology, but that the mechanical philosophy *demands* that there is a God. The essay begins by noting that the mechanical philosophy might well be thought to lead us to atheism:

Through the admirable improvement of mathematics and the approaches which chemistry and anatomy have opened into the nature of things, it has become apparent that mechanical explanations—reasons from the figure and motion of bodies, as it were—can be given for most of the things which the ancients referred only to the Creator or to some kind (I know not what) of incorporeal forms. The result was that truly capable men for the first time began to try to save or to explain natural phenomena, or those which appear in bodies, without assuming God or taking him into their reasoning. Then, after their attempt had met with some little success, though before they arrived at foundations and principles, they proclaimed, as if rejoicing prematurely at their security, that they could find neither God nor the immortality of the soul by natural reason, but that in these matters faith must rest either on civil laws or on historical records.[32]

This, of course, is not satisfactory for Leibniz. In the rest of part I of the essay, Leibniz attempts to argue that when we go deeper into the mechanical philosophy and attempt to arrive at the foundations and principles themselves, then we are forced to turn to God. → Principles of Mech P

In brief, Leibniz proceeds as follows. He begins with a definition of body: "a body is defined as that which exists in space."[33] But, he notes, from the definition of body we cannot derive anything about the specific shape of a given body. And while it may follow from the definition of a body that it is mobile, we cannot infer from the definition that a given body is actually in motion, or that it has a specific motion. Leibniz then turns to the *consistentia* of bodies, by which he means their resistance to acquiring new motion, the coherence of their parts, and the fact that a hard body is reflected when it encounters another immovable body. Here

---

[30] This essay was given to Boineburg, who, in turn, gave it to Gottlieb (Theophilus) Spitzel, who published it anonymously in 1669. See Aiton (1985), 26–7 and Antognazza (2008), 101ff.

[31] A6.1.489 (L 109).   [32] A6.1.489 (L 109–10).   [33] A6.1.490 (L 110).

he notes that these properties cannot be explained in terms of the shape, size or motion of bodies, or, presumably, in terms of the nature of body. How, then, can we explain these features of body? Leibniz's conclusion is that it is by appeal to God: "For through the ultimate analysis of bodies, it becomes clear that nature cannot dispense with the help of God."[34] Or, as he puts it more fully:

Interaction between bodies exp. by recourse to God [handwritten marginalia]

M. Mory [handwritten]

But since we have demonstrated that bodies cannot have a determinate figure, quantity, or motion, without assuming an incorporeal being, it readily becomes apparent that this incorporeal being is the one [cause] for all [these phenomena] because of the harmony of things among themselves, especially since bodies don't derive their motion each from its own but mutually. But no reason can be given why this incorporeal being chooses one magnitude, figure, and motion rather than another, unless he is intelligent and wise with regard to the beauty of things and powerful with regard to their obedience to his command. Therefore such an incorporeal being will be a mind ruling the whole, that is, God.[35] *Sparse ontology of mech phil. cannot occ. For these* [handwritten]

This is not the usual way to bring God into the picture. In this concluding paragraph of part I of the "Confessio," there is a gesture toward God's reasons for choosing the specific shape and motion that he does for things in the world. However, Leibniz is definitely not presenting a standard argument from design for the existence of God, an argument from the order of the world to the existence of a wise and beneficent designer. The basic form of the argument is an infinite regress:

Either the body in question must be assumed to have been a square from all eternity, or it has been made square by the impact of another body. . . . But if you say that it was made square by the motion of another body. . . .

For if they say this body moves from eternity, there is no clear reason why it should not rather have rested from all eternity . . . But if they say that this body is being moved by another body contiguous to it and in motion. . . .

---

[34] A6.1.492 (L 112). Leibniz appears to be alluding to this argument from the "Confessio" at the end of his April 1669 letter to Thomasius: "The nature of body therefore evidently is constituted by extension and antitypy, and since there is nothing in things without a cause, and nothing ought to be supposed in bodies whose cause cannot be discovered in their first or constitutive principles..." [A2.1².36 (L 101)].

[35] Ibid. Cf. also the outline of the "Demonstrationes catholicae" of the same period. There, in part I chs. 2 and 3, Leibniz includes demonstrations of the existence of God "from the principle: that the origin of motion is not in bodies" and "from the principle: that the origin of *consistentia* is not in bodies" (A6.1.494).

[T]hese interlocking instruments must be hard and tenacious in order to do their work of holding together the parts of bodies. Whence this tenacity? Must we assume hooks on hooks to infinity? . . .[36]

The divine reasons are considered only in order to establish that first cause inferred in each of these three regress arguments, the agent who creates bodies with shape, motion and *consistentia* is a single first cause, an intelligent agent, i.e. God as understood in the Christian tradition. Since the particular sizes, shapes, motions, etc. are created in a harmonious way, their (efficient) cause must be one, must be wise, and therefore must be God. But the specific details of *why* God creates what he does, the purposes, the final causes play no role at all in the arguments that establish the *existence* of a first cause. In this way the role of God in the "Confessio" seems much more like the Cartesian God, a God whose specific ends play no role in our reasoning. Divine wisdom is here subordinated to God as the *efficient* cause of shape, motion, and *consistentia*: without an immaterial agent such as God, there is no other agent who could fix these elements of the physical world.

Before Paris: Leibniz's First Physics

These early indications of Leibniz's interest in the new mechanical philosophy are largely unsystematic and largely subordinated to his theological interests. The first indication of any systematic interest in natural philosophy on Leibniz's part independent of his theology isn't found until late 1669.[37] This first physics embodies a conception of body that will be central for us to understand when we consider Leibniz's later thought in successive chapters.

---

[36] A6.1.490–2 (L 111–12).

[37] Goldenbaum (1999a) argues that the theological works are primary for understanding his intellectual program in these years, and that his interest in physics is, in a sense, subordinated to his theological writings. I agree that his views on substance are quite closely connected with his theological investigations, but I think that at least after his first acquaintance with the Huygens/Wren laws of impact and the genesis of his projects in the *TMA* and *HPN*, his interest in physics is an independent strand in his thought. In fact, as I shall argue later in this chapter, Leibniz's mechanist view of body and the physical world is at least somewhat in tension with the more Aristotelian view of substance that arises out of his theological views. That said, I still find Goldenbaum's analysis striking and illuminating.

In August 1669, in Bad Schwalbach with his then patron Baron von Boineburg, Eric Mauritius, a scientific amateur and friend of Boineburg's, showed Leibniz the recent publication of the laws of collision due to Christiaan Huygens in the *Philosophical Transactions of the Royal Society*.[38] This almost chance event begins Leibniz's serious engagement with physics. Leibniz began working on his own thoughts on motion and its laws, a series of notes that led up to his first substantial writings in natural philosophy, the *Hypothesis physica nova* (*HPN*) or *Theoria motus concreti*, presented to the Royal Society of London in 1671, and the *Theoria motus abstracti* (*TMA*), presented to the French Académie Royale des Sciences that same year.[39] Leibniz, then only twenty-five years old, quickly developed ambitions to join the premier scientific societies of his age. These two works were intended to be his admission tickets.[40]

These works together constitute an interesting system of natural philosophy. In the *TMA* Leibniz gives an abstract account of motion. The subtitle, *Rationes Motuum universales, à sensu & Phaenomeniis independentes*, *The Universal Reasons for Motions, Independent of Sense and the Phenomena*, suggests that it is meant to be an account of motion grounded purely in reason. As I shall later argue, it is, in fact, grounded as much in the natural philosophy of Thomas Hobbes as it is in reason; in an obvious way it is a variant on the system that Hobbes presented in his *De corpore* of 1655.

[38] See the textual note at A6.2.157 and Leibniz to Oldenburg, 10/20 August 1670, A2.1².97f. What Leibniz seems to have seen is the *Philosophical Transactions of the Royal Society*, vol. 4, where Huygens's laws were published on pp. 925–8. Leibniz begins his own study of impact by copying out Huygens's text: see A6.2.157–9. Huygens had previously published his laws in French in the *Journal des scavans*, 18 March 1669. Christopher Wren's very similar laws had been published earlier in the *Philosophical Transactions*, vol. 3 (1668); they can also be found in Oldenburg (1965–86), vol. 5, 320–1 (English). Huygens's main work on bodies in impact was started as early as 1656, though not published until after his death; see "De motu corporum ex percussione," in Huygens (1888–1950), vol. 16, 29–168. On Huygens, see Dijksterhuis (1961), 373–6. On Huygens and Wren, see Westfall (1971b), 146–57 (on Huygens), and 203–5 (on Wren). For an account of Leibniz's first reactions to the Huygens/Wren laws, see Goldenbaum (2008), 57–9. On the early development of Leibniz's physics, see Antognazza (2008), 106ff.

[39] The notes are found in A6.2.157–218; the *HPN* and *TMA* are found in that same volume. The *HPN* and *TMA* are also found in GM VI and G IV, though there are some confusing differences in the numbering of the sections. The alternative title, "Theoria motus concreti," is not found on the title page of the *HPN*, but on the first page of the text.

[40] Leibniz did manage to become a member of the Royal Society just two years later, in 1673, which he maintained all his life, but it took him almost thirty years, until 1700, to get through the door of the Académie Royale des Sciences. See Aiton (1985), 48, 218, 244, 248 and Antognazza (2008), 386.

Leibniz himself acknowledged as much in a letter he wrote to Hobbes during the period in which he was working out his *TMA*: "I have been thinking about the abstract principles of motion, where the foundations which you have laid seem to me remarkably justified."[41] But such an account of motion is radically in contradiction with the everyday experience of bodies and with the more exact experiments of other investigators. Leibniz's solution to this apparent inconsistency between reason and the empirical world is a hypothesis about the state of the universe God created which, together with the abstract laws, yields something close to what it is that we observe in the world; this is the task of the *HPN*, or the theory of concrete motion, which is, as the subtitle suggests, a theory of motion for *our* world.[42]

The heart of the abstract theory of motion that Leibniz gives in the *TMA* is an account of the collision of two bodies; for Leibniz, as for other mechanists, collision is the only way in which the motion of a body can be changed naturally. But unlike Descartes, for example, who derives his laws of motion and collision from the activity of God on the world, Leibniz's laws of motion and collision are supposed to be derived from the very definition of the terms. As he wrote in one of the preliminary studies for the *TMA*:

[E]xperiments must be eliminated from the science of the abstract reasons for motion, just as they should be eliminated from geometrical reasonings. For they are demonstrated not from fact and sense, but from the definitions of the terms.[43]

Leibniz's inspiration here, as I suggested above, is Thomas Hobbes. In his *De corpore* (1655), the principal exposition of his account of the physical

---

[41] Leibniz to Hobbes, July 1670, A2.1^2.92 (L 106). On the importance of Hobbes for the young Leibniz, see Bernstein (1980).

[42] The subtitle of the work on its first page is given as: "Hypothesis de rationibus phaenomenorum nostri Orbis," A6.2.223. For a fuller account of these writings, see Hannequin (1908), esp. 59–148; Duchesneau (1994), ch. 1; Beeley (1996a), chs. 7–13. On the distinction between an abstract and a concrete physics, see Leibniz's *Nova methodus discendae docendaeque jurisprudentiae*, A6.1.288, discussed in Duchesneau (1994), 23. Duchesneau emphasizes the extent to which Leibniz's physics in this period is grounded in more general methodological precepts. He notes that even though the details of Leibniz's hypothesis have to be established empirically, through experience, the general outlines are governed by a conception of Divine Wisdom. See *HPN* § 51 (A6.2.244) and Duchesneau (1994), 85–6.

[43] A6.2.160. Cf. Beeley (1995). On Descartes's derivation of the laws of motion from God, see Garber (1992), chs. 7–9.

world, Hobbes tells us that all true philosophy (science) begins with definitions:

The end of science is the demonstration of the causes and generations of things; which if they be not in the definitions, they cannot be found in the conclusion of the first syllogism, that is made from those definitions; and if they be not in the first conclusion, they will not be found in any further conclusion deduced from that; and, therefore, by proceeding in this manner, we shall never come to science; which is against the scope and intention of demonstration.[44]

Leibniz was very impressed with Hobbes on this point. In a contemporary text he attempts to demonstrate a variety of propositions in physics, mathematics, and even metaphysics starting with definitions of the terms involved in the propositions.[45] In general, though, the claim to be able to derive everything in his physics from initial definitions is more of a program (or an empty boast) in Leibniz, as it was in Hobbes; in general it is a promissory note that Leibniz never redeems.[46]

But Hobbes's influence goes deeper still, and permeates his account of motion. Following Hobbes, Leibniz's account of impact is given in terms of the notion of a conatus, an indivisible, non-extended part of motion, the beginning or end of motion, as he puts it.[47] Leibniz constructs his abstract theory of motion on the conviction that the outcomes of collisions are determined by simply combining the instantaneous motions (conatus) of the two bodies at the moment of collision; body as such offers no resistance to motion and so the mass or size of the bodies in question plays *no role whatsoever* in the outcome of a collision. As Leibniz put it in the *HPN*,

[44] *De corpore* 6.13. In citing *De corpore*, I give the chapter and section number, and the translation from Hobbes (1656). The Latin can be found either in Hobbes (1655) or in the modern critical edition in Hobbes (1999).

[45] See A6.2.479–86. Among the propositions in question is the Principle of Sufficient Reason: "Nihil est sine ratione, seu quicquid est habet rationem sufficientem."

[46] There is a delicious irony hidden in this particular Hobbesian influence. Hobbes's position on the foundations of physics in definition is, I would argue, intended as an atheist alternative to Descartes's attempted derivation from God. But Leibniz's program is precisely to show how the mechanical philosophy leads us to God.

[47] A6.2.264–5 (L 139–40); Loemker's otherwise fine translation should be treated with extreme caution in these passages. Hobbes develops the concept of conatus (or 'endeavour,' as it is translated in Hobbes (1656)) in *De corpore* 15. On the relation between Hobbes and Leibniz on the notion of conatus, see Kabitz (1909) and Bernstein (1980). More recently, Ursula Goldenbaum has argued that Leibniz was first attracted to the notion of conatus in Hobbes through its connection with the latter's account of sensory perception. See Goldenbaum (2008), 60–6. This notion of conatus should not be confused with the very different notion of conatus that Leibniz later defines in the "Specimen dynamicum" of 1695, "the speed taken with the direction [of a body]" [GM VI 237 (AG 120)].

"all power in bodies depends on the speed."[48] And so, from his earliest studies for the *TMA*, Leibniz held the view that rest cannot be a cause, and that a resting body cannot act.[49] In fact, Leibniz thought that he had established this from the definition of the terms alone.[50] In this respect, the physics of Leibniz's *TMA* resembles Hobbes's physics much more than it resembles Descartes's or any other available model. For Hobbes, as for Leibniz, bodies as such can offer no resistance to the motion of another body. As Hobbes puts it in the *De corpore*, "it is therefore manifest, that rest does nothing at all, nor is of any efficacy; and that nothing but motion gives motion to such things as be at rest, and takes it from things moved."[51] If two bodies with unequal speed collide, then, Leibniz argues, the two will move together after the collision with a speed that is the difference between the two, and in the direction of the faster. Since all the force a body has is a matter of its motion, a body at rest can offer no resistance to a moving body that strikes it. As a consequence, if a moving body A hits a body B at rest, then they both move off in the direction the body A has, no matter how small A is, and no matter how large the resting B might be; in this case, the body B offers no resistance whatsoever to being set into motion. When the two speeds are equal, then "the directions of both will be destroyed, and a third will be chosen intermediate between the two, the velocity of the conatus being conserved," a conclusion that Leibniz argues is "the peak of rationality in motion," a conclusion that he justifies by appeal to the principle that "there is nothing without a reason," an early appeal to what will later emerge as the most fruitful of his principles.[52] An interesting special case of this is when two bodies with the same speed collide directly. In this case, both come to a halt, in violation

---

[48] A6.2.228.   [49] A6.2.161, 169.

[50] See Leibniz's attempt at a formal derivation of this conclusion from definitions in A6.2.483–4.

[51] *De corpore* 15.3. Cf. also *De corpore* 9.7: "There is one that has written that things moved are more resisted by things at rest, than by things contrarily moved; for this reason, that he conceived motion not to be so contrary to motion as rest. That which deceived him was, that the words rest and motion are but contradictory names; whereas motion, indeed, is not resisted by rest, but by contrary motion." The "one" in question is, of course, Descartes. See *Principia philosophiae* II.49 and the account of that in Garber (1992), ch. 8.

[52] The account of collision is given on A6.2.268 (L 142), §§ 20–4; the consequences are presented in a series of theorems that immediately follows: A6.2.268f (not translated in L). Note that Leibniz distinguishes between the case of collision, where conatus cannot be compounded, and a new conatus must be determined, and the case in which the conatus can be compounded and the body can retain both conatus. For example, when a sphere rolls along a plane, a point on the surface has both circular and rectilinear motion. See §§ 19f of the "Fundamenta Praedemonstrabilia."

of the Cartesian conservation principle, in accordance with which the total quantity of motion (size times speed) is conserved in the world in general and in every individual collision.[53]

These laws of motion, reasonable as they might be in the abstract, fit very poorly with the world we see around us, as Leibniz knew; in particular, the bodies of our world do seem to offer resistance to being set into motion. In the *HPN* these abstract laws are reconciled with experience through a hypothesis about the make-up of the world. As his earlier writings might suggest, the spirit behind the *HPN* is thoroughly mechanistic. Leibniz writes:

I agree completely with the followers of those excellent gentlemen, Descartes and Gassendi, and with whomever else teaches that in the end, all variety in bodies must be explained in terms of size, shape, and motion.[54]

Leibniz's procedure in the *HPN* is very reminiscent of the creation story that Descartes told some years earlier.[55] Descartes's strategy was to derive the present state of the world from an initial creation and the laws of motion. Leibniz, too, starts at the beginning with an assumed first state, a solar and a terrestrial globe (he ignores here the other planetary bodies, large and small), all infused with a universal aether. These two globes are set into motions of various sorts, resulting in these two bodies rotating each around its own axis, and revolving around each other, with light streaming from the sun to the earth.[56] (As in Descartes, light seems to be the centrifugal pressure of the aether as it turns.) Leibniz argues that the pressure of the light against the surface of the earth results in the production of tiny bubbles ("bullae") of matter. This is a crucial step in the theory. For,

---

[53] A6.2.269 § 12. According to Descartes's conservation principle, the sum over all bodies of size times speed (quantity of motion) is a quantity conserved by God; see Descartes, *Principia philosophiae* II.36. For a discussion, see Garber (1992), ch. 7. It should be noted here that Descartes's principle differs from the conservation of momentum. Momentum is a vector quantity, size (mass) times *velocity*, and a change of direction entails a change in momentum, even if the speed remains the same. Not so for Descartes's quantity of motion, which remains the same even if the direction is changed. For Leibniz's comments on Descartes's conservation law, see Leibniz to Oldenburg, 15/25 October 1671, A2.1^2.272.

[54] *HPN* § 57; A6.2.248; cf. A6.2.249–50.

[55] Descartes's creation story can be found in ch. 7 of *Le monde*, and in his *Principia philosophiae* III.46. These two accounts differ somewhat; the initial state of the world in *Le monde* is a complete chaos, while in the *Principles*, Descartes imagines God to have created particles of approximately equal size. In the opening of part V of the *Discours de la méthode*, Descartes outlines the whole program of deriving the present state of the world from creation; see AT VI 42ff.

[56] *HPN* §§ 1–10; A6.2.223–6.

Leibniz argues, "these . . . bubbles are the seeds of things, . . . the foundation of bodies, and the ground of all of the variety that we admire in things, and all of the impetus we find in motions."[57] These bubbles contain smaller bubbles, which contain bubbles smaller still, and so on to infinity.[58] The project, then, is to explain the main phenomena of the world in terms of these tiny bubbles or corpuscles. And so, for example, Leibniz discusses the Aristotelian four elements (earth, water, air, and fire), showing how each can be generated from his theory (*HPN* §§ 13–14), gravity (*HPN* §§ 15f), color, sound, and heat (*HPN* §§ 30f), the magnet (*HPN* §§ 33bis f), chemical reactions (*HPN* §§ 37f), density and rarity (*HPN* §§ 56), among many other things.

These tiny bubbles are held together and have their hardness by virtue of their internal motion. In some preliminary notes for the *TMA*, dated August to September 1669, Leibniz made the following remarks about hardness:

Hardness and softness are not real differentia in bodies (unlike size, shape and motion), but only sensual differentia, as are all sensible qualities. Moreover, that hardness which is perceived by sense is nothing but resistance; all resistance is motion, and therefore, only those things are hard whose surface parts are so moved by a strong motion in such a way that they oppose the impetus of things impelled from the outside.[59]

Hardness is resistance, and resistance derives from motion alone. Now, the motion relevant to the bubbles can only be the internal motion of the aether that makes them up. Presumably, then, the faster the motion, the more the resistance is, and the harder the body is. And so, he asserts that

[57] *HPN* § 12; A6.2.226.

[58] *HPN* §§ 43–4; A6.2.241–2 (RA 338–9). It should be noted that this is not fully asserted, but presented somewhat hypothetically, as something that is quite possible. Leibniz at this stage seems unsure that he has a real argument for it, though other contemporary passages do suggest more certainty. See, e.g., an untitled fragment from 1670 or 1671: "Matter is actually divided into infinite parts. There are infinitely many creatures in any body whatever" [A6.2.280 (RA 344)]. Leibniz connects this view to alchemical theories, to the contemporary microscopical investigations of Hooke and Kircher, and to Anaxagoras's view of matter. On these connections, see Beeley (1996a), ch. 8. If these bubbles are understood as the elements into which bodies are infinitely divided, then it would support the reading discussed below that the ultimate elements in the infinite division are material points, not mathematical points. On the relation between this view of Leibniz's, classical atomism and chemical atomisms have been explored in an excellent article by Richard Arthur (2003). Arthur links Leibniz's view here in the period, which he sometimes characterizes as a kind of atomism, with the various chemical atomisms that were then under discussion. See also the discussion in Arthur (1998b), 119–23.

[59] A6.2.161.

"a body is harder to the extent that it moves more quickly around its own axis."[60] These ultimate constituents of larger bodies, then, are swirls of fluid matter, rotating around an axis, what Descartes called and what Leibniz himself will later call vortices. These, in turn, contain smaller vortices to which motion is imparted by the motion of the larger vortices of fluid that contain them.[61]

But most of interest to us in this context is how exactly the abstract laws of motion concerning bodies in impact come out on the new hypothesis of the *HPN*. As I noted earlier, according to the abstract theory of the *TMA*, size or mass, the quantity of matter can play no role in the determination of the outcome of a collision. Furthermore, since at the moment of impact the two bodies in impact will have exactly the same conatus, they will always move in the same direction at the same speed. But, Leibniz argues, through the discontinuity of bodies and through the elasticity that he thinks his physical hypothesis entitles him to assume in bodies, he can show how bodies that obey the abstract laws of the *TMA* at the lowest level can appear to behave as if size were a factor in their behavior in collision: "A discontinuous body resists more than a continuous one does."[62] And so, for example, let us imagine a horizontal row of n tiny discrete balls, $a_1, a_2, \ldots, a_n$, colliding with a single ball B, moving in the opposite direction. Let us further suppose that B moves faster than the balls in row A. Consider, for example, the first ball, a_1, hitting B. By the laws of the *TMA*, the post-collision speed of B will be its pre-collision speed, minus the speed of a_1, and the two balls will go off in the same direction at the same speed after the collision, i.e., the direction in which B originally moved. The pair of balls, a_1 and B, will then hit a_2, and the same thing will happen; that is, the speed of B will be further reduced. In this way, the

[60] A6.2.164. Catherine Wilson traces this view back to Hobbes. See Wilson (1997), 341–3.

[61] See the development of these ideas in a piece that Leibniz entitled "Summa hypotheseos physicae novae," written in the second half of 1671, A6.2.363–7. Thanks to Philip Beeley for some very helpful correspondence on this question. In connection with the vortex theory of atoms from a few years later, Catherine Wilson notes that Leibniz is probably not talking about vortices in the strict technical sense. Rather, she suggests that, for Leibniz, "the presence of a body indicates the presence of a unity-preserving set of motions analogous to those of the typical 'whirlpool' shape" [Wilson (1999a), 238]. I suspect that she is right. Interestingly enough, vortex atoms not unlike what Leibniz posited will come up again in the nineteenth century in the work of the physicists William Thomson (Lord Kelvin) and Joseph Larmor. See Dear (2006), 128–9 and 136.

[62] *TMA*, "Theoremata" § 21, A6.2.270.

speed of B will be reduced in the collision; if there is a sufficient number of balls, it can even be reversed. And so, in a discontinuous body, size (or, at least, the number of particles in the line of direct collision) *can* play a role in the outcome of a collision.[63] Similarly, Leibniz can appeal to his physical hypothesis (here the discontinuity of bodies, together with the ether that flows around their parts) to introduce elasticity in the world, thus enabling bodies to reflect from one another on occasion.[64] And so he wrote in the *HPN*:

But by means of the wonderful handiwork of the creator, or through his gift, necessary for life, on our hypothesis all sensible bodies are elastic, due to the circulation of the ether, and therefore all sensible bodies reflect or refract. . . . Everything is discontinuous, from which it follows that other things equal, the greater mass accomplishes more; everything is elastic, that is, when compressed, and left to itself, it soon restores itself to its prior state on account of the circulating ether.[65]

Indeed, Leibniz thought that together his abstract laws and his physical hypothesis yielded the Huygens/Wren laws of impact recently discovered, and widely discussed. Writing on 13/23 July 1670 to Henry Oldenburg, secretary of the Royal Society in whose *Philosophical Transactions* were published the Huygens/Wren laws and to which the *HPN* had been dedicated, Leibniz noted:

For I have established certain elements of the true laws of motion, demonstrated in the geometrical method from the definitions of terms alone, . . . and this has also shown that those rules of motion, which the incomparable Huygens and Wren have established, are not primary, not absolute, not clear but, no less than gravity, follow from a certain state of the ter-aqueous globe, not demonstrable by axiom or theorem, but from experience, phenomena, and observation, however fertile and admirable . . . they might be.[66]

And so, the laws bodies appear to obey in our world are the result of abstract and geometrical laws, very different from what we experience in day-to-day life, operating in a complex world that follows from God's

---

[63] See on this A6.2.164 (§ 33); *HPN* §§ 22–3; A6.2.228–32. For a more detailed discussion, see Hannequin (1908), 103–7; Duchesneau (1994), 63f. This may well have been inspired by Hobbes, *De corpore* 15.8. (I would like to thank Kathryn Morris for this observation and for the reference.)

[64] For a more detailed discussion of this, see Hannequin (1908), 120–2.

[65] *HPN* § 22; A6.2.229, 230. Cf. *TMA* "Problemata Specialia" § 11; A6.2.271.

[66] A2.1².95. See also *HPN* § 23; A6.2.231–2.

initial creation. Leibniz frames his hypothesis in such a way that in the world of the *HPN*, bodies acting in accordance with the laws of motion outlined in the *TMA* will behave as we see them behave. Indeed, because what we see is due to the interaction between the abstract laws, a result of reason, and the contingent facts that obtain with respect to the make-up of bodies in our world, experience cannot be used as a guide to the true laws of motion.[67]

God's role here is interesting. Divine wisdom and plan are not entirely missing from the world of the *HPN*: Leibniz does acknowledge in one inconspicuous place that the complex architecture of the world that allows the abstract laws to be reconciled with experience, "the great craftsmanship of the universal arrangement," is a consequence of God, and "arises from the admirable wisdom of the creator of things."[68] But this appeal to God seems like an afterthought in his text; it is hardly a central theme, as it will later become. As with the "Confessio naturae," it is God's power, his role as an efficient cause, the creator of the world that is most in prominence, not his wisdom.

Impenetrability, Motion, and the Nature of Body

In many of the texts from this period, the late 1660s and very early 1670s, Leibniz is concerned most with his theory of motion and with the physical hypothesis that mediates the abstract and geometrical theory of motion and the phenomena that we observe in the world. But scattered through the texts there are some indications of his metaphysical conception

---

[67] Cf. A6.2.166. Cf. Beeley (1995). In a personal communication, Domenico Bertoloni Meli informed me that this view can also be found in Ignace Gaston Pardies, *Discours du mouvement local* (Paris, 1670). According to Bertoloni Meli, Pardies denies any resistance in bodies, any causal efficacy to rest, and draws a distinction much like Leibniz's between abstract and concrete laws of motion. But, so far as I can see, Leibniz would have had no acquaintance with this book until he got to Paris. Müller and Krönert (1969), 31, claim that Leibniz associated with Pardies in 1672 and 1673, though they give no documentation. The earliest reference that I can find to Pardies in letters is in 1673, while Leibniz was in Paris. See A2.1².369 (critical apparatus and note) and A3.1.43.

[68] *HPN* § 46; A6.2.242–3. See also *HPN* § 51; A6.2.244, where Leibniz also appeals to divine wisdom in connection with a principle of parsimony to justify the schematic representation of the different kinds of bubbles in the world. So far as I can see, these two brief passages are the only mention of divine wisdom in the *HPN*.

of body. In this period, Leibniz seems to begin with the view that bodies are extension and impenetrability or antitypy alone. For example, he writes the following in the important letter to Thomasius from 20/30 April 1669, which we discussed earlier:

It remains therefore to seek some sensible quality which occurs in all bodies and only in bodies and by which men may distinguish body from nonbody, as if by a criterion. Beyond any doubt this is mass or antitypy, together with extension.... The nature of body therefore evidently is constituted by extension and antitypy, since there is nothing in things without a cause, and nothing ought to be supposed in bodies whose cause cannot be discovered in their first or constitutive principles.[69] *Mass + extension alone are essential to body*

The addition of impenetrability (antitypy) to extension here is important: it allows Leibniz to differentiate between body and empty space. Indeed, at this point, Leibniz wants to admit the real existence of vacua in the physical world. In his notes leading up to the TMA, he writes: "Note well that we seem to be able to demonstrate from our principles that there is some sort of vacuum, and that the phenomena in the world cannot be saved if everything were full."[70] This is the conception of body that Leibniz seems to have in mind when he sometimes characterizes body as that which is in space, or that which fills space: "a *body* is something in space (that is, something not apart from some space), which we perceive we cannot think of without space, though we can think of space without it.... Moreover, space and body are distinct."[71]

In the HPN and the TMA of 1671 and related texts, Leibniz holds that a body at rest can offer no resistance to new motion, as I have argued. In addition, he comes to the view that the cohesion of bodies arises through internal pressure: "Therefore bodies which push or impel each other are in a state of cohesion, for their boundaries are one...."[72] From these it

---

[69] A2.1².36 (L 101). Cf. the characterization of matter in terms of extension and antitypy, and form in terms of shape at A2.1².26–7 (L 95–6).

[70] A6.2.185. See also A6.2.270 (§ 22), A2.1².104; A2.1².271: A2.1².278 (L 148). On Leibniz's views on the vacuum in this period, see Beeley (1996a), 178–82.

[71] A6.2.305 (L 143); cf. A6.2.167–8.

[72] TMA Praedem. § 16. Cf. A2.1².103; A2.1².271; etc. On Leibniz's theory of cohesion, see Arthur (1998b), 113–19.

1669: Nature of body = mass + extension
1671:   ''   '' ''   ~ Motion

would seem to follow that a body at rest is indistinguishable from empty space insofar as it has neither resistance nor cohesion: "A resting body is nothing . . . nor does it differ from an empty space. . . ."[73] From this Leibniz draws the conclusion that the essence of body is not extension, or even extension and impenetrability, as he had believed only a little while earlier, but motion, as he writes to Arnauld in 1671:

First, there is no cohesion or consistency in bodies at rest . . . furthermore, whatever is at rest can be impelled and divided by motion, however small. This proposition I later extended still further, discovering that there is no body at rest, for such a thing would not differ from empty space. . . . The other proposition is that all motion in a plenum is homocentric circular motion and that no rectilinear, spiral, elliptical, oval or even circular motion around different centers can be understood to exist in the world, unless we admit a vacuum. . . . From the later principle it follows that the essence of body does not consist in extension, that is, in magnitude and figure, because empty space, even though extended, must necessarily be different from body. From the former it follows that the essence of body consists rather in motion, since the concept of space involves nothing but magnitude and figure, or extension.[74]

Though in this and other similar texts Leibniz focuses on motion as what characterizes bodies, bodies are still extended and, I am inclined to say, essentially so: there is nothing in these texts that says that bodies are *not* extended.[75] But Leibniz has clearly come to the view that extension is not enough; space, too, is extended, though it is distinct from body. A body must have motion in order to exhibit resistance to the motion of other bodies, and, in that way, differentiate itself from bare space; with motion comes coherence as well, the property by which the parts of the body cohere with one another and make a tactile whole.[76] And

---

[73] A6.2.340; cf. A6.2.280; A2.1².101–2; A2.1².271.

[74] Leibniz to Arnauld, early November 1671, A2.1².278 (L 148). See also Leibniz to Oldenburg, 15/25 October 1671, A2.1².271. In this respect Leibniz seems to depart from Hobbes, who asserts that the essence of body is extension, though by that he means something a bit different than either Descartes or the younger Leibniz meant. See *De corpore* 8.1 and 8.23. This was the only letter Leibniz was to write to Arnauld before the famous exchange in 1686 and 1687. However, he did know Arnauld in Paris. See Antognazza (2008), 141.

[75] Christia Mercer seems to take this chacterization of body in terms of motion as a move toward the elimination of what she calls "passive matter" and towards a kind of idealism; see Mercer (2001), 271–2. Given the argument that Leibniz offers in terms of motion required to differentiate body from space, I don't see how this could be right.

[76] Impenetrability, as distinct from coherence, would seem to drop out of the picture here. Impenetrability, the property of excluding other bodies, is distinct from coherence, that by virtue

insofar as without motion a body lacks such resistance (and coherence), motion must be essential to body as such; it is, perhaps, *the* essential property of body insofar as body shares its extension with space and thus extension cannot differentiate it from bare space. This seems to be the sense of the position that Leibniz takes here and expresses to Arnauld.[77] But even so, it seems a bit confused: *what exactly is it* that is doing the moving here and that constitutes body? And whatever it is that is doing the moving would certainly be a part of the nature of body, one would think. *[handwritten: Isn't it a body that is moving? Chicken/egg, etc.]*

 In addition to the passages that express a fairly straightforward mechanist conception of body as extended and impenetrable, there are others that suggest something somewhat different. In an untitled fragment probably written sometime in 1671, Leibniz writes the following:

Whatever is sensed, exists. Indemonstrable.

Whatever exists is sensed. To be demonstrated.

Indeed, it is not true that whatever is sensed, exists, but that whatever is clearly and distinctly sensed, exists.[78] *[handwritten: Also false, depending on what kind of existence he means. If he means "exists as sensation," then this applies to unclear sensations as well]*

In the paragraphs that follow, Leibniz then tries to make an argument for the claim that what exists is sensed. The identification of existence and being sensed comes up again in some notes on John Wilkins from 1671 or 1672. Here is what he writes:

(Existence) is the distinct sensibility of anything

(Essence) is the distinct thinkability (*cogitabilitas*) of anything

THE REAL is whatever is not only apparent. *[handwritten: The real is whatever's sensibility is not distinct, plus something more?]*
The APPARENT is that whose sensibility is not distinct.[79]

A later addition to the first line reads as follows:

or the Existing [*Existens*] is what can be sensed or perceived distinctly[,] distinctly, that is by using distinct concepts, just as Being [*Ens*] is what can be conceived distinctly.[80]

---

of which the parts of bodies stick together to form durable wholes. Perhaps Leibniz thought that coherence, which follows directly from motion, was enough to ground bodies, and that impenetrability need not be considered explicitly in this context.

[77] For a very different reading of this doctrine that connects it more to Leibniz's struggle over mentality in the world, see Bassler (2002).
[78] A6.2.282.   [79] A6.2.487–8.   [80] A6.2.487.

In another passage still from this period, Leibniz suggests that for a body to exist is for it to be sensed by God. In a piece entitled 'De minimo et maximo. De corporibus et mentibus,' Leibniz writes:

Since to be a body is to move, it must be asked what it is to move. If it is to change place, then what is place? isn't this determined by reference to bodies.... So what in the end are body and motion really, if we are to avoid this circle? What else, but being sensed by some mind.[81]

From this Leibniz concludes: "For the existence of bodies, it is certain that some mind exempt from body is required, different from all the others we sense."[82] As Leibniz makes clear in the summary of the argument that immediately follows, that mind is God.[83]

What exactly is going on in these passages?[84] There isn't much to go on, unfortunately; these texts that I have quoted are all there is he has to say along these lines. One possibility is that in these passages (except for the last, of course) Leibniz is advancing a Berkeleyan kind of phenomenalism. On that view, bodies exist insofar as they are sensed by minds, but the kinds of minds at issue here are the conscious minds of rational creatures.[85] In the fragment 'De conatu et motu, sensu et cogitatione,' Leibniz suggests paraphrasing "body is sensed" by "Body is that which *I* sense" [my emphasis] and even further to "Body is that which *I* am sensing."[86] This Berkeleyan phenomenalism is exactly the kind of position that Leibniz flirted with starting in the mid-1670s and continued to play with in his later years, as we shall discuss below in Chapter 7. Insofar as Leibniz sometimes had doubts about whether or not one had good reason to believe in an external world, he toyed with the position that the world of bodies is nothing beyond the organized and coherent sensations of conscious minds.

But this may not be what Leibniz has in mind. It is important to remember here that the Epicurean atomists also defined body in terms of the property of being sensible in order to distinguish it from empty space,

---

[81] A6.3.100 (RA 17).   [82] Ibid.   [83] A6.3.101 (RA 19).

[84] Mercer sees these passages as committing Leibniz to a kind of proto-monadological idealism; see Mercer (2001), 319–21. I think that she is reading too much into the text.

[85] I am, of course, leaving aside here the aspect of Berkeley's view that relates to the divine cause of these sensory ideas in finite minds.

[86] A6.2.283, my emphasis.

which is not sensible. Leibniz could have read such a position in Epicurus
or Lucretius,[87] or in Gassendi,[88] or even in an important letter from Henry
More to Descartes that was available to Leibniz in Clerselier's edition of
Descartes's correspondence.[89] Certainly these thinkers didn't intend this
conception of body to lead them to any kind of phenomenalism, either
Berkeleyan or monadological, and it is not out of the question that Leibniz
is here recalling that position. This seems rather plausible in the letter to
Thomasius from April 1669. Leibniz ends the argument with an attempted
demonstration of the claim that body is just extended and impenetrable.
But where he begins is just where these other passages quoted above
begin: "Everyone calls that a body which is endowed with some sensible
quality."[90] And where he ends is with the conclusion he seeks:

> Whether learned and ignorant, therefore, men find that the nature of body consists
> in two things—extension and antitypy together. The former we derive from sight,
> the latter from touch, and by the combination of both senses we usually ascertain
> that things are not phantasms.[91]

We shall later return to the question of Leibniz's phenomenalisms, but
there is good reason to believe that Leibniz hadn't yet signed on to any
kind of phenomenalism in the early 1670s.

The Real Division to Infinity

One interesting feature of Leibniz's view in the period of this first physics,
a view that will persist through his entire career in one or another way,
is that body is actually divided to infinity.[92] This is the way he begins the
"fundamenta praedemonstrabilia," the postulates, as it were, of his system
in the *TMA*:

(1) There are actually parts in the continuum, though the learned Thomas White
believes the contrary.[93]

(2) And they are actually infinite, for the indefinite of Descartes is not in the thing
but in the thinker.[94]

---

[87] *De rerum natura* I.304.   [88] *Syntagma* 2.1.3.1, in Gassendi (1658), vol. I, 231.
[89] AT V 239–40.   [90] A2.1².35 (L 101).   [91] A2.1².36 (L 101).
[92] This point gets particular emphasis in Beeley (1999).
[93] See White (1647), book II, lect. I, esp. § 4.
[94] See Descartes, *Principia philosophiae* II.34–5.

(3) There is no minimum in space or in body, that is, that whose magnitude or part is nothing; for such a thing cannot have any position, since whatever has a position can be in contact at the same time with several things which do not touch each other and hence will have many faces. Nor can a minimum be assumed without it following that there are as many minima in the whole as in the part, which implies a contradiction.

(4) There are indivisibles or unextended beings, for otherwise we could conceive neither the beginning nor the end of motion or body. . . . ⟶ Points

(5) A point is not that which has no part, or whose parts are not considered, but rather it is something whose extension is nothing, that is, whose parts are indistant, whose magnitude is inconsiderable, unassignable, less than any ratio with a sensible quantity, unless infinite, less than can be given. . . .[95]

⟶ Contra Hobbes

These passages are somewhat obscure.[96] The claim is that the (physical) continuum[97] is actually divided to infinity, in opposition to the standard Aristotelian view that the continuum is only potentially divisible to infinity. Leibniz also claims that there must be "indivisibles or unextended beings," presumably points, "something whose extension is nothing." One might infer from this that the infinite parts of which the continuum is made up are these unextended points. But, at the same time Leibniz holds that "there is no minimum in space or in body." How can we put all of this together?

One possible way would be to identify the ultimate parts of bodies with the unextended points whose existence he proves in §§ 4–5. Such points are unextended, to be sure, but since they have parts, and since they have magnitude, though that magnitude is "inconsiderable," we can talk about some points being greater than others, as Leibniz acknowledges later in § 18 of the "fundamenta praedemonstrabilia." In that way, even though bodies are actually divided into points, there is still "no minimum in space or in body," as Leibniz requires in § 3.

Alternatively, though, Leibniz might have wanted to distinguish between the physically smallest parts in body that he refers to in § 3, what we might call physical points, and the unextended points of §§ 4–5, what we might call mathematical points. The distinction between physical and

---

[95] A6.2.264 (L 139–40). The definition of a point is directed explicitly against the definition Hobbes gives in *De corpore* 8.12. Cf. Beeley (1996a), 245ff.

[96] For a helpful historical commentary on these and related texts, see Beeley (1996a), ch. 10.

[97] On the relation between Leibniz's views on the mathematical continuum and the physics of the *HPN*, see Beeley (1996a), 235f.

mathematical points is made in a letter to the Duke Johann Friedrich from 21 May 1671, almost contemporary to the *TMA*. He writes:

This kernel of substance, consisting in a physical point (which is the proximate instrument and as it were the vehicle of the soul, which is located in a mathematical point) endures forever.[98]

This bears on his theory of mind at that moment, in accordance with which mind is located in mathematical points. But my interest here is in the distinction he makes between the mathematical point in which mind is located (without extension) and the physical point (body) in which the mind is placed. It is these physical points, one might claim, into which bodies are actually divided to infinity in the *TMA*. This view might be connected with the position in the *HPN*, discussed above, that the little bubbles into which Leibniz thinks that bodies are divided contain smaller bubbles, "worlds in worlds to infinity."[99] → But never reaching

non-extension (math. points)

Mentality and the Physical World: the *TMA* and Before

This last passage raises the question of mind and mentality in this period.[100] Leibniz's early thoughts on matter and mentality have suggested to some commentators that behind the apparent Hobbesian physics of the early years lurks something like the later monadology. My own view is that the monadological metaphysics enters only much later in Leibniz's career, as the 1714 letter to Remond suggests, and I shall argue this at length in the following chapters. But we must examine these earlier texts with some care.

Mentality enters in crucial ways in the theological works that precede the first physics of the *TMA* and *HPN*, particularly in the person of God. In the

[98] A2.1².176. Beeley (personal communication) argues that physical points have no place in the *TMA*, suggesting that the first view is closer to being correct. His argument is that the distinction between physical and mathematical points arises only after the drafting of the *HPN*, when Leibniz is attempting to introduce mind into the world of the *TMA/HPN*. While he may be right, the texts seem open to both readings.

[99] *HPN* §§ 43–4; A6.2.241–2 (RA 338–9). Such a view is suggested in Beeley (1996b), esp. 25–6.

[100] For fuller accounts of this question, see Hannequin (1908), 149–78; Beeley (1996a), ch. 14, and Beeley (1996b).

"Confessio naturae contra atheistas," Leibniz argues that the phenomena of the physical world cannot be explained by matter alone, but that we have to appeal outside of matter to spirit, in particular to God. In a passage we saw earlier in this chapter Leibniz writes: *eg who determines?*

But since we have demonstrated that bodies cannot have a determinate figure, quantity, or motion, without assuming an incorporeal being, it readily becomes apparent that this incorporeal being is the one [cause] for all [these phenomena] because of the harmony of things among themselves, especially since bodies don't derive their motion each from its own incorporeal being, but mutually. But no reason can be given why this incorporeal being chooses one magnitude, figure, and motion rather than another, unless he is intelligent and wise with regard to the beauty of things and powerful with regard to their obedience to his command. Therefore such an incorporeal being will be a mind ruling the whole world, that is, God.[101] *⟹ Proto-BOAPW?*

Here Leibniz appeals to a variety of features of the world, the size and shape of bodies, their motion and their coherence to argue for the need to appeal beyond matter to God. But motion seems to be the most important reason to appeal to mind.

This is what Leibniz focuses on in his important letter to Thomasius from April 1669. At the end of the letter, Leibniz makes the following observation:

[W]e can assume nothing in bodies which does not follow from the definition of extension and antitypy. But from these concepts are derived only magnitude, figure, situation, number, mobility, etc. Motion itself is not derived from them. Hence there is no motion, strictly speaking, as a real entity in bodies. I have demonstrated, instead, that whatever moves is continuously created and that bodies are nothing at any time midway between the instants in motion—a view that has never been heard of until now but which is clearly necessary and will silence the atheists.[102]

Here the appeal is, again, to God, who causes motion by continually recreating bodies at different places at different times.[103] When Leibniz

[left margin handwritten, vertical:] Time seems divisible, but motion not. Why? E.g. I.H. is motion on the part of God?

[101] A6.1.492 (L 112).

[102] A2.1².36 (L 102). This echos Leibniz's views in the "De transsubstantione" of the same period. See A6.1.508-9 (L 115-16).

[103] See also the "Demonstrationum catholicarum conspectus" from 1668-9, an outline of the program he intended to follow, where Leibniz includes a chapter he entitles: "demonstration [of the existence of God] from the principle that there could be no motion without continuous creation" (A6.1.494).

[handwritten note at bottom:] ⟹ Gd creates in one place and time, then another. But each time B determinate, only so motion cannot be inf divs even if space/time are. But that doesn't seem continual. Ie, Gd creates at all times.

[handwritten, left:] ⟹ Should be fine.

printed this letter in the introduction to his edition of Marius Nizolius, *De veris principiis* roughly a year later, this passage was considerably altered:

[W]e can assume nothing in bodies which does not follow from the definition of extension and antitypy. But from these concepts are derived only magnitude, figure, situation, number, mobility, etc. (Motion itself is not derived from them, whence bodies have motion only from incorporeal things.)[104] *Less specific! no "continual creation",*

Here the claim seems to be more generally that motion in bodies requires an incorporeal cause. But why did he change this passage when the letter went into print? And what kind of "incorporeal things" did Leibniz have in mind? The doctrine of continual recreation and the kind of occasionalism that seems to follow from it were familiar themes in Cartesian tracts (not to mention earlier versions of occasionalism in the scholastic literature), and it is rather surprising that Leibniz would have thought his view at all original, as he brags to Thomasius.[105] Perhaps between the time he first wrote the letter and the time he published it, someone pointed that out to him and he consequently toned the passage down a bit. Or, perhaps the alteration represents a change in view, a rejection of the view that motion requires an incorporeal cause *external* to body, that is, God, and the adoption of the view that there is some *internal* incorporeal principle (or principles) responsible for motion in body.[106] But this passage is too vague by itself to draw any definite conclusions about what the young Leibniz might have had in mind.

Leibniz's advances in his conception of the physical world in the *TMA* and *HPN* brought with them further attention to the question of mentality in the world, now focused squarely and unambiguously on finite minds. In a letter Leibniz wrote in May 1671, the same year as he sought admission to the Royal Society and the Académie des sciences, he wrote the following to Duke Johann Friedrich:

Geom. over fonr-d

Indeed the doctrine of the point and angle, instant and conatus. . . will be, for me, the key to explaining the nature of thought. For I shall demonstrate that mind consists in a point, that thought is conatus or a smallest motion, and that

---

[104] A6.2.443.   [105] See, e.g., Garber (2001b) and Garber (2001c).
[106] See the discussions of this question in Garber (1982), 171 and Mercer (2001), 137–44.

there can be several conatus in the same [mind] at the same time, though not with motion.[107] *[handwritten: → Conatus: int. small motion? Point motion?]*

This is very interesting. Like Hobbes before him, Leibniz seems to identify thought with motion, in this case conatus, "a smallest motion." Further-more, mind is located in a point, a mathematical point rather than a physical point, as an earlier remark in the same letter suggests, as quoted above.[108] This suggests that to the Hobbesian world of bodies in motion, really divided into an infinity of *physical* points, Leibniz wants to add minds, different from bodies, located at *mathematical* points. They are like Cartesian minds, in a sense, insofar as they are non-extended things. However, they are like Hobbesian minds insofar as their thought is understood in terms of conatus, the infinitesimal motions that are the foundation of his theory of motion. While the history of Leibniz's view here is clear enough, as is the motivation, one might be a bit puzzled by Leibniz's identification of thought and conatus. When Hobbes identifies thought and motion, it is within the context of a materialistic theory of the human being in which thought is identified with the motions of the parts of the brain. But it is unclear how exactly thought is to be identified with conatus for Leibniz, who seems to want to introduce non-extended minds into his world.[109]

The waters are muddied further still by one way that Leibniz sometimes characterizes this position. In the *TMA* and related writings, the young Leibniz characterizes bodies as what he calls "momentary minds":

(17) No conatus lasts beyond a moment without motion except in minds. For what in a moment is conatus, in time is the motion of a body.... For every body

---

[107] Leibniz to Johann Friedrich, 21 May 1671, A2.1².181. Cf. Leibniz's remark to Arnauld, November 1671: "Thought consists in conatus, as body consists in motion" [A2.1².279 (L 149)].

[108] "This kernel of substance, consisting in a physical point (which is the proximate instrument and as it were the vehicle of the soul, which is located in a mathematical point) endures forever" (A2.1².176).

[109] In these texts from 1671, Leibniz seems clearly to identify thought with conatus conceived of as a very tiny motion. However, in texts written slightly later, the connection between conatus and motion seems to become rather more metaphorical. For example, in the "Confesio philosophi" of 1672/3, he writes that "what a conatus is in a body, an affect is in a mind." He then goes on to compare the resolution of conatus in the motion of bodies with the resolution of different affects. But the example he gives of the resolution of affects doesn't look at all as if he is dealing with motions: "Hence, someone frustrated in a desire cannot help suffering at that moment, but he cannot continue to suffer if he is content with the governance of the world..." [A6.3.141 (Leibniz [2005], 89)].

[handwritten margin note, left side: How does conatus differ from non-motion?]

[handwritten margin note, left side: How can a mathematical point move, even in infinitesimally?]

[handwritten note at bottom: Conatus: Motion within a time slice. The body is moving, yet within a time-slice gets numbers, therefore its motion at a time is infinitesimal.]

is a momentary mind, that is, a mind lacking recollection, since it does not retain its own conatus and the other contrary one together for longer than a moment. For two things are necessary for sensing pleasure or pain—action and reaction, opposition and the harmony—and there is no sensation without them. Hence body lacks memory; it lacks the perception of its own actions and passions; it lacks thought.[110]

Now, it is quite tempting to read Leibniz here as subscribing to a position like this. Bodies are actually divided into tiny parts, (physical?) points, which are their ultimate constituents. These points are of two sorts. Some of them are genuine minds, those where contrary conatus are retained; others are just momentary minds, those where the contrary conatus are resolved into motions after an instant. But even so, one is tempted to read Leibniz as holding that all the world is mind. On the issue of the momentary minds it can look as if Leibniz is rejecting Hobbes's celebrated materialism, and replacing it with a thoroughgoing idealism. We seem to have something strikingly like the later monadology. And it seems to be there as early as 1671!

I once thought so.[111] But this is, in a way, reading Leibniz's later position back into his very early years. (Remember, Leibniz is only twenty-four or twenty-five years old when he is writing this.) When reading these lines it is better to look backwards to where Leibniz was coming from rather than forwards, to where he is going. Here, as with several other doctrines of the period, the inspiration is Hobbes.

For Hobbes, of course, sensation is just motion or endeavor (conatus):

Now that all mutation or alteration is motion or endeavour (and endeavour also is motion) in the internal parts of the thing that is altered, hath been proved. . . . Sense, therefore, in the sentient, can be nothing else but motion in some of the internal parts of the sentient. . . .[112]

More strictly speaking, a phantasm (sensation) arises when a motion in the sense organ reaches resistance (reaction) in the sentient creature, which reaction is itself a motion.[113] But Hobbes's account of sensation doesn't end there. If sensation were only motion, then wherever there was motion there would be sensation, and the world would be alive with sentient

---

[110] A6.2.266 (L 141); cf. Leibniz to Oldenburg, 11 March 1671, A2.1².147.
[111] See Garber (1982).   [112] De corpore 25.2.   [113] De corpore 25.3.

creatures. Hobbes wants to block that conclusion. And so he fills out his account of sensibility as follows:

But though all sense, as I have said, be made by reaction, nevertheless it is not necessary that every thing that reacteth should have sense. I know there have been philosophers, and those learned men, who have maintained that all bodies are endued with sense. Nor do I see how they can be refuted, if the nature of sense be placed in reaction only. And, though by the reaction of bodies inanimate a phantasm might be made, it would nevertheless cease, as soon as ever the object were removed. For unless those bodies had organs, as living creatures have, fit for the retaining of such motion as is made in them, their sense would be such, as that they should never remember the same. And therefore this hath nothing to do with that sense which is the subject of my discourse. For by sense, we commonly understand the judgment we make of objects by their phantasms; namely, by comparing and distinguishing those phantasms; which we could never do, if that motion in the organ, by which the phantasm is made, did not remain there for some time, and make the same phantasm return. Wherefore sense, as I here understand it, and which is commonly so called, hath necessarily some memory adhering to it, by which former and later phantasms may be compared together, and distinguished from one another. Sense, therefore, properly so called, must necessarily have in it a perpetual variety of phantasms, that they may be discerned one from another.[114]

For Hobbes, one cannot have genuine sensation and thought without memory: motion by itself, without the structures necessary to retain motion and make comparison possible, is not sensation for Hobbes. What that structure is for Hobbes is just the complex structure of the brain and the nervous system, including the heart, which, once put into motion, will retain the motion (that is, sensation). Now, it is not unreasonable to see Leibniz's account of mind and body in these years as a direct extension of Hobbes's view.[115] The earliest appearance of the momentary minds view I know of comes up in a context that suggests its origin in reflections on Hobbes on sensation, in the letter to Hobbes of July 1670. He writes:

I wish also that you had expressed yourself more distinctly about the nature of mind. For although you have rightly defined sensation as an enduring [permanens] reaction, ... there is no truly enduring reaction in the nature of mere corporeal things. It only appears so to the senses but is in truth discontinuous and is always

---

[114] De corpore 25.5.   [115] Cf. Wilson (1997), 343.

stimulated by a new external cause. So I fear that when everything is considered, we must say that in beasts there is no true sensation, but only an apparent one, any more than there is pain in boiling water. . . .[116]

Note that the point of Leibniz's remarks here is precisely to distinguish minds from bodies, which he doesn't yet call momentary minds. But he will be a bit clearer about that a few months later, in the *TMA*. In later texts he will be more explicit about the nature of the structure that retains conatus and is therefore genuinely sentient: the structure that retains motion is not the brain or the nervous system, *but something that exists at a point, a mind.* As Leibniz wrote to Duke Johann Friedrich in May 1671:

Indeed the doctrine of the point and angle, instant and conatus . . . will be, for me, the key to explaining the nature of thought. For I shall demonstrate that mind consists in a point, that thought is conatus or a smallest motion, and that there can be several conatus in the same [mind] at the same time, though not with motion.[117]

Bodies have motion, of course: but they don't retain contrary motions. At the moment of collision the contrary conatus are resolved into a single conatus, which is immediately realized as motion in time. In this way they lack a "memory" of the motions that have gone into their present state. At the moment of collision they may have as many contrary conatus as there are bodies in collision; at that moment they are, in that sense *like* minds. But insofar as the multiplicity of conatus in the single thing lasts only a moment, bodies are just *momentary* minds. Which is to say, they are not really minds at all. In this way Leibniz's account of body as momentary mind should *not* be understood as a way of bringing mentality to the world of bodies, but quite the contrary: it is a way of drawing a *real distinction* between body and mind. The ellipsis in the quotation from *TMA* § 17 above reads as follows: "This opens the door to the true distinction between body and mind, which no one has explained before."[118] Or, as he explains at greater length to the Duke Johann Friedrich on October 1671, "In Natural Theology I can demonstrate from the nature of motion I have discovered in physics that . . . there is incorporeal mind, that mind acts on

---

[116] A2.1^2.93–4 (L 107). There is another reference to the denial of sensation to animals in a short essay "De usu et necessitate demonstrationum immortalitatis animae," attached to his letter to Johann Friedrich, 21 May 1671, A2.1^2.178.

[117] A2.1^2.181; cf. A2.1^2.279 (L 149).   [118] A6.2.266 (L 141).

➡ *Mind acts on itself*

itself, that no action on itself is motion, but that there is no action of a body except motion, and *thus that mind is not body*."[119]

But how many minds are there, and what is it that they do? Well, there is certainly God, and there are certainly human minds. But there are a few texts that suggest that there may be numerous other minds as well. Earlier in this chapter we discussed the bubbles (*bullae*) that are the ultimate particles of which the physical world is composed. In the *HPN* these *bullae* are purely material, made hard by virtue of their internal motion. However, in at least a few passages that may be contemporary with the first physics, Leibniz argues that we must add minds to these tiny vortices. In a fragment that the Akademie editors date from 1670–71, after introducing the idea of particles hard by virtue of their internal motion, Leibniz continues:

[P]*rimary matter is nothing if it is at rest*. And this is what certain scholastics said obscurely when they said that primary matter even obtains its existence from form. There is a demonstration of this. For whatever is not sensed is nothing. But that in which there is no variety is not sensed. Similarly: *If all primary matter were to move in one direction, that is, in parallel lines, it would be at rest*, and consequently would be nothing. *Everything is a plenum*, since primary matter and space are the same. Therefore *every motion is circular*, or is composed of circular motion, or at least joins back up with itself. The several circulations will mutually obstruct each other, or act one upon another. *Several circulations will endeavour to unite into one*, that is, all bodies tend towards rest, i.e. annihilation. *If bodies are devoid of mind, it is impossible for motion to have been eternal*.[120] *The conflicting universal circulations give rise to the particular ones, i.e. bodies. Matter is actually divided into infinite parts. There are infinitely many creatures in any body whatever*. . . .[121]

Leibniz's idea here is somewhat obscure, but it does look as if he is arguing that we somehow have to introduce minds into the swirls of matter

---

[119] A2.1².265, my emphasis; cf. A2.1².147. Here is another interesting passage. After giving this account of mind and its distinction from body in an untitled essay from 1671, Leibniz adds: "If anyone denies this because I have demonstrated that body is [identical to] mind, he would certainly be forced to admit that it is something completely different from other bodies, and that from this all the phenomena of mind can be clearly and distinctly explained" (A6.2.285).

[120] The Akademie editors remark that Gerhardt notes that over the last words Leibniz wrote: "it would diminish without end."

[121] A6.2.280 (RA 344). Cf. also the "Propositiones quaedam physicae" (1672), A6.3.66–8, where Leibniz offers a similar argument for the necessity of introducing mind into the mechanist's world. This text looks much like the earlier "Confessio naturae," discussed above, where Leibniz tries to show that if we take the mechanical philosophy seriously, we are led to posit God and mind rather than to deny them.

that make up the ultimate parts of bodies in order to save motion from diminishing continually.[122] A version of this idea will come up again later in the mid-1670s, as we shall see below in Chapter 2. But it is interesting that this idea doesn't seem to make its way into the *HPN*. There is every reason to believe that at this moment, it was a philosophical speculation that Leibniz considered, but did not consider sufficiently sound to include in his published writings. But on this view, Hobbesian bodies would contain not only human minds, but minds everywhere. Such minds would not explain human cognition and reason, but the persistence of motion in the world.

Let me sum up my reading of Leibniz so far. There are non-extended minds, distinct from extended bodies. These minds exist in mathematical points in body. And body is made up of a real infinity of extended parts, though some of them small enough to be considered *physical* points. Furthermore, there is a real relation between body and mind insofar as both are understood in terms of the unifying notions of motion and conatus, its instantaneous part. Furthermore, while every mind is *in* a body, as I read him, Leibniz does not want to *reduce* body to mind: to say that every body is a momentary mind is to say precisely that it is *not* a mind. In this way, as I read him, Leibniz seeks only to introduce genuine mentality into Hobbes's world without subverting it.[123] I do not want to deny the importance of mentality in Leibniz's world in this early "mechanist" period. It is very obviously of great importance to him in the *TMA* and related writings. And it continues to be of importance to him in still other ways throughout this decade, even before, as he tells Remond in 1714, he was led back "from the material to the formal." But I also don't want to read too much into these mentalistic intrusions into his early mechanism: this is *not* the monadology, or any anticipation of the monadology. I want to interpret Leibniz's first view of the physical world as a kind of heterodox Hobbesianism, a kind of Hobbesian mechanical philosophy to which Leibniz has added mind, not to *replace* body but to *supplement* it.

Christia Mercer has advanced a monadological reading of Leibniz's early texts on somewhat different grounds. According to Mercer, "by

[122] Since 'mind' here is singular, one might argue that he has God in mind as the preserver of motion. However, in the parallel passage in A6.3.67, he is clearly talking about adding minds in the plural: "Therefore it is necessary to add mind to matter, that is, it is necessary for us to assume incorporeal substances."

[123] Catherine Wilson offers a similar reading of the young Leibniz in Wilson (1997).

the winter of 1670–71, Leibniz has decided to reject the reality of inert extended matter, to conceive the passive principle in corporeal substance as a collection of mind-like substances, and to describe the interrelations among the latter in panorganic terms."[124] In short, she holds that Leibniz had adopted something very close to the mature monadology by 1671. Mercer's case is based on a number of specific texts that can be read as putting forward her view, as well as a general claim that Leibniz's thought in the period must be read in the context of the neo-Platonism of his teachers and his theological commitments. While her carefully developed case deserves a more careful examination than I can give it here, I can indicate some of the reasons why I don't follow her interpretation.

Some of her case is based on the passages discussed earlier in this chapter that identify existence with being sensed.[125] As I argued earlier, these can be given a rather different interpretation than the one that she gives. In other cases, I think some of Mercer's arguments rest on misreadings of key texts. For example, she wants to read Leibniz's appeal to an all-pervading aether in the *HPN* and related texts in terms of a neo-Platonic and vitalistic World Soul.[126] But writing about this aether to Pierre Carcavy on 22 June (?) 1671, Leibniz notes:

For even if several interpreters have absurdly peddled the view that this [i.e., the universal spirit] is incorporeal, nevertheless, it is sufficiently well established that for those who are sensible, this spirit (to which it is not necessary to attribute an intellect) is nothing but a subtle body.[127]   → Aether is a body.

Similarly, she argues that "Leibniz's solution to the Problem of Cohesion depends on the insertion of an infinity of momentary minds into matter."[128] But when you look at texts where Leibniz discusses the coherence of bodies, it is the coincidence or interpenetration of their boundaries that is at issue; minds don't enter at all.[129] In support of her reading, she quotes the following excerpt from a letter to Oldenburg, 28 September 1670:

Nor is it possible that there be any other convincing explanation of the connection among things other than that which refers to incorporeal beings and

---

[124] Mercer (2001), 298; cf. 256.   [125] See ibid., 319–21.
[126] See ibid., 270ff.   [127] A2.1^2.209–10.   [128] Mercer (2001), 267.
[129] See, e.g., *TMA*, "fundamenta praedemonstrabilia" §§ 15–16, A6.2.266 (L 141).

their extraordinary activity which is perpetual. . . . Nor is it possible that the world . . . lacks or has lacked incorporeal beings.[130]

Actually, the last phrase ("Nor is it possible . . .") comes from somewhat later in the letter, where Leibniz is listing some further consequences of his larger physical theory, and is not connected with his account of cohesion. Returning to the beginning part of the passage, the Latin reads:

Nec possibilis est alia ratio solida connexionis in rebus, nisi entibus incorporalibus evocatis perpetuoque extra ordinem concursu alligatis.[131]

Hall and Hall translate this as follows in their edition of the Correspondence of Oldenburg:

Nor is any other sound theory of the connection between things possible, unless some incorporeal entities are evoked and they are bound together in some perpetual praeternatural arrangement.[132]

On this more plausible reading of the Latin, Leibniz's point is that if you reject his purely physical account of coherence, you will have to introduce minds in an implausible way to explain the physics of coherence.

This, of course, does not refute Mercer's argument. The only real answer is to give an alternative reading of Leibniz's development that better coheres with the texts of the period and with the larger story of the development of his thought, which is what I have tried to do in this chapter and in this book.

There are very important methodological reasons for being cautious about readings that pick out elements of his earlier thought that seem to us suggestive of the later monadology, and give them special prominence. While *we* may know where Leibniz was ultimately heading, at that moment Leibniz himself didn't. It is not surprising that we can find in the young Leibniz hints of where he will ultimately wind up; indeed, it would be surprising if we couldn't. They can be used retrospectively, perhaps, to illuminate the origin of views that Leibniz will later come to hold. But these hints have a significance for us that they almost certainly did *not* have for the young Leibniz at the moment when he wrote them. To pull them out, and give them special prominence because of our own perspective

---

[130] A2.1².104, quoted in Mercer (2001), 267.   [131] A2.1².104.
[132] Oldenburg (1965–86), vol. 7, 168–9.

on Leibniz's career is fundamentally to distort those earlier writings, to see them from the point of view of where they will lead, and not from the point of view of whence they derive. The burden of proof is clearly on any commentator who wants to read later views back into earlier texts. It is, of course, impossible completely to erase from our consciousness what we now know about where Leibniz went, and where philosophy went. But even so, that hardly justifies abandoning all attempts at reading Leibniz's earlier writings in an objective and non-teleological way.

Substance, Substantial forms, and the Mysteries of Faith

Before leaving for Paris with the young Leibniz, I want to return briefly to the early theological writings that I have mentioned a few times already. In general, I have been emphasizing the extent to which Leibniz was a heterodox Hobbesian in these years before going to Paris—a Hobbesian in physics, though, unlike Hobbes, he admitted minds. However, Leibniz's early theological musings lead us in an interestingly different direction. Leibniz's physics led him to an ontology of bodies and minds, and a physics in which everything is explicable in terms of size, shape, and motion. However, despite his conversion to mechanism, there is a sense in which his Aristotelian heritage continued to exert considerable influence on his theological views.

This comes out clearly in Leibniz's essay, "De transsubstantione" (1668?), part of the early "Demonstrationes catholicae" project discussed above.[133] In that text Leibniz is attempting to make sense of the possibility of transubstantiation: the idea that at the moment that it is consecrated, the host is transformed from one kind of substance into another, from bread to body of Christ. Now, in order to deal with this problem, Leibniz needs to make clear what it is to be a substance. He proposes that "a substance is a being which subsists within itself," and "a being which subsists in itself is that which has a principle of action within itself." Now, "the essence or definition of a body is being in space," from which it follows that "every action of a body is motion." But "no body has a principle of motion

---

[133] On Leibniz's early thought about the Eucharist, see, e.g., Fouke (1992).

within itself apart from a concurrent mind." And "therefore, no body is to be taken as a substance, apart from a concurrent mind." And so, Leibniz concludes this part of the argument with the following conclusion:

Something is substance when taken together with a concurrent mind; something taken apart from concurrent mind is accident. Substance is union with mind, Thus the substance of the human body is union with the human mind, and the substance of bodies which lack reason is union with the universal mind, or God. . . . Thus the substance of body is union with a sustaining mind.[134]

This view seems to persist even after the composition of the *TMA* and the *HPN*. A couple of years after writing the "De transsubstantione," in November 1671, after the publication of the *TMA* and the *HPN*, Leibniz explicitly refers back to this discussion in explaining to Arnauld how, on his view, transubstantiation can be made intelligible.[135] There he explains his position in similar terms:

[T]he essence of body doesn't consist in extension . . . but in motion, and thus the substance or nature of body is the principle of motion (for there is no absolute rest in bodies), something also consistent with Aristotle's definition. Moreover, the principle of motion or substance of body lacks extension.[136]

And from this, the account of transubstantiation follows directly:

If a body consecrated and appropriated by the mind of Christ has the same concurrent mind as the glorious body of Christ who suffered for us . . . it has numerically the same substantial form or the same substance as the body of Christ who suffered for us. . . . Accordingly the bread and wine in transubstantiation are the numerically identical substance as the body of Christ who suffered for us.[137]

And thus transubstantiation is possible. → *But this has the consequence that anything appropriated by God is substantially identical to Christ's body, all blessing is Eucharistie, Totally wrong!*

---

[134] A6.1.508–9 (L 115–16).

[135] A2.1².281. There he talks about how four years earlier he had explained to Boineburg the possibility of transubstantiation. There is every reason to think that he is referring to the "De transsubstantione" in this connection.

[136] Ibid.

[137] A6.1.509 (L 116). Basically the same account of transubstantiation is given in the Arnauld letter. The main idea seems to be that in transubstantiation, when the host is consecrated, the "concurrent mind" that makes the host a substance is replaced by the mind of Christ. But it is difficult to reconcile this with the fact that Christ is one of the three persons of the Trinity that makes up God. Does the sustaining God have a mind different from each of the three persons who make him up? Does each of the persons of God also have a separate mind? Is it God the Father who is the concurrent mind for non-human things, while Christ replaces God the Father at the moment of the consecration? It seems that this is an issue that the young Leibniz hasn't exactly thought through.

Theologically confused: the Three Persons of the Trinity don't "make up" God as parts, but each is fully God.

Leibniz's account of transubstantiation involves an appeal to substantial form and to an Aristotelian conception of substance. He writes, again in the "De transsubstantione":

I demonstrate the numerical identity of substance from the numerical identity of substantial form, in conformity with the principles of the noblest scholastic and Aristotelian philosophers, those for whom substantial form is the principle of individuation. I define transubstantiation as change of substantial form. . . . To make the consistency appear even greater, the same interpretation of substantial form follows from another principle of Aristotle and the scholastics. For Aristotle himself, and the noblest of his followers, agreed that substantial form is the nature. The nature is the principle of rest and motion. Therefore, even in Aristotle's sense, substantial form is the principle of rest and motion.[138]

The claim that the "substance of body" is incorporeal might suggest, again, that Leibniz is subscribing to a kind of monadological idealism here. But that isn't what is going on in these passages. The "substance of body" is the substantial form, that which transforms the body into a genuine substance; while it is incorporeal, the union of body and soul (form) as a whole is certainly not. Leibniz is emphasizing his orthodox Aristotelianism here, and Aristotle and his followers were certainly not idealists.

Leibniz articulates a similar theory to deal with the problem of understanding the resurrection of the body at the Second Coming. This view is articulated in a letter to Johann Friedrich, 21 May 1671, to which he attaches an appendix, "De resurrectione corporum."[139] On that view, "every body, both man and beast, plants and minerals have a kernel of substance," which he calls the "flower of substance."[140] This kernel of substance is extremely small, though finite in size, a physical point in which the soul resides at a mathematical point:

This kernel of substance, consisting in a physical point (which is the proximate instrument and as it were the vehicle of the soul, which is located in a mathematical point) endures forever.[141]

This kernel of substance is so small and hard that it cannot be destroyed by any physical means: "it is not diminished by teeth or by stomach acid"

---

[138] A6.1.511 (L 117–18).   [139] A2.1².175 and 183–5.
[140] A2.1².175, 185.   [141] A2.1².176.

and is "so subtle that it even remains in the ashes when the thing is burned."[142] By virtue of containing our soul, this kernel, the flower of substance, will be at the core of our resurrected body, and will identify us as the individuals that we are. While he doesn't explicitly use the term "substantial form" to characterize the soul that resides in the kernel of substance, the view is intended to provide an alternative to the "philosophia Democritica" according to which "the entire essence of bodies is explained through magnitude, shape and motion,"[143] and bears more than a passing resemblance to the more explicit appeal to the Aristotelian conception of substance at work in his account of transubstantiation. *More heresies: soul remains in body at death*

In this way, Leibniz's attempt to articulate a metaphysics adequate to account for the mysteries of faith in a way satisfactory to a spectrum of different and competing views led him to hang tightly to the scholastic notion of a substantial form. This would seem to sit rather uncomfortably with his adherence to the mechanical philosophy, one would think. But uncomfortable as it might be, Leibniz's position is not formally inconsistent. It is fully consistent for Leibniz to hold that *bodies* are roughly as mechanist physics conceives of them, as extended, impenetrable, and mobile entities, and all of the phenomena that pertain to physics proper can be explained entirely in terms of size, shape, and motion, while at the same time holding that, for the purposes of theology, bodies are constituents of *substance*, bodies together with substantial forms. *Substance* so explained allows us to understand the supernatural and miraculous happenings that Catholic theology posits, the transformation of the host into body of Christ, while leaving *body* to the physicist. In this way Leibniz can subscribe to a mechanist conception of body and physics while at the same time he holds a kind of Aristotelian account of substance. There is no contradiction: physics deals with bodies, and theology deals with substances. But while not inconsistent, the two domains, physics and theology, seem to pull in somewhat different directions.[144]

---

[142] A2.1².185, 175.   [143] A2.1².183.

[144] Lea Schweitz in personal correspondence also suggested that this separates the domains of theology and physics in a very un-Leibnizian way, reminiscent of Stephen J. Gould's theory of the two non-overlapping magisteria. Fouke (1992) also argues for a closer connection between the two domains. The two domains are connected, as the "Confessio naturae" argues. But even so, there does seem to be something of a metaphysical disconnect between the mechanical philosophy and the theology, a gap waiting to be bridged in his later years.

Leibniz goes to Paris: Continuity and Transition (1672–1678)

In March 1672, the young Leibniz arrived in Paris, under the sponsorship of his patron, the Baron von Boineburg. The people he met and the ideas that he encountered there were to change his views considerably. In Paris and beyond, after he returned to Germany in 1676, Leibniz seems to have been working at a fever pitch; the notes that remain from these years are rich with speculation and reflection about a variety of topics. As we document some of Leibniz's later views, we shall come back and examine more carefully their roots in the speculations of this fertile period. But even though there is a great deal of ferment and experiment, and notable discoveries, as we shall see, at least some of his views about body and substance remain reasonably stable through the period. At very least one can say that even though he is experimenting with many new ideas, there is reason to believe that his considered views about the physical world remain largely unchanged through much of his stay in Paris.

While there are various notes and drafts, Leibniz didn't attempt a major statement of his views on physics in his Paris years or in the years that immediately followed.[145] Even so, there is reason to believe that he

---

[145] At the beginning of A6.3 the Akademie editors give a number of texts from the early to the mid-1670s that relate to Leibniz's physics. The most important are:

(1) 'Propositiones quaedam physicae' (A6.3.4–72), an extensive series of manuscripts tentatively dated between early in the year and fall 1672.

(2) A series of manuscripts that they date to fall 1672, and group under their title 'Demonstratio substantiarum incorporearum' (A6.3.73–93). The title comes from Leibniz's own title for the first of the series. While it is appropriate for that ms., in general these manuscripts are more concerned with questions about physics and the physical world.

(3) A manuscript that the editors entitle 'Principia mechanica' and date tentatively 1673–76 (A6.3.101–11). The title here is not altogether appropriate; the main subject is rather motion than mechanics. We shall discuss this in some detail below in Ch. 3, where I shall argue that various elements of the text suggest innovations in Leibniz's thought that appear only in 1676.

Also of note is Leibniz's long letter to Honoratus Fabri from early 1677 (A2.1².441–66), where he reaffirms the spirit of his earlier approach to physics in the HPN and the TMA. However, unlike in his earlier writings, Leibniz here argues that there is no vacuum: see esp. A2.1².450. See also a note from 12 December 1676, where he writes: "there is no vacuum, whether interspersed or great, since it is possible for all things to be filled" [A6.3.585 (SR 109)]. But his position is actually rather complex. In a note from 11 February 1676, Leibniz argues that there is a metaphysical vacuum, but that that is consistent with a physical plenum. See A6.3.473 (SR 23–5.) Leibniz's position seems to be that

continued to hold the view of body in terms of extension, impenetrability, and motion.[146] For example, in a set of notes on Descartes's *Principia Philosophiae*, probably written in late 1675, Leibniz scolds Descartes for not recognizing that in addition to extension, one needs to place impenetrability in bodies:

To me it seems that there is a certain quality besides extension that cannot be taken away from body, namely, impenetrability, i.e. what makes one body yield to another; and I do not see how this could be derived from extension.[147]

In those same notes, he also refers to the view he had expressed earlier in the decade, that the essence of body is motion:

He defines motion by the translation of bodies from the vicinity of other bodies, but it seems to me that the nature of body should be explained through motion.[148]

As in the earlier years, he continues to hold that bodies are divided to infinity. He writes in the dialogue "Pacidius Philalethi":

[T]here is no portion of matter that is not actually divided into further parts, so that there is no body so small that there is not a world of infinitary creatures in it. . . . This does not mean, however, either that a body or space is divided into points, or time into moments, because indivisibles are not parts, but the extrema of parts. And this is why, even though all things are subdivided, they are still not resolved all the way down into minima.[149] *Approach minima*

while space and body are distinct from one another, there is (almost) no empty space. See A6.3.526 (SR 89) and A6.3.585 (SR 111). On Leibniz's views of the vacuum at the end of the Paris years, see Beeley (1996b), 29–30. Leibniz's first letters with Malebranche, which date from early 1676, are concerned with the existence of a vacuum and the distinction between body and space. See A2.1².398–401 and A2.1².403–6.

[146] This isn't to say that there weren't changes and important conceptual innovation in the period. On Leibniz's views on body in this period and his early critiques directed specifically at Descartes, see Fouke (1991). Among the most important discoveries, Leibniz first articulated the principle of the equality of cause and effect in the summer of 1676, and the conservation of mv^2 in January 1678, as we shall discuss below in some detail in Ch. 3. But it wasn't for a few years until Leibniz put these together and articulated a new conception of the physical world.

[147] A6.3.215 (RA 25).   [148] Ibid.

[149] A6.3.565–6 (RA 209–11). See also earlier in the dialogue, A6.3.555 (RA 185–7); A6.3.513 (RA 119); A6.3.524 (RA 61). Sam Levey argues that the "folded matter" view of infinite divisibility dates from the "Pacidius Philalethi"; see Levey (1998) and Levey (1999). While I find his analysis of these texts very illuminating and convincing, I suspect that the view goes back at least as far as the infinitely nested "bubbles" of the *HPN*. Note, though, at least one passage from 1676 in which Leibniz says that the infinite division of bodies entails that bodies are divided into points: A6.3.474 (RA 49). It may be that Leibniz was experimenting with this position, or it may be that by 'point' here he means *physical* point, and not mathematical point.

During these years it is also reasonable to think that Leibniz never gave up one of the central features of the physics of the *TMA* and *HPN*, the view that bodies in and of themselves offer no resistance to the acquisition of new motion, and that the only such resistance can arise from motion itself. In a fragment dated December 1675, he wrote: "We have assumed by a kind of prejudice that a greater body is harder to move, as if matter itself resisted motion."[150] In another fragment, probably from the same period, Leibniz makes an attempt to explain the apparent resistance of bodies to the acquisition of motion in collision through physical hypotheses about elasticity and the division of matter into smaller parts, a strategy much like the one that he used in the *HPN* to reconcile the phenomena with the underlying laws of motion.[151] In general, throughout this period he seems to hold to the view that everything can be explained mechanically, and that the substantial forms of the schoolmen have no role to play at all in physics. As he wrote to Herman Conring on 19/29 March 1678:

I recognize nothing in the world but bodies and minds, and nothing in minds but intellect and will, nor anything in bodies insofar as they are separated from mind but magnitude, figure, situation, and changes in these, either partial or total. Everything else is merely said, not understood; it is sounds without meaning. Nor can anything in the world be understood clearly unless it is reduced to these.[152]

Leibniz did experiment with using mind to explain various features of the physical world during these years, as we shall later see, but there is no reason to believe that in these years he abandoned his considered view that the heterodox Hobbesian view of the mechanical philosophy that he adopted before leaving for Paris is, in its essentials, correct.

There seems to be even less in the way of theology later in the 1670s. Leibniz's earlier interests in theology had been fueled by his relations with Boineburg, and after Boineburg's death in 1672, he seemed to put

---

[150] A6.3.466 (RA 31).

[151] A6.4.1959–60. The Akademie editors date this fragment from 1677, entirely on the basis of content. However, it seems to me more plausible that this fragment should come from sometime before summer 1676 for reasons I will discuss below in Ch. 3, when we return to this text.

[152] A2.1².604–5 (L 189); cf. A6.4.1972–3 (L 173). Cf. Leibniz to Conring, 3/13 January 1678, A2.1².580–1.

these issues aside.[153] While his interest in the "Demonstrationes catholicae" project was to revive only in 1679, there is every reason to believe that his basic positions on issues relating to the metaphysical grounds of real presence, transubstantiation, and resurrection remained the same. In an untitled piece, which the Akademie editors date at 1673–75, Leibniz offers an account very reminiscent of his earlier theological metaphysics. Leibniz complains that a purely mechanist account of body in terms of absolute impenetrability such as Gassendi proposed "contradicts both the decrees of our faith and the doctrine of polytopia [i.e., being in several places at the same time], and it is just as difficult to see how a body can be in several places as it is to see how several bodies can be in the same place."[154] To address this difficulty, Leibniz suggests adding to body a principle of activity or, "as the scholastics called them, substantial forms, things which also illuminate Natural Theology and the mysteries of faith. . . ."[155] Once we have the true concept of substance, Leibniz thinks, just as he earlier did, that we can make sense of the theological doctrine of multipresence, the presence of the Christ in the host in many places at once. Similarly, in a note from February 1676, Leibniz refers explicitly to the earlier note that he had written for Duke Johann Friedrich on the possibility of resurrection of the flesh.[156] In that note he repeats the doctrine that he had explained to the Duke, that the soul is contained in a small part of the body that cannot be destroyed through natural means, and that this soul united to a tiny piece of the body is what fixes the identity of the person: "I think that the flower of substance is our body. This flower of substance subsists perpetually in all changes. . . . It is easily seen from this why cannibals, devouring a man, have no power over the flower of substance. This flower of substance is diffused through the whole body, and in a way it alone contains form."[157]

---

[153] I consider the "Confesio philosophi" of 1672/3, discussed below in Ch. 6, as belonging to this earlier period of his theological interests.

[154] A6.3.158. The word 'polytopia' is in Greek in Leibniz's text. Originally Leibniz had written 'Eucharistia.'

[155] Ibid.

[156] "Six years ago his Serene Highness the Duke of Hanover, who was in the habit of meditating about religion, instructed Boineburg to seek out my opinion about the resurrection of the flesh. I put this together in a short paper, which I then sent to the Duke" A6.3.478 (SR 33).

[157] Ibid.

A New Direction: Substantial Forms
and the Mechanical Philosophy

But in the late 1670s, in 1678 or 1679, Leibniz seems to make a decisive break with his past views, and starts on what is substantially a new direction. A number of commentators characterize the change as the revival of substantial forms.[158] This is not altogether incorrect. Some of Leibniz's own announcements in this period suggest that he thought of it in this way too. In autumn 1679, Leibniz announces dramatically in a letter to Duke Johann Friedrich (by then his employer at Hanover), "I reestablish substantial forms with demonstrative certainty [*démonstrativement*] and explain them intelligibly . . ."[159]

But matters are more complex than this simple account would suggest. In a way, substantial forms go back at least a decade to the end of the 1660s; there is a sense in which he never abandoned them, despite what he would tell Remond many years later about his philosophical development. Indeed, Leibniz's comments to Johann Friedrich are in the context of an attempt to interest his patron in his project for unifying the churches under the Leibnizian philosophy, and a revival of the project of the "Demonstrationes catholicae" that he had worked on for Boineburg a decade or so earlier. But throughout this period, substantial forms were largely restricted to theology: in theology what was important was substance, transubstantiation, and multipresence, and for this one needs substantial form. But in physics substantial forms were largely left behind.[160] This is how he explains his revival of substantial forms to Johann Friedrich in another letter from the same months:

Now, it is well-known that without these forms and without the difference that there is between them and real accidents, it is impossible to maintain our

---

[158] Robinet (1986), ch. 5; Fichant (1993a) and Fichant (1993b).

[159] A1.2.225; cf. A2.1².754.

[160] This is certainly true of Leibniz's thought before he went to Paris, but things may have changed during his years on the Seine. As we shall later see, in various of the notes from Paris and the years that immediately follow, Leibniz is playing with the idea that mind, soul, and form are needed to explain particular physical phenomena, as I mentioned earlier. Hannequin (1908), 159ff argues that mentality has a central role in his physics even before the Paris years. But separating out Leibniz's considered view from his philosophical experiments is a delicate business.

mysteries: for if the nature of body consists in extension, as Descartes proposes, it is certainly a contradiction for a body to exist in many places at the same time.[161] *→ Discomfort w/ the idea that the Eucharist is the same body in many places. Why?*

Understood in this way, there would seem to be nothing really new in Leibniz's position: substantial forms had been a central part of his theological metaphysics for at least a decade at the time that he wrote this.

But even so, there *is* a radical change in Leibniz's thought at just that moment. In 1678 or 1679, Leibniz seems to extend substantial forms from theology to physics: substantial forms are important now for body itself, for the concept of body that we need to understand the physical world. He continues to believe, as he had for some time and as he will for the rest of his career, that everything must be explicable mechanically, through size, shape, and motion. But starting in 1678 or 1679, Leibniz begins to articulate a new doctrine: even though everything is explicable mechanically, the foundations of the mechanical philosophy require us to appeal to soul or form.

The earliest documents in which this new program appears form a project for a new book on physics, now dated at summer 1678 to winter 1678/9. In apparent haste, excited by the new view he had just come to, Leibniz scribbled out the plan for a new book, what the Akademie editors have entitled the 'Conspectus libelli,' "an outline of a little book."[162] But the book doesn't look so small to me. It was to have been a book on the elements of physics, a comprehensive treatise giving his new view of the subject, a physics to replace the now-abandoned physics of the *HPN* and the *TMA*,[163] from the most general parts of physics to the study of magnets, elasticity, "meteors, crystals, and other bodily configurations." Connected with the sketch are some paragraphs intended for the introduction to the book. Leibniz never got around to writing the book. Indeed, this is quite typical of his style of working: in his papers there are many such prefaces, outlines, and sketches of books he contemplated writing, vast

---

[161] A2.1².754.

[162] Fichant (1993a) underscores the importance of this work in his translation and commentary.

[163] For Leibniz's later comments on his youthful physics, see his remarks to Foucher in a letter probably written in early 1693, G I 415: "They may contain some good things, since you, among others, have judged them so, Sir. But there are many domains in which I believe that I am better informed at present. . . ."

All in terms of substantial form

projects that he contemplated but never started in earnest. In the preface he sketched there is a bold statement of his new view of a mechanical philosophy grounded in the once-discredited substantial forms of the schoolmen:

Here it will be well, however, to explain a little more distinctly how a middle way can be found, in my opinion, between the scholastic and the mechanistic basis for philosophy; or better, in what sense there is truth on both sides. . . . The mechanists condemn the scholastics . . . as ignorant of what is useful for living, while the scholastics and the theologians who cultivate the scholastic philosophy hate the mechanical philosophers as harmful to religion. . . . This is what I think. Everything is by nature to be understood clearly and distinctly and could be manifested to our understanding by God if he willed to do so. And the operation of a body cannot be understood adequately unless we know what its parts contribute; hence we cannot hope for the explanation of any corporeal phenomenon without taking up the arrangement of its parts. But from this it does not at all follow that nothing can be understood as true in bodies save what happens materially and mechanically, nor does it follow that only extension is to be found in matter. . . . Mathematical science provides magnitude, figure, situation, and their variations, but metaphysics provides existence, duration, action and passion, force of acting, and end of action, or the perception of the agent. Hence I believe that there is in every body a kind of sense and appetite, or a soul, and furthermore, that to ascribe a substantial form and perception, or a soul, to man alone is as ridiculous as to believe that everything has been made for man alone and that the earth is the center of the universe. But on the other hand, I think that when once we have demonstrated the general mechanical laws from the wisdom of God and the nature of the soul, then it is as improper to revert to the soul or to substantial forms everywhere in explaining the particular phenomena of nature as it is to refer everything to the absolute will of God.[164]

This sentiment is repeated over and over again in the years that follow, as Leibniz begins to work out the details of this middle way between the schoolmen and the mechanical philosophers. Everything is explicable mechanically, but the mechanical philosophy itself must be grounded in something that goes beyond the resources that the mechanical philosopher allows himself.[165]

---

[164] A6.4.2009–10 (L 289).

[165] See, e.g., 'Contemplatio de historia literaria' (1682?), A6.4.464–5; 'Discours de métaphysique' §§ 10, 18; letters with Arnauld (G II 58, 78); "Elementa rationis" (1686), A6.4.722; "Spongia exprobrationum" (1686/7), A6.4.735; "Animadversiones in partem generalem Principiorum Cartesianorum"

In the 'Conspectus libelli' Leibniz suggests a few more details about how exactly the appeal to substantial form is supposed to address the inadequacies of the purely mechanist world:

There follows now a discussion of incorporeal things. Certain things take place in body which cannot be explained from the necessity of matter alone. Such are the laws of motion, which depend upon the metaphysical principle of the equality of cause and effect. Therefore we must deal here with the soul and show that all things are animated. Without soul or form of some kind, a body would have no being, because no part of it can be designated which does not in turn consist of more parts. Thus nothing could be designated in a body which could be called 'this thing,' or a unity.[166] *Soul the seat of substance/identity*

This seems to be the crucial moment to which he is referring in the 1714 letter to Remond:

But when I looked for the ultimate reasons for mechanism, and even for the laws of motion, I was greatly surprised to see that they could not be found in mathematics but that I should have to return to metaphysics. This led me back to entelechies, and from the material to the formal. . . .[167]

Though substantial forms had never left Leibniz's thought, a significant milestone is passed when he admits them not only in connection with his theological metaphysics, but also in connection with his natural philosophy. In later chapters we will have to go more deeply into the arguments that lie behind this passage and others like it, and talk in more detail about how exactly the revival of substantial forms in physics is supposed to ground the mechanical philosophy. But it is clear that something has changed fundamentally in Leibniz's thought at this moment.

The Aristotelian account of substance had, for a decade or so, sat uneasily next to a rather radical Hobbesian mechanism. With this new project they come together. Substantial forms, retained perhaps from his earliest years to deal with problems in theology but elsewhere rejected, are

(1692), G IV 391–2 (L409–10); "De primae philosophae emendatione . . ." (1694), GIV 470 (L 433); "Système nouveau," first draft (1694?), G IV 472 (WF 22); "Système nouveau" (1695), GIV 478 (AG 139); etc.

[166] A6.4.1988 (L 278–9). Cf. A6.4.1398–9 (RA 245), which may be from the same period. In connection with this, Goldenbaum (1999a), 81 notes that Leibniz has gone from thinking that animals are mere machines to the view that they have souls. Since souls are substantial forms, this is another manifestation of the new view that Leibniz comes upon at this moment in his development.

[167] G III 606 (L 654–5).

now reintroduced into his physics; the Aristotelian substances that grounded his irenic theology are now the selfsame substances that will ground his physics. With this, the conception of substance needed in theology and the conception of body that grounds the physics are united into one. With this begins the view of corporeal substance that will dominate his thought for some years to come.

The 'Conspectus libelli' suggests two motivations for introducing substantial forms into physics: (i) without a "soul or form of some kind...nothing could be designated in a body which could be called 'this thing,' or a unity," and (ii) soul or form is necessary to explain the laws of motion, "which cannot be explained from the necessity of matter alone." These two considerations will be discussed in the chapters that follow.

Before entering into that discussion, though, let me introduce a brief remark about Leibniz's target in these discussions. His critique is directed at two somewhat different positions. First of all, there is his own earlier view on the nature of body, not always easy to characterize, as we have seen in this chapter. Before the revolution, sometime in the second half of the 1670s, Leibniz clearly believed that bodies contained no internal principle from which resistance could arise, and even though he may have believed in substantial forms for theological reasons, forms played no role in the physics of body. But even so, it was not always clear how exactly Leibniz understood the essence of body. This earlier conception of body is clearly one of Leibniz's targets in the years that follow. In numerous passages, Leibniz will begin the exposition of his own views on body with what is represented as a historical recitation of his previous views, and how he came to reject them: "Once, many years ago, when a callow youth, I believed that...but now, I have come to see the error of my ways—and you should too."[168] These passages have a particular audience, of course. Leibniz thought that his own earlier views on body shared a great deal with the views of the Cartesians, those who followed Descartes in holding that the essence of body is extension, and that bodies are the objects of geometry made real. This view is another target of Leibniz's later critiques, a point

---

[168] A very conspicuous passage is in part I of the "Specimen dynamicum" (1695), GM VI 240f (AG 123f). The "Système nouveau," also from 1695, the first publication of his metaphysical system, is also set out as a kind of intellectual autobiography.

of contrast against which he presented his own view of the make-up of body. Leibniz didn't always carefully distinguish these two targets, and in what follows we won't either. Increasingly, I suspect, it is the Cartesians that he has in mind, and even when he uses his own earlier view as a whipping boy, it is really a stand-in for his Cartesian contemporaries.

2

Reforming Mechanism: Unity

Outline of the little book

In the 'Conspectus libelli' Leibniz wrote:

Without soul or form of some kind, a body would have no being, because no part of it can be designated which does not in turn consist of more parts. Thus nothing could be designated in a body which could be called 'this thing,' or a unity.[1]

In another writing that is probably from the same years, he wrote:

Substantial form, or soul, is the principle of unity and of duration, matter is that of multiplicity and change.[2]

In this chapter we shall explore the notion of unity and individuality in Leibniz's early and middle years, and the way in which it leads him to one conception of corporeal substance as the foundation of his metaphysics.

Earliest Thoughts: Individuality and Identity

Questions of identity and individuation are among the very first topics in philosophy that attracted the attention of the young Leibniz. Leibniz's first philosophical publication was entitled "Disputatio metaphysica de principio individui," published in 1663 at the tender age of 17.[3] The "Disputatio" was a scholastic exercise, a dissertation written under the supervision of his professor, Jacob Thomasius, required for his bachelor's degree at the University of Leipzig. Might Leibniz's later interest in unity and individuality be traced back to this very first philosophical exercise?

The "Disputatio" treats a classical problem in scholastic philosophy, the "principle of the individual": what is it that differentiates individuals

---

[1] A6.4.1988 (L 278–9).   [2] A6.4.1398–9 (RA 245).   [3] A6.1.5–19.

from one another and makes them the individual things that they are?[4] In the course of the short essay, Leibniz considers four different positions: entities can be individuated by way of (1) the whole entity; (2) negation; (3) existence; and (4) *haecceity*. The first is Leibniz's position, as well as that of his teachers. We will return to it after a brief discussion of the three other positions that he rejects.

Position (2), individuation by negation, is somewhat puzzling, and is made more so by the fact that it seems to have no takers: "But I doubt strongly whether it has anyone to defend it, except, perhaps, some obscure nominalist."[5] In its most general form it seems to be the view that things are individuated by intrinsic properties that they lack, rather than intrinsic properties that they have. In particular, they get their identity from their non-identity with another: "Therefore let there be two individuals—Socrates and Plato. Then the principle of Socrates will be the negation of Plato and the principle of Plato will be the negation of Socrates."[6] In another more specific form it seems to go as follows:

[T]he position can be defended in the following manner. From the *summum genus* through differences determined by the subaltern, one should descend to the *infima* species. But there you cannot [descend] further and the negation of further descent would be the formal, intrinsic [principle] of the individual.[7]

Leibniz dismisses this rather quickly.

The third position is that things are individuated by their existence. Leibniz considers this in two cases. If existence is really distinct from essence, then the position is indefensible; if there is only a distinction of reason between the two, then Leibniz claims that this position collapses into the first, that things are individuated by their "whole entity":

But this [position] can be taken in two ways. In one way, existence might be some real mode, intrinsically individuating the thing and distinct *a parte rei* from its essence. If this is the case, it can by no means be defended, as will become clear

---

[4] For a detailed study of the "Disputatio," see chs. 1–4 of McCullough (1996). A briefer account, with reference to modern ways of viewing the problem, can be found in Cover and O'Leary-Hawthorne (1999), ch. 1. Mugnai (2001) begins with the "Disputatio", but discusses aspects of Leibniz's thought about individuation from then up until the 1680s.

[5] "Disputatio" § 11, A6.1.14, translated in McCullough (1996), 37.

[6] Ibid. § 12, A6.1.14 [McCullough (1996), 38].

[7] Ibid. § 11, A6.1.14 [McCullough (1996), 37].

shortly [in §§ 14–15]. But if [existence] differs only in reason from essence, [this position] agrees uncommonly well with us.[8]

In either case, the third position is refuted.

The fourth postion is that things are individuated through their *haecceities*. The idea, which derives from Scotus, is that none of the properties that a thing has in common with other things (so-called "common natures") could individuate it. And so, the claim is, a thing is individuated by its special "thisness" or "haecceitas."[9] Leibniz devotes the largest part of the "Disputatio" to the refutation of this view, presumably because he thought it to be the most serious rival to his own view. In a long series of arguments, he argues against both the view that there is any such thing as common natures, natures that can be instantiated in different individuals, and against the view that there is any such thing as primitive "thisness."[10]

What Leibniz supports in the "Disputatio" is that a thing is individuated "by its whole entity."[11] What exactly does this mean? In 1663, Leibniz seems still to be assuming the scholastic Aristotelian conception of substance understood as matter and form, though he does seem willing at least to entertain the possibility that angels have no matter. And so, the claim is that things are individuated both by the particular form that they have, and by the particular matter that they have, if they have matter at all:

Ramoneda erroneously attacks those who claim that the individual individuates itself and those who say that matter and form supply it [i.e. the principle of individuation], as contradicting each other, since they could instead be understood to be subordinate views, as special instances under the general view. For what is matter and form united except the whole entity of the composite? Add that we here abstract from bodies and angels, so that we preferably employ the term 'whole entity' rather than 'matter and form.'[12]

---

[8] Ibid. § 13, A6.1.14–15 [McCullough (1996), 46].

[9] The position is referred to in ibid. § 16, A6.1.15–16 [McCullough (1996), 54]. The view was so familiar to Leibniz's readers that he doesn't feel the need to give a full exposition of the position. For a discussion of Scotus's conception of haecceity, see McCullough (1996), 51ff.

[10] "Disputatio" §§ 16–26, A6.1.15–18. See the discussion of this view in McCullough (1996), 51–69.

[11] Ibid. § 4, A6.1.11 [McCullough (1996), 100].

[12] Ibid. § 4, A6.1.12 [McCullough (1996), 101]. Leibniz seems to leave accidents out of the picture here; see ibid. § 10, A6.1.14 [McCullough (1996), 103]. This passage gives us good reason to be suspicious of Leibniz's boast to Remond that he was converted to the mechanical philosophy as early as his fifteenth year, which he would have reached in 1661. See G III 606 (L 654–5).

In this way, it would seem that for Leibniz, both matter and form, its 'whole entity' constitutes its principle of individuation.[13]

How seriously should we take this bit of juvenilia? In an often-quoted remark, Benson Mates wrote:

But on the fundamental points of his philosophy, his constancy over the years is little short of astonishing. For instance, from the first of his publications, at age seventeen, to the end of his life he never wavered in holding the rather unusual and implausible doctrine that things are individuated by their "whole being"; that is, every property of a thing is essential to its identity.[14]

But I am skeptical. For one, we must remember that the "Disputatio" was the bachelor's project of a 17-year-old student. As Roger Ariew has emphasized, the point of the disputation was not to defend an original position, but to show off the young student's learning. Ariew also notes that it is no accident that the position that Leibniz defends in the "Disputatio" is that of his teachers. In the "Disputatio" Leibniz defends the nominalists against the Scotists, but "if Thomasius had preferred the Scotist position over that of the nominalists, Leibniz would surely have done the same."[15] Indeed, on the title page of the published "Disputatio," the teacher Thomasius's name is above that of the candidate "Gottfredus Guilielmus Leibnuzius" [sic] and in larger type.

But even so, might one defend the view that this position is what Leibniz held for the remainder of his career? It does, indeed, resemble the view that Leibniz later came to hold in his monadological writings, that monads are individuated by their "whole entity," that is, by virtue of having different internal properties, by differing in their perceptions and appetitions.[16] However, the resemblance is only superficial. When in 1663 the young Leibniz says that things are individuated by their "whole entity," he means that they are to be individuated not by matter alone or by form alone, but by both; contrary to what Mates implies, properties or accidents have no role to play.[17] Even this superficial resemblance holds only if one

---

[13] For more detailed discussions of Leibniz's positive view in the "Disputatio", see McCullough (1996), 6; Cover and O'Leary-Hawthorn (1999), 40–50; and Angelelli (1994).

[14] Mates (1986), 7. In a note Mates adds the following clarification: "Or, perhaps, that every accident of an individual is unique to that individual." This is quoted with full approval in McCullough (1996), 133. Cover and O'Leary-Hawthorne (1999), 3 cite this as well, though the extent to which they agree isn't entirely clear.

[15] Ariew (forthcoming), 5.   [16] See, e.g., 'Monadologie' §§ 8–13.

[17] Again, see "Disputatio" § 10, A6.1.14 [McCullough (1996), 103].

thinks, as some do (but I don't), that Leibniz came to his monadological metaphysics very early in his career.

Relations with the later monadology aside, by the end of the decade, Leibniz had clearly abandoned the "whole entity" conception of individuation for a conception grounded in the substantial form alone.[18] In the essay "De transsubstantione" (1668?), discussed above in Chapter 1, Leibniz writes:

> If a body consecrated and appropriated by the mind of Christ has the same concurrent mind as the glorious body of Christ who suffered for us...it has numerically the same substantial form or the same substance as the body of Christ who suffered for us.... Accordingly the bread and wine in transubstantiation are the numerically identical substance as the body of Christ who suffered for us.[19]

In this way what individuates a substance is not the "whole entity," matter *and* form, but just its form, clearly a rejection of the position adopted in the "Disputatio."[20] And again, as pointed out above in Chapter 1, Leibniz takes a similar position in his discussion of the resurrection of the body in a piece that he wrote on that question for Duke Johann Friedrich in May 1671.[21] There it is the soul, permanently attached to a small bit of matter, too hard to break or destroy, that is the seat of our personal identity. It is by virtue of containing that "flower of substance" that my resurrected body is mine, despite what may have happened to the particular bits of matter that had belonged to me in this first life. Though Leibniz doesn't put it quite as explicitly as he did in the "De transsubstantione," it is not unreasonable, again, to see form as what determines identity. This conception of identity will persist in Leibniz's theological writings through the rest of his career.

The question of a principle of individuation makes another appearance a few years later in an an interesting but somewhat singular fragment found among the notes that have come to be known as *De summa rerum*, notes

---

[18] On this, see, again, Ariew (forthcoming).   [19] A6.1.509 (L 116).

[20] McCullough reads this essay differently, a move, perhaps the first, from an Aristotelian conception of substance to one on which all there are are immaterial substances. Commenting on a passage from "De transsubstantione," he writes: "The extension of substance has been reduced from both material and non-material individuals to the latter alone" [McCullough (1996), 135]. Clearly I think that he is mistaken, and is reading Leibniz's view from rougly thirty years later back into this earlier and rather Aristotelian text.

[21] A2.1.108–9 and 115–17. Note also the reaffirmation of this view in the Paris notes in February 1676, A6.3.478–9 (SR 33–5).

on metaphysical topics that Leibniz wrote in 1675 and 1676 while he was in Paris.[22] One of the pieces, dated 1 April 1676, is entitled "Meditatio de principio individui."[23] Leibniz begins with the assumption that

the effect envelops its cause; that is, in such a way that whoever understands some effect perfectly will also arrive at the knowledge of its cause. For it is necessary that there is some connection between a complete cause and the effect.[24]

However, Leibniz notes, "different causes can produce an effect that is perfectly the same." The example he gives is that of a square, which can be formed from two right triangles, or from two rectangles of appropriate size. Since what appears to be the same effect—a square—can be produced in these two ways, the principle would seem to be violated.[25] Leibniz concludes:

So if we are certain, from some other source, that the effect does envelop its cause, then it is necessary that the method of production must always be discernible in the squares that have been produced. And so it is impossible that two squares of this kind should be perfectly similar; for they will consist of matter, but that matter will have a mind, and the mind will retain the effect of its former state. And indeed, unless we admit that it is impossible that there should be two things which

---

[22] I don't mean to imply that this is the next occasion on which the question of individuation arises in the texts. As Mugnai (2001), 38–40 notes, individuation is at issue in the "Confessio philosophi" of 1672–3. See A 6.3.147. The issue comes up in connection with a theological question, and Leibniz there seems to take the position that he takes nowhere else, that things can be individuated extrinsically by space and time alone. See also Cover and O'Leary-Hawthorne (1999), 60f, where this passage is discussed in connection with their account of Leibniz on relations. I pass over this Leibnizian text because of its apparent singularity.

[23] A6.3.490–1 (SR 51–3).

[24] A6.3.490 (SR 51). I am translating 'involvere' as 'envelops', which captures the sense of the term better than 'involves' does. This seems to echo Spinoza's axiom 4 from part I of the *Ethica*: "The knowledge of an effect depends on, and envelops, the knowledge of its cause." While Leibniz would visit Spinoza later in November of that year and discuss his philosophy, it isn't clear exactly how much he knew of Spinoza's thought when he wrote this essay. There is a summary of some doctrines from the *Ethica*, which the Akademie editors date from October 1675–February 1676, which shows that he had some acquaintance with Spinoza's thought by that time, through Tschirnhaus; see A6.3.384–5. However, that summary doesn't mention the causal axiom. Note, though, Leibniz's comment on a letter from Spinoza to Oldenburg, which he was probably given by Oldenburg in November 1676, on his way to Holland: "In any case, it can be said that all things are one, and all things are in God, in the same way the effect is contained in its full cause, and the property of a subject [is contained] in the essence of the same subject. For it is certain that the existence of things is a consequence of God's nature, which has brought it about that only the most perfect things could be chosen" [A6.3.370. trans. and commented on in Curley (1990), 294]. Hobbes is another possible source for this idea. See A6.3.388, a fragment dated 12 February to April 1676, which gives the causal axiom and attributes the idea to Hobbes.

[25] Leibniz used exactly the same example to make a different point in 1671; see A6.2.327–8.

are perfectly similar, it will follow that the principle of individuation is outside the thing, in its cause.... But if we admit that two different things always differ in themselves in some respect as well, it follows that there is present in any matter something which retains the effect of what precedes it, namely a mind. And from this it is also proved that the effect envelops the cause.[26]

The causal principle that Leibniz adopts ("the effect envelops its cause"), together with the idea that the principle of individuation has to be something internal to a thing, entails that in any material instantiation of a geometrical object, there must be something over and above its geometrical properties, something that retains its causal history and defines the thing as the individual that it is. That something is mind.

I know of no place where Leibniz repeats this argument in this particular form; it may well be a kind of philosophical experiment, an idea sketched in haste and later abandoned. However, the argument resonates with a number of other strands in Leibniz's thought that we will explore in later chapters.[27] It shows the extent to which Leibniz considered mind, soul, and form as central to the identity of an individual in his mechanist 1670s, even before the official reintroduction of substantial forms into physics in 1678-9.

After these early discussions, the scholastic problem of the principle of individuation largely drops out of Leibniz's writings; it is not this strand, after all, that will lead to his mature concerns on unity and individuality. His early concern is with what makes an individual, Gottfried or René, the particular individual that he is. In his later years, the identity of indiscernibles is all that one needs to know about individuation in this sense; the scholastic worries about individuation are, for Leibniz, simply a muddle that derives from the fact that the schoolmen thought that two things could be identical in every way but differ in number alone.[28] But even if Leibniz lost his interest in the abstract metaphysical problem of

---

[26] A6.3.490-1 (SR 51-3).

[27] In particular, it will be connected with Leibniz's principle of the equality of cause and effect, a basic principle that underlies his derivation of the laws of motion, as we shall see in Ch. 3 below. It is also closely connected with the complete concept argument given in 'Discours de métaphysique' § 8, which we shall discuss below in Ch. 5.

[28] See NE2.27.3 and Leibniz's Fifth Paper to Clarke, § 26. Mugnai (2001), 42f links the problem of individuation in Leibniz with his complete concept account of the individual substance. While one might debate the question as to whether the complete concept view is to be seen primarily in connection with the problem of individuation, it is certainly quite important for Leibniz's views in the 1680s. We shall discuss it below in Ch. 5.

individuality, individuals and individuality, and the closely related notion of unity, remained at the center of his thought. Indeed, by the mid- or late 1670s Leibniz came to ground his metaphysics of body and the natural world on the view that there must be genuine individuals, genuine unities, if there is to be anything at all in the world. His concern turns away from what makes individuals the individuals that they are to questions about what makes them individuals at all, and the metaphysical necessity for there to be such individuals in the world.

Unity and Coherence in the 1670s

The worries about unity and individuality that ultimately lead Leibniz to the revival of substantial forms in physics seem first to arise in some reflections on views like those of Descartes, for whom matter is indefinitely divisible. In a passage from the *De summa rerum* dated 18 March 1676, Leibniz wrote:

Whatever is divisible, whatever is divided, is altered—or rather, is destroyed. Matter is divisible, therefore it is destructible, for whatever is divided is destroyed. Whatever is divided into minima is annihilated; but that is impossible.[29]

In another passage written some weeks later, in April 1676, he wrote that "every body which is an aggregate can be destroyed."[30] This is what we might call the "division-to-dust" problem. Leibniz saw a solution to this problem in a kind of atomism.[31] He continues this last passage as follows: "There seem to be elements, i.e. indestructible bodies...."[32] Another passage, probably from the same year, makes the same point: "If there were no atoms, then, given a plenum, all things would be dissolved."[33]

This argument is hardly original with Leibniz. It is, in fact, one of the classical arguments for atomism.[34] But the atoms that Leibniz posits in this context are rather different from the atoms of classical atomism.

---

[29] A6.3.392 (SR 45).   [30] A6.3.521 (SR 81).

[31] For another perspective on Leibniz's early atomism, see Arthur (2006). Arthur's lovely essay connects Leibniz's atomistic speculations in the 1670s to a number of earlier traditions in atomism, particularly that of Daniel Sennert and Pierre Gassendi. See also Arthur (1998a) and Arthur (2003).

[32] A6.3.521 (SR 81).   [33] A6.3.525 (SR 87).

[34] For Epicurus, see the Letter to Herodotus, Diogenes Laertius, *Lives of the Eminent Philosophers* X.41 and X.54, in Diogenes Laertius (1925), vol. 2, 571, 585. The same argument is also found in Lucretius, *De rerum natura* I 215ff.

The atoms in the Paris notes are the direct descendants of the bubbles (*bullae*) of his first physics. Though Leibniz seems not to have been motivated by the division-to-dust problem in the physics of 1671, he was clear there that the world is made up of small coherent parts, in terms of which all the phenomena of nature are to be explained. As briefly discussed above in Chapter 1, in the *HPN* Leibniz held that in the beginning, light streaming from the sun onto the earth produced bubbles of matter. While these bubbles are hard, they are made up of smaller bubbles, which are made up of bubbles smaller still, and so to infinity.[35] As noted above, these bubbles are made hard by virtue of their internal motion. While there are suggestions that these swirls of matter may have been connected with mind, the dominant view, as expressed in the *HPN* and related texts, seems to be that these bubbles are purely material.

This earlier world is very close to the world that Leibniz outlines a few years later in the Paris notes, now in response to the "division-to-dust" problem. In these later texts, individual hard bodies are swirls of matter, what he now explicitly calls vortices, tiny vortices in distinction to the larger vortices that are at issue in cosmology.[36] But in 1676 it seems quite central to Leibniz's view that such individual finite vortices have minds. As Leibniz wrote on 11 February 1676:

Every mind is indissolubly implanted in matter; this matter is of a certain magnitude. Every mind has a vortex around itself. All the globes of the world are perhaps endowed with a mind, nor do the intelligences seem absurd. . . . There are innumerable minds everywhere. . . .[37] ——➤ ie, the vortices are substantial,

In what may be an expression of the same view, following the statement of the "division-to-dust" problem from the fragment of 18 March 1676 quoted above, Leibniz continues with the remark: "Matter in some way has its being from form."[38]

---

[35] The relation between Leibniz's atomism here and the claim that every body is made up of bodies smaller still, to infinity, is explored in Arthur (2003). Arthur argues that this is a paradox only if we think of atomism in the classical Epicurean sense. If we understand that there was also a variety of chemical atomisms available, then the paradox is resolved.

[36] On the "general infinite vortex," see A6.3.474 (SR 25); A6.2.480 (SR 35–7). On the atoms as vortices, see, e.g., A6.3.525 (SR 87): "There are as many unsplittable bodies as there are vortices. . . ."

[37] A6.3.476–7 (SR 31). Cf. also a chapter heading for a project Leibniz was contemplating in early 1676: "On souls; that all things are animated, but that only the immortal soul remembers itself" [A6.3.527 (SR 89)]. Leibniz considered this important enough to put "NB" in the margin. On Leibniz's vortex theory in the Paris notes, see Wilson (1999a).

[38] A6.3.392 (SR 45).

Earlier, when Leibniz contemplated adding mind to the swirls of fluid, it was to preserve their motion, as we saw above in Chapter 1. But by the mid-1670s, Leibniz's reasons for placing minds in these elemental bodies have changed. In one interesting passage from the Paris notes, Leibniz suggests that minds are placed in every hard particle (that is, in every vortex) in order to increase the harmony of the world. Earlier in the fragment dated 11 February 1676 from which we quoted above, Leibniz wrote:

It seems that there is some centre of the entire universe, and some general infinite vortex; also some most perfect mind, or God. This mind, like a soul, exists as a whole in the whole body of the world; the existence of things is also due to this mind. It is the cause of itself. Existence is simply that which is the cause of consistent sensations.... Particular minds exist, in sum, simply because the supreme being judges it harmonious that there should exist somewhere that which understands, or, is a kind of intellectual mirror or replica of the world. To exist is nothing other than to be harmonious; consistent sensations are the mark of existence.[39]

Here Leibniz suggests that the minds scattered throughout nature are a consequence of divine wisdom.

More typical in the Paris notes is the claim that mind is now needed to account for the very hardness of these elemental bodies. A statement of the "division-to-dust" argument that we earlier saw thus goes as follows:

Every body which is an aggregate can be destroyed. There seem to be elements, i.e. indestructible bodies, *because there is a mind in them.*[40]

He writes at greater length in a note from March 1676:

Since therefore I agree, on other grounds, that there is some solid and unbreakable portion of matter, and nothing that holds things together can be admitted in the basic origins of matter, as I believe can easily be proved; and since, again, connection cannot be explained by means of matter and motion alone, ... from all this it follows that thought enters into the formation of matter, and there comes into existence a body which is one and unsplittable, i.e., an atom of whatever size it may be, whenever it has a single mind. Further, there are necessarily produced, simply by the motion of firm bodies, as many vortices as there are firm bodies in nature. And there are as many minds, or little worlds, or perceptions, as there are vortices in the world.... [41]

[39] A6.3.474 (SR 25).   [40] A6.3.521 (SR 81), emphasis added.   [41] A6.3.393 (SR 47).

The view is a little puzzling, though. In the physics of the *HPN* and *TMA*, the internal motion of the *bullae* was posited in order to explain their hardness: hardness is resistance, and the only possible source of resistance that Leibniz had available to him is motion. But when hardness is explained now not in terms of motion, but in terms of mind, why does Leibniz need the internal motion of the particles at all?[42] Perhaps what Leibniz assumes here is that mind causes the motion, which in turn is the cause of the hardness of the particle.

I don't have an answer to this particular puzzle; Leibniz simply doesn't say enough about what he is thinking here for us to do any more than make conjectures. But there are some elements of the mind-in-a-vortex view of the Paris notes that suggests that an interesting transition is in progress. In the passage I just quoted from March 1676, Leibniz talks about "a body which is *one* and unsplittable" coming into existence. And in a fragment dated 15 April 1676, Leibniz offers the following remark:

So my opinion is this: that the solidity or unity of the body comes from the mind; that there are as many minds as there are vortices; that there are as many vortices as solid bodies; that a body resists, and that this resistance is sensation. . . .[43]

A few lines later, Leibniz adds: "It is my view that all true entities or minds, which alone are one, always increase in perfection. . . ."[44] What is interesting here is that the solidity of a body is linked with its *unity*. Unity, in turn, is linked with mind: minds alone are one; they alone are "true entities." I don't want to make too much of a few isolated words, which go against the general drift of Leibniz's thought in these few months as his thoughts are pouring out into these remarkable notes. But they do lead in an interesting direction, away from the problems of coherence and solidity that suggest a kind of physical atomism, and toward problems of unity and genuine individuality that will take him toward what he will later call a metaphysical or substantial atomism in the years to come.

The metaphysics of body we will later see in the 1680s emerges from the Paris notes when he realizes that what he needs is not *physical*

---

[42] The view Leibniz advances here goes back, in a way, to views that he had held before the first physics of the *HPN* and *TMA*. In his earlier writings, Leibniz had appealed directly to God to explain the coherence of bodies, as we discussed above in Ch. 1. See the "Confessio naturae . . .," A6.1.491–2 (L 111–12).

[43] A6.3.509–10 (SR 61).   [44] A6.3.510 (SR 61).

unity—hardness—but *metaphysical* unity, that is, genuine individuality. This transformation seems to have been made by the time of the 'Conspectus libelli':

> Without soul or form of some kind, body would have no being, because no part of it can be designated which does not in turn consist of more parts. Thus nothing could be designated in a body which could be called 'this thing,' or a unity.[45]

These brief sentences seem to stand in for a more complex argument that Leibniz was working out at the time. It was obvious to Leibniz that there is something wrong with a world in which all there is is extended and indefinitely divisible body. Leibniz's worry here is articulated in a number of passages from these years. He argues, for example, that, lacking genuine individuals, extended matter must lack reality:

> For since we have said that body is actually divided into parts, each of which is agitated with a different motion, and since for the same reason each part is again divided, then certainly if we consider matter alone, no point will be assignable that will remain together with another, nor a moment at which a body will remain identical with itself; and there will never be a reason for saying that a body is a unity over and above a point, and the same for longer than a moment. And since points and moments themselves are not things, but bounds, i.e. modes, of things, it follows that if there were only matter in body, there would be no reality or perfection in it.[46]

In another fragment from just a few years later (1682/3), he sets out this worry as an argument:

> (1) I suppose that what has no greater unity than the logs in a bundle of firewood or log pile, or bricks placed one on top of the other, is not properly one entity, but rather entities, although one name can be supposed for them all. And this is true whether they are close together or far apart, and likewise whether those bricks or logs in the pile are arranged together in an orderly way or not, for this does not give them greater unity. . . .
> (2) I also suppose that nothing is intelligible in a body other than extension. . . .
> (3) Finally, I suppose that every body is actually divided into several parts, which are also bodies.

---

[45] A6.4.1988 (L 278–9). Cf. A6.4.1398–9 (RA 245), which may be from the same period. In connection with this, Goldenbaum (1999a), 81 notes that Leibniz has gone from thinking that animals are mere machines to the view that they have souls. Since souls are substantial forms, this is another manifestation of the new view that Leibniz comes upon at this moment in his development.

[46] A 6.4.1399 (RA 245).

From this it follows...that either bodies are mere phenomena, and not real entities, or there is something other than extension in bodies.[47]

What seems to save the reality of the material world is form or soul; as he writes in a fragment contemporaneous with the 'Conspectus libelli': "Substantial form, or soul, is the principle of unity and of duration."[48] In particular, the genuine individual that will ground the reality of the physical world will be a union of body and soul that constitutes an animate creature, what he will call a corporeal substance. As he writes in another fragment that the Akademie editors date as 1683 to 1685: "unless it is animated, or contains within it a certain single substance, corresponding to the soul, which they call a substantial form or primary entelechy, body is no more one substance than a woodpile...."[49] In another note, scribbled on the back of a bill dated 29 March 1683, Leibniz refers to the unities in question as "substantial atoms": "There are as many souls as there are substantial atoms or corporeal substances."[50] In yet another untitled note, dated from 1684 to 1686 by the Akademie editors, Leibniz writes:

An *entity (unity) in itself* [*per se*] is, for instance, a man; an *accidental entity (unity)*—for instance, a woodpile, a machine—is what is only a unity by aggregation, and there is no real union in it other than a connection: perhaps a contact or even a running together into the same thing, or at least an agreement observed by a mind gathering it into a unity. But in an entity in itself some real union is required, consisting...in some unique individual principle and subject of its attributes and operations, which in us is called a soul, and in every body a substantial form....[51]

Leibniz seems to have moved from physical atoms to what he will later call substantial atoms, unities forged not from solidity but from substantial form.

Unfortunately we don't have the documents where Leibniz makes the transition from the division-to-dust argument, which leads to physical atomism, and the more metaphysical considerations that are supposed to take us from the divisibility of body to substantial atoms or corporeal substances. But the nature of the shift is nicely articulated in some

[47] A6.4.1464 (RA 257–9). The Akademie editors date this as winter 1682/3; RA prefers 1678–79.
[48] A 6.4.1399 (RA 245).
[49] A6.4.559 (RA 265). See also A6.4.576; A6.4.627; A6.4.1506 (RA 283).
[50] A6.4.1466 (RA 265).   [51] A6.4.1506 (RA 283).

notes that Leibniz made on the French atomist Gerauld de Cordemoy in 1685.

Leibniz had met Cordemoy in Paris during his visit in the early 1670s.[52] Though a follower of Descartes in most respects, Cordemoy was an atomist as well, something as puzzling to his contemporaries as it is to us. Basic to Cordemoy's view is a distinction between body or bodies on the one hand, and matter on the other. In his *Six discours sur la distinction et l'union du corps et de l'âme* (1666),[53] Cordemoy writes:

Bodies are extended substances. . . . Since each body is only one single substance, it cannot be divided: its shape cannot change, and it is so necessarily continuous, that it excludes every other body.[54]

Matter, on the other hand, is something quite different:

Matter is an assemblage of bodies. Every body, considered as composing this assemblage, is what one properly calls *a part of matter*. . . . Since each body cannot be divided, it can't have parts: but since matter is an assemblage of bodies, it can be divided into as many parts as there are bodies. . . . Every mass is a collection of several substances, and not a substance; . . . it has no extension of its own, but only appears to have it, because every body which composes it, has extension.[55]

The kind of indivisibility that Cordemoy has in mind is *physical* indivisibility: his bodies, his extended substances, are indivisible in the sense that they cannot be split. They are atoms in the classical sense.

The position for which Cordemoy is arguing is not unlike the position that Leibniz himself seems to have held in 1676, though unlike Leibniz, Cordemoy didn't seem to hold that the hard particles he recognized contained smaller particles to infinity, nor did they contain minds. But the resemblance makes Leibniz's comments particularly interesting: his critique of Cordemoy can be read as a kind of reflection on his own earlier position.

---

[52] See A1.2.428–9; Antognazza (2008), 167.

[53] The *Six discours* can be found in a modern edition in Cordemoy (1968). References will be to this edition. Leibniz's notes can be found in A6.4.1797–1800 (RA 274–81). According to the Akademie editors, Leibniz's notes are on Cordemoy (1679), a Latin translation of the work.

[54] Cordemoy (1968), 95–6.

[55] Ibid., 96–7. By 'mass' Cordemoy means here an assemblage of bodies that are intertwined with one another, and (almost) at rest with respect to one another so that they cannot be detached from one another; cf. ibid., 96. Cordemoy distinguishes a mass from a heap (*tas*) or a liquid, but all three are varieties of matter.

Commenting on the *Six discours* in 1685, Leibniz summarizes Cordemoy's view as follows: "It is true that body is an extended substance, but false that matter is a substance. For each and every substance in itself cannot be divided." Leibniz's comment on this summary shows his appreciation for Cordemoy's insights: "The excellent gentleman saw the truth confusedly and through a cloud, but could not set it out [*demonstrare*] clearly."[56] On Leibniz's view, Cordemoy has correctly observed that matter is just an aggregate of substances, substances that have true unity. But Leibniz thinks Cordemoy (and himself at an earlier moment as well) was mistaken in holding that the unity derives from *physical* unsplittability; matter is ultimately made up of unities, but things that are unified in quite a different way. Leibniz writes, again commenting on Cordemoy:

It is notable that first the ordinary Cartesians, who call every extended thing divisible, then the semi-Gassendist Cordemoy, who judges that every substance is indivisible, and truly one, appeal to ideas, perhaps both of which are true, on my view. For if all organic bodies are animated, and all bodies are either organic or collections of organic bodies, then it follows that all bulk [*molis*] is divisible, but that substance itself can neither be divided nor can it be destroyed.[57]

Like the Cartesians, Leibniz wants matter to be infinitely divisible. Yet, at the same time, like Cordemoy, he wants matter to be made up of genuine substances that are genuinely unified. These genuinely unified substances are not the unsplittable atoms that Cordemoy posits, though;

---

[56] A6.4.1798 (RA, 277).

[57] Ibid. Leibniz makes a similar remark in his letter to Arnauld on 28 November/8 December 1686:

I recall that M. Cordemoy, in order to preserve substantial unity in bodies in his treatise about the discrimination between the soul and the body, thought himself obliged to admit atoms, or indivisible bodies possessing extension, so that he could find some regular basis for the creation of a simple entity.... It appears that M. Cordemoy had recognized some part of the truth, but he had not yet seen wherein lies the true concept of a substance, and moreover it is there that the key to the most important knowledge is to be found. (G II 78)

One must be very careful with the notion of an organic body in Leibniz. In Leibniz's vocabulary, an organic body is simply one that is divided into parts or organs, one that has an internal organization. In an unpublished paper, Justin Smith refers to a passage from Anne Conway in this connection: an animal is not "a mere Organical body like a Clock, wherein there is not a vital Principle of Motion" [Conway (1996), 64]. He also cites the following passage from the "Principes de la nature et de la grace" (1714) § 3: "And this body is organic when it forms a kind of automaton or natural machine, which is not only a machine as a whole, but also in its smallest distinguishable parts." For Leibniz what is involved is not only that the body is organized, but that it is infinitely organized, what he calls a "natural machine" to distinguish it from an artificial machine, like a clock. This notion will be discussed below in Ch. 8.

rather, they are the organic bodies Leibniz remarks on in the quotation, organized bodies that are connected with souls. Together with their souls, we can infer, they constitute genuine individuals. But yet, at the same time, insofar as their bodies are made up of smaller parts, smaller organic bodies (corporeal substances), they can be divided still further. Cordemoy made the same mistake that Leibniz himself had made earlier, in the mid-1670s, perhaps even under the influence of the Parisian atomist. By 1685 or so, when he wrote these notes, Leibniz had seen the light.[58] But even though he saw the light, he didn't fail to appreciate that there is something very right about atomism, and that there are elements of atomism that deserve a place in the reformed philosophy that he is attempting to articulate. When he later calls his view a substantial or metaphysical atomism, we should not dismiss the notion as a mere turn of phrase. As with his views on Aristotelianism, Leibniz is eager to take what is true from a variety of sources in fashioning his own view, as he will tell Remond many years later.

Leibniz first seems to have arrived at this view on unity, substance, and the make-up of body as early as 1678 or 1679, as we saw in the 'Conspectus libelli.' But the first clear and extensive exposition of Leibniz's new view would not come until 1686 or 1687, when he renewed his correspondence with Antoine Arnauld.[59]

The Correspondence with Arnauld: Body, Form, and Unity in the Later 1680s

The biggest obstacle to Leibniz's philosophical work in the early 1680s was probably his scheme for draining the silver mines in the Harz mountains,

---

[58] Cf. also Leibniz's remarks in a response to Bossuet (?) from November/December 1692 (?): "La difficulté qu'il y a sur l'unité des corps ne doit point être imprimée. Elle a embarassé Mons. Cordemoy et l'a forcé de recourir aux atomes" [Costabel (1966), 281].

[59] In a famous remark he made to Thomas Burnett in a letter of 8/18 May 1697, Leibniz notes that it has "only been for about 12 years that [he] found [himself] satisfied" with his philosophical thoughts (A.1.14.244). That would put it at 1685 or so. One might suspect that he had the 'Discours de métaphysique' in mind here. But it is the letters with Arnauld that he mentions earlier in the paragraph, and not the 'Discours.' Furthermore, while he certainly must have thought about publishing the 'Discours' while he was writing it, given the care he put into it, there is no later indication that he ever seriously attempted to publish it, or even expressed the intent to publish it. Instead, his first publication of the ideas expressed in the 'Discours' comes in the "Système nouveau" in 1695. For whatever reason, the 'Discours' seems to have been abandoned by its author.

which occupied a great deal of his time from late spring of 1678, when he first broached the subject with his employer, Duke Johann Friedrich, until April 1685, when Duke Ernst August, Johann Friedrich's successor, finally called a halt to the project. (This must have been a great disappointment to Leibniz, who stood to make a great personal fortune from this project, had he been able to get the windmills to work as planned.)[60] But there were many other obstacles as well, other projects such as the first publication of the calculus and his intensive work on formalized languages and logics. There were also various political projects under Duke Ernst August, who became Elector of Hanover when Johann Friedrich died in December 1679, and who, unlike his predecessor as Elector, was largely uninterested in Leibniz's intellectual projects.[61]

It wasn't until early 1686 that Leibniz seems to have had an opportunity to pull some of the threads from the philosophical revolution of 1678/9 together and try to produce a coherent statement of his philosophy. On 1/11 February 1686, in a letter to the Landgrave Ernst von Hessen-Rheinfels, a Catholic convert with whom Leibniz had been exchanging views for some time, Leibniz remarks that he had been "at a place where for some days I had nothing to do," and took the opportunity to compose "a short discourse on metaphysics."[62] The work in question was, of course, the famous 'Discours de métaphysique,' which seems to have been drafted in just a few days. This, in turn, was the starting point of his correspondence with Antoine Arnauld. Arnauld was, at that moment, one of the most celebrated

[60] On Leibniz's project in the Harz mountains, see Aiton (1985), 87–90, 104, 107–14; and Elster (1975), ch. 3.

[61] See Aiton (1985), ch. 5.

[62] G II 11. Throughout I have consulted the excellent Mason translation of the correspondence with Arnauld; Leibniz and Arnauld (1967). Since Mason gives references to the pagination in G II, I will not cite it independently. I often use his translations, frequently with my own silent emendations. I cite the French text in the pagination given in the Gerhardt edition, as is customary. It should be noted that Gerhardt's text is quite obsolete at this point. Geneviève Rodis-Lewis discovered the manuscripts of the letters as Arnauld actually received them and published them in Leibniz (1952). There are important variants between what Arnauld received and what are found in the copies that Leibniz kept of the same letters, the version that Gerhardt published. It is generally thought that the additional text in Leibniz's own copies is, for the most part, later additions, added when he later contemplated publishing them. The text of the letters in Leibniz and Arnauld (1993) is the Gerhardt text, with the variants from Leibniz (1952) indicated. Reinhardt Finster has produced a new edition of the correspondence from the manuscripts; Leibniz and Arnauld (1997), which includes texts not available in the other editions. We still await the definitive text from the Akademie edition.

philosophers in Europe.[63] He had known Descartes, commented on the *Meditations*, and had corresponded with him when only a very young man. (His *Objections* to the *Meditations* were written before he was 30.) Though initially skeptical, he became converted to Descartes's philosophy. Arnauld had, in later years, been the co-author of a Cartesian logic, *La Logique, ou l'art de penser* (known as the *Port-Royal Logic*, published in 1662, with many later editions), which would be widely read for almost two centuries after its first publication. He was also a participant in a celebrated controversy with Nicolas Malebranche, which was the talk of philosophical circles in the early 1680s.[64] It could not have been unproblematic for Leibniz that Arnauld was also associated with the Jansenist movement, and for that reason not entirely representative of Catholic orthodoxy. But even so, Arnauld's fame and accomplishments made it highly desirable for Leibniz to link his name with Arnauld's. It is in the correspondence with Arnauld that we find the most developed statement of this central thread of Leibniz's thought, the emphasis on unity and the way in which unity requires us to posit substantial forms in bodies. This document was so important to Leibniz that for years afterwards he referred to it in both letters and published writings; indeed, he contemplated publishing it as late as 1707.[65]

As we saw above in Chapter 1, Leibniz first started writing to Arnauld in 1671, when he was also cultivating other celebrated people, such as Hobbes, Oldenburg, the secretary of the Royal Society, and Duke Johann Friedrich. Leibniz had little to offer then, as an unknown young man of 25 years from the wilds of Germany. In Paris he actually met Arnauld, and claimed to be on intimate terms.[66] Now, in 1686, Leibniz was a well-known mathematician, the author of the first published article on the differential calculus, and the counselor to the House of Hanover. Leibniz the Lutheran had hoped to convince Arnauld the Catholic of the truth of his own philosophy, as part of a campaign to unify the Churches in Europe. This is the important subtext behind their exchanges.

---

[63] For an elegant summary of Arnauld's philosophy, career, and significance for Leibniz as a correspondent at this moment, see Sleigh (1990a), ch. 3. In ch. 2, Sleigh treats the Landgrave Ernst von Hessen-Rheinfels, who was the intermediary in the correspondence. In general, Sleigh's is a lovely examination of this important exchange.

[64] On this, see Nadler (1989) and Moreau (1999).

[65] See Mason's introduction in Leibniz and Arnauld (1967), xiii–xiv.

[66] See A2.1².358–9. See Antognazza (2008), 141.

The correspondence begins rather inauspiciously. To the best of our knowledge, Arnauld never saw the complete 'Discours de métaphysique'; in his first letter destined for Arnauld, sent to the intermediary in the correspondence, the Landgrave Ernst von Hessen-Rheinfels on 1/11 February 1686, Leibniz sent only a summary of each of the thirty-seven articles into which it was divided. But the summary was enough to disturb Arnauld deeply. In a letter of 13 March 1686 to Hessen-Rheinfels, Arnauld wrote:

I find in these thoughts so many things that frighten me and that almost all men, if I am not mistaken, will find so shocking, that I do not see what use such a work can be, which will clearly be rejected by everybody.[67]

Arnauld's frank opinion about Leibniz was not flattering. Writing, again to Hessen-Rheinfels, presumably not for Leibniz's eyes, he remarked:

Would it not be better if he abandoned these metaphysical speculations which cannot be of any use to him or to others, in order to apply himself seriously to the greatest business that he can ever have, the assurance of his salvation by returning to the Church. . .?[68]

In the letters that immediately follow, Leibniz attempted to defend himself against the charge of necessitarianism that Arnauld (not to mention many later readers) saw in the position that he was advancing. But Leibniz was obviously frustrated that some themes that he thought were important were passing by without mention. So, at the very end of a letter from 4/14 July 1686, Leibniz abruptly changed the subject:

If the body is a substance and not a simple phenomenon like the rainbow, nor an entity united by accident or by aggregation like a heap of stones, it cannot consist of extension, and one must necessarily conceive of something there that one calls substantial form, and which corresponds in a way to the soul. I have been convinced of it finally, as though against my will, after having been rather far removed from it in the past.[69]

Arnauld took the bait. In the next letter he sent Leibniz, on 28 September 1686, he responded to Leibniz's proposal to revive substantial forms. After

---

[67] G II 15.

[68] G II 16. Paul Lodge has suggested to me that this might have been an invitation to Hessen-Rheinfels to discourage Leibniz from any future work on metaphysics.

[69] G II 58.

a short discussion of Leibniz's hypothesis of concomitance (what was later to be called the hypothesis of pre-established harmony), Arnauld wrote:

The second matter on which I should like enlightenment is the following remark: 'that in order that the body or matter not be a simple phenomenon, like the rainbow, nor an entity united by accident or by aggregation like a heap of stones, it cannot consist of extension, and there must necessarily be something there that one calls substantial form and that corresponds to what one calls the soul'.[70]

He continued: "There are many things to ask about that." And indeed there were. Arnauld continued with a series of seven objections to substantial forms, many of them standard to the new philosophy, exactly as Leibniz had no doubt expected. The letters that follow give him the opportunity to develop his position in greater detail.

In his correspondence with Arnauld, Leibniz's main motivation for introducing substantial forms and the corporeal substances that, together with body, they make up is an argument that I shall call the *aggregate argument*.[71] Leibniz writes:

I believe that where there are only entities through aggregation, there will not even be real entities; for every entity through aggregation presupposes entities endowed with a true unity. . . . I do not grant that there are only aggregates of substances. If there are aggregates of substances, there must also be genuine substances from which all the aggregates result. One must necessarily arrive either at mathematical points from which certain authors make up extension, or at Epicurus's and M. Cordemoy's atoms (which you, like me, dismiss), or else one must acknowledge that no reality can be found in bodies, or finally one must recognize certain substances in them that possess a true unity.[72]

The claim, which we already saw in some of the pieces from earlier on in the 1680s, is a rather simple one: the reality that an aggregate of individuals has derives from the reality of its parts. To use an example Leibniz often appeals to, a pile of stones can only be real if the stones of which it is composed are real. As Leibniz puts it, "I deduce that many entities do not exist where there is not a single one that is genuinely an

[70] G II 65.
[71] The development of Leibniz's position in the following pages is essentially that given in Garber (1985). For another careful development of this argument, see Levey (2003).
[72] Leibniz to Arnauld, 30 April 1687, G II 90. See also G II 58, 72, 97, 118.

entity and that every multiplicity presupposes unity."[73] Leibniz takes this general argument to have an obvious application to bodies. If we conceive of extended bodies, as the Cartesians argued, as indefinitely divisible and as containing extended parts which, in turn, contain further extended parts, ad infinitum, then it follows that bodies must therefore have no reality (in a sense we shall later discuss). Leibniz writes:

Now each extended mass [*masse étendue*] can be considered as composed of two or a thousand others; there exists only an extension achieved through contiguity. Thus one will never find a body of which one can say that it is truly a substance. It will always be an aggregate of many. Or rather, it will not be a real entity, since the parts making it up are subject to the same difficulty, and since one never arrives at any real entity, because entities made up by aggregation have only as much reality as exists in their constituent parts.[74]

But *if* a body is to be real, if, as he puts it, body is to be more than "a phenomenon, lacking all reality as would a coherent dream,"[75] then "one must recognize certain substances [in bodies] that possess a true unity."[76] Leibniz is sometimes a bit tentative in inferring the existence of these true unities from the aggregate argument, suggesting that we are only entitled to them under the assumption that there is, indeed, something real in bodies, an assumption about which we cannot be absolutely certain.[77] But as the argument progresses, Leibniz becomes more and more confident of the conclusion that bodies must contain something substantial. When Arnauld, for example, questions the necessity for unities in bodies,[78] Leibniz replies:

You say you do not see what leads me to admit these substantial forms or rather these corporeal substances endowed with true unity; but it is because I cannot conceive of any reality without true unity.[79]

---

[73] Leibniz to Arnauld, 10 September 1687, G II 118. Gerhardt dated this as 9 October 1687. It has recently been redated by the Akademie editors. In what follows I will refer to it using the current dating.

[74] Draft of Leibniz to Arnauld, 28 November/8 December 1686, G II 72.

[75] G II 97. We shall discuss what Leibniz means by phenomenal in this context below in Ch. 7. There we shall also discuss in more detail Leibniz's worries about the real extra-mental existence of bodies in this period, which are a kind of undertone to his discussion with Arnauld.

[76] G II 96.

[77] Sleigh emphasizes Leibniz's hesitations; see Sleigh (1990a), 103–6. These, I argue, are connected with some of the skeptical worries that had concerned Leibniz since the mid-1670s, as we shall discuss in Ch. 7.

[78] G II 86–7.   [79] G II 97.

The implication here, and throughout these later letters, is that such a conception of the world of bodies is just not credible. Though Leibniz never claims to have a demonstrative argument that will establish the real existence of the world of bodies beyond all doubt, he is clear that if there is to be something real in the world of bodies, then there must be something in body that is, unlike bare extension, a genuine unity.

The Correspondence with Arnauld: Corporeal Substances

But what, *in concreto*, are the unities that Leibniz has in mind? A passage I quoted earlier makes clear that neither mathematical points nor atoms will do for Leibniz.[80] Leibniz wants something more, something substantial. What he tells Arnauld is what we have seen in the notes from the late 1670s on: this something substantial essentially involves mind, soul, or form. Leibniz writes, for example:

If the body is a substance and not a simple phenomenon like the rainbow, nor an entity united by accident or by aggregation like a heap of stones, it cannot consist of extension, and one must necessarily conceive of something there that one calls substantial form, and which corresponds in a way to the soul.[81]

Or, even more explicitly, Leibniz writes:

The substance of a body, if bodies have one, must be indivisible; whether it is called soul or form does not concern me.[82]

These passages might suggest that the unities that ultimately ground the reality of bodies, the genuine substances into which the aggregate is resolved, are merely minds, forms, souls, the incorporeal substances we discussed earlier. This, in turn, might suggest the view Leibniz will take explicitly in his later writings whereby bodies are simply aggregates of

---

[80] G II 96. Later we shall discuss Leibniz's claim that extension and thus bodies cannot be made up of points. For Leibniz's argument against atomism, the claim that bodies are made up of uniform, infinitely hard small bodies, see Garber (1995), 321–5.

[81] Leibniz to Arnauld, 4/14 July 1686, G II 58.

[82] G II 72. The curious phrase, "the substance of a body," was used earlier in the theological writings from the late 1660s and early 1670s to designate the substantial form. See the discussion above in Ch. 1.

mind-like monads, families of tiny souls, to use Russell's colorful phrase.[83] But this cannot be precisely what is going on here in these earlier texts. Arnauld at one point argues, appealing to the authority of St Augustine, that true unity may well be lacking in body, and found only in spirit. He writes:

St. Augustine feels no difficulties about recognizing that bodies possess no true unity, because unity must be indivisible and no body is indivisible. Hence there is no true unity except in spirits, anymore than there is a true 'self' [except in spirits].[84]

Leibniz's answer is instructive. He does *not* reply that the unities that make up bodies are themselves minds. Rather, he replies:

You object, Sir, that it may be of the essence of body to be devoid of true unity; but it will then be of the essence of body to be a phenomenon, lacking all reality as would a coherent dream.[85]

Whatever these unities are that make up real bodies, they do not seem to be souls *simpliciter*. Rather, they seem to be corporeal substances. But how are these to be understood? Leibniz's conception of unity as it pertains to the substances that make up real bodies is, perhaps, best appreciated in contrast with cases in which the appropriate sort of unity is lacking. Consider, first, an illuminating example Leibniz gives Arnauld where, he claims, we have no unity and thus no substance:

Let us assume that there are two stones, for instance the diamonds of the Grand Duke and of the Grand Mogul; one and the same collective name may be given to account for both, and it may be said that they are a pair of diamonds, although they are to be found a long way away from each other; but it will not be said that these two diamonds compose one substance. Matters of degree have no place here. If therefore they are brought closer to one another, even to the point of contact, they will not be more substantially united on that account; and even if after contact one were to add some other body calculated to prevent their separating, for example, if one were to set them in a single ring, all that will make only what is called *unum per accidens*. For it is as though by accident that they are forced into one and the same movement.[86]

In this case, no physical glue, however strong, could make the two diamonds into a single substance. Leibniz continues this passage a few lines

[83] Russell (1972), 583.   [84] G II 86. See also G II 87, 106.
[85] G II 97.   [86] G II 76.

later by suggesting that somehow or other the appeal to a soul or form is in order if we are to have the genuine unity a substance requires:

Substantial unity requires a complete, indivisible and naturally indestructible entity . . . which cannot be found in shape or motion . . . but in a soul or substantial form on the example of what one calls 'self'.[87]

But what does Leibniz have in mind here? Though the passage suggests, once again, that the ultimate unities are just souls, what Leibniz has in mind is something quite different, I think. To see how the soul or form is supposed to bring about unity, let us turn briefly to Leibniz's account of how the soul produces unity in human beings. In human beings, Leibniz thinks, "the soul is truly the substantial form of our body."[88] Or, as Leibniz tells Arnauld at somewhat greater length:

man . . . is an entity endowed with a genuine unity conferred on him by his soul, notwithstanding the fact that the mass of his body is divided into organs, vessels, humors, spirits . . .[89]

An obvious suggestion is that the human body, despite its complex parts, is unified and enters into a genuine substance by virtue of the fact that it is appropriately connected to an immaterial substance, a soul. It is in this way, it seems, that the soul brings about unity; it is in this way that, for human beings, at least, "substantial unity requires . . . a soul or substantial form."[90] The soul is, as it were, a kind of incorporeal glue that unites the different parts of the body and makes them all belong to one genuine individual, one genuine substance. And, consequently, a corpse, a human body not so connected with a soul, cannot be a substance, properly speaking, as Leibniz tells Arnauld.[91] But, Leibniz argues, it is similar in the world of non-human corporeal substances.[92] That is, the substantial form can provide a non-human body with substantial unity in just the way our soul does for us, by being appropriately connected to that body. Returning now to the discussion of the two diamonds, Leibniz concludes:

I accord substantial forms to all corporeal substances that are more than mechanically united. . . . If I am asked for my views in particular on the sun, . . . the earth, the

---

[87] G II 76.
[88] G II 75. The position is attributed to the "last Lateran Council" in this text, but clearly with Leibniz's approval.
[89] Leibniz to Arnauld, 10 September 1687, G II 120.   [90] G II 76.
[91] See G II 73, 75.   [92] See Leibniz to Arnauld, 10 September 1687, G II 120.

Can this happen in the case of a corpse?
Replacement of substantial form?

moon, trees and similar bodies, and even on animals, I cannot declare with absolute certainty if they are animate or at least if they are substances or even if they are simply machines or aggregates of many substances. . . . [E]very part of matter is actually divided into other parts as different as the diamonds [of the Grand Duke and the Grand Mogul]; and since it continues endlessly in this way, one will never arrive at a thing of which it may be said: 'Here really is an entity,' except when one finds animate machines whose soul or substantial form creates substantial unity independent of the external union of contiguity. And if there are none, it follows that apart from man there is apparently nothing substantial in the visible world.[93]

The presence of a substantial form makes no empirical difference

So, it seems, corporeal substances, the unities of which the bodies of everyday experience are composed, are to be understood on analogy to human beings, a mind or something mindlike (a substantial form), connected with a body. And this, then, is the proper conclusion of the aggregate argument: for the extended things in the material world to be real, they must, ultimately, be made up of corporeal substances, unities composed of soul and body. Thus while bodies must contain something mental or analogous to the mental, a form that will unite discrete bodies and create genuine unity, it is these unities, these corporeal substances, that constitute the basic building blocks that ground bodies, and not the incorporeal substances themselves.[94]

Earlier I talked about how a body becomes a substance by virtue of being "appropriately connected" to a soul or form. What exactly does this mean? This is, of course, a problem that is not peculiar to Leibniz's metaphysics; it is a problem faced by the scholastics of Leibniz's day,[95] and is, in a way, just the problem of what connects the mind to the body so familiar from Descartes and later Cartesians. An obvious candidate for an answer to this question is Leibniz's doctrine of pre-established harmony or, as it was called in the mid-1680s, the hypothesis of concomitance. That is,

---

[93] G II 77. See also G II 72–3, 75, 76–7.

[94] Michel Fichant sees the emphasis on unity as the central criterion of substantiality in the Arnauld letters and as the starting place of Leibniz's monadological metaphysics. See Fichant (2003a), 8, 17; Fichant (2004), 78ff; Fichant (2005). While I think that the letters to Arnauld represent an important stage in Leibniz's development, where themes found earlier in his writings come together and get a clearer and more systematic articulation, I don't think that there is anything in the letters substantially different from the corporeal substance position that he had been developing from the late 1670s on. While, as I will later argue, the notion of unity that is so central in the letters will be an important element that will later move Leibniz in the direction of the monadological metaphysics, I don't think that he is there yet in 1686/7. We shall address Fichant's thesis again below in Ch. 8.

[95] See, on this, Boehm (1938), 35–58.

it is a certain harmony between the states of the immaterial substance that is the form, and the states of the corporeal substances that make up its body that seem to unite the form to its organic body in corporeal substances at every level. Leibniz is not *absolutely* clear about this, and later he will deny that he ever intended pre-established harmony to account for unity in any strong sense.[96] But in the correspondence with Arnauld, and in the 'Discours de métaphysique' with which it is connected, it certainly looks as if this is exactly what Leibniz has in mind.[97]

This is clearest when Leibniz is discussing the human being. When Leibniz first presents the hypothesis of concomitance in 'Discours' § 33, it is presented as an "unexpected clarification of the union of the mind and body." Since the result of a union is a unity, and a genuine unity is, for Leibniz, a substance, this suggests that the hypothesis of concomitance is supposed to account for the fact that mind and body together constitute a substance. And consider a passage that Leibniz wrote to Arnauld in concluding an extended discussion of the hypothesis of concomitance. Leibniz wrote:

The soul, however, is nevertheless the form of its body because it is an expression of the phenomena of all other bodies in accordance with the relationship to its own.[98]

The claim is that it is because of the special relation that the human soul bears to the human body, the fact that the soul expresses the universe by expressing its body, the relation that constitutes harmony, that the soul is the form that belongs to the body to which it is attached. The suggestion is that it is the harmony which attaches the soul to the body in such a way

---

[96] These later denials are in response to an attack on Leibniz's doctrine of pre-established harmony that Boehm (1938) argued is central to Leibniz's later thought on the *vinculum substantiale* in particular and to his thought on composite substance in general. The attack is found in Tournemine (1703). Tournemine's objection is quite simple. Calling to mind Leibniz's often repeated two-clock example for illustrating pre-established harmony [see, e.g., G IV 498–500 (AG 147–8)], Tournemine writes: "Thus correspondence, harmony, does not bring about either union or essential connection. Whatever resemblance one might suppose between two clocks, however justly their relations might be considered perfect, one can never say that the clocks are united just because the movements correspond with perfect symmetry" (pp. 869–70). Leibniz's first reaction was to deny that there is anything to union over and above harmony. See, e.g., his remarks to de Volder in 1708, G II 281. But in the response he published in the *Mémoires de Trévoux* in 1708 [G VI 595–6 (AG 196–7)], he suggests that the union, like the mysteries of faith, surpasses philosophical understanding.

[97] For a subtle and penetrating discussion of Leibniz's problems with the unity of corporeal substance, focusing on the issue of pre-established harmony and mind/body unity, see Rutherford (1995), ch. 10.

[98] G II 58.

as to make it the form of the body, and to make it a form with respect to the substance, which is the human being.

Leibniz says nothing *explicit* to suggest that harmony is what unites form to matter in the more general case of a non-human corporeal substance. But if, indeed, harmony is what is supposed to unite the human soul to the human body in such a way as to form a genuine corporeal substance, then there is every reason to think that Leibniz would extend the account to the more general case, at least in the correspondence with Arnauld. Leibniz emphasizes in a number of places that his hypothesis of concomitance is not a *special* hypothesis about human minds and human bodies, but a "consequence of the concept of an individual substance."[99] Furthermore, as I noted earlier, Leibniz suggests a number of times to Arnauld that corporeal substances, both their constituents (form and matter) and their unity, can be understood on analogy with the corresponding aspects of human beings. Thus form is somewhat like the human mind, matter like the body. And, to extend the analogy, one would suppose that their unity consists in a harmony between what goes on in the one and in the other.

The Correspondence with Arnauld: Substantial Atomism and Infinite Divisibility

This resolution of the bodies of everyday experience into fundamental unities, corporeal substances, suggests a kind of atomism, what Leibniz sometimes calls *substantial* atomism to distinguish it from the more familiar Epicurean atomism of Cordemoy, for example, a world of basic things distinguished by virtue of their extreme hardness.[100] But there is a crucial difference between Leibniz's substantial atomism and any other atomism current in the seventeenth century. For the physical atomist, there is a rock-bottom level of analysis: when we divide a body into its ultimate parts, we arrive at atoms, beyond which we cannot go. But not so for Leibniz's substantial atomism. The real existence of an inanimate body, an aggregate

[99] G II 75. See also G II 112, 136.
[100] As we saw earlier, Leibniz uses the term "substantial atom" in 1683; see A6.4.1466 (RA 265). See also the "Système nouveau," G IV 482 (AG 142) and "De ipsa natura" § 11, G IV 511 (AG 162).

that itself lacks a soul, is grounded in the existence of constituent corporeal substances. But, it is important to note, we needn't stop with the first layer of corporeal substances we come upon. Leibniz's basic building blocks themselves contain further corporeal substances, and so on ad infinitum. In this respect they would seem to be the direct descendants of the *bullae* of the *HPN*. Leibniz writes to Arnauld, implicitly appealing to the so-called principle of plenitude:

I also believe that to wish to restrict genuine unity or substance to man almost without exception is to be as limited in metaphysics as were in physics those who enclosed the world in a ball. And since genuine substances are as many expressions of the whole universe considered in a certain sense and as many duplications of the works of God; it is in keeping with the greatness and beauty of God's work, since these substances do not impede one another from making as many [substances] in this universe as possible and as higher reasons allow.[101]

These bodies with souls, corporeal substances that, in recognition of the mentality of form, are analogous to animate beings, are, thus, everywhere in Leibniz's world, in its smallest part. "The whole of matter must be full of substances animate or at least living," Leibniz writes.[102] And thus Leibniz responds to Arnauld's common-sense objection that animate bodies are but a miniscule proportion of the world:

From that I see, Sir, that I have not yet expressed my ideas clearly so as to make you understand my hypothesis. For apart from the fact that I do not remember saying that there is no substantial form except souls [*ames*], I am very far removed from the belief that animate bodies are only a small part of the others. For I believe rather that everything is full of animate bodies, and to my mind there are incomparably more souls than there are atoms for M. Cordemoy, who makes a finite number of them, whereas I maintain that the number of souls or at least of forms is quite infinite, and that since matter is endlessly divisible, one cannot fix on a part so small that there are no animate bodies within, or at least with forms [*informés*], that is to say, corporeal substances.[103]

---

[101] G II 98. The phrasing here echoes a passage from an ms. dated as contemporary with the 'Conspectus libelli' that the Akademie editors have entitled 'Definitiones cogitationesque metaphysicae': "But to attribute a soul only to man and to a few other bodies is as inept as believing that everything is made for the sake of man alone" [A6.4.1399 (RA 245)]. Cf. also the 'Conspectus libelli': "It is improper to try to ascribe perception to man alone...." [A6.4.1989 (L 279)]. See also A6.4.2008–9 (L 289).

[102] G II 161. This was not in the text sent to Arnauld. See Leibniz (1952), 93.

[103] Leibniz to Arnauld, 10 September 1687, G II 118. Here I follow the text as received by Arnauld, and as given in Leibniz (1952), 85–6. The version of this passage given in G II gives the final phrase as

Thus, even an individual corporeal substance, a body united by a form or soul, must *itself* contain other corporeal substances. So, Leibniz writes about human beings, in a passage that we have already seen in part:

man . . . is an entity endowed with a genuine unity conferred on him by his soul, notwithstanding the fact that the mass of his body [*la masse de son corps*] is divided into organs, vessels, humours, spirits, *and that the parts are undoubtedly full of an infinite number of other corporeal substances endowed with their own entelechies.*[104]

Or, Leibniz writes about corporeal substances in more general terms:

If one considers the matter of the corporeal substance not mass without forms but a secondary matter which is the multiplicity of substances of which the mass [*masse*] is that of the entire body, it may be said that these substances are parts of this matter, just as those [substances] which enter into our body form part of it, for as our body is the matter and the soul is the form of our substance, it is the same with other corporeal substances.[105]

In this way Leibniz's view is of a world of corporeal substances, bugs in bugs, on to infinity.[106]

---

follows: "since matter is endlessly divisible, one cannot fix on a part so small that there are no animate bodies within, or at least bodies endowed with a basic entelechy or (if you permit one to use the word 'life' so generally) with a vital principle, that is to say corporeal substances, about which it may be said in general of them all that they are living." This change was almost certainly introduced later, when Leibniz was revising the text for possible publication. See also a note Leibniz wrote in April–October 1686, A6.4.1615.

[104] G II 120. Cf. Leibniz to Malebranche, 22 June/2 July 1679, A2.1².719.

[105] G II 119. This is a passage not found in the letter Arnauld received. See Leibniz (1952), 87, n. (1). Secondary matter will be discussed below in Ch. 4.

[106] This is not to say that the view is not without its complexities, and, perhaps, its serious problems. As Ohad Nachtomy emphasizes, living things, corporeal substances, have a definite structure where the lesser corporeal substances are subordinated to the soul of the whole animal by what he argues are "degrees of activity." On this, see Nachtomy (2007), ch. 9. But even on Nachtomy's sophisticated account of what he calls "nested individuals," problems remain. We certainly want to distinguish the worm in the blood, which is not an integral part of the corporeal substance from the blood which is. (To this extent, the bugs-in-bugs analogy that I use may not be entirely appropriate; what we are talking about is interconnected bugs in bugs.) But we also want to distinguish the arm from the heart: while both are, in a sense, integral parts of an animal, say, the arm can be removed while the heart cannot. This structure is what Leibniz will later, in the "Système nouveau" of 1695, call "machines de la nature." On this notion see especially Fichant (2003). Fichant implies, incorrectly, I think, that these natural machines only arise in the mid-1690s. While the basic idea goes back somewhat earlier in Leibniz's thought, he is probably correct in arguing that it is only in the mid-1690s that it takes a central place in Leibniz's thought as defining the difference between artificial machines and living things.

But it was also important to Leibniz that these substances, though complex and made up of smaller substances, bugs in bugs, are, nevertheless, indivisible. As he writes to Arnauld:

Only indivisible substances and their different states are absolutely real. This is what Parmenides and Plato and other Ancients have indeed recognized. Besides, I grant that the name of "one" can be given to an assembly of inanimate bodies, although no substantial form links them together, just as I can say: there is *one* rainbow, there is *one* flock; but it is a phenomenal or mental unity [*unité de phenomene ou de pensée*], which is not enough for the reality in phenomena.[107]

But how can that be if what is at issue here is corporeal substances, souls *and* their bodies, made up of smaller substances? Arnauld, naturally enough, finds the indivisibility claim somewhat puzzling. He objects:

Is it the substantial form of a marble tile that makes it one? If that is the case, what becomes of this substantial form when it [i.e. the tile] ceases to be one because it has been broken into two?[108]

Leibniz answers:

I believe that a marble tile is perhaps only the same as a heap of stones and thus cannot be considered a single substance but a collection of many.[109]

Arnauld's mistake is in thinking that Leibniz intended inanimate objects, like marble tiles, to be genuine substances, with their own substantial forms.[110] If this were Leibniz's position, then it would indeed be puzzling to consider corporeal substances as indivisible, since a single marble tile can, indeed, be split into two pieces, each of which is, it seems, a marble tile in its own right. But Leibniz's answer is straightforward: the marble tile lacks a single unifying form, and thus is not a corporeal substance, but an aggregate of corporeal substances. Consequently, Leibniz sees no problem here; the indivisibility claim only applies to the usually rudimentary animate organic bodies that Leibniz considers genuine corporeal substances.

More relevant to Leibniz's position is a second question that Arnauld raises:

For what reply can one make about those worms which are cut into two, each part of which moves as before?[111]

[107] G II 119. See also G II 76.   [108] G II 66.   [109] G II 76.
[110] See G II 85, where Arnauld gives his mistaken first impression of Leibniz's position and acknowledges his mistake.
[111] G II 87.

Arnauld may have had in mind here something like planarians, a kind of worm that is capable of regenerating lost parts, including its head. With such a worm, one can cut off a section of the tail, and in time, the tail section will generate a new head, thus, apparently, producing two animals where there was originally only one.[112] If the planarian is a genuine corporeal substance, then it would seem that a single corporeal substance could be split into two. Leibniz answers:

As regards an insect which one cuts in two, the two parts do not necessarily have to remain animate, although a certain movement remains in them. At least the soul of the whole animal will remain only in one part. . . .[113] → The other part is inanimate; no empirical difference

Leibniz's position seems to be that when we are dealing with a genuine corporeal substance, like he supposes Arnauld's worm to be, then it must be indivisible: one cannot split one living thing to make two living things, both of which are identical to the original one, Leibniz claims. When the body of a living thing is split, its soul, that which makes it the corporeal substance it is, must remain in one half or the other. → Thus, in the case of Arnauld's worm, at most one half of the worm divided can remain the same as the original worm; the motion that remains in the other half cannot be the motion of the same worm as that with which we started.[114] Leibniz is in no way intending to deny that one can divide the body of a corporeal substance into smaller parts: one can take out a person's appendix, cut a flower off a rose bush, or split a worm into two wriggling parts. But dividing the body of a corporeal substance is altogether different from dividing the *substance* itself: hard as one may try, Leibniz insists that the knife cannot make two living worms from one, two *substances* out of one. That is, corporeal substances are indivisible in the sense that one cannot take a corporeal substance and split it into two parts, each of which is equally well a corporeal substance, soul or form unifying a body, and each of which

(margin handwriting: So it is the soul which is indivisible. But the body united to the soul being substantial is divisible despite)

---

[112] Alternatively, he may just have had in mind a kind of worm that has vital motion in both parts, when cut in half. Whether he had the one or the other in mind is not really important for the example at hand.

[113] G II 100. See also Arnauld's similar objection from the fact that plants can be propagated from cuttings and tree limbs can be grafted (G II 85), and Leibniz's answer (G II 92).

[114] It is possible, too, that neither half of the worm is animate, strictly speaking. That is, it is possible that splitting kills the worm (cf. Leibniz's theory of death below) and that the motion of both parts is purely mechanical.

can be properly said to be *the same* corporeal substance that existed before the split.[115]   ⟹ Ecclesiological analogy?

And just as corporeal substances are indivisible, Leibniz claims that they are indestructible as well. This claim, too, is somewhat paradoxical. Corporeal substances are all, in a very general sense, living things, and Leibniz certainly cannot deny that living things die. But, Leibniz claims, the death of an animal is not the destruction of a corporeal substance, but only its transformation. Thus, when Arnauld asked what becomes of worms and their souls when burned in a fire, Leibniz replies:

> Those who conceive that there is almost an infinite number of little animals in the smallest drop of water, as the experiments of M. Leeuwenhoek have made known, and who do not find it strange that matter is everywhere full of animate substances, will not find it strange either that there is something animate even in ashes and that fire can transform an animal and reduce it in size instead of totally destroying it . . . [Such animals are] little organic bodies, wrapped up as they are because of a sort of contraction from a larger body which has undergone corruption . . .[116]

Thus, "corruption or death is nothing other than the diminution and envelopment of an animal which nevertheless goes on surviving and remaining alive and organic."[117] Corporeal substances, thus, do not perish in Leibniz's world, but only grow or shrink.[118]

This, in brief, is Leibniz's position on indivisibility and indestructibility of corporeal substances. The position is grounded in a number of intertwined positions on souls and forms, the relation between souls and forms and their bodies, and the individuation of corporeal substances. The first and most

[Margin note, left side: Compare w/ Monadology: "only fuzzily perceiving"; "dead substance is"]

---

[115] Later, as we shall see below in Ch. 8, Leibniz will argue from the indivisibility of substance to the claim that genuine substances are simple, and from that to the claim that they are unextended. Adams (1994), 335–6 wants to attribute this view to Leibniz in the middle years as part of his case for arguing that he held something close to the monadology in these years. But in these texts, Leibniz had a very different conception of indivisibility, as the planarian example shows.

[116] G II 122. For Arnauld's question, see G II 108. Leibniz was deeply interested in the microscopy of his day, which he found quite relevant to a number of metaphysical issues. On this see Wilson (1997) and Fouke (1989).

[117] G II 123. See also G II 100.

[118] This is certainly connected with Leibniz's earlier speculations starting in 1671 about the resurrection of the body, discussed above in Ch. 1. Leibniz's account of generation is the exact mirror of his account of death. The natural ingenerability of souls and forms entails that generation must proceed by the transformation of a very small animal into a larger one, from an animal seed, so to speak, to animals large enough for us to see.

important of these positions is the claim that forms and souls are indivisible and naturally indestructible, a claim that he repeats a number of times in the correspondence with Arnauld.[119] Leibniz never attempts to produce an argument for that conclusion, though, perhaps because it is a position that he considers generally accepted by a wide variety of philosophers, ancient, medieval, and modern.[120] Secondly, Leibniz claims that while souls and forms taken apart from any bodies are genuine substances, immaterial substances, and, as such, can in principle exist without being attached to any body in nature, in *this* possible world every soul is the soul of some body: "there is naturally no soul without an animate body,"[121] Leibniz writes. Leibniz's motivation for this doctrine is somewhat obscure. It is possible that it derives from a simple application of the principle of perfection. The world Leibniz outlines in his correspondence with Arnauld is a tightly organized world, a world of corporeal substances nested in one another to infinity. A bare soul, existing in this order but detached from a body, would seem to detract from the orderliness of the world. Another possible motivation for this doctrine, one found explicitly in somewhat later writings, derives from the role of the form as active principle and the body or its primary matter as passive. On this account, soul or form cannot exist in nature without body because the active is incomplete without the passive, or because only God can be completely active and non-passive. Given the lack of attention to notions of activity and passivity in the correspondence, and given the attention Leibniz gives the principle of perfection there, this motivation seems less likely than the former, though. A third doctrine relevant here concerns the individuation of corporeal substances. While Leibniz is not explicit, he seems to take for granted throughout the discussion of corporeal substances that they are individuated by their forms, a view unsurprising given what we have seen earlier in this chapter. That is, a corporeal substance or animal can change its body as much as nature will allow, but as long as it has the form or soul it has, it is the same corporeal substance or animal.

Together these three doctrines entail the indivisibility and indestructibility of corporeal substances. Since forms are indivisible, so must be the corporeal substances that they serve to individuate. In fact, it is because

---

[119] See G II 72, 75, 76, 116–17, 124.   [120] See G II 116–17.   [121] G II 124.

corporeal substances as substances must be indivisible that they must have forms, Leibniz sometimes argues:

I think I have shown that every substance is indivisible and that consequently every corporeal substance must have a soul or at least an entelechy which is analogous to the soul, since otherwise bodies would be no more than phenomena.[122]

The indivisibility of corporeal substances thus derives from the indivisibility of their forms. Similarly, the indestructibility of corporeal substances derives from the indestructibility of the forms attached to their bodies. Since forms are indestructible, since they are always attached to some body, and since they are what identifies the corporeal substance as the substance it is, it follows that corporeal substances must also be indestructible. *But they are diminishable*

Even though corporeal substances are indivisible and immortal, they are not simple.[123] Indeed, they are infinitely complex, bugs in bugs that go to infinity. Leibniz opens the 'Monadologie' with the following famous lines:

The monad, which we shall discuss here, is nothing but a simple substance that enters into composites—simple, that is, without parts. . . . And there must be simple substances, since there are composites; for the composite is nothing more than a collection, or aggregate, of simples. . . . But where there are no parts, neither extension, nor shape, nor divisibility is possible. These monads are the true atoms of nature and, in brief, the elements of things.

This is quite clearly a version of the aggregate argument that we have seen in connection with Leibniz's correspondence with Arnauld. But there is a crucial difference. The conclusion here is that there must be *simple* substances. Leibniz's conclusion in the correspondence with Arnauld is that there must be *individual* substances or *corporeal* substances in the world.[124] Generations of readers of the correspondence have assumed that Leibniz was ultimately presenting Arnauld with the same metaphysics that he would

Note: it is not the corporeal substance but the form that is complete.

But their substantiating forms are simple.

[122] G II 121.

[123] Leibniz *never* tells Arnauld that genuine substances have to be simple or without parts. However, the term "simple" does appear a small handful of times in the 1680s, as we shall see below in Ch. 8 when we discuss the first systematic introduction of the notion into Leibniz's thought in the mid-1680s. As I shall argue there, those uses are rather different than the later use of the term, as in the 'Monadologie.'

[124] The significance of the later notion of simplicity will be discussed at length below in Ch. 8.

later present to de Volder, Des Bosses, and in the 'Monadologie.' But I see no reason to think that that is true: hard as I try, I cannot see the metaphysics of the monadology in Leibniz's words to Arnauld. While the notion of a simple substance will become central in Leibniz's later thought, in this period it occurs almost not at all. There is, of course, a sense in which souls might be considered as simple substances, substances without parts. But, as I noted earlier, Leibniz is absolutely clear that "there is naturally no soul without an animate body."[125] And so, in nature *every substance is complex,* made up of a soul joined to a body, a substantial form that makes some portion of organized matter into a unified complex being. And since this goes to infinity—bugs in bugs—there is no bottom layer of organization within the world. This is a radical contrast to classical atomism.

There is a way of posing the question of corporeal substance in Leibniz in some recent literature that leads to confusion. On that view, the question is posed as choice between a world in which all there is are simple substances, and a world in which there are also corporeal substances made up of simple substances.[126] Now, while this is the way Leibniz may have posed the question of corporeal substances later in life, after adopting the monadology, in the Des Bosses correspondence, for example, as we shall discuss in some detail below in Chapter 9, this was *not* the way Leibniz thought of things in the period that we have been examining. In the correspondence with Arnauld and in related texts, while the substantial form of a corporeal substance *might* be construed as a "simple substance" (Leibniz does not adopt that terminology until somewhat later, though), corporeal substances are not construed as complexes made up entirely of simple substances. At this moment Leibniz isn't working within an

[handwritten margin note: Because the body is complex]

[125] G II 124.

[126] This is the way the question is posed in Cover and O'Leary-Hawthorne (1999), 50–5. Though they concede that Leibniz may actually have believed in such things as corporeal substances, the view seems to them to be "rather a botch" (p. 53) and they choose to treat only simple substances in their account of Leibniz's metaphysics. Jonathan Bennett takes a similar view of Leibniz and assumes throughout his discussions that, from very early on, it's all monads in Leibniz's metaphysics; see Bennett (2001), vol. 1, 306–7 for his very brief discussion of corporeal substance. For this reason their readings of Leibniz's doctrines are difficult to relate to the approach taken in this book. Hartz (2007), *passim* has a similar conception of corporeal substance (animals) as collections of monads. But unlike Cover, O'Leary-Hawthorne, and Bennett, Hartz thinks that Leibniz took animals seriously, and argues that Leibniz was a theory pluralist who recognized both idealism and realism at the same time. We will return to Hartz's view below in Ch. 9.

ontology of simple substances, and debating whether or not to accept complex substances as something in addition to simple substances; he is working rather within an ontology of corporeal substances, in which the question of ultimate underlying simple substances doesn't really come up. For Leibniz at this moment it is a world without grounding, a world of infinite complexity and regress to infinity.

Leibniz's position as articulated in the correspondence with Arnauld is exceedingly elegant. Like the atomist, but unlike the Cartesian, Leibniz believed that bodies are made up of smaller parts that have real entity, real individuality, and real unity. In fact, Leibniz's substantial atoms are even more genuinely indivisible than the atomist's atoms in a certain substantial sense. But like the Cartesian's material substance, Leibniz's bodies are infinitely divisible. Indeed, even more than the Cartesian's bodies, they are *actually* divided to infinity. In this way he manages to get both genuine indivisible individuals without sacrificing infinite divisibility. Neat trick.

The Fardella Memo: Souls and Corporeal Substances

Leibniz's views in this period are further clarified in an interesting exchange he had with Michel Angelo Fardella in 1690.[127] Fardella was an Italian Cartesian or Malebranchist, teaching in Venice, whom Leibniz met during his Italian voyage, shortly after the exchange with Arnauld from which we have been quoting. The two seemed to hit it off quite nicely, and continued to correspond for some years afterwards. In a very rich document that seems to have been written shortly after their meeting, Leibniz describes their encounter as follows:

I communicated several of my metaphysical thoughts to the Reverend Father Michel Angelo Fardella of the Order of Friars Minor, because I saw that he combined meditation on intellectual things with an understanding of mathematics, and because he pursued truth with great ardor. And so, after he grasped my views, he wrote out certain propositions at home to remember them in order to master what he heard from me, along with objections, which, it so happens, he sent to me for my examination.[128]

---

[127] For a fuller account, see Garber (2004).   [128] A6.4.1666 (AG 101).

What follows then is a series of texts, presumably Fardella's version of what Leibniz told him, together with his objections and Leibniz's answers to those objections. Fardella begins with what looks like a summary of some of the arguments from the correspondence that we have been examining. His objection is as follows:

When dealing with a multitude of stones ABC, either stone A or B or C must be understood first. But it is not the same with a soul which, with other souls, does not constitute body. And it seems that there is some difficulty in the argument that, given that there are bodies composed of substances in the world, there must necessarily be something which is a single indivisible substance. Now, this can legitimately be inferred if the unity, as a part of the same sort, intrinsically composed the aggregate. But the substantial unity in question does not intrinsically constitute the aggregate, and is not a portion of it, but is understood to be essentially altogether different from it. How, then, is it required in order for this aggregate to subsist?[129]

What is Fardella worried about here? As I read this passage, Fardella has problems both with Leibniz's position, as he understands it, and with the argument Leibniz offers for it. He takes Leibniz to be arguing from the fact that bodies are divisible and thus aggregates of smaller parts, to the fact that they must contain indivisible substances. It seems to me that the assumption he makes here is that the indivisible substances that Leibniz has in mind in the initial passage are something like Cartesian souls, an assumption that isn't surprising given his own Cartesian background and Augustinian proclivities. This is the position he attributes to Leibniz, something not unlike what Leibniz will later hold in the classical monadological writings, and something not unlike what many later commentators have read into others of Leibniz's writings in the period. (In 1690, of course, Leibniz has yet to use the word "monad" in this connection.) Fardella wants to disagree with Leibniz about this position: souls taken together don't make up bodies. Secondly, he wants to argue that the argument Leibniz uses here, the argument from the existence of an aggregate to the existence of unities that ground the existence of that aggregate, doesn't work here. As I read this passage, Fardella argues that from the fact that a *body* is an aggregate of smaller parts, one cannot infer the existence of an indivisible substance (a *mind* or *soul*, Fardella thinks Leibniz has in mind) that is

[129] A6.4.1670 (AG 104).

altogether different in kind from a body. From the fact that body is a multiplicity, we can infer only the necessity of *bodily* parts, parts of the same *kind* as the aggregate; we cannot infer the existence of parts of an altogether different sort.

Here is Leibniz's reply:

I do not say that the body is composed of souls, nor that body is constituted by an aggregate of souls, but that it is constituted by an aggregate of substances. Moreover, the soul, properly and accurately speaking, is not a substance, but a substantial form, or the primitive form existing in substances, the first act, the first active faculty.[130]

Leibniz here is commenting on Fardella's understanding of the argument in question. He is clarifying what he takes to be a misinterpretation of his position. And what he seems to be holding is that bodies are *not* collections of souls, as Fardella seems to have interpreted Leibniz as holding. He then goes on to say that, strictly speaking, *souls aren't substances*. Instead, he asserts, souls are the *substantial forms of substances*. I don't want to pause over the fact that this is inconsistent with what Leibniz says elsewhere about souls. Nor is there an argument for the view given here. But Leibniz feels it is necessary first of all to clarify his view: bodies are made up of corporeal substances that are not *themselves* souls but which *have* souls.

Corporeal Substances and Monads

When Leibniz talks about corporeal substances in the texts that we have been examining, he *means* corporeal substances: the unity of a soul or form and a body or matter, understood in very roughly the way the terms would have been used by an Aristotelian of his day. Leibniz has some idiosyncrasies in his use of the terminology, of course, but when he talks about the revival of substantial forms the allusion to the standard Aristotelian conception of substance is unmistakable. It is reasonable to presume that this is how a correspondent such as Arnauld or a discussant such as Fardella would have understood him. In the next two

---

[130] A6.4.1670 (AG 105).

chapters we will refine what Leibniz meant by 'body' and 'matter' here: these terms aren't understood by Leibniz exactly the way they would be understood by the Cartesians or the schoolmen. However, it seems clear that in the texts we have been examining, corporeal substances are not monads, or even complex aggregates of monads; the Fardella memo would seem to make this especially clear. But there are commentators who disagree.

In later chapters we shall examine some other arguments that attempt to establish that Leibniz held a monadological metaphysics during the years that we have been examining, from the late 1670s through to the end of the 1690s. But here I would like to examine an argument advanced by Robert Adams.

One strategy Adams uses can be illustrated by his treatment of the Fardella memo. Let us focus for a moment on what I take to be the most striking line of the text: "the soul, properly and accurately speaking, is not a substance, but a substantial form. . . ." Adams writes:

One might certainly be tempted to take the statement that the soul is not a substance, strictly speaking, because it is a substantial form, as expressing the Aristotelian one-substance theory, in which a corporeal substance has its organic body as a constituent and does *not* have a simpler substance as a constituent. The statement does not compel us to this interpretation, however. In saying that the soul is not a substance Leibniz certainly has in mind that it is only an aspect of, or abstraction from, a concrete substance. The question is, What is that concrete substance of which it is an aspect? Is it a substance of which the organic body is a constituent, as in the Aristotelian one-substance conception? Or is it an unextended monad, as in the qualified monad and two-substance conceptions?[131]

This calls for a bit of background; in particular, what Adams means by the qualified monad, one-substance and two-substance interpretations. The two-substance conception is the view that there are two kinds of substance, the simple substance (or monad, as Leibniz was later to call it) and the composite or corporeal substance. On this view, the soul or form of the corporeal substance is a monad that unites a collection of other monads that constitute the organic body of the corporeal substance.[132] Adams recognizes two kinds of one-substance theories that might be attributed

---

[131] Adams (1994), 275.   [132] Ibid., 265–7.

to Leibniz. First there is the standard Aristotelian conception of substance, form and matter, where the form is not itself a substance but simply a constituent of substance, and the substance as a whole is, presumably, a full-fledged extended substance, something other than a monad. Second, there is what Adams calls the "qualified monad conception." On this conception, there is just one kind of substance in the world, the non-extended monad. But a monad can be called a corporeal substance insofar as it has a body: "A corporeal substance, on this view, is not a monad *plus* a body, but a monad *as having* a body."[133] Though Adams doesn't say so explicitly, the body in question is, presumably, a collection of other monads.

Adams goes on in his discussion to argue that there are considerations that count strongly against attributing to Leibniz the Aristotelian one-substance conception. On the other hand, he argues that the passages that we examined above from the Fardella memo are "quite consistent with both the two-substance and the qualified monad conception."[134] The two interpretations that Adams considers as live candidates for Leibniz's view both understand corporeal substance in terms of monads, either as a collection of monads united by a dominant monad, or as a "qualified" monad.[135] These readings have to be understood in the context of Adams's larger interpretation of Leibniz's metaphysics. Adams wants to downplay the importance of corporeal substance talk in Leibniz's writings in the middle period. He seems to think that Leibniz's interest in corporeal substance was "usually rooted in an interest in accommodating within his system, at least verbally, and if possible more than verbally, a common sense or traditional realism about bodies."[136] He claims:

Leibniz never had a deep personal commitment to the view that there are corporeal substances, one per se. His attempt to find a place for that idea in his philosophy was heteronomous, an accommodation to traditionalist concerns of others, especially Roman Catholics.[137]

[133] Ibid., 267–9. The quotation is from p. 269. Adams attributes this view to Cassirer.
[134] Adams (1994), 275–6.
[135] Cf. ibid., 285, where Adams clarifies his view further by suggesting that "the two-substance conception is the only one that we can be certain that Leibniz held at any time," though "some of his writings, especially before 1703, may have been influenced by something like the qualified monad conception."
[136] Ibid.   [137] Ibid., 307.

In this way, Adams argues, corporeal substance is not really part of Leibniz's core metaphysics; rather, it is something just added onto a basically monadological metaphysics, in both the middle and the late writings.

Adams's larger view about corporeal substance and its place (or lack thereof) in Leibniz's thought can be answered only by showing the ways in which the notion first enters his philosophy, and how it then functions in his thought. This is one of the main tasks of this book as a whole. But the specific readings that he proposes for the notion of corporeal substance in the Fardella memo and in other texts of this period can be answered more directly.

Now, Adams's dismissal of the Aristotelian one-substance reading of the Fardella memo seems rather hasty to me.[138] However, I don't want to dwell on that since I am not sure that what he calls the Aristotelian conception is the only alternative to the views he supports; nor do I think that it is an entirely accurate conception of what I take to be Leibniz's position.[139] But I would like to challenge the two interpretative options that Adams thinks remain: the Aristotelian two-substance view, as he understands it, and the qualified monad account.

As I noted above, Fardella was a Cartesian scientist, mathematician, and philosopher. But he would originally have been educated in scholastic Aristotelianism. Now, when Leibniz uses Aristotelian language to talk about substances and their substantial forms, it is reasonable to expect that Fardella will understand him in the way he had been educated. For example, when Leibniz says to such a person that "the soul, properly and accurately speaking, is not a substance, but a substantial form, or the primitive form existing in substances, the first act, the first active faculty," this is going to be understood most naturally in terms of a traditionally Aristotelian conception of substance. It is a virtual paraphrase of what

[138] The considerations advanced in ibid., 275–6 relate to an analogy Leibniz draws in a later passage between substances and souls on the one hand, and lines and points on the other. I have difficulty seeing how exactly they lead Adams to reject the Aristotelian one-substance conception.

[139] While, in the Fardella memo, Leibniz does argue that the soul is not a substance but a substantial form, in most other texts of the period he treats the soul as a substance. Furthermore, I don't think that Leibniz's conception of matter is necessarily going to be that of any standard Aristotelian account. There are lots of versions of the Aristotelian conception of substance available in the scholastic literature of the period, as Adams (and Leibniz) certainly knows. While Leibniz's view is definitely inspired by Aristotelian ideas, some considerable work will need to be done in the chapters below to flesh out exactly how he conceives of corporeal substance.

one could read in any Aristotelian textbook.[140] I don't doubt that Leibniz's language could be read in a more idiosyncratically Leibnizian way, as Adams does in attributing to him either the two-substance or the qualified monad conception of substance in this context. But if so, one would suppose that Leibniz would have explained his view to Fardella in a somewhat different way since these conceptions of substance make sense only in the context of a monadological metaphysics. After all, what would the point have been for Leibniz to have said a string of words to Fardella that he *knew* would be interpreted in one way, an Aristotelian way, when what he *really* meant was something altogether different, something that Fardella could not possibly have understood without further explanation? How would that have constituted a conversation? Now, it is always possible that the Fardella memo was meant for Leibniz's eyes only, and was not intended to explain his view to Fardella, in which case Adams's possible readings have more plausibility. But this cannot be said about his letters to Arnauld, which also use the language of corporeal substance extensively, as we have seen, and which were without a doubt intended to convince Arnauld of his position. When in these texts and in others of this period Leibniz uses Aristotelian language and talks about bodies and souls, matter and form, I think we have to assume that he has in mind something that his intended audience will comprehend. At the very least, there is a strong presumption that Leibniz was using philosophical language in a more-or-less standard way, and a considerable burden of proof rests on anyone who wants to read the monadology into these passages. In later chapters we shall consider some further arguments that Adams and other commentators have advanced for thinking that Leibniz really had monads on his mind in these texts. But I don't find convincing the readings of Adams that we have just been considering.

This is not to say that the interpretative job is done. Leibniz's conception of substance still remains somewhat murky. As I understand it, it is something close to the Aristotelian one-substance view that Adams sketches, but not

---

[140] Eustachius a Sancto Paulo, for example, characterizes the substantial form as "the primary and principal principle of acting," "agendi principium ... primarium ac principale." See his *Summa philosophiae quadripartita*, part III (Physica), Eustachius a Sancto Paolo (1609), vol. 2, 29. Note that each of the four parts of the book is paginated separately. This was a very popular textbook, and was republished numerous times throughout the century, in both Catholic and Protestant countries. On Leibniz's acquaintance with Eustachius, see, e.g., Leibniz to Des Bosses, 2 February 1706, LDB 8.

exactly, insofar as Leibniz sometimes conceives of the form or soul as itself a genuine substance. But what exactly is this body to which the soul is attached? What exactly is the matter that, united with form, constitutes a corporeal substance? One solution is to see Leibniz's proposal in the context of the Cartesian alternative against which he is reacting. It may look here as if Leibniz's solution to the problem of unity in Cartesian bodies is simply to add forms to Cartesian matter; it may look as if Leibnizian bodies are just Cartesian animal bodies to which a soul has been added to transform them into single corporeal substances. But this is not quite right. As we shall see in the next chapters, when Leibniz revives Aristotelian forms, he also means to revive an Aristotelian conception of matter.

3

Reforming Mechanism: Body and Force, Matter and Form (I)

The argument from unity discussed in the previous chapter is one of the most important in Leibniz's arsenal. It will appear again and again in various forms in later texts. But Leibniz has other reasons for introducing substantial forms into the world. Let me return briefly to the passage from the 'Conspectus libelli' that has been guiding this discussion to pick up the other prominent theme in that passage:

Certain things take place in body which cannot be explained from the necessity of matter alone. Such are the laws of motion, which depend upon the metaphysical principle of the equality of cause and effect. Therefore we must deal here with the soul and show that all things are animated....[1]

Forms must be introduced into bodies in order to ground an adequate natural philosophy; in particular, as we shall see, they are needed for grounding activity in the world. ——> Motion

Remember: Nature of body only gives us mobility.

Resistance and Conservation

Let's return to the physical world as Leibniz understood it in the early 1670s. At that moment, the world seems to have been made up of extended bodies, actually divided to infinity, along with minds. The only kind of activity that Leibniz, like Hobbes before him, recognized was motion. In particular, bodies had no resistance to motion from other bodies, so the laws of impact, at the most basic level, involved appropriate combinations

Motion: only change in bodies

[1] A6.4.1988 (L 278-9).

of velocity alone. There were certain obvious inconveniences with this view. For one, it seemed obviously at odds with what we experience in the world. For example, if this picture of the physical world is right, then when a small body (say a pea shot from a pea shooter) hits a large body at rest (say a giant boulder), then it will set the larger body into motion at whatever speed it hits, without losing any of its own speed. This is certainly not what we experience in everyday life. Leibniz's solution was to reconcile experience and theory by way of hypotheses about the make-up of the world that served to allow size to play a role. A second kind of problem comes from the fact that on this view of basic physics, motion can be lost in the world when, say, two bodies collide directly with one another. This would seem to undermine the possibility of any conservation law. Despite the evident problems, though, Leibniz was generally satisfied with this conception of the physical world through much of the first part of the 1670s.

Leibniz's first years in Paris were largely occupied with other matters; this is the period of his mathematical apprenticeship, among other things, the time in which the smart and ambitious young man from the wilds of Germany came to take his place on the international stage.[2] But by the mid-1670s, Leibniz had returned to physics and began to worry about some of the consequences of his Hobbesian physics of bodies without resistance. In a number of short pieces from the period, Leibniz is obviously experimenting with different ways of dealing with the consequences of his earlier views. While few of these writings suggest that he has arrived at any final and settled views, they are nevertheless indicative of the fact that Leibniz was thinking hard about the apparent resistance bodies exhibit toward acquiring new motion.

In a fragment dated December 1675, Leibniz wrote:

That the same quantity of motion is conserved, i.e., that if the magnitude of a moving body is increased, its speed is diminished, has been observed by Galileo, Descartes, and Hobbes, and even by Archimedes. This fact has been derived from the phenomena, but no one has shown its origin in nature itself.[3]

But even so, Leibniz seems unwilling to abandon his earlier view of body and resistance:

---

[2] See Antognazza (2008), 140ff, Hofmann (1974) and Hall (1980), ch. 4.   [3] A6.3.466 (RA 31).

We have assumed by a kind of prejudice that a greater body is harder to move, as if matter itself resisted motion. But this is unreasonable, for matter is indifferent to any place whatever, and thus also to change of place, or motion.[4]

In the text that follows, Leibniz tries to derive the conservation of Cartesian quantity of motion (size times speed) from the claim that the physical world is a plenum, and from the claim that a body moving faster occupies more space in a given instant than a body moving more slowly does. He writes:

Now, if a part of matter should begin to move faster than before, it follows that it will have occupied more space during the time AB than it would otherwise have occupied. But the [amount of] space in the world is definite, that is, certain and determinate, even if it is assumed to be infinite, and if everything is a plenum, something could not occupy more space than before unless something else occupied less space than before, otherwise bodies would be understood to penetrate each other. And therefore something could not move more quickly than before unless something else moved more slowly—by an amount sufficient for matter as a whole to be understood as having occupied precisely the same amount of space in the same time. That is, the same quantity of motion will be conserved in the whole, since the total quantity of motion is the same as the quantity of space successively occupied by a determinate quantity of matter in a determinate time.[5]

The basic idea is this. Given that the amount of space is fixed, even if it is infinite, if faster things occupy more space in a given time interval than slower things do, then if one body increases its speed, other bodies must slow down. In this way, Leibniz claims, we can have a principle of the conservation of motion even though, strictly speaking, matter doesn't actually resist motion.

In another passage written a few months later, in April 1676, Leibniz tries out a different way of understanding this apparent resistance:

The nature of body or matter . . . contains a secret marveled at until now: namely, that magnitude compensates for speed, as if they were homogeneous things. And this is an indication that matter itself is resolved into something into which motion is also resolved, namely, a certain universal intellect. For when two bodies collide, it is clear that it is not the mind of each one that makes it follow the law of compensation, but rather the universal mind assisting both, or rather all, equally.[6]

---

[4] Ibid.   [5] A6.3.467–8 (RA 33–5).   [6] A6.3.493 (RA 77).

Here it is God who adjusts speed to mass, and makes it more difficult to set a larger body in motion than a smaller one.[7]

In yet another short piece, probably from the same period, Leibniz returns to the general strategy of the *HPN* and attempts to explain why larger bodies are harder to set into motion through a series of elaborate physical hypotheses about aether, elasticity, and the division of matter into smaller parts.[8] But at the end of the text, Leibniz makes an interesting suggestion, one quite different than anything he had been willing to admit before: "However, everything would proceed more simply if we assumed the inertia of matter, namely that a greater thing would resist more."[9] At that moment, though, he did not seem to be ready to abandon his earlier commitments and take up that suggestion in a serious way.

But by a few months later, in the summer of 1676, Leibniz had a major breakthrough in his physics, one that finally forced him radically to reevaluate his view on body and resistance. Leibniz had been in contact with the English mathematical community mediated by the German secretary of the Royal Society of London, Henry Oldenburg. In mid-August, through Oldenburg he had finally received a long letter from the young Isaac Newton, the so-called *First Letter* in which the reclusive and somewhat secretive English mathematician told Leibniz about some of his discoveries. At the end of his hasty reply, addressed to Oldenburg, Leibniz added a few lines about his recent work in physics, in his usual modest and self-effacing style:

I have decided to proceed as follows so as to reduce all mechanics to pure geometry, as soon as I have the leisure, and I shall settle problems about elasticity and fluids, and pendula and projectiles, and the resistance of solids and friction,

---

[7] In this passage Leibniz is not worried about conservation of motion as such, but only about the apparent fact that larger bodies are harder to set into motion than smaller ones. He continues: "On the other hand, it is not necessary for the same quantity of motion always to be conserved in the world, since if one body is carried by another in a certain direction, but is moving of its own accord equally in the contrary direction, it will certainly come to rest, i.e. it will not leave its place. From this it follows that the conservation of the quantity of motion must be asserted of the action, i.e. relative motion by which one body is related to or acts on another" [A6.3.493 (RA 77–9)]. Cf. Leibniz's remarks on conservation in his first notes on Descartes's *Principia philosophiae* II.36, A6.3.215–16 (RA 25–7), where he takes a similar position.

[8] 'Regulae motus systematicae praestari mechanice,' A6.4.1959–60. The Akademie editors date this fragment from 1677, entirely on the basis of content. However, it seems to me more plausible that this fragment should precede the essay "De arcanis motus..." from summer 1676 that I am about to discuss.

[9] A6.4.1960.

which hitherto no one has succeeded in doing. And I believe that the whole business is now in my power. Within this area I have satisfied myself concerning the rules of motions by way of demonstrations that are utterly flawless, nor do I desire anything further in this domain. *However, what is amazing is that the matter turns entirely upon a very pretty metaphysical axiom concerning motion, which is of no less importance for motion than the axiom that the whole is greater than the part is with respect to magnitude.*[10]

The "very pretty metaphysical axiom" to which he refers here is no doubt the principle of the equality of cause and effect, that the entire effect must have the same ability to do work as its full cause, the principle to which he refers in the excerpt from the 'Conspectus libelli' quoted at the beginning of this chapter.

The equality principle, as we shall call it, first emerges in Leibniz's writings in mid-1676.[11] It is not entirely clear where it came from. At about the time it emerged Leibniz was reading Wallis's *Mechanica*, in which he argues that "effects are proportional to their adequate causes."[12] This is not exactly Leibniz's principle, insofar as Wallis holds that the effect is *proportional* to its cause rather than *equal*.[13] But it is close. Another possible source comes from some of Leibniz's early reflections on cause and effect. The essay entitled "Meditatio de principio individui" (1 April 1676), discussed above in the previous chapter, begins as follows:

We say that the effect envelops [*involvere*] its cause; that is, in such a way that whoever understands some effect perfectly will also arrive at the knowledge of its cause. For it is necessary that there is some connection between a complete cause and the effect.[14]   ⟶ This is not equality, but only derivability

---

[10] Leibniz to Oldenburg, 17/27 August 1676, A3.1.586, trans. in Oldenburg (1965–86), vol. 13, 49, emphasis added. This important letter was to be one of the key documents in the later priority fight between Leibniz and Newton. See Hofmann (1974), ch. 17.

[11] For a very subtle account of the equality principle and its origin in Leibniz's thought in the mid-1670s, see Carraud (2002), 399–416. Carraud is particularly interested in the way the principle connects with the notion of reason in Leibniz's thought in general, and with the Principle of Sufficient Reason in particular. In the end, though, I think that he connects it too closely with final causality; see esp. pp. 413f.

[12] See Hofmann (1974), 140; Fichant (1978), 229; Fichant (1990), 55–6; Fichant (1994), 280n. Thanks to Philip Beeley for sharing with me a copy of Leibniz's ms. notes on Wallis. Thanks also to Beeley for pointing out the connection.

[13] Cf. Leibniz to Bayle, 9 January 1687: "Elle [i.e. the equality principle] ne dit pas seulement que les Effects sont proportionnels aux causes, mais de plus, que chaque effect entier est equivalent à sa cause" (G III 46).

[14] A6.3.490 (SR 51). Cf. A6.3.111.

This is not the equality principle, to be sure, but it is very reminiscent of the considerations that Leibniz will later advance for that principle.

The first extensive statement of the equality principle is found in a remarkable piece, which Leibniz entitled "De arcanis motus et mechanica ad puram geometriam reducenda," "On the secrets of motion and the reduction of mechanics to pure geometry," probably written in the summer of 1676, sometime shortly before the letter to Oldenburg from 17/27 August.[15] There he wrote: "Just as in geometry, the principle of reasoning usually cited is the equality between the whole and all of its parts, so in mechanics everything depends on the equality of the whole cause and the entire effect."[16] Leibniz went on to offer rather elaborate explanations of his new principle. He noted:

Hence it is necessary that the cause be able to do as much as the effect and vice versa. And thus any full effect, if the opportunity offers itself, can perfectly reproduce its cause, that is, it has forces enough to bring something back into the same state that it was in previously, or into an equivalent state. (For being able to measure equivalent things, it is therefore useful that a measure be assumed, such as the force necessary to raise some heavy thing to some height.).... Hence it happens that a stone which falls from some height constrained by a pendulum can climb back to the same height, but no higher, if nothing interferes and it acts perfectly, and if nothing of the forces are removed, no lower either....[17]

Leibniz claims that this principle can play the same role in physics that the axioms play in geometry:

Just as geometry depends on metaphysics concerning whole and part, so mechanics depends on metaphysics concerning cause and effect. Indeed, it is an a priori metaphysical principle that the effect is of the same strength as the whole cause, or the cause produces the same thing, neither more nor less, as long as it is neither helped nor hindered.[18]

---

[15] It is published in Hess (1978), 202–5. It is discussed, and its significance underscored, in Fichant (1978). Note also the elegant discussion of the equality principle in Fichant's commentary on the "De corporum concursu," Fichant (1994), 277ff.

[16] Hess (1978), 203. Note other early statements of the principle: A6.3.400 (SR 115); A6.3.584 (SR 107); A6.4.1963.

[17] Hess (1978), 204.

[18] Ibid. While the notion of the a priori is in some flux at this moment, I am assuming that Leibniz means it here in the modern epistemological sense, that is, knowable without appeal to experience. It is very interesting to note here that when it is first introduced, Leibniz considers the equality principle

This principle is a metaphysical principle (whatever exactly that means for Leibniz at that moment), which, he thinks, can ground all of mechanics (whatever exactly that means for Leibniz at that moment). It is, in essence, a very general conservation principle that mandates the constancy of the ability to do work in the world.

Leibniz quickly realized that this principle has important consequences for the laws of motion. In what is quite clearly a reference to his meeting with Spinoza in November 1676, Leibniz reports having set Spinoza right about the Cartesian laws of motion:

> Spinoza did not see the mistakes in Descartes' rules of motion; he was surprised when I began to show him that they violate the equality of cause and effect.[19]

But though he saw some of the negative consequences of his new principle, it took him a little while longer to grasp the laws that he was eventually to derive. It is exactly this approach that, combined with the Galilean law of free fall, led Leibniz to the conclusion less than a year and a half later that it is mv^2 that is conserved in collision in some notes on the theory of impact, "De corporum concursu" of January 1678.[20]

Later in the next chapter we shall return to the equality principle and examine the way in which it led Leibniz to his famous principle of the conservation of mv^2 in much greater detail. But here I want to emphasize another consequence Leibniz quickly drew directly from his "very pretty metaphysical axiom." Even before Leibniz used the equality principle to arrive at a mathematical measure of force, the new metaphysical principle led him to adopt something he had been trying to avoid for a number of

to be necessary, something that he soon abandons. Below in Ch. 6 we shall discuss this issue in more detail.

[19] Quoted in Foucher de Careil's introductory essay to Leibniz (1854), LXIV. Unfortunately, Foucher de Careil gives no identifiable source for the quotation, and I have not been able to verify it in any more reliable source, so some uncertainty attaches to the dating of the passage. Indeed, the ms. itself may have been lost by Foucher de Careil! Cf. Laerke (2008), 368–9. In a personal communication, Laerke suggested that this must be a later—and somewhat inaccurate—recollection of the conversation. By the time of the conversation with Leibniz, Spinoza had already distanced himself from Descartes's physics, as he reported in two letters to Tschirnhaus; see Spinoza (1925), vol. 4, 332, 334. Given their close relations, it is likely that Leibniz knew about these exchanges. However, it is also possible that Spinoza's doubts about Descartes's physics didn't extend to the laws of motion. For more on the relations among Leibniz, Tschirnhaus, and Spinoza, see Goldenbaum (1994) and Kulstad (1999) and (2002).

[20] Fichant (1994), 152–8. See also Fichant (1974) and Fichant (1990).

Inertia

years, positing a genuine force of resistance in bodies. Leibniz ends the
"De arcanis motus" with the following passage:

It has been established through experience that the cause why a larger body is
moved with difficulty even on a horizontal plane is not [always] heaviness, but
massiveness.[21] Unless body were to resist, perpetual motion would follow, since
a body resists in proportion to its bulk [*moles*], since there is no other factor that
would limit it [*nulla alia ratio determinandi*]. That is to say, since there is no other
factor [*ratio*] which would hinder it from rebounding to less than its [original]
height, since in itself, without an extrinsic impediment through the impulse of
[another] body, it would give [the other body] its whole motion, and retain it as
well.[22]

The equality principle almost certainly rules out the strategy of the *HPN*,
where the apparent resistance of heavy bodies can be explained by way of
a hypothesis about the structure of the world. While such a strategy may
save appearances at the macroscopic level, we would still have problems at
the microscopic level. Consider two elementary bodies moving at the same
speed and colliding directly. After the collision, all motion would cease
and both would be at rest, arguably resulting in a decrease in the ability to
do work in the system composed of the two bodies. But, it would seem,
it is still open to Leibniz to explain the apparent resistance bodies exhibit
in terms of the direct activity of God, as he had done as recently as April
1676 in the text quoted above. In this way we might say that the equality
principle doesn't seem to *demand* that we recognize a force of resistance in
bodies. But be that as it may, as a matter of fact, by the summer of 1676 the
equality principle led Leibniz to recognize that bodies must contain some
force by which they resist the acquisition of new motion in collision.

Motion and Activity

While Leibniz was grappling with the question of resistance in the mid-
and late 1670s, he seems also to have become aware of another problem,
that of motion.

---

[21] The word here is 'soliditas.' According to Robert Estienne's *Dictionarium latinogallicum* (Paris, 3rd
edn, 1552), 'soliditas' means "massivité, solidité, fermeté." Of these, I think that the first is closest to
what Leibniz has in mind here.

[22] Hess (1978), 205.

One of the earliest discussions of problems raised by the notion of motion can be found in a curious document that dates from early on in Leibniz's Paris visit, from sometime in the autumn or winter of 1672/3, a grab-bag of reflections on infinity and infinitesimals, minds and bodies. The reflections on the notion of motion in the document are connected with a theme that we discussed earlier in Chapter 1, Leibniz's early attempt to link the notion of body with the notion of motion. Leibniz concludes the first part of the argument with the claim that "*to be a body* is nothing other than *to move*."[23] But this, in turn, raises another question: what does it mean to move? Leibniz goes through a number of definitions that others have suggested for what motion is, ultimately concluding that none of them work. He writes: *Metaphysical or epistemological*

Since to be a body is to move, it must be asked what it is to move. If it is to change place, then what is place? Isn't this determined by reference to bodies? If to move is to be transferred from the vicinity of one body to another body, the question returns, what is body? Thus body will be inexplicable, that is, impossible, unless motion can be explained without body entering into its definition. It is no good saying that to move is to change space, when we have concluded that there is no distinction between space and body. So what in the end are body and motion really, if we are to avoid this circle?[24]

Leibniz's answer: "What else, but being sensed by some mind."[25] But Leibniz doesn't mean just any mind; finite minds are insufficient for grounding the reality of motion (and thus body), he claims.[26] And so he concludes: "we vindicated the necessity of minds, but from among minds,

---

[23] A6.3.100 (RA 17).

[24] Ibid. The reference to the transference of a body from the vicinity of one body to that of another is a reference to Descartes's definition of motion in *Principia philosophiae* II.25.

[25] Ibid.

[26] Leibniz's reasoning here is somewhat obscure. Here is the passage in which he appears to make the argument:

For the existence of bodies, it is certain that some mind free of body is required, different from all the others we sense. For it is clear that these minds we sense, such as anyone experiences in himself, confer nothing towards the existence of things. For it is known from experience that everything is not sensed any the less by others because I am absent, and the same is true of every individual. Therefore this will also be the case in the aggregate of all things, which combines them only by considering them together. On the other hand, it is clear that that mind that is free from body, i.e. does not need a body in order to exist, must exist per se.... [A6.3.100–1 (RA 17)]

What is particularly puzzling is the phrase "everything is not sensed any the less by others because I am absent....," "omnia ab aliis non ideo minus sentiri, quod ego abfui...." Perhaps the sense of this is: "I'm not the only individual that doesn't sense everything; and this is true of every other individual too." The last sentence suggests that the reason that finite things can't sense everything is

only God's."[27] The view seems to be that motion is to be understood as grounded in divine perception: motion is change as perceived by God. The view is somewhat puzzling, though: if place, body, and change of place are indefinable without God, how does the appeal to God help us out? What is it that God can perceive that we cannot? This essay seems to be less an exercise in physics and more in the spirit of the other theological essays from 1668 and 1669 which we examined above in Chapter 1, essays connected with the "Demonstrationes catholicae," where the point is to use problems from physics as a way of introducing mind and God into the mechanist's world.

The problem of motion resurfaces around 1675 or 1676, when Leibniz begins to turn to physics again. The problem is particularly visible in a long document that the Akademie editors name 'Principia mechanica,' but which is probably better titled 'Principia scientiae motus.'[28] The document is somewhat rambling, Leibniz thinking on his feet rather than presenting his finished thoughts in a polished essay. He begins with some general remarks about mechanics and about the notions of situation (*situs*) and distance, before finally approaching the question of motion. Motion is introduced as change of place. But very quickly he focuses on a problem raised by that definition: "Indeed, the change of place is not yet sufficient for us to judge to which of those things which change place among themselves motion should be ascribed."[29] And this is the question that Leibniz attacks for the rest of the manuscript: when bodies are changing place with respect to one

---

that they are connected with finite bodies. The conclusion would be that only God, unconnected to a finite body, could sense everything, and so only God can be the foundation of motion and thus of body itself, insofar as bodies are defined in terms of motion. It is interesting to note that if this is, indeed, what Leibniz has in mind here, it is in contradiction with the position that he will later adopt, that every individual reflects the entire world in which it exists. But even though his reasoning is obscure here, the conclusion Leibniz draws is clear.

[27] A6.3.101 (RA 19).

[28] The opening lines are: "Scientiae Motuum quam Mechanicen vocant, principia tradere constituimus" (A6.3.101). Though he begins by talking about mechanics in general, he never manages to get beyond a lengthy discussion of the concept of motion. The Akademie editors date it tentatively at 1673–76 (?). Various elements of the text resonate strongly with other texts that are securely dated to 1676, which suggests that this piece dates to this period as well. For example, the text begins by talking about the project of reducing mechanics to pure geometry, suggesting the title of the "De arcanis motus..." from the summer of 1676; cf. A6.3.102, ll. 2–3. The ending (A6.3.111, ll. 26–8) asserts that the full cause must produce a unique effect, and alludes to the example of shape, here characterized as an incomplete concept. This suggests the discussion in the "Meditatio de principio individui" from 1 April 1676 [A6.3.490f (SR 51f)] and the discussion of shape and other incomplete concepts in some notes on metaphysics dated December 1676 [A6.3.400 (SR 115)].

[29] A6.3.104.

another, how do we decide which is really in motion, and which is really at rest? While he considers various strategies, in the end he arrives at the following conclusion:

Therefore, it is obvious from this that from the phenomena of change of situation alone we can never have any certain knowledge of absolute motion and rest. But if absolute motion cannot be discerned from other phenomena, not even by those to whom all phenomena have been revealed, it follows that motion and rest taken absolutely is an empty name, and whatever is real in them consists only in relative change. For since no hypothesis can be refuted with respect to others through certain demonstration, even by someone who is omniscient, it follows that none is false with respect to others. That is (since they cannot be consistent) all are false, nor can they be admitted except as different appearances of the same thing, that is, as optical tricks, like an eye placed now in one, now in another position.[30]

[handwritten: Motion / rest = illusions]

In this way, what is real in motion is simply the change in mutual distance between two bodies: there simply is no fact of the matter about whether one or another body is *really* in motion or *really* at rest. But Leibniz does not want to give up the distinction between motion and rest altogether. Because there is no real fact of the matter about motion and rest, he claims, we are free to attribute motion or rest to whichever bodies we like in a system of moving bodies, as long as the phenomena are respected. And so Leibniz continues the above quotation with the following remark:

However, here we will be permitted to choose the simpler way of explaining which relates to a particular cause from which the other changes can be derived more easily.[31]

Such an attribution of motion and rest involves telling different causal stories about the phenomena. But Leibniz doesn't think that it is clear that there is any such thing as the *correct* causal story in any absolute sense:

thus we say that the stone descends to the earth rather than saying that the globe of the earth, together with the whole universe, leaps up toward it. But even if, perhaps either the descent of the stone or the leaping up of the earth were likewise alien to nature, nothing really happens but a certain relative change of place, or a translation from a distant place into a neighboring one.[32]

[handwritten: → This is metaphysical, not only epistemological]

[30] A6.3.110–11.   [31] A6.3.111.   [32] Ibid.

In this way, all that is real in motion is just the mutual separation or approaching of two bodies.[33]

Other writings on motion in this period reflect a similar point of view. In a piece dated from early 1677, Leibniz argues as follows:

in reality...motion is not something absolute, but consists in relation. And therefore if two bodies collide, the speed must be understood to be distributed between them in such a way that each runs into the other with the same force. Thus if two colliding bodies are understood to be equal, then all the phenomena consistent with experiments will at once be deduced from this fact alone.[34]

In contrast to the earlier text that we have been examining, although Leibniz claims that motion is purely relational, here he offers a definite answer to the question of where the motion is: we should attribute speeds to the two moving bodies in such a way that they act on one another with equal force. (The problem here, of course, is in determining what 'force' means and how it is measured. Leibniz doesn't really address the question in the text.) In another fragment from the same period (this one is dated February 1677), Leibniz draws a somewhat different conclusion from the relativity of motion:

A remarkable fact: motion is something relative, and one cannot distinguish exactly which of the bodies is moving. Thus if motion is an affection, its subject will not be any one individual body, but the whole world. Hence all its effects must also necessarily be relative.[35]

In this way, the subject of motion is not in either of the moving bodies, nor is it in their relative distance, but in the world as a whole.

While these texts all seem to agree that motion is relative in some sense, it is clear that Leibniz is searching for a way of understanding motion and its subject. Indeed, there is some reason to think that he thought this to be a pressing problem. In a fragment difficult to date, but quite possibly from the late 1670s, Leibniz writes:

That matter and motion are only phenomena, or contain in themselves something imaginary, can be understood from the fact that different and contradictory hypotheses can be made about them, all of which nevertheless satisfy the phenomena perfectly, so that no reason can be devised for determining which of them

---

[33] This conception of motion winds up rather close to the view that Descartes adopted in the *Principia philosophiae*. See Garber (1992), ch. 6.

[34] A6.4.1968 (RA 225).

[35] A6.4.1970 (RA 229). See the discussion of this view in Lodge (2003), 284−5.

should be preferred. In real things, on the other hand, every truth can be accurately discovered and demonstrated. Thus concerning motion I have shown elsewhere that it is not possible to determine which subject it is in. . . .[36]

In this way the lack of a fact of a matter about whether a given body is in motion or at rest is itself a reason for thinking that motion itself isn't real, but only phenomenal.[37]

But this cannot be an altogether comfortable position for a mechanist to take. If everything is explicable in terms of body in motion, then the reality of physics would seem to demand that we be able to find something real in motion. Perhaps as a result of this, Leibniz sometimes qualifies his claim that motion is just relational. To ground the reality of motion, Leibniz turns away from the purely geometrical, and to the underlying cause of change. In the fragment from February 1677 quoted above, for example, after advancing the claim that motion is in its nature relative, Leibniz adds:

It should be noted, however, that when we consider motion not formally as it is in itself, but with respect to cause, it can be attributed to the body of that thing by whose contact change is brought about.[38]

Given the larger context of this passage, the speculations about the relativity of motion in the preceding paragraph, one might infer that Leibniz may not have been quite ready to sign on to this position in February 1677. But within a couple of years, at about the time he announces his revival of substantial forms in physics, Leibniz seems to take this conception of the subject of motion in terms of proximate cause more seriously.[39] This view is set out in a series of fragments that the Akademie editors date from summer 1678 to winter 1680/1, exactly the period of the 'Conspectus libelli.' One fragment in the series begins with a definition of motion:

A body is in motion, when it is the proximate efficient cause why some part or another of it changes with respect to other bodies; otherwise it is said to be at rest.[40]

---

[36] A6.4.1463 (RA 257). The Akademie editors date this to winter 1682/3 based entirely on internal evidence. Richard Arthur, on the other hand, prefers the date 1678/9, also for internal evidence. I tend to agree with Arthur on this one, though the evidence is slim.

[37] We will discuss Leibniz's notion of the phenomenal below in Ch. 7.   [38] A6.4.1970 (RA 229).

[39] On this conception of motion see Lodge (2003), 285ff. Lodge goes on to discuss (pp. 297ff) a further criterion that Leibniz uses in later writings, the simplicity of hypotheses.

[40] A6.4.2011.

Leibniz fills this out with an example. Consider the sun and some particular star with respect to which it is changing its distance. To which should we attribute motion? "If we were to know what was the proximate cause of the change of place, then we would attribute the motion to it," Leibniz writes.[41] If the star were found to be moved by an intelligence, or if it were moving a moment before (since motion does not stop by itself), or if it were pushed along by an ambient medium (as it would be in a vortex theory), then the star would properly be said to be moving; if none of these factors were found with respect to the sun, then the sun would be at rest; if causes for change were found in both the sun and the star, then both would be said to be moving.

Another fragment in this same series of texts, presumably from the same period of time, attacks the problem in a slightly different way. As earlier, Leibniz writes:

If we consider change of position alone, that is, what in motion is merely mathematical, then it cannot be said to which of a number of bodies changing position with respect to one another we should ascribe motion.[42]

As in astronomy, Leibniz notes, any hypothesis, that is, any assignment of motion and rest consistent with the phenomena, will do in these circumstances. But, Leibniz continues, "if we go to physical causes, then we can more easily establish to which [body] motion should be ascribed."[43] Leibniz illustrates with an example. He posits a number of bodies, moving with respect to one another. (See Figure 3:1.) When we consider only their change of position with respect to one another, there is no way to determine which is in motion, and which is at rest. But the consideration of *impact* breaks the relativity for Leibniz.

---

[41] Ibid.   [42] A6.4.2017–18.

[43] A6.4.2018. Cf. 'Definitiones cogitationesque metaphysicae' (1678–81): "When two bodies approach each other, it can only be decided from the cause of motion, not from the motion itself, which of the two is at rest or moves, or whether both are moving. It is the same with several bodies" [A6.4.1400 (RA 249)]; "Mira de natura substantiae corporeae" (29 March 1683): "And just as color and sound are phenomena, rather than true attributes of things containing a certain absolute nature without relation to us, so too are extension and motion. For it cannot really be said just which subject the motion is in. Consequently, nothing in motion is real besides the force and power vested in things, that is to say, beyond their having such a constitution that from it there follows a change of phenomena constrained by certain rules" [A6.4.1465 (RA 263)].

whatever is acted on
the change of position
is actual or
is the cause of
moving

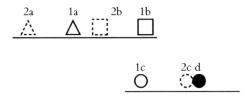

Figure 3:1. From A6.4.2017.

All the hypotheses with respect to motion and rest are equally valid, he writes,

> unless we assume some new body *d* such that if *c* is assumed to move from 1*c* to 2*c*, it is necessary that it collide with *d*, for then we pass from the simple mathematical consideration of the change of situation to physics, namely, to some action. For some communication of motion will follow [the collision with *d*], from which it will be obvious that some action is to be ascribed to *c*.[44]

What makes *c* the body in motion and *d* the body at rest is the fact that *c* exerts a certain *physical action* and that, as a consequence, *c* must be the cause of the motion in *d*. Indeed, Leibniz claims, if it is physical action that is the criterion for motion, then a body can be in motion *even when it is not changing its place with respect to bodies regarded at rest*. In the paragraph that follows he gives an example in which a person is walking along a deck of a ship, while, at the same time, that same ship is moving with the same speed that the person is moving, but in the opposite direction.[45] (See Figure 3:2.)

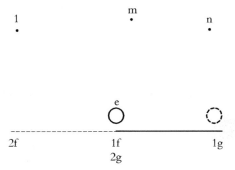

Figure 3:2. From A6.4.2018.

---

[44] A6.4.2018.   [45] A6.4.2018−19.

The person is at rest with respect to the fixed points l, m, and n in Leibniz's diagram. Yet, at the same time, the person *feels* the effort of walking, and thus is moving, says Leibniz:

> However, we should say that he is in motion: for, at any rate, that man will feel that he is becoming tired by walking, and he will be able to push or pull something by means of his motion. And thus, he acts. Therefore, since we attribute motion to that in which the cause of change of situation is found, that is, to that which acts, we will, at any rate, say that the body e moves, even if the place it has in the world, and which is taken with respect to fixed points does not change.[46]

True motion seems, in a way, almost entirely divorced from change of geometrical place. In another fragment from the series, he unambiguously rejects the position that he himself once held, and along the way gives the cause a general name:

> And so we attribute motion to that thing which has a force of acting [*vis agendi*]. Whence it is also obvious that those who have said that what is real and positive in motion belongs equally to both of two continuous bodies receding from one another have spoken falsely. For there can be a force of acting (and thus also the cause of the change of situation) in only one of them.[47] —⟩ Why is that

The '*vis agendi*,' the force of acting, then, is what will enable us to say that there is a distinction between motion and rest.[48]

It is important to observe that the force or activity in question, this '*vis agendi*,' is *not* reducible to size, shape, and change of place, the sorts of things that a Cartesian mechanist thinks make up the world of bodies. But even though it is not a mode of extension, it is something that we can conceive of in a very vivid way through sensation and imagination. We can *feel* the effort that we make when we work, we can conceive of the effort that the heavenly intelligences might make, turning the planets in their

---

[46] A6.4.2019.

[47] Ibid. First among those who have spoken falsely here in saying that motion belongs equally to two bodies receding from one another is Descartes. See *Principia philosophiae* II.29–30. Note that the words "change of situation" in the last sentence are conjectures by the editors. Note also that in the marginal note to the very beginning of the fair copy of "Pacidius Philalethi" (1676), Leibniz remarks: "Still to be treated are, first, the subject of motion, to make it clear which of two things changing their mutual situation motion should be ascribed to, and second the cause of motion, i.e. motive force [*vis motrix*]." This might be as early as 1676, but it might also be a later addition [A6.3.529 (RA 129)].

[48] For a careful development of this view, appealing to later texts and contemporary mathematical and philosophical ideas, see Roberts (2003) and Slowik (2006).

orbits. Leibniz even thinks that we can see, in collision, one body acting on another, exerting a force, and acting as a genuine cause of change. I do not want to suggest that this position is unproblematic for a mechanist or for someone who, like Leibniz, is sympathetic to the mechanist position. It isn't. We may feel our efforts well enough, but can we *really* see motion pass from one body to another in collision, and can we *really* determine which body is the actor, and which body is the patient? But, without hiding the difficulties in Leibniz's view, I want simply to set out the position Leibniz takes in these texts. When we consider only the geometrical properties of bodies, all questions of motion and rest are open, and all hypotheses are equally good. But when we consider force and activity as well, we can actually assign motion and rest.

The question of the real cause of motion and the extent to which it can be identified in the physical world becomes much more complex and tangled in later years. But for the moment I want to turn to examine some of the consequences that Leibniz drew from the studies of motion and resistance he made in these years.

Force and Form

By the late 1670s, then, Leibniz had come to the view that bodies have a passive force for resisting the acquisition of new motion, and a '*vis agendi*,' an active force by which motion and rest can be distinguished from one another. The recognition of forces, active and passive, led Leibniz, by a different path, to the same position that he was led to by considerations of unity and individuality, to the revival of substantial form in the physical world:

Certain things take place in body which cannot be explained from the necessity of matter alone. . . . Therefore we must deal here with the soul and show that all things are animated. . . .[49]

To put the argument very simply, physics requires that we admit forces, active and passive.[50] But Cartesian (or Hobbesian) bodies, the objects of geometry made real, have nothing in them from which such active and

[49] A6.4.1988 (L 278–9).   [50] Presuming, of course, as Leibniz does, that occasionalism is false.

passive forces could arise. So, Leibniz concludes, *there must be something to bodies over and above their geometrical properties*. To ground these forces in bodies we must revive the forms that the schoolmen had posited and that the mechanists had rejected.

The argument is set out in a text contemporary with the 'Conspectus libelli' that has all of the marks of an essay Leibniz was preparing for publication.[51] Leibniz didn't give the text a title, but had he done so, it might have been something like 'De natura corporis et de legibus motus'; I shall refer to it as 'De natura corporis' for short. Leibniz, by then in his early thirties, begins the essay by recalling a position that he had taken in his callow youth, that is, seven or eight years earlier:

There was a time when I believed that all the phenomena of motion could be explained on purely geometrical principles, assuming no metaphysical propositions, and that the laws of impact depend only on the composition of motions....[52]

The reference here is, of course, to the *TMA* of 1671. But, he tells his reader, "through more profound meditation, I discovered that this is impossible...."[53] Leibniz then goes through some cases of impact in detail, and shows how the initial assumption that bodies in collision offer no resistance to the acquisition of new motion leads to absurd results: "What we concluded in this way about the collision of bodies differs from experience, especially [in one of the cases discussed] when the magnitude of the body to be moved is increased, it is not thereby determined that the speed is decreased."[54] Referring to the strategy of the *HPN*, Leibniz does admit that this consequence can be reconciled with experience by way of a hypothesis about the make-up of the physical world:

And furthermore, even if what I concluded were to hold with respect to the condition of bodies placed outside of an organized system, bodies in their untamed condition, so to speak, so that the greatest body at rest would be carried off by the smallest colliding body, with the same speed it has, however little that might be, I believed that in an organized system, that is, with respect to the bodies around us, such a thing would be utterly absurd, for in this way the slightest bit of work would produce maximal disorder. And thus, I believed, this result is blocked by various

---

[51] A6.4.1976–80 (AG 245–50). Note that the text is incorrectly dated in the earlier printings of AG. The Akademie editors date it summer 1678–winter 1680/1, exactly the range as the 'Conspectus libelli.'

[52] A6.4.1976 (AG 245).   [53] Ibid.   [54] A6.4.1980 (AG 249).

devices. For, I believed, bodies are endowed with elasticity and are flexible, and often a part is impelled without the whole being impelled.[55]

But Leibniz came to see that this kind of ad-hoc device is not really satisfactory. He continues:

But when I considered how, in general, we could explain what we experience everywhere, that speed is diminished through an increase in bulk [*moles*] as, for example, when the same boat carried downstream goes more slowly the more it is loaded down, I stopped, and all my attempts having been in vain, I discovered that this, so to speak, inertia of bodies cannot be deduced from the initially assumed notion of matter and motion, where matter is understood as that which is extended or fills space, and motion is understood as change of space or place. But rather, over and above that which is deduced from extension and its variation or modification alone, we must add and recognize in bodies certain notions or forms that are immaterial, so to speak, or independent of extension, which you can call powers [*potentia*], by means of which speed is adjusted to magnitude. These powers consist not in motion, indeed, not in conatus or the beginning of motion, but in the cause or in that intrinsic reason for motion, which is the law required for continuing.[56]

The ad-hoc hypotheses of the *HPN* are able to save macroscopic phenomena. But at the microscopic level, the problems persist: the resistance to the acquisition of new motion is something that we experience *everywhere*, which suggests that it must hold at the most fundamental levels as well.[57]

But how does it help to introduce forms? Leibniz's idea seems to be this. Resistance and the ability to do work are kinds of activity in bodies, and therefore cannot be derived from bare matter, which is entirely passive, or from motion, which is just change of place. Indeed, the assumption here seems to be that resistance is, itself, a kind of activity. As he writes

---

[55] Ibid.

[56] Ibid. Cf. also the following passage from a letter to de La Chaise (April/May 1680), where Leibniz goes as far as to identify activity and active force with the essence of body: "[j'ai trouvé . . .] Qu'il y a des formes substantielles, et que la nature du corps consiste non pas dans l'étendue, mais dans une action qui se rapporte à l'étendue, car je tiens qu'un corps ne sçauroit estre sans effort: d'ou il s'ensuit *non corpus necessario determinata extensionis esse, sed ad eam habendam inclinari nisi superior potentia impediat*" (A2.1².798). See also the notes on Simon Foucher (1676) : "L'essence des substances consiste dans la force primitive d'agir, ou dans la loy de la suite des changemens, comme la nature de la *series* dans les nombres" (A6.3.326). But both the textual notes and the contents suggest that this is a later addition.

[57] Given the infinite divisibility of matter, this may not be strictly speaking true. If matter is infinitely divisible, then we may be able to follow the strategy of the *HPN* at ever lower levels. However, Leibniz does not pursue this as a possibility.

in an important document from the period (to which we shall return shortly), "a resisting thing is that which acts on that by which it is acted upon."[58] And, therefore, to inert extended matter we must add something that can be the source of this activity. One solution, of course, would be to ground that activity in God, as the occasionalists do, and as Leibniz himself had suggested with respect to the problem of resistance in an earlier text, discussed above. Leibniz wants to reject this possible solution. In the essay we have been examining, 'De natura corporis,' Leibniz writes:

> And investigators have erred insofar as they considered motion, but not motive power or the reason for motion, which even if derived from God, author and governor of things, must not be understood as being in God himself, but must be understood as having been produced and conserved by him in things.[59]

This is obviously unsatisfactory as an argument; later, in Chapter 5, we shall come back to the question of Leibniz's rejection of occasionalism and look at the arguments that he offers for the activity of bodies. Leibniz's preferred solution is to ground force and activity directly in body itself. That is, to inert matter we must add "powers" or forces, that "by which speed is adjusted to magnitude." In 'De natura corporis,' at least, these forces or powers are identified with the forms that Leibniz wants to attribute to bodies: forms just *are* powers or forces. And if forms are understood in this way, then adding force and activity to body *is just* to add form.

The focus in this passage (indeed, in the whole essay 'De natura corporis') is on the force by which bodies resist new motion; it is the necessity of introducing resistance into bodies that seems to motivate the introduction of form to bodies. But the '*vis agendi*' that we saw in connection with Leibniz's studies of motion and rest is there too, even if it is a bit below the surface. These forces or powers that the phenomena of resistance leads Leibniz to posit "consist not in motion, indeed, not in conatus or the beginning of motion, but in the cause or in that intrinsic reason for motion."[60] That is to say, the forces or powers, the immaterial forms that account for resistance, are the same as that which distinguishes motion

---

[58] A6.4.1394 (RA 237). Leibniz is not altogether consistent on this question. In the 'Conspectus libelli' he writes: "Corpus est extensum, mobile, resistens. Id est quod agere et pati potest quatenus extensum est; agere si sit in motu, pati si motui resistat" (A6.4.1987).

[59] A6.4.1980 (AG 249).   [60] A6.4.1980 (AG 250).

from rest: Leibniz doesn't seem to draw a radical distinction here between the force by which a moving body acts on another through its motion and the force by which a body reacts to another body acting on it. Though he doesn't explicitly mention the role force plays in grounding motion as distinct from rest as one of the motivations for introducing form into body, that will emerge as an explicit consideration in the following years. Just a few years later, in 'Discours de métaphysique' § 18, this will be one of the arguments that Leibniz advances for the rehabilitation of substantial forms. He writes:

For if we consider only what motion contains precisely and formally, that is, change of place, motion is not something entirely real, and when several bodies change position among themselves, it is not possible to determine, merely from a consideration of these changes, to which body we should attribute motion or rest, as I could show geometrically, if I wished to stop and do this now. But the force or proximate cause of these changes is something more real, and there is sufficient basis to attribute it to one body more than to another. Also, it is only in this way that we can know to which body the motion belongs. Now, this force is something different from size, shape, and motion, and one can therefore judge that not everything conceived in body consists solely in extension and in its modifications, as our moderns have persuaded themselves. Thus we are once again obliged to reestablish some beings or forms they have banished.[61]

Given the importance of the '*vis agendi*' for distinguishing between motion and rest in the texts on motion from the years when Leibniz was reviving substantial forms, I am somewhat inclined to think that though he didn't emphasize arguments of this kind in the late 1670s, they may well have been on his mind and constituted one of his motivations for reviving substantial forms in physics.

Leibniz never did publish the essay 'De natura corporis.' But even so, the strategy that he used in that essay is remarkably similar to a number of texts from later years, both published and unpublished. Among texts that Leibniz drafted with the intention of publishing, versions of this argument appear in the 'Discours' and in the "Phoranomus" of 1689 (to which we shall turn in the next chapter).[62] The argument appeared in print in a separate piece Leibniz published in French in the *Journal des sçavans* in 1691

[61] A6.4.1558–9 (AG 51).   [62] See 'Discours' § 21 and Leibniz (1991), 803–9.

and in part I of the "Specimen Dynamicum," published in 1695, a central text that we shall discuss in detail later in the next chapter.[63] It also appears in numerous letters, where Leibniz was trying to convince contemporaries of his somewhat heterodox views on the nature of the physical world.[64] He obviously felt that this kind of autobiographical argument was very effective in making his case and convincing the reader of the necessity of reviving substantial forms.

But despite the apparent simplicity of the argument, it hides a metaphysical view that is complex and not altogether satisfactory.

The complexity of the initial metaphysics connected with activity, passivity, and the revival of substantial forms in 1678/9 is illustrated by a long and rambling series of notes that the Akademie editors have dubbed 'Definitiones cogitationesque metaphysicae,' and dated as being exactly contemporaneous with the 'Conspectus libelli.' The document is obviously not a finished essay: it seems to be Leibniz working out on paper some of the metaphysical and physical problems that concerned him at that moment. You can see early statements of themes that will appear in more fully developed form in later writings, such as the 'Discours de métaphysique' and the correspondence with Arnauld, and other things that will drop out altogether. While it is difficult to infer any stable doctrines from such a document as this, the passages on body and substance can give us a pretty good idea of the kinds of considerations that were motivating Leibniz at this crucial moment.

The document begins with some propositions (or, perhaps, definitions) that pertain to body:

> *Body* is a resisting extended thing.

For from this alone it can be distinguished from space, which we conceive as that which is extended, absolutely, without the addition of anything else.

The *extended* is that which has magnitude and situation.

A *resisting* thing is that which acts on that by which it is acted upon.[65]

---

[63] *Journal des sçavans*, 18 June 1691, G IV 464–6; GM VI 240–2 (AG 123–5). On some background to the publication in 1691, see Costabel (1966). Costabel situates this text in what he calls "une véritable offensive du philosophe de Hanovre contre les thèses cartésiennes" (Costabel (1966), 264).

[64] See, e.g., Leibniz to Alberti (early 1690s?), G VII 447–8; Leibniz to Foucher, 1693 (?), G I 415; Leibniz to Malebranche (1693–94?), G I 350–1; Leibniz to de Volder, 24 March/3 April 1699, G II 170 (L 516–17); Leibniz to de Volder, 23 June 1699, G II 186–7.

[65] A6.4.1393–4 (RA 237).

So far there is nothing about substance. But a few things are interesting to note. First of all, resistance is now part of the definition of body. And secondly, as I noted above, *resistance is itself a kind of activity*: it is the activity by which a thing "acts on" something else that has acted on it. Leibniz at this point takes off in a number of different directions. But a few pages later he comes back to body:

Body is a movable extended thing, or body is extended substance.

It can be demonstrated that these definitions coincide, for I define substance as that which can act; but the action of an extended thing is by motion, namely, local motion.[66]

Substance has entered now, and bodies are taken to be substances.[67] More importantly, being a substance is identified with being active, with being able to act. He continues:

Every body is actually in motion.
For every substance is actually operating, as is demonstrated in Metaphysics.
Every body is organic, i.e. is actually divided into smaller parts endowed with their own particular motions, so that there are no atoms.
For every finite substance is actually acted upon (for, although it is actually acting, it is also finite, i.e. imperfect, and its action is always checked, that is, to some extent impeded); moreover every passion of a body involves division.
Every body is animate, i.e. has sensation and appetite.
For every substance is as perfect as it can be through all the others. But it cannot depend on all the other bodies without there being in each one a soul, i.e. as much appetite as there is in it a force of acting, and as much sensation as there is in it a force of being acted upon. But to attribute a soul only to man and to a few other bodies is as inept as believing that everything is made for the sake of man alone.
Substantial form, or soul, is the principle of unity and of enduring [*duratio*], matter is that of multiplicity and change.[68]

duratan

---

[66] A6.4.1398 (RA 245).

[67] The Latin is somewhat malleable here. The first sentence could also be read "A body is a movable extended thing, or, a body is an extended substance." That is, it isn't clear whether he is talking about substance generically, or whether he is talking about individual bodies as substances. In either case, the view doesn't seem to be entirely consistent with what he asserts elsewhere, but we have to remember that these are just notes to himself.

[68] A6.4.1398–9 (RA 245).

At this point Leibniz heads off into a discussion of unity and substance, which we have already discussed above in Chapter 2. A number of lines later he returns to these themes, perhaps with the intention of beginning this section of the essay over again:

> *Body* is a substance that can act and be acted upon.
>
> *Matter* is the principle of passion.   ~~Matter — Acted upon~~
>
> *Form* is the principle of action.   ~~Pattern — Acting on~~
>
> Pure intelligences can act, but cannot be acted upon. Thus only God is a pure intelligence; all the rest are in matter, as is our mind, and so also an angel's.
>
> Because a principle of passion must contain within itself a potential multiplicity [*multitudinem in se potestate continere*] matter is a continuum containing a plurality of things at the same time, i.e. an *extended thing*.
>
> Every form is a *soul*, i.e. capable of sensation and appetite.
>
> Even though all things are animate, nonetheless they all act according to the laws of mechanics, for sensation and appetite are determined by organs (i.e. parts of a body) and objects (i.e. by surrounding bodies).
>
> Every body is actually acting and being acted upon.
>
> Every body acts on all others and is acted upon by all others, i.e. perceives all others. . . .
>
> When two bodies approach each other, it can only be decided from the cause of motion, not from the motion itself, which of the two is at rest or moves, or whether both are moving. It is the same with several bodies.[69]

The view that he is trying to articulate here seems to be that for there to be activity—both resistance and the positive activity by which one body acts on another—there must be form in bodies. Form is the source of this activity, both resistance and positive activity. But unlike in the essay 'De natura corporis,' Leibniz is also attempting to articulate a doctrine of matter. Form is contrasted here with matter, which is conceived of as extended and divisible, the principle of passion and multiplicity. As in the approach to form through unity that we examined in more detail earlier in Chapter 2, form here is quite explicitly characterized in mentalistic terms: it is a kind of soul, indivisible, immaterial, and a source of unity in bodies. Furthermore, it contains both sensation and appetite. Leibniz seems to associate appetite with the ability a body has to act on another,

---

[69] A6.4.1399–1400 (RA 247–9). The last paragraph doesn't seem to be consistent with what Leibniz says in the earlier passage, that "every body is actually in motion."

Sensitive

Appetitive   *Passive*

presumably both the positive activity by which a body imposes its motion on another, and the resistance by which it actively opposes the motion of another. Sensation, on the other hand, is associated with being acted upon. This sensation is not, itself, the passion of the body: "every passion of a body involves division." That is, when one body acts on another, it imparts motion to the other, thus resulting in further divisions of the body acted upon. The sensation is the effect on the form or soul of the action of another body on the body in question. (The picture here seems deeply influenced by Hobbes. For Hobbes, as we discussed earlier, sensation arises when there is an internal resistance to a motion imposed on an organized body; without resistance, there is no sensation. But this sensation is also the origin of a volition (appetition), which is the action of a body of sufficient complexity in response to the impingement of a motion from outside.)

But there is an obvious problem with the passivity of bodies in this view that I have been sketching. Passivity appears in two distinct and different places in the theory. First of all, it appears in extended matter. Bodies act on one another by imparting motion to their parts, and thus causing divisions within them: "every passion of a body involves division." And as a consequence, a body capable of being acted upon must be capable of being divided: "a principle of passion must contain within itself a potential multiplicity." But there is also another kind of passivity, the force of resistance, that by virtue of which a body acted upon by another body poses an opposition to it. Leibniz places this other passivity in the soul-like principle that he posits in body, its form: "this, so to speak, inertia of bodies cannot be deduced from the initially assumed notion of matter and motion ... but rather ... we must add and recognize in bodies certain notions or forms that are immaterial."

Sometime in the early 1680s, Leibniz seems to have addressed this problem by putting all passivity, including resistance, into matter, and all genuine activity into form. In a passage from the essay "De modo distinguendi phaenomena realia ab imaginariis," now dated as between summer 1683 and winter 1685/6, Leibniz wrote:

Concerning bodies I can demonstrate that not merely light, heat, color and similar qualities are apparent but also motion, figure, and extension. And that if anything

Secondary qualities
The feminists freak out

is real, it is solely the force of <u>acting and suffering</u> [*vim agendi et patiendi*], and hence that the substance of a body consists in this (as if in matter and form). Those bodies, however, which have no substantial form are merely phenomena or at least only aggregates of the true ones.[70]

Leibniz is somewhat more expansive on this theme in another essay that probably dates from the same period, just before the composition of the 'Discours de métaphysique,' an essay that the Akademie editors have entitled 'De mundo praesenti':

Corporeal substances have parts and species. The parts are matter and form. Matter is the principle of being acted on [*principium passionis*] that is, the primitive force of resisting, which is commonly called bulk or antitypy, from which flows the impenetrability of body. The substantial form is the principle of action or the primitive force of acting. Furthermore, there is in every substantial form a certain knowledge [*cognitio*] that is an expression or representation of external things in a certain individual thing, in accordance with which a body is *per se* one, namely in the substantial form itself. This representation is joined with a reaction or conatus or appetite which follows this thought of acting. This substantial form must be found in all corporeal substances which are *per se* one.[71]

What is important here is that matter now unites both forms of passivity, the force of resistance that a body exerts against being put into motion, as well as the grounds of extension and divisibility.

And with this we have a basic outline of this second strand in Leibniz's thought. Like the arguments from unity that were discussed above in Chapter 2, these arguments lead Leibniz to a new conception of body, one grounded in the ideas of form and matter, interpreted here in terms of

[70] A6.4.1504 (L 365). The essay continues with the celebrated last line: "Substances have meta-physical matter or passive power insofar as they express something confusedly; active, insofar as they express it distinctly." This would seem to suggest a kind of idealistic underlying metaphysics, though I shall argue below that it isn't obvious what this last line really means, or even when exactly it was written. This is a complicated essay, and we shall have to return to it a number of times.

[71] A6.4.1507–8 (RA 285–7). It is somewhat mysterious just what the species are: "As for the species of body, we may now neglect the consideration of substantial form, and whether a body is a unity in itself, and shall consider only the differentiae of *matter*" [A6.4.1508 (RA 287)]. Presumably, the species are just the different sorts of things in the material world, individuated by the different kinds of sizes and shapes of bodies, i.e. horses vs cows vs rocks.

active and passive forces. But in order to understand this new conception of body, we must turn to the notion of force itself, and the science of dynamics in which Leibniz treats the notion of force. This will be taken up in the next chapter. With this in hand, we shall return to the question of the nature of body.

4

Reforming Mechanism: Body and Force, Matter and Form (II)

When looking at the corporeal substance from the point of view of the problem of unity, as we did in Chapter 2, it can look as if Leibniz simply wants to add substantial forms to Cartesian organic bodies. From the point of view of the argument from unity, it looks as if the only thing wrong with Cartesian bodies is that they lack genuine unity, and the addition of substantial form seems to be able to supply that lack. In the earliest versions of the argument from activity, as we discussed in the previous chapter, Leibniz seems to be pursuing a similar strategy. Here the main lack of Cartesian bodies is activity, both the active force that bodies exert when they are in motion, and the resistance that they exhibit when they are acted upon by other bodies. Here, again, the appeal to form is supposed to remedy a deficiency found in Cartesian bodies. However, the more sophisticated later view that Leibniz seems to have adopted in the early 1680s suggests something rather different. Insofar as all of the passive forces are to be united in the notion of matter, it looks as if Leibniz has stepped beyond the Cartesian conception of matter. With this it appears as if Leibniz has completely rejected the view of corporeal substance as the union of a quasi-Cartesian soul and a largely Cartesian body for a conception of corporeal substance grounded in the union of active and passive force. In a certain way, Leibniz can be seen as reviving not only the substantial forms of the schoolmen, but the entire hylomorphic framework, both substantial form and matter.[1] *→ Early 1680s: revisa Cartesian conception of body in favor of hylomorphism.*

---

[1] Cf. A6.4.1504–5. In speaking in the way I do in this paragraph I don't mean to imply that Leibniz was ever a Cartesian about the nature of body, strictly speaking. As I noted earlier, Hobbes was by far the more important influence on his earlier view, though by the period under discussion, the early 1680s, Cartesianism has become a central opponent.

But, at the same time, it isn't a simple revival of Aristotelian scholastic hylomorphism either. When Leibniz first announced that he wanted to revive substantial forms in the autumn 1679 letter to Duke Johann Friedrich, he put his claim as follows: "I reestablish substantial forms with demonstrative certainty [*démonstrativement*] *and explain them intelligibly* . . ."[2] We can now understand what he meant when he said that he could explain them intelligibly. A standard criticism of the scholastic notions of matter and form is that they are obscure and unintelligible. But in Leibniz's system, they are connected directly with notions of active and passive force that play evident and intelligible roles in his physics. This, he claims, is precisely what makes them intelligible in a way in which they weren't in the philosophy of the schools. As he writes in the "Système nouveau" of 1695:

Hence, it was necessary to restore, and, as it were, to rehabilitate the substantial forms which are in such disrepute today, but in a way that would render them intelligible, and separate the use one should make of them from the abuse that has been made of them.[3]

Forces manifest themselves in the motions that they cause. Active force manifests itself in the ability that bodies have to do work, say raise a given weight to a given height. The resistance by which bodies oppose the acquisition of new motion is evident in the way in which one body colliding with another will have its motion slowed as it imparts new motion to the body with which it collides. In this way, Leibniz writes in an important essay he published in 1694, "De primae philosophiae emendatione, et de notione substantiae,"

the concept of *forces* or *powers* . . . for whose explanation I have set up a distinct science of *dynamics*, brings the strongest light to bear upon our understanding of the true concept of *substance*.[4]

In this way the very laws of nature reveal the active and passive forces of bodies that make intelligible the notion of substance that Leibniz advances and the notions of form and matter that compose his conception of substance. I do not at all mean to suggest that Leibniz's view is in any way unproblematic. Leibniz's physics, and the metaphysical foundations

---

[2] A1.2.225; cf. A2.1².754.   [3] G IV 478–9 (AG 139).
[4] G IV 469 (L 433); cf. Leibniz to Paul Pellisson-Fontanier, July 1691, A1.6.226–7.

that he gives his physics in the notions of form and matter, presuppose a radical distinction between activity and passivity, between the active forces that ground motion and the passive forces that ground resistance and impenetrability. This distinction will prove very difficult for Leibniz to make. But even so, one can understand why he thought what he was doing was not merely reviving a discredited old metaphysics. *Passive force = capacity for an active / resistive force*

This shift in Leibniz's metaphysics of body from the late 1670s, where all activity, both active force and resistance, is in form, to the more sophisticated position that he adopts by the mid-1680s, where resistance is now grounded in matter, has profound consequences for his view. As we shall see later in Chapter 8, this reconfiguration of the notion of substance will seriously destabilize Leibniz's metaphysics, and, I shall argue, it will be one of the factors that leads him away from the metaphysics of corporeal substance and towards the more idealistic monadological metaphysics. But here I would like to emphasize another interesting consequence of this change. In the argument that Leibniz offers in 'De natura corporis,' he says that because bodies exhibit resistance and impenetrability, we must posit that they have form in addition to matter. This kind of argument is predicated on the view that the force of resistance is grounded in form; otherwise it is difficult to see how Leibniz could infer the existence of forms from the need for a force of resistance. But once resistance is moved from form to matter, it would seem as if that kind of argument could no longer be used. Interestingly enough, however, even though he is no longer entitled to it, Leibniz seems to continue to use that form of argument until the end of the 1690s, at least. In this way, the 'De natura corporis' argument is very much like the aggregate argument, which continues to be used until the end of Leibniz's life, even though the corporeal substance view that it was originally designed to support has been modified almost beyond recognition, as we shall later see in Chapter 9. The arguments persist even though the metaphysical ground underneath shifts and changes.

→ One reason to think that the similarities between Monadology and earlier works don't imply a similar metaphysics

Dynamics and a Metaphysics of Force

The metaphysical view of body conceived in terms of form and matter understood as active and passive force, which complements and, as I shall argue, completes the view of body grounded in unity that we saw in

Chapter 2, seems to have been firmly in place by the mid-1680s. Insofar as Leibniz's conception of body is grounded in force, it is deeply connected with the development of his new science of dynamics.

As we have seen, Leibniz's notes and correspondence in the late 1670s and early 1680s show considerable interest in questions of motion, physics, and, more generally, natural philosophy.[5] But the foundations of Leibniz's new physics was not publicly revealed until March 1686, when he published his important "Brevis demonstratio erroris memorabilis Cartesii et aliorum..." in the *Acta eruditorum*.[6] In this essay, Leibniz presented for the first time in public what he had been telling friends and correspondents in private for some years, that the Cartesian law of the conservation of quantity of motion (size times speed) is false, and leads to paradox, an argument we shall discuss in more detail later in this chapter.

While not without challenge, the Cartesian law of the conservation of quantity of motion was still held as fundamental by many in the 1670s, 1680s, and 1690s. It was the Cartesian conservation principle that Leibniz had to confront—and refute—in the late 1670s when formulating his own physics, and it was Leibniz's published critique of the Cartesian conservation principle in the "Brevis demonstratio" of 1686 that raised one of the most visible public controversies in Leibniz's career, as Cartesians came out of the woodwork to defend what many took as the foundation of their own physics. Leibniz was not the first to attack Descartes's conservation principle, and the specifics of his arguments owe much to others, particularly Huygens.[7] But the liveliness of the exchanges that followed the "Brevis demonstratio" suggest that Leibniz's point was still news to many. This controversy, the so-called *vis viva* (living force) controversy, which continued well beyond Leibniz's death, resulted in

[5] It is difficult to identify all of the sketches from the period from 1679 to 1686 or so that might be relevant; much remains to be published, and of the notes on physics that are available, the dating is often very problematic. For some notes relating to Leibniz's interests in the foundations of physics that the editors of the Akademie edition also date to the period 1678–82, see A6.4.1976–2026. It should be noted that these papers include only material that the editors deem to be of philosophical interest; the more technical papers remain largely unedited, and await the appearance of the volumes of series 8 of the Akademie edition.

[6] A6.4.2027–30 (L 296–301).

[7] Though there is not sufficient space to enter into the question here, it should be noted that Leibniz owes a considerable debt in his laws of motion to other thinkers of the period. For a more detailed account of Leibniz's borrowings, and the way in which he transformed the work of others, see Gueroult (1967), ch. 4; Westfall (1984); Bos (1978).

numerous refinements and variants on the original argument, as formulated in the late 1670s and published in 1686.[8]

While the "Brevis demonstratio" emphasized what is wrong with Cartesian physics, it deals with only one issue, the correct conservation law, and gave only a hint of Leibniz's full program. But shortly after the appearance of that essay, Leibniz began to work out the details of his larger program in physics, almost certainly goaded by the appearance of Isaac Newton's *Philosophiae naturalis principia mathematica* in 1687.[9] There were a number of technical essays intended to respond to Newton's planetary theory and opposition to the vortex theory of planetary motion. Important here are the "Schediasma de resistentia medii et motu projectorum gravium in medio resistente" and the "Tentamen de motuum caelestium causis," both published in the *Acta eruditorum* in 1689.[10] These essays deal with questions in cosmology and related questions concerning the motion of bodies in a resisting medium. (This is an issue that Newton had taken up in book II of his *Principia* in his attack on vortex theories, theories that explain planetary motion in terms of a rotating vortex of aether.) But Leibniz also turned his attention to the very foundations of physics, to the notions of force and motion and to the laws that govern these fundamental notions, what he dubbed dynamics, the science of force.

The first attempt at a detailed account of the dynamics was a long dialogue, the "Phoranomus seu de potentia et legibus naturae," written in July 1689 while Leibniz was in Rome.[11] This was quickly followed by the

[8] For accounts of the controversy, see especially Iltis (1971); Costabel (1973); Papineau (1977); Ranea (1989); Freudenthal (2002).

[9] Leibniz claims not to have seen the full text of Newton's *Principia* until he arrived in Rome in April 1689, and claims to have seen only a review in the *Acta eruditorum* before that; see GM VI 189 and GM VII 329. But Bertoloni Meli (1993) very convincingly establishes that this is not true, and that Leibniz had read crucial sections of the *Principia* before composing his "Tentamen de motuum caelestium causis," which he had claimed was written only with the knowledge of the review published in the *Acta eruditorum* in June 1688. Cf. Aiton (1985), 153, which gives Leibniz's version of the story.

[10] The "Schediasma" was published in the *Acta eruditorum* in January 1689, 38–47 (GM VI 135–44) and the "Tentamen" was published in the *Acta* in February 1689, 82–96 (GM VI 144–61); the "Tentamen" is translated in Bertoloni Meli (1993), 126–42. In addition, Leibniz published a short third essay, "De lineis opticis" [*Acta eruditorum*, January 1689, 36–8 (GM VII 329–31)]. Bertoloni Meli characterizes this as "little more than an introduction to the two following memoirs," that had as its main purpose to inform the reader of the other two more substantial pieces that they had all been written without knowledge of the full text of Newton's *Principia*. [See Bertoloni Meli (1993), 7.]

[11] See Leibniz (1991), which gives the text with a very helpful introduction and commentary by André Robinet. See also Duchesneau (1998a), which challenges some of Robinet's readings.

composition of the massive *Dynamica de potentia et legibus naturae corporeae* (1689–90), a text written in Euclidean style, with definitions, axioms, and theorems. Though it was written with the intention of publication, and though Leibniz worked at publishing it, he never considered it entirely finished and it remained unpublished during his lifetime.[12] This work is a systematic treatise on motion and its laws, presenting in a rigorous fashion the foundations and conclusions of the new science of dynamics.

While Leibniz never published the *Dynamica*, he did reveal some tantalizing hints of the larger project. In 1692, he sent an "Essay de dynamique" to Paris, for discussion in the Académie Royale des Sciences, with only moderate success; while the essay was received, it wound up, virtually unread, buried in the archives of the Académie, lost until late in the twentieth century.[13] Then later, goaded by friends (so he claims) to publish more of his thought, he finally revealed some of the metaphysical foundations of the project in an essay entitled "Specimen dynamicum," published in the *Acta eruditorum* in 1695.[14] Its title suggests a summary of or a selection from the earlier work, and Leibniz's opening words suggest that the new work will present some hint of what the *Dynamica* contained. However, it actually contains something in a way rather more interesting: a careful exposition of the metaphysical foundations of the new science, something that is hard to find in the old *Dynamica* or any of the more technical pieces that had been

---

[12] The text of the *Dynamica* was published for the first (and only) time in GM VI 281–514. On his reservations about publishing, see his remarks in a letter to L'Hospital, 15/25 January 1696, A3.6.617. For a discussion of Leibniz's plans to publish the book, see Robinet (1988), 261ff. Though the bulk of the work may have been completed in Italy, the prefatory "specimen" of arguments was probably written after January 1691, when Leibniz had returned to Hanover; see AG 105–6.

[13] See Costabel (1966) and Costabel (1973).

[14] Though Leibniz had intended to publish the text in two parts, only part I appeared in the *Acta* in April 1695; part II, intended for May 1695, never appeared in Leibniz's lifetime. The complete "Specimen dynamicum" can be found in GM VI 234–54. Leibniz (1982) also contains the full text in a new transcription, along with variants and the text of a previously unpublished preliminary version of part I, though this edition is somewhat controversial; see Knobloch (1983). For an account of the composition of the "Specimen dynamicum," see Most (1984). Some of the most philosophically interesting content of the "Specimen dynamicum" is repeated in an important untitled essay dated May 1702 by Leibniz himself, but unpublished in his lifetime; see GM VI 98–106 or G IV 393–400 (AG 250–6). For convenience I shall call it 'Contra philosophiam Cartesianam,' picking up a few words from the opening sentence. It is not clear why Leibniz wrote this essay, but it may be connected with the correspondence that he was then having with Burcher de Volder on physics and its metaphysical foundations. The opening sentence of the "Specimen dynamicum" is where he claims that many have asked for details of the new science of dynamics: "Ever since we made mention of establishing a New Science of Dynamics, many distinguished persons have requested a fuller explanation of this doctrine in various places. . . ."

published in the earlier 1690s, and no less valuable than the more technical physics of the *Dynamica*. Indeed, this more metaphysical perspective on the project may represent the material that Leibniz was struggling to work out for the unfinished portions of the *Dynamica*.[15]

In the "Specimen dynamicum" and related writings Leibniz presents a conception of body and force that involves two important distinctions, the distinction between primitive and derivative forces, and the distinction between active and passive forces. Leibniz writes:

Active force (which might not inappropriately be called *power* [*virtus*], as some do) is twofold, that is, either *primitive*, which is inherent in every corporeal substance *per se* . . . or *derivative*, which, resulting from a limitation of primitive force through the collision of bodies with one another, for example, is found in different degrees. Indeed, primitive force (which is nothing but the first entelechy) corresponds to the soul or substantial form. . . . Similarly, passive force is also twofold, either primitive or derivative. And indeed, the *primitive force of being acted upon* [*vis primitiva patiendi*] or of *resisting* constitutes that which is called *primary matter* in the schools, if correctly interpreted. This force is that by virtue of which it happens that a body cannot be penetrated by another body, but presents an obstacle to it, and at the same time is endowed with a certain laziness, so to speak, that is, an opposition to motion, nor, further, does it allow itself to be put into motion without somewhat diminishing the force of the body acting on it. As a result, the *derivative force of being acted upon* later shows itself to different degrees in *secondary matter*.[16]

So in all, there are four principal varieties of force, primitive active and passive force, and derivative active and passive force. (There is also a reference here to the distinction between primary and secondary matter, to which we shall later return.)

Let us begin by examining the notions of (derivative) active and passive force. Leibniz's development of the notion of active force begins with some reflections on the notion of motion. He begins with some definitions and distinctions:

Motion is the continual change of place, and so requires time. However, just as a mobile thing in motion has motion in time, so too at any given moment it has a speed [*velocitas*], which is greater to the extent that more space is traversed in less

[15] Most (1984), esp. 155-7 emphasizes this aspect of the "Specimen dynamicum."
[16] GM VI 236-7 (AG 119-20). Cf. the account given in the earlier draft, Leibniz (1982), 66. A very similar account is given in 'Contra philosophiam Cartesianam' (May 1702); see G IV 395 (AG 252).

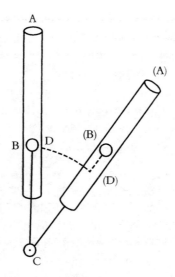

Figure 4:1. From GM VI.

time. Speed taken together with direction is called *conatus*. Furthermore, *impetus* is
the product of the bulk [*moles*] of a body and its speed. . . .[17]

Leibniz then uses the example of a ball in a rotating tube to illustrate the
distinction between acceleration and the actual motion that it gives rise to.
(See Figure 4:1.) He writes:

Consider tube AC rotating around the immobile center C on the horizontal plane
of this page with a certain uniform speed, and consider ball B in the interior of
the tube, just freed from a rope or some other hindrance, and beginning to move
by virtue of centrifugal force. It is obvious that, in the beginning, the conatus
for receding from the center, namely, that by virtue of which the ball B in the
tube tends toward the end of the tube, A, is infinitely small in comparison with
the impetus which it already has from rotation, that is, it is infinitely small in
comparison with the impetus by virtue of which the ball B, together with the
tube itself, tends to go from place D to (D), while maintaining the same distance
from the center. But if the centrifugal impression deriving from the rotation were
continued for some time, then by virtue of that very circumstance, a certain
complete centrifugal impetus (D) (B), comparable to the rotational impetus D

---

[17] GM VI 237 (AG 120). One has to be a bit careful with the terminology here. Leibniz's *'velocitas'*
corresponds to the modern conception of speed, the scalar quantity, while *'conatus'* corresponds to the
modern notion of velocity, the vector quantity.

(D), must arise in the ball. From this it is obvious that the *nisus* is twofold, that is, elementary or infinitely small, which I also call *solicitation*, and that which is formed from the continuation or repetition of elementary nisus, that is, *impetus* itself.[18]

It is important to understand that, in this passage, Leibniz is distinguishing between two kinds of motion: actual motion, and the acceleration whose repetition results in actual motion. He uses this distinction to introduce a parallel distinction between two kinds of active force:[19]

From this it follows that [derivative active] *force* is also twofold. One force is elementary, which I also call *dead force*, since motion does not yet exist in it, but only a solicitation to motion, as with the ball in the tube or a stone in a sling while it is still being held in by a rope. The other is ordinary force, joined with actual motion, which I call *living force [vis viva]*. An example of dead force is centrifugal force itself, and also the force of heaviness [*vis gravitatis*] or centripetal force, and the force by which a stretched elastic body begins to restore itself. But when we are dealing with impact, which arises from a heavy body which has already been falling for some time, or from a bow that has already been restoring its shape for some time, or from a similar cause, the force in question is living force, which arises from an infinity of continual impressions of dead force.[20]

This suggests that there are two kinds of derivative active force, one connected with speed or velocity and the other with acceleration, more specifically, dead force with acceleration, and living force with actual motion. In the first draft of the "Specimen dynamicum," Leibniz distinguishes them in a rather more colorful way:

Therefore, the force by which bodies act on one another, is twofold, in my way of speaking: the one is *dead or slumbering [sopita] force*, or, if you prefer, inchoate

---

[18] GM VI 238 (AG 121). Interestingly enough, Leibniz doesn't offer a formal definition of 'nisus.' Its ordinary meaning in Latin is effort or endeavor.

[19] Actually, there is an interesting complication there. In the original ms. Leibniz moves directly from the distinction between motion and acceleration to the distinction between living and dead force, suggesting a direct parallelism between the motion concepts and the corresponding force concepts. But the published version of "Specimen dynamicum" part I adds the following sentence in between, which breaks the continuity: "Nevertheless, I wouldn't want to claim on these grounds that these mathematical entities are really found in nature, but I only wish to advance them for making careful calculations through mental abstraction." [See here the textual note to lines 162–5 in Leibniz (1982), 12.] It seems that Leibniz had a later worry about moving from motion to force. This is discussed in more detail in Garber (2008).

[20] GM VI 238 (AG 121–2).

force; the other is living or awakened force, or if you prefer, formed force. And dead force is to living force as a point is to a line, or as conatus is to motion.[21]

But though force is closely connected to motion, active forces must not be *identified* with motion or acceleration: motion and change in motion (acceleration) are not forces themselves, but the *effects* of forces.

(Derivative) passive force is something quite different. As the earlier passage quoted from the "Specimen dynamicum" suggests, passive force is connected not with motion, but with the resistance to motion. This resistance is of two sorts.[22] First there is impenetrability, "that by virtue of which it happens that a body cannot be penetrated by another body." But in addition to that there is a kind of passive force by virtue of which bodies actively oppose the motion other bodies try to impose on them in impact, what Leibniz calls "a certain laziness." This resistance is something quite different from the mere tendency bodies have to remain in a given state, a notion basic to the thought of Descartes, Hobbes, and Spinoza. Leibniz writes to the Cartesian de Volder:

I admit that each and every thing remains in its state until there is a reason for change; this is a principle of metaphysical necessity. But it is one thing to retain a state until something changes it, which even something intrinsically indifferent to both states does, and quite another thing, much more significant, for a thing not to be indifferent, but to have a force and, as it were, an inclination to retain its state, and so to resist changing.[23]

---

[21] Leibniz (1982), 66.

[22] See 'Contra philosophiam Cartesianam' (May 1702), G IV 395 (AG 252), where Leibniz makes the distinction more explicitly than he does in the "Specimen dynamicum."

[23] Leibniz to de Volder, 24 March/3 April 1699, G II 170 (AG 172). Leibniz here probably has in mind a formulation Descartes gives of the principle in his *Principia philosophiae* II.37, something with which the Cartesian de Volder would have been intimately familiar:

From God's immutability we can also know certain rules or laws of nature, which are the secondary and particular causes of the various motions we see in particular bodies. The first of these laws is that each thing, in so far as it is simple and undivided, always remains in the same state, as far as it can, and never changes except as a result of external causes. Thus, if a particular piece of matter is square, we can be sure without more ado that it will remain square for ever, unless something coming from outside changes its shape. If it is at rest, we hold that it will never begin to move unless it is pushed into motion by some cause. And if it moves, there is equally no reason for thinking it will ever lose this motion of its own accord and without being checked by something else. Hence we must conclude that what is in motion always, so far as it can, continues to move.

Leibniz wants to argue that, properly speaking, the notion of resistance goes beyond what Descartes has in mind here, that there is a difference between remaining in a given state unless there is a reason for change, and actively opposing that change. Later in Ch. 8 we shall discuss Leibniz's relations with de Volder in more detail, and give some of the context of this discussion. I am deeply indebted to Paul

It is this force of resistance that slows the body in motion colliding with the body at rest, allowing Leibniz to avoid the result that so tainted his own early physics. As with the active forces, Leibniz differentiates passive forces from the behavior in bodies that they cause. In the "Specimen dynamicum" Leibniz is careful to characterize passive force as "that by virtue of which it happens" that bodies have impenetrability and resistance; the passive forces are the causes of this behavior in just the way that the active forces are the causes of motion.

Let us now look more closely at the distinction between primitive and derivative forces. In the passage from the "Specimen dynamicum" quoted above, Leibniz characterizes the primitive active force as corresponding to "the soul or substantial form"; the primitive passive force, on the other hand, is characterized as constituting "that which is called *primary matter* in the schools, if correctly interpreted." Form and matter join together to constitute a (corporeal) substance. Leibniz writes in 'Contra philosophiam Cartesianam' (May 1702):

Primitive active force, which Aristotle calls first entelechy and one commonly calls the form of a substance, is another natural principle which, together with matter or [primitive] passive force, completes a corporeal substance. This substance, of course, is one *per se*, and not a mere aggregate of many substances, for there is a great difference between an animal, for example, and a flock.[24]

And so, it seems, the primitive forces, active and passive, come together to make up the corporeal substance, the genuine unity that, Leibniz claims, underlies the extended bodies of the physical world. In this passage it is interesting to see how the dynamical point of view joins the view of

Lodge for generously sharing with me his edition and translation of the de Volder correspondence to be published in the Yale Leibniz series. While I have introduced some changes in his draft, the new edition of the Latin text and his English translations have been enormously helpful.

[24] G IV 395 (AG 252). The dating of this passage is quite curious. Below in Ch. 8 we shall discuss the transition from the view Leibniz took in the middle period, grounded in the notion of a corporeal substance, to the monadological view that he advanced in his later years. I shall argue that by 1700 he had made the transition from the one to the other. This passage, which seems connected with the earlier corporeal substance view, seems then to have been written after the transition. However, it is written just before he revealed his new views to de Volder, as we shall see in Ch. 8; earlier letters seem to be advancing the earlier corporeal substance view that, on my reading, he had already set aside as his fundamental metaphysics. This would seem to support the conjecture that I made above in n. 14 that this piece had originally been written in the context of the correspondence with de Volder. It does, though, leave unexplained the fact that Leibniz hid his true views from de Volder for the first years of his correspondence. But however one understands the essay 'Contra philosophiam Cartesianam', this is something that needs explanation.

substance that derives from considerations of unity: the two approaches to substance are, at root, concerned with a single notion of substance for Leibniz.

Derivative forces, in contrast, are the forces most of interest to the physicist, those connected with motion. Leibniz writes in the "Specimen dynamicum":

> Therefore, by derivative force, namely, that by which bodies actually act on one another or are acted upon by one another, I understand...only that which is connected to motion (local motion, of course), and which, in turn, tends further to produce local motion. For we acknowledge that all other material phenomena can be explained by local motion.[25]

Derivative force is, furthermore, that in terms of which we can frame the laws of physics. Leibniz writes, again in the "Specimen dynamicum":

> It is to these notions [i.e., the derivative forces] that the laws of action apply, laws which are understood not only through reason, but are also corroborated by sense itself through the phenomena.[26]

(The laws in question are the laws that deal with the conservation of *force*, not the laws of *motion*.)

Leibniz uses a number of terms to describe the relation between primitive and derivative forces. In the "Specimen dynamicum" he talks of derivative force as resulting from "a *limitation* of primitive force through the collision of bodies with one another."[27] In the first draft of the "Système nouveau" (1694?) he writes:

> [I call form or entelechy] the primitive force in order to distinguish it from the secondary [i.e. derivative force], what one calls moving force, which is a limitation or accidental variation of the primitive force.[28]

Similarly, he writes to Bernoulli in 1698:

> If we conceive of soul or form as the primary activity from whose modification secondary [i.e. derivative] forces arise as shapes arise from the modification of extension, then, I think, we take sufficient account of the intellect. Indeed there can be no active modifications of that which is merely passive in its essence, because modifications limit rather than increase or add.[29]

---

[25] GM VI 237 (AG 120).   [26] Ibid.
[27] GM VI 236 (AG 119).   [28] G IV 473 (WF 23).
[29] Leibniz to Johann Bernoulli, 17 December 1698, GM III 552 (AG 169).

And finally, Leibniz writes in 'Contra philosophiam Cartesianam' (May 1702) that "active force is twofold, primitive and derivative, that is, either substantial or accidental."[30] These passages suggest that derivative forces are to be understood as modes, accidents or the like, modifications of the primitive forces, which are understood as substances, or, better, as constituents of corporeal substances. Primitive active and passive forces, then, are the substantial ground of the derivative active and passive forces, which are their accidents or modes, as shape is an accident or mode of an extended thing.

The distinction between active and passive forces goes back to at least the late 1670s, as we saw in the last chapter. It is unclear when exactly the distinction between primitive and derivative forces arises. Leibniz seems to talk about primitive forces long before he explicitly introduces the coordinate notion of a derivative force. In a note on Simon Foucher dated 1676, we find the following text: "The essence of substances consists in the primitive force of acting [la force primitive d'agir], or in the law of the series [suite] of changes, just as the nature of the series consists in the numbers."[31] The content together with the textual note in the Akademie edition strongly suggest that this was a much later addition to the text. But by the middle of the 1680s, the terminology seems to enter Leibniz's vocabulary in a stable way. In 'De mondo praesenti' of 1685/6, he writes: "*Matter* is the principle of passion, or primitive force of resisting, which is commonly called bulk or antitypy, from which flows the impenetrability of body. *Substantial form* is the principle of action, or primitive force of acting."[32] Similarly in the "Specimen inventorum . . ." (1688?) he writes: "And this principle of actions, or primitive force of acting, from which a series of various states results, is the form of the substance."[33] In a note connected with the Fardella Memo of 1690 Leibniz writes: "In every substance there is nothing but the nature, or the primitive force, from which follows the series of its internal operations."[34] Although the notion of a derivative force would seem to be coordinate with the notion of a primitive force, the latter is not in general found before the mid-1690s. In Gerhardt's text of the letter from Leibniz to Arnauld, 10 September 1687, there is the following phrase: "when I say that a corporeal substance

---

[30] G IV 395 (AG 252).   [31] A6.3.326.   [32] A6.4.1507-8 (RA 285-7).
[33] A6.4.1625 (RA 321).   [34] A6.4.1673.

imparts to itself its own movement, or rather what is real in the movement at each moment, that is to say, the derivative force, of which it is a consequence, since every present state of a substance is a consequence of its preceding state."[35] But the phrase "that is to say, the derivative force, of which it is a consequence" is not in the text Arnauld received, and is considered to be a later addition.[36] The earliest reliably datable text I know of where Leibniz explicitly contrasts primitive and derivative forces is the first draft of the "Specimen dynamicum," probably written in 1694.[37] Though the distinction between primitive and derivative forces may be new to the mid-1690s, it is arguably just further clarification of earlier distinctions that Leibniz had made between force and the motion it causes, and between the momentary state of the force and its ontological ground in corporeal substance.

It is important to mention one more distinction, that which Leibniz draws between primary and secondary matter. Leibniz makes reference to 'materia prima' a number of times in early texts, though it seems to be understood in a traditional Aristotelian sense.[38] But what may be the earliest discussion of the distinction between primary and secondary matter as Leibniz understands it is a very interesting text, appended to a letter destined for Arnauld of 10 September 1687. There Leibniz introduces the notion of "a second matter [*une matiere seconde*]" which he contrasts with other notions of matter, presumably primary matter. He writes:

Extended mass, considered without a substantial form . . . is not a corporeal substance, but an entirely pure phenomenon like the rainbow; therefore philosophers have recognized that it is form which gives determinate being to matter. . . . Only indivisible substances and their different states are absolutely real. . . . But if one considers as matter of corporeal substance not mass without forms but a second matter which is the multiplicity of substances of which the mass is that of the total body, it may be said that these substances are parts of this matter, just as those which enter into our body form part of it, for as our body is the matter, and the soul is the form of our substance, it is the same with other corporeal substances. . . . But if one were to understand by the term 'matter' something always essential to the same substance, one might in the sense of certain scholastics understand thereby

---

[35] G II 115.   [36] Cf. the text of the letter given in Leibniz (1952), 82–3.

[37] See Leibniz (1982), 66.

[38] See, e.g., Leibniz to Thomasius, 20/30 April 1669, A2.1².26f (L95f); 'De materia prima' (1670–71?), A6.2.279f; 'Definitiones: aliquid, nihil' (1679?), A6.4.310; etc.

the primitive passive power of a substance, and in this sense matter would not be extended or divisible, although it would be the principle of divisibility or of that which amounts to it in the substance. But I do not wish to argue over the use of terms.[39]

The first kind of matter that he mentions, "extended mass, considered without a substantial form," would seem to be Cartesian matter, stuff that is extension and extension alone; we shall discuss this at greater length below when we discuss extension in connection with Leibnizian bodies. The secondary matter in this passage would seem to be the body of a corporeal substance, a collection of other, smaller corporeal substances, each of which, in turn, has an organic body and a soul. This is the conception of body that came up above in Chapter 2 in connection with the "unity" conception of the corporeal substance. The third conception of matter Leibniz introduces here is the "primitive passive power," "something always essential to the same substance." Presumably this is primary matter, in contrast with the secondary matter that he had just introduced. But is it not entirely clear that Leibniz fully endorses this conception of matter in this text. In an earlier draft of the letter he wrote:

One can give yet another definition of matter which corresponds rather to the meaning the schoolmen give it, but doesn't much correspond to ordinary usage. According to this explanation, though it is the principle of divisibility, matter isn't any more divisible than form. But that would be to dispute about words.[40]

This may be a different way of characterizing what I suggested was intended as primary matter in the later passage, though it isn't clear. The passages are problematic in other ways as well. The long passage that I first quoted is a marginal addition to the letter, and was never sent to Arnauld. While it may correspond to the earlier draft, which we can presume to have been written in September 1687 or thereabouts, there is no telling when exactly the later addition was made; it may date from as late as 1706 or 1707, when Leibniz was still considering publishing the correspondence. In any case, the distinction he draws between primary and secondary matter is neither explicit nor clear.

The first clear and clearly datable exposition of a distinction between two different conceptions of matter that I could find appears only in 1695,

---

[39] G II 119–20.   [40] Leibniz and Arnauld (1997), 300.

interestingly enough, at just the moment that Leibniz is beginning to think about simple substances and monads, as I shall argue below in Chapter 8. The text in question here is one that we just saw from the "Specimen dynamicum":

Similarly, passive force is also twofold, either primitive or derivative. And indeed, the *primitive force of being acted upon* [*vis primitiva patiendi*] or of *resisting* constitutes that which is called *primary matter* in the schools, if correctly interpreted. This force is that by virtue of which it happens that a body cannot be penetrated by another body, but presents an obstacle to it, and at the same time is endowed with a certain laziness, so to speak, that is, an opposition to motion, nor, further, does it allow itself to be put into motion without somewhat diminishing the force of the body acting on it. As a result, the *derivative force of being acted upon* later shows itself to different degrees in *secondary matter*.[41]

Primary matter is the primitive passive force, that which manifests itself in the derivative passive forces of resistance and impenetrability.

Leibniz leaves somewhat mysterious here just what secondary matter is. But the question is addressed in other contemporary texts. In the "De ipsa natura" of 1698 Leibniz writes:

I understand matter as either secondary or primary. Secondary matter is, indeed, a complete substance, but it is not merely passive; primary matter is merely passive, but it is not a complete substance. And so, we must add a soul or a form analogous to a soul, or a first entelechy, that is, a certain urge [*nisus*] or primitive force of acting, which itself is an inherent law, impressed by divine decree.[42]

Here primary matter, an incomplete entity, the passive principle in substance, is contrasted with secondary matter, a complete substance, presumably the corporeal substance, the soul or form together with its body. But in his letters to Johann Bernoulli from 1698 he offers a different view, something closer to what he had suggested in the letter to Arnauld

---

[41] GM VI 236–7 (AG 119–20). The distinction also appears in what is likely an almost exactly contemporary document, Leibniz's notes on Christian Thomasius on substance. See Utermöhlen (1979), 88. However, Leibniz's account there is relatively uninformative: "Scil. distingu[endum] inter [materiam] primam et secundam, prima non est. Cum sit Ens incompletum, ejusque notio constat in relatione."

[42] "De ipsa natura" § 12, G IV 512 (AG 162–3).

from which I quoted above. In a letter from August/September 1698 (?) he writes:

Matter in itself, or bulk [*moles*], which you can call primary matter, is not a substance; indeed, it is not an aggregate of substances, but something incomplete. Secondary matter, or mass [*massa*], is not a substance, but [a collection of] substances; and so not the flock but the animal, not the fish pond but the fish is one substance.[43]

Secondary matter is not a single complete corporeal substance, but rather a collection of corporeal substances, not the individual animal but the flock or the fish pond. In this way, the animal body, a machine of infinite complexity, but a machine nevertheless, comes out as secondary matter.

Understood in this second way, the distinction between primary and secondary matter seems to reflect a deep ambiguity in Leibniz's conception of matter, one that can be traced back to Leibniz's first introduction of the hylomorphic model of substance into his physics in the late 1670s. From early on, matter is conceived of in two rather different ways, corresponding to the two principal arguments that Leibniz uses to establish this view in the period. Corresponding to the argument from unity, discussed above in Chapter 2, matter is conceived of as the organic body of the corporeal substance: by adding form to an organic body, we transform it into a genuine unity. This would seem to correspond to what he later calls secondary matter in the sense in which he explained it to Bernoulli. But, of course, Leibniz also introduces corporeal substances because "certain things take place in body which cannot be explained from the necessity of matter alone," as he wrote in the 'Conspectus libelli,' and as we discussed in this chapter and the last. When we think of corporeal substances in terms of force rather than unity, then the matter in question is conceived of as the passive force of a corporeal substance, in distinction from the active force that Leibniz identifies with its form. This would seem to correspond to what he later calls primary matter.

---

[43] GM III 537 (AG 167). Leibniz begins the passage as follows: "By monad I understand a substance truly one, namely, one which is not an aggregate of substances." I shall argue below in Ch. 8 that when Leibniz first introduces the term 'monad' in 1695 and 1696, he often uses it to refer not to the non-extended and mind-like entity of his later thought but to the corporeal substance.

At first I suspect that Leibniz identified these two notions of matter, and assumed that they were just two aspects of one notion, just as unity and active force were just two aspects of a single and unitary notion of form. In a fragment now dated as coming from the same years as the 'Conspectus libelli,' Leibniz has the following sentences within a few lines of one another:

The substantial form or soul is the principle of unity and duration, while matter is the principle of multitude and mutation. . . . Matter is the principle of passion. Form is the principle of action.[44]

While the ambiguity in the notion of matter is evident to the discerning eye in texts dating from the late 1670s onward, from the moment that Leibniz "revives" substantial forms in physics, the explicit distinction between the two notions of matter only emerges fairly late, in the texts that we have just been examining; in the late 1670s and early 1680s, Leibniz's attention was on what he thought of as the novel elements of his position, the revival of substantial forms, and he seems to have taken the notion of matter for granted as being relatively uncontroversial and unproblematic.[45] But this ambiguity will cause him some difficulty, as I shall later argue in Chapter 8.

The Conservation of mv^2 and the Distinction Between Motion and Force

In the previous chapter I argued that the discovery of the equality principle in a way marks the start of Leibniz's mature physical thought, and emphasized the role that it played in the crucial introduction of resistance into bodies. But also important is another consequence Leibniz drew from that principle, the refutation of the Cartesian law of the conservation of quantity of motion. This argument, which he gave in a number of different forms, is very important for the history of Leibniz's physics. But what was its significance for his metaphysical view of body and corporeal substance? What was the connection between the technical results of Leibniz's account of the mathematical laws of motion and force, and

---

[44] A6.4.1499.
[45] For a somewhat different exposition of what amounts to the same tension in Leibniz's view, see Look and Rutherford's comments in their introduction to LDB, xlii–xliv.

his metaphysical characterization of corporeal substance in terms of form and matter, primitive active and passive force? There are texts from the period that would seem to suggest a direct connection between the two. In 'Discours de métaphysique' § 17, Leibniz gives a version of the argument he published in the "Brevis demonstratio." This is followed immediately in 'Discours' § 18 with the following statement: "The distinction between force and quantity of motion is important, among other reasons, for judging that one must have recourse to metaphysical considerations distinct from extension in order to explain the phenomena of bodies." How is it that the distinction between the proper mathematical measure of force and quantity of motion is supposed to lead us to this metaphysical conclusion?

It will be helpful to begin with a few words about the Cartesian conservation principle that Leibniz opposed. Basic to Descartes's physics, of course, was the view that the essence of body is extension. By this he meant that bodies are the objects of geometry made real, and that the only thing that really is in bodies is size, shape, and motion.[46] As a consequence, all of the laws that govern the physical world must be understood in these terms. Now, Descartes holds that God must sustain the world from moment to moment for it to continue in its existence. And from the fact that he is constant in his activity, Descartes holds that it follows that the total quantity of the motion that he sustains must be constant. This is how he puts the argument in the *Principia philosophiae*:   D is an occasional BT

In the beginning he created matter, along with its motion and rest; and now, merely by his regular concurrence, he preserves the same amount of motion and rest in the material universe as he put there in the beginning. Admittedly motion is simply a mode of the matter which is moved. But nevertheless it has a certain determinate quantity; and this, we easily understand, may be constant in the universe as a whole while varying in any given part. Thus if one part of matter moves twice as fast as another which is twice as large, we must consider that there is the same quantity of motion in each part; and if one part slows down, we must suppose that some other part of equal size speeds up by the same amount. For we understand that God's perfection involves not only his being immutable in himself, but also His operating in a manner that is always utterly constant and immutable. . . . Thus, God imparted various motions to the parts of matter when He first created them, and he now preserves all this matter in the same way, and

---

[46] Impenetrability turns out to be a bit of a disputed issue on the Cartesian view. On this, see Garber (1992), 144–8.

by the same process by which he originally created it; and it follows from what we have said that this fact alone makes it most reasonable to think that God likewise always preserves the same quantity of motion in matter.[47]

What God conserves, Descartes suggests, is size times speed, m|v|.

It is important here not to read into Descartes's conservation principle the modern notion of momentum, mass times *velocity*, a vector quantity. While Descartes was certainly aware of the importance of considerations of directionality,[48] directionality does not enter into the conservation principle at all. What is conserved is size times speed *simpliciter*, a scalar magnitude, so that when a body reflects off a surface and changes its direction, then as long as there is no change in its speed, there is no change in the quantity of motion.[49] It is important to realize that the issue is *not* over the conservation of momentum (mv) vs the conservation of force (motive force, motive power, living force)[50] as expressed by mv², but between the conservation of motion as expressed by a scalar quantity, m|v|, and the conservation of force as expressed by mv².[51]

---

[47] *Principia philosophiae* II.36 (Descartes (1984–91), vol. 1, 240). See Garber (1992) chs 7 and 9 for a fuller discussion of Descartes's views.

[48] On the question of determination and directionality in Descartes's physics, see Garber (1992), 188–93.

[49] This feature has lead to a "Cartesian" theory of mind/body interaction, and the claim that mind acts on body by changing the direction of the motion of a body without changing its speed, in that way allowing for mind/body interaction without violating the conservation principle. For a discussion of this, as well as a discussion of the general scope of the laws of nature, and the question as to whether they govern animate bodies or not, see Garber (2001a).

[50] Leibniz uses different terms in different places. In the opening paragraph of the "Brevis demonstratio" he uses 'vis,' 'potentia motrix' and 'vis motrix' interchangeably; see A6.4.2027–8. In 'Discours de métaphysique' § 17, he uses 'force' and 'force mouvante' indifferently; see A6.4.1556–8. In the version of the argument that Leibniz gives in the "Specimen dynamicum" he talks about force (*vis*) *simpliciter* (see "Specimen dynamicum," GM VI 243–6 (AG 127–30)), but it is clear that in the language of the earlier paragraphs of the "Specimen dynamicum," he is dealing with *vis viva*, the variety of active derivative force that is associated with a body that is in actual motion.

[51] Leibniz, of course, also thinks that what we call momentum (and what he called "common progress") is also conserved. (He also argued for the conservation of a vector quantity he called "respective speed.") For a discussion of Leibniz's different conservation laws, see Garber (1995), 316–19. See also Leibniz's explanation to L'Hospital of the difference between quantity of motion and momentum (there called "quantité de progrés vers un certain costé") in his letter of 15 January 1696, A3.6.622. But he did think that the conservation of mv² has a kind of priority over the others. In the "Essay de dynamique" from 1698–1700, he wrote:

This equation [i.e., the conservation of mv², what he calls 'absolute force' there] has an excellent feature, that all of the variations in sign which can only come from the different direction of the speeds v, x, z, y, cease, because all of the letters which express these speeds are here raised to the square. For −y and +y have the same square, +yy, so that all of the different directions mean nothing here. And it is also for this that this equation gives something absolute, independent of respective speeds or of

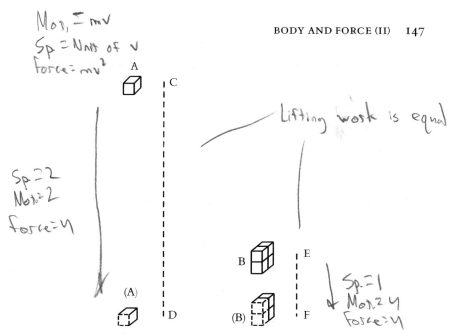

Figure 4:2. From A6.4.2028.

Leibniz offers two kinds of arguments against the Cartesian conservation law, an a posteriori argument (in a variety of different forms) and an a priori argument. The a posteriori argument first emerges in January 1678, a direct consequence of combining the Galilean law of free fall with the principle of equality that Leibniz discovered in the summer of 1676. Consider two bodies; let A be one unit in size, and B be four. (See Figure 4:2.) Now, Leibniz reasons, it takes exactly as much work to raise A four feet (from D to C) as it does to raise B one foot (from F to E), since one can regard the larger body B as being made up of four smaller bodies, each identical to A, and each of which is being raised one foot. And so, when A and B fall through those respective distances, and their speeds are converted to the horizontal, they should have exactly the same force, that is, ability to do work, for by the principle of the equality of cause and effect, the speed that

the progress in a certain direction. We have only to estimate the different masses and speeds, without taking account of the direction of these speeds. (GM VI 227–8)

In this way, even though there is a variety of different mathematical conservation laws that hold in the world, Leibniz thinks that the conservation of mv^2 has a kind of priority over the others insofar as it is "absolute" in the sense that directionality plays no role in determining its value. This is somewhat disingenuous insofar as the exact value is determined by the choice of a reference frame, and Leibniz thinks that the reference frame can be chosen at will.

A and B acquire in falling is sufficient to raise those bodies to their original heights, and we have assumed that it takes as much work to raise A four feet as it does to raise B one. Now, Leibniz argues, when A falls, by the Galilean law of free fall it will acquire two degrees of speed, while B acquires one. But if that is the case, then after the fall, <u>A will have two units of quantity of motion while B will have four.</u> So, since A and B have the same ability to do work (force), it follows that force and quantity of motion cannot be the same.[52] Now, as I noted above, Leibniz understood the principle of the equality of cause and effect to have the consequence that force, the ability to do work, must be conserved in the universe as a whole.[53] The conclusion that Cartesian quantity of motion is not conserved then follows directly out of the conservation of force together with the conclusion that force and quantity of motion are distinct and different.[54] But the result can also be established directly from the principle of the equality of cause and effect. For, Leibniz can show, if it is the Cartesian's quantity of motion that is conserved, one could build a perpetual motion machine, a machine that would create the ability to do work out of nothing at all, in obvious violation of the principle of the equality of cause and effect.[55] That mv^2 is the correct measure of force, and thus that it is mv^2 that is conserved in the world, can also be established using a variant of this argument. Consider bodies A and B as above. It is evident that in the case at hand, where after falling A will have two degrees of speed and B will have one, while A and B have different quantities of motion (two units in the case of A and four

[52] This is a paraphrase of the argument in the "Brevis demonstratio," A6.4.2028–30 (L 296–8) and in 'Discours de métaphysique' § 17 (AG 50). Brown (1984) correctly notes that it is the main point of the "Brevis demonstratio" argument to show simply that force is distinct from quantity of motion, and not that mv^2 is what is actually conserved in nature. However, it is important to point out that elsewhere Leibniz uses the basic argument form for other purposes, as we shall see.

[53] In the *Dynamica*, Leibniz argues for the conservation of the ability to do work (*potentia*) from the principle of the equality of cause and effect, both in the universe as a whole and in any closed system ("in quovis Systemate corporum cum aliis non communicantium"); see GM VI 440–1.

[54] This argument is suggested in the opening paragraph of the "Brevis demonstratio," for example; see A6.4.2027–8 (L 296).

[55] Such a machine is described, for example, in the "Specimen praeliminare" to the *Dynamica*, GM VI 289–90 (AG 108–9). In that place, Leibniz is concerned not only to show that quantity of motion differs from force, but that quantity of motion is not conserved; he gives three different a posteriori arguments to that conclusion. See GM VI 288 (AG 107) for a statement of the proposition proved, followed by three alternative demonstrations. As Desmond Hogan reminded me, the argument against perpetual motion depends on the assumption that at a crucial moment in the argument, the quantity $m|v|$ can be completely transferred from one body to another, something that is physically impossible. This was also pointed out to Leibniz by Denis Papin. See Iltis (1971), 31 and Freudenthal (2002), 611ff.

in the case of B), their size times the square of their speeds will be equal, that is, four units in both cases. It is easy to generalize this, and show that *whenever* they have equal force, the size times the square of their speed will be equal, and that whenever this is violated, the ability to do work will be either gained or lost, in violation of the principle of the equality of cause and effect.[56] Similarly, one can show that if mv^2 is allowed to increase, a perpetual motion machine can always be constructed.

But as striking as the a posteriori argument is, it has an obvious imperfection. Insofar as it depends on the behavior of heavy bodies in free fall, it depends on certain contingent features of our world that would appear to have nothing to do with the basic laws of physics. This sort of criticism is particularly problematic for Leibniz and his contemporaries, many of whom (including Leibniz himself) believed that gravity derives from the particular configuration of ethereal vortices that surround the earth; were the vortices to move differently, the law of free fall might also be altogether different, resulting in a different quantity conserved, it would appear.[57] In response to such a difficulty, Leibniz attempted to formulate an a priori demonstration of his conservation law. The a priori demonstration first appears in the "Phoranomus" of July 1689, then in the *Dynamica* of 1689–90, and in Leibniz's correspondence starting in 1696.[58] Leibniz gives a particularly simple exposition of the argument in a letter to Bayle from the late 1690s:

In the uniform motion of a single body (1) the action of traversing two places in two hours is double the action of traversing one place in one hour (since the first action contains the second precisely two times); (2) the action of traversing one place in one hour is double the action of traversing one place in two hours (or better, actions which produce the same effect are proportional to their speeds). And thus (3) the action of traversing two places in two hours is four times the action of traversing one place in two hours. This demonstration shows that a moving body receiving a double or triple motion so as to be able to

---

[56] See, for example, "Specimen dynamicum," GM VI 244 (AG 128).

[57] See Johann Bernoulli's comments to this effect in his letter to Leibniz, 8/18 June 1695, A3.6.409–10.

[58] See Leibniz (1991), 817–20; the "Specimen praeliminare" to the *Dynamica*, GM VI 291–2 (AG 110–11); in the body of the *Dynamica*, GM VI 345–67; Leibniz to de Volder, 24 March/3 April 1699, G II 172–4; Leibniz to Bayle, 1699–1701?, G III 59–60. It is also mentioned in the "Specimen dynamicum," GM VI 243 (AG 127). On the genesis of the a priori argument, see Duchesneau (1998a).

accomplish a double or triple effect in a given time, receives a quadruple or nine fold action. Thus, actions are proportional to the square of speeds. Thus it turns out, most happily, that this accords with my measure of force derived either from experience, or on the grounds of the avoidance of perpetual mechanical motion.[59]

Though it is not at all obvious that "action" as understood in this argument is equivalent to force as understood in the a posteriori arguments, as the ability to do work, Leibniz closely connects the two,[60] and takes this a priori argument to establish the same conclusion as some of the a posteriori arguments do, that force is measured by mv^2, and not by Cartesian quantity of motion. Once this is established, the conservation of mv^2 follows directly from the principle of the equality of cause and effect, as above with the a posteriori arguments. Despite its surface simplicity, this argument hides a tangle of complexity.[61] Even so, it is obvious why such a strategy should be attractive to Leibniz.

But what does this technical physics have to do with the nature of body? 'Discours de métaphysique' § 18 begins as follows: "The distinction between force and quantity of motion is important, among other reasons, for judging that one must have recourse to metaphysical considerations distinct from extension in order to explain the phenomena of bodies." Now, in 'Discours' § 17 Leibniz begins by asserting that "it is extremely

---

[59] G III 60.

[60] Indeed, in the "Specimen praeliminare" to the *Dynamica* he goes so far as to suggest that the equivalence of the two notions enables us to *demonstrate* Galileo's law of free fall! See GM VI 292 (AG 111). Presumably what he has in mind is this. If the proper measure of force (the ability to do work) can be established a priori, then we can use the fact that, in a given body, the force is proportional to the square of its speed to establish that the height to which a given body can raise itself then must be proportional to the square of its speed. From which it would follow by the principle of the equality of cause and effect that the speed it would acquire in free fall would be proportional to the square root of the distance fallen. Though action and force are closely connected, they are not identical. As Paul Lodge pointed out to me, Leibniz holds that "action is nothing other than the operation of force over time, or proportional to force multiplied by time. So actions are calculated by the products of times and forces. . . ." (Leibniz to de Volder, 24 March/3 April 1699, G II 174).

[61] For more detailed discussions of the argument, see Gueroult (1967), 118–54, Stammel (1984); and Duchesneau (1994), ch. 4. Gueroult (1967), 153–4 complains that were this argument to succeed (which he thinks it doesn't), then Leibniz would be in the position of holding that the conservation of mv^2 is necessary, in contradiction with his claim that the laws of motion are contingent. This does not follow. What the argument would show, if successful, is that the proper measure of force is proportional to the square of speed. But the conservation of mv^2 requires the additional assumption that force is conserved in the world, an assumption that depends on the principle of the equality of cause and effect, which, for Leibniz, is the result of God's wise choice and is thus contingent. We shall discuss this at greater length in Ch. 6.

reasonable that the same force is always conserved in the universe." By 'force,' of course, Leibniz means the ability to do work. Where Descartes goes wrong is to think that force understood in this way can be identified with quantity of motion (m|v|), Leibniz claims, and thus Descartes wrongly infers that quantity of motion is conserved in the world. However, since force is correctly measured by mv^2, one can take Leibniz also to have established that what is conserved is mv^2 and not m|v|. And one might think that the particular mathematical measure of force is what is at issue here, and that the fact that what is conserved is measured by mv^2 and not by m|v| is what gives Leibniz his metaphysical conclusion about the nature of body. This is how Robert Sleigh interprets Leibniz's reasoning. Sleigh cites the following suggestive passage from a letter to Bayle Leibniz wrote on February 1687:

I would like to add a remark of consequence for metaphysics. I have shown that force ought not to be estimated by the product of speed and size, but by the future effect. However, it seems that force or power is something real at present, while the future effect is not. From which it follows *that we must admit in bodies something different from size and speed, at least unless one wants to refuse bodies all power of acting.*[62]

Sleigh quite reasonably interprets Leibniz here as holding that the force a body has at some time *t* must be some non-dispositional and occurrent property that body has at that time. Here is how he then reads the argument:

Of properties identifiable with some mode characterizable in terms of size, shape, and motion, the only plausible candidate [for an intrinsic occurrent property grounding its future effects] is [quantity of motion]. . . . But the point of the argument at ['Discours de métaphysique'] § 17 is just that this identification yields incorrect results. So there is no property identifiable with a mode characterizable in terms of size, shape, and motion that yields the right results, which is the conclusion Leibniz set out to establish here. So motive force is not a physical mode of corporeal substance, if by physical mode we mean a mode of extension. The product of a body's mass at *t* and the square of its velocity at *t* serves to measure its motive force at *t*. But no one who utilized the machinery of a substance-mode ontology in our time period would have viewed the abstract composite entity

[62] G III 48; quoted in Sleigh (1990), 118. For the dating of the letter, see Müller and Krönert (1969), 80.

consisting of a body's mass at t and the *square* of its velocity at t as a mode of anything.[63]

And hence, according to Sleigh, Leibniz establishes that because force is measured in terms of mv^2 rather than $m|v|$, it follows that there must be something in body that goes beyond the geometrical.

Interesting as this reading is, I think that it misses Leibniz's point. I think that it is very significant that in 'Discours de métaphysique' § 17, Leibniz never explicitly draws the conclusion that what is conserved is mv^2; the conclusion of his argument, and what he appeals to in the beginning of 'Discours' § 18 is quite simply that it is "*the distinction between force and quantity of motion*" that is important for introducing something beyond the geometrical into body. Let me suggest a different way of understanding the connection. Leibniz's point, I think, is not fundamentally about *quantity* of motion and force, but about *motion itself* and force: it is a point not about *mathematical measures* but about the *basic underlying metaphysical reality*. The Cartesian conceptualization of the situation ("all there is in body is size, shape, and motion...") leads one—mistakenly—to believe that one can make do with a physical ontology of geometrical concepts; it seduces us into thinking that it is *motion itself* that is conserved. Hence it is the Cartesian metaphysics that is behind Cartesian physics and the idea that it must be the quantity of motion that is conserved: what else could it be? If you think that what is conserved is *literally* motion, the geometrical mode of body, then you will be led to Descartes's conservation law. Discovering that Descartes's *conservation law* is false leads us to see that his *metaphysical premise* might also be false. In this way the technical argument of the "Brevis demonstratio" or 'Discours de métaphysique' § 17 can lead us to the *metaphysical* point that there must be something more to body than size, shape, and motion: in this way, understanding that the conservation of *force* is different than the conservation of *motion* can lead us to reject the Cartesian metaphysics of body.

In general, I think that as important as the specific mathematical form of the conservation principle was for Leibniz's program in physics, it was not as important as one might think for his metaphysics. About a dozen years

---

[63] Sleigh (1990), 118.

after writing the 'Discours de métaphysique,' Leibniz wrote the following to Johann Bernoulli:

And in whatever way we quantify [*aestimemus*] that power which is conserved, we can conclude from the fact that force or action does not perish that there is something other than those two things, namely extension and impenetrability in bodies.[64]

While it is possible that his earlier views were different, here Leibniz is quite clear that the issue is not the mathematical expression, but the fact there is something about the force that persists. Also interesting in this context are some remarks that Leibniz made in a letter written roughly ten years after the 'Discourse' to the Marquis de L'Hospital. Leibniz writes:

I remain in agreement with you that a body acts by its mass and by its speed, and also that it is only by these things that I determine the moving force. But it doesn't at all follow that forces are directly proportional to the product of the masses and the speeds.[65]

Leibniz does agree—like any good mechanist—that the only physical magnitudes that enter into physical law are things like size and speed.[66] But, he would argue, though force *gives rise* to speed, they are distinct notions, and there is not necessarily going to be a direct proportionality between the one and the other, as Descartes thought.

While Leibniz himself may not always be clear about the question, in the end I think that what is important for his metaphysics of body is less the refutation of the Cartesian conservation law, and more the crucial distinction between force, that is, the ability to do work, and motion. It is true that the one, force, is conserved, and the other, motion, is not. But in the end what does the real metaphysical heavy lifting for Leibniz is the fact that force has a kind of greater reality for him than motion and the other geometrical qualities do, and as a consequence, if bodies are to be

---

[64] Leibniz to Bernoulli, 29 July 1698, GM III 521. I would like to thank Paul Lodge for calling this passage to my attention. Lodge (1997) is a very thoughtful and convincing critique of Sleigh's position. My own response to the problem of 'Discours de métaphysique' § 17–18 is similar to his.

[65] Leibniz to L'Hospital, 15/25 January 1696, A3.6.617.

[66] As we shall discuss in detail below in Ch. 6, for Leibniz everything in nature can be explained in terms of size, shape, and motion, *except* for the laws of nature themselves, which require metaphysical laws such as the equality principle, and are grounded in divine wisdom, which goes beyond the geometrical.

real, they must be understood in terms of force and not just in terms of the geometrical properties of bodies.[67] ⟶ F is substantial

This is the strategy Leibniz appeals to immediately after the passage we have been working over in 'Discours de métaphysique' § 18, a passage that we discussed in the previous chapter:

For if we consider only what motion contains precisely and formally, that is, change of place, motion is not something entirely real, and when several bodies change position among themselves, it is not possible to determine, merely from a consideration of these changes, to which body we should attribute motion or rest, as I could show geometrically, if I wished to stop and do this now. But the force or proximate cause of these changes is something more real, and there is sufficient basis to attribute it to one body more than to another.

Why is force more real? Here the point seems to be that motion considered purely in terms of change of place with respect to other bodies is unreal _subjective_ insofar as it has no well-defined subject: it is only when we move from the level of the geometrical to the level of cause and force that we get something that genuinely belongs to one or another body, and is thus a genuine reality. As he wrote in an essay from 1683, "it cannot really be said just which subject the motion is in. Consequently, nothing in motion is real besides the force and power vested in things . . ."[68]

The quotation from the letter to Bayle that Sleigh cites suggests a somewhat different argument to what is substantially the same conclusion. Leibniz writes:

I would like to add a remark of consequence for metaphysics. I have shown that force ought not to be estimated by the product of speed and size, but by the future effect. However, it seems that force or power is something real at present, while the future effect is not. From which it follows _that we must admit in bodies something different from size and speed, at least unless one wants to refuse bodies all power of acting._[69]

This is clarified by some things that he says in another text written not long after. In a letter to Paul Pellisson-Fontanier in July 1691:

The notion of force is as clear as that of action and passion, because it is that from which action follows when nothing prevents it. . . . On the other hand, motion is a successive thing, which, consequently, never exists, any more than time does,

---

[67] This, in a way, is a kind of dynamical parallel to the arguments for unity discussed above in Ch. 2.
[68] A6.4.1465 (RA 263).   [69] G III 48; quoted in Sleigh (1990), 118.

since all of its parts never exist together. Unlike that, I say, force or effort exists completely at each moment, and must be something true and real. And since nature takes account of that which is true rather than that which exists only entirely in our mind, one finds (as I have demonstrated) that it is also the same quantity of force, and not the same quantity of motion (as Descartes thought) that is conserved in nature. And it is from this principle alone that I draw everything that experience has taught about motion and about the impact of bodies, against Descartes' rules, and that I have established a new science which I call dynamics, whose elements I have set out.[70]

Here the point seems to be that insofar as motion never really fully exists at any given time, it isn't really real. But, Leibniz suggests, force *is* really there at any given moment.[71] As such, force must be distinct from motion, the reality that undergirds motion; indeed, the reality that undergirds body itself.

Body and Extension

Leibniz took great pains to distinguish his conception of body and corporeal substance from the Cartesian conception of body as extended substance. In numerous texts, he attempted to distance himself from the claim commonly made by his mechanist contemporaries that extension is the essence of body. In the last few chapters we have been examining the view that extension alone is insufficient to characterize body, and that we need to add substantial form or soul in order to account both for the unity of body as well as the forces that bodies exert in motion and collision. But there are other texts from this period that suggest an attack on the Cartesian notion of body as extension that is more radical still. In a number of those texts, it looks as if Leibniz is arguing that there is a clear sense in which bodies aren't really extended *at all.*

For example, in a passage from the essay, "De modo distinguendi phaenomena realia ab imaginariis," now dated 1683–86, Leibniz wrote:

Concerning bodies I can demonstrate that not merely light, heat, color, and similar qualities are apparent but also motion, figure, and extension. And that if anything

[70] A1.6.226–7. See also Costabel (1973), 130–1; and "Specimen dynamicum," GM VI 235 (AG 118).

[71] Cf. the discussion of Leibniz's notion of force in the 1694 "De primae philosophiae emendatione, et de notione substantiae," G IV 469–70 (L 433).

is real, it is solely the force of acting and suffering, and hence that the substance of a body consists in this (as if in matter and form).[72]

Force

This seems closely connected to something Leibniz argues in the 'Discours de métaphysique':

That the Notions Involved in Extension Contain Something Imaginary and Cannot Constitute the Substance of Body.... I believe that anyone who will meditate about the nature of substance, as I have explained it above, will find that the nature of body does not consist merely in extension, that is, in size, shape, and motion, but that we must necessarily recognize in body something related to souls, something we commonly call substantial form, even though it makes no change in the phenomena, any more than do the souls of animals, if they have any. It is even possible to demonstrate that the notions of size, shape, and motion are not as distinct as is imagined and that they contain something imaginary and relative to our perception, as do (though to a greater extent) color, heat, and other similar qualities, qualities about which one can doubt whether they are truly found in the nature of things outside ourselves.[73]

How does this erode extension

In these striking passages, and many others like them, Leibniz claims that the mechanist's basic notions of extension, shape, motion, and the like are not so basic as they thought, and that there is something imaginary in them. This would seem to undermine the claim that bodies are really extended. Just as a mechanist might say that the apple isn't really red or tasty, Leibniz would seem to be saying that the apple isn't really round; indeed, that it isn't even really extended!

Behind these bold claims stand at least two different kinds of argument. The idea that matter is really just passive force seems to be one of the important elements that leads Leibniz to his apparent denials that bodies are really extended. As we have seen in the long passage from the letter to Arnauld quoted earlier in this chapter, he argues that insofar as matter is just passive force, "in this sense matter would not be extended or divisible, although it would be the principle of divisibility or of that which amounts to it in the substance."[74] Similarly, in another passage dated at 1685(?)

---

[72] A6.4.1504 (L 365). Cf. Leibniz's remark to Tschirnhaus in a letter from June 1682: "neither thought nor extension are primitive notions nor are they perfectly understood" (A2.1².831).

[73] 'Discours' §12. There are many other passages in which Leibniz claims that our ideas of extension contain something imaginary. See, e.g., A6.4.1622 (RA 315); A6.4.1465; A6.4.1612–13; Leibniz and Arnauld (1997), 234.

[74] G II 120.

Leibniz writes that "matter is the force of being acted upon or of resisting in any body whatsoever, from which follows a certain extension in body, unless the Author of things desires otherwise."[75] The passage is primarily concerned with the problem of the Eucharist; he continues by noting: "hence a way of defending the sacrament of the Eucharist is open to us." In this context, the fact that God can create passive force without thereby creating something extended can only happen by miracle.[76] But even so, it is interesting to note the way in which extension seems to be distanced from what is real in bodies: Leibniz can say that even though extension and divisibility arise from passive force, there is a real sense in which bodies are not extended or divisible. Is, then, to say that force is what really underlies body to say that bodies are really not extended? Or that they are *un*extended, and in this way something analogous to souls?[77]

I think not. It is important to note that in the passage at issue, when Leibniz calls matter "the principle of divisibility" and denies extension to bodies, he represents this conception of matter as a simple paraphrase of a scholastic conception, "in the sense of certain scholastics."[78] There is something in that. While one can find different conceptions of matter among the scholastics, a number of thinkers held that primary matter is not itself extended but is that which gives rise to extension.[79] Surely none of them could be held to be presenting the view that bodies are genuinely unextended. And, I would claim, neither is Leibniz. His point is simply that extension is not basic to body, but derives from the passive force in body; in particular, one would suppose, from impenetrability by virtue of which one body excludes other bodies from occupying the same place. $=Ext.$ Regarding the second passage under discussion, it is very difficult to know what to say about the relation between extension and force when it is only through the supernatural act of God that extension can be withdrawn. It

---

[75] A6.4.2326.

[76] Adams (1994), 349ff discusses passages like these as part of an argument that Leibniz was an idealist in the period under discussion. However, the fact that extension can be separated from force only supernaturally makes these passages problematic for his case.

[77] Cf. Adams (1994), 337–8 and 348–9. We shall discuss Adams's views in more detail below in this chapter.

[78] G II 120. This is clearer still in an earlier version of the passage: "One can also give another definition of matter which conforms well enough to the meaning of the scholastics, but which doesn't especially conform to ordinary usage" [Leibniz and Arnauld (1997), 300].

[79] See, e.g., Garber (1992), 151 for a discussion of this issue in the scholastic commentator Franciscus Toletus. → Descartes Metaphysical Physics

certainly isn't obvious that his remarks would commit him to the view that under normal circumstances, that is, without the special and miraculous intervention of God, bodies are not extended.

But there is another consideration that Leibniz has in mind when he claims that there is "something imaginary" in our conception of the modes of extension. What underlies this claim is the observation that, in reality, bodies do not and cannot have the geometrical shapes that we attribute to them: in reality, their boundaries are infinitely complex, and cannot be captured by geometry as it was known in Leibniz's day.[80] The ground of this view is a doctrine that we have seen developed in previous chapters, that the bodies of everyday experience are composed of corporeal substances, which, in turn, are composed of corporeal substances smaller still, bugs in bugs to infinity.[81] Because of that, the surfaces of ordinary objects are of infinite complexity, not unlike a modern fractal, as Sam Levey has suggested. Thus Leibniz writes in the important "Specimen inventorum" of 1688(?):

Indeed, even though this may seem paradoxical, it must be realized that the notion of extension is not as transparent as is commonly believed. For from the fact that no body is so very small that it is not actually divided into parts excited by different motions, it follows that no determinate shape can be assigned to any body, nor is a precisely straight line, or circle, or any other assignable shape of any body found in the nature of things, although certain rules are observed by nature even in its deviation from an infinite series. Thus shape involves something imaginary, and no other sword can sever the knots we tie for ourselves by misunderstanding the composition of the continuum.[82]

Similarly, Leibniz writes in the 'Primae veritates' of 1689(?):

There is no determinate shape in actual things, for none can be appropriate for an infinite number of impressions. And so neither a circle, nor an ellipse, nor any

---

[80] On this question I am drawing on passages cited in Levey (2005) and Levey (forthcoming), as well as on Sam Levey's insightful analyses.

[81] Leibniz also offers a very strange and difficult argument to the unreality of shape from considerations drawn from the nature of time. This argument seems to be found in a single piece, a short fragment that the Akademie editors date at 1686, A6.4.1613−14 (RA 297−9). It is discussed at length in Levey (forthcoming). I suspect that it was more of a philosophical experiment on Leibniz's part than a position that he seriously considered adopting.

[82] A6.4.1622 (RA 315).

other line we can define exists except in the intellect, nor do lines exist before they are drawn, nor parts before they are separated off.[83]

The suggestion here is that the geometrical shapes that we attribute to bodies when we perceive them as spheres or cubes or any other geometrical shape, bounded in lines and planes and curved surfaces, is just our imposition onto a reality that in itself is much more complex. This comes out most explicitly in a passage from a letter Leibniz wrote to Princess Sophie in 1705:

It is our imperfection and the defects of our senses which makes us conceive of physical things as mathematical entities. . . . And one can demonstrate that there is no line or shape in nature that has the properties of a straight or circular line or of any other thing whose definition a finite mind can comprehend, or that retains it uniformly for the least time or space. . . . However, the eternal truths grounded on limited mathematical ideas don't fail to be of use to us in practice, to the extent to which it is permissible to abstract from inequalities too small to be able to cause errors that are large in relation to the end at hand. . . .[84]

In this way one may say that the extensionality of bodies is, in a way, phenomenal, the result of our imperfect senses, which impose geometrical concepts onto bodies that are, in their real nature, something quite different and that don't fit them exactly. Some commentators have been tempted to read the no-exact-shape argument as an attempt to establish the claim that the world is made up of non-extended simple substances, and that the extension of bodies is an illusion in a strong sense. But I think that it is more plausible to see Leibniz's intention here to point out the difference between what Sellars has called the manifest view of the world, the world as it appears to us, bodies with real geometrical shapes, and the scientific image of the world, bodies of infinite complexity, beyond our power to grasp in sense.[85]

---

[83] A6.4.1648 (AG 34).

[84] Leibniz (1873), vol. 3, 152f or G VII 563–4. There is a good discussion of this passage in Hartz and Cover (1988), 501. Although I would claim that Leibniz's metaphysics of body and the ultimate make-up of substance is somewhat different when he wrote this letter than it was earlier in the 1680s and early 1690s, the view expressed in the passage quoted is very much continuous with the earlier period.

[85] Robert Sleigh, in particular, sees this as the central argument for his reading of the 'Discours' and the correspondence with Arnauld in monadological terms. Although he finds the kind of reading I am proposing, which makes a metaphysics of corporeal substance basic in the period, somewhat plausible, in the end Sleigh argues that "all things considered, the account of extension offered in the *Discourse*

Closely connected with these two positions, the grounding of extension in passive force and the no–real–shape argument, is a very sophisticated conception of the relation between geometry and the physical world. In response to Leibniz's "Système nouveau" of 1695, Simon Foucher published a brief commentary. One of the issues that Foucher addressed was the question of the composition of the continuum. In response to these comments, Leibniz wrote one of the clearest accounts of the relation between the world of geometrical objects and the real world of bodies.[86] (Unfortunately, he chose not to publish the longer comments, making do with a short summary in the response he published.) In that text, Leibniz draws a clear distinction between the world of mathematical entities (lines, surfaces, numbers), and the world of concrete things. The problem of the composition of the continuum is concerned with the parts from which continua can be constructed. Leibniz's point is that the mathematical continuum does not have such parts, nor does it need them: its parts come from the division of the line, and these parts are not properly elements of that line. However, in real concreta, the whole is indeed composed of parts, though those parts don't make up a genuine mathematical continuum. The problem of the composition of the continuum is thus solved: the objects of geometry, which exist in the realm of the ideal, are continuous, but not composed of parts; the real objects that exist in the physical world are composed of parts, but they are not continuous.

It may look here as if Leibniz is denying that geometry truly represents bodies. But this cannot be right. It is important to remember that his metaphysics is intended to ground a fundamentally mechanistic conception of the physical world. From his earliest years, Leibniz consistently held that everything can be explained through size, shape, and motion, but that this mechanistic conception of the world requires a foundation in something that goes beyond extension and motion. In response to the Cartesians, who

and correspondence is closer to the monadological theory than any version of the corporeal substance theory" [Sleigh (1990), 101; the detailed argument is set out on pp. 112–15]. Donald Rutherford also emphasizes these considerations in his argument for a monadological reading of these texts. See Rutherford (1995), 156–7. While Adams doesn't put as much weight on these arguments, he agrees with Sleigh and Rutherford that they do strongly support a monadological reading of these texts; see Adams (1994), 229–32. For an excellent discussion of these arguments and a response to Adams and Sleigh, see Levey (2005), 84–92.

[86] See G IV 491–2 (AG 146–7).

want to say that bodies *just are* the objects of geometry made real, Leibniz wants to emphasize the difference between real concrete bodies and the ideal world of geometrical objects. But this is not to say that Leibniz wants to deny extension to bodies altogether. In the course of this discussion, Leibniz makes the following observation: "However, number and line are not *chimerical* things, even though there is no such composition, for they are relations that contain eternal truths, by which the phenomena of nature are ruled."[87] Or, to return to the quotation from the letter to Princess Sophie discussed above:

However, the eternal truths grounded on limited mathematical ideas don't fail to be of use to us in practice, to the extent to which it is permissible to abstract from inequalities too small to be able to cause errors that are large in relation to the end at hand. . . .

The view seems to be that geometrical extension is something ideal that exists outside the world of concrete things. However, concrete things in the world *instantiate* geometrical relations, at least approximately, insofar as real extension is infinitely complex and not genuinely continuous. Real extension is thus both more and less than geometrical extension: more insofar as it is infinitely complex, and less insofar as it is not continuous. But yet geometry is applicable to the world of concreta, a world that by its nature is ultimately characterized in terms of force. That is, there are real forces in the world, which give rise to infinitely complex structures that instantiate geometrical relations, at least approximately. Bodies are extended insofar as geometry is (approximately) true of them. However, in a metaphysical sense, what is really there is force. Thus he says, again in the notes on Foucher, "Extension or space and the surfaces, lines, and points one can conceive in it are only relations of order or orders of coexistence. . . ."[88] Geometry in this way can be said to represent something that is really in body, even if it has properties that the concrete body it represents does not, such as continuity: mathematical representation is not identity. Indeed, this is one way of putting Leibniz's point, and this is exactly where Descartes erred, in confusing the mathematical representation of bodies in geometrical terms with their concrete reality. To say that bodies are not extended, in the strictest sense, is meant to say something not only about

---

[87] Ibid.   [88] G IV 491 (AG 146).

body but also about the metaphysical status of geometry and extension, and their relation to the material world.

At this point we can return to the analogy that Leibniz draws between extension and its modes, and the so-called secondary qualities, such as color, or taste, or sound. What does an adherent of the standard mechanical philosophy mean when he says that the apple isn't really red or gold isn't really yellow? One thing that he often means is simply that the color that we sense in bodies is a causal consequence of something more basic in bodies: the size, shape, and motion of the smaller parts that make up the surface of the bodies and cause the light to be reflected in a particular way. His point is that color, understood as a particular felt quality, distinct from extension and its modes, isn't really in the physical world, and that only size, shape, and motion are. In another sense, though, the mechanist should be happy to say that a ripe apple is red, if by this we understand only that it has the particular surface texture that characteristically causes the sensation of red in sentient creatures.[89] (Actually, it is a bit more complicated than that, but this will do for our purposes here.[90]) The mechanist certainly does not want to deny that there is a difference in color between a ripe apple and an unripe apple, or between gold and lead. This is one of the ways in which we tell things apart, and without such cues, life would be much more difficult. Color, like other kinds of sensation, is given to us to preserve life, after all.[91] But these differences in color are just signs to us of deeper differences in corpuscular substructure.[92]

Leibniz wants to extend this picture to extension itself. What he wants to say is that, like color, extension is grounded in something metaphysically more basic: passive force, impenetrability, resistance. Furthermore, because of the division to infinity, things in the real world have infinite complexity and thus don't fit neatly into geometrical shapes. But even so, just as we might want to say that there is a sense in which the apple is red, there is also a sense in which the apple is extended. It isn't *really* extended, perhaps,

[89] This is exactly what Leibniz himself suggests about color in the "Notiones generales" (1683/5), A6.4.555.

[90] For a survey of some recent views on color, see Byrne and Hilbert (1997).

[91] "For the proper purpose of the sensory perceptions given me by nature is simply to inform the mind of what is beneficial or harmful for the composite of which the mind is a part; and to this extent they are sufficiently clear and distinct" (Descartes, *Meditation* VI, AT VII 83).

[92] See, e.g., Descartes, *Principia philosophiae* I.66, 70; IV.198.

any more than it is *really* red. But nevertheless, as long as we understand the basic metaphysics here, we can talk with the vulgar; that is, we can talk about bodies as extended.——⟶ w/out meaning ¿!?

Descartes's target is a common-sense view of color on which one holds that there is a real sense in which the apple is red, that redness is a quality distinct from the size, shape, and motion of anything, that pertains to red apples but not to green apples. When Leibniz asserts that the notions of size, shape, and motion "are not as distinct as is imagined," his target is the Cartesian orthodoxy that bodies are *really* extended; in fact, that they are nothing but extended, that they are extended substances, the objects of geometry made real. Just as Descartes wants to take us below the surface of the bodies of ordinary experience, below their sensory qualities and to the modes of extension that underlie them, Leibniz wants to take us below the surface of Cartesian bodies, to the forces that underlie the extension that the mechanical philosopher appeals to in his science and to their infinite complexity. And just as the mechanist doesn't want to deny that there is a real sense in which bodies have these sensory properties, Leibniz, too, doesn't want to deny that bodies are extended. Indeed, as we have seen, and will continue to see, Leibniz is perfectly happy calling himself a mechanical philosopher, and continuing to explain the phenomena of the physical world in terms of size, shape, motion, and the laws of nature, as long as we recognize that these are all grounded in something more basic still.

So far we have been examining two classes of arguments against the Cartesians: a group of arguments, examined in previous chapters, that claim that extension by itself is insufficient for body, leading to the addition of substantial form or soul; and a pair of arguments, examined in this chapter, that advance the view that, in themselves, bodies are not geometrical, either because they are really constituted by force, or because they are too complex to be characterized in terms of simple geometrical figures. But in the 1690s, Leibniz adds a new and interesting strategy to his repertoire: two arguments intended to show the absurdity of the notion of a body that is extended and extended alone. In the first of these arguments Leibniz wants to hold that extension is not the kind of thing that could possibly exist by itself in the way in which the Cartesians hold that it does, and in the second that a Cartesian universe of purely extended body without empty space is also without division or change.

So far as I can determine, the first of these arguments makes its initial appearance in the 1692 "Animadversiones in partem generalem Principiorum Cartesianorum":

> the notion of extension is not a primitive one but is resolvable. For an extended being implies the idea of a continuous whole in which there is a plurality of things existing simultaneously. To speak of this more fully, there is required in extension, the notion of which is relative, a something which is extended or continued as whiteness is in milk, and that very thing in a body which constitutes its essence; the repetition of this, whatever it may be, is extension.[93] ⟵ Loemker 390

The argument is clearer still in a letter that Leibniz wrote to de Volder in 1699:

> I don't think that substance consists of extension alone, since the concept of extension is incomplete. And I don't think that extension can be conceived through itself, but I think it is a notion that is resolvable and relative. . . . Something must always be assumed which is either continued or diffused, as whiteness is in milk, color, ductility and weight are in gold, and resistance is in matter. For continuity taken by itself (for extension is nothing but simultaneous continuity) no more constitutes a complete substance than does multitude or number, where there must be something numbered, repeated, and continued. And so I believe that our thought is completed and terminated more in the notion of the dynamic [i.e., force] than in that of extension. . . .[94]

One cannot intelligibly talk about numbers made real, something that is *just* three, or twenty, *and nothing else*: one must talk about three persons, or twenty loaves of bread. Similarly, one cannot talk about something *just* being extended, *and nothing else*: the concept of extension presupposes something that is extended, and the idea of a thing that is extended and extended alone is simply absurd and incoherent.

The other such argument can be found in Leibniz's essay "De ipsa natura," a polemic against J. C. Sturm, published in the *Acta eruditorum* in 1698. This ingenious argument seems to have pleased Leibniz greatly, since he referred to it a number of times in later correspondence. Leibniz first

---

[93] G IV 364 (L 390).

[94] G II 169–70 (AG 171–2). Leibniz repeats the same basic argument a number of times in his correspondence with de Volder: see G II 234, 269, 277. It is also found in later writings, e.g. G IV 393–4 (AG 251) and G VI 584 (AG 261).

notes that if all there is in body is extension, and if there is a plenum and thus no empty places in the world, then:

at the present moment (and furthermore, at any moment whatsoever) a body A in motion would differ not at all from a resting body B, and the view of that distinguished gentleman [i.e. Sturm] (if his view of the matter is different from mine) would entail that there is no clear criterion in bodies for distinguishing them, since in a plenum, the only criterion for distinguishing between masses uniform in themselves is connected with motion.[95]

In such a world, there is no distinction between a body in motion and one at rest at a given moment, nor can we even distinguish one body from another, presumably in the sense of their being ways of distinguishing the two from one another; being hunks of indistinguishable material substance, there could be no qualitative features to distinguish them from one another. But, Leibniz argues, we couldn't appeal to motion either to distinguish the two. Leibniz writes:

For if no portion of matter whatsoever were to differ from equal and congruent portions of matter (something that the distinguished gentleman should admit, since he has eliminated active forces or impetus, and with them all other qualities and modifications except 'existing in this place' and 'successively coming to exist in some other place'), and furthermore, if one momentary state were to differ from another in virtue of the transposition of equal and interchangeable portions of matter alone, portions of matter in every way identical, then, on account of this perpetual substitution of indistinguishables, it obviously follows that in the corporeal world there can be no way of distinguishing different momentary states from one another.

The argument here is that since from one moment to the next, any change could only involve the "transposition of equal and interchangeable portions of matter alone," motion couldn't help in any way to distinguish bodies from one another. Indeed, there is no way that we, in the corporeal world, could establish that there had been genuine motion, that is, genuine change: since we cannot distinguish between different portions of matter, motion would be undetectable, since "under the assumption of perfect uniformity in matter itself, one cannot in any way distinguish one place from another,

---

[95] All these texts are taken from "De ipsa natura" § 13, G IV 513–14 (AG 163–4).

or one bit of matter from another bit of matter in the same place." But the situation is even worse:

And since everything substituted for something prior would be perfectly equivalent, no observer, not even an omniscient one, would detect even the slightest indication of change. And thus, everything would be just as if there were no change or discrimination in bodies, nor could we ever explain the different appearances we sense.

And if not even God could understand there to be a change, then there is no change: "absolutely nothing would change in bodies, and . . . everything would always remain the same." Once again, the supposition of a Cartesian world leads to absurdity, an unchanging world of indistinguishable objects.[96]

Oh, Dear, What Can the Matter Be?

In these last few chapters we have been concerned with the notions of form and matter in Leibniz's middle years, from the late 1670s through to the mid-1690s or so. In his writings in this period, Leibniz gives a great deal of attention to the notion of form: it is his great innovation to return substantial form to physics. Matter, though, gets somewhat less attention. Matter is identified with force, primitive passive force. But what exactly is its metaphysical status? Is it a metaphysical principle genuinely distinct from the form or soul that gets the bulk of Leibniz's attention? Or is it to be understood somehow in terms of the perceptions and appetitions of a non-extended simple substance?

In Leibniz's later monadological metaphysics, he certainly recognizes something that he calls matter. As he wrote to de Volder:

I therefore distinguish: (1) the primitive entelechy or soul; (2) matter, namely primary matter or primitive passive power; (3) the monad completed by these two things. . . .[97]

If we understand by 'monad' here the unextended mind-like simple substance of his later metaphysics, then it would seem that primary matter is just a constituent of an unextended substance. And insofar as he seems to

---

[96] For a somewhat different reading of Leibniz's argument here, see Lodge (1998b).
[97] Leibniz to de Volder, 20 June 1703, G II 252.

hold that "there is nothing in things except simple substances and in them perception and appetite,"[98] as he later wrote to de Volder, this matter must be understood in terms of monadic perception and appetite. This raises an important question. If primary matter can be so easily accommodated into a monadological view in Leibniz's later writings, might he have had such a conception of matter in mind in his earlier writings as well? Might Leibniz have been a monadological metaphysician even in the middle period when corporeal substances seem to be so much in evidence?

R obert Adams has attempted to make just such a case. Fundamental to his argument is a passage from the essay "De modo distinguendi phaenomena realia ab imaginariis" (1683/6). The final sentence of the text as we now have it reads as follows:

Substances have metaphysical matter or passive power to the extent that [quatenus] they express something confusedly, and active power to the extent that they express something distinctly.[99]   — Loemker

This would seem strongly to support the view that, for Leibniz, primary matter is to be understood in an entirely mentalistic way, as the confused perception of a non-extended substance. Adams supports this view with two further arguments. The kinds of forces that Leibniz associates with primary matter are the passive forces of resistance and impenetrability. Adams notes that both of these forces are relational: they are reactive, forces that bodies exert only when acted upon by other bodies. Adams argues that it would be unsatisfactory for Leibniz to consider such forces as basic pieces of furniture in the world:

I find it hard to believe that Leibniz did not intend to postulate the diffusion of an *intrinsic* property, and also hard to believe that he regarded the tendency to resist penetration and motion as an intrinsic rather than a relational property.[100]

And so Adams argues:

If resistance or passive force must include intrinsic properties, what can they be? I think that for Leibniz they can only be qualities of *perception*, or tendencies to

[98] Leibniz to de Volder, 30 June 1704, G II 270.

[99] "Substantiae habent materiam Metaphysicam seu potentiam passivam quatenus aliquid confuse exprimunt, activam quatenus distincte" A 6.4.1504 (L 365). This passage is discussed first in Adams (1994), 325; he returns to it on pp. 329, 364, and 393. Donald Rutherford is also impressed by this passage and sees it as supporting a monadological reading of primary matter. See Rutherford (1995), 158.

[100] Adams (1994), 328.

such qualities. Here the identification of passive force as a function of confusedness of perceptions satisfies Leibniz's conceptual needs. Resistance, insofar as it is a nature prior to the system of spatiotemporal relations and can ground extension by its repetition or diffusion, will be a tendency to have confused perceptions. The entities in which the system of spatiotemporal relations is grounded will be perceiving substances. . . .[101]

This argument, then, supports the view that is apparently advanced in the "De modo . . ." Adams advances yet another argument in support of this view, from the indivisibility of primary matter. This argument starts off with a passage from the Arnauld correspondence that we saw earlier, where it is plausible to suppose that Leibniz is characterizing primary matter: "in this sense matter would not be extended or divisible."[102] Adams concludes:

We are left with the conclusion that the primary matter of a substance, on Leibniz's view, is indivisible—and hence as unextended—as the substantial form. . . . If a substantial form unites with such a primary matter to form a substance (a perceiving substance . . .), it is hard to see why the primary matter would not be an internal aspect of an unextended, perceiving substance. In other words, the primary matter seems to be, thus far, an internal aspect of what Leibniz would ultimately call a 'monad'. . . .[103]

In this way, Adams wants to argue, the unities of form and matter that concern Leibniz in this middle period are virtually the same as the monads that he will later posit.

Should we follow Adams? I think not. Let me begin with the arguments from the relativity of passive force and from the claim that primary matter is indivisible and non-extended. The fact that the passive forces associated with primary matter—resistance and impenetrability—are relative is not really to the point. To understand Leibniz's view, we have to distinguish between primitive and derivative forces, as discussed earlier in this chapter. Resistance and impenetrability are, indeed, relative in the sense that Adams notes. But they are also derivative forces. And primary matter is characterized as *primitive* passive force. That is to say, primary matter is the ground of the derivative forces of resistance and impenetrability, that which gives rise to them. One can, and probably should, suppose that the

101 Ibid., 327.   102 G II 120.
103 Adams (1994), 338. Essentially the same argument is given on pp. 347–9.

primitive passive force is absolute and non-relational, even though the derivative passive forces are relational.[104] As for the second argument, that primary matter is indivisible and non-extended, that has already been addressed earlier in this chapter. The full passage reads as follows: "in this sense matter would not be extended or divisible, although it would be the principle of divisibility or of that which amounts to it in the substance."[105] As I argued earlier, Leibniz's point is not that primary matter is non-extended in the sense of being a mere constituent of a non-extended substance; it is simply that extension is not basic to corporeal substance, but is a consequence of the diffusion of resistance and impenetrability. As I argued, his target is the Cartesian identification of body and extension, for Leibniz the conflation of the concrete, whose real nature is force, with the mathematical, which exists in the realm of the ideal.

But both of these arguments of Adams's get considerable support from the passage from "De modo . . .," which seems to assert that primary matter is nothing but the confused states of a perceiving substance. However, this passage is much more complicated than it looks on its surface. We shall come back to this passage and the essay in which it is contained a number of times later in this book. But let me outline briefly some of the problems that it poses for the commentator who wants to use it to support an idealistic reading of Leibniz's metaphysics in this period. First of all, it is not at all clear to me that it dates from the same period as the rest of the essay. We shall discuss the essay as a whole in some detail below in Chapter 7, when we discuss Leibniz's phenomenalisms. When we understand the full context, it seems to me that this sentence is somewhat out of place. The main theme of the essay is the distinction between real and imaginary phenomena, i.e., the phenomena connected with the tables and chairs in my office vs the experiences I had while dreaming last night. After discussing this distinction, Leibniz then turns to the question of "those things which do not appear but which nevertheless can be inferred from

---

[104] *Primitive* passive force is not relational in the sense at issue in Adams's argument, that is, relative to the impact of another body in motion and to its attempt to penetrate the body in question. However, it is relative in another sense insofar as primary matter is incomplete and can't exist without form. This is the sense at issue in the characterization of substance written in response to Thomasius, and quoted above in note 41: "Cum sit Ens incompletum, ejusque notio constat in relatione" [Utermöhlen (1979). 88]. For a discussion of the notion of an incomplete substance, see Adams (1994), 269ff. Of course I don't follow Adams in his attempt to make this consistent with his monadological reading.

[105] I do not mean to suggest that Adams is unaware of the full citation. He discusses it at Adams (1994), 338, though he offers a reading of it consistent with his monadological interpretation.

appearances."[106] After discussing minds, he then turns to bodies, which are characterized in a way quite typical for the period, as we saw earlier in this chapter:

Concerning bodies I can demonstrate that not merely light, heat, color and similar qualities are apparent but also motion, figure and extension. And that if anything is real, it is solely the force of acting and suffering, and hence that the substance of a body consists in this (as if in matter and form). Those bodies, however, which have no substantial form, are merely phenomena or at least only aggregates of the true ones.[107]

And then, immediately following, is the passage at issue, which ends the essay. The passage isn't entirely unrelated to what had come before; it does pick up on the notions of matter and form mentioned in the penultimate paragraph, and offers an account in terms of confused and distinct expression. But it does seem to take the essay abruptly in a rather different direction. And when you look at the ms. of this passage, it is in a somewhat different handwriting than the rest of the ms., rather neater and less rushed.[108] This suggests to me that the sentence in question was a later addition. Even if it were to be contemporaneous with the original drafting of the essay, there is a further complication for someone like Adams who wants to use this as a support for a monadological reading of the middle years. The passage talks about confused and distinct *expression*, and *not* confused and distinct *perception*. As we shall discuss in more detail in Chapter 5, perception is a kind of expression, one that can take place only in a subject capable of perception. But expression is a more general notion that simply involves appropriate correspondence between two objects, one that expresses and the other that is expressed. And so, for example, a map expresses the territory that it represents. In this way, expression has no particular mentalistic implications.

Over and against the passage from "De modo...," of uncertain date, difficult to interpret, and apparently unique in the period (if it is, indeed, from the period), there are a number of very clear passages where Leibniz takes quite a different line. In the March 1694 issue of the *Acta eruditorum*, Leibniz published an essay entitled "De primae philosophiae emendatione,

---

[106] A6.4.1503 (L 365).   [107] A6.4.1504 (L 365).
[108] See LH IV 6, 8b Bl. 2. I would like to thank Philip Beeley for providing me with a copy of the ms. page.

et de notione substantiae." In the essay, Leibniz emphasizes the conception of substance as grounded in force. He writes:

the concept of *forces* or *powers*, which the Germans call *Kraft* and the French *la force*, and for whose explanation I have set up a distinct science of *dynamics*, brings the strongest light to bear upon our understanding of the true concept of *substance*.[109]

There is no hint here that he isn't giving the reader the full story about the grounds of his notion of substance. There is every reason to believe that Leibniz thought of active and passive forces not only as the ground-level *physical* realities, but as the ultimate *metaphysical* realities that ground the created world, and which do not need further explication in terms of monadic perceptions, distinct or confused. This view is supported in other texts from the period. A correspondent, Jacques Lenfant, wrote to Leibniz with the following remark on 7 November 1693:

The whole question is thus to know if the force to act in bodies is in matter something distinct and independent of everything else that one conceives there. Without that, this force cannot be its essence, and will remain the result of some primitive quality or another.[110]

What Lenfant is asking, in essence, is whether force is metaphysically basic, or whether it requires a deeper account. This is part of Leibniz's reply:

And since everything that one conceives in substances reduces to their actions and passions and to the dispositions that they have for this effect, I don't see how one can find there anything more primitive than the principle of all of this, that is to say, than force.[111]

That is to say, force would seem to be metaphysically fundamental. This is what he wrote even more clearly to Bossuet in a letter from 2 July 1694: "I find nothing so intelligible as force."[112] These passages suggest that we should take force in general, and primitive passive force—primary matter—at face value. Later Leibniz may want to give a deeper account of force in terms of the distinct and confused perceptions and the appetitions of non-extended and mind-like monads; later the metaphysics of force may

---

[109] G IV 469 (L 433).   [110] Tognon (1982), 326.

[111] Leibniz to Lenfant, 25 November 1693, Tognon (1982), 327. It is interesting to observe that even though Lenfant had written to Leibniz about *body*, his reply is quite clearly about *substance*.

[112] A1.10.144 (WF 30).

be subsumed into a metaphysics more fundamental still. But at this moment there is every reason to believe that he thought of primary matter and the passive forces of resistance and impenetrability in a thoroughly realistic way, as existing outside of the internal states of non-extended perceiving substances, and grounding a world of genuinely extended things. While it may be tempting to impose Leibniz's later monadology back onto his thought in this period, and read primary matter as the confused perception of a non-extended perceiving substance, I see no good reason for doing so.

Force, Leibnizian and Newtonian[113]

Leibniz's doctrine of force and body is directed solidly against the mechanist doctrines of Descartes, Hobbes, and their followers. There is every reason to think that it was largely in place by 1686 when, seemingly out of nowhere, Newton published his *Philosophiae naturalis principia mathematica*, what came to be known simply as the *Principia*, and articulated a conception of force that was very different from what Leibniz had developed. The ultimate success of the Newtonian program has all but driven Leibniz's conception of force off the playing field. But I would like to reflect a bit about the places in which the two conceptions of force come together, and the ways in which they differ.

Now, there are at least two sets of notes Leibniz wrote on Newton's *Principia* that survive, in addition to the numerous comments that he made in letters and essays on his great contemporary and rival.[114] Interestingly enough, none of them are addressed directly to the relation between their accounts of force. My account here is thus less a report on how each saw the other in relation to his own views, than it is the remarks of a modern commentator trying to make historical and philosophical sense of the relations between them on this issue.

---

[113] This section is taken from a lecture presented at a conference on Newton and/as Philosophy organized by Eric Schliesser at the University of Leiden in June 2007. I would like to thank the audience there for a lively and very helpful discussion that forced me to rethink some key aspects of the position for which I was arguing.

[114] Leibniz (1973a) was thought to be the only such set of notes for quite a while. Then Bertoloni Meli (1993) published another set of notes in his appendix 1, and in ch. 5 argued very convincingly that Leibniz had read Newton's *Principia* before writing his "Tentamen de motuum caelestium causis," as discussed above in n. 9.

The various notes we have that precede the final composition of the *Principia* show that Newton struggled with the articulation of the notion of force. Though it would be interesting to trace the development of Newton's conception and compare it with the considerations that drove Leibniz,[115] I am going to limit myself to a consideration of the final account as it appears in the *Principia*.

The star of the *Principia* is Newton's notion of impressed force. Newton defines it as follows in the *Principia*:

Impressed force is the action exerted on a body to change its state either of resting or of moving uniformly straight forward.

This force consists solely in the action and does not remain in a body after the action has ceased. For a body perseveres in any new state solely by the force of inertia. Moreover, there are various sources of impressed force, such as percussion, pressure, or centripetal force.[116]

(The reference to the force of inertia is significant here, and I shall get to that in a moment.) It is this kind of force that is at issue in Newton's second law: "A change in motion is proportional to the motive force impressed and takes place along the straight line in which that force is impressed."[117] The project of book I of the *Principia* is to give us the general tools that we need to infer the existence of various impressed forces from the phenomena. As Newton writes in the preface to the first edition, "the basic problem of philosophy seems to be to discover the forces of nature from the phenomena of motions and then to demonstrate the other phenomena from these forces."[118] In book III Newton works out one important example, that of gravitational force. But there is an explicit assumption from the beginning that this is not the only kind of force in nature. Again, in the preface to the first edition Newton writes:

For many things lead me to have a suspicion that all phenomena may depend on certain forces by which the particles of bodies, by causes not yet known, either are impelled toward one another and cohere in regular figures, or are repelled from one another and recede. Since these forces are unknown, philosophers have hitherto made trial of nature in vain.[119]

---

[115] For an elegant account of the last stages of Newton's development of the notion of force, see Bertoloni Meli (2006), § 2.

[116] Newton (1999), 405.   [117] Ibid., 416.   [118] Ibid., 382.   [119] Ibid., 382–3.

In the *Principia*, Newton gives us the methods we need to find these other forces, perhaps chemical forces, electrical forces, magnetic forces, etc. All of these other impressed forces can be handled by the same mathematical tools, etc., but they are in their nature rather different. What they have in common is simply that they are causes of the change in velocity of bodies. Force answers the question not of what bodies are, but how they behave.

This conception of force seems importantly different from Leibniz's conception. For Newton, the focus is on the impressed force that changes the motion of a body. His interest in the *Principia* is in the common cause of the impressed forces that explain the trajectories of the heavenly bodies, as well as the fall of bodies on earth. That cause is what he calls gravity. Newton is thus interested in causes in the *Principia*, but only in determining that there is a common cause for a variety of phenomena: otherwise the cause in question remains unknown in its nature, though one can, perhaps, read him as entertaining the possibility that gravitation (i.e., the underlying cause of the impressed forces that are examined in the *Principia*) is essential to body as such. At the same time, Newton recognizes other forces in nature (chemical, electrical, magnetic, etc.) that will have their own distinctive (but as yet unknown) causes, causes that might be present in some bodies but not in others. These other causes will impress other forces on bodies in other circumstances.

Now, it is not impossible that all of the Newtonian impressed forces can be given a mechanical explanation, as Descartes or Hobbes or Leibniz would want to do. That is, it is not impossible that all of the causes of the impressed forces that explain the different phenomena of interest to Newton are, at root, mechanical causes. It is also possible for Newton that gravitation could be an essential property of body as such. While one can find many apparently tentative speculations about this question in his notes and papers,[120] this wasn't Newton's interest, at least not in the *Principia*: his first problem was to establish the existence of the forces of different kinds. It was only after that that one should investigate the underlying causes, and that only to the extent that experience and experiment reveal them to us. To the best of our knowledge, Newton never got to that part of his investigation. He was certainly attracted by the mechanical

---

[120] See the introduction to part III in Newton (1962).

philosophy. But the framework of the *Principia* doesn't commit him to that: it is an open framework that allows one to entertain a larger vision.

Leibniz, unlike Newton, is doing what we might call fundamental physics, trying to characterize the physical world at its physically most basic level. And in this connection, Leibniz's interest in the notion of force is linked to a strict and rigorous version of the mechanist program: at root there is one kind of material stuff, all of which obeys the same laws. Leibniz is working within a rigidly mechanist framework. And as for Descartes and Hobbes before him, his problem is grounding the physical world in an appropriate conception of that material stuff. This is where the notion of force enters into his project. Force is not just a tool to explain the empirically observed behavior of bodies; the conception of force that interests Leibniz operates at the physically most fundamental level and reveals the underlying nature of body as such. In Newton's world one can contemplate different *kinds* of forces, with different underlying causes. Leibniz begins with the commitment that, in the world, there is just body of one sort. And in this world, there is force of one sort, at root. Again, it might turn out for Newton that all the different forces can be reduced to one kind of force, the mechanist's force that acts through collision. But while Newton is not committed to that position for a priori reasons, Leibniz is. It is this one, unitary conception of force that he identifies with body as such. For Newton, the force treated in the second law and the focus of attention in the rest of the *Principia* is a generic notion, as it were, a general kind of thing, characterized by its mathematical structure and connection with other notions such as mass and acceleration: it can thus come in different varieties, gravitational, chemical, electrical, magnetic, and perhaps others. For Leibniz, on the other hand, force is something very specific and very concrete: it is what is ultimately grounded in the fundamental make-up of a mechanist world. It is force with a capital 'F', the ultimate stuff that grounds the physical world. ——> & comes in at least eight varieties.

Indeed, in a very strict sense, there *are* no external, impressed forces for Leibniz. It is well known that, for Leibniz, there is no genuine causal communication between substances; as we shall see in more detail below in Chapter 5, all of the activity of a corporeal substance derives from its own internal states. Thus Leibniz writes in part II of the "Specimen dynamicum": "*every passion of a body is of its own accord*, that is, *arises from*

ie, no derivative forces

an internal force, even if it is on the occasion of something external."[121] In this way, from a metaphysical point of view, at least, the central notion of force, that of an impressed force, is strictly speaking unintelligible from the point of view of a Leibnizian conception of force.

But even if Newton's impressed force doesn't have much in common with Leibniz's conception of force, there is another Newtonian notion that seems much closer. In the *Principia* Newton writes:

Inherent force of matter is the power of resisting by which every body, so far as it is able, perseveres in its state either of resting or of moving uniformly straight forward.
This force is always proportional to the body and does not differ in any way from the inertia of the mass except in the manner in which it is conceived. Because of the inertia of matter, every body is only with difficulty put out of its state either of resting or of moving. Consequently, inherent force may also be called by the very significant name of force of inertia. . . .[122]

The inherent force of matter is very closely identified with matter itself: it is something that pertains to body as such, by virtue of which body is capable of resisting an impressed force imposed upon it. In this respect it is rather different from the more central notion of impressed force in Newton, as commentators have noted with some puzzlement. In his recently published commentary on the *Principia*, I. B. Cohen remarks that this definition is "in many ways the most puzzling of all the definitions in the *Principia*." He continues:

Today's reader will . . . be struck by the fact that Newton uses the word "force" in relation to 'inertia' ('*vis inertiae*'), although—as Newton is at pains to explain—this is an internal force and not the kind of force which (according to the second law) acts externally to change a body's state of rest or of motion. Unless we follow Newton's instructions and make a sharp cleavage between such an internal 'force' and external forces, we shall fail to grasp the Newtonian formulation of the science of dynamics.[123]

The fact that Cohen consistently puts this use of force into scare-quotes suggests that he doesn't think that it is really force, properly speaking. If what we mean by force is a physical magnitude that satisfies Newton's second law, then the *vis insita* certainly isn't a force.

---

[121] GM VI 251 (AG 134–5).   [122] Newton (1999), 404.   [123] Cohen (1999), 96.

But Newton's inherent force of matter is very similar to Leibniz's primitive passive force: both are expressions of the basic nature of body as such.[124] And both are connected with the resistance to change in a body's state of motion or rest. Here is how Leibniz characterizes primitive passive force in the "Specimen dynamicum," as quoted above:

And indeed, the *primitive force of being acted upon* [*vis primitiva patiendi*] or of *resisting* constitutes that which is called *primary matter* in the schools, if correctly interpreted. This force is that by virtue of which it happens that a body cannot be penetrated by another body, but presents an obstacle to it, and at the same time is endowed with a certain laziness, so to speak, that is, an opposition to motion, nor, further, does it allow itself to be put into motion without somewhat diminishing the force of the body acting on it. As a result, the *derivative force of being acted upon* later shows itself to different degrees in *secondary matter*.[125]

And here is Newton, from Definition 3 of the *Principia*:

Moreover, a body exerts this force only during a change of its state, caused by another force impressed upon it, and this exercise of force is, depending on the viewpoint, both resistance and impetus: resistance insofar as the body, in order to maintain its state, strives against the impressed force, and impetus insofar as the same body, yielding only with difficulty to the force of a resisting obstacle, endeavors to change the state of that obstacle. Resistance is commonly attributed to resting bodies and impetus to moving bodies, but motion and rest, in the popular sense of the terms, are distinguished from each other only by point of view, and bodies commonly regarded as being at rest are not always truly at rest.[126]

Let me begin by emphasizing some striking similarities between these two conceptions. First of all, Leibniz's passive force seems to be responsible for doing pretty much what Newton's *vis insita* is supposed to do: it is the force that resists change both in bodies at rest and bodies in motion. In this way it is the force that breaks the speed of a colliding body. Unlike Leibniz, Newton does not emphasize the difference between primitive and derivative forces. But one can say that something very like Leibniz's distinction is inherent in Newton's definition insofar as he distinguishes between the "inherent force" which is "always proportional to the body"

---

[124] On the relation between Newton's *vis insita* and Leibniz's notion of inertia, see Bernstein (1981).
[125] GM VI 236-7 (AG 119-20). [126] Newton (1999), 404-5.

and "inherent" in it, and the *exercise* of this force on the occasion of an impact.

But despite the similarities, there are some profound differences as well. One profound difference concerns the relation between resistance and impetus, the force exerted by a body resisting change in its motion, and the force exerted by a body in motion on another body. For Newton, the two are the same force, and differ only in our point of view:

this exercise of force is, depending on the viewpoint, both resistance and impetus: resistance insofar as the body, in order to maintain its state, strives against the impressed force, and impetus insofar as the same body, yielding only with difficulty to the force of a resisting obstacle, endeavors to change the state of that obstacle.

Though Newton, of course, recognizes a real distinction between absolute motion and absolute rest, this distinction does not enter into his account of the *vis insita*: it is both resistance and impetus. But, for Leibniz, the arch-relativist in other respects, there is a real distinction between resistance and impetus, between (primitive) passive force and (primitive) active force. Indeed, this distinction is identical for Leibniz to a fundamental distinction in his metaphysics between matter and form, the two distinct principles that make up corporeal substance. Though a relativist about space and time, Leibniz is *not* a relativist about motion and rest, and thus not a relativist about impetus and resistance. For him they are radically distinct, and ground a fundamental dichotomy in his metaphysical account of body.

There is another, perhaps more subtle, difference between Newton and Leibniz on this issue worth noting. Newton's is a *vis insita*, a force inherent in body. This is important to Newton, no doubt. But Newton is less interested in the contribution this makes to the understanding of the *nature* of body, and more interested in the consequences that it has for our understanding of the *behavior* of body. What is important about it being an *inherent* force is simply that it is always available to us in understanding the behavior of bodies. Impressed forces come and go as bodies find themselves in different external circumstances. But you can *always* count on a body to resist the change in its state. For Leibniz, though, the inherence of passive forces, important as it is for understanding the behavior of bodies, is also central for his account of their nature. The primitive passive force of a body is a central constituent of its underlying nature.

And with this we reach what is a very deep difference between Leibniz and Newton regarding their conception of force. In the *Principia*, Newton is interested in demonstrating certain theorems about force and motion and in demonstrating from them and from certain empirical phenomena the existence of a universal law that explains planetary motion and terrestrial gravitation and the connection between the two. While in various places he speculates about the nature of matter, his thoughts about matter are just that, speculations, and in the *Principia*, at least, he does not want to advance a solid doctrine of body and its make-up. But Leibniz's project is quite different. Leibniz, too, is interested in motion and the behavior of bodies in motion. But his interest in force is broader than that. What Leibniz seeks is the big picture: the nature of body as a grounding for an account of motion and its laws. Force plays a role in Leibniz's account of the behavior of bodies. But he is just as interested, if not more, in the way the notion of force can illuminate the *nature* of body. In that way, force plays a central role in his proposed replacement for the Cartesian/Hobbesian account of the nature of body.

Let me put this difference in broader terms still. Earlier in the century, there is a tension between two great traditions in thinking about the natural world. Descartes is working in a broadly Aristotelian tradition of natural philosophy. His aim is ultimately to give a view of the world that includes an account of the behavior of bodies as such, but grounded in an understanding of the true first causes: the nature of bodies, the causes of their motion, the way in which the laws that govern their behavior are grounded in the first cause, i.e. God. A different strand was the Galilean project. Galileo's project was within the domain of mixed mathematics, as it was called, a quantitative account of the world that favored mathematical description over an account of the ultimate first causes. I would claim that Leibniz is an inheritor of the natural philosophical tradition of Descartes, and Newton is an inheritor of the mathematical tradition that Galileo followed. The very different ways in which Leibniz and Newton treat the notion of force are, I would claim, reflections of that fundamental difference.

5

Complete Individual Concepts, Non-Communication, and Causal Connection

In the last three chapters we have been exploring two paths that led Leibniz to the revival of substantial forms in natural philosophy, starting at the end of the decade of the 1670s, arguments around the notion of unity in Chapter 2, and in Chapters 3 and 4 considerations connected with force, activity, and the grounding of physics. In later chapters we shall find tensions within and between these two approaches that will challenge the view of the world that dominates the 1680s and 1690s. But in this period, Leibniz sees the two as converging into one grand view. That these two very different considerations appear to converge on the revival of substantial forms must have seemed to Leibniz a great confirmation of both approaches and of the conclusion to which both seem to point. Indeed, more than twenty years later, in the essay 'Contra philosophiam Cartesianam' (May 1702), from which we quoted in the previous chapter, Leibniz still sees these two themes as closely linked. He writes:

Primitive active force, which Aristotle calls first entelechy and one commonly calls the form of a substance, is another natural principle which, together with matter or passive force, completes a corporeal substance. This substance, of course, is one *per se*, and not a mere aggregate of many substances, for there is a great difference between an animal, for example, and a flock.[1]

---

[1] G IV 395 (AG 252). The conception of corporeal substance as unity is also joined explicitly with the dynamical conception of corporeal substance in "Specimen Demonstrationum Catholicarum" (1685(?)), A6.4.2326; the "Système nouveau" (1695), G IV 478–9 (AG 139); and in many other passages.

Leibniz really thinks of this as one philosophy, arrived at from different directions. He believed in the underlying unity of knowledge, as he believed in the underlying unity of religion.[2]

But there is yet another approach to the notion of substance in this period, through the notion of a Complete Individual Concept and Leibniz's celebrated Predicate-in-Notion principle. While this conception of substance seems somewhat less important to Leibniz than the approaches to the notion of substance through unity and force that we have been examining in earlier chapters, it is this approach that he features in the 'Discours de métaphysique,' a text drafted with some care in the mid-1680s.[3] In that text, and others that start from this conception of substance, Leibniz draws out many of the same kinds of consequences that he drew from the other approaches to substance that we have already seen. But, Leibniz thought, this conception of substance is especially useful for leading us to certain insights about activity and causality in the world of created substances. In particular it will lead Leibniz to the somewhat surprising view that there is no genuine interaction among substances. We shall end the chapter with an extended discussion of the difficult doctrine of causality in terms of distinct and confused expression that is closely linked to that view.

Complete Individual Concepts and Individual Substances

In his letter to the Landgrave Ernst von Hessen-Rheinfels of 1/11 February 1686, Leibniz wrote: "Being at a place where for some days I had nothing

---

[2] Here I would differ strongly from the approach taken, in different ways, in Robinet (1986), Wilson (1989), and Wilson (1999b). Robinet and Wilson argue for distinct and independent strands in Leibniz's thought, of which he was not fully aware, and which pull him (unconsciously?) in different directions. I agree that the strands that I have been tracing, the "unity" strand and the "activity" strand, do, indeed, wind up being not entirely consistent with one another. However, there is every reason to believe that Leibniz was fully aware of both, and genuinely believed that they were completely consistent with one another.

[3] For an extended discussion of the argument, with copious references to earlier related texts and to the secondary literature, see Di Bella (2005a). For a good discussion of the historical roots of Leibniz's conception of substance in terms of the Complete Individual Concept, see Rutherford (1995), 119–24. Rutherford argues that while there are "rudimentary" versions of the doctrine in the late 1670s, it is only in the 1680s that it gets its full articulation. In this way it seems to be subsidiary to the characterization of substance in terms of unity or activity that we have been examining, at least historically speaking.

to do, I have lately composed a short discourse on metaphysics.''[4] So begins the letter that transmits to Hessen-Rheinfels the summary of the 'Discours de métaphysique,' which begins the correspondence with Arnauld examined above in Chapter 2. While Arnauld never saw the 'Discours' itself, it was a work to which Leibniz devoted much care and attention, and it went through a number of drafts with numerous changes and corrections. For all that, Leibniz never published it, nor is there any evidence that he contemplated publishing it in the years following, unlike the correspondence with Arnauld. But for whatever reason, except for the summaries he shared with Arnauld, it remained unknown to the larger world until it was finally published in the middle of the nineteenth century.[5] Even so, it is an important attempt to articulate and summarize his views on metaphysical questions that had been developing over the previous decade or so.

The question of substance is raised in the 'Discours' in the context of another problem, that of occasionalism. These are the summary paragraphs that Leibniz attaches to the first seven sections of the 'Discours':

1. On Divine Perfection, and That God Does Everything in the Most Desirable Way.
2. Against Those Who Claim That There Is No Goodness in God's Works, or That the Rules of Goodness and Beauty Are Arbitrary.
3. Against Those Who Believe That God Might Have Made Things Better.
4. That the Love of God Requires Our Complete Satisfaction and Acquiescence with Respect to What He Has Done without Our Being Quietists as a Result.
5. What the Rules of the Perfection of Divine Conduct Consist in, and That the Simplicity of the Ways Is in Balance with the Richness of the Effects.
6. God Does Nothing Which Is Not Orderly and It Is Not Even Possible to Imagine Events That Are Not Regular.
7. That Miracles Conform to the General Order, Even Though They May Be Contrary to the Subordinate Maxims; and about What God Wills or Permits by a General or Particular Volition.

These sections, then, obviously deal with the activity of God in creating the world and acting on it after he created it. In § 8, then, Leibniz turns

---

[4] G II 11.

[5] The first publication is as an appendix to Grotefend's edition of the Leibniz–Arnauld correspondence in Leibniz and Arnauld (1846).

away from God and his activity and towards the activity of finite things. That section has the following summary:

8. To Distinguish the Actions of God from Those of Creatures We Explain the Notion of an Individual Substance.

It opens as follows:

It is rather difficult to distinguish the actions of God from those of creatures; for some believe that God does everything, while others imagine that he merely conserves the force he has given to creatures. What follows will let us see the extent to which we can say the one or the other.

Leibniz quite clearly has occasionalism on his mind: to what extent can we say that God is the real active power in the world, and to what extent can we say that things themselves are genuinely active?

Later in this chapter we shall return to the question of occasionalism. But at this point, I would like to turn to the account of substance that Leibniz offers in 'Discours' § 8. Leibniz begins by announcing a logical premise:

Now it is evident that all true predication has some basis in the nature of things and that, when a proposition is not an identity, that is, when the predicate is not explicitly contained in the subject, it must be contained in it virtually. That is what the philosophers call *in-esse*, when they say that the predicate is in the subject. Thus the subject term must always contain the predicate term, so that one who understands perfectly the notion of the subject would also know that the predicate belongs to it.

This premise, the so-called Predicate-in-Notion principle, is taken to be uncontroversial; as he writes to Arnauld, "the predicate is contained in the subject, or else I do not know what truth is."[6] From this Leibniz draws in § 8 the conclusion that every individual substance must have associated with it a concept that contains everything that can be predicated of it, past, present, and future:

Since this is so, we can say that the nature of an individual substance or of a complete being is to have a notion so complete that it is sufficient to contain and to allow us to deduce from it all the predicates of the subject to which this notion is attributed. . . . God, seeing Alexander's individual notion or haecceity, sees in

---

[6] Leibniz to Arnauld, 4/14 July 1686, G II 56.

it at the same time the basis and reason for all the predicates which can be said truly of him, for example, that he vanquished Darius and Porus; he even knows a priori (and not by experience) whether he died a natural death or whether he was poisoned, something we can know only through history.

The contrast here is with an incomplete concept, one that does not contain "the basis and reason for all the predicates which can be said truly" about an individual. In his notes on Arnauld's letter of 13 May 1686, Leibniz contrasts the concept of the specific sphere on Archimedes' tomb, which he assumes to have a complete concept, with the simple concept of a sphere:

So the concept of the sphere in general is incomplete or abstract, that is to say that one considers only the essence of the sphere in general or in theory without regard to the particular circumstances, and consequently it does not in the least contain what is required for the existence of one individual sphere, but the concept of the sphere that Archimedes had placed on his tomb is complete and must contain all that pertains to the subject of that form.[7]

So far the argument is rather trivial, from a logical point of view, at least: from the Predicate-in-Notion principle it follows that every individual substance has what can be called a Complete Individual Concept (CIC), a concept that is so complete that it contains everything true of the individual in question.[8] But from this in § 8 Leibniz draws a remarkable conclusion:

Thus when we consider carefully the connection of things, we can say that from all time in Alexander's soul there are vestiges of everything that has happened to him and marks of everything that will happen to him and even traces of everything that happens in the universe, even though God alone could recognize them all.

How in the world did Alexander's *soul* get into this, not to mention the rest of the universe?

What is going on here is this, I think. The universe enters from the fact that each individual bears some relation to all of the other things in the world in which it exists. Furthermore, Leibniz argues, there are no purely extrinsic denominations: every relational property is in some sense

[7] G II 39.

[8] Of course, it doesn't follow from this that *we* have access to this concept and could draw out the truths it entails about any subject.

If y is true, then it is true of x that y.

(which we cannot explore here) grounded in the non-relational properties of things. As Leibniz writes in the 'Primae veritates' paper of 1689:

Every individual substance contains in its perfect notion the entire universe and everything that exists in it, past, present, and future. For there is no thing on which one cannot impose some true denomination from another thing, at very least a denomination of comparison and relation. Moreover, there is no purely extrinsic denomination. I have shown the same thing in many other ways, all in harmony with one another.[9]

That the CIC, both Alexander's properties and those that pertain to the world in which he exists, must be grounded in marks and traces in his *soul* is a bit more difficult to understand. But not much. First of all, Leibniz reasons that if the CIC is truly predicated of Alexander, then there must be something *in Alexander himself* by virtue of which his CIC is true of him; the attribution of a property to a subject requires not just a foundation in the *concept* of the subject, but *in the subject itself*. But why in his *soul*? Leibniz explains to Arnauld:

Substantial unity requires a complete, indivisible and naturally indestructible entity, since its concept embraces everything that is to happen to it, which cannot be found in shape or in motion (both of which embrace something imaginary, as I could prove), but in a soul or substantial form after the example of what one calls Self.[10]

While this passage is not without its own obscurities, we might fill it out as follows. Suppose that it is now (at t_1) true of individual substance S that S will at some future time (at t_2) have property P. Leibniz *seems* to be reasoning that if it is true at t_1 that S will have P at t_2, then there must be something at t_1 which will be P at t_2, and something at t_2 which is P, and these two somethings must be the same thing. If we are now to have a truth about something in the future, then there must be some one thing to which both the present and future facts attach: an enduring truth requires an entity that endures, for Leibniz. A similar argument can be given from the present truth of facts about the past. Since a CIC includes facts about the future (and past) states of a substance, there must be something that persists from the past, to the present, and into the future, something that is

And souls endure

---

[9] A6.4.1646 (AG 32–3).
[10] Leibniz to Arnauld, 28 November/8 December 1686, G II 76.

present whenever the substance is, something to which the past, present, and future properties can attach themselves. This something is, of course, the form or soul that unites the corporeal substance, and creates a genuine persisting individual: the matter in the body, fluctuating and changing from moment to moment just will not do, Leibniz thinks.[11]

The elements that make up this remarkable argument go back a few years in Leibniz's history. The idea of substance as a complete being that involves all of its properties appears as early as a note written shortly after leaving Paris. In a piece dated December 1676, Leibniz writes:

In my view a substance, or, a complete being, is that which by itself involves all things, or, for the perfect understanding of which the understanding of nothing else is required. A shape is not of this kind; for in order to understand from what a shape of such and such a kind has arisen, we need to have recourse to motion. Each complete being can be produced in only one way; the fact that figures can be produced in various ways is a sufficient indication that they are not complete beings.[12]

But the Predicate-in-Notion principle with which it is closely associated in the 'Discours' and related texts seems to emerge only a bit later, in the logical writings of 1679. Leibniz's project was to build a symbolic calculus in which reasoning could be represented by arithmetic relations. In one of the early pieces in the ground-breaking series of papers from April 1679, Leibniz writes:

To make evident the use of characteristic numbers in propositions, it is necessary to consider the fact that every true universal affirmative categorical proposition simply shows some connection between predicate and subject. . . . This connection is, that the predicate is said to be in the subject, or to be contained in the subject; either absolutely and regarded in itself, or at any rate in a stated fashion. This is to say that the concept of the subject . . . involves the concept of the predicate, and therefore that subject and predicate are related to each other either as whole and part, or as whole and coincident whole, or as part to whole.[13]

---

[11] In an earlier draft of 'Discours' § 8, Leibniz uses a different example, that of the ring of Gyges or Polycrates, claiming that while the shape of the ring is not a substance that has a CIC, the ring itself may be conceived of as having a CIC that contains all of its properties. But, Leibniz notes, this can hold only under the assumption that the ring "has a consciousness," i.e. a soul that makes it into a substance, a soul to which the CIC can attach. It is obvious why the example was dropped. See the textual notes in A6.4.1540.

[12] A6.3.400 (SR 115).

[13] A6.4.197 [Leibniz (1966), 18–19]. This quotation omits a clause that is inserted to deal with applying the formula to the case of particular affirmatives, such as "some wealthy person is wretched."

The claim that the concept of the predicate must be in the concept of the subject in every true predication is basic to the formalization of logic that Leibniz was attempting in that period, and, indeed, in all of the work that he did in logic ever after.[14]

Leibniz very quickly realized that his Predicate-in-Notion principle entails that an individual substance must have a Complete Individual Concept. In a piece thought to have been written in early or mid-1679, Leibniz writes:

In order to investigate the nature of substance or of a subsisting thing, we must reflect on the fact that even if many different attributes can be said of the same subject, none of them is a subsisting something, as, for example, when hot and bright and situated here today is said about this same fire. Moreover, the concept of a subsisting thing, for instance this fire, is what includes all those attributes which can be said of the thing, about which we can speak. And so, just as a subsisting thing is nothing but a complete term, or that in which everything is, which can be attributed to it or to the same thing, so if the same A is B and C and D and E etc., then A will be a substance, that is, a complete term. Hence nothing is in a complete term *per accidens*, that is, all of its predicates can be demonstrated from its nature.[15]

This observation, that individual substances have concepts that contain all of their properties, can be found in numerous texts leading up to the argument of 'Discours' § 8.[16] But it seems to be only in the mid-1680s that Leibniz tried to make this argument do significant philosophical work for him in any systematic way.

In later sections of the 'Discours,' Leibniz draws a number of striking conclusions from this argument:

Several notable paradoxes follow from this; among others, it follows that it is not true that two substances can resemble each other completely and differ only

---

In this case, the concept of the predicate is contained in the concept of the subject "with some further addition."

[14] It should be noted that in the passage quoted, it is only universal affirmative propositions that are at issue. But Leibniz thinks that the principle can suitably be generalized to cover all propositions in all forms.

[15] A6.4.306.

[16] Summer 1678–winter 1680/81, A6.4.2770; summer 1680–winter 1684/5, A6.4.389; summer 1683–early 1685, A6.4.553–5; summer 1683–early 1685, A6.4.559–60; summer 1683–winter 1685/6, A6.4.575–6; early 1684–winter 1685/6, A6.4.1506–7 (RA 283–5); mid-1685, A6.4.625; winter 1685/6, A6.4.672.

in number [*solo numero*], and that what Saint Thomas asserts on this point about angels or intelligences (that here every individual is a lowest species) is true of all substances. . . . It also follows that a substance can begin only by creation and end only by annihilation; that a substance is not divisible into two; that one substance cannot be constructed from two; and that thus the number of substances does not naturally increase and decrease, though they are often transformed.[17]

It also follows from this remarkable argument, Leibniz thinks, that we must revive the substantial forms of the schoolmen:

It seems that the ancients, as well as many able men accustomed to deep meditation who have taught theology and philosophy some centuries ago (some of whom are respected for their saintliness) have had some knowledge of what we have just said; this is why they introduced and maintained the substantial forms which are so decried today. But they are not so distant from the truth nor so ridiculous as the common lot of our new philosophers imagines.[18]

As I noted above, insofar as an individual substance has a CIC, it must have a persisting seat for the CIC, a something that persists of which the CIC is true. That, Leibniz argues, can only be a soul. And once again we rejoin the conclusion, arrived at through the other arguments that we have been examining, that we must reintroduce substantial forms into the world.

But, as I pointed out, in the 'Discours,' this conception of substance is supposed to address the question of occasionalism in some way. How exactly does that work?

Leibniz and Occasionalism

The doctrine of occasionalism was, of course, central to seventeenth-century metaphysics, particularly among the Cartesians. On this widely held view, the changes that one body appears to cause in another upon impact, the changes that a body can cause in a mind in producing a sensation, or a mind can cause in a body in producing a voluntary action are all due directly to God, moving bodies or producing sensations in minds on the occasion of other appropriate events. The doctrine of occasionalism is sometimes presented as having been primarily a solution to the problem

---

[17] 'Discours' § 9.   [18] 'Discours' § 10.

of mind/body interaction; since it is inconceivable how minds and bodies can interact, it is argued, seventeenth-century philosophers held that it is God who connects the motion of the sensory organs with the sensation in the mind, and the volition in the mind with the voluntary motion of the body. But in reality, the motivation for the doctrine among most seventeenth-century philosophers is somewhat different.[19]

Descartes, of course, famously held that God must keep the world in existence from moment to moment with a power equivalent to that by which he recreated it in the beginning.[20] Louis de La Forge, one of his important followers, takes this view quite literally, and uses it as the basis of an argument in his *Traité de l'esprit de l'homme* for the claim that only God can cause motion:

I hold that there is no creature, spiritual or corporeal, that can change [the position of a body] or that of any of its parts in the second instant of its creation of the creator does not do it himself, since it is he who had produced this part of matter in place A. For example, not only is it necessary that he continue to produce it if he wants it to continue to exist, but also, since he cannot create it everywhere, nor can he create it outside of every place, he must himself put it in place B, if he wants it there, for if he were to have put it somewhere else, there is no force capable of removing it from there.[21]

For many of Descartes's later followers, what is central to the doctrine of occasionalism is the denial of the efficacy of finite causes simply by virtue of their finitude. Clerselier, for example, a correspondent of Descartes's and his literary executor, argues for occasionalism by first establishing that only an incorporeal substance can cause motion in body. But, he claims, only an infinite substance, like God, can imprint new motion in the world "because the infinite distance there is between nothingness and being can only be surmounted by a power which is actually infinite."[22] Cordemoy argues similarly. Like Clerselier, he argues that only an incorporeal substance can be the cause of motion in a body, and that this incorporeal substance can only be infinite; he concludes by saying that "our weakness informs us that it is not our mind which makes [a body] move," and so he concludes

---

[19] See Lennon (1974); Garber (2001b); Garber (2001c).

[20] See, e.g., *Meditation* III, AT VII 48–9; *Principia philosophiae* I.21, II.36.

[21] La Forge (1974), 240. Malebranche also uses this argument in Dialogue Seven § X of the *Entretiens sur la métaphysique et sur la religion*. For a discussion of this argument, see Garber (2001c).

[22] Clerselier to de La Forge, 4 December 1660, in Descartes (1667), vol. 3, 642.

that what imparts motion to bodies and conserves it can only be "another Mind, to which nothing is lacking, [which] does it [i.e., causes motion] through its will."[23] And finally, the infinitude of God is crucial to the main argument that Malebranche offers for occasionalism in his central work, *De la recherche de la vérité*. The title of the chapter in which Malebranche presents his main arguments for the doctrine is "The most dangerous error in the philosophy of the ancients."[24] And the most dangerous error he is referring to is their belief that finite things can be genuine causes of the effects that they appear to produce, an error that, Malebranche claims, causes people to love and fear things other than God in the belief that they are the genuine causes of their happiness or unhappiness.[25] But why is it an error to believe that finite things can be genuine causes? Malebranche argues as follows:

> As I understand it, a true cause is one in which the mind perceives a necessary connection between the cause and its effect. Now, it is only in an infinitely perfect being that one perceives a necessary connection between its will and its effects. Thus God is the only true cause, and only he truly has the power to move bodies. I further say that it is not conceivable that God could communicate to men or angels the power he has to move bodies.....[26]

For these occasionalists, then, God must be the cause of motion in the world because only an infinite substance can be a genuine cause of anything at all.

Leibniz seems to have flirted with some variety or another of occasionalism in his youth. As I noted above in Chapter 1, Leibniz advanced what we can recognize as an occasionalist view on motion in physics in the important letter to his teacher Jacob Thomasius from 20/30 April 1669, though when the letter is published a year or so later, the reference to occasionalism is considerably weakened.[27] But Leibniz comes back to occasionalism later in the decade. It is quite possible that he had become acquainted (or, perhaps, re-acquainted) with the doctrine during his Paris years, though this is surprisingly difficult to document; interestingly enough, the doctrine

---

[23] Cordemoy, *Six discours*, in Cordemoy (1968), 143.

[24] Malebranche, *Recherche de la vérité* VI.II.III, in Malebranche (1979–92), vol. 1, 643 [Malebranche (1997a), 446].

[25] Malebranche (1979–92), vol. 1, 643–6 [Malebranche (1997a), 446–8].

[26] Malebranche (1979–92), vol. 1, 649 [Malebranche (1997a), 450].

[27] See A2.1².36 (L 102) and A6.2.443, and the discussion above, pp. 30–1. As I noted earlier in Ch. 1, it isn't entirely clear that Leibniz himself saw the connection to Cartesian occasionalism here.

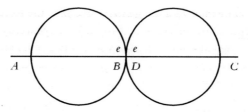

Figure 5:1. From A6.3.567.

does not seem to appear in any of the texts from that period.[28] However, in the dialogue "Pacidius Philalethi," written in October 1676 at the very end of his time in Paris and on his way to take up his new post in Hanover, Leibniz clearly presents a version of occasionalism. He writes:

And therefore the action by which a moving point is transferred from one sphere into another one contiguous to it—that is, the action by which a moving body *e* which was in one sphere at one moment is caused to be in another contiguous sphere at the next moment afterward—does not belong to the very body *e* which is to be transferred. For at the moment when it is at point *B* it is not in motion, as shown above [see Figure 5:1] and therefore it does not act by motion; similarly it does not act when it is already at point *D*. Therefore what moves and transfers the body is not the body itself, but a superior cause which by acting does not change, which we call God. Whence it is clear that a body cannot even continue its motion of its own accord, but stands in continual need of the impulse of God, who, however, acts constantly and by certain laws in keeping with his supreme wisdom.[29]

While this is sometimes represented as an aberration in Leibniz's view, a momentary lapse in judgment, it probably wasn't. A clear statement of the same view appears as late as January 1678, in connection with the "De corporum concursu," where Leibniz first announces the conservation of mv^2. He writes:

[B]ut it is necessary that they [i.e. bodies] are either carried by a general mover (which, however, is unsatisfactory, since they would also have their own force,

---

[28] In his letters with Malebranche from the mid-1670s, the subject is not occasionalism, but the vacuum. See A2.1^2, letters 123–5. While Leibniz met Cordemoy in Paris, he may not have read his *Six discours* until much later; the notes we have on that work are on the Latin translation of 1679, and probably date from 1685. See the discussion of Leibniz and Cordemoy above in Ch. 2. Leibniz met Clerselier, who gave him access to the Descartes *Nachlass*, but there is no record of any philosophical conversations between them. And strangely enough, there is no record of his ever having met Louis de La Forge. That said, it would be strange indeed if Leibniz spent almost four and a half years in Paris and never heard of the doctrine of occasionalism.

[29] A6.3.566–7 (RA 211–13).

which would be combined with the general force [i.e., the force imparted by the general mover]), or, rather, that they are continually impelled by that wisest cause, which remembers all and cannot fail. Therefore, the laws of motion are nothing but the reasons for the divine will, which matches [*assimilat*] effects to causes, to the extent that the reason of things allows.[30]

In this way Leibniz seems to have flirted with occasionalism for a fair period of his early years.

But that seems to change when Leibniz abandons his earlier metaphysics of body. The revival of substantial forms in physics, the transformation of physical body into corporeal substance, seems to lead Leibniz to abandon his earlier occasionalism, and put activity into body itself.[31] In the essay 'De natura corporis,' discussed above in Chapter 3 and written sometime between summer 1678 and the winter of 1680/1, Leibniz argues:

And they have erred in considering motion, but not motive power or the reason for motion, which *even if derived from God, author and governor of things, must not be understood as being in God himself, but must be understood as having been produced and conserved by him in things.* From this we shall also show that it is not the same quantity of motion (which misleads many), but the same powers that are conserved in the world.[32]

Leibniz understood his new dynamical account of body in terms of active and passive force as a direct challenge to occasionalism: rather than inert extended bodies, shuffled about by a God who is the only source of genuine activity in the world, Leibniz posits genuinely active bodies, bodies that are the source of their own activity; bodies, in short, that genuinely embody forces.

But how exactly is the conception of substance in 'Discours' § 8 relevant here? If every individual substance contains in its soul marks and traces of every property it will ever have, then, Leibniz seems to have inferred,

---

[30] Fichant (1994), 134; see the commentary on 269f.

[31] There is an extensive literature on Leibniz's refutation of occasionalism, an issue that strays outside of the main themes of this book. See, e.g., Woolhouse (1988); Sleigh (1990), 161–70; Rutherford (1993); Jolley (2005b), and the references cited there for accounts of Leibniz's refutation of occasionalism.

[32] A6.4.1980 (AG 249), emphasis added. Note, though, a curious phrase in a letter to Weigel from September 1679: "For I think that it is not our mind that acts on things as much as it is God, in accordance with his will..." (A2.1².747). This passage, which suggests an occasionalist position on mind and body, would seem to place the passage quoted from 'De natura corporis' sometime after September 1679.

God need not produce these properties in the substance; each individual substance already contains within itself all of its properties, past, present, and future: "all the things that can ever happen to us, are only consequences of our being."[33] In this way, Leibniz concludes, individual substances must be the sources of all of their properties: in this way they must be genuine agents in the world, and not mere inert things, shuffled about by God, as they are for the occasionalists. And so, it would seem, the activity of individual substances is derived from what appears to be purely logical premises.

But more follows from 'Discours' § 8 than just the refutation of occasionalism.

The Non-Communication Thesis

In 'Discours' § 8 Leibniz addresses the question as to the activity of created things. In 'Discours' § 14 he turns to another related question:

After having seen, in some way, what the nature of substances consists in, we must try to explain the dependence they have upon one another and their actions and passions.

Individual substances do, of course, for Leibniz (as for every other Christian philosopher of his era), depend on God:

Now, first of all, it is very evident that created substances depend upon God, who preserves them and who even produces them continually by a kind of emanation, just as we produce our thoughts.[34]

But, Leibniz claims, other than that, substances don't depend on anything else at all. In particular, he claims, they have no genuine causal relations with any other finite substances:

[E]ach substance is like a world apart, independent of all other things, except for God; thus all our phenomena, that is, all the things that can ever happen to us, are only consequences of our being. . . . We could therefore say in some way and properly speaking, though not in accordance with common usage, that one

[33] 'Discours' § 14. This and following passages strongly suggest a kind of phenomenalism, and have suggested to some that, at this stage, Leibniz already is working within a metaphysics essentially identical to that of the later monadology. These passages will be discussed below in Ch. 7.
[34] 'Discours' § 14.

particular substance never acts upon another particular substance nor is acted upon by it, if we consider that what happens to each is solely a consequence of its complete idea or notion alone, since this idea already contains all its predicates or events and expresses the whole universe.[35]

And so, one might say, the argument that establishes the activity of an individual substance establishes it to such an extent that there is no room for another (finite) substance to act on it. In this way, the non-communication thesis can be seen to derive directly from the refutation of occasionalism and the argument for the inherent activity of substance in 'Discours' § 8.[36]

One consequence of the occasionalist doctrine that God is the only genuinely active agent in the world is that finite things are not the genuine causes of changes in one another: minds cannot be the genuine causes of voluntary motions, and bodies cannot be the genuine causes of either perceptions in minds or motions in other bodies. Apparently causal connections among minds and bodies are just what came to be called the *occasional* causes of changes in one another. Even though Leibniz rejects the full occasionalist doctrine, he does agree with it in this. As Leibniz wrote in a note from 1689 or so:

The system of occasional causes should be admitted in part, and rejected in part. Each and every substance is the true and real cause of its immanent actions, and has a force of acting [*vis agendi*], and though it is granted that it is sustained by divine concourse, yet it cannot happen that it is only passive; this is true both for corporeal and incorporeal substances. But, on the other hand, each and every substance (except for God alone) is only the occasional cause of its transeunt actions on other substances. . . .[37]

The particular way in which Leibniz made individual substances genuinely active, the sources of their own states and changes, cut off all genuine causal

---

[35] Ibid.

[36] Mendelson (1995), 52ff also sees a connection between the non-communication thesis and the doctrine of the Complete Individual Concept, though he develops it in a rather different way than I do here.

[37] A6.4.1640–1 (RA 313). Richard Arthur argues for an earlier date, 1686, but the exact dating doesn't matter for my purposes. Leibniz characterizes his conception of the causal relation in terms of occasional causes in earlier versions of 'Discours' § 32; see A6.4.1581, textual notes to ll. 2 and 7. However, he did change his mind before the final draft. In a letter to L'Hospital, 30 September 1695, Leibniz presents his own pre-established harmony in a sense deriving out of Malebranche's occasionalism: "On peut dire que ce n'est pas tant un renversement, qu'un avancement de sa doctrine, et que c'est à luy que je suis redevable de mes fondemens sur ce sujet" (A3.6.506). However, it isn't clear the extent to which this is just a rhetorical flourish.

interaction: each substance is, in his colorful phrase, "like a world apart."[38] This is what I will call the non-communication thesis.

It is difficult to say when exactly Leibniz first came to hold the thesis that there are no genuine causal relations among substances. By the late 1670s, he seems convinced that there is no direct communication between minds and bodies. Leibniz writes to Malebranche in January 1679:

I am entirely of your opinion concerning the impossibility of conceiving that a substance which has nothing but extension, without thought, can act upon a substance which has nothing but thought, without extension. But I believe that you have gone only halfway and that still other consequences can be drawn than those which you have made.[39]

A few months later he writes, again to Malebranche:

I approve most heartily these two propositions which you advance: that we see all things in God and that, strictly speaking, bodies do not act upon us. I have always been convinced of this for important reasons which seem to me indisputable and which rest on certain axioms which I do not as yet see used anywhere....[40]

It isn't at all clear what axioms Leibniz has in mind here. Nor is it clear that he really had "always" been convinced of the view in question. But there is some evidence that Leibniz held views that entail something like the non-communication of mind and body as early as December 1676, shortly after leaving Paris for Hanover:

If it could be supposed that a body exists without a mind, then a man would do everything in the same way as if he did not have a mind, and men would speak and write the same things, without knowing what they do, just as when they are playacting. But the supposition that the body exists without a mind is impossible.[41]

In another similar passage from an essay that Leibniz is thought to have written in 1677/8, and which he entitled "Anima quomodo agit in corpus":

How the soul acts on the body. As God acts on the world: that is, not in a miraculous way, but through mechanical laws. And so if minds were eliminated

---

[38] "Each substance is like a world apart, independent of all other things, except for God...." ['Discours' § 14]

[39] Leibniz to Malebranche, 13/23 January 1679, A2.1².678 (L 209).

[40] Leibniz to Malebranche, 22 June/2 July 1679, A2.1².724 (L 210).

[41] A6.3.400 (SR 115). The Latin of the first phrase reads as follows: "Si fingi posset mentem esse sine corpore...." I follow Parkinson in seeing this as a slip of the pen for: "Si fingi posset corpus esse sine mente...."

leaving the laws of nature (which would be impossible), the same thing would happen as if there were minds: books would even be written and read by human machines, though they would understand nothing.[42]

While these passages are somewhat obscure, they do suggest quite strongly certain elements of the later doctrine of pre-established harmony: even if what happens in mind and in body correspond with one another, everything that happens in the body can be given a purely mechanical explanation. While he doesn't say in these passages that mind and body are causally independent, the explanatory independence of body would seem to cohere well with its causal independence from mind as well.[43]

But the causal independence of mind and body is not the full non-communication thesis. Indeed, given the fact that the body taken without a soul isn't a substance at all, it would seem to be something of a rather different order. If the body taken without a soul is an aggregate of substances, then the non-interaction of mind and body would seem to be a consequence of the thesis that there are no genuinely causal relations among substances, but the entailment wouldn't necessarily go the other way.

The earliest statement I know of where Leibniz adopts the full non-communication thesis is in an essay that the Akademie editors have entitled 'De libertate et gratia,' and dated between summer 1680 and summer 1684:

No substance is capable of transeunt action, but only of immanent action, except for God alone, on whom all other substances depend.[44]

ie no substance acts outside itself

---

[42] A6.4.1367.
[43] There is a lively debate on when the doctrine of pre-established harmony was first articulated. The general consensus seems to put the date at about 1679; see, e.g., Kulstad (1993) and Lodge (1998a). Mendelson (1995) doesn't give a definite date, but the texts he cites in that connection are all from the mid-1680s. Mercer and Sleigh (1995), 100f put the date at 1676, but Lodge (1998a) convincingly argues against the evidence cited. In her more recent book, Mercer (2001), ch. 8, pushes the date back to as early as 1671. I think that the evidence is even slimmer than her 1676 dating. However, there are some interesting hints of the pre-established harmony from 1676 that Mercer doesn't mention. One is a passage from a note on Simon Foucher from 1676: "But perhaps the nature of our mind is the immediate cause of our perceptions of material things, and that God, author of everything, is the cause of the agreement which there is between our thoughts and that which is outside of us" (A6.3.318–19). I am very impressed by the passage from December 1676 [A6.3.400 (SR 115)] and the similar passage from the year or two afterwards (A6.4.1367), both quoted earlier in this paragraph, which haven't been discussed in the literature. But however suggestive they may be of certain elements of pre-established harmony, it is unlikely that Leibniz had the full doctrine that early; account must also be taken of Leibniz's apparent commitment to occasionalism in those years, the idea that God is the ultimate causal agent in the world.
[44] A6.4.1458.

But as clear a statement as this is, Leibniz gives no grounds for this general statement in this passage. However, in a familiar passage from the 'Primae veritates' paper now thought to have been written in 1689, Leibniz suggests two arguments:

Strictly speaking, one can say that no created substance exerts a metaphysical action or influx on any other thing. For, not to mention the fact that one cannot explain how something can pass from one thing into the substance of another, we have already shown that from the notion of each and every thing follows all of its future states. What we call causes are only concurrent requisites, in metaphysical rigor.[45]

The first argument is derived from the simple unintelligibility of an influx from one substance into another, the passing of certain physical magnitudes from one substance to another.[46] However, Leibniz doesn't seem to put much weight on it. The second argument recalls the Complete Individual Concept argument that we have been discussing. As I noted earlier in this chapter, the observation that individual substances have concepts that contain all of their properties can be found in numerous earlier texts. But only in the mid-1680s do we find Leibniz drawing the consequence from this view that substances have no genuine commerce with one another. The logical considerations behind the CIC argument of 'Discours' § 8 seem to be what led Leibniz to the thesis that there is no transeunt causality between substances.

But interesting as this argument is, Leibniz seems to have abandoned it rather quickly. While the claim that individual substances have complete individual concepts is one of the enduring theses of Leibniz's philosophy, and while Leibniz continues to hold the non-communication thesis to the end of his life, the argument for it from the CIC seems to drop out of his

---

[45] A6.4.1647 (AG 33). See also Leibniz's remark in the "Specimen inventorum" thought by the Akademie editors to be from the same period: "From the notion of individual substance it also follows in metaphysical rigor that all the operations of substances, both actions and passions, are spontaneous, and that with the exception of the dependence of creatures on God, no real influx of them on one another is intelligible" [A6.4.1620 (RA 311)]. Given that the essay begins with the conception of individual substance to which Leibniz is alluding in the 'Primae veritates' paper, I take this to say the same thing. See also Leibniz's remark in the *Dynamica* (1690), part II, sect. III, prop. 18: "each and every singular substance is so constituted that it envelopes the entire universe in its complete notion, and in a certain sense it can be said to do everything through itself and as it were spontaneously" (GM VI 507). The argument from 'Primae veritates' is repeated almost word for word at the end of Leibniz's life, in his letter to Des Bosses, 19 August 1715, LDB 348. For an excellent discussion of the notion of a requisite as it relates to the notion of a cause, see Futch (2005); for a more general account of the notion of a requisite, see Di Bella (2005b).

[46] On the influx theory, particularly as Leibniz understands it, see O'Neill (1993).

repertoire rather quickly, by the early or mid-1690s.[47] When Leibniz first publishes his philosophical thoughts on body and substance in 1695 in the "Système nouveau" and in the "Specimen dynamicum," the argument of 'Discours' § 8 from the Predicate-in-Notion principle and the Complete Individual Concept seem to play no role in any of the arguments. Perhaps Leibniz was afraid of making too public a doctrine that had obvious implications with respect to Spinozistic necessitarianism: if each individual substance contains all of its properties, past, present, and future, then it would seem that everything is necessary, as Arnauld immediately accused Leibniz of believing. Or perhaps Leibniz realized that the argument simply didn't succeed in establishing its conclusion with respect to the activity of substance. Since God must sustain bodies for them to persist in their existence, as Leibniz knew full well and often admitted, placing all their properties in them doesn't at all settle the question of whether they are genuinely active or whether it is really God who is responsible for them doing what they do. Leibniz will address this question later, particularly in the "De ipsa natura" of 1698. But there it is more purely metaphysical considerations and not logical considerations that come to the fore. The 'Discours de métaphysique,' in the end, may have been only one of a number of attempts to systematize his philosophy that Leibniz tried but ultimately abandoned as unsuccessful.

In the texts that we have been examining, Leibniz has been pretty careful in formulating his thesis in terms of *substances*: in the strictest sense, *substances* don't have genuine causal interactions with one another. But once it has been articulated in the mid-1680s, Leibniz extends the thesis more generally to *bodies*, which, of course, are understood as aggregates of substances. There is a sense in which the extension of the thesis is unnecessary: if substances don't interact, then neither should aggregates of substances.[48] But in texts

No. int. between bodies.

[47] The last appearance I know of the argument from the CIC conception of substance to the non-communication thesis is in the passage from the *Dynamica* quoted in the previous note. Interestingly enough, though, the Predicate-in-Notion principle appears in what seems to be a rather late piece as an argument against action at a distance! See Leibniz (1903), 11f. On the more general demise of the characterization of substance in terms of the CIC see Rutherford (1995), 150ff.

[48] Miller (1988) argues that Leibniz does allow for genuine interaction at the level of bodies, though he works on the assumption that Leibniz adopts something like the monads even in the 1680s. Miller is answered effectively in Brown (1992). Brown argues: "Speaking in metaphysical rigor, then, what we perceive as interaction is only the confused representation of an underlying harmony of spontaneous, substantial activity" (p. 68).

that seem to start in the late 1680s, Leibniz introduces some rather different considerations for thinking that there are no genuine causal interactions specifically among bodies, considerations that arise from the notion of elasticity.[49]

The notion of elasticity was quite fundamental in Leibniz's thought about the physical world from the earliest physics of the *HPN* in 1671.[50] Various considerations in his mature writings led Leibniz to the view that all bodies, however small, *must* be elastic.[51] And so, for example, if there were any bodies that weren't elastic, then in collision, they would change their speed instantaneously, violating the principle of continuity, the principle that there are no leaps in nature. And because of that, Leibniz held that there can be no atoms in nature, nothing perfectly solid and hard, since elasticity entails the existence of smaller parts that can move with respect to one another.[52] But then in the late 1680s, Leibniz appeals to the notion of elasticity as part of his extension of the non-communication thesis to bodies.

The thesis is announced, among other places, in the "Specimen inventorum" of 1689(?). Leibniz begins with a statement of the non-communication

---

[49] There is an earlier text from 1677/8 that has suggestions of the later view; see A6.4.1965. That text, part of a slightly longer text on the conservation of conatus, argues that the communication of conatus in collision is impossible. It ends as follows: "Therefore, this transference is not real. However, we can admit hypothetically that everything happens in this way [i.e. through the transference of conatus?], and thus other things following with the help of the force of elasticity, a rebound arises." However, suggestive as this may be, it isn't evident that this is the thesis that he will later adopt. We cannot be entirely sure that there are no texts before the late 1680s that advance the thesis of the non-communication of bodies. The problem is that while the papers from the earlier 1680s that the Akademie editors have identified as "philosophical" have been published in A6.4, those that are identified as scientific and technical have not, and await the publication of series 8 of the edition. Among those manuscripts are many that deal with impact and elasticity. Unless one is willing to wade through the technical manuscripts (which I am not in the context of this book), one cannot be entirely sure that there isn't something earlier in the 1680s that bears on this question. Indeed, I am certain that when those papers are made available, we shall be able to trace the history of the thesis of the non-communication of bodies in the way in which the publication of A6.3 and A6.4 have allowed us to trace the history of other of Leibniz's ideas.

[50] See, e.g., *HPN* § 22: "omnia corpora sensibilia ob aetheris circulationem per *hypothesin nostram* sunt Elastica..." (A6.2.229). See also Leibniz to Mariotte, July 1673: "ce grand principe du Ressort, qui est la cause veritable de tous les phenomenes du choc de corps" (A2.1².370). There is no hint of the non-communication thesis in these early texts.

[51] In Leibniz's sense, a body is elastic if it is deformable. In the modern sense, a collision is said to be elastic if kinetic energy is preserved. Characteristically, it is perfectly hard bodies, i.e., bodies incapable of being deformed, that enter into perfectly elastic collisions.

[52] On the importance of elasticity for Leibniz's thought about the physical world, see Breger (1984) and Garber (1995), 321–5.

thesis for substances: "From the notion of individual substance it also follows in metaphysical rigor that all the operations of substances, both actions and passions, are spontaneous, and that with the exception of the dependence of creatures on God, no real influx of them on one another is intelligible. . . ." After a long discussion of the non-communication of substances, Leibniz continues:

These things are true to the extent that in physics too, on careful investigation of the matter, it is evident that no impetus is transferred from one body to another, but each body moves by an innate force, which is determined only on the occasion of, i.e., with respect to another. For it has already been acknowledged by eminent men that the cause of the impulse one body gets from another is the body's elasticity itself, by means of which it recoils from the other.[53]

This thesis is repeated in a number of other texts from the period, most often without argument.[54]

However, in his main work on dynamics in the period, the unfinished and unpublished *Dynamica* (1690), he offers the following argument in the context of his general account of impact:

Proposition 6: Bodies don't act immediately on one another through their motion, nor are they immediately moved except through their own elasticity [elastra].

Since all bodies are pliant (by the preceding proposition) and it is easier to deform [*flectere*] a firm body to some extent than it is to give impetus to it or take impetus away from it (by prop. 30 of the chapter on cause and effect), a body is thus deformed to some extent before any determinate degree of speed or impetus can be accepted from another [body] or received by its action. And since the same reason always remains, and given that once the deformation has happened a new deformation is easier than pushing it . . . we can always assume a smaller deformation, until the force for pushing is completely consumed. Therefore a body is not impelled unless it is deformed by another. Moreover, it is not impelled except through its own elasticity for restoring itself, which immediately begins to act towards separating the bodies from one another.[55] ——→ *But here interaction is the cause of the deformation*

---

[53] A6.4.1620 (RA 311). Philip Beeley pointed out to me that among the "eminent men" is probably John Wallis. Evidently, it was a theme in Wallis's *Mechanica, sive de motu tractatus geometricus* (London, 1670–1). However, again, there seems to be no hint of the "non-communication" thesis there.

[54] See, e.g., 'Primae veritates' (1689), A6.4.1647 (AG 33); 'Motum non esse absolutum quiddam' (1688/9), A6.4.1638.

[55] GM VI 492.

Leibniz clearly takes this to establish the non-communication of bodies. In a later passage in the *Dynamica* he rehearses the CIC argument for the non-communication of substances:

each and every singular substance is so constituted that it envelops the entire universe in its complete notion, and in a certain sense it can be said to do everything through itself and as it were spontaneously.[56]

Immediately following on this passage Leibniz makes reference to the proposition just quoted ("Adde prop. 6") before moving on ("But this is not the place for these matters.")[57]

This must be the argument that Leibniz has in mind in the "Specimen inventorum" and other texts that date from the same period. But even so, the argument is a bit puzzling. Why does Leibniz think that it is easier to deform a body than to set it in motion? In the demonstration, he refers to another proposition, proposition 30 from the chapter on cause and effect. That proposition reads: "The force of gravity and elasticity is dead force, that is, it is to the power of speed as the finite is to the infinite."[58] Leibniz distinguishes living force (*vis viva*), the force associated with bodies that are actually in motion, from dead force, which is the force associated with acceleration, such as the force of gravity and the force that a bow exerts while it is restoring itself. His claim is that dead force is to living force as the finite is to the infinite. Alternatively, it is often said to be an infinitesimal magnitude with respect to living force.[59] But how is this proposition relevant here, and how does it justify the claim that, on impact, one body causes another to be deformed rather than to move? Furthermore, one might also object that even if the impacting body doesn't actually cause the other to move, it may be the genuine cause of its deformation.

This thesis also comes up later in the "Specimen dynamicum" of 1695. There he suggests a somewhat different argument:

Something else wonderfully follows from what I have said, that every passion of a body is of its own accord, that is, arises from an internal force, even if it is on the occasion of something external. I understand here the body's own passion, the passion that arises from collision, that is, the passion that remains the same, whichever

---

[56] GM VI 507.
[57] There is another reference to prop. 6, in the demonstration of the proposition following. It isn't clear how that reference relates to this issue, though.
[58] GM VI 452.   [59] On the relation between living and dead force, see Garber (2008).

hypothesis we finally adopt, that is, to whatever things we ascribe absolute rest or motion in the end. For, since the impact is the same, wherever the true motion in the end belongs, it follows that the effect of the impact is equally distributed between the two, and thus that in impact, both bodies are equally acted upon, and equally act, and that half the effect arises from the action of the one, and half from the action of the other. And since half the effect or half of the passion is in one, and half in the other, it is also sufficient for us to derive the passion in the one from its own action, and we do not need any influx of the one into the other, even if the action of the one provides the occasion for the other to produce a change in itself.[60]

Here the argument seems to be grounded in the claim that there is a frame in which we can regard both bodies as acting equally, and, as a consequence, "we do not need any influx of the one into the other." A kind of Occam's razor argument gets Leibniz the conclusion.

These arguments are quite different from the arguments that we saw earlier for the non-communication of substances. Nor is it clear how they are supposed to be related to one another. The passage cited above from the *Dynamica* suggests that there *is* a relation, though what it is remains unsaid there. When the thesis of the non-communication of bodies comes up in the 'Primae veritates' paper, it is presented as an "illustration" of the more general (and more basic?) thesis of the non-communication of substances:

Strictly speaking, one can say that no created substance exerts a metaphysical action or influx on any other thing. For, not to mention the fact that one cannot explain how something can pass from one thing into the substance of another, we have already shown that from the notion of each and every thing follows all of its future states. What we call causes are only concurrent requisites, in metaphysical rigor. This is also illustrated by our experience of nature. For bodies really rebound from others through the force of their own elasticity, and not through the force of other things, even if another body is required in order for the elasticity (which arises from something intrinsic to the body itself) to be able to act.[61]

In another essay, probably from the same year, Leibniz suggests that the physical theorem "confirms" the metaphysical thesis:

Furthermore, there isn't any influx of a substance into another, in metaphysical rigor (except for in the dependence of creatures [on God], which is a continuous

---

[60] G VI 251 (AG 134–5). This passage appears in part II, a section of the essay that was prepared for publication, but, for reasons that remain obscure, never published.

[61] A6.4.1647 (AG 33).

production), nor is any impetus really transferred from one body to another, but as the phenomena also confirm, every body recedes from another by virtue of its own elastic force. This happens through the motion of its own internal parts.[62]

But in the "Specimen inventorum," the relation seems closer. Immediately after discussing the non-communication of substances, he writes:

These things are true to the extent that in physics too, on careful investigation of the matter, it is evident that no impetus is transferred from one body to another...[63] ⟶ (e) in a certain frame

It is quite possible that Leibniz himself didn't have a definite view on how the two theses related to one another.

One question remains, though, with respect to the non-communication thesis. It is obvious how the non-communication thesis might work with respect to incorporeal substances, such as the mind-like monads of Leibniz's later philosophy. But Leibniz's world in this period is much more complex than that. If I am right, the basic entities are corporeal substances, souls linked with bodies that, in turn, are composed of smaller corporeal substances, and so on to infinity. How can we imagine that the non-communication thesis works for these corporeal substances as well? Well, however it might work, it is clear that Leibniz did think that the non-communication of substances thesis holds for corporeal substances as well as for incorporeal substances. This is strongly suggested by the connection that he repeatedly draws between the non-communication of substance thesis and the thesis of the non-communication of bodies. But it is clearly implied in a text from 1689 or so that we have already seen earlier in this chapter:

The system of occasional causes should be admitted in part, and rejected in part. Each and every substance is the true and real cause of its immanent actions, and has a force of acting [*vis agendi*], and though it is granted that it is sustained by divine concourse, yet it cannot happen that it is only passive; *this is true both for corporeal and incorporeal substances*. But, on the other hand, each and every substance (except for God alone) is only the occasional cause of its transeunt actions on other substances. . . .[64]

---

[62] A6.4.1638. Thanks to Graeme Hunter for correcting a mistranslation in an earlier version.
[63] A6.4.1620 (RA 311).   [64] A6.4.1640–1 (RA 313), emphasis added.

But It's the body+soul that is subs., not the soul alone

In the first part of this passage, Leibniz is absolutely clear that he is speaking of substance quite generally, both incorporeal and corporeal; there is no reason to think that he means to introduce any restrictions in the second part of the passage.

But even if we grant that the non-communication thesis holds for corporeal substances as well, mysteries still remain. In particular, how can we understand how the soul of a corporeal substance can determine the behavior of its own body, if the soul is a substance, the body an aggregate of substances, and there can be no communication? The only place I know of where Leibniz addresses this question is in a passage from a letter he wrote to Burcher de Volder on 9/20 January 1700.[65] He writes:

When I say that the soul or entelechy can do [*posse*] nothing in the body, then I understand by 'body' not the corporeal substance of which it is the entelechy, which is one substance, but the aggregate of the other corporeal substances constituting our organs. For one substance cannot influence another [*influere in*] let alone an aggregate of others. Therefore, I intend this: Whatever happens in a mass [*massa*] or in an aggregate of substances in accord with the laws of mechanics, is expressed in the soul or entelechy . . . through its own characteristic laws. But the force of change in any substance is from itself or its entelechy, and this is true to such an extent that whatever is going to happen in an aggregate even can be inferred [*colligi*] from those things that are now in the aggregate. However, since there are so many separate [*privatae*] entelechies in the mass [*massa*] of our body, it obviously follows that not everything that happens in our body is to be derived from the entelechy, even if it agrees [*conspiret*] with it.[66] Without doubt entelechy or force, or activity differs from resistance or passivity. You could take the former for form and the latter for primary matter; however they do not differ in such a way that they should be considered as two distinct substances, but as constituting one. And the force changing the primary matter is certainly not a force that belongs to it, but is the entelechy itself.[67]

This is a difficult and obscure passage. In it, Leibniz seems to suggest that one can regard the corporeal substance in two ways. In one way, it

[65] The date may seem a bit awkward, since, as I shall later argue, he had by that time already adopted a thoroughly monadological point of view, and replaced corporeal substances as the basis of his metaphysics with non-extended and mind-like monads. But, as we shall later discuss in some detail in Ch. 8, he hadn't clued de Volder into that fact yet, and so was writing to him firmly in the context of the earlier view. Furthermore, as I shall also argue, even in the later period there is no reason to think that he had given up on the view of the physical world in terms of corporeal substances.

[66] Sentence is missing in G.

[67] G II 205–6. I would like to thank Paul Lodge for calling this passage to my attention. The emendation of Gerhardt's text is due to him. I have introduced some changes into his draft translation.

is a composite of two elements: a single soul or entelechy that bears a special relation with an aggregate of corporeal substances that constitute its body. Understood in this way, everything that happens in the body can be explained mechanically, and is "expressed" in the soul or entelechy, which is in harmony with the body. Also, understood in this way, the soul and the body are not causally connected in the true full-blooded sense: "For one substance cannot influence another let alone an aggregate of others...." But there is another way to look at the corporeal substance, not as a composite of two elements, but as a single unity. Understood in this way, "the force of change in any substance [including, presumably, any *corporeal* substance] is from itself or its entelechy...." But even understood in this way, as a single substance, not everything that happens in the corporeal substance is to be derived from its entelechy. The entelechies in the corporeal substances that make up the organic body of a given corporeal substance have their own contributions to make to the state and behavior of the whole: "However, since there are so many separate entelechies in the mass of our body, it obviously follows that not everything that happens in our body is to be derived from the entelechy...."

Thus Leibniz. But even so, I still find myself somewhat puzzled. Leibniz gives us two ways of looking at a corporeal substance, as a union of a soul, itself a substance with a collection of other substances with which it cannot communicate, strictly speaking, or as a single coherent whole, form and primary matter that constitute a single genuinely unsplittable whole. But nowhere in this rich and complex passage does he tell de Volder (or us) how these two perspectives are to be reconciled with one another.

Understanding Cause and Effect[68]

According to the non-communication thesis, substances don't really interact with one another, in all metaphysical rigor. However, in some key texts

[68] This section benefited considerably from the discussion of earlier and much cruder versions of this material at the Seminar for Early Modern Philosophy at Yale in December 2006, at the Montreal Interuniversity Workshop in the History of Philosophy in February 2007, at the Università di Lecce in March 2007, and at the Early Modern Study Group at Harvard in May 2007. I would like to give special thanks to the audiences there, including especially Larry Jorgensen, Michael Della Rocca, Justin Smith, François Duchesneau, and Don Rutherford. While none of them may be satisfied with how the account turned out in the end, it is immeasurably improved because of their discussion.

from the mid-1680s, Leibniz articulates an extended sense in which we can say that what happens in one substance can be understood as the cause of what happens in another, what Robert Sleigh has called a "quasi-cause," something generally taken to be a causal relation when we are doing physics, but which falls short of a full, metaphysical cause whereby the cause actually brings about the effect.[69] The doctrine is nicely summarized in § 15 of the 'Discours de métaphysique':

> The Action of One Finite Substance on Another Consists Only in the Increase of Degree of its Expression Together with the Diminution of the Expression of the Other, Insofar as God Requires Them to Accommodate Themselves to One Another.[70]

From this and similar passages it would seem as if causal relations in the world of finite substances are for Leibniz simply a matter of the distinctness or confusion of the expression of the substances in question, where this is understood mentalistically in terms of some quality of the internal states of representation in souls or soul-like entities. It is tempting to read this account of cause and effect, activity and passivity,[71] as entailing a view in accordance with which the only substances are immaterial and incorporeal substances, rather like the monads of Leibniz's later years. Indeed, this view might cause one to doubt that Leibniz took corporeal substances seriously, and that the real ground of his metaphysics in these years is soul-like entities, unextended perceivers. But I think this would be to misread Leibniz's intentions. Read in the context of Leibniz's larger view here, a somewhat different and rather more complex picture emerges. But what exactly does Leibniz mean here? And where does it come from?

Leibniz begins the exposition of his idea in § 15 by remarking that he will give only an abbreviated account of his view: "But, without entering into a long discussion. . . ." This suggests that there is more to be said than what follows. And indeed there is. In an earlier version of the section, he goes on at much greater length. That is a good place to begin looking into Leibniz's account of activity and passivity.

This text, found at the end of § 14 of an earlier draft of the 'Discours,' gives a much more leisurely account of the matter than Leibniz gives in § 15.

---

[69] See Sleigh (1990), ch. 7 §§ 3–4 passim.   [70] A6.4.1552–3 (AG 48).

[71] In the passages we are considering, Leibniz talks indifferently about cause and effect, and that which acts as opposed to that which is acted upon (i.e., is passive). Consequently, I won't distinguish between the problem of causality and the problem of activity and passivity.

In order to make discussion easier, I shall divide the text into a number of parts, and label each individually. I shall first set out the bulk of the passage in detail, and then discuss the individual parts of the argument. (Later we shall add the concluding paragraph.) First the text:

[A] It is certain, above all, that when we desire some phenomenon, and that phenomenon happens at a given moment, and that happens ordinarily, we say that we have acted and that we are its cause, as when I will that which one calls moving my hand. Also, when it appears to me that at my will, something happens to what I call another substance, and that this happens by that means (as I judge by frequent experiences), even though the other substance didn't will it, I judge that this substance is acted on [patit], as I admit of myself, when this happens to me following the will of another substance. Also, when we have willed something which happens, and when something else follows which we didn't will, we don't fail to say that we did it, as long as we understood that that followed from it.

[B] There are also some phenomena relating to extension which we attribute to ourselves more particularly and whose foundation in reality is called our body. And since everything significant that happens to it [i.e., the body], that is, all of the notable changes which appear to us there make themselves strongly sensed, at least ordinarily, we attribute to ourselves all of the passions of this body, and this with very good reason, since even if we are not aware of them [i.e., the passions], we don't fail to perceive the consequences, as when we are transported from one place to another while asleep. We also attribute to ourselves the actions of this body, as when we run, strike, fall, and when our body, continuing the motion already started, produces some effect. But I don't at all attribute to myself what happens to other bodies, since I notice that there can happen great changes which aren't at all sensible by me, unless my body finds itself exposed to them in a certain way that I find appropriate for them. Thus one sees that although all bodies in the universe appear to us in a certain way, and sympathize with ours, we don't at all attribute to ourselves what happens to them. Since when my body is pushed, I say that someone has pushed my own, but when someone pushes another, I don't say that I have been pushed, even though I perceive it and this gives rise to a certain passion in me, since I measure the place where I am by that of my body. And this language is quite reasonable, since it is appropriate for expressing oneself clearly in ordinary practice.

[C] One can say briefly that with respect to the mind, our volitions and our judgments are actions, but that our perceptions or sensations are passions, and with respect to the body, we say that the change which happens is an action when it is the consequence of a preceding change, but otherwise it is a passion.[72]

In general, the structure here is pretty clear. In [A] Leibniz is talking about voluntary motion and situations in which we are acted upon; in [B] Leibniz discusses when our body can be said to be the cause of an event, and when it can be said to be an effect; and in [C], Leibniz summarizes the two cases. But let us look more carefully at what Leibniz is saying here.

Let us begin with passage [A]. In this passage, Leibniz deals with the sense in which we can be taken to be the cause of voluntary motions. The example Leibniz gives of an action is my moving my hand: when I have a volition, and the motion of my hand follows in a regular way, it "happens ordinarily" that the one follows the other; that constitutes an action. Here it is the volition, and its regular connection with a motion of my arm, that makes it an action. We seem to be dealing with a kind of regularity account: when we will to raise our arm, and that happens regularly, then we are said to be the cause.[73] If when I voluntarily raise my arm, and, say, knock over a glass and spill the wine in it as an unintended consequence of raising my arm, Leibniz would say that I acted and the glass was acted upon, insofar as I understand that knocking over the glass was a consequence of raising my arm. Leibniz doesn't seem to want to say that the volition is a true metaphysical cause of the raising of the hand in the body; presumably, that would violate the non-communication thesis with respect to the relation between the soul, considered as a non-extended substance, and the collection of corporeal substances that make up the organic body. Leibniz doesn't talk about passions in [A], the ways in which the soul is acted on by other substances, but passions come up in the summary text [C]: "with respect to the mind, our volitions and our judgments are actions, but . . . our perceptions or sensations are passions. . . ." That is, when the mind is acted on, this passion, a being acted on, constitutes a perception or sensation in the mind. Again, one supposes here that direct, metaphysical causality is not at issue. Rather, there is a regular relation between the body being acted upon, and its mind registering an appropriate perception or sensation. There is a bit of a difficulty here, which we discussed earlier

---

[72] A6.4.1551−2.
[73] Note that, in this passage, Leibniz isn't careful to distinguish between a desire and a volition.

in this chapter: even though the soul and the body can be construed as different substances, together they constitute a single corporeal substance. How can Leibniz apply the non-communication thesis *within* the confines of a single substance, the human being? But here, in this text, Leibniz treats the corporeal substance as the union of a soul (itself a substance) with a body, presumably an aggregate of smaller corporeal substances; he holds that the fact that the volition in the mind is regularly attended with the motion in the body is what makes the volition a physical or quasi-cause of the motion. It is clear here that while we are dealing with our souls and their volitions, the souls are definitely connected with bodies: only an embodied soul can succeed in raising an arm. We are dealing with ourselves considered as corporeal substances, minds connected with bodies.

In text [B], Leibniz turns to the sense in which we can attribute actions and passions to our bodies. Here Leibniz wants to distinguish between the cases in which we can say that our bodies act, our bodies are acted upon, and our bodies are just neutral observers, as it were, to the action of other bodies on one another. It is interesting to note here that Leibniz limits his attention to us and our bodies: he is dealing not with bodies in general, but only with our (ensouled) human bodies. It is important here that we are dealing with bodies connected with souls: as such, they constitute substances, and it is the activity and passivity of substances that interests Leibniz in these sections of the 'Discours.' In [B], Leibniz first deals with the passions that pertain to the human body. The claim is that when we feel the sensation of another body acting on us, then we attribute a passion to our body. But we must be careful here. Consider a pin prick in my finger. When my finger is pricked by a pin, I feel a sensation of pain. What Leibniz is saying here is that the passion in my soul (the pain) is an indication that there is a passion that should be attributed to the body (the separation of the flesh in my finger as the pin penetrates it). The passion at issue in [B] pertains to the body itself, not to the soul, but it is because we *have* a sensation that we *know* that the passion pertains to the body: the sensation in the soul is the criterion by which we judge that the body has been acted upon. This, in a way, is a kind of internal criterion of what it means to be acted on. Leibniz is *not* characterizing a passion of the body in terms of another body that acts upon it from the outside: the sign of a passion of the body is a sensation in the soul that is appropriately related to that body. After discussing passions of the (ensouled) body, Leibniz then turns to the actions of bodies. He says that when we "run, strike, fall" and the like, we attribute an *action* to our body. That is, our body is the cause of some effect in other bodies. The inclusion of running here among the circumstances that count as actions suggests the kind of voluntary motions that Leibniz had in mind in [A]. The other instances he gives in [B], striking and falling, suggest something a bit different, that when we collide with other bodies, or bring about changes in other bodies by falling, we (i.e. our bodies) are the cause of the changes in other bodies. But even so, it isn't evident just what the criteria are by which we determine when a body is acting, and when it is acted upon. Indeed, Leibniz characterizes the activities of bodies in terms of that which "produces some effect [*fait quelque effect*]." This seems particularly unhelpful.

One can see in these passages reflections of a certain strand of Leibniz's thought on causality that starts quite early in his career, and continues long after the period of the 'Discours.' There are many discussions of cause and effect where Leibniz is quite concerned to sort out the way in which a cause might be necessary and/or sufficient for the existence of an effect, and the way in which the existence of a cause might be part of a complex of factors that goes into producing an effect in a particular situation.[74]

But then Leibniz introduces something that seems to be rather different, rather more metaphysical, if you will. The crossed-out text ends with the following passage, which follows immediately upon the conclusion of [C]:

[D] In general, to give our terms a sense which reconciles metaphysics with practice, when several substances are affected by a single change (since, in fact, every change touches them all) one can say that that which through this passes immediately to a greater degree of perfection or continues in the same degree of perfection acts, but that which becomes by that immediately more limited, so that its expressions become more confused, is acted upon [*patit*].[75]

Then this entire passage, [A]–[D], is crossed out, and replaced by what is § 15 in the definitive draft of the 'Discours,' a passage that seems to extend what Leibniz proposed as an account of cause and effect in passage [D]:

15. *The Action of One Finite Substance on Another Consists Only in the Increase of Degree of its Expression Together with the Diminution of the Expression of the Other, Insofar as God Requires Them to Accommodate Themselves to One Another.*

[74] For a very thorough and lucid account of this strand of Leibniz's thought, see Futch (2005).
[75] A6.4.1552.

But, without entering into a long discussion, in order to reconcile the language of metaphysics with practice, it is sufficient for now to remark that we ascribe to ourselves—and with reason—the phenomena that we express most perfectly and that we attribute to other substances the phenomena that each expresses best. Thus a substance, which is of infinite extension insofar as it expresses everything, becomes limited in proportion to its more or less perfect manner of expression. This, then, is how one can conceive that substances impede or limit each other, and consequently one can say that, in this sense, they act upon one another and are required, so to speak, to accommodate themselves to one another. For it can happen that a change that increases the expression of one diminishes that of another. Now, the efficacy [vertu] a particular substance has is to express well the glory of God, and it is by doing this that it is less limited. And whenever something exercises its efficacy or power, that is, when it acts, it improves and extends itself insofar as it acts. Therefore, when a change takes place by which several substances are affected (in fact every change affects all of them), I believe one may say that the substance which immediately passes to a greater degree of perfection or to a more perfect expression exercises its power and acts, and the substance which passes to a lesser degree shows its weakness and is acted upon [patit].[76]

This seems to be a new way of looking at causal relations between substances. Indeed, the context of this passage, the way in which it replaces a discussion of causality that seems altogether different, suggests to me that this may well be the very moment when Leibniz abandons his earlier ways of trying to characterize causal relations and replaces them with the formula that he will use from then on, where cause and effect are understood in terms of relations of expression.[77] But what does this formula mean?

Let me begin the discussion by setting out a few other passages from the period in which Leibniz attempts to elaborate what appears to be much the same idea. First there is a nice summary of the view in a passage that appears, curiously enough, both in a letter to Simon Foucher in 1686 and in Leibniz's letter to Arnauld, 4/14 July 1686:

One [substance] acts on another, since one expresses more distinctly than the other the cause or reason of the changes, a bit like we attribute motion to a boat rather than to the entire sea, and correctly so.[78]

---

[76] A6.4.1552–3 (AG 48).

[77] The passage from the essay "De modo distinguendi phaenomena realia ab apparentiis" (1683/6), discussed above in Ch. 4 in connection with the notion of primary matter, may be earlier, though, as I noted there, it is not easy to date. We shall return to that passage at the end of this chapter.

[78] G I 383 and G II 57.

This is what Leibniz says in a letter to Arnauld in November/December 1686:

However, there is good reason to say that my volition is the cause of the motion of my arm, and that a dissolution of the continuity of the matter in my body is the cause of my pain, since the one expresses distinctly what the other expresses more confusedly, and one should attribute action to the substance whose expression is the more distinct.[79]

The doctrine is also nicely summarized in the "Specimen inventorum" of 1689(?):

From the notion of individual substance it also follows in metaphysical rigor that all the operations of substances, both actions and passions, are spontaneous, and that....no real influx of them on one another is intelligible....However, that whose expression is more distinct is deemed to act, and that whose expression is more confused to be acted upon, since to act is a perfection, and to be acted upon is an imperfection. And that thing from whose state a reason for the changes is most readily provided is adjudged to be the cause.[80]

With these we can begin to look into what exactly Leibniz has in mind in his account of cause and effect.

It should be noted, first of all, that there are some real differences among these different articulations of what is apparently the same basic doctrine. The passages are consistent in characterizing the relation between cause and effect, that which acts and that which is acted upon in terms of the notion of *expression*. But Leibniz sometimes talks about increase and decrease in the perfection of expression, sometimes about "degree" of expression, and sometimes in terms of the distinctness and confusion of the expression. Also, for the most part, the passages leave vague just what the object of the expressions in question is, though in one of the passages, Leibniz specifies that we are dealing with the expression of "the cause or reason of the changes." Another theme is the cause or reason for the change, though that is treated differently in different passages. That suggests to me that, at this stage, Leibniz doesn't yet have a real grasp on what exactly he is doing here: he may have a vision of where he is going, but he doesn't really have a well-worked-out doctrine in mind, at least not yet. ——— Which he would have if he already had the M.

---

[79] G II 71.   [80] A6.4.1620 (RA 311).

Let me begin with the strand in these texts that deals with the question of the reason for change. This strand is at best only implicit in passages [A]–[C], particularly in the discussion of volition in [A]. But it is quite explicit in some of the other passages. In the Arnauld/Foucher passage, he talks about one substance expressing more distinctly than the other "the cause or reason of the changes, a bit like we attribute motion to a boat rather than to the entire sea, and correctly so." The passage from the "Specimen inventorum" also makes reference to the reason for change: "And that thing from whose state a reason for the changes is most readily provided is adjudged to be the cause." Its continuation involves essentially the same example Leibniz uses in the Arnauld/Foucher passage:

Thus if one person supposes that a solid moving in a fluid stirs up various waves, another can understand the same things to occur if, with the solid at rest in the middle of the fluid, one supposes certain equivalent motions of the fluid (in various waves); indeed, the same phenomena can be explained in infinitely many ways. And notwithstanding the fact that motion is really a relative thing, nonetheless, that hypothesis which attributes motion to the solid and from this deduces the waves in the liquid, is infinitely simpler than the others, and for this reason the solid is adjudged to be the cause of the motion. Causes are not derived from a real influence, but from the providing of a reason.[81]

Consider a ship in water ("a solid moving in a fluid") surrounded by waves. (It is interesting to note here that we are dealing with inanimate bodies, and not with corporeal substances; this doesn't seem to matter to Leibniz.) We can understand the motion of the ship as the reason for the waves, or we can consider the motion of the water (i.e., the motion of "entire sea," as in the Arnauld/Foucher letter) with respect to a stationary ship as the reason for the waves. In the former case, the ship is acting and the water is acted upon, while in the latter, the water is acting and the ship is acted upon. Leibniz claims that the hypothesis of the moving boat and the stationary water is "infinitely simpler" than the hypothesis of the stationary boat and the moving water, so in this case, we should attribute activity to the boat, and not to the water.

In this discussion, the question of what is in motion and what is at rest is really a matter of choice, and the rule to choose that hypothesis which is simpler is more a rule of thumb than it is a rule that tells us which is

[81] A6.4.1620 (RA 311).

really in motion, and which *really* at rest. Given Leibniz's worries about relativity and the reality of motion, as discussed above in Chapter 3, he must have found this way of distinguishing between cause and effect to be not altogether satisfactory. But there is another way of thinking about the cause as the reason for the effect in these texts. In both the summary and the body of 'Discours' § 15, Leibniz talks about God requiring substances "so to speak, to accommodate themselves to one another." This suggests that the state of one, the cause, is the reason for God to create the other, the effect, in the state that it is. This, of course, goes back to Leibniz's account of creation, in accordance with which God creates the best of all possible worlds. On that view, God creates a world of individual substances that harmonize with one another in appropriate ways. The view here seems to be the following. God may first decide to create a given substance A, say, with some particular properties at a given time. Then, having made that decision, he must figure out how to create other substances (B, C, D, etc.), or better, how to choose other possible individual substances to create from among the infinity of choices available in such a way that they harmonize appropriately with what he has already decided to create in A. In that case, A can be construed as the cause of the particular properties in B, C, D, etc., insofar as A is the reason why B, C, D, etc. have the properties that they do. (The relations of priority and posteriority are, presumably, something other than temporal priority and posteriority, though what exactly they are is a bit obscure.)

It unclear how these two ways of construing cause as reason are related, and which is more basic. But it does seem to me that Leibniz is struggling to articulate a rather powerful vision, which is clearly summarized at the end of the "Specimen inventorum" passage: "Causes are not derived from a real influence, but from the providing of a reason." But there is something else in these passages, of course: cause and effect, the active and the passive, are understood in terms of the notion of expression, and its perfection or its distinctness or confusion. What does Leibniz have in mind here? This is my conjecture and my strategy for explicating Leibniz's view: the account of cause and effect in terms of relations of expression can be understood as a restatement of the "reasons" view of cause and effect.[82] Let me try to make this plausible.

---

[82] Cf. Di Bella (2002), 423–5.

Leibniz discusses the notion of expression in an essay, "Quid sit idea?" that probably dates from 1677. He writes:

That is said to express a thing in which there are relations [*habitudines*] which correspond to the relations of the thing expressed. But there are various kinds of expression; for example, the model of a machine expresses the machine itself, the projective delineation on a plane expresses a solid, speech expresses thoughts and truths, characters express numbers, and an algebraic equation expresses a circle or some other figure. What is common to all these expressions is that we can pass from a consideration of the relations in the expression to a knowledge of the corresponding properties of the thing expressed. Hence it is clearly not necessary for that which expresses to be similar to the thing expressed, if only a certain analogy is maintained between the relations.[83] Structuralism?

The same basic idea is found in Leibniz's letter to Arnauld of 10 September 1687:

One thing *expresses* another (in my terminology) when there exists a constant and fixed relationship between what can be said of one and of the other. This is the way that a perspectival projection expresses its ground-plan. Expression is common to all forms, and it is a genus of which natural perception, animal sensation and intellectual knowledge are species.[84]

There may well not be a single explication that captures what Leibniz has in mind here. At the very least, expression is a relation between two things A and B by virtue of which there is a function that takes us from A to B.[85] But it is certainly more than just this. One commentator suggests that "one thing *expresses* a second just in case there is a structure-preserving mapping from either to the other."[86] This conception makes good sense of the geometrical examples Leibniz offers, as well as the way a model of a machine expresses a machine. But it is difficult to see how it can account for the way in which an equation expresses a curve or a word expresses an object. Another commentator suggests that when A expresses B, then we can derive features of B from A "by some sort of calculation based on a law."[87] However construed, it is clear that the expression relation is quite general, and can hold not only between a perceiver and the things that it perceives, but between

---

[83] A6.4.1370 (L 207).   [84] G II 112.
[85] In more elaborate form, this is the view advanced by Kulstad, first in Kulstad (1977) and then defended in Kulstad (2006).
[86] Swoyer (1995), 82.   [87] Mates (1986), 38.

any two objects. In particular, it is quite clear that the notion of expression is more general than the more obviously mentalistic notion of perception. The examples of expression that Leibniz gives in the passages cited suggest that it can be a relation between two bodies, between a perceiver (presumably a perceiver of any kind—human, animal, or below) and a body, or, to be sure, between two perceivers.[88] Given the way it is defined, the expression relation would seem to be symmetric: if A expresses B, then B expresses A.

Now, the relation between a cause and an effect would seem to be a case where "there exists a constant and fixed relationship between what can be said of one and of the other," to use the formula that Leibniz used in the letter to Arnauld. That is, the relation between cause and effect would seem to be an instance of the expression relation. This is exactly what Leibniz himself suggests in the 1686 letter to Foucher from which Arnauld/Foucher passage quoted above is taken:

Every individual substance expresses the universe in its way, a bit like the same city is expressed differently from different points of view. Every effect expresses its cause, as well as the cause of every substance, that is the resolution that God took to create it.[89]

But it also seems reasonable to suppose that the cause expresses its effect: if there is a "constant and fixed relation" between the effect and the cause,

---

[88] In one interesting passage that the Akademie editors date as being from 1686, Leibniz suggests, interestingly enough, that organic things can only be represented by other organic things:

The general and exact relation of all things among themselves proves that all parts of matter are full of organism. Since every part of matter must express the others, and among the others there are many organic things [beaucoup d'organiques], it is obvious that there must be something organic [il y ait de l'organique] in that which represents the organic.   (A6.4.1615)

It may seem as if this is saying that something alive can be expressed only by something else that is alive. But as noted in Ch. 2, something is organic in virtue of having an inner structure of organs. Note here that 'organisme' is in the singular, and not in the plural, something characteristic of Leibniz's usage. Justin Smith suggested to me that one might read "organisme" as parallel to "mechanism," as calling attention to the organization of matter. On the concept of organism in Leibniz, see Duchesneau (1998b), 334–44. When we take this into account, the text should properly be understood as saying that something with complex organization can only be expressed by something else that has complex organization. Duchesneau (1998b), 341 suggests that this passage is almost certainly later than the Akademie editors date it because of its use of the term 'organique.' He dates it to the first decade of the eighteenth century. Because of its use of the term 'expression' rather than 'perception' I would put it a bit earlier, perhaps in the mid- or late 1690s, though it would be earlier than any other occurrences of the term 'organisme' than in any other texts. (Thanks to Justin Smith and Christian Leduc for these observations.)

[89] G I 383. Cf. 'Discours' § 28. As I read this passage, each substance expresses both its finite cause and God, the cause of all creation. Cf. also Leibniz's observations about the relation between an effect and its cause in two texts from April 1676, A6.3.490–1 (SR 51) and A6.3.514–15 (SR 71).

then there should be a "constant and fixed relation" between the cause and the effect.

The cause/effect relation is a special case of the expression relation. But what especially characterizes it and differentiates it from the general case? Leibniz characterizes the difference in a number of different ways. In passage [D] from 'Discours' § 14 and in 'Discours' § 15 he talks about an "increase in the degree" of expression, or what is expressed "most perfectly" as opposed to a "diminution in the degree" of expression and a "less perfect manner of expression." But in what I take to be later versions of the same doctrine, in the Arnauld/Foucher passage, in the letter to Arnauld, and in the passage from the "Specimen inventorum," Leibniz talks about cause and effect, the active and the passive, in terms of distinctness and confusion. This makes more explicit a suggestion that can be found as early as passage [D], where Leibniz seems to identify the passage to a lesser state of perfection with confused expressions.

The *locus classicus* for the distinction between the distinct and the confused is an essay that Leibniz published in the *Acta eruditorum* in 1684, the "Meditationes de cognitione, veritate, et ideis." The main focus for the essay is not the notion of expression, but the very notion of a notion. In the essay, Leibniz begins with the distinction between clear and obscure notions:

A notion which is not sufficient for recognizing the thing represented is obscure, as, for example, if whenever I remember some flower or animal I once saw, I cannot do so sufficiently well for me to recognize that flower or animal when presented and to distinguish it from other nearby flowers or animals, or, for example, if I were to consider some term insufficiently explained in the schools, like Aristotle's entelechy, or his notion of a cause insofar as it is something common to material, formal, efficient and final causes. . . .[90]

A clear notion, on the other hand, is one that *is* sufficient for recognizing the thing represented: "Therefore, knowledge [*cognitio*] is clear when I have the means for recognizing the thing represented."[91] The distinction between distinct and confused notions is then introduced as follows:

---

[90]   A6.4.586 (AG 23–4).

[91]   A6.4.586 (AG 24). Note here that the word for knowledge, '*cognitio*,' doesn't mean knowledge in the propositional sense of knowing that p, but in the sense of being able to identify something that we are presented with. *Recognitional knowledge*

Clear knowledge, again, is either confused or distinct. It is confused when I cannot enumerate one by one marks [*nota*] sufficient for differentiating a thing from others, even though the thing does indeed have such marks and requisites into which its notion can be resolved. And so we recognize colors, smells, tastes, and other particular objects of the senses clearly enough, and we distinguish them from one another, but only through the simple testimony of the senses, not by way of explicit marks [*notis enuntiabilibus*]. . . . But a distinct notion is like the notion an assayer has of gold, that is, a notion connected with marks and tests sufficient to distinguish a thing from all other similar bodies.[92]

Distinct notions, then, involve "explicit marks" of the things of which they are notions, *notae enuntiabiles*, marks that can be explicitly articulated; confused notions do not.[93]

The distinction in the "Meditationes" is between distinct and confused *notions*, not *expression*, and it is not obvious how the distinction might be interpreted in terms of expression. But here is an idea of how to understand it. When Leibniz says that the cause expresses more distinctly than the effect, he usually omits saying just what exactly it is that the cause expresses, its object. I presume, first, that he is talking about the cause and effect expressing each other.[94] What differentiates the cause from the effect in this relation of mutual expression, then, is the fact that we can recognize the effect through the cause, but not vice versa. That is, one can infer the state of the effect from the state of the cause, but not vice versa. One

---

[92] A6.4.586–7 (AG 24).

[93] The distinction between the distinct and the confused is somewhat less clear than it may seem on the surface. What exactly is an "explicit mark" and how exactly is it different from a non-explicit mark? The case of the assayer's notion of gold seems clear enough: there are explicit tests that one can frame to tell whether or not something is gold: is it appropriately malleable? does it melt at the right temperature? is it soluble in aqua regia? This seems to be rather different from the case of recognizing the color 'red', where we aren't normally in a position to give explicit criteria. But there seem to be lots of intermediate cases. I can recognize my friend's face by his nose, his mouth, his eyes, etc. Do these count as explicit marks? I can recognize a street as being in Paris based on certain features of its architecture, some of which I can explicitly specify, and some of which I can't: the height of the buildings, the characteristic windows, etc. Because I have some training in music I can recognize the music excerpted from a Puccini opera by the shape of the melodic line, the characteristic orchestration, etc. Do these count as "explicit marks"? Here it isn't simply a question of whether there is a continuum of cases between distinct and confused notions, which, of course there are: the very notion of an "explicit mark" in terms of which confusion and distinctness are characterized doesn't itself seem to be very distinct. But for the moment, at least, I will set this worry aside and for the purposes of discussion, at least, proceed as if the notions at issue are clear enough.

[94] This does go against the specific language in the Arnauld/Foucher passage, where he talks about that which acts expressing "more distinctly than the other the cause or reason of the changes," but I would have to say that he was being a bit careless there.

Obscure notion: no recognition

clear notion: recognition ⟋ Confused: Unable to enumerate marks of difference
⟍ Distinct: Able to enumerate marks of difference

might say that in an extended sense of the term, the substance A in state S_A (the cause) expresses B in state S_B (the effect) distinctly insofar as grasping A allows us to grasp B. In that extended sense, one might hold that A contains "explicit marks," "*notae enuntiabiles*" of B, and we might say that A expresses B distinctly. But how is it that we can recognize the effect from the cause? In what way does the one have an "explicit mark" for recognizing the other? Perhaps it is this: because *the cause constitutes the reason for the effect*. In this way, the "explicit mark" of the effect in the cause is just the fact that the one provides the reason for the other. In this way the account of cause and effect in terms of distinct and confused expression reduces directly to the "reasons" account.[95]

While I hesitate to bring in texts from Leibniz's later monadological writings, there is one passage from the 'Monadologie' that strongly supports the reading that I am offering here. There he writes:

49. The creature is said to act externally insofar as it is perfect, and to be acted upon [*patir*] by another, insofar as it is imperfect. Thus we attribute action to a monad insofar as it has distinct perceptions, and passion, insofar as it has confused perceptions. . . .

50. And one creature is more perfect than another insofar as one finds in it that which provides an a priori reason for what happens in the other; and this is why we say that it acts on the other.

51. But in simple substances the influence of one monad over another can only be ideal, and can only produce its effect through God's intervention, when in the ideas of God a monad rightly demands that God take it into account in regulating the others from the beginning of things. For, since a created monad cannot have an internal physical influence upon another, this is the only way in which one can depend on another. . . .

52. It is in this way that actions and passions among creatures are mutual. For God, comparing two simple substances, finds in each reasons that require him to adjust the other to it; and consequently, what is active in some respects is passive from another point of view: active insofar as what is known distinctly in one serves

---

[95] It should be noted here that this does not undermine the symmetry of the expression relation. One can say that substance A in state S_A (the cause) expresses B in state S_B (the effect) if and only if B in state S_B expresses A in state S_A while at the same time saying that A's state constitutes the reason for B's state.

to explain what happens in another; and passive insofar as the reason for what happens in one is found in what is known distinctly in another. . . .[96]

While this text is much later than the ones that we have been examining, and involves monads or simple substances rather than substances taken more generally, it is obviously of a piece with the doctrine that he first seems to announce in the 'Discours.' What is most interesting to me in this context, though, is the last sentence of § 52: "what is active in some respects is passive from another point of view: active insofar as what is known distinctly in one serves to explain what happens in another; and passive insofar as the reason for what happens in one is found in what is known distinctly in another." Leibniz seems explicitly to explicate the distinctness of perception by way of the fact that what happens in the one serves as a reason for what happens in the other. But despite the close similarities between this text and the ones that we have been looking at from the second half of the 1680s, there is also a crucial difference. All of the texts in the 1680s characterize the active/passive or cause/effect relation in terms of relations of *expression*; the 'Monadologie' characterizes it in terms of relations of *perception*.[97] 'Perception' is a frankly mentalistic term that pertains exclusively to non-extended simple substances, to monads; 'expression' is a term that applies to any two things, including extended things. This subtle difference between the two texts marks an important change in Leibniz's thought as he moves from one metaphysical framework and into another. Or, at least, that is what I shall argue below in Chapters 8 and 9.

I have argued that the formula Leibniz adopts to distinguish cause and effect, that the cause is the more distinct expression and the effect the more confused, is a simple restatement of the view that when the changes in two substances are regularly correlated, then the cause is that which constitutes the reason for the effect. But this leaves us with a bit of a

---

[96] 'Monadologie' §§ 49–52 (AG 219).

[97] See 'Monadologie' § 49: "we attribute *action* to a monad insofar as it has distinct perceptions, and *passion*, insofar as it has confused perceptions." In remarking on this difference between early and late, I don't mean to deny that the notion of perception comes up in his earlier writings. Of course it does. For example, in 'Discours' § 14 Leibniz writes: "it is very true that the perceptions or expressions of all substances mutually correspond. . . ." But it is clear that in this passage he means to include both corporeal substances and their souls, the latter of which have perceptions properly speaking.

puzzle: why would Leibniz adopt the more complex formulation if the simpler one is all that he means? Here is one possible explanation. Basic to the philosophical view in the 'Discours' and in other texts of this period is Leibniz's thesis that everything mirrors everything else. The mirroring thesis is often advanced using the language of expression: "that each singular substance expresses the whole universe in its own way...."[98] Given that any two substances express one another, it would be quite reasonable for Leibniz to want to understand causal relations in terms of his notion of expression, and in terms of what is special about the expression relation as it applies to substances that are said to be in the relation of cause and effect with respect to one another. Or, to put it in another way, given that everything expresses everything else, Leibniz would want to know what exactly distinguishes those things that express one another and bear the special relation of cause and effect from those things that merely reflect one another, without being in any special causal relations, an issue that he raises explicitly in passage [B] above, as well as in the body of 'Discours' § 15 and in the 1686 letter to Foucher from which I have been quoting. Were it to succeed, his account of causality would allow him to do exactly that.[99]

Before ending this section, I would like to return to the passage from "De modo distinguendi phaenomena realia ab apparentiis" (1683/6) that we discussed above in Chapter 4 in connection with the notion of primary matter. It reads as follows:

Substances have metaphysical matter or passive power to the extent that [quatenus] they express something confusedly, and active power to the extent that they express something distinctly.[100]

In that context, I argued that its context and dating undermine the view that the passage supports a monadological reading of Leibniz's middle period, and suggested that, when properly interpreted, it supports that reading even less. Now, after having examined Leibniz's views on causality and activity, we may be in a better position to understand the significance

---

[98] 'Discours' § 9.
[99] I owe this suggestion to Larry Jorgensen. But cf., again, Di Bella (2002), 423–4, who makes a similar observation.
[100] A 6.4.1504 (L 365).

of this much-discussed passage, which has served as a major support of monadological readings of Leibniz's middle period.

The view presented obviously resonates with the passages on cause and effect that we have been examining. As in many of the texts that we have been discussing, activity and passivity are explicated in terms of distinct and confused expression. It is important to note that, as in those passages, it is *expression* that is at issue. As I have emphasized, insofar as the expression relation can hold between two extended bodies or corporeal substances, it is clear that there are no mentalistic implications in this claim. But what is different in this passage in relation to the others we have examined earlier in this chapter is the explicit connection with matter, and because of that, the implicit connection with the coordinate principle of form. Insofar as substances have distinct expressions and act, they are said to have active power (form); insofar as they have confused expressions and are acted on, they have passive power, that is, "metaphysical" (i.e. primary) matter. There is all the vagueness and imprecision that we have found in other such passages from the mid- and late 1680s; in particular, Leibniz doesn't say what exactly it is that is supposed to be expressed distinctly or confusedly. Why does he make the connection between his account of activity and passivity and the metaphysical notions of form and matter? We may never know for sure; this is the only passage I know written in the middle years (if it is written in the middle years) that links distinct and confused expression with form and matter, primitive active and passive force. But from the late 1670s on, Leibniz was definitely worried about understanding corporeal substance in terms of the Aristotelian notions of form and matter. And, if I am right, from 1686 or so, the period of the 'Discours,' he is interested in understanding cause and effect, activity and passivity, in terms of distinct and confused expression. The remark from 'De modo' can be read simply as an attempt to link the two perspectives and produce a unified metaphysical view. As such, it is a natural comment, likely a later reflection on what comes in the preceding paragraph of the text: "if anything is real, it is solely the force of acting and suffering, and hence that the substance of a body consists in this (as if in matter and form)."[101] In later years it may lead Leibniz to a monadological interpretation of form and matter in terms of distinct and confused *perception*. But at the moment when he penned

[101] Ibid.

the lines at the end of 'De modo,' it is simply an attempt to put together two strands of his metaphysical view. Insofar as neither pair of distinctions, form/matter or distinct/confused expression, itself commits Leibniz to a mentalistic or monadological view of the world, neither does the unified view that he is attempting to build from them. And we should remember that if it is indeed from the period, it is the unique passage in those years in which he identifies active power (form) with distinct expression and passive power (matter) with confused. This suggests that Leibniz was not altogether happy with the resulting view. So far as I can see, it will not appear again in the middle years.

I don't deny that the words Leibniz wrote in the 1680s can be taken out of their context and made consistent with what he wrote ten or fifteen or twenty years later in his more unabashedly monadological writings. But they can also be made consistent with his views in writings of the same period, and it seems much more sensible to do that than to try to argue that these few passages are, in some way, glimpses of a hidden doctrine or prefigurings of what he will later think.

6

Divine Wisdom and Final Causes

In the last few chapters we have emphasized the notion of substance and the role that the various conceptions have in shaping Leibniz's view of the world of bodies. But there is yet another element in the mix: theology. As I pointed out in Chapter 1, from his earliest years, Leibniz saw theology as central to his larger intellectual project. In that context, he saw the Aristotelian view of body as matter and form as central to any account of the Eucharist that would be acceptable to a wide variety of Christians. And so, in its first incarnation in the late 1660s, the "Demonstrationes catholicae" project was closely connected with the defense of substantial forms. Because of that, it is fair to say that the revival of substantial forms that started in the late 1670s was, strictly speaking, not so much the revival of the position as it was the extension of a metaphysical view that Leibniz was already committed to in theology into his natural philosophy. Writing to Duke Johann Friedrich in the fall of 1679, in a passage that we alluded to at the end of Chapter 1, Leibniz outlines the broad new philosophy he intends to compose while in the employ of the House of Hanover. In this context, he emphasizes the connection between the revival of substantial forms in physics and certain questions in theology:

There is one more thing that is quite important in my philosophy, which gives it a way of approaching the Jesuits and other theologians. It is that I reestablish the substantial forms, which the atomists and Cartesians claim to have eliminated. Now, it is known that without these forms, and without the difference there is between them and real accidents, it is impossible to maintain our mysteries: since if the nature of body consists in extension, as Descartes claims, it would be contradictory to maintain that a body exists in many places at the same time. But since that which has been said up until now about the essence of body has not been intelligible, one shouldn't be astonished if these substantial forms have passed for chimeras among the best minds. In place of this, that which I will say will be as intelligible as everything which the Cartesians have ever said about other things.[1]

In this way, theology joins the mix of arguments that could only have reinforced Leibniz's view that he was on the right path.

The letter to Johann Friedrich might lead one to think that the main theological pay-off for Leibniz's new conception of the physical world comes in the way in which it makes it possible to reconcile physics with an acceptable account of the Eucharist. But there is much more to it than that. Integral to Leibniz's new view of the physical world was the revival of final causes.

Final Causes and the Mechanical Philosophy

The final cause was, of course, a central notion in Aristotelian natural philosophy; indeed, for many, including perhaps Aristotle himself, it was the most important of the four causes. The final cause is the purpose for which something exists or is done, the end or goal that explains why it is the way it is.[2] But when the philosophy of the schools came under attack, one of the things that was attacked was the idea that there are final causes in nature.[3] Descartes, for example, argued in his *Principia philosophiae*:

When dealing with natural things we will, then, never derive any explanations from the purposes which God or nature may have had in view when creating

---

[1] A2.1².754; cf. A1.2.225–6. This letter is followed by another sketch of one (A2.1².760f), where Leibniz gives his intellectual autobiography, in the third person, as if he were talking about a friend. It ends with a curious passage in which he says that "his friend" is interested in physics and mathematics only for their theological implications:

I surprised him one day, reading books of [theological] controversies, and I showed my astonishment, since we all thought of him as a mathematician by profession, since he did hardly anything else in Paris. He told me that people were mistaken, that he had many other perspectives, and that his principal meditations were on theology, and that he had applied himself to mathematics as he did to things scholastic, that is, only for the perfection of his mind and to learn the art of discovery and demonstration. (A2.1².761)

[2] See, for example, Aristotle, *Physics* II.8; St Thomas Aquinas, *De principiis naturae* IV.25.

[3] Carraud (2002) gives a brilliant and sweeping account of the elimination of final causes in favor of efficient causes in some key thinkers of the sixteenth and seventeenth centuries, starting with the Jesuit scholastic Suarez and ending with the revival of final causes in Leibniz.

them [and we shall entirely banish from our philosophy the search for final causes]. For we should not be so arrogant as to suppose that we can share in God's plans.[4]

For Descartes, then, our ignorance of God's intentions prevents us from appealing to final causes in physics. Spinoza goes one better than Descartes, and denies that God has any intentions at all. He writes in his *Ethics*:

[There is] a widespread belief among men that all things in Nature are like themselves in acting with an end in view. Indeed, they hold it as certain that God himself directs everything to a fixed end; for they say that God has made everything for man's sake and has made man so that he should worship God. . . . There is no need to spend time in going on to show that Nature has no fixed goal and that all final causes are but figments of the human imagination. For I think that this is now quite evident [from discussions earlier in the *Ethics*] . . . that all things in Nature proceed from an eternal necessity and with supreme perfection.[5]

Not all mechanical philosophers followed Descartes and Spinoza in rejecting final causes, of course.[6] Robert Boyle, in particular, was quite insistent on the fact that final causes were an important part of the mechanist's world view.[7] But final causes were clearly under attack by at least some visible advocates of the new mechanical philosophy, and Leibniz saw his role as defending them.

In the earlier writings that we examined, Leibniz seems not to have been much interested in final causes and the divine wisdom on which they are grounded. As we saw above in Chapter 1, in the late 1660s, in essays such as the "Confessio naturae contra atheistas," written in connection with the "Demonstrationes catholicae" project, Leibniz was definitely interested

---

[4] *Principia philosophiae* I.28. The phrase in brackets was added to the French translation of 1647. See also Meditation IV, AT VII 55.

[5] Elapp, Spinoza (1925), vol. 2, 78–80. Translations of the *Ethics* are taken from E. M. Curley's translations in Spinoza (1985), vol. 1. Since Curley's edition is keyed to the pagination of Spinoza (1925), I shall not add special references to his translation.

[6] See, e.g., Gassendi's objection to Descartes, AT VII 308–9; and Boyle (1688), in Boyle (1999–2000), vol. 11.

[7] For a study that emphasizes those who wanted to keep final causes, see Osler (1996). For Leibniz's reading notes on Boyle in the Paris years, see A6.3.218ff. Leibniz had actually met Boyle during his visit to England in 1673. For Leibniz's relations with Boyle, intellectual and personal, see Loemker (1955). Boyle was clearly an influence on Leibniz's thought about the reconciliation of the mechanical philosophy with piety. However, Leibniz had already signed on to such a program in the late 1660s, before he became acquainted with the theological themes in Boyle's work, and, as Loemker points out, Leibniz's approach to the reconciliation of faith and natural philosophy is somewhat different.

in reconciling the atheistic tendencies of the mechanical philosophy with piety. His strategy then was to argue that when we examine the foundations of the mechanical philosophy, we shall see that we have to introduce God as an efficient cause of various features of the world that are otherwise unintelligible, features such as shape, motion, and *consistentia*. Leibniz wasn't entirely uninterested in final causes in physics at that moment; as I pointed out in Chapter 1, he does make appeal to divine wisdom in both the "Confessio naturae" and in the *HPN*. However, there final causes seem at best an afterthought, and are hardly central to his vision of how God enters into physics. Leibniz's basic strategy there is to appeal to God as the first cause to explain shape, motion, and *consistentia* by way of an infinite regress argument. Divine wisdom enters only in a subordinate way, in order to explain why we should think that the God who explains these features of the world is the God of the Christian tradition. The argument is not an inference to an intelligent designer: the specific details of *why* God creates what he does, the final causes that flow from divine wisdom, play no role in the argument. Divine wisdom is simply not a factor in explaining the specific details of the current state of the physical world.

Interestingly enough, final causes and divine wisdom are not much in evidence even in the "Confessio philosophi," an important work in philosophical theology that Leibniz composed in his early Paris years. The focus of the dialogue is the question of divine justice: if God is just, why are so many damned?[8] The basic answer that Leibniz offers is that sin is a part of the harmony of things, and that God loves harmony. So, when he creates a harmonious world, sin is necessarily a part of it.[9] But it is interesting how little a role divine wisdom plays in the "Confessio philosophi." Though the solution to the problem of divine justice does involve divine choice, in a broad sense, wisdom has a very subordinate role to play in his account. Leibniz's basic strategy is to argue that God is the *ground* (*ratio*) of sin, but that he is not the *author* of sin, and that he thus does not will sin. And in his account of God as the ground of the world, and thus of sin, choice and wisdom have no substantive role to play:

For let God be *A*, and let this series of things be *B*. Now if God is the sufficient ground of things, that is, the self-sufficient being [*ens a se*] and the first cause, it follows that, God having been posited, this series of things exists, otherwise,

---

[8] See A6.3.116–17 (CP 27–33).   [9] See, e.g., A6.3.130–1 (CP 63–5).

God is not the sufficient ground, but rather some other requisite, independent of God, must be added in order to bring it about that just *this* series of things exists.... Therefore, it must be held that God having been posited, this series of things follows, and, accordingly, this proposition is true: *if* A *exists, then* B *will also exist*. Moreover, it is well known from the logical rules of the hypothetical syllogism that conversion by contraposition holds, from which it can be inferred that *if* B *does not exist, then* A *will not exist*. Therefore, it follows that were this series of things, sins included, taken away or changed, God would be taken away or changed—which is what was to be demonstrated. Therefore, the sins included in this total series of things are due to the ideas themselves of things, i.e., to the existence of God.[10]

And thus Leibniz notes:

Sins occur to bring forth a universal harmony of things.... However, the universal harmony is a result not of the will of God but the intellect of God, or of the idea, that is, the nature of things. Therefore, sins are to be ascribed to the same thing; accordingly sins follow from the existence of God, not the will of God.[11]

In this way, Leibniz's central theodicean argument in the "Confessio philosophi" doesn't involve choice or divine wisdom at all. It is, I think, significant that the word 'wisdom' is altogether missing from the "Confessio philosophi"; it enters the text only with later remarks on Steno's marginal notes in the later 1670s.[12] In this respect, the view in the "Confessio philosophi" is quite strikingly different from later accounts, such as the account in the "De rerum originatione radicali" (1697),[13] where the domain of alternative possible worlds and God's choice among them is front and center.

I don't want to suggest that Leibniz doesn't have a conception of divine wisdom and final causes in these texts and in these years. They are certainly there. But they are in the background, and not very visible.

---

[10] A6.3.123–4 (CP 45–7).

[11] A6.3.122 (CP 45); cf. A6.3.133 (CP 69). It is interesting here that even Leibniz's account of will in the "Confessio philosophi" doesn't seem to involve wisdom or even what we would consider real choice: "*To will in favor* of something is to be delighted by its existence; *to will against* something is to be sad at its existence or to be delighted at its nonexistence.... *To be the author* is by one's will to be the ground of something else" [A6.3.127 (CP 55)].

[12] See A6.3.121 (CP 41n.) and A6.3.123 (CP 47n.). Leibniz seems to have shown a copy of the ms. of the "Confessio philosophi" to Nicholaus Steno in 1677 or 1678; Steno's marginal comments together with Leibniz's answers are preserved. On this see Sleigh's comments in his introduction to the text, CP xxi–xxii.

[13] G VII 302–8 (AG 149–55).

It may well have been his confrontation with the philosophy of Spinoza in late 1675 and 1676 that led Leibniz to see the importance of defending final causes in a more explicit way than he did in his earlier writings.[14] There is considerable evidence of Leibniz's struggles with Spinoza's thought in reading notes and letters, not to mention the actual visit Leibniz made to The Hague in November 1676, where he met Spinoza and discussed philosophy with him at some length.[15]

As numerous commentators have argued, much of Leibniz's thought about the issue of necessity and contingency can be traced back to this source.[16] Spinoza's necessitarianism made a great impression on the young Leibniz. For Spinoza, "in nature there is nothing contingent, but all things have been determined from the necessity of the divine nature to exist and produce an effect in a certain way."[17] As a consequence, "a thing is called contingent only because of a defect of our knowledge," from the fact that we don't *know* that it is necessary.[18] Spinoza takes it to follow from God's omnipotence that everything that is possible is actual. Spinoza writes:

Indeed—to speak openly—my opponents seem to deny God's omnipotence. For they are forced to confess that God understands infinitely many creatable things, which nevertheless he will never be able to create. For otherwise, if he created everything he understood he would (according to them) exhaust his omnipotence and render himself imperfect. Therefore to maintain that God is perfect, they are driven to maintain at the same time that he cannot bring about everything to which his power extends. I do not see what could be feigned which would be more absurd than this or more contrary to God's omnipotence.[19]

If everything that is possible is actual, then things could not be other than they are.

The young Leibniz found this idea extremely seductive. Leibniz later writes about his youthful views in an important essay that probably dates from a dozen years or so later in 1689:

---

[14] See Antognazza (2008), 167–9.

[15] On Leibniz's visit with Spinoza, see ibid., 177–8.

[16] For a detailed account of Leibniz's confrontation with the philosophy of Spinoza that is likely to be the standard account for some years to come, see Laerke (2008), as well as the extensive references cited there.

[17] E1p29.   [18] E1p33s1.   [19] E1p17s1 [Spinoza (1925), vol. 2, 62].

When I considered that nothing happens by chance or by accident (unless we are considering certain substances taken by themselves), that fortune distinguished from fate is an empty name, and that no thing exists unless its own particular conditions are present (conditions from whose joint presence it follows, in turn, that the thing exists), I was very close to the view of those who think that everything is absolutely necessary, who judge that it is enough for freedom that we be uncoerced, even though we might be subject to necessity, and close to the view of those who do not distinguish what is infallible or certainly known to be true, from that which is necessary.

But it ends happily. He continues:

But the consideration of possibles, which are not, were not, and will not be, brought me back from this precipice. For if there are certain possibles that never exist, then the things that exist, at any rate, are not always necessary, for otherwise it would be impossible for others to exist in their place, and thus, everything that never exists would be impossible.[20]

This story, which can be substantiated in its essentials in the papers that Leibniz left behind, is by now well known, and there is a considerable literature on the development of Leibniz's ideas about necessity and contingency.[21]

But there is a twist in the story that has not been so carefully explored. Closely connected with Spinoza's necessitarianism is his denial of final causes in nature. This is one of the central foci of the Appendix to part I of the *Ethics*, a long diatribe against what he considers the superstition that God acts for an end. He writes:

All the prejudices I here undertake to expose depend on this one: that men commonly suppose that all natural things act, as men do, on account of an end; indeed, they maintain as certain that God himself directs all things to some certain end, for they say that God has made all things for man, and man that he might worship God.[22]

Spinoza goes on to characterize the will of God as a "sanctuary of ignorance," and argues that "Nature has no end set before it, and . . . all final causes are nothing but human fictions."[23]

---

[20] A6.4.1653 (AG 94).

[21] This, for example, is central to the very careful account Noel Malcolm gives of Leibniz's encounter with Spinoza in 1676. See Malcolm (2003). For classic accounts of the development of Leibniz's views on necessity and contingency, see Sleigh (1990), ch. 4 and Adams (1994), ch. 1.

[22] E1app. [Spinoza (1925), vol. 2, 78].   [23] Ibid., 81, 80.

Leibniz took close notice of this doctrine of Spinoza's: it appears in a number of the summaries he gives of Spinoza's thought, and in the notes he kept on Spinoza's doctrines.[24] But though the issue of final causes is closely related to that of necessity and contingency, Leibniz seems to have distinguished the two; even though he found Spinoza's position on necessity tempting for a time, he never seems to have followed him to the denial of final causes. In his copy of the *Ethics*, which he seems to have read carefully in 1678, Leibniz had underlined the passage from the Appendix in which Spinoza asserts that "all final causes are nothing but human fictions," adding the comment "*male*," that is, "badly" or "wickedly."[25] Leibniz's position comes out in more detail in some comments written by him on a letter Spinoza wrote to Oldenburg, a text that Oldenburg himself shared with Leibniz as he passed through London on his way to The Hague in October 1676. Spinoza had written: "For I do not subject God to Fate in any way, but I conceive that everything follows from the nature of God with an inevitable necessity...." Leibniz then offers the following comment:

This should be explicated as follows. The world could not have been produced otherwise, since God couldn't have worked in a way that is not the most perfect. For since He is most wise, He chooses the best. It is hardly to be thought that everything follows from the nature of God without any intervention of will....[26]

In a comment on another passage from the same series of letters, Leibniz remarks: "it is certain that the existence of things is a consequence of the nature of God, which brings it about that only the most perfect things can be chosen."[27] In this way Leibniz seems to agree that everything is *necessary*, since God in his perfection could not have chosen otherwise. But, at the same time, he also holds that there are reasons for things, that God's choice is governed, indeed, determined by his wisdom. As a consequence, at least at that moment, *Leibniz wants to hold that even though everything is necessary, there are still final causes in the world.*[28]

---

[24] See, e.g., A6.3.364; A6.4.1710; A2.1².593; A1.2.318.   [25] A6.4.1710.

[26] A6.3.364. The passage of the letter to Oldenburg on which Leibniz is commenting can be found in Spinoza (1925), vol. 4, 311–12. For a discussion of the larger context of Leibniz's comments on these letters of Spinoza to Oldenburg, see Curley (1990).

[27] A6.3.370.

[28] Cf. Adams (1994), 20–1; Friedmann (1962), 117–21. In a monograph currently in progress, Michael Griffin argues a similar point, that Leibniz was a necessitarian in the 1670s, but that what was important to him was final causes.

My conjecture is that Leibniz's brush with Spinozism awoke him to the importance of final causes in the physical world.[29] As I have already noted a number of times, in the late 1660s Leibniz was eager to introduce God into the mechanical philosophy as the ground of such features as motion, shape, and *consistentia*. A decade later, in the late 1670s, Leibniz is still very much concerned to get God into the mechanical philosophy. But what is interesting is that a new perspective seems to have entered: Leibniz is now concerned to get divine wisdom and God's choice of the best into his account of the physical world. This comes out nicely in a passage from a theological dialogue entitled "Conversation du Marquis de Pianese . . ., et du Pere Emery Eremite . . .," which the Akademie editors date as being from between the second half of 1679 and the first half of 1681. He writes:

There are two extremes to avoid when we are dealing with the laws of the universe. Some believe that everything happens with a mechanistic necessity, as in a watch; others are persuaded that the sovereignty of God consists in a freedom without rule. The proper middle position is to consider God not only as the first principle, and not only as a free agent, but to recognize in addition that his freedom is determined by his wisdom. . . . When one has this idea of God, one can love him and honor him.[30]

The introduction of divine wisdom and final causes into the physical world is explicitly linked with Spinoza's philosophy in an essay that Leibniz drafted between 1678 and 1680. The subject of this essay is an examination of the "two sects of naturalists" then in fashion. The first sect, whom Leibniz characterizes as Epicureans, is led by Hobbes and his followers, who deny immaterial substance, argue that everything is material, and, Leibniz claims, go so far as to deny the existence of God.[31] But it is the second group,

[29] Douglas Jesseph pointed out to me that the anti-finalist position is also found in Hobbes: why didn't his earlier acquaintance with Hobbes raise the same reaction? Hard to say; perhaps the young Leibniz simply didn't notice the position there. In a paper in progress that he shared with me ("Leibniz's Optics and Contingency in Nature"), Jeffrey McDonough has argued that the change in Leibniz's position here is to be explained not through his acquaintance with Spinoza, but through his work in optics. Given the importance of optics to Leibniz in his discussion of final causes, as we shall see later in this chapter, this has a kind of plausibility. However, as of the time I am writing this note, Leibniz's optical papers from the 1670s are yet to be fully catalogued, dated, and transcribed. When we have studied them, McDonough may well turn out to have a good case. But even if the optical investigations are as important as McDonough thinks that they are, I strongly suspect that Leibniz's acquaintance with Spinoza at that moment will also turn out to be an important part of the story.
[30] A6.4.2269.   [31] A6.4.1384–5 (AG 281–2).

the new Stoics, led by Spinoza, that gets most of Leibniz's attention in the essay. And what disturbs him most about them is their denial of final causes:

> The sect of the new Stoics believes that there are incorporeal substances, that human souls are not bodies, and that God is the soul of the world, or, if you wish, the primary power of the world, that he is the cause of matter itself, if you wish, but that a blind necessity determines him to act; for this reason, he will be to the world what the spring or the weight is to a clock. They further believe that there is a mechanical necessity in all things, that things really act because of his power and not due to a rational choice of this divinity, since, properly speaking, God has neither understanding nor will, which are attributes of men. They believe that all possible things happen one after the other, following all the variations of which matter is capable; that we must not seek final causes. . . . If they knew that all things are ordered for the general good and for the particular welfare of those who know how to make use of them, they would not identify happiness with simple patience.[32]

What follows is a paraphrase of Plato's *Phaedo*. In this paraphrase, Leibniz emphasizes the importance of final causes for physics, the claim that "final causes are the principles in physics and that we must seek them in order to account for things":[33]

> Those who only say, for example, that motions of bodies around the earth keep it here, where it is, forget that divine power disposes everything in the finest way, and do not understand that it is the good and the beautiful that join, form, and maintain the world.[34]

This idea, that natural philosophy is grounded in final causes and the wisdom of God, becomes one of Leibniz's central ideas from the late 1670s on. It is nicely summarized in a passage that Leibniz wrote somewhat later, in an essay he called the "Tentamen anagogicum" (1696(?)):

> This consideration gives us the middle term needed to satisfy both truth and piety . . . .: all natural phenomena could be explained mechanically if we understood them well enough, but the principles of mechanics themselves cannot be explained geometrically, since they depend on more sublime principles which show the wisdom of the Author in the order and perfection of his work.[35]

---

[32] A6.4.1385 (AG 282).   [33] A6.4.1386 (AG 283).
[34] A6.4.1388 (AG 284).   [35] G VII 272 (L 478).

The "sublime principles" Leibniz has in mind here, which help to reconcile the mechanical philosophy with piety, are the reasons for which God chooses the laws that he imposes on mechanical nature. Leibniz wants to reform the mechanical philosophy, and bring it back to piety by emphasizing God's wisdom, and not just his power; God as final cause in the world, and not just as efficient cause.

Leibniz is not always careful in setting out this theme in his thought. However, there seem to be a number of different ways in which final causes enter his conception of the mechanical philosophy. First, they enter in connection with the grounding of the laws of motion. As Leibniz often emphasizes, the laws of motion are not geometrically necessary, but are a consequence of God's choice, grounded in reasons. In this way, the ultimate explanation for the laws of motion is grounded in final causes. But Leibniz also argues for the importance of final causes *within* the mechanist's world: while everything can be understood mechanistically, through efficient causes, Leibniz also argues that everything can be explained in terms of final causes as well. This doctrine seems to mean at least two different things. Leibniz argues that, parallel to the understanding of the world in terms of efficient causes, there is an explanatory structure grounded in principles that must be understood in terms of final causes as well. In this way final causes are useful in physics itself, and enable us to discover things that are too complex for us to discover if we limit ourselves to the study of efficient causes. And finally, while Leibniz argues that everything in the world is explicable mechanically, at least sometimes he wants to hold that everything can also be explained in terms of the will (appetite) of the souls or forms that pertain to the corporeal substances that make up the world, and that there is a perfect harmony between the two ways of explaining the behavior of bodies. Let us explore these issues one by one.

Divine Wisdom and the Laws of Nature

Late in his life, Leibniz wrote the following words to Nicolas Remond:

My dynamics requires a work of its own. . . . You are right, sir, to judge that it is in large part the foundation of my system, since there one learns the difference between truths whose necessity is brute and geometric and those truths which have their source in fitness and final causes.[36]

This conception of the laws of nature as grounded in the will of God is fundamental to Leibniz's mature thought. In texts too numerous to cite, Leibniz shows how the laws of nature in this best of all possible worlds are grounded in such principles as the principle of the equality of cause and effect and the principle of continuity, principles that are chosen by God as part of his creation of this best of all possible worlds.

It is important to note here that the issue is *not* a simple question about whether the laws of nature are necessary or contingent. As I pointed out earlier in this chapter, for Leibniz the problem of necessity is distinct from the problem of final causes: Leibniz at least entertains the position that God might have *chosen* the best of all possible worlds *necessarily*. If so, one might hold that what God chose, he chose necessarily, but that, nevertheless, there is a *reason* why things are the way they are and not otherwise. The contrast that Leibniz is drawing in the passage quoted from the letter to Remond is between truths that are grounded in "fitness and final causes" and truths "whose necessity is brute and geometric," that is, truths that don't involve divine wisdom. The distinction is nicely drawn in a text from the *Théodicée*, published in 1710, shortly before the letter to Remond:

Now, the truths of reason are of two sorts. Some are those which one calls eternal truths, which are absolutely necessary in the sense that their contrary implies a contradiction: these are the truths whose necessity is that of logic, metaphysics, or geometry, and which one cannot deny without our being led to absurdity. There are others which one can call positive, since they are the laws which it has pleased God to give nature, or which depend on him. We learn them either through experience, that is a posteriori, or by reason, and a priori, that is through considerations of the suitability which made them be chosen. This suitability also has its rules and reasons, but it is the free choice of God, and not a geometrical necessity which makes him prefer the suitable, and carries them toward existence. Thus one can say that physical necessity is grounded on moral necessity, that is, on the choice of the wise, worthy of his wisdom, and that both should be distinguished from geometrical necessity. This physical necessity is that which makes up the order of nature. It consists in the rules of motion, and

---

[36] Leibniz to Remond, 22 June 1715, G III 645.

in certain other general laws, which it pleased God to give to things in giving them being. It is thus true that it isn't without reason that God imposed these rules and laws, since he chooses nothing capriciously or by chance, or from pure indifference.[37]

Leibniz's point is that the laws of nature are a result of divine wisdom, *physically* necessary, which, in turn, is grounded in the *morally* necessary: but the laws of nature are *not geometrically* necessary. Geometrical necessities, unlike physical or moral necessities, are absolutely necessary, and their contrary implies a contradiction.

In Leibniz's mature philosophy, the laws of nature are grounded in divine wisdom. But, of course, it wasn't always so. As I noted in Chapter 1, Leibniz's first physics, the physics of the *TMA* and the *HPN*, was grounded in a very different conception of physical law. While contingent hypotheses about the state of the world had a major role to play in that early system, the view was grounded in a conception of the laws of motion as geometrically necessary. In these early writings, Leibniz's laws of motion and collision are supposed to be derived from the very definition of the terms.[38]

Now, the foundations of Leibniz's physics changed radically when in mid-1676 Leibniz discovered his principle of the equality of cause and effect, which led directly to the discovery of the conservation of mv^2 in the "De corporum concursu" in January 1678. But it is interesting to observe that, at its first appearance, Leibniz held that the equality principle ("that the cause be able to do as much as the effect and vice versa") follows directly from the very definition of the terms involved, and is thus in its way also of geometrical necessity. Let us return to the first statement of the equality principle in the "De arcanis motus" of 1676:

Just as in geometry, the principle of reasoning usually cited is the equality between the whole and all of its parts, so in mechanics everything depends on the equality of the whole cause and the entire effect. Hence just as the primary axiom in geometry is that the whole is equal to all its parts, so the primary mechanical axiom is that the whole cause and the entire effect have the same power [*potentia*].[39]

---

[37] *Théodicée*, disc. prélim. § 2, G VI 50. See also *Théodicée* § 349, G VI 321.

[38] Though, as I pointed out there, this is more of a program and a promissory note than it is a description of his actual practice in physics.

[39] Hess (1978), 203.

Leibniz continues this as follows:

Both axioms must be demonstrated from metaphysics, and just as the one depends on the definition of whole, part, and equal, the other depends on the definition of cause, effect, and power.[40]

A few lines later he continues:

Hence, at any rate, it is necessary that this connection can be demonstrated, for every necessary proposition is demonstrable, at least by someone who understands it. Moreover, every demonstration takes place through the resolution into identical propositions. Therefore, it is necessary that in the end, 'cause' and 'effect' wind up perfectly resolved into the same thing.[41]

This is not the only text in which Leibniz claims that the principle can be demonstrated. It is also reflected in a text that the Akademie editors date from 1677 or 1678, which Leibniz entitled "De aequipollentia causae et effectus." He writes:

Since the whole effect envelops the full cause, and, in turn, the full cause envelops the whole effect, that is, in order that someone be able to gain knowledge of the cause from knowledge of the effect alone, and from the knowledge of the cause alone knowledge of the effect, it follows that no cause can produce an effect altogether similar which differs only in magnitude.[42]

Writing to a correspondent (conjectured to be Jean Bertet) in September 1677, Leibniz declares that he has found the true laws of motion, and expresses the confidence that he is able to prove them demonstratively: "I see a way to get there demonstratively. . . ."[43]

But within two or three years of first announcing the principle, Leibniz retreats from the claim that it is geometrically necessary. The earliest securely dated passage is a letter that Leibniz wrote to Herman Conring on 19/29 March, 1678:

Everything happens mechanically in nature, that is, by certain mathematical laws prescribed by God.[44]

---

[40] Hess (1978), 203.   [41] Ibid.   [42] A6.4.1963.

[43] A3.2.235. Interestingly enough, the quotation continues as follows: "but beforehand I have to do certain experiments, which I have projected. . . ." One has to wonder about what kinds of experiments Leibniz has in mind and how they would relate to the demonstrations.

[44] A2.1².604. There is a passage that may be a few months earlier. After having recognized that the equality principle entails the conservation of mv^2, in January 1678, Leibniz went back and corrected

Insofar as the mathematical laws of motion follow from the equality principle, one must assume that the equality principle too is grounded in divine choice. Similarly he writes in a letter to Christian Philipp sent in December 1679:

For my part, I believe that the laws of mechanics which serve as foundation for the whole system depend on final causes, that is to say, on the will of God determined to do what is most perfect, and that matter takes on not all possible forms but only the most perfect ones. . . .[45]

This view is echoed in a number of other pieces that are less securely datable, but seem to have been written in the same period.[46] This, of course, raises a serious question: why did Leibniz change his mind and come to hold that the equality principle, initially introduced as geometrically necessary, a consequence of the meaning of the terms 'cause' and 'effect', is a consequence of the divine wisdom and the decision to create the best?

Let's begin by looking at the inverse of my main question: why did Leibniz ever think that the equality principle was geometrically necessary? And what kind of proof did he have in mind when he said that it was demonstrable from definitions?

In the "De arcanis motus," Leibniz asserts that there must be a demonstration of the necessity of the equality principle from the meanings of the terms. He writes in a passage I quoted earlier:

Just as in geometry, the principle of reasoning usually cited is the equality between the whole and all of its parts, so in mechanics everything depends on the equality

---

earlier passages of the manuscript that are based on mistaken assumptions and arguments. In one such passage he writes:

Furthermore, it follows from this that bodies usually are carried by themselves, through the impetus that they have received, as if they could have remembered from what height they descended or as if they could understand in what system they had been carried. But it is necessary that they are either carried by a general mover (which, however, is unsatisfactory, since they would also have their own force, which would be combined with the general force [i.e., the force imparted by the general mover]), or, rather, that they are continually impelled by that wisest cause, which remembers all and cannot fail. Therefore, the laws of motion are nothing but the reasons for the divine will, which matches [*assimilat*] effects to causes, to the extent that the reason of things allows.   [Fichant (1994), 134]

This last phrase may be interpreted as suggesting that God chooses the laws of nature. But it is probably more natural to read it as expressing a version of occasionalism, as discussed above in Ch. 5.

[45] A2.1².767 (L 272).

[46] E.g., "For the general laws of mechanics are decrees of the divine will. . . ." (A6.4.1367), dated by the Akademie editors at early 1677 to early 1678; preface to the book outlined in the 'Conspectus libelli,' quoted above, dated by the Akademie editors at summer 1678 to winter 1678/9, A6.4.2009–10

of the whole cause and the entire effect. . . . Both axioms must be demonstrated from metaphysics, and just as the one depends on the definition of whole, part, and equal, the other depends on the definition of cause, effect, and power. . . . Hence, at any rate, it is necessary that this connection can be demonstrated, for every necessary proposition is demonstrable, at least by someone who understands it. Moreover, every demonstration takes place through their resolution into identical propositions. Therefore, it is necessary that in the end, 'cause' and 'effect' wind up perfectly resolved into the same thing.[47]

Leibniz here compares the equality principle with a geometric principle, the equality of the whole and all of its parts, another principle that Leibniz thought could be proven from definitions.

A formal proof of a closely related proposition, that the whole is greater than its part, can be found in a curious document that the Akademie editors date as having been written a few years earlier, sometime between the autumn of 1671 and the early part of the following year.[48] In this document, briefly discussed above in Chapter 1, Leibniz sets out formal demonstrations of a number of propositions that he considers fundamental. In addition to the proposition that the whole is greater than its part, Leibniz proves the principle that will become central to his later philosophy, that "nothing is without a reason," as well as a central proposition in the early physics of the *TMA* and *HPN*: "there is no resistance in something at rest." This is how Leibniz proves the proposition about whole and part, giving an argument that is substantially borrowed from Hobbes:

Proposition:

The whole *cde* is greater than the part *de*

Definition: The greater is that whose part is equal to another whole [i.e., X is greater than Y =df a proper part of X is equal to Y]. . . .

Demonstration:

That whose part is equal to another whole is greater [than that whole] *by the definition of 'greater'*

(L 289); "Principium mechanicae universae novum," LH 35. 10. 5. 3r in Fichant (1994), p. 287 n.1, dated by Fichant at 1679–80.

[47] Hess (1978), 203.   [48] See A6.2.479–86.

The part of the whole *cde* (namely *de*) is equal to the whole *de* (namely, to itself)

Therefore, *cde* is greater than *de*; the whole [is greater] than the part.[49]

Whatever one thinks of this proof,[50] what is interesting to me is the big picture: Leibniz seemed to think that a proper science should be grounded in propositions based on the definitions of terms. This vision, like much of Leibniz's earliest thought, is derived from Hobbes, as I noted above in Chapter 1. For Hobbes, a true science begins with definitions: this is the true "first philosophy" for him. Still inspired by this conception, when Leibniz discovered a new fundamental principle for his physics in 1676, the equality principle, his first assumption seems to have been that, like the other principles that he thought that he had found, it must be provable from the definitions of the relevant terms. However, much as Leibniz would like to establish such a principle by an analysis of the terms, I don't see anything in the "De arcanis" that I can identify as such an argument in that central text, nothing parallel to his borrowed proof of the geometrical axiom.

But Leibniz didn't give up; there are other texts from those years in which he is clearly trying to supply the missing argument. One such argument is found in the "De corporum concursu" of January 1678, the manuscript in which Leibniz first enunciates the conservation of mv^2, in a text that was written, presumably, before the passage from the same manuscript in which he announces that the laws of motion derive from the will of God. After stating the principle and illustrating it with a geometrical example, Leibniz enters into what appears to be an argument. It begins with an observation borrowed from mechanics, that "the present state of any machine differs from the preceding state in the placement of the powers, but not in their sum." He goes on:

The full effect arises from the full cause, and the concept of the effect arises from the concept of the cause, insofar as it also envelops the necessity of change. Moreover, change is always understood to be as little as possible. Hence, the full effect is equipollent with the full cause, that is, it has the same power. This is a

---

[49] A6.2.482−3. Cf. Hobbes, *De corpore* 8.25. For a more general attempt to prove the axioms of Euclidean geometry, see A6.4.265ff.

[50] Johann Bernoulli, for example, didn't think much of it. See his objection to substantially the same argument in his letter of 22 September 1696, GM III 329−30.

corollary of what precedes, since there can be no need for a change of power, even if there is a need for a change in its situation.[51]

Here the presumption is that the concept of the effect must be contained in the concept of the cause, as Leibniz had already argued in the "Meditatio de principio individui" of April 1676.[52] But here he adds that the idea of the effect is contained in the concept of the cause, *along with* the idea of change. The implication here is that a cause, by definition, envelops its effect, and involves the stipulation that the effect is different from the cause and thus that it constitutes a change. However, Leibniz presumes here that the idea of change in question must be the idea of *minimal* change: "change is always understood to be as little as possible." This is a curious condition. How can it be justified? *Why* is the change always understood to be minimal? Assuming this seems tantamount to assuming something very close to what we are trying to prove, that is, the equality principle, that whatever change there might be, the ability to do work must remain unaffected by the change.

Another attempt to prove the equality principle is found in the essay entitled "De aequopollentia causae et effectus" (1678/9), mentioned earlier in this chapter. The main argument reads as follows:

Since the whole effect envelops the full cause, and in turn, the full cause envelops the whole effect, that's to say from the knowledge of the effect alone someone can come to know the cause, and from the knowledge of the cause alone, one can come to know the effect, it follows that no cause can produce an effect that is altogether similar but differs only in magnitude. And so an effect [cause?] like *a* cannot produce a cause [effect?] like *b*, assuming that *a* and *b* differ only in magnitude, since two things that differ in magnitude alone cannot envelop one another. [See Figure 6:1.] For by virtue of the fact that they are similar, a lack of magnitude cannot be offset by anything outside, nor can *b* envelop [*a*] except as its part.[53]

Though it is clear that the argument is somehow based on the claim that the concept of the cause envelops the concept of the effect, I find it difficult to say what exactly the argument is here. The point seems to be that if *a* and *b* differ only in magnitude (presumably, in the magnitude of the work that they are capable of doing) and are otherwise altogether similar, there

(margin annotation: Min. change related to divis. of matter)

---

[51] Fichant (1994), 145.   [52] A6.3.490 (SR 51).   [53] A6.4.1963.

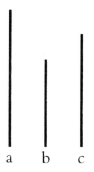

a   b   c

Figure 6:1. From A6.4.1963.

is no sense in which we can know the effect from the cause, or the cause from the effect: what could there possibly be in our conception of *a* that told us how much less than it *b* is, or how much magnitude to add to *b* in order to get *a*?[54]

Leibniz's second try at an argument in this text is as follows:

> Also, the same thing can be proved in a different way from the fact that *no reason can be given* why *a* produces *b* rather than *c*. For everything is similar, and differ only in magnitude, and so either *a* produces nothing at all, or it produces something infinite,[55] which two [outcomes] differ maximally from the magnitude itself [i.e., the magnitude of *a*], or else [it produces] what differs minimally from itself, that is, what is equal to it. And from this it can be demonstrated that the cause and the effect are altogether equipolent.[56]

This second argument is much clearer. But it seems to be based on the Principle of Sufficient Reason. This adds a bit of complication to the argument. Now, much later in Leibniz's career, the Principle of Sufficient

---

[54] Leibniz seems to come back to this way of formulating the question later on in the same essay, where he reflects further on the consequences of the 'envelopment' relation between cause and effect:

And the same cause cannot produce homogeneous effects which are different, that is, similar but unequal. This follows from the fact that if the effect envelops the cause, and the cause envelops the effect, it follows that the effects of the same cause envelop one another mutually. For, let *a* be a cause, and *b* and *c* be effects. *b* envelops *a* (the effect envelops the cause), *a* envelops *c* (the cause envelops the effect). Therefore *b* envelops *c*. In the same way, different causes of the same effect mutually envelop one another. Indeed, more broadly, [I wonder whether] diverse effects of different causes, or diverse causes of the same effects have been or could be their common effect or cause.   (A6.4.1964)

[55] Cf. a principle that Leibniz articulates in March 1676: "For if there is something to which something is to be given, and there is no reason why you should give it some particular thing, then you have given everything to it" [A6.3.392 (SR 45)].

[56] A6.4.1963–4.

Reason will be pretty clearly identified as the principle that underlies divine choice and thus contingent truth.[57] But matters aren't so clear at the time Leibniz proposed this argument. Earlier, in 1671/2, Leibniz had offered a demonstrative argument for the Principle of Sufficient Reason from the definition of its terms, as I noted above.[58] While it isn't altogether clear that Leibniz still held this view at the time he wrote the "De aequopollentia . . .," he may well have thought that the principle is geometrically necessary, making the equality principle that follows from it geometrically necessary as well. But however one goes on this question, it seems clear that this isn't an argument for the equality principle that follows from the definitions of cause and effect, as he had hoped to find in the "De arcanis."

There is a possible third argument for the equality principle in this same essay. The very last paragraph reads as follows:

If a power is fixed [certus], that is, if it can be measured by the quantity of the effect in something homogeneous, then it is necessary that it always remain the same in the same things [i.e., the equality principle holds]. Moreover, it follows from the nature of God that there is a fixed power of a definite magnitude [non vagam] in anything whatsoever, otherwise there would be no reasonings about these things.[59]

Here the argument seems to be that if force is stable and measurable, then it necessarily follows that it must be conserved. Here it seems that the equality principle is taken to follow from the very conception of what it is to attribute a force to a body. However, it is not clear that this is the same as saying that the equality principle is true by the definitions of the terms in which it is framed.

Now, at the very same time that Leibniz was struggling with the metaphysical status of the equality principle (and, with it, the metaphysical status of the laws of nature that follow from it), he was struggling with the question of final causes in nature, as we discussed earlier in this chapter. My conjecture, then, is that it was the new-found importance of final causes in Leibniz's thought, together with the difficulties that he was having in formulating a genuine demonstration of the equality principle from definitions, as he had originally hoped to do, that led Leibniz to the view that it, together with the mathematical laws of motion that follow out of it, are not geometrically necessary, but instead follow from the divine

---

[57] See, e.g., 'Monadologie' §§ 33ff.   [58] See A6.2.483.   [59] A6.4.1964.

wisdom. At that moment, in early 1678, the failure of the program to offer a demonstration of the geometrical necessity of the equality principle from definitions in the Hobbesian style may have been quite welcome to him, and given him yet another proof of the consistency between piety and the mechanical philosophy. Understood in this way, Leibniz's discovery of the divine origin of the basic laws of nature resulted from the confluence of two different philosophical projects, and surely gave him confidence that he was on the right track in both physics and theology.

Coming just at the moment when he was eager to reintroduce final causes into his mechanical philosophy, the impossibility of formulating an argument that exhibits the necessity of the equality principle must have been a sign to Leibniz that he was on the wrong track, and must have coaxed him to see the principle as a consequence not of geometrical necessity but of divine choice. This, of course, falls short of being a real *argument* in any proper philosophical sense for why the laws of nature *must* be grounded in divine wisdom. Indeed, it also falls short of substantiating the claim that Leibniz makes to Remond later in his career, that from the laws of nature one can learn "the difference between truths whose necessity is brute and geometric and those truths which have their source in fitness and final causes."[60] But it does give us an understanding of what may have motivated Leibniz to reject his first instinct, that the equality principle is geometrically necessary, and adopt the position that he was to hold for the rest of his life.

On my reading, the important issue that Leibniz faced in his early physics, and the issue that he continued to come back to in later expositions of his view, is whether the laws of nature are geometrically necessary, or whether they are what he calls "physically necessary," and follow from divine wisdom.[61] But, of course, another issue is whether the laws of nature are contingent. In the passage that I quoted from the *Théodicée* earlier in this chapter, Leibniz seems to be quite clear that the laws in question are genuinely contingent: "it is the free choice of God, and not a geometrical necessity which makes him prefer the suitable, and carries them toward existence."[62] Though there are a number of passages that suggest that

---

[60] Leibniz to Remond, 22 June 1715, G III 645.
[61] See, e.g., "Specimen demonstrarum catholicarum," A6.4.2326; "Tentamen anagogicum," G VII 278 (L 484), etc.
[62] *Théodicée*, disc. prélim. § 2, G VI 50. See also *Théodicée* § 349, G VI 321.

physical necessity is a kind of necessity, insofar as it is genuinely necessary for God to choose the best, there are many passages from the early 1680s on that suggest the view that the choice of the laws of nature is a free choice on the part of God, and thus that the laws of nature are contingent. For example, in an essay on necessity, contingency and truth that Leibniz drafted in 1685 or 1686, he wrote:

these same laws [i.e., laws of nature] are not necessary and essential, but are contingent and existential. For since the fact that the series itself exists is contingent and depends on the free decrees of God, its laws also will be contingent in the absolute sense; but they will be hypothetically necessary and will only be essential given the series.[63] — *ie, since God created anything at all*

In this way, what Leibniz calls physical necessity in the passage from the *Théodicée* is really hypothetical necessity, that is, necessary *given* what God has (freely) decided to create; in this way what is physically necessary is contingent.[64] The issue of contingency in Leibniz's thought is, of course, central, particularly in the 1680s and 1690s, when he devoted much effort to making room for such contingency, and struggled to find ways of rejecting Spinoza's radical necessitarianism.[65] But however significant this issue was for Leibniz, what seemed to be of central importance for Leibniz in connection with the laws of nature was not the issue of contingency, but the issue of divine wisdom and the specific denial of *geometrical* necessity.

It is interesting to note that even on this new account of the laws of nature, Leibniz still thinks that they are, in a way, demonstrable—not from definitions and identities, as he once thought, but precisely from the divine wisdom in which they are grounded. The appeal to divine wisdom puts the laws of nature in a rather interesting epistemological category. Even though they are metaphysically grounded in God's choice, insofar as we have some insight into how God chooses, we can know a priori the laws of nature that God chooses for this best of all possible worlds. In this way, it is possible to have genuine a priori knowledge of contingent truths.

Demonsh. not from the defs of phy. nature, but from div. wisd,

[63] A6.4.1518 [Leibniz (1973b), 100]. See also some passages in the correspondence with Arnauld (1686) G II 40, 41, 51; "sur un principe general utile à l'explication des lois de la nature..." (1687) G III 53–4 (L352); "Principium quoddam generale..." (1688) A6.4.2038–9; etc.

[64] The idea of hypothetical necessity as contingency is developed at greater length in, e.g., 'Discours de métaphysique' § 13.

[65] There is an enormous literature on necessity and contingency in Leibniz's thought. Since it turns out to be (surprisingly!) marginal to the questions that interest me in this book, I shall not go into this issue here.

Leibniz seems to have recognized the importance of this insight almost as soon as he realized the importance of divine wisdom and final causes for his natural philosophy. In the draft preface to the 'Conspectus libelli' of 1678/9 he writes:

> *The most perfect method involves the discovery of the interior constitution of bodies a priori from a contemplation of God, the author of things. But this method is a difficult one and not to be undertaken by just anyone.*

Just as there is a twofold way of reasoning from experiments, one leading to the application, the other to the cause, so there is also a twofold way of discovering causes, the one a priori the other a posteriori, and each of these may be either certain or conjectural. The a priori way is certain if we can demonstrate from the known nature of God that structure of the world which is in agreement with the divine reasons, and from this structure, can finally arrive at the principles of sensible things. This method is of all the most excellent and hence does not seem to be entirely impossible. For our mind is endowed with the concept of perfection, and we know that God works in the most perfect way.[66]

The question at hand here is the interior constitution of bodies, but there is no reason why this observation shouldn't apply equally well to knowledge of the laws of nature. A decade or so later Leibniz uses such reasoning to show why another of his basic principles, the principle of continuity, must be observed in nature. The issue is the argument that he advanced against Descartes's laws of impact: they result in egregious violations of that principle. In the essay, "Lettre de M. L. sur un principe general utile à l'explication des loix de la nature par la consideration de la sagesse divine...," which Leibniz published in the *Nouvelles de la république des lettres* in July 1687, he wrote:

The Rev. Father Malebranche admits in a way that there is some difficulty in them [i.e. the violations of continuity in Descartes's laws] but he continues to believe that since the laws of motion depend on the good pleasure of God, God could therefore have established laws as irregular as these. But the good pleasure of God is ruled by his wisdom, and geometricians would be nearly as surprised to see irregularities of this kind occur in nature as to see a parabola to which the properties of a ellipse with an infinitely remote focus could not be applied.[67]

---

[66] A6.4.1998–9 (L 283).
[67] G III 53–4 (L 352). A Latin version can be found at A6.4.2038. See also the "Tentamen anagogicum," G VII 279 (L 484).

This observation is, of course, also found in the passage quoted from the *Théodicée* above, where Leibniz admits a class of truths of reason that he calls "positive," which are "the laws which it has pleased God to give nature, or which depend on him." We can know these positive laws through reason and a priori, Leibniz holds, "through considerations of the suitability which made them be chosen."[68]

In this way, the laws of nature for Leibniz are a kind of contingent a priori, truths that can be known without the aid of experience, even though they are not necessary.[69] This, of course, brings to mind the Kantian category of the synthetic a priori, which is at the heart of the project of the *Critique of Pure Reason*. Some commentators have suggested that the laws of nature for Leibniz are, indeed, synthetic a priori in something like the Kantian sense.[70] Strictly speaking, I think that this is an anachronistic way of thinking about Leibniz's project. The analytic/synthetic distinction, central to Kant's project, is not found in Leibniz or his contemporaries.[71] This is how Kant characterizes the distinction in the *Critique of Pure Reason*:

In all judgments in which the relation of a subject to the predicate is thought (if I consider only affirmative judgments, since the application to negative ones is easy), this relation is possible in two different ways. Either the predicate B belongs to the subject A as something that is (covertly) contained in this concept A; or B lies

---

[68] *Théodicée*, disc. prélim. § 2, G VI 50.

[69] One must be somewhat careful with the notion of the a priori and a posteriori in this period. The standard medieval and earlier seventeenth-century usage of the distinction involves cause and effect: an a priori account goes from cause to effect, while an a posteriori account goes from effect to cause. See, e.g., the the *Logique Port-Royal* IV.1: "soit en prouvant les effets par les causes, ce qui s'appelle démontrer *à priori*, soit en démontrant au contraire les causes par les effets, ce qui s'appelle prouver *à posteriori*" [Arnauld and Nicole (1970), 367]. However, by Leibniz's time, the terms could also be used in the modern sense, to distinguish between knowledge that can be acquired independent of experience, and knowledge that comes to us through experience. See, e.g., Leibniz in the "Meditationes de cognitione, veritate, et ideis":

The possibility of a thing is known a priori when we resolve a notion into its requisites, that is, into other notions known to be possible, and we know that there is nothing incompatible among them.... The possibility of a thing is known a posteriori when we know through experience that a thing actually exists, for what actually exists or existed is at very least possible. [A6.4.589 (AG 26)]

See also the Leibniz's Fifth Paper to Clarke, § 129, where the experimental philosophy is said to proceed a posteriori, whereas a priori justifications proceed "par la pure raison."

[70] See, e.g., Poser (1984), 173f; Freudenthal (1999), 9–10.

[71] Indeed, it is not found in Kant before the *Critique of Pure Reason*, and many of Kant's contemporaries found it difficult to understand and problematic. See the editors' note in Kant (1998), 717 n. 4. and Hogan (forthcoming).

entirely outside the concept *A*, though to be sure it stands in connection with it. In the first case I call the judgment analytic, in the second synthetic.[72]

First of all, if we were to import Kant's distinction to Leibniz's thought, then it would seem that *all* propositions must be analytic for him. If, as Leibniz often says, in a true predication, the concept of the subject is contained in the concept of the predicate, then on Kant's strict definitions, there can be no synthetic propositions for Leibniz. But even more importantly, the equality principle and the conservation principles that follow from it do not play the role that synthetic a priori judgments play for Kant in his transcendental philosophy. In the *Critique of Pure Reason*, synthetic a priori judgments have a central role in the program: they are intimately linked with the way that we experience the world. They are expressions of the innate apparatus by which we see the world in terms of space and number, cause and effect. While this innate apparatus doesn't represent the world as it is in itself, it constitutes the framework through which we perceive the world, the glasses through which we view the world. Without these synthetic a priori principles, experience is literally impossible for us, according to Kant. But the laws of nature simply do not have that status for Leibniz.[73] Important as they are, they are not connected with any necessary preconditions for experience as such.

That said, from time to time Leibniz does make interesting remarks about the centrality of the laws of nature in our conceptual scheme. In a couple of places, Leibniz suggests that the equality principle is necessary in order for forces to be measurable. For example, in the *Dynamica* of 1690, Leibniz writes:

The whole effect is equivalent to the full cause, and therefore there is no mechanical perpetual motion. . . . Nature observes this law in the most constant way. Its truth can also be understood from this, that if it were eliminated, there would remain no way of measuring powers, or of establishing the magnitude of an effect from its causes.[74]

---

[72] *Critique of Pure Reason* A6/B10 [Kant (1998), 130].

[73] For a contrary view, see Freudenthal (1999), 23ff. Freudenthal attempts a detailed argument that, in regard to the laws of nature, Leibniz anticipated Kant's transcendental philosophy. While he has found some very suggestive passages, some of which are discussed below, in general I don't find his case entirely convincing.

[74] GM VI 437, discussed in Freudenthal (1999), 23. See also Fichant (1994), 284f and Carraud (2002), 405. Carraud argues that "par le principe d'équipollence, la causalité physique devient géométrisable. . . . C'est à ce titre que l'équipollence de la cause et de l'effet assure l'intelligibilité entière

More radically still, Leibniz suggests that if the equality principle were not satisfied, then the very notion of a force would be undermined. In a letter to Johann Bernoulli from 29 July 1695, Leibniz wrote:

These reasonings always work out and are satisfied. If, indeed, things didn't come out in this way, and if a different proportion of forces between two bodies of a given speed were to arise from consuming the force by stretching an elastic band than was produced in raising weights or in imposing motion, the entire science of dynamics would fall. It would be impossible to estimate forces; indeed, power would not have a defined quantity, but would be something vague and non-harmonious.[75]

These remarks suggest that, for Leibniz, the equality principle has a special metaphysical and epistemological status in his thought. But they seem more like interesting isolated remarks than hints of a genuinely developed doctrine that anticipates Kant's transcendental idealism in any serious way.

Miracles and the Laws of Nature: A Brief Digression

As I have argued, Leibniz came to see the importance of final causes and divine wisdom for the laws of nature by the late 1670s, and by the early 1680s, this had become a central part of his conception of the physical world. However, in the mid-1680s, he introduced a somewhat more elaborate version of this view. This elaboration of his earlier view seems to arise from a renewed interest in the notion of a miracle, and, in particular, from the question as to whether miracles involve the violation of the laws of nature.

From his earliest theological writings, Leibniz could not avoid the notion of a miracle. Leibniz was certainly interested in miracles in the early writings connected with the "Demonstrationes catholicae": miracles have always

de la physique; autrement dit, cette *aequatio* est un *ratio*. . . ." (405). It is interesting that in a passage quoted above from the essay "De aequopollentia causae et effectu" (1677/8), written when Leibniz still believed that the equality principle was geometrically necessary, the inference goes in the other direction: from the stability of the measure of force to the necessity of the equality principle. See A6.4.1964. Related to this is another argument from the essay "De legibus naturae . . ." (1691) that unless we have a measure of force that is invariant under the choice of a measure, nature would lack laws (GM VI 209–10). This is discussed in Freudenthal (1999), 23–4.

[75] A3.6.471.

been one of the important supports of faith in Christianity, and insofar as he was interested in Christian theology, he had to be interested in the kinds of miracles that ground Christianity.[76] But interestingly enough, in these early writings, Leibniz seems relatively unclear about just what it is that constitutes a miracle. Here is how he characterizes miracles in a text that may be from 1669–70:

def

All miracles in bodies consist in creating, in annihilating, in sustaining motion, in exciting, in moving in an instant, in deflecting from the ordinary course of things.[77]

In a list of definitions from 1671/2 in connection with the project for a universal characteristic, Leibniz offers an explicit definition of the miraculous:

The natural is what follows from motion and rest, for nature is the principle of motion and rest. That is, [the natural is] what is consonant with experience or reason. . . . A miracle is a non-natural actuality [*actus*].[78]

This is not very informative, but even so, it seems that Leibniz doesn't characterize miracles as violations of the laws of nature.

This comes out even more clearly in some of Leibniz's writings from a few years later, in 1676, particularly those written in response to his early contact with Spinoza. Leibniz's first acquaintance with Spinoza was in 1670/1, when he first read the *Tractatus Theologico-Politicus*, then just published. His initial interest in the *TTP* was largely in questions relating to Spinoza's view of the Bible and biblical interpretation.[79] But later brushes with Spinoza involve his views on miracles as well. In the *TTP*, Spinoza argues that what are commonly interpreted as miracles are not violations of the laws of nature, but are simply unusual events of whose causes we are ignorant.[80] In a letter to Oldenburg, which Leibniz saw in 1676, Spinoza summarizes this position by remarking that "miracles and ignorance are the same." This is Leibniz's comment on that characterization:

If we conceive of miracles as if God violently laid his hands on the world, like a workman on an automaton which tries to run off in another direction, I think

---

[76] See, e.g., A6.1.495f; A6.1.533; A6.2.146–7.

[77] A6.1.533. This is a marginal comment on a text dated at 1669–70, and thus may be later than the text itself.

[78] A6.2.494.   [79] See Goldenbaum (1999b), 105–7 for Leibniz's first notes on the *TTP*.

[80] Miracles are treated in ch. 6 of the *TTP*.

that miracles would be consistent with neither divine wisdom nor with the divine nature. If we believe that all things are already preordained from eternity in such a way that wonders happen at certain particular times through a singular conjunction of causes, then I think that miracles can be reconciled with philosophy, if, that is, we understand miracles, not as what are above the nature of things, but as what are above the nature of sensible bodies. For I don't see what would prevent there from being certain minds, more powerful than ours, clothed in a certain body, granted, with whose help marvels can be accomplished. Therefore, I don't see what prevents us from understanding the resurrection and ascension of Christ in a literal sense.[81]

Here Leibniz seems to understand miracles in much the way that Spinoza does, as being consistent with natural law, as being accomplished through natural causes that are hidden from us.

It is, in a way, not surprising that Leibniz would take this view of miracles at this moment. Remember that Leibniz's view before early 1678 was that the laws of nature are geometrically necessary, and could be proved demonstrably from definitions. If that is the case, then not even God could cause a violation in the laws of nature, any more than he could decide to make two plus three equal anything but five. But, of course, when Leibniz changes his view, and begins to argue that the laws of nature are a consequence of divine wisdom, then this changes, and it becomes possible to understand miracles as violations of the normal laws of nature. This is the view that Leibniz begins to press sometime in the mid-1680s.

The view is expressed at greatest length in an unpublished essay that Leibniz seems to have written sometime between the end of 1685 and early

---

[81] A6.3.365. Cf. the remarks on this in Curley (1990), 302ff. Also interesting here is a fragment from December (?) 1676: "Miracles are performed with the help of certain minds. Certain minds can be united uniquely with God: namely, those to which there is granted perfect action in accordance with reason, and whose bodies are granted so much power [*vis*] of motion that they cannot be overcome by those which surround them" [A6.3.588 (SR 113)]. Like the passage just quoted, this suggests that God might perform miracles not by violating the laws of physics, but by giving certain bodies sufficient (physical) force to overcome the physical force that other bodies might have. Cf. also Leibniz's remarks in the Paris fragment "De arcanis sublimium vel de summa rerum" from 11 Feb. 1676: "Nor is there any need of miracles to explain the grace of God, even though many rare things concur in such a way that it is evident that they occur by God's decision. For God arranged all things from the beginning in this way" [A6.3.477 (SR 31)]. This view also appears in a fragment dated early 1677 to early 1678, "Anima quomodo agat in corpus": "Souls don't act on bodies outside of the order. Nor does God act on nature [outside of the order], even if things appear to happen outside of the order, things having been constituted from the beginning in such a way that the general order involves something extraordinary in appearance" (A6.4.1367).

1686, at roughly the same time as he wrote the 'Discours de métaphysique.' In this essay, which the Akademie editors have named 'De natura veritatis, contingentiae et indifferentiae atque de libertate et praedeterminatione,' Leibniz writes:

But it must not be thought that only particular propositions are contingent, for there are . . . certain propositions which are for the most part true; there are also propositions which are almost always true, in the course of nature at any rate, so that an exception would be ascribed to a miracle. Indeed, I think that in this series of things there are certain propositions which are true with absolute universality, and which cannot be violated even by a miracle. This is not to say that they could not be violated by God, but rather that, when he chose this series of things, by that very act he decreed that he would observe them, as the specific properties of just this chosen series. And through these propositions, once they have been established by the force of the divine decree, a reason can be given for other universal propositions, or even for many of the contingent things which can be observed in this universe. For from the first essential laws of the series—true without exception, and containing the entire purpose of God in choosing the universe, and so including even miracles—there can be derived subordinate laws of nature, which have only physical necessity and which are not repealed except by a miracle, through consideration of some more powerful final cause. Finally, from these there are inferred others whose universality is still less; and God can reveal even to creatures the demonstrations of universal propositions of this kind, which are intermediate to one another, and of which a part constitutes physical science. But never, by any analysis, can one arrive at the absolutely universal laws nor at the perfect reasons for individual things; for that knowledge necessarily belongs to God alone.[82]

Leibniz's view here is that there is a general order in nature, which is absolutely without exception, including by miracle. This is the basic order of the world, and contains the "entire purpose of God in choosing the universe." But in addition, Leibniz holds, there are "subordinate laws of nature." These subordinate laws are subject to exception, and when they are violated, we have a miracle. Understood in this way, miracles are, indeed, violations of the laws of nature, though these violations are made

[handwritten margin notes: Essential laws indemons. | Universal laws | Universal laws demonst. | Particulars indemonst | → Final Cause]

---

[82] A6.4.1518 [Leibniz (1973b), 99–100]. See similar developments of this idea at about the same time in 'Discours' §§ 7, 16; notes on a letter of Arnauld, G II 41; Leibniz to Arnauld, 4/14 July 1686, G II 51. Jolley (2005b), 124–5 correctly points out that while miracles may involve violations of the laws of nature, strictly speaking they are defined in terms of that which goes beyond the causal powers of created things.

for the sake of "some more powerful final cause." In that way, the world never fails to be governed by reason.[83]

It is not entirely certain what exactly these "subordinate laws" were that Leibniz had in mind in this context. In a passage from the 'De natura veritatis' that follows the passage just quoted, Leibniz writes as follows:

That this stone tends downwards when its support has been removed is not a necessary but a contingent proposition, nor can such an event be demonstrated from the notion of this stone by the help of the universal notions which enter into it, and so God alone perceives this perfectly. For he alone knows whether he will suspend by a miracle that subordinate law of nature by which heavy things are driven downwards; for others neither understand the absolutely universal laws involved, nor can they perform the infinite analysis which is necessary to connect the notion of this stone with the notion of the whole universe, or with absolutely universal laws. But at any rate it can be known in advance from the subordinate laws of nature that unless the law of gravity is suspended by a miracle, a descent follows.[84]

This suggests that Leibniz thinks that something like the law of gravity counts as a law of nature of this subordinate sort. Indeed, gravitation does have a subordinate status for Leibniz, insofar as it isn't a basic law of nature (as it is for some Newtonians). Rather, the heaviness of bodies is to be explained in terms of the interaction between the heavy body and the vortex surrounding the earth.[85] This would allow God to suspend the free-fall of heavy bodies by altering some of the contingent conditions on earth, without violating more basic laws, say, the law of the conservation of

---

[83] On this see especially the elegant account in Carraud (2002), 440–53. Carraud emphasizes the extent to which even miracles do not violate the Principle of Sufficient Reason, even if we cannot understand how. Leibniz's view here comes rather close to the general idea behind the hierarchy of laws that Malebranche presents in dialogue XIII of his *Entretiens sur la métaphysique et sur la religion* (1688). There Malebranche outlines five levels of laws, beginning at the bottom with the "general laws of the communication of motion," followed by the laws of the union of the soul and body, the laws of the union of the soul with God, the general laws which give good and evil angels power over their bodies, and the laws that give Jesus Christ power over heaven and on earth. See Malebranche (1958–84), vol. 12–13, 319–20 [Malebranche (1997b), 252–3]. On Malebranche's view, the requirements of higher-order laws can cause violations in lower-order laws. While the canonical presentation of the system of laws only occurs in the *Entretiens* of 1688, the scheme is suggested as early as some of the Eclaircissements to the *Recherche de la vérité* and the *Traité de la nature et de la grace*; on this see Pellegrin (2006), 42–7. I have not been able to establish a direct connection between Leibniz's views on this issue and Malebranche's, but it is quite possible that the two philosophers may have influenced one another.

[84] A6.4.1519 [Leibniz (1973b), 100].

[85] On Leibniz's reaction to Newton's account of gravitation, see Garber (1995), 333–5.

mv². Indeed, in a letter to Bayle from 1687, Leibniz does suggest that the equality principle, from which the conservation of mv² is taken to follow, is among the laws that are genuinely inviolable. He writes:

This is why I believe that instead of the Cartesian principle, one can establish another law of nature that I hold the most universal and the most inviolable, namely, that there is always a perfect equality between the full cause and the entire effect.[86]

But, on the other hand, in the 'Discours de métaphysique,' where Leibniz also introduces the distinction between the inviolable general order of nature and what he calls there the subordinate maxims, which can be violated by miracles, Leibniz identifies his equality principle as a prime example of one of the subordinate maxims of nature.[87] So, in the end, it rests a bit unclear just which are the subordinate laws that God can suspend in performing a miracle.

Two Kingdoms: Parallel Ways of Explaining Nature

We have seen one way in which final causes enter into Leibniz's mechanical philosophy. Leibniz argues that the laws of nature were (freely) chosen by God in accordance with his wisdom. In this way the laws of nature *must* be understood in terms of final causes, God's choice of the best. But there is another way in which Leibniz wants to reintroduce final causes into the world. Though he agrees with mechanists such as Hobbes, Descartes, and even Spinoza that everything *can* be explained mechanically, he also wants to argue that everything can be explained through final causes as well. He often expresses this view through the metaphor of the two kingdoms. As he puts it in the "Specimen dynamicum" of 1695:

In general, we must hold that everything in the world can be explained in two ways: through the kingdom of power, that is, through efficient causes, and through the kingdom of wisdom, that is, through final causes, through God, governing

---

[86] G III 45–6.
[87] See 'Discours' § 17. In addition to the question of the relation between miracles and the laws of nature, in 'Discours' § 16 Leibniz is also concerned about the relation between his thesis that each individual substance contains everything past, present, and future in the whole universe, and the fact that miracles are still possible for God.

bodies for his glory, like an architect, governing them as machines that follow the laws of size or mathematics, governing them, indeed, for the use of souls, and through God governing for his glory souls capable of wisdom, governing them as his fellow citizens, members with him of a certain society, governing them like a prince, indeed like a father, through laws of goodness or moral laws. These two kingdoms everywhere interpenetrate each other without confusing or disturbing their laws, so that the greatest obtains in the kingdom of power at the same time as the best in the kingdom of wisdom.[88]

What exactly does Leibniz have in mind here?

One thing he has in mind is directly connected with some questions in optics that he worked on from the late 1670s. The passage just quoted from the "Specimen dynamicum" begins as follows:

Indeed, one can even bring final causes to bear from time to time with great profit in particular cases in physics (as I showed with the clearly remarkable example of an optical principle, which that most celebrated Molyneux greatly applauded in his *Dioptrics*), not only the better to admire the most beautiful works of the Supreme Author, but also in order that we might sometimes discover things by that method [*via*] that are either less evident or follow only hypothetically on the method of efficient causes. Perhaps philosophers have not yet sufficiently seen just how useful this is.[89]

The reference here is to an essay Leibniz wrote some years earlier, "Unicum opticae, catoptricae et dioptricae principium," published in the *Acta eruditorum* in June 1682. There Leibniz proposed a new principle for understanding the behavior of light: "Light travels from the radiating point to the point illuminated by the easiest of all paths."[90] Using this principle,

---

[88] GM VI 243 (AG 126). On the two kingdoms and the importance of the distinction between efficient and final causes, see Carraud (2002), 391–9, McDonough (forthcoming-a) and (forthcoming-b). It is important here not to confuse the distinction between the kingdoms of efficient and final causes with other uses Leibniz makes of the kingdom analogy. There is, first of all, the distinction he makes between the kingdom of nature and the kingdom of grace: Leibniz to Johann Bernoulli, 17 December 1698, GM III 561 (AG 170), "Principes de la nature et de la grâce" § 15; "Causa Dei" § 46 (G VI 446); "Addition a l'explication du système nouveau . . ." G IV 573; *Théodicée* I § 18, II §§ 112, 118, III § 340. And then there is the use he makes of the notion of the kingdom of heaven: 'Discours' § 37; cf. A6.4.1587–8; A6.4.2237.

[89] GM VI 243 (AG 126). See Molyneux (1692), 192ff.

[90] Leibniz (1682), 185. Later statements of the principle give it as requiring "the path most determined in length of time" ["Tentamen anagogicum," G VII 278 (L 483)]. McDonough (forthcoming-a), 8 paraphrases the rule as follows: "Put simply, Leibniz's principle is tantamount to the claim that from among all the possible paths between a source and a sink, a ray of light will travel along the path which is unique with respect to ease; where 'ease' is understood as the quantity obtained by multiplying

Leibniz then went on to show how one could derive the laws of both reflection and refraction for light.

Leibniz immediately realized the philosophical significance of this technical discovery. Earlier in the century, Descartes had proposed to derive these laws from considerations of purely efficient causes. Using models of light conceived as streams of particles, Descartes appealed to the laws of motion to argue for laws that govern the behavior of light when it is reflected from an immobile surface, or when its speed changes as it passes from one medium into another.[91] What he has shown, Leibniz thinks, is that these same laws can be derived not only from efficient causes, but from divine wisdom and final causes as well. As he announced in his first public statement of the principle:

Therefore we have reduced all laws concerning [light] rays, justified through experience, to pure geometry and calculation, having made use of this singular proposition, obtained through a final cause, if you consider the matter correctly. . . . And so those who reject *final causes* in physics with *Descartes* greatly err (not to say something more serious still), since besides providing admiration for divine wisdom, final causes also give us a most beautiful principle for finding the properties of those things whose inner nature is not yet known clearly by us. . . .[92]

As Leibniz was later to repeat, on the basis of this example from optics, considerations of final causes lead us not only to piety, but can even help us discover new laws in nature. As he wrote much later in the "De ipsa natura" of 1698:

For I believe that God came to decree those laws observed in nature through considerations of wisdom and reasons of order. And I think that it is apparent from this (something that I once noted, using an opportunity afforded by the laws of optics, something that was afterwards greatly applauded by the distinguished Molyneux in his *Dioptrics*) that final causes not only advance virtue and piety in ethics and natural theology, but also help us to find and lay bare hidden truths in physics itself.[93]

the distance of the path by the resistance of the medium(s)." See McDonough (forthcoming-a) more generally for an account of the optical example and its historical context. See Duchesneau (1993), 263–4 for an account of the change in Leibniz's terminology from the "easiest" to the "most determined" path.

[91] See Descartes, *La dioptrique* (1637), disc. 2, AT VI 93ff.   [92] Leibniz (1682), 186.

[93] "De ipsa natura," § 4, G IV 506 (AG 157). Cf. the preliminary draft of the "Système nouveau," G IV 472 (WF 22); "Reponse aux reflexions . . ." (1697), G IV 340; etc.

But Leibniz, from the start, saw the particular example as leading to a metaphysical truth deeper still. In the context of the long and rambling 'Definitiones cogitationesque metaphysicae' (1678–80/1), discussed at some length above in Chapter 3, Leibniz precedes a brief account of his emerging proof of the law of refraction with the following very general statement:

All the phenomena of nature can be explained solely by final causes, exactly as if there were no efficient cause; and all the phenomena of nature can be explained solely by efficient causes, as if there were no final cause.[94]

This is expressed somewhat more clearly, but no less dramatically, in a passage from a fragment composed in 1677/8:

Everything in the whole of nature can be demonstrated either by final causes, or by efficient causes. Nature does nothing in vain, nature acts through the shortest paths, as long as they are regular.[95]

In this way, Leibniz seems to be advancing the very general thesis that not just in optics, but in *every* case, there are parallel modes of explanation: anything that can be explained in terms of efficient causes can also be explained in terms of final causes.

This view gets its fullest expression in the 1690s, in the "Specimen dynamicum" and especially in the essay, "Tentamen anagogicum," an extended exposition of the importance and utility of appealing to final causes in physics, with a full exposition of the optical work that originally led Leibniz to this view. There he writes:

The most beautiful thing about this view seems to me to be that the principle of perfection is not limited to the general but descends also to the particulars of things and of phenomena.... [T]he smallest parts of the universe are ruled in accordance with the order of greatest perfection; otherwise the whole would not be so ruled.... It is for this reason that I usually say that there are, so to speak, two kingdoms even in corporeal nature, which interpenetrate without confusing or interfering with each other—the realm of power, according to which everything can be explained *mechanically* by efficient causes when we have sufficiently penetrated into its interior, and the realm of wisdom, according to

[handwritten margin note: this seems to be a different issue.]

---

[94] A6.4.1403 (RA 253).

[95] A6.4.1367. Leibniz goes on to write: "Hence the shortest paths should be sought not in the refracting surfaces themselves, but in tangents. But this is just in passing." This suggests that Leibniz had the optical case in mind here.

which everything can be explained architectonically, so to speak, or by final causes when we understand its ways sufficiently.[96]

In the principal expositions of this view of parallel modes of explanation, Leibniz puts great weight on the optical examples that go back to the late 1670s. This might lead one to think that these are the only examples he has. But there are others as well. Jeffrey McDonough notes three classes of problems where Leibniz thinks that teleological principles are useful.[97] The first involves maximization of an area or volume for a given perimeter or surface area. This can explain "the case of a liquid placed in another of a different kind, which forms itself into the most capacious shape, namely that of a sphere."[98] A second class involves the shape of the catenary, the curve made by a cord or chain suspended at two points. This is "the case in common mechanics where the struggling of many heavy bodies with one another finally gives rise to a motion through which there results the greatest descent, taken as a whole."[99] And finally, there is the problem of the brachistochrone, the curve of shortest descent between two given points. Leibniz notes here that "if in the case of the curve of shortest descent between two given points, we choose any two points on this curve at will, the part of the line intercepted between them is also necessarily the line of shortest descent with regard to them."[100]

There are, to be sure, significant difficulties in Leibniz's view here. Even if the optical case is not the only one Leibniz has on which to base his thesis, it does seem to be a bold hypothesis that *all* phenomena in nature can be explained through either efficient or final causes: the idea of parallel explanatory structures everywhere in nature seems a kind of speculative program for a natural philosophy, grounded in a metaphysical vision rather than in detailed argument, empirical or otherwise. And secondly, recent commentators have legitimately asked whether Leibniz's principles are genuinely teleological at all: in what way is the principle that light follows the easiest or most determined path a genuine appeal to final causes?[101]

---

[96] "Tentamen anagogicum," G VII 272–3 (L 478–9). On the role of architectonic principles in Leibniz's thought, see Duchesneau (1993), 259–379.

[97] See McDonough (forthcoming-a), 24ff.

[98] "De rerum originatione radicali," G VII 304 (AG 151).   [99] Ibid.

[100] "Tentamen anagogicum," G VII 272 (L 478).

[101] See, e.g., Bennett (2005), 138ff; McDonough (forthcoming-a), 27ff. Couturat made this observation as early as 1902. See also Couturat (1972), 28, 35. Thanks to Desmond Hogan for calling this last reference to my attention.

There seem to be two somewhat different issues here. On the one hand, there is the question as to whether principles of maxima and minima, such as the optical principle that Leibniz introduces, are, themselves, intrinsically teleological; that is, whether they involve a kind of appeal to an end toward which nature in general or the individual light ray itself tends. And secondly, there is the issue of whether the existence of such modes of explanation requires an appeal to God as having chosen such laws for reasons of their perfection and harmony. There are reasons to think that Leibniz had both senses in mind.[102] Of the two senses, the latter is probably easier to establish, since it is tolerably obvious that such principles do not admit of geometrical proof. However, if all Leibniz is saying is that his optical principle, for example, requires divine wisdom, then that doesn't seem to differentiate it from any of the other laws of nature, as we saw earlier in this chapter. For the optical principle to support the two-kingdoms view, and introduce final causes into nature itself, it is the intrinsic teleology that is at issue, and this is much harder to establish. It is beyond the scope of my project in this book to settle this question. It is enough for my own more limited purposes that Leibniz thought that his principles were teleological, and that he saw his approach to optics and other areas as a way of introducing final causes into natural philosophy.

Two Kindgoms: Bodies and Souls

One thing that Leibniz has in mind by the two-kingdoms view is that there are, everywhere, parallel explanatory structures for phenomena in the physical world, one appealing to the laws of motion and impact, that is, to efficient causes, and the other to final causes, understood as teleological principles such as the ones he made use of in his optics. But Leibniz sometimes seems to have something rather different in mind by the two-kingdoms metaphor.

The view I want to discuss seems first to emerge in a fragment that we have already seen, "Anima quomodo agat in corpus," which the Akademie editors date as having been written in 1677/8, during the exciting period

---

[102] For the latter, see, e.g., Leibniz (1682), 186: "but the originator of things created light in such a way that from its nature that most beautiful outcome arises."

when Leibniz's new physics of substantial form and corporeal substance is emerging. The passage reads as follows:

How the soul acts on the body. As God does on the world, that is, not by way of miracle, but through the mechanical laws. And so, if (though impossible) minds were eliminated, leaving the laws of nature, the same things would come about as if there were minds, and even books would be written and read by human machines, understanding nothing. Indeed, it should be known that it is impossible to eliminate minds while preserving the mechanical laws. For the general mechanical laws are decrees of the divine will, and the individual [*speciales*] laws in each and every body (which follow from the general laws) are the decrees of its soul or form, striving towards its good, that is, towards perfection. And so God is that mind which leads everything toward general perfection. Furthermore, the soul is that sentient force which strives in each and every thing toward individual perfection. . . . Everything in nature as a whole can be demonstrated both through final causes and through efficient causes. . . .[103]

Everything in body can be explained mechanically, through the laws of motion. But yet mind enters in two ways. One mind required is God's, needed to ground the mechanistic laws of nature which explain the behavior of bodies without appeal to the souls or forms. But, Leibniz suggests, there is also a role for individual souls, from which come the "individual laws" that govern bodies, which are "the decrees of its soul or form, striving towards its good. . . ." Each individual corporeal substance has its own soul or form, Leibniz suggests in this passage. From that soul or form derive other, particular laws that govern the individual to which the soul or form are attached. And so, he concludes that "everything in nature as a whole can be demonstrated both through final causes and through efficient causes."[104] Here the final causes in question would seem to involve both God's choice for the best and the volitions made by the individual souls

---

[103] A6.4.1367. The beginning of this passage resonates with a text written in December 1676, and discussed above in Ch. 5:

If it could be supposed that a body exists without a mind, then a man would do everything in the same way as if he did not have a mind, and men would speak and write the same things, without knowing what they do, just as when they are playacting. But the supposition that the body exists without a mind is impossible. [A6.3.400 (SR 115)]

[104] The statement in this text seems linked with the optical example discussed earlier. It continues: "Hinc viae brevissimae quaerendae non in superficiebus ipsis refringentibus sed in tangentibus." This suggests that Leibniz didn't distinguish the two readings of the "two-kingdoms" doctrine (the appeal to general teleological principles vs the appeal to the activity of souls or forms) as carefully as I do here.

in their own striving for the good. It isn't clear, though, exactly what the relation is between the general laws grounded in God and the individual laws grounded in the soul, or, for that matter, what exactly the individual laws are supposed to be.

Somewhat clearer is the view expressed in the 'Definitiones cogitationesque metaphysicae' (1678–1680/1), a text that we have already seen a number of times. Leibniz writes:

Even though all things are animated and act with sense and appetite, they nevertheless act according to the Laws of Mechanics.

I see that in this matter most people go to extremes. For some who think that everything is governed by the laws of mechanics, do away with all incorporeal substances and final causes. On the other hand, those who admit them see them as being able to bring anything about by their direct instigation alone [*sibi solo instinctu quidvis efficere posse*], and do not try to find out how things are governed. I believe that both efficient and final cause should be conjoined, for everything happens because of the pleasure of souls [*voluptatis animarum causa*]. Thus souls act by willing, but again, each of their forces going to infinity is determined by mechanical laws. . . .[105]

As in the two-explanatory-systems account discussed earlier in this chapter, Leibniz claims here that everything can be explained in terms of the laws of motion and impact. But here the alternative he wants to highlight is not some sort of teleological principle, as in the optical case, but an explanation in terms of the activity of souls: "everything happens because of the pleasure of souls. . . ."

The view that Leibniz articulates in the texts that we have just examined is closely connected to his doctrine of pre-established harmony, what he had earlier called the doctrine of concomitance, which came up earlier in Chapters 2 and 5 in other connections. This doctrine, as presented in the 'Discours de métaphysique' or the "Système nouveau," focuses on the problem of mind–body causality, and is framed as an alternative to Descartes's view that the mind and the body interact directly with one another, or to the occasionalism of many of Descartes's followers, in accordance with which God is the intermediary between mind and

---

[105] A6.4.1402 (RA 251). Note a remark Leibniz makes a few pages earlier: "Even though all things are animate, nonetheless they all act according to the laws of mechanics, for sensation and appetite are determined by organs (i.e. parts of a body) and objects (i.e. by surrounding bodies)" [A6.4.1400 (RA 247)]. Cf. also A6.4.464–5, a text from roughly the same period.

body. This is how Leibniz presents the doctrine to Arnauld, in a letter of 28 November/8 December 1686:

when I wish to raise my arm, it is precisely at the moment when everything is arranged in the body so as to carry this out, in such a manner that the body moves by virtue of its own laws; although it happens through the wonderful but unfailing harmony between things that these laws conspire towards that end precisely at the moment when the will is inclined to it, since God took it into consideration in advance, when he made his decision about this succession of all things in the universe.[106]

Leibniz articulates the same view in the first public statement of the doctrine in the "Système nouveau" of 1695:

[T]he organized mass, in which the point of view of the soul lies, being expressed more closely by the soul, is in turn ready to act by itself, following the laws of the corporeal machine, at the moment when the soul wills it to act, without disturbing the laws of the other—the spirits and blood then having exactly the motions that they need to respond to the passions and perceptions of the soul. It is this mutual relation, regulated in advance in each substance of the universe, which produces what we call their communication, and which alone brings about the union of soul and body.[107]

Leibniz also expresses this view in terms of the metaphor of the two kingdoms, in a way similar to what we saw earlier in the chapter. This is how Leibniz articulates it in the first such version that I could find, in the 1692 "Animadversiones in partem generalem Principiorum Cartesianorum":

Nature has, as it were, an empire within an empire, a double kingdom, so to speak, of reason and necessity, or of forms and of the particles of matter, for just as all things are full of souls, they are also full of organic bodies. These kingdoms are governed, each by its own law, with no confusion between them, and the cause of perception and appetite is no more to be sought in the modes of extension than is the cause of nutrition and of the other organic functions to be sought in the forms or souls. But that highest substance which is the universal cause of all things brings it about, by its infinite wisdom and power, that two very different series in the same corporeal substance correspond to each other and perfectly harmonize with each other, just as if one were ruled by the influence [influxus] of the other.[108]

---

[106] G II 74.   [107] Leibniz (1695), 303 (AG 144).
[108] G IV 391 (L 409–10). Cf. the statement of this view in the 1702 reply to Bayle, G IV 558–61 (L 577–8). By 1705 or so, Leibniz seems to have identified this version of the two-kingdoms view

In all of these passages, Leibniz is quite clear that the mind goes its way, governed by its laws, and that the body goes its way, governed by *its* laws: the harmony, due to God, is that even so, the two entities, the mind and the body, correspond in an appropriate way, as if they actually influenced one another. So, when the mind, in the course of its development, has a volition, to grasp an ice-cream cone, for example, the state of the body is such that the arm moves in an appropriate way, and the fingers grasp the cone, all the while behaving strictly in accordance with the mechanical laws of nature. This can be thought of as a coordination between the realm of the mind, governed by final causes (that is, formulating volitions to satisfy certain ends), and the realm of the body, governed by the laws of motion. But viewed from a perspective only slightly different, we can say that in the human being, body and soul, the voluntary motion involved in grasping the ice-cream cone can be explained either in terms of the laws of motion that govern the body, or in terms of the volition in the mind. That is, the event in question, the physical grasping of an ice-cream cone, can be explained either in terms of mechanical causes, the physical state of the body and its surrounding causal context, or in terms of a final cause, a volition formed for certain ends. And insofar as nature is full of life, this account is quite general, and there is a divinely established harmony between the "two very different series *in the same corporeal substance*" *everywhere* in nature.

Now, this view has a kind of plausibility when we are dealing with voluntary motions, such as the grasping of an ice-cream cone, or with

with pre-established harmony. See the "Considerations sur les principes de vie et sur les natures plastiques" (1705):

Therefore souls or vital principles, according to my system, change nothing in the ordinary course of bodies and do not even give God the occasion for doing so. The souls follow their laws, which consist in a definite development of perceptions according to goods and evils, and the bodies follow theirs, which consist in the laws of motion; nevertheless, these two beings of entirely different kind meet together and correspond to each other like two clocks perfectly regulated to the same time. It is this that I call the theory of *pre-established harmony*. . . . [G VI 540–1 (L 587)]

The view seems to extend all the way to the end of Leibniz's career. See, e.g., the following passage from the 'Monadologie' of 1714:

79. Souls act according to the laws of final causes, through appetitions, ends, and means. Bodies act according to the laws of efficient causes or of motions. And these two kingdoms, that of efficient causes and that of final causes, are in harmony with each other. . . .

81. According to this system, bodies act as if there were no souls (though this is impossible); and souls act as if there were no bodies; and both act as if each influenced the other.

the parallel case in lesser animals, corporeal substances with souls and bodies. (This, of course, assumes that we understand what it is for a lesser, that is, non-rational corporeal substance to have something like a volition.) But in the earlier texts we were examining, it looks as if Leibniz wants to claim that *all the activity of bodies can be explained both mechanically and in terms of the volitions of souls and forms*. This seems much less plausible. While my voluntary motions might be explicable in terms of the volitions of my soul, in what sense can my involuntary motions be understood in those terms? What sense can be made of that?

Here is one possible way of understanding the stronger claim. Remember some of the arguments that we discussed earlier in Chapters 3 and 4. What, in the end, does it mean for bodies to behave in accordance with the laws of nature? If all there were in the physical world were extension, then they wouldn't obey the laws of nature they do: they would behave in accordance with the laws of geometrical necessity. So, to say that bodies behave in accordance with the laws of nature is to say that they have more than the purely material, that they have forms. So, in this way, even when we are talking about bodies following only the laws of nature, bodies whose behavior is explicable entirely in terms of efficient causes alone, we are making tacit appeal to forms and souls as well. Perhaps what Leibniz had in mind is that while we can explain the behavior of bodies entirely in terms of the laws of nature, we could also go directly to the forms and souls that underlie the mechanical laws that they obey, and, at least in principle, explain their behavior directly in those terms. And explaining the behavior of bodies in terms of the activity of their souls would, presumably, be explaining it in terms of final causes.[109] Perhaps this is what Leibniz has in mind when he says that everything in nature can be explained either in terms of the volitions of souls ("everything happens because of the pleasure of souls"), or in terms of efficient causes. But even so, it still seems a bit of a stretch, a bit of rhetorical excess.

Even if everything could be explained in terms of the activity of souls or forms, Leibniz is generally clear that it isn't a good idea to do so. In

---

[109] In this respect Hirschmann (1987–8), 147–8 may not be entirely wrong when he relates the two kingdoms to the distinction between the phenomenal world of bodies and the world of monads. For a discussion and critique of Hirschmann, see McDonough (forthcoming-b).

Can Leib. say that bodies' motions ca be explained mechanically? What about the inderivability of particular motions from mobility?

the preface to the unwritten physical treatise Leibniz sketched out in the 'Conspectus libelli' he wrote:

I believe that there is in every body a kind of sense and appetite, or a soul, and furthermore, that to ascribe a substantial form and perception, or a soul, to man alone is as ridiculous as to believe that everything has been made for man alone and that the earth is the center of the universe. But on the other hand, I think that when once we have demonstrated the general mechanical laws from the wisdom of God and the nature of the soul, then it is as improper to revert to the soul or to substantial forms everywhere in explaining the particular phenomena of nature as it is to refer everything to the absolute will of God. . . .[110]

Even though in principle the behavior of bodies is grounded in the activities of forms or souls, Leibniz is generally pretty clear that the appropriate way to explain things is either through efficient causes, or through the large-scale final causes that are traceable back to God; we are not to explain things in terms of the activities of the souls or forms, except when we are dealing with living things, such as us, and then only when we are dealing with voluntary behavior.[111]

The reintroduction of teleology and final causes is very important to Leibniz's project. However, this aspect of his thought turns out to be somewhat more complicated than it might look at first glance. There are a number of threads in his position, a number of rather different things that he means to claim when he presses his contemporaries to recognize finality in nature.

---

[110] A6.4.2009–10 (L 289). This theme is repeated in numerous passages. See, e.g., 'Discours' § 10.

[111] An interesting apparent exception to this is found in the following curious passage from a text, "Origo animarum et mentium," dated at 1681:

Insofar as God relates the universe to some particular body, and regards the whole of it as if from this body or, what is the same thing, thinks of all the appearances or relations of things to this body considered as immobile, there results from this the substantial form or soul of this body, which is completed by a certain sensation and appetite. For there is in all things a certain sensation and a natural appetite which does not at all detract from the laws of mechanism; for the latter is not so much a cause as an occasion for God's acting.   [A6.4.1460 (RA 261)]

Here the account of the behavior of bodies in terms of forms and final causes seems to be basic, while the account in terms of the laws of the mechanical philosophy seem to be "occasions" for God to act. Also, this passage contains a very different idea of where forms come from and why from any of the other texts we have examined. There is every reason to think that this constitutes a kind of philosophical experiment for Leibniz, and does not present a doctrine that Leibniz ever seriously held.

7

Leibnizian Phenomenalisms

It is a standard view that Leibniz held a broadly idealistic view of the world from at least the early 1680s until the end of his life, and that the 'Discours de métaphysique' and correspondence with Arnauld, along with other texts of that era that we have been discussing in earlier chapters, offer fundamentally the same doctrine that his later writings do, a world grounded in mind-like monads, in which "there is nothing in things except simple substances and in them perception and appetite."[1] This differs from the position I have been developing in earlier chapters of this book. On the view that I favor, in the 1680s and probably through much of the 1690s Leibniz's view of body and the physical world is grounded in a world of corporeal substances, substances understood on analogy with organisms, not minds, organic bodies transformed into substances by virtue of containing souls. For me the best argument for this position is the developmental story that I have been telling in earlier chapters. The world of corporeal substances is the world that emerges from the conception of body and the physical world that Leibniz held in the 1670s, when he faced certain problems in that largely Hobbesian conception of the world. These problems of unity and activity are largely resolved to his satisfaction by giving substantial forms, which earlier had a mainly theological role to play in his thought, work to do in the physical world. These substantial forms, understood on analogy with souls, transform organic bodies into genuine unities, and give them a source of activity. If this is the right story, there would seem to be no toehold for a monadological metaphysics in this period of Leibniz's thought: a world grounded in corporeal substance is an elegant solution to the knotty problems that he faced with his earlier view of the world.

---

[1] G II 270 (AG 181). As we shall discuss below in Ch. 9, there are those who question whether even the monadological view should be regarded as idealistic.

But this is not to deny that there are other lines of argument in the texts of the middle period that are more suggestive of the later monadological view. It is hard not to notice that in the texts of this period, Leibniz often appears to suggest that bodies are in some sense phenomenal, or that they are less than fully real. This, of course, calls to mind the formula Leibniz uses in his later years, that the bodies of everyday experience are well-founded phenomena, and that only monads and their perceptions and appetitions are truly real. This might suggest that behind the talk of bodies and corporeal substances Leibniz is really endorsing the monadological view that is so prominent in his later texts. I think that this amounts to reading later views back into Leibniz's thought in this period. But nonetheless, there is something very interesting going on here, something significant in itself, and something significant for his later philosophy. In this chapter we shall examine this strand in his thought.

Simon Foucher and the Problem of the External World in 1675

On 2 May 1674, while Leibniz was living in Paris, the first of two volumes of Nicolas Malebranche's *Recherche de la vérité* appeared in Paris. Seven months later, on 10 December 1674, officials approved the publication of the first critique of what was to become a classic in the history of philosophy.[2] The short work was entitled *Critique de la Recherche de la verité. Où l'on examine en méme-tems une une [sic] partie des Principes de Mr Descartes.* While published anonymously ("*Lettre par un Academicien*"), the author was Simon Foucher, honorary canon of the Sainte Chapelle of Dijon, but a regular habitué of the Paris intellectual scene.[3] Foucher was an unremarkable young man (he was 30 at the time) who had the year before published a book, now lost, entitled *Dissertations sur la recherche de la verité, ou sur la logique des academiciens.* Foucher's skeptical orientation can be inferred both from the title of the work, and from the very explicit defenses of skepticism that will characterize his later writings.

---

[2] See Watson (1987), 71.
[3] For a brief account of Foucher's life, see Richard Watson's introduction to Foucher (1995), 4–5.

Foucher was under the perfectly reasonable assumption that Malebranche's published volume was the whole of the work: the book ends with the word "FIN," there was certainly no indication on the title page that this was the first of two volumes, and very little in the text to indicate that there is more to follow.[4] In a response to Foucher that Malebranche appended to the beginning of the second volume of the *Recherche* when it appeared the following year, Malebranche mocked Foucher for jumping the gun: "When you offer a critique of a book, it seems to me that you should at least have read it."[5] Malebranche also complained that Foucher hadn't understood what he had read of the *Recherche*. But be that as it may, the *Critique* contains some very interesting arguments, arguments that were to catch Leibniz's attention at this crucial moment in his philosophical development.

Foucher begins with some general remarks about why he is undertaking the critique, and about his own general philosophical orientation. As someone who "philosophize[s] in the manner of the ancient Academy,"[6] Foucher complains that, in general, philosophers go for the novel and that which will win them the admiration of the masses. But, he claims, the first principles on which all knowledge has to be based remain obscure and in need of clarification: "It is...true that these primary principles are still unknown, and that they are encumbered with nearly insurmountable difficulties, so far are we from finding the evidence necessary to establish true demonstrations."[7] In particular, he suggests (though doesn't exactly assert) that Malebranche goes wrong in assuming the principles of Descartes's philosophy, "on whose principles he wholly grounds himself."[8] The pamphlet is then organized under fourteen headings, seven assumptions ("*suppositions*") that Foucher attributes to Malebranche, and seven "assertions" that he finds in the volume.

This is not the place to go through Foucher's *Critique* in full detail. But three of the assumptions that Foucher discusses are of particular interest, and turn out to be important for Leibniz's reaction. All deal in one

---

[4] Watson (1987), 57 notes one sentence in I.4 that indicates a list of topics to be treated that goes beyond what is contained in the published volume. But even if Foucher had noticed that, how often do authors promise more than they deliver in a book?

[5] Malebranche (1958–84), vol. 2, 496.

[6] Foucher (1675), Avertissement, 4 [Foucher (1995), 14]. Although I refer to Richard Watson's very handy translation of this text, I don't always follow his readings.

[7] Foucher (1675), 4 [Foucher (1995), 16].   [8] Foucher (1675), 8 [Foucher (1995), 18].

way or another with our knowledge of an external world of extended bodies.

The fifth assumption that Foucher attacks is the assumption that "we have two kinds of ideas, ideas that represent to us what is outside of us, and ideas that represent to us only what is within us." But the marginal summary is blunter: "Assumption of ideas that represent what is outside of us."[9] The sixth assumption is "of ideas that represent without being likenesses."[10] The seventh is "the assumption that we know by the senses that there is extension outside of us."[11] In the explanatory text, Foucher offers a number of arguments that are intended to lead us to question the confidence that we have in the existence of an external world of extended bodies. Foucher's arguments aren't easy to follow: the text and the reasoning wander and digress a good bit, and contain a number of subsidiary arguments directed against what he takes to be specific claims that he finds in Malebranche's text. But Foucher advances two main considerations against the claim that we can know the existence of material things outside of us.

Foucher begins his discussion of the fifth assumption as follows:

For, as the author rightly recognizes, all our ideas are only modes of our soul. We know immediately and truly only these ideas, as he [Malebranche] remarks again very judiciously on those occasions when he means by the word *idea, what the mind perceives immediately.*[12]

But, Foucher argues, modes of the soul cannot in any way resemble modes of body:

The author has very well remarked that our senses do not acquaint us [*ne nous font pas connoistre*] with things that are outside us. Because these objects have nothing in themselves *like* what they produce in us, for matter cannot have modes that are *like* those of which the soul is capable.[13]

Thus since an idea can only represent what it resembles, ideas can give us no access to an external world of extended bodies.

---

[9] Foucher (1675), 44 [Foucher (1995), 29].   [10] Foucher (1675), 50 [Foucher (1995), 31].
[11] Foucher (1675), 61 [Foucher (1995), 35].
[12] Foucher (1675), 44 [Foucher (1995), 29]. The word translated here as "mode" is "façon d'estre" in the French, literally "way of being" as Watson translates it. However, Descartes often uses "façon" or "façon d'être" to translate his Latin technical term "modus." I am assuming that Foucher is making reference to that notion.
[13] Foucher (1675), 45 [Foucher (1995), 30].

1) Ideas are modes of the soul
2) Modes of the soul cannot resemble modes of the body
3) Nothing represents what it does not resemble
4) ∴ Ideas do not represent bodies.

Foucher is perfectly well aware that, in language, we seem to have a domain of things that represent without resembling their objects. But this is how he understands what is going on in this situation:

Properly speaking it is not the word that represents the tree, but it is the idea this word excites in us that represents it. The idea represents the tree because the idea is like the tree, and this is obvious because when one pronounces the word *tree*, we imagine something that is very like what we see when a tree is actually present before our eyes. I do not say that the image that this word excites in us is like a tree in itself, but I say that the image is like the effect this object produces in us through our senses.[14]

Foucher's claim is that the word doesn't really represent anything: it just excites an image (an idea of imagination) that does represent the tree. But what is represented is not the tree itself, but rather the idea of sense that we would have if we were actually seeing the tree. And it accomplishes this representation by way of resemblance.

There is a second kind of argument that weaves its way through Foucher's text. This argument turns on the supposed distinction between the ideas of sensible qualities, such as color and sound, which exist only in the mind, and the ideas of size, shape, and motion, which are supposed to exist outside of ourselves in extended bodies, a distinction familiar from the Cartesians and found in virtually all the mechanists. In connection with his discussion of the seventh assumption, Foucher relates the question he put to the famous Cartesian physicist Jacques Rohault:

[A]ll that we know by the senses are only modes of our soul that belong entirely to us, and there is nothing at all *like* these modes in material objects. Now, is it the case that if we know extension by the senses, therefore we must conclude that extension is a mode of our soul, and that there is nothing *like* this mode in material objects?[15]

The answer that Foucher expects, of course, is that the distinction cannot be maintained. He writes:

Because all our sensations being nothing other than experiences of several modes of which our soul is capable, we know truly by the senses only what objects produce in us, from which it follows that if one admits that we know extension and figures by the senses as well as light and colors, one must conclude necessarily

---

[14] Foucher (1675), 57 [Foucher (1995), 34].   [15] Foucher (1675), 65 [Foucher (1995), 36].

that this extension and these figures are no less in us than are that light and those colors.[16]

The conclusion, again, is that from experience we can have no access to a world of extended bodies that exist independently from mind.

The resemblance between these arguments of Foucher's and Berkeley's arguments for immaterialism here is obvious. Like Berkeley, Foucher holds that there is nothing like an idea but another idea. And like Berkeley, Foucher argues for the untenability of the distinction between the ideas, such as extension, size, motion, etc. that represent things supposedly outside of us and the ideas, such as color, heat, taste, etc. that represent things that are only states of the mind. Unlike Berkeley, Foucher doesn't explicitly draw the conclusion that the world of mind-independent material things simply does not exist. But the epistemological question is certainly raised: how *do* we know that extended bodies exist outside of us?

As I noted earlier, Malebranche was not at all happy with Foucher's critiques, and objected that he had been misunderstood. This gave rise to a number of exchanges over the issues raised in Foucher's *Critique*.[17] But Malebranche's reaction to Foucher and the question as to whether Foucher correctly understood the *Recherche* is less interesting for us than another feature of this exchange. It was probably through reading Foucher's critique of Malebranche in 1675 and possibly discussing those issues with him while the two were together in Paris that Leibniz began to worry about how we can know the existence of the external world.

Leibniz and Foucher in 1675

Among the many philosophers and savants that Leibniz got to know when he was in Paris was Simon Foucher.[18] Perhaps they first got together over scientific questions. A few years before publishing the *Critique*, Foucher had written and published a little pamphlet called *Nouvelle façon d'hygrometres* (1672).[19] There is a brief ms. in the Leibniz archives that has written at

---

[16] Foucher (1675), 79 [Foucher (1995), 38].   [17] On this see Watson (1987), ch. 5.

[18] For an account of Foucher's relations with Leibniz, see S. Brown (2004).

[19] Foucher's interest in the subject continued for some years after this publication; see his *Traité des hygrometres ou machines pour mesurer la secheresse et l'humidité de l'air* (Paris: Estienne Michallet, 1686).

the top, "Expérience de Mons. l'Abbé Foucher, de Dijon, qu'il m'a dit l'an 1675, mois d'Avril," and which contains the record of an experiment that may be connected with those kinds of questions.[20] In addition, there is another manuscript dating from a few years later that gives a charming, but brief, account of a chance meeting between Leibniz and Foucher in a Paris bookshop in which was displayed a copy of Foucher's newly published *Critique*.[21] Leibniz and Foucher were to remain in cordial epistolary contact until Foucher's death in 1696. The very first letter we have is from Leibniz to Foucher, and was probably written in mid-1675, after the publication of the *Critique*. It is addressed "To Mons. l'Abbé Foucher, auteur de la *Critique de la recherche de la verité*,"[22] and discusses the pamphlet in some detail. It is interesting and significant that Leibniz chose to write Foucher a letter rather than meeting him in person to discuss the book, suggesting that he took the issues quite seriously.

Leibniz discusses a number of themes from Foucher's pamphlet. He begins by complimenting Foucher on his commitment to examining the ultimate principles on which our thinking is based: "I agree with you that it is important once and for all to examine all of our assumptions in order to establish something solid."[23] But Leibniz sees the question of our knowledge of the external world as central to Foucher's concerns: "Your aim, so far as I can see, is to examine all the truths which affirm that there is something outside of us."[24] Leibniz interprets this question in a very broad sense. He argues, for example, that "we cannot deny that the very truth of hypothetical propositions is something outside of us, something that does not depend on us."[25] Similarly, he argues that necessities, such as we find in geometry, also have an external existence:

Thus the nature of the circle with its properties is something existent and eternal. That is, there is a constant cause outside us which makes everyone who thinks carefully about the circle discover the same thing.[26]

But Leibniz is also concerned with how we can know the existence of a world of bodies external to the mind.

---

[20] LH 38. 144r.   [21] A6.4.2715. See Antognazza (2008), 170.

[22] A2.1².387. In addition to the letter we also have Leibniz's notes on Foucher's response to Malebranche's response to his pamphlet, Foucher (1676), though, unfortunately, many of the marginal notes were mutilated when the pamphlet was bound and trimmed, and the editors had to make many conjectures about the text. See A 6.3.311–26.

[23] A2.1².387 (AG 1).   [24] Ibid.   [25] Ibid.   [26] A2.1².388 (AG 2).

Leibniz begins by offering a kind of proof for the existence of an external world. He begins with the following observation:

Thus there are two absolute general truths, that is, two absolute general truths which speak of the actual existence of things: the first, that we think, and the second, that there is a great variety in our thoughts. From the former it follows that we exist, and from the latter it follows that there is something else besides us, that is, something else besides that which thinks, something which is the cause of the variety of our appearances.[27]

But why should the variety of thoughts require an external cause? Leibniz notes:

Now, this variety cannot come from that which thinks, since a single thing by itself cannot be the cause of the changes in itself. For everything would remain in the state in which it is, if there is nothing that changes it; and since in itself it is indeterminate with respect to having these changes rather than others, one cannot begin to attribute any variety to it without saying something which, we must admit, has no reason—which is absurd.[28]

The point seems to be that things left to themselves remain in the same state, *including minds*. Furthermore, he argues, the mind is indeterminate with respect to the particular change in our thoughts, so if it were the source of the variety of phenomena, the particular nature of the variety would be without a reason, in violation of the Principle of Sufficient Reason. And thus, he concludes, there must be an external cause of the variety of our thoughts:

Therefore there is some cause outside of us for the variety of our thoughts. And since we conceive that there are subordinate causes for this variety, causes which themselves still need causes, we have established particular beings or substances certain of whose actions we recognize, that is, things from whose changes we conceive certain changes in us to follow.[29]

And from this, the argument moves directly to bodies: "And we quickly proceed to construct what we call matter and body."[30]

---

[27] A2.1².388 (AG 2).

[28] A2.1².390 (AG 3). Note that the translation in AG is inaccurate on this point.   [29] Ibid.

[30] Ibid. This argument is also suggested in Leibniz's notes on Foucher (1676); see A 6.3.313, 318–19. The same argument also appears in texts from 1678/81; see A6.4.1395 and A6.4.2262. However, it

As it stands, this argument isn't altogether satisfying. There may be a way of arguing from the variety of our thoughts to an external world; this is somewhat similar to the strategy of Descartes's Meditation VI argument for the existence of an external world. But for Descartes it is more the involuntary character of sensation (together with a number of other assumptions) that is at work, rather than just the variety of thoughts. The assumptions that Leibniz makes to get this argument going seem to stand in contradiction with any notion of the mind as in some sense self-determined, if not free, an issue that Leibniz does not even raise in this connection. And even if the reasoning gets us a cause for thought external to the mind, it is very difficult to see how it gets us all the way to bodies. The argument proceeds to them quickly, *too* quickly one is inclined to say.

Leibniz acknowledges problems with this reasoning. He continues the letter by calling to mind some of the considerations that Foucher had advanced in his pamphlet:

> But it is at this point that you are right to stop us a bit and renew the criticisms of the ancient Academy. For, at bottom, all our experience assures us of only two things, namely, that there is a connection among our appearances which provides us the means to predict future appearances with success, and that this connection must have a constant cause. But it does not strictly follow from all this that matter or bodies exist, but only that there is something that presents well-sequenced appearances to us.[31]

Leibniz doesn't address the specific arguments Foucher proposes here: he does not discuss the claim that an idea can only be like another idea, or Foucher's argument for the untenability of the distinction between the ideas of extension, size, motion, etc. and the ideas we have of color, heat, taste, etc.[32] But he clearly grasps Foucher's central point, that the senses give us no direct access to an external world of mind-independent bodies. In

---

would seem to be somewhat problematic to hold, insofar as it is in tension with the conception of minds as spontaneous.

[31] A2.1^2.390 (AG 3–4).

[32] Some of the specific arguments are discussed in Leibniz's comments on Foucher (1676); see A6.3.311ff. Since Foucher (1676) is a response to Malebranche's attack on Foucher (1675), Leibniz's comments on it are more focused on addressing particular claims and arguments that Foucher makes, though nowhere there does he address the question of the external world in the general and almost systematic way he does in the 1675 letter.

discussing Foucher's position, in fact, Leibniz goes beyond what Foucher himself advanced:

For if an invisible power took pleasure in giving us dreams that are well connected with our preceding life and in conformity among themselves, could we distinguish them from realities before having been awakened? And what prevents the course of our life from being a long well-ordered dream, a dream from which we could be wakened in a moment? . . . [W]hat prevents a vision from passing for a reality?[33]

Leibniz here does still seem to think that we can infer from the variety of our thoughts to an external cause, but he does admit that that cause need not be a world of external extended bodies, as opposed to some "invisible power."[34] (The Cartesian overtones are obvious here: the allusion is, of course, to Descartes's hypothesis of the evil genius from the *Meditations*.) Indeed, not even the coherence of our thoughts helps much:

It is true that the more we see some connection in what happens to us, the more we are confirmed in the opinion we have about the reality of our appearances; and it is also true that the more we examine our appearances closely, the more we find them well-sequenced, as microscopes and other aids in making experiments have shown us. This constant accord engenders great assurance, but after all, it will only be moral assurance until somebody discovers the a priori origin of the world we see and pursues the question as to why things are the way they appear back to the ground of essence. For having done that, he will have demonstrated that what appears to us is a reality and that it is impossible that we ever be deceived about it again.[35]

By "reality" here Leibniz seems to mean the assumption that our sensations derive from external extended and mind-independent bodies, and his claim is that not even the coherence of our experience allows us to infer the "reality of our appearances." That could only be established with real certainty, he claims, by establishing a priori what the world must be like (e.g., the nature of body) and why bodies appear the way in which they do. Until then, our knowledge of the material world has only moral certainty, not metaphysical. And the prospects of attaining such knowledge are quite

---

[33] A2.1².390, 391 (AG 4).

[34] In the notes on Foucher (1676), Leibniz suggests that "perhaps the nature of our soul is the immediate cause of our perception of material things, and that God, the author of everything, is the cause of the relation that there is between our thoughts and that which is outside of us" (A6.3.318–19).

[35] A2.1².391 (AG 4).

dim, Leibniz thinks: "But I believe that this would nearly approach the beatific vision and that it is difficult to aspire to this in our present state."[36] This is more than a mere metaphysical worry for Leibniz. Should we be able to attain to such knowledge, "we would learn from this how confused the knowledge we commonly have of body and matter must be...."[37] If we cannot know for certain whether bodies even exist, how can we know with any certainty what they are really like?

Considering Foucher's critique of Malebranche seems to have led Leibniz to reflections about how it is that we know about the existence of an external world. But Leibniz's reflections didn't end with the skeptical conclusion to which he comes in the letter to Foucher. In an interesting series of reflections from the Paris notes dated 15 April 1676, Leibniz takes the ideas a step further. The focus of the piece is Descartes, and Foucher's name does not come up. But the considerations Foucher had raised are central to the reflections on the existence of an external world of bodies. Early in the essay Leibniz makes the following observation:

Since what we can judge about the existence of material things is no more than the consistency of our senses, one has a sufficient basis for judging that we can ascribe nothing to matter apart from being sensed in accordance with some certain laws, the reason for which (I admit) remains to be sought.[38]

But later in the piece he offers a more radical position:

On due consideration, only this is certain: that we sense, and that we sense in a consistent way, and that some rule is observed by us in our sensing. For something to be sensed in a consistent way is for it to be sensed in such a way that a reason can be given for everything and everything can be predicted. This is what existence consists in—namely, in sensation that involves some certain laws; for otherwise, everything would be like dreams. Further, it consists in the fact that several people sense the same, and sense what is coherent; and different minds sense themselves and their own effects.... Therefore there is no reason why we should ask whether there exist certain bodies outside us, or whether space exists, and other things of this sort; for we do not explain adequately the terms that are involved here. Unless, that is, we say that we call a "body" whatever is perceived in a consistent way, and say that "space" is that which brings it about that several perceptions cohere with each other at the same time.... As this is so, it does not follow

---

[36] Ibid.   [37] Ibid.   [38] A6.4.508 (SR 59). I have altered Parkinson's translation.

that there exists anything but sensation, and the cause of this sensation and of its consistency. . . .[39]

Here the suggestion is that for a body to exist is just for us to have experience that is coherent in a certain way: the existence of body is just "sensation that involves some certain laws," and bodies are just "whatever is perceived in a consistent way." Leibniz has not given up the idea that this coherence needs a cause and an explanation. But whatever that cause and explanation is, it need not be anything like the extended bodies represented in our experience. In any case, whatever that cause may be, it isn't what we mean when we talk about bodies. In this way the reality of bodies is tied simply to the fact that we can reliably predict the perceptions we will have in different circumstances. Their reality is thus tied to the consistency of our perceptual world, and not to the existence of anything outside of us.

It is important here to recognize that we are dealing with *minds*, presumably *human* minds, minds like ours that have sensations and that belong to other persons, conscious and rational perceivers like us. What is pressing Leibniz to this position here and in the 1675 letter to Foucher is the epistemological difficulty of inferring mind–independent material bodies on the basis of our sensory experience; what we are left with when we bracket mind-independent material bodies is just the mind that perceives them and its sensations.

There are a number of different themes in these texts. There are skeptical worries about the knowability of an external world of extended bodies on the basis of our sensory experience; there is the claim that we can infer the existence of an external cause from the variety of our experiences, though we may not know what exactly that cause is like and it may well turn out to be some "invisible power" that is spiritual and not material; there is the claim that we can distinguish between dreams and reality on the basis of the coherence of our experience and our ability to predict the future; there is the suggestion that our idea of body is somehow to be identified with our coherent experiences. I think that it would be wrong to suggest that Leibniz has a single and well-worked-out position in mind here; Leibniz is exploring new ideas here, not setting them out in a rigorous and final way. It would be even more incorrect to suggest that Leibniz unambiguously subscribes to such a position; there are plenty texts from the period that

---

[39] A6.4.511 (SR 63–5).

suggest a less skeptical and more realistic conception of the world at this same time. But quite loosely, in these texts, it looks as if Leibniz is playing with a position that we might call phenomenalism (though Leibniz does not), not entirely unlike Berkeley's immaterialism.[40] I hesitate to push this comparison too far. Unlike Berkeley, Leibniz never tells us in these texts how exactly bodies are to be understood in terms of sensory perceptions. But even so, one cannot deny that these texts show a Leibniz who is attracted by the view that all may be minds and their ideas. To distinguish this somewhat imprecise position from what Leibniz will later adopt, I shall call it *human-mind phenomenalism*.

Phenomenalism and Corporeal Substances

In earlier chapters I have emphasized the significant moment of change in Leibniz's views in 1678/9, when he introduces corporeal substances into his account of the physical world and when substantial forms begin to play a more central role in his physics and metaphysics. But despite this important change, many of the skeptical themes from 1675/6 wind their way through Leibniz's texts in the years that follow. In a number of texts, Leibniz repeats the observation that, on the basis of our sensory experience, we cannot know whether or not there is an external world of extended material things, though he usually asserts that we can know that there must be *some* external cause for the variation in our perceptions. In a piece from 1677 or 1678 that Leibniz entitled "Distinctio mentis et corporis," Leibniz bases an argument for the distinction between mind and body on the fact that we can never be certain that there are bodies outside of us.[41] In a letter to Malebranche from 22 June/2 July 1679, he writes:

As for the existence and nature of what we call body, we deceive ourselves even more than you say, and I agree with you that it would be hard to prove that there is extension outside of us in the sense in which this is usually understood.[42]

Similarly, in the "De modo distinguendi phaenomena realia ab apparentiis" (1683/6), which we have already discussed and to which we shall soon

---

[40] Cf. Adams (1994), 235. More generally, Adams draws out broader comparisons between Leibniz and Berkeley in his ch. 9 *passim*.

[41] A6.4.1368–9. [42] A2.1².724 (L 210).

return, Leibniz notes that "by no argument can it be demonstrated absolutely that bodies exist...."[43]

Also, in a number of later texts, Leibniz repeats the observation that we can distinguish dreams from reality on the basis of the coherence of our experience. In a dialogue from 1679/81, Leibniz writes:

And our interior experiences give us the means to judge things which subsist outside of us. For when the appearances that we sense in ourselves are coherent in a way that allows us to make successful predictions from them, it is by this that we distinguish periods of wakefulness [les veilles] from that which we call dreams. And furthermore, knowing by axioms that all changes must come from some cause, by this we arrive at the knowledge of things which subsist outside of us.[44]

But there are also numerous passages that go beyond this observation and assert that the coherence of appearances is, in some sense, all there is to body. In another piece, this one dated between 1678 and 1681, Leibniz offers a pretty close reprise of his letter to Foucher from 1675. In the course of the essay, he gives the same argument for the existence of an external cause of the variety of perceptions that he had offered Foucher, and offers the same criterion for distinguishing dreams from reality that he had proposed to Foucher, the coherence of our perception.[45] But as in the paper of 15 April 1676, he also argues that there may be nothing more to bodies than coherent appearances:

For he who can finally make predictions with success must be said to have become sufficiently proficient in nature. And so the objections the Skeptics make against observations are inane. Certainly, they may doubt the truth of things, and if it pleases them to call the things that occur to us dreams, it suffices for these dreams to be in agreement with each other, and to obey certain laws, and accordingly to leave room for human prudence and predictions. And granting this, it is only a question of names. For apparitions of this kind we call true, and I do not see how they could be either rendered or chosen truer.[46]

This suggests that all there is to the world of body is the sensations we have.

It is with the kind of human-mind phenomenalism suggested in his early letter to Foucher and in later texts that we should read the famous

---

[43] A6.4.1502 (L 364).   [44] "Conversation...du Pere Emery Ermite...," A6.4.2262.
[45] A6.4.1395–7 (RA 239–41). Richard Arthur sees this as Leibniz's refutation of phenomenalism; see RA 416, n. 2 to 28. But reading the whole text, Leibniz's position seems much more ambiguous to me.
[46] A6.4.1398 (RA 243–5).

passages in 'Discours de métaphysique' § 14 that are so suggestive of the later theory of monads. Leibniz begins by reminding the reader what had been established earlier in the text, that each individual substance is the source of all of its properties:

Now we said above, and it follows from what we have just said, that each substance is like a world apart, independent of all other things, except for God; thus all our phenomena, that is, all the things that can ever happen to us, are only consequences of our being.

When Leibniz talks about "each substance" being "a world apart," he must include substances of all kinds, including both corporeal substances as well as their souls, insofar as they can be considered substances. But when we are dealing with our own minds, the soul that pertains to us as corporeal substances, the properties in question will just be their phenomena. Later in the section Leibniz elaborates on this claim:

In fact, nothing can happen to us except thoughts and perceptions, and all our future thoughts and perceptions are merely consequences, though contingent, of our preceding thoughts and perceptions. . . .

→What do bodies have to do w/ this.

It is important to remember here that the "us" in question is "us"—you and me, minds that have conscious perceptions. But, Leibniz notes:

And since these phenomena maintain a certain order in conformity with our nature or, so to speak, in conformity with the world which is in us, an order which enables us to make useful observations to regulate our conduct, observations justified by the success of future phenomena, an order which thus allows us often to judge the future from the past without error, this would be sufficient to enable us to say that these phenomena are true without bothering with whether they are outside us and whether others also perceive them.

And this, of course, is the observation that he made as early as the 1675 Foucher letter, that the coherence of our phenomena is grounds enough for us to conclude that they are in an important sense real. This regularity can be counted upon absolutely, whether or not there is an external world: "This would never fail, and it would happen to me regardless, even if everything outside of me were destroyed, provided there remained only God and me." But despite the hint of the phenomenalism that is more pronounced in other texts, Leibniz does not really question the existence of an external world here. Though the coherence of the phenomena "would be sufficient" for us to say that the phenomena are "true" whether or not they represent something outside of us, Leibniz doesn't here question that they are, I think. As I emphasized earlier in Chapter 5, in the passage on cause and effect that ends § 14 in an earlier draft of the 'Discours,' Leibniz is explicitly concerned with both souls and bodies and their relations among one another, suggesting that he doesn't think that the earlier passages seriously called into question the existence of an external world of bodies.

In these texts, Leibniz suggests a kind of human-mind phenomenalism very much like the position he argued in 1675/6 in connection with the response to Foucher. But there is another text from this era that suggests a very interesting extension of that picture.

Perhaps the most careful working out of some of these phenomenalistic themes in the 1680s is in the essay "De modo distinguendi phaenomena realia ab apparentiis" from 1683/6, which we have already seen a number of times in earlier chapters. Leibniz's project there is to figure out "which phenomena are real," and how they differ from imaginary phenomena, such as dreams.[47] While he goes through a number of contributing criteria, the one that he arrives at is the kind of coherence that he had proposed in the Foucher letter:

> Yet the most powerful criterion of the reality of phenomena, sufficient even by itself, is success in predicting future phenomena from past and present ones, whether that prediction is based upon a reason, upon a hypothesis that was previously successful, or upon the customary consistency of things as observed previously. Indeed, even if this whole life were said to be only a dream, and the visible world only a phantasm, I should call this dream or this phantasm real enough if we were never deceived by it when we make good use of reason.[48]

Leibniz then goes on to discuss things that go beyond the appearances, things that "do not appear but which nevertheless can be inferred from appearances."[49] This is, apparently, in the service of seeking a cause for the phenomena and their regularity: "It is indeed certain that every phenomenon has some cause."[50] Could such a cause be ourselves?

---

[47] A6.4.1500 (L 363).   [48] A6.4.1501–2 (L 364).   [49] A6.4.1503 (L 365).
[50] Ibid.

But if anyone says that the cause of phenomena is in the nature of our mind which contains the phenomena, he will affirm nothing false, but nevertheless he will not be telling the whole truth.[51]

Why isn't it the whole truth? First of all, one must account for the very existence of the mind that is having those perceptions. But there is something else that needs accounting for: the correspondences that exist between the phenomena in different minds. (How do we know that there are other minds? We shall return to this in a moment.) Leibniz argues that all these other minds are interrelated:

[S]ince all existents must be interrelated, there must be a cause of their interrelations; indeed, everything must necessarily express the same nature but in a different way. But the cause which leads all minds to have intercourse with each other or to express the same nature, and therefore to exist, is that cause which perfectly expresses the universe, namely God.[52]

Leibniz's claim here is that while the perceptions in our minds (and in all other minds) derive from the depths of our own existence, it is God who is the ultimate cause of our existence, the existence of all of the other minds, and of the existence of all the perceptions in all the minds and their coordination. (This, in essence, is the hypothesis of concomitance, or pre-established harmony, as it later came to be called.) But this is not to say that bodies have been eliminated. The penultimate paragraph of the essay (which we discussed above in Chapters 3 and 4) reads as follows:

Concerning bodies I can demonstrate that not merely light, heat, color and similar qualities are apparent but also motion, figure and extension. And if anything is real, it is solely the force of acting and suffering, and hence that the substance of a body consists in this (as if in matter and form).[53]

When we discussed this passage in earlier chapters, it was for the analysis of body in terms of force, matter, and form that it offered. But in this context we can appreciate another facet of this passage. Leibniz very carefully remarks that *if* anything is real in body, it is just the force of acting and suffering. *If* there really are bodies on the other side of our sensations, Leibniz argues, then they *must* be thus and so. But we can't know for certain that anything *is* real, as he noted earlier in the essay. And if they are

[51] Ibid.   [52] Ibid.   [53] A6.4.1504 (L 365).

not real, then bodies are just the phenomena of minds: *real* phenomena, *coherent* phenomena, phenomena that allow for the prediction of the future and the regulation of life. But phenomena nonetheless.

The essay is noteworthy for the care with which Leibniz works out the position. But it is also noteworthy for the discussion of other minds, how we know that they exist, and what they are, one of the very few places where he addresses this question. The discussion is not altogether easy to follow. Its main emphasis is on establishing the existence of the minds in other human beings. Leibniz begins by making the following remarks:

> And certainly there is nothing to prevent innumerable other minds from existing as well as ours, although not all possible minds exist. This I demonstrate from the fact that all existing things have interconnections with one another [*inter se habent commercium*].[54]

He goes on from here to give a rather obscure argument for why all existing things must be interrelated.[55] (The claim is very close to the famous mirroring thesis that Leibniz held for much of his career, the thesis that every individual mirrors all aspects of the possible world in which it exists, including other individuals, from its own point of view.) Leibniz then continues: "Now, if some possible minds exist, the question is: Why not all?" Taken more or less literally, as the expression of the presumption that all possible minds exist, this would seem to be inconsistent with what he wrote a few lines earlier, that not all possible minds can exist. But if we interpret this second statement as restricted to possible minds that do have interconnections with ours, or at least are capable of such interconnections, then there is no contradiction at all: what Leibniz is suggesting is that all minds *capable of such interconnection* exist.

What Leibniz has in mind, first and foremost, is other *human* minds. After the brief remarks about God as a cause of the interconnection between minds quoted above, Leibniz writes:

> Hence it is at once clear that there exist many minds besides ours, and, since it is easy to think that men who converse with us can have exactly the same reason to doubt our existence as we have to doubt theirs; and since no reason operates more strongly for us than for them, they will also exist and have minds. Thus both

---

[54] A6.4.1503 (L 365).
[55] For an interesting attempt to make sense of these very condensed arguments and how they establish the existence of other minds, see Westphal (2001).

sacred and profane history, and indeed whatever pertains to the status of minds, that is [*seu*] rational substances, may be considered confirmed.[56]

But even if human minds are the focus of his attention, there is a curious sentence that Leibniz sticks early on in the argument. Here is the passage, preceded by the sentences I quoted earlier that give it some context:

And certainly there is nothing to prevent innumerable other minds from existing as well as ours, although not all possible minds exist. This I demonstrate from the fact that all existing things have interconnections with one another. However, one can conceive of minds of a nature other than ours [*Possunt autem intelligi Mentes alterius naturae quam nostra*], having [no] interconnections with this mind of ours.[57]

The "no" in brackets is an editorial insertion, filling in what the Akademie editors seem to construe as a mistaken omission of the negation on Leibniz's part.[58] And in the context of the argument, it makes a certain amount of sense. One can read the passage as asserting that Leibniz is giving an example of the sort of possible minds whose existence he wants to deny, that is, those that are not properly interconnected with ours. But there is nothing grammatically or philosophically wrong with the passage as it stands, without the editorially added negation. Construed as it is without the editorial "correction," what Leibniz is saying is that there *are* other possible minds, different in nature from our own, but which nevertheless bear the appropriate interconnection with our own. These might well be the forms of the corporeal substances that make up the bodies of everyday experience, should they really exist, as Leibniz himself remarks in the paragraph following, as quoted above, though they might also be spirits of another kind, such as angelic minds.

If we read Leibniz in this way, as acknowledging in this context minds "of a nature other than ours," then this would seem to imply a somewhat different kind of phenomenalism. What it means for minds, ours and others', human and "of another nature than ours," to "have interconnections with one another" is for them to "express the same nature but in a different way." That is to say, each must experience, each in its own way, the same world of bodies. Though Leibniz doesn't explicitly draw this conclusion,

<hr/>

[56] A6.4.1503 (L 365).   [57] Ibid.

[58] Originally Leibniz wrote: "one can conceive of minds having nothing in common with ours . . ." and replaced it with "one can conceive of minds of a nature other than ours. . . ." But this doesn't bear on the question of the appropriateness of adding the "no" in the clause following.

this, in turn, suggests that bodies are now to be construed as the coherent perceptions of a multitude of minds, both rational minds like our own, and minds "of a nature other than ours," the souls attached to corporeal substances that are not human, like us. As I have argued in earlier chapters, in 1678/9, Leibniz came to realize the importance of substantial forms in bodies of all sorts as part of the foundations of his conception of the physical world. And with that, it seems, came the possibility of an expanded kind of phenomenalism as an alternative to that conception of the physical world, an idea of what the world would be like if, as a matter of fact, there were no bodies on the other side of our sensory perceptions. On this view, which we might call *extended-mind phenomenalism,* bodies are conceived in terms of the regular perceptions of minds taken in the broadest sense, the souls of corporeal substances, and not just the rational minds of other creatures like us.

Again, I don't want to suggest that Leibniz's position is any better worked out than it is: he has not worked out the details in any systematic way. Nor do I want to suggest that Leibniz is fully committed to such a position. Indeed, there is even less reason to think that he is committed to an extended-mind phenomenalism than to think that he is committed to a human-mind phenomenalism. Important as it is, the "De modo . . ." is the only text I know of from the middle years where there is even a suggestion of the position, and I wouldn't want to say that there is anything more than a bare suggestion of it in this text. But given Leibniz's commitment to minds or souls spread throughout nature as the forms of corporeal substances, after the introduction of the corporeal substance metaphysics in the late 1670s extended-mind phenomenalism would be an attractive position for him to explore in response to the kinds of skeptical worries that had let him to consider human-mind phenomenalism in the mid-1670s.

Metaphysical Phenomenalisms

The phenomenalisms we have been examining—both human-mind and extended-mind—are varieties of veil-of-perception phenomenalism. In this way the push for phenomenalism is mainly epistemological, the impossibility of our knowing for sure that there are bodies on the other side of our perceptions. But in the decade of the 1680s, the grounds of Leibniz's phenomenalism broaden as he considers other more metaphysical reasons for calling the existence of the external world into question. Once formulated, the idea that there may not be anything to bodies over and above our perceptions came to be regarded as a player in a number of other games.

There is one passage, dated by the Akademie editors at 1683–85, where Leibniz offers the following argument:

> It seems to me that all bodies are only modes, for there is no argument by which it can be shown that they act and are acted upon; they are nothing but our sensations. Therefore body is nothing but the object of sensation; the cause of actions which we attribute to bodies without reason is God. All actions belong to God, except ours, that is, except those of our minds. Therefore the reality of bodies is no different from the reality of dreams, except for the fact that they are constant and depend on certain rules; moreover these rules derive from the will of God, that is, from understanding the best. Therefore the reason why Descartes found a difficulty in the union of the mind and the body is because he considered bodies as substances; I consider them as modes of mind, and the reason why different minds sense things in the same way is because they all communicate with the same Entity, namely God. . . .[59]

The argument here seems to be that since bodies are capable of neither acting nor being acted upon, they cannot be real. And if they are not real, then, he reasons, they must be modes of mind. It isn't at all clear why Leibniz thinks that bodies cannot act or be acted upon; perhaps Leibniz is dealing here with Cartesian bodies. But the position to which he turns upon judging that bodies are not real things (substances) is the position that he developed in reaction to skeptical doubts about the real existence of body: the reality of bodies is grounded in the coherence of the sensations in our minds. (Note here that we are talking about *our minds* and their *sensations*.) And as in a number of other texts, the coherence of those sensations is grounded in God.

This is, admittedly, something of an eccentric text. I don't know of another such text in the corpus that argues from the causal inertness of bodies to their status as phenomena; in that way, this may have been a failed philosophical experiment. But Leibniz uses a similar strategy in a number of other texts, arguing from metaphysical problems with the notion of body to a kind of phenomenalism.

[59] A6.4.1467.

Consider, for example, the following, from a piece that Leibniz entitled "Calculus ratiocinator" (1679?):

The whole, if it is assumed to be body or matter, is nothing other than all of its parts; but this is absurd, since there aren't any smallest parts. Therefore there really exist only minds and their perceptions. Bodies are coherent appearances. A mind has each and every appearance of the world, and from an appearance there only follows another appearance. . . .[60]

There is a similar argument in a piece that Leibniz entitled "Corpus non est substantia" from 1689/90:

A body is not a substance but a mode of an entity or a coherent appearance. . . . By 'body,' however, I do not mean what the scholastics compose out of matter and a certain intelligible form, but what the Democriteans elsewhere call bulk [*molis*]. This, I say, is not a substance. For I shall demonstrate that if we consider bulk as a substance, we will fall into contradiction as a result of the labyrinth of the continuum. In this context we must above all consider: first, that there cannot be atoms, since they conflict with divine wisdom; and second, that bodies are really divided into infinite parts, but not into points. Consequently, there is no way one can designate one body, rather, any portion of matter whatever is an accidental entity, and, indeed, is in perpetual flux. . . . Now this is the nature of bodies, for if God himself wished to create corporeal substances of the kind people imagine, he would have done nothing, nor could even he perceive himself to have done anything, since in the last analysis nothing but appearances are perceived. So coherence is the sign of truth, but it's cause is the will of God. . . .[61]

It is important here that the corporeal substances in question are Cartesian or Democritean corporeal substances, "corporeal substances of the kind people imagine," "what the Democriteans . . . call bulk," and *not* form and matter composites, i.e. Leibnizian corporeal substances. What is Leibniz's argument here? Take a body. It is divisible into parts. Now, a given body, a whole, can be nothing but the sum of its parts. But this cannot be, since there is no smallest part of a body. That is given any part of the original body, it is itself a body, and thus made up out of the sum of *its* parts. Unless

---

[60] A6.4.279.

[61] A6.4.1637 (RA 259–61). Both Adams (1994), 236 and Arthur date this from the late 1670s. That dating is important to their case that Leibniz gave up his so-called phenomenalism by 1679, when he adopted substantial forms. But the Akademie edition dating is based on a watermark, in addition to internal arguments, and seems more secure to me.

there is a minimal part, Leibniz is assuming, we can never constitute the body as the sum of its ultimate parts. This, in essence, is the problem of the composition of the continuum. The argument, then, is that the very notion of an extended body, a body understood as extended bulk alone, is itself incoherent, and so there cannot be such things *in rerum natura*. And so, Leibniz argues, what we take to be mind-independent external bodies understood in that way must just be "coherent appearances." Again, this kind of phenomenalism, originally introduced in 1675/6 in reaction to skeptical doubts about the reality of the external world, is the position to which Leibniz turns as an alternative to the reality of body when confronted with the metaphysical problem of the composition of the continuum.

Note here, particularly in the second and chronologically later passage, that Leibniz is quite careful to clarify that the argument in question applies not to body understood as the unity of matter and form, that is to corporeal substances, but to matter considered as "bulk," that is to say, matter considered without forms. And so, for example, it would apply to the Cartesian conception of body as pure extension. As I argued earlier in Chapter 2, Leibniz's revival of substantial forms in the physical world is intended to address the problem of the composition of the continuum: with the revival of substantial forms and the introduction of corporeal substances, we have a way of understanding how bodies can be made up of smaller parts that are genuine unities, while, at the same time, bodies remain divisible to infinity. But, Leibniz argues, if there *weren't* such substantial forms in matter, then bodies *would* just be phenomenal in the sense that we have been exploring, "coherent appearances" in some sense that Leibniz leaves imprecise.

This argument is given in an interesting fragment that the Akademie editors date to 1682/3:

(1) I suppose that what has no greater unity than the logs in a bundle of firewood or log pile, or bricks placed one on top of the other, is not properly one entity, but rather entities, although one name can be supposed for them all. And this is true whether they are close together or far apart, and likewise whether those bricks or logs in the pile are arranged together in an orderly way or not, for this does not give them greater unity. . . .

(2) I also suppose that nothing is intelligible in a body other than extension. . . .

(3) Finally, I suppose that every body is actually divided into several parts, which are also bodies.

From this it follows . . . that either bodies are mere phenomena, and not real entities, or there is something other than extension in bodies.[62]

This is also an especially important theme in the correspondence with Arnauld. At one point Arnauld makes the following remark:

I see no drawback to believing that in the whole of corporeal nature there are only 'machines' and 'aggregates' of substances, because of none of these parts can one say, accurately speaking, that it is a single substance. That indicates only what it is very proper to note, as did St. Augustine, that thinking or spiritual substance is in that respect much more excellent than extended or corporeal substance, that only the spiritual has a true unity and a true self, which the corporeal does not have. . . . [I]t may be of the essence of matter not to have true unity, as you admit of all those bodies which are not joined to a soul or substantial form.[63]

This is Leibniz's response:

You object, Sir, that it may be of the essence of body to be devoid of true unity; but it will then be of the essence of body to be a phenomenon, lacking all reality as would a coherent dream, for phenomena themselves like the rainbow or a heap of stones would be wholly imaginary if they were not composed of entities possessing true unity.[64]

Or, as he expressed himself somewhat more bluntly in an earlier letter: "if there are no corporeal substances such as I can accept, it follows that bodies will be no more than true phenomena like the rainbow. . . ."[65]

---

[62] A6.4.1464 (RA 257–9). RA dates this to 1678/9, but for my purposes the exact dating is not crucial.

[63] Arnauld to Leibniz, 4 March 1687, G II 87.   [64] Leibniz to Arnauld, 30 April 1687, G II 97.

[65] Leibniz to Arnauld, 28 November/8 December 1686, G II 77. Phenomenalism also appears as an alternative to the existence of corporeal substances in other letters; see G II 58, 96, 118. See also A6.4.555.

These passages raise the question as to how Leibniz is thinking of the rainbow. In the correspondence with Arnauld and many other texts, Leibniz generally considers the rainbow as a kind of "real phenomenon," and groups it with dreams and parhelia. Leibniz gives some explanation of the way he is thinking about the rainbow in this connection in a long piece from 1684/6 which the Akademie editors have entitled 'De mundo praesenti.' Here is what he writes:

Every Being is either real or imaginary. A real Being is outside the operation of the mind, such as the sun, about which we judge from the agreement of several perceptions. An imaginary Being is one that is perceived to be like a real Being, but only through one mode of perception, such as a rainbow, a parhelion, a dream, but isn't perceived through other modes nor does it hold up under examination, which it would have to do, if it were a real Being. [A6.4.1506 (RA 283, translated differently)]

In some of the letters and in earlier drafts of the *Discours*, Leibniz hesitates about the existence of corporeal substances and thus about the reality of the world of bodies, since if there are no corporeal substances in the world, there cannot really be bodies. For example, the first draft of 'Discours' § 34 opens as follows:

I do not attempt to determine if bodies are substances in metaphysical rigor or if they are only *true* phenomena like the rainbow and, consequently, if there are true substances, souls, or substantial forms which are not intelligent.[66]

In the final text, he does make that determination, and sets aside the phenomenalist alternative for a more realistic conception of body: "Assuming that the bodies that make up an *unum per se*, as does man, are substances. . . ." In a draft of a letter that Leibniz was sending to Arnauld, he similarly wrote:

The other difficulty is incomparably greater, concerning substantial forms and the souls of bodies; and I confess that I am not satisfied about it. In the first place one would have to be sure that bodies are substances and not merely true phenomena like the rainbow.[67]

In *Leibniz and Arnauld*, Robert Sleigh called attention to these and other passages in these texts where Leibniz seems to vacillate between a realistic view of the world as corporeal substances, and a view of the world of

---

The claim here is that imaginary beings are perceptible only through one sense modality. This can't be quite right: dreams, for example, might involve sights, sounds, kinesthetic feelings, all mixed together. Better, perhaps, is Leibniz's claim that imaginary phenomena don't "hold up under examination." By this he presumably means that when we go up in a balloon to find the rainbow, it disappears, or when the next morning, we try to continue a conversation we had with someone in a dream, they give us odd looks. In a certain important sense, rainbows and other imaginary beings aren't *really* there.

But Leibniz isn't always consistent about this. In a long essay that Leibniz entitled "Notiones generales" (1683/5), he writes:

The rainbow is an aggregate of drops which jointly produce certain colors that are apparent to us. . . . Hence the rainbow is of diminished reality under two headings, both because it is a Being by aggregation of drops, and because the qualities by which it is known are apparent or at least of that kind of real ones that are relative to our senses. [A 6.4.555; translated in Adams (1994), 247]

In this same text he also reclassifies the parhelion as an entity by aggregation, putting both of them on the side of "real beings" as opposed to "apparent beings." In this text, at least, the prime example of apparent beings are dreams

not so much because their cause is in us or because nothing external corresponds to them . . . than because what we dream is not congruent with other phenomena, nor are they even coherent among themselves. (A6.4.555)

To put it another way, what makes dreams apparent beings is the fact that they don't "hold up under examination," to use the phrase Leibniz uses in the passage quoted earlier.

[66] A6.4.1583 (AG 65).   [67] G II 71.

bodies as being, in some sense phenomenal.[68] He interprets this as an attempt to "pique Arnauld's interest in the possibility that there are no corporeal substances, so that he and Arnauld might engage in a serious discussion of alternative theories, including, one would conjecture, the spiritual theory."[69] But I don't think that Leibniz was actively promoting any kind of phenomenalism in this context. Phenomenalism was, as it were, the stick that lies behind the carrot: if you don't accept the existence of substantial forms and the corporeal substance view that I am advocating, Leibniz says, this is what you are stuck with. If there are no substantial forms to define genuine individuals in the world of extended bodies, then the problems of the composition of the continuum will drive us to this kind of phenomenalism.

This is important and worth re-emphasizing. Phenomenalism of this kind, the world of bodies considered as a kind of coherent dream, seems to be a general alternative to any reason for doubting the existence of an external world of mind-independent bodies. But it is almost always *just* an alternative, and is rarely asserted.[70] While we might not know for certain about the external world of bodies, while our senses might not assure us of its real existence, while we cannot be certain that the metaphysical prerequisites for its real existence are met, Leibniz almost never claims to know for certain that it *doesn't* exist, and almost always assumes that it *does*. Although the world of bodies wouldn't have genuine existence if there were no corporeal substances, Leibniz generally takes this as an argument for why there have to be such entities in the world.

Aggregates, Corporeal Substances, and Inanimate Bodies

So far we have been talking about phenomenalism—human-mind and extended-mind—as an alternative to a real world of corporeal substances

---

[68] See Sleigh (1990), 103–6.

[69] Ibid. 103. As Sleigh understands it, the spiritual theory, which he distinguishes from the monadology, is the view that "there are no substances (in concreto) except spirits," and is linked with a phenomenalistic account of bodies. (See ibid., 98.) It is, as I understand it, very similar to what I called human-mind phenomenalism. For an argument against Sleigh's position, see Phemister (2001).

[70] Robert Adams makes a similar suggestion: "his earlier, more austere phenomenalism is sometimes visible behind the complex theory of his later years, as a rejected but respected alternative, or even as a fall-back position kept in reserve" [Adams (1994), 240; cf. 259].

existing outside the mind. If there are no real bodies on the other side of our sensory experiences, then bodies must be understood in terms of the coherent perceptions of mental substances. But there is another, very different kind of phenomenalism in Leibniz's thought in the middle years. This variety of phenomenalism isn't an alternative to the existence of an external world of mind-independent bodies; in fact it *presupposes* the existence of such a world. In calling bodies (or their properties) phenomenal in this somewhat different and weaker sense, Leibniz is eager simply to emphasize the contribution that the mind makes to the constitution of bodies and their properties. This kind of phenomenalism comes in two principal varieties, which I shall call *aggregate phenomenalism* and *primary-quality phenomenalism*.

As we discussed at length in earlier chapters, the basic constituents of Leibniz's world in the period are corporeal substances, unities of matter and form, genuine individuals from a metaphysical point of view. Each of these corporeal substances can be regarded as a living thing, a soul that unites the parts of a body and makes it into one. But, of course, most of the bodies in our everyday experience are inanimate. Such bodies are aggregates of corporeal substances. Such aggregates can be considered as unities of a sort too, but one *per accidens* rather than one *per se*. Leibniz summarizes the view in the following passage from the 'De mundo praesenti,' an essay that the Akademie editors date to 1683/6:

Every real Being is either one *per se* or one *per accidens*. A Being one *per se*, such as a man, and a Being one *per accidens* such as a pile of wood or a machine, which is only one through aggregation, nor is there any real union in it except for the connection or contact or even the coming together in the same [pile] or at least the conscious bringing them together by a mind collecting them into one. But in a Being one *per se* a certain real union is required consisting not in the situation or motion of parts, as in a chain, a house, or a boat, but in a certain unique individual principle and subject of attributes and operations, which in us is called a soul and in every body is called a substantial form, as long as it is one in itself.[71]

Leibniz's view here is that what makes something one *per accidens* a unity is a result of the activity of the mind, "the conscious bringing them together

[71] A6.4.1506 (RA 283, but translated differently).

by a mind collecting them into one." Leibniz is even more explicit about this in a passage he wrote to Arnauld:

I agree that there are degrees of accidental unity, that an ordered society has more unity than a confused mob, and that an organized body, or rather a machine, has more unity than a society, that is to say, it is more appropriate to conceive them as a single thing, because there are more relations among the constituents. But in the end, all these unities become realized [reçoivent leur accomplissement] only by thoughts and appearances; like colors and other phenomena, which, nevertheless, are called real. . . . We can therefore say of these composites and similar things what Democritus said so well of them, namely, they depend for their being on opinion or custom. And Plato held the same opinion about everything which is purely material. Our mind notices or conceives some true substances which have certain modes; these modes involve relations to other substances, so the mind takes the occasion to join them together in thought and to make one name account for all these things together. This is useful for reasoning, but we must not allow ourselves to be misled into making substances or true beings of them; this is suitable only for those who stop at appearances, or for those who make realities out of all abstractions of the mind, and who conceive number, time, place, motion, shape, as so many separate beings. Instead I hold that philosophy cannot be better reestablished and reduced to something precise, than by recognizing only substances or complete beings endowed with a true unity, together with the different states that succeed one another; everything else is only phenomena, abstractions, or relations.[72]

Here Leibniz speaks of "appearances" or "phenomena" to characterize the situation: the unities in question are one because the mind *makes* them one by considering them together as constituting a single thing.[73] This comes out clearly in other passages he wrote to Arnauld:

There is as much difference between a substance and such an entity [i.e. an aggregate] as there is between a man and a community, such as a people, army, society or college, which are moral entities, where something imaginary exists, dependent upon the fabrication of our minds.[74]

I have already said in another letter that the composite of the Grand Duke's and the Grand Mogul's diamonds can be called a pair of diamonds, but it is merely

---

[72] Leibniz to Arnauld, 30 April 1687, G II 100–1 (AG 88f). Cf. also "Mira de natura substantiae corporeae" (1683): "A pile or entity by aggregation such as a heap of stones should not be called a corporeal substance, but only a phenomenon" [A6.4.1466 (RA 265)].

[73] For accounts of the way in which the mind aggregates individual things into complex individuals, see, e.g., Hartz (1992) and Lodge (2001a), 476ff.

[74] Leibniz to Arnauld, 28 November/8 December 1686, G II 76.

an entity of reason, and even if one of them is brought close to the other, it will be an entity of the imagination or perception, that is to say a phenomenon; for contiguity, common movement, concurrence towards one and the same end make no difference to substantial unity.[75]

Note here that Leibniz is somewhat obscure about the sense in which these entities are phenomenal. Most of the passages suggest that what makes aggregates of corporeal substances (which is to say, inanimate bodies) phenomenal is the fact that it is an act of mind that unites them and makes them one.[76] This last passage suggests something a bit different, in the case of the diamonds of the Grand Duke and the Grand Mogul. When they are separate from one another, in different treasuries in different countries, and united by an act of thought, then the single thing constructed from the two constitutes is an "entity of reason." But when they are put in physical proximity to one another, then it is the "imagination or perception" that unites them, and the unity *per accidens* in question constitutes a phenomenon. Despite the small differences among the passages, the underlying picture is clear enough: aggregates, inanimate bodies, unities *per accidens* are not phenomenal in the way in which bodies are phenomenal on the view of human-mind or extended-mind phenomenalism, which are simply the regularities in the experience of perceiving entities, be they human minds or minds in a broader sense. Aggregates have their being by virtue of containing corporeal substances that are genuinely real, and exist independently of our perceiving them. They are phenomenal in a somewhat more extended sense insofar as the mind participates in their being considered unified. In a certain important sense they are only unities in relation to us. Unlike unities *per se*, which are one in the fullest sense, aggregates are unified only with respect to the mind that conceives them as unified. Aggregates depend for their real existence on the things of which they

---

[75] Leibniz to Arnauld, 30 April 1687, G II 96.

[76] For a very detailed account of the criteria by which aggregates are constituted, see Hartz (1992). Though Hartz's title indicates that the focus is to be Leibniz's phenomenalism, the real goal is to define the conditions that must be satisfied for there to be a body (aggregate) at a given time, or a body (aggregate) that endures over time; see ibid., 513. Though the analysis is very impressive, Hartz assumes that Leibniz's doctrine is unified and coherent throughout his career. Though Hartz recognizes corporeal substances, he treats them on a par with monads, and generally assumes that the conditions for aggregates of corporeal substances are the same as the conditions for aggregates of monads. While Hartz (2007) also deals extensively with aggregates, here the question is different than the ones taken up in Hartz (1992): the focus is now on the question of realism and idealism, which we shall address below in Ch. 9.

are aggregated: were there no corporeal substances, there would be no aggregates; were there no animate bodies, there would be no inanimate bodies. But it is by virtue of the mind that such entities become entities, even if they are only entities *per accidens*.[77] This is what might be called aggregate phenomenalism.

But there is yet another way in which Leibniz considers bodies to be phenomenal in the period. I can be very brief here, since this question was, in essence, already discussed above in Chapter 4. There we discussed Leibniz's claims in a number of places that the so-called primary qualities, the modes of extension, are, in their way, dependent on the imagination, just as secondary qualities are. And so, once again, the passage from

---

[77] There is some confusion in the literature about a parallel issue that arises in the interpretation of Leibniz's conception of bodies in the monadological metaphysics. A number of commentators raise the question as to how a body can both be a (well-founded) phenomenon, and at the same time be identified with an aggregate of monads. See Adams (1983); Adams (1994), 218–19; McGuire (1985); Rutherford (1990); Jolley (1986); Wilson (1989), 190ff; Lodge (2001a); Hartz (2007), chs. 6–7; Phemister (2005), ch. 7. There is a parallel question that can be raised in the context of the view of inanimate bodies as aggregates of corporeal substances, which, Leibniz says, are both phenomenal and aggregates. (In the literature only Arthur (1998a) seems to focus on that specifically, though there is also some discussion of it in Phemister (2005).) Adams gives an elaborate answer, which gave rise to much discussion in the literature. On Adams's view, phenomena are intentional objects, the representational content of our perceptions, Cartesian objective realities rather than formal realities (220). "... corporeal phenomena are perceptions considered with regard to their objective reality or representational content, or insofar as they *express* some nature, form or essence" (221). In this respect, corporeal phenomena must be *in* the mind: "Leibniz does not believe that phenomena have any being except *in* the existence or occurrence of qualities or modifications of perceiving substances" (223). But, Adams argues, *aggregates* can be in the mind, even if the elements aggregated are not: "The apparent conflict between the thesis that bodies are phenomena and the thesis that they are aggregates of substances springs from the assumption that an aggregate of Fs must have the same ontological status as the Fs. This is at best a controversial assumption" (244). "Since Leibniz adhered to the Scholastic maxim that 'being' and 'one' are equivalent ..., he inferred that aggregates that have their unity only in the mind also have their being in the mind" (245–6). "Leibniz's claim is that aggregates have their unity, and therefore their being, only in the mind, and that this is true even of aggregates of real things" (246). I find myself in most agreement with a very sensible response from Paul Hoffman (Hoffman (1996)). Hoffman rejects the view that "Leibniz's theory is phenomenalistic in the full-blown sense that it identifies aggregates with merely intentional objects or with the objective reality of ideas. I do not even think it follows that his theory is phenomenalistic in a weaker sense of maintaining that the being of aggregates consists entirely in their being perceived as unified" (118). He notes that the being of bodies on this monadological view is dependent on the being of the constituent monads, but that Leibniz's point is simply that the unity of the body comes from the mind. If one substitutes "corporeal substance" here for "monad," then this is very close to my own reading of what is going on in the earlier period. In general, though, the literature doesn't distinguish carefully enough between the kind of phenomalism at issue in connection with human-/extended-mind phenomenalism and the very different kind at issue in connection with aggregate- and primary-quality phenomenalism.

"De modo..." that we have already seen a number of times. Leibniz writes:

Concerning bodies I can demonstrate that not merely light, heat, color and similar qualities are apparent but also motion, figure and extension. And if anything is real, it is solely the force of acting and suffering, and hence that the substance of a body consists in this (as if in matter and form).[78]

And, again, in 'Discours de métaphysique' § 12 Leibniz writes:

That the Notions Involved in Extension Contain Something Imaginary and Cannot Constitute the Substance of Body. . . . It is even possible to demonstrate that the notions of size, shape, and motion are not as distinct as is imagined and that they contain something imaginary and relative to our perception, as do (though to a greater extent) color, heat, and other similar qualities, qualities about which one can doubt whether they are truly found in the nature of things outside ourselves.[79]

In these striking passages, and many others like them, Leibniz claims that the mechanist's basic notions of extension, shape, motion, and the like are not so basic as they thought, and that there is something imaginary in them. Though he rarely uses the word 'phenomenal' in this context, this thesis would seem to belong in the family of Leibnizian phenomenalisms, positions that emphasize the mind-dependence of body and certain properties of body. Insofar as Leibniz is concerned here with what some mechanists, such as Locke have called the primary qualities, I shall call this view 'primary-quality phenomenalism.' On this view, the claim is that the primary qualities of body—shape, size, motion—contain "something imaginary and relative to our perception," and in this respect, are not that different from the so-called secondary qualities, such as color.[80]

---

[78] A6.4.1504 (L 365). Cf. Leibniz's remark to Tschirnhaus in a letter from June 1682: "neither thought nor extension are notions that are primitive or perfectly understood" (A2.1².831).

[79] 'Discours de métaphysique' § 12. There are many other passages in which Leibniz claims that our ideas of extension contain something imaginary. See, e.g., A6.4.1622 (RA 315); A6.4.1465 (RA 263); A6.4.1613–14 (RA 297–9); Leibniz (1997), 234.

[80] While Levey (2005) traces this thesis back to the "Placidius Philalethi" of 1676 and related writings, it doesn't get fully articulated until the early 1680s. The earliest explicit statements of primary-quality phenomenalism I know are 'Materiam et motum esse phaenomena tantum' (1682/3) [A6.4.1463 (RA 257)] and "Mira de natura substantiae corporeae" (1683) [A6.4.1465 (RA 263)]. It is interesting that Leibniz's thesis here—that there is no radical distinction between primary and secondary qualities—is close to one of the most radical theses in Foucher (1675).

As discussed above, there are two somewhat different motivations that underlie primary-quality phenomenalism. The first is suggested by the passage quoted from "De modo..." Here Leibniz's point seems to be that, in themselves, bodies, or, more properly, the corporeal substances that are the elements of which inanimate bodies are aggregated, are by their nature not extension, but force, active and passive. As I argued above in Chapter 4, Leibniz holds that the extension of body is derived from the passive force of corporeal substances. And secondly, as I also argued above, Leibniz argues that because they are made up of an infinity of corporeal substances, bugs in bugs to infinity, they have no definite shape of the sort that is treated in geometry; they are, as Sam Levey has suggested, fractals, infinitely complex shapes that vary from moment to moment.[81] Thus Leibniz writes in the "Specimen inventorum" of 1688(?):

> Indeed, even though this may seem paradoxical, it must be realized that the notion of extension is not as transparent as is commonly believed. For from the fact that no body is so very small that it is not actually divided into parts excited by different motions, it follows that no determinate shape can be assigned to any body, nor is a precisely straight line, or circle, or any other assignable shape of any body found in the nature of things, although certain rules are observed by nature even in its deviation from an infinite series. Thus shape involves something imaginary, and no other sword can sever the knots we tie for ourselves by misunderstanding the composition of the continuum.[82]

Insofar as we see bodies as having geometrical shapes, we are imposing something from our imagination onto them, as it were. In themselves, bodies are altogether different.

It is clear here that in advancing the thesis that extension and its modes are phenomenal, Leibniz doesn't mean to deny completely the reality of extra-mental bodies. Rather, he wants to call attention to what he thinks the bodies of everyday experience *really* are—infinite aggregates of corporeal substances which, in turn, are to be understood in terms of forces, active and passive—in contrast to what the Cartesians claim them to be, the extended objects of geometry made real. And Leibniz wants to underscore the role that the mind plays in constituting the primary qualities of the mechanist's bodies. Bodies still exist in the world, independent of us and any other perceiver. It is just that their geometrical properties

---

[81] See Levey (2005), 76–7.   [82] A6.4.1622 (RA 315).

are not intrinsic, but imposed by the minds that perceive them. In this way primary-quality phenomenalism is phenomenalistic in the somewhat weaker way in which aggregate phenomenalism is phenomenalistic.

While they differ in many ways, aggregate phenomenalism and primary-quality phenomenalism have a number of features in common, features that differentiate them from the kind of human-mind or extended-mind phenomenalism that we discussed earlier in the chapter. In human-mind or extended-mind phenomenalism, the motivation is doubt—doubt grounded either in epistemological or in metaphysical considerations—about the real existence of an external world of mind-independent bodies. Furthermore, the resolution of the problems rests on the view that bodies are to be understood, broadly speaking, in terms of the regularity of experience. But it is important that Leibniz rarely, if ever, actually asserts that all there is to body is coherent experience. This kind of phenomenalism is (almost) always just the position that we are forced to, should an external world of bodies fail to exist. However, the situation is quite different with respect to aggregate phenomenalism and primary-quality phenomenalism. Here the thesis is *not* that bodies are just in minds, human or understood in an extended sense to encompass minds of a broader sort. Rather, the point of these phenomenalisms is to make salient the contribution that mind makes to the constitution of bodies. But mind only contributes the unity and geometrical properties to the aggregate of corporeal substances that constitutes a body. Far from eliminating a mind-independent external world of bodies, this second and weaker variety of phenomenalism *presupposes* an external world of corporeal substances; without such a world there aren't any aggregates to which we can attribute either unity or extension and its modes. And finally, unlike the stronger human-mind and extended-mind phenomenalisms, Leibniz clearly and unambiguously *asserts* the truth of aggregate phenomenalism and primary-quality phenomenalism: inanimate bodies really are phenomenal in the sense that the mind contributes unity, extension and its modes onto the physical world.

Conclusion

In this chapter we have explored some of the phenomenalistic strains in Leibniz's thought mostly in the 1670s and 1680s. While these positions are suggestive of the monadological metaphysics that Leibniz will later adopt, none of them is exactly what Leibniz will come to adopt in later years when he interprets the world of bodies in terms of the infinity of mind-like monads. The view closest to the monadology among the views that we have been examining is what I called extended-mind phenomenalism, the view that bodies are to be understood in terms of the coherent perceptions of an infinity of minds, including human minds as well as others "of a nature different than ours." But even here it is important to note the significant differences. In particular, the main motivation for the view, as presented in "De modo . . .," is the epistemological worry about whether we can infer the real existence of an external world of bodies on the basis of our sensory experiences. As we shall later see, Leibniz's motivations for the monadology are rather different. Furthermore, we must remember that the evidence for attributing extended-mind phenomenalism to Leibniz is slim at best, even as a position that he contemplated holding in this period, and there is no evidence at all that he actually adopted it. Human-mind phenomenalism is, in its way, not unlike certain versions of the monadological account of body, but insofar as it is limited to human minds, it is more like a version of Berkeleyan phenomenalism than it is like Leibniz's own later thought. And what I have called aggregate phenomenalism and primary-quality phenomenalism are rather different: both actually presuppose a world made up of corporeal substances that exist apart from mind.

There are indeed passages from this era, from the 1670s to the early 1690s, that are suggestive of the later monadology, long before Leibniz announces it unambiguously in some of his later writings. And it is not implausible to see in these earlier texts some ideas that will come to be important later. But we must be very careful. With the benefit of hindsight, knowing his later writings, *we* can see exactly where Leibniz was going. But Leibniz himself may not always have been able to do so. *We* can pick out the elements that may suggest or imply the monadology in his early work, interpret them in terms of his later view, and see them as especially prominent. But that isn't to say that *Leibniz* could have done so at the time, or that he could have connected the dots and made the inferences that we do or that he himself will later make. Had Leibniz's thought gone in a different direction (which it might well have done), we would probably ignore those prescient passages, and focus on others that reflect the path he actually took. Reading Leibniz teleologically, in terms of the positions we know he will eventually take, has caused some to misunderstand his earlier writings, and in focusing on the anticipations of his later views, we have missed the complexities, not to mention the somewhat different positions that he actually took in earlier periods in his thought. Just as we humans can't see what God can in our souls, how what we are now will lead naturally to our future state, there is no reason to believe that Leibniz could have seen what *we* can in his earlier writings, the doctrines that his earlier commitments eventually led him to accept.

But even though I resist attributing a monadological metaphysics to Leibniz at this moment, these phenomenalisms will have major roles to play in the constitution of the monadology in later years.

8

Enchanting the World: "After Many Corrections and Forward Steps in my Thinking..."

Let us return to the letter that Leibniz wrote to Remond in 1714, the letter discussed at the beginning of Chapter 1. There Leibniz recalls the path that he took to his mature philosophy. He begins with his discovery of the mechanical philosophy when, he claims, he was only 15. He then notes:

But when I looked for the ultimate reasons for mechanism, and even for the laws of motion, I was greatly surprised to see that they could not be found in mathematics but that I should have to return to metaphysics. This led me back to entelechies, and from the material to the formal, and at last brought me to understand after many corrections and forward steps in my thinking, that monads or simple substances are the only true substances and that material things are only phenomena, though well founded and well connected.[1]

In previous chapters we concentrated on the earlier steps in this process: how, in the late 1670s, Leibniz introduced corporeal substances, body and soul, the first step from the more purely material world of Leibniz's earlier thought to the introduction of forms into his understanding of the physical world. It is time, now, to take the next step and, finally, enter the world of monads.

Leibniz Astonishes de Volder

In mid-1698, Leibniz made contact with the Leiden physicist and mathematician Burcher de Volder. In 1674 de Volder had visited England,

---

[1] G III 606 (L 655).

where he met Newton and probably Boyle, and returned to Leiden with an enthusiasm for the new experimental philosophy. But even though he was impressed with English experimental philosophy, he remained a Cartesian in spirit.[2] At first, in July 1698 the mathematician Johann Bernoulli conveyed messages between the two, but by December, Leibniz was writing directly to the Dutch professor, though Bernoulli continued to transmit the letters. The correspondence was to last until 1706, and contains some of the most important statements of Leibniz's views on body and substance.[3]

The first issues that concern Leibniz and de Volder are in physics. Bernoulli reports to Leibniz ou de Volder's doubts concerning his, Leibniz's, views on collision, elasticity, and the proper conservation law in physics, issues growing out of the disputes concerning the "Brevis demonstratio" of 1686.[4] But at the end of the very first letter that Leibniz sent directly addressed to de Volder, he mentions his "Système nouveau" and some of the replies, as well as the newly published "De ipsa natura."[5] This introduces the topic of the nature of body and substance, a question that will occupy the two through the rest of their correspondence.

In reading the correspondence, we have to remember that in 1698 the public knowledge of Leibniz's philosophy was somewhat limited. In the last chapters we have been discussing Leibniz's private letters and papers from the late 1670s up to 1690 or so. This is where Leibniz developed the new view on body and the metaphysics of the material world that he came to in the late 1670s. But little of the new view was published. On the side of Leibniz's technical work in physics, there was the "Brevis demonstratio," published in the *Acta eruditorum* in 1686, where he offered a refutation of the Cartesian principle of the conservation of quantity of motion. This gave rise to a flurry of responses and counter-responses. Then, in 1689, Leibniz published a series of technical essays on cosmology and planetary theory, in response to Newton, most notably the "Tentamen de

---

[2] De Volder has been accused of being a crypto-Spinozist by recent commentators. For a discussion and rejection of this view, see Lodge (2005b).

[3] In my account of Leibniz's exchanges with de Volder I owe an enormous debt to Paul Lodge's writings and to the important translations of the letters that he has shared with me. His new edition and translation of the texts will, hopefully, soon replace the texts that we now have in GM III and G II. But for the moment, even though I have made use of Lodge's edition and quote from his translations, I shall give references to the older editions.

[4] Johann Bernoulli to Leibniz, 5 July 1698, GM III 505–6.

[5] Leibniz to de Volder, 17/27 December 1698, G II 162.

motuum caelestium causis," as I mentioned above in Chapter 4. In 1695 there was the "Specimen dynamicum," part I of which was published in the *Acta eruditorum*, containing brief sketches of some of Leibniz's ideas about the physical world. But the book outlined in the 'Conspectus libelli' of 1678/9 never seems to have gotten beyond a draft of the introduction. Leibniz certainly intended to publish his *Dynamica*, but that project never came to fruition. In what we might think of as the more philosophical side of Leibniz's thought, there was, if anything, even less available to the reader. The 'Discours de métaphysique' certainly shows signs of having been polished, presumably for publication. And we know that from early on Leibniz had the idea of publishing his correspondence with Arnauld, a project that he still had in mind as late as 1707.[6] But it is very interesting that none of these publication projects (nor, no doubt, other contemplated publications) was ever completed. In 1684 he had published the "Meditationes de cognitione, veritate et ideis" in the *Acta eruditorum*. But important as it was, this essay focused on logic, reasoning, and ideas, and said nothing at all about body and substance. It was a decade later, in 1694, before he published his next philosophical work, the essay "De primae philosophae emendatione, et de notione substantiae" in the *Acta eruditorum*, at best a short promissory note for a new conception of substance grounded in the notion of force. Leibniz's first extended philosophical essay in print was the "Système nouveau pour expliquer la nature des substances et leur communication entre elles," published in the *Journal des sçavans* in 1695. In 1698, at just about the time that Leibniz and de Volder were beginning their exchange, he published the "De ipsa natura" in the *Acta eruditorum*, as well as a reply to Bayle's objections to the "Système nouveau" in the *Histoire des ouvrages des savants*, under the title "Lettre de M. Leibnits à l'Auteur, contenant un Eclaircissement des difficultez que Monsieur Bayle a trouvées dans le système nouveau de l'Union de l'âme et du corps."

De Volder probably started with little idea of what exactly Leibniz's view of the world was, but very quickly he came to see in his correspondent something very close to the kind of corporeal substance view that we have been developing in earlier chapters of this book. As I remarked earlier, much of their discussion concerned physics, collision, and conservation of

---

[6] On Leibniz's later plans to publish the correspondence with Arnauld, see Leibniz to Foucher, 6/16 April 1695, G I 420; Leibniz to Basnage de Beauval, 3/13 January 1696, G IV 499 (AG 149), and Leibniz to Quesnel, 12 March 1707, in Leibniz and Arnauld (1952), 107.

motion and force, in which discussions Leibniz emphasized the importance of introducing forces over and above mere extension.[7] As in his earlier writings, Leibniz took this to imply that we must introduce souls, forms, or entelechies into nature in order to provide a source of activity. And also as in the earlier writings, Leibniz emphasized the importance of unity to the notion of substance.[8] De Volder was at least to some extent aware of Leibniz's claims and his position, though his Cartesian instincts led him in somewhat different directions. In his letter of 18 February 1699, for example, he told Leibniz that "I have read through what you say in the *Journal des sçavans*, the *Acta eruditorum*, and the *Histoire des ouvrages des savants* concerning the nature of substances, the communication between them, and their forces." And while he modestly told Leibniz that "I dare not persuade myself that I have understood what you mean," he went on to offer criticisms that show that he knew perfectly well what Leibniz was up to. He understands Leibniz to "deny that extension is a substance," and to hold that "in extension alone there is no real unity, but only an aggregate of many parts."[9] But for de Volder, the problem was the opposite:

on the contrary, it is more difficult to conceive of really distinct parts in extension than unity. For if there is indeed no empty space, as you submit, it will not be possible for one part, which anyone might imagine for themselves, to be conceived without the others. From this it seems to follow that there is no real distinction between them but that the distinction between parts that is imagined in these things consists not so much in a difference of substance as in a difference of modes.

De Volder also understood Leibniz's concerns about force:

You add that, besides extension, a certain force is required that is like the soul, and that you think that it does not fall under the imagination but is nonetheless clearly understood.

---

[7] See, e.g., Leibniz to de Volder, 24 March/3 April 1699, G II 169ff; Leibniz to de Volder, 1/11 September 1699, G II 194f, etc.

[8] See, e.g., Leibniz to de Volder, 1/11 September 1699, G II 193. Leibniz uses the word "monad" there to characterize the unities in question. However, as I shall argue later in this chapter, when Leibniz first introduces the term in the second half of the 1690s, it often means nothing more than what he earlier meant by unity. The example he uses in this text is that of a flock of animals, an army made up out of individual soldiers, a cheese made of worms, etc., the examples that he had earlier used in contrasting corporeal substances to aggregates of corporeal substances.

[9] On the debate between de Volder and Leibniz over extension and body, see Lodge (2001b).

As a Cartesian, though, de Volder had great problems understanding this notion of force:

For me it does not even fall under the intellect as long as I do not know the cause or foundation of force. When I talk about forces, I do not understand the cause of the forces. I am talking about nothing other than the effect. I would finally understand the forces themselves when I knew what they were, where they arose from, and how they produced an effect necessarily.[10]

And so it goes, with Leibniz advancing much the same view that we saw in the earlier texts, and de Volder countering with his own kind of Cartesianism.[11]

But then there was a rather radical shift in the discussion. It begins when de Volder proposed a definition of the notion of substance. De Volder wrote:

If I consider my concepts, I seem to find this difference among them: either the concept represents one thing to me, and I can remove nothing from the representation without the whole thing perishing, or it represents two things to me, one of which I can conceive separately, the other of which I cannot. If the first occurs, I say that the concept is the concept of a thing or substance, and I call the object corresponding to it a thing or substance. However, if the second occurs, I call those concepts the concepts of modes, and the objects of those concepts I call modes.[12]

This applies to the notion of extension as follows:

When I conceive of extension one thing is represented to me. I can indeed conceive of it as greater or less, but, whatever the magnitude, I conceive of extension of one kind, and I either conceive of the whole of it, as it were, or none of it. However, in figure and motion I also conceive of extension, which I can conceive without motion or figure, and I conceive of either a certain boundary or a translation of extension, which cannot be conceived without extension. They will therefore be modes.[13]

---

[10] G II 166.

[11] For a general account of Leibniz's correspondence with de Volder, see Lodge (2004). See also Antognazza (2008), 422–5.

[12] De Volder to Leibniz, 18 October 1700, G II 215.

[13] De Volder to Leibniz, 18 October 1700, G II 216.

And so, he argues, extension is a substance

since all the remaining things belong to it, and we will have either no concept of it, and it will be a mere word signifying nothing, or we will have a concept that represents one thing.[14]

De Volder's idea is none too clear here, but this is what he seems to have in mind. Take the notion of being square. This is a complex notion that includes the notion of having a shape; having a shape, in turn, is a complex notion that includes the notion of being extended. But being extended is basic in this series: it is, he claims, a notion that is not decomposable into any other notions. Such notions pertain to substance; the other, complex notions pertain to modes. In this respect de Volder takes himself to be offering a version of Descartes's criterion of substancehood:

This is my notion of substance, which I think agrees very well with the common, albeit more obscure, definitions of substance. It exists through itself, i.e. it needs no subject in which to exist, and it will sustain accidents. And, except for an efficient cause, it will need nothing else in order to exist, which in brief is Descartes' view.[15]

Indeed, both of these conceptions of substance can, in some way, be traced back to Descartes.[16]

Leibniz replied with some arguments against de Volder's conception of substance. But the most interesting is the following:

You say that a substance is that whose concept represents one thing in such a way that nothing can be taken away from the representation without the whole thing perishing. . . . I may observe that your notion of substance does not seem to apply to those things that are commonly so called, but only to the most simple substance. The same is true when you say that substance is that which is conceived through itself, to which I opposed the maxim that the effect cannot be conceived better than through the cause, but that every substance apart from the first has a cause. . . .[17]

---

[14] De Volder to Leibniz, The definition is repeated in de Volder to Leibniz, 13 February 1701, G II 222.

[15] De Volder to Leibniz, 18 October 1700, G II 217.

[16] On the first, see, e.g., Descartes's reply to Hobbes in the "Objectiones tertiae cum responsionibus authoris" appended to the *Meditationes*, AT VII 176; for the second, see *Principia philosophiae* I.51.

[17] Leibniz to de Volder, 6 July 1701, G II 224–5. In the phrase "the most simple substance," the reader should remember that Latin has no articles, and the Latin could just as well be translated as "a

The language is somewhat indirect here, but what Leibniz is suggesting is that de Volder's conception of substance applies only to "the most simple substance"—note the singular here—that is, to the "first" substance, that is, to God. Clearly that is what Leibniz has in mind in connection with the characterization of substance as conceived through itself: insofar as anything must be conceived through its cause, if a substance is that which is conceived through itself, then only God, who alone lacks a cause external to itself, can satisfy the definition. Leibniz certainly held that the notion of extension is not simple in the sense that de Volder requires for his first characterization: "Nor do I think that extension is conceived through itself but that it is a resolvable and relative notion."[18] While he doesn't offer an argument here, there is every reason to believe that Leibniz thought that only God can meet that condition too. Which is to say, in this context, the "most simple substance" that, Leibniz claims, is the only thing that satisfies de Volder's definition must be God.

De Volder doesn't seem to pick up on Leibniz's meaning. His reply seems rather naive, given the seriousness of the charge:

You add that my "notion of substance does not seem to apply to those things that are commonly so called, but only to the most simple substance." . . . And what if every substance were simple insofar as it is a substance?[19]

Leibniz replies by making more explicit the objectionable consequences of de Volder's position:

If the notion of substance in general does not apply to anything except the most simple or primary substance, then this alone will be a substance. I admit that you are within your rights to understand the word 'substance' so that God alone is a substance, and the other things are called something else. But it is my intention to look for a notion which will apply to the others as well, and which agrees with ordinary ways of speaking, according to which you and I and others are counted as substances. . . .[20]

most simple substance." However, since Leibniz clearly has God in mind, as he will make explicit in his next letter, the definite article seems appropriate here.

[18] Leibniz to de Volder, 24 March/3 April 1699, G II 169.
[19] De Volder to Leibniz, 8 October 1701, G II 229.
[20] Leibniz to de Volder, 27 December 1701, G II 232.

Leibniz implies here that de Volder is in the embarrassing position of agreeing with Spinoza! But then he says something very surprising:

I concede that every substance is simple, in a certain sense. I say substance, not aggregate of substances.[21]

De Volder interpreted this as a concession to his own view:

You concede that every substance is simple in a certain sense. If I understand these words properly they favor my view.[22]

But that isn't what Leibniz had in mind. He wrote:

When I say that every substance is simple, I understand by this that it lacks parts.[23]

De Volder didn't immediately recognize that something important happened here.[24] His next letter, sent 25 July 1702, didn't mention Leibniz's claim about simple substances. But in the letter that follows he does note it, with some puzzlement:

A mass of matter, as long as it is divisible to infinity and there is no empty space, has no unity. As long as it is merely passive, impenetrable, and resists motion, it can do nothing unless there is added a motive force, an entelechy, which, together with the mass, will make a corporeal substance, a unity, a monad, since you maintain that it is indivisible. However, every single corporeal substance contains in it infinite machines, each equipped with its own forces, and each of these again contains infinite others, and so on in this way to infinity. Given this, it seems to me that the unity that you had established before disappears again. For by this reckoning, every single corporeal substance will be not so much a substance as an aggregate of infinite substances, and it will never be possible to reach a simple substance that has not been joined together out of many. . . .[25]

---

[21] Leibniz to de Volder, 27 December 1701, G II 233.
[22] De Volder to Leibniz, 3 April 1702, G II 236.   [23] Leibniz to de Volder, April 1702, G II 239.
[24] It seems to me that this marks a significant confession, and a moment of change in what Leibniz had been telling de Volder before. In personal communications, Paul Lodge has expressed some skepticism about that. He points to a passage from the letter to de Volder, January 1705:

You say that you "noticed many very new and unexpected things" in my most recent letter. But perhaps you will find that the same things were already adequately introduced in previous letters, and that only prejudice prevented you from reaching the same point before now. . . .   (G II 275)

But, of course, Leibniz doesn't say here which previous letters he has in mind here. On my reading, he had been presenting his new doctrine to de Volder for more than two and a half years at the time he wrote those sentences.

[25] De Volder to Leibniz, 7 October 1702, G II 244–5. De Volder's understanding of Leibniz's view here may also have been influenced by his reading of Leibniz's reply to Bayle's critique in the second

As de Volder understood it, Leibniz's position was essentially the one that we have been outlining in earlier chapters, a world grounded in corporeal substances, entities understood on analogy with animals. On that view, every corporeal substance would seem to be composite, not simple, and to be composed of parts, smaller corporeal substances that, in turn, contain parts smaller still, and so on to infinity. Given this understanding, de Volder is understandably a bit puzzled about what exactly Leibniz means when he says that every substance is simple.

In his reply to this letter of de Volder's, written in winter 1702/3, though not received by de Volder until the following June, Leibniz began to sketch out a somewhat different conception of the world. At first it isn't easy to figure out that there is something different going on. In explaining himself to de Volder, Leibniz began with something that looks very much like an exposition of the corporeal substance view that we saw in the letters with Arnauld and that de Volder could have read in Leibniz's published writings:

When I say that a substance, a corporeal one, contains an infinity of machines, at the same time I think that it must be added that it embraces the one machine composed from them and that it is actuated by one entelechy without which there would be no principle of true unity in it.[26]

But pretty soon it is clear that things are a bit different. On the corporeal substance view, the individual substance, the ground of reality is the whole corporeal substance, soul and organic body. But now Leibniz seems to be saying something else. Later in that letter he writes, using his recently coined term, "monad":

For the rest, in the Monad, or complete simple substance, I do not unite anything with the entelechy except a primitive passive force, which is related to the whole mass of the organic body. Indeed, the remaining subordinate monads placed in the organs do not make up a part of [the substance], although they are immediately required for it, and they come together with the primary monad for the organic corporeal substance, or animal or plant. I therefore distinguish: (1) the primitive

edition of his *Dictionaire historique et critique* (1702), which Bayle had sent him, along with a brief reply. See de Volder to Leibniz, 7 October 1702, G II 244. (Leibniz's text was not to be published until 1716; see WF 70–1.) However, de Volder's comments on Leibniz don't include anything that couldn't have been gleaned from Leibniz's publications, particularly the "Système nouveau," or from the previous discussions.

[26] Leibniz to de Volder, 20 June 1703, G II 250.

entelechy or soul; (2) matter, namely primary matter or primitive passive power; (3) the monad completed by these two things; (4) the mass or secondary matter, or organic machine for which innumerable subordinate monads come together; and (5) the animal, or corporeal substance, which the monad dominating in the machine makes into one thing.[27]

Here the body of the corporeal substance is sharply distinguished from the "monad or complete simple substance," something that seems rather different from the corporeal substance view. Earlier in the letter he had written:

I regard substance itself, endowed with primitive active and passive power, like the 'I' or something similar, as the indivisible or complete monad. . . .[28]

Together with the passage I earlier quoted, it now seems that Leibniz is conceiving of the unities that ground his world on the model of souls rather than animals. At the end of the letter Leibniz confirms this by informing de Volder that, strictly speaking, his monads or simple substances are non-extended:

For even if monads are not extended, they nonetheless have a certain kind of situation in extension. . . . [T]hings that are simple, even if they do not have extension, must have a situation in extension, although it may not possible to designate it precisely, as with incomplete phenomena.[29]

And if, as Leibniz had written, all substances are simple in this sense, then these mind-like monads are now what there really is in the world: these, not the corporeal substances, are the active unities that ground reality.

In the letters that follow Leibniz expands on his position. In January 1704 he writes to de Volder:

Bodies, which are commonly taken for substances, are nothing but real phenomena, and are no more substances than perihelia or rainbows, and this is not something that is overturned by touch any more than by sight. The monad alone is a substance, a body is substances not a substance.[30]

---

[27] Leibniz to de Volder, 20 June 1703, G II 252. Here I depart slightly from Paul Lodge's reading, following a suggestion by Graeme Hunter about what is to be placed in the brackets.

[28] Leibniz to de Volder, 20 June 1703, G II 251.

[29] Leibniz to de Volder, 20 June 1703, G II 253.

[30] Leibniz to de Volder, 21 January 1704, G II 262.

On 20 June 1704 he is even more explicit:

Indeed, considering the matter exactly, it should be said that there is nothing in things except simple substances and in them perception and appetite; moreover, matter and motion are not so much substances or things as phenomena of perceivers, whose reality is situated in the harmony of perceivers with themselves (at difference times) and with other perceivers.[31]

At first, de Volder simply didn't see what Leibniz was doing: a comment he makes as late as May 1704, almost a year after Leibniz first announces this position, suggests that he thought that Leibniz continued to hold the corporeal substance view that had been under discussion from the beginning of the correspondence. In his letter of 31 May 1704, de Volder wrote:

Next, if we compare the view of bodies according to which they can be infinitely divided with your entelechy, I do not see as much difference as there appeared to be at first glance. Each body is composed of parts, and these again from others, and so on in this way to infinity. Each corporeal substance has an infinity of others under it, and these again have others under them, and so on in this way to infinity,[32] so that in neither case can we reach a substance not containing many substances in itself. There is only this difference: You add to each of these substances an indivisible entelechy producing everything successively. If I were able to form a clear and distinct notion of this entelechy, it would help me greatly in grasping the thing itself. Now I seem to perceive nothing except the name, unless I consider the general notion of force that attends it.[33]

In this way he attributes to Leibniz essentially the same view that he had earlier held.

But Leibniz's last and very explicit statement from June 1704 woke him up. In a letter sent on 14 November 1704, de Volder wrote:

It now seems to me that you do away with bodies altogether, in as much as you put them only in the appearances, and that you substitute forces alone for things; and not even corporeal forces, but "perception and appetite." These things certainly filled my mind with confusion, so that even now, after having read and reread your letters many times, I dare not say with any confidence that I understand the things that you say satisfactorily.[34]

---

[31] Leibniz to de Volder, 30 June 1704, G II 270.
[32] Lodge notes that Gerhardt mistakenly omits "to infinity [*in infinitum*]" here.
[33] G II 265–6.   [34] G II 272.

De Volder seemed quite astonished to discover that things were not as he had imagined them. Leibniz replied in his next letter, in January 1705, with a direct answer to de Volder's anguished remarks, and a summary of his new philosophy:

I do not really do away with body, but reduce it to what it is. For I show that corporeal mass that is believed to have something besides simple substances, is not a substance, but a phenomenon resulting from simple substances, which alone have unity and absolute reality. I relegate derivative forces to the phenomena, but I think that it is clear that primitive forces can be nothing other than the internal strivings of simple substances, by which they pass from perception to perception[35] by a certain law of their nature and at the same time agree with each other, representing the same phenomena of the universe in a different manner, something that necessarily arises from a common cause. It is necessary that these simple substances exist everywhere and that they are self-governing (each as far as itself is concerned), since the influence of one on another cannot be understood. Anything more beyond this in things is posited in vain and added without argument.[36]

De Volder's next letter to Leibniz wasn't sent until 5 January 1706, more than a year after his last, and in it he admitted that he was still "stuck on the same difficulties that I posed in my last letter." He continued: "Moreover, there has fallen upon me a despair of ever understanding correctly certain of your opinions."[37] De Volder never really regained his equilibrium: that was the last letter he ever wrote to Leibniz.

A World Enchanted: A Preliminary Account

The position that Leibniz outlines in these letters to de Volder starting in April 1702 would seem to be a very significant change in the position we saw in Leibniz's earlier writings.[38] We shall return to the question as to

---

[35] Originally Leibniz wrote: "from sensation to sensation [de sensione in sensionem]."

[36] Leibniz to de Volder, January 1705, G II 275.   [37] G II 279.

[38] My main target in this chapter (and, more generally in this book) is a widely held view that Leibniz's philosophy remains constant over his career, from the late 1670s or early 1680s to the end of his life. Usually, this means attributing the monadological metaphysics to Leibniz's earlier years. However, in Phemister (2005), Pauline Phemister has made the somewhat surprising claim that there is continuity in the other direction. That is, on her reading, the monads that dominate his later thought are to be identified with corporeal substances. As a consequence, there is an important sense in which

how exactly Leibniz's later metaphysics differs from his earlier view later in Chapter 9, after we have explored it in greater detail. But it will be helpful here to have at the very least a preliminary and rough-and-ready characterization of the difference between the view that Leibniz articulated in his later letters with de Volder and the earlier view that we have seen in the 1680s and early 1690s. At least until recently, it was often simply taken for granted that Leibniz's later view was a variety of idealism.[39] But since this label has been contested by some recent commentators, as we shall discuss in more detail in Chapter 9, I shall refer to the later position as a monadological metaphysics,[40] in contrast with what I shall call the corporeal substance metaphysics of the middle period so as to remain neutral on the question. To add an extra layer of complexity, in using the term I do for the middle period metaphysics, I don't mean to deny that corporeal substances play a significant role in Leibniz's later monadological metaphysics, as we shall see in the remainder of this chapter and in the following one.[41] But a bit of explanation is in order.

At the root of Leibniz's new metaphysics as I want to understand it is the notion of a monad, a substance that is simple in the sense that it has

Leibniz never gives up the corporeal substance metaphysics of his middle years. Referring to the conception of a monad advanced in Leibniz's letter to de Volder 20 June 1703 (G II 252), as quoted in the text above, she claims that "each De Volder monad, in its created complete state, is equivalent to a complete corporeal substance" [Phemister (2005), 40]. (If I understand him correctly, Justin Smith makes a similar suggestion in Smith (2002), linking Leibniz's thought to later eighteenth-century biological thought inspired by Leibniz's views.) Addressing her subtle reading in detail deserves an essay of its own, and would take us too far afield from the concerns of this book. But briefly, I can't agree with her identification of monads and corporeal substances: there are too many passages, including the one on which she bases her reading of monads, in which Leibniz carefully distinguishes monads from corporeal substances to identify the two. And as I shall try to establish more clearly in this and the following chapter, there really is a breaking-point between Leibniz's middle and late metaphysics of body that happens sometime in the mid- and late 1690s. But that said, there is something very right in her reading. Phemister is absolutely correct to note that the corporeal substances of Leibniz's middle years can be found in his thought all the way to the end of his life; in this sense there is a real continuity. However, monads as metaphysical posits distinct from corporeal substances do enter at a certain point, and also have an important role to play in his thought. But, as we shall see in the next chapter, the role that they play is not easy to pin down, and the distinction between the middle and late Leibniz is more difficult to articulate than many have thought, including me.

[39] This, for instance, is the view that is taken in part III of Adams (1994).

[40] Let me remind the reader here about the convention that I adopted at the beginning of the book. I use 'monadology' uncapitalized to designate the general metaphysical doctrine that takes monads to metaphysically fundamental in some sense (to be discussed in detail, of course). 'Monadologie' designates the specific writing of 1714 in which Leibniz sets out one version of the monadology.

[41] In addition to Phemister (2005), this is a point emphasized in Hartz (1998); Smith (1998); Arthur (1989); and Arthur (2006).

no parts and is therefore unextended. As he writes in the opening of the 'Monadologie':

The monad, which we shall discuss here, is nothing but a simple substance that enters into composites—simple, that is, without parts. . . . But where there are no parts, neither extension, nor shape, nor divisibility is possible. These monads are the true atoms of nature and, in brief, the elements of things.[42]

In contrast to this, on Leibniz's earlier position, the corporeal substance metaphysics that we have seen developed in earlier chapters, the basic entities in the world are corporeal substances.

Each of these corporeal substances on the earlier view is made up of smaller parts, and so on to infinity: bugs in bugs forever. These corporeal substances are the active unities that ground the reality of the world around us, genuine unities insofar as they are indivisible and unified by virtue of a substantial form, and active insofar as they are the sources of their own activity. These substances are *indivisible*, yet they are *not* simple in the sense of having no parts, it would seem. Remember here the example of the planarians that Arnauld brought up in objection to Leibniz's claims about the indivisibility of corporeal substances.[43] If planarians are, indeed, corporeal substances, then they would seem to undermine that claim insofar as the tail cut off a planarian can grow a new head, apparently creating two animals (corporeal substances) where there was originally only one. Leibniz quite clearly rejects this as a counterexample to his claim. Though the body of the planarian can be cut, at most one of the two pieces can count as the continuation of the original planarian, the one in which the original soul continues to function as the form. This is the sense in which they count as indivisible, even though they have parts. More generally, pieces of a corporeal substance can be separated off without the corporeal substance itself being divided, strictly speaking. While corporeal substances are genuine unities and genuinely indivisible for Leibniz, they are not simple and without parts: they are composed of corporeal substances smaller still, to infinity. And insofar as corporeal substances are the basic unities of which the world is composed at the most basic metaphysical level, *there is no bottom level of substances in the world, no metaphysical level that is the ultimate foundation of reality.*

---

[42] 'Monadologie' §§ 1, 3.   [43] See the discussion above on pp. 84–6.

But in the world of simple substances that Leibniz outlines to de Volder, things seem rather different. The basic units of the world (in whatever sense they turn out to be basic) are now not corporeal substances but monads or simple substances. These monads are not composed of anything more basic: they are the ultimate bottom layer of things. They are also non-extended and endowed with perception and appetition alone: "Indeed, considering the matter carefully it should be said that there is nothing in things except simple substances and in them perception and appetite."[44] In this way monads can be called mind-like. Unlike in the corporeal substance metaphysics, in the monadological metaphysics simple substances constitute a bottom level of things, things that ground the reality of the world and are not, in turn, grounded in anything else. Now, one of the things that makes it a bit tricky to characterize the difference between the two views is the fact that, as we shall later see, in this later monadological view, Leibniz has certainly not eliminated the complex world of corporeal substances, nested in one another to infinity. This world is still very much a part of Leibniz's picture. Indeed, he often (though not always) continues to use the terminology that he had used in his earlier writings, calling its constituents composite substances, compound substances, or even corporeal substances. But in the monadological metaphysics there is something new, a metaphysical sub-basement of simple substances added to the earlier view of bugs in bugs, a kind of absolute grounding for that world, a domain of genuine metaphysical unities that don't themselves contain any further unities. Whether he wants to argue that non-extended and mind-like monads are the *only* genuine substances in the world, or, as he will sometimes hold, that there are, in addition, composite substances made up out of monads, it is a key doctrine of the monadological metaphysics, as I shall understand it, that monads are "the true atoms of nature and, in brief, the elements of things."[45] Whatever else there might be—be they bodies, corporeal substances, composite substances or whatever—they must ultimately be grounded in some way in simple substances or monads.[46]

Another important contrast concerns the notion of force. As we saw in earlier chapters, Leibniz offers at least two complementary conceptions of corporeal substance. Corporeal substance can be interpreted either in

---

[44] Leibniz to de Volder, 30 June 1704, G II 270.   [45] 'Monadologie' § 3.

[46] As we shall see in Ch. 9, this doctrine is stretched to the limit by the end of the Des Bosses correspondence. But even so, this statement is true to a first approximation.

terms of soul and body, as in the "unity" approach to corporeal substance outlined in Chapter 2, or in terms of the notions of primitive active and passive force, as outlined in Chapters 3 and 4. On that conception of corporeal substance, form is identified with the primitive active force and matter with the primitive passive force. In this context, there is every reason to believe that Leibniz thought of primitive active and passive forces not only as the ground-level *physical* realities, but as the ultimate *metaphysical* realities that ground the created world. A correspondent, Jacques Lenfant, wrote Leibniz with the following remark on 7 November 1693:

The whole question is thus to know if the force to act in bodies is in matter something distinct and independent of everything else that one conceives there. Without that, this force cannot be its essence, and will remain the result of some primitive quality or another.[47]

This is part of Leibniz's reply:

And since everything that one conceives in substances reduces to their actions and passions and to the dispositions that they have for this effect, I don't see how one can find there anything more primitive than the principle of all of this, that is to say, than force.[48]

Or, as he wrote even more clearly to Bossuet from 2 July 1694, "I find nothing so intelligible as force."[49] It is also the message of the 1694 essay "De primae philosophae emendatione" that the notion of force is all we need to ground the metaphysics of substance. If the active and passive forces that ground body in the physical world also ground Leibniz's fundamental metaphysics of substance, then it would seem as if the reality of extended body is assured, at least if we understand extended body in the way Leibniz does, the way we have discussed it above in Chapter 4.

Leibniz's conception of force here is very closely connected with his physics, his program for understanding the nature and behavior of extended bodies in the physical world. These forces, active and passive, are connected with motion, though not identified with it, as I earlier emphasized. Active force is connected with the ability bodies in motion have to act on one another in collision, or to accomplish some effect, such as raising themselves

---

[47] Tognon (1982), 326.
[48] Leibniz to Lenfant, 25 November 1693, Tognon (1982), 327. It is interesting to observe that even though Lenfant had written Leibniz about *body*, his reply is quite clearly about *substance*.
[49] A1.10.144 (WF 30).

a certain distance. Passive force is associated with the resistance bodies exert toward acquiring new motion or the resistance to penetration that they exhibit in response to collision with other bodies. And so, as I also pointed out earlier, it is from passive force, primary matter, impenetrability in particular, that the extension of body derives. That is to say, bodies are said to be extended insofar as they exclude other bodies from certain regions that are said to be in their extension. In that way, one can say, corporeal substances are, in a sense, genuinely extended, even though they are not extended in the way in which Cartesian bodies are extended, the objects of geometry made real. They are extended in the sense that the passive force of bodies gives rise to structures that instantiate geometrical relations, at least approximately, as we discussed earlier.

In his new monadological metaphysics, Leibniz doesn't abandon his doctrine of force. However, the primitive active and passive forces, the form and matter that in the earlier view have a fundamental metaphysical status, are, in the monadological view, understood as features of the perceptions of these monads. As he writes in a draft of a letter to de Volder from 1706:

Arguments, in my opinion, cannot prove the existence of anything besides perceiving things and perceptions (if you subtract their common cause [i.e., God]), and the things which should be admitted in them. . . . There is an active force and a passive force in every perceiving thing; the active in the transition to the more perfect, the passive in the opposite. And there are innumerable perceiving things, that is, as many as there are simple substances or monads.[50]

In this way the notion of force, which seemed to be at the root of Leibniz's metaphysics in the earlier texts that we have been examining, loses its foundational status: primitive force gets folded into the perceptual life of non-extended perceiving things. Remember the passage from the letter to de Volder, 20 June 1703, quoted above:

I therefore distinguish: (1) the primitive entelechy or soul; (2) matter, namely primary matter or primitive passive power; (3) the monad completed by these two things. . . .[51]

In this conception there is still form (entelechy) and matter, but both are now embodied in the monad, explicitly identified as non-extended later

---

[50] G II 281.   [51] Leibniz to de Volder, 20 June 1703, G II 252.

in the same letter. In another text written for de Volder he makes clear that kinds of force relevant to the monad are understood in terms of their perceptions and appetitions:

it is clear that primitive forces can be nothing other than the internal strivings of simple substances, by which they pass from perception to perception by a certain law of their nature. . . .[52]

And in response to a question from Des Bosses, Leibniz writes:

You ask why there is a need for primary matter if there is no need for real extension, and why an entelechy alone does not constitute a monad? I would respond that, if there are only monads with their perceptions, primary matter will be nothing other than the passive power of the monads, and an entelechy will be their active power; if you add composite substances, I would say that in these things a principle of resistance must be added to the active principle or motive force.[53]

A full explication of this passage will have to await our discussion in the next chapter of Leibniz's later conception of the substantial bond and the notion of corporeal substance that he develops in his letters with Des Bosses. But briefly, Leibniz here is distinguishing between the kind of matter that pertains to non-extended monads, their primitive passive force, and resistance and impenetrability, the kind of matter that pertains to extended corporeal substances. The primary matter of a monad is internal to the perceptions and appetitions of a non-extended monad, and does not give rise to extension in the same way as does the resistance and impenetrability of the passive force that he attributes to corporeal substances.

This in very brief outline is the world that Leibniz is trying to explain to de Volder in his later letters. We shall come back to it later and try to fill out the picture of what the new view comes to. In particular, we must address changes in Leibniz's conception of body from the earlier period to the later, a matter of some complexity that will occupy us for much of the next chapter. But at the moment, I would like to turn to another kind of question.

It is implausible to suppose that Leibniz is inventing this new metaphysics at the very moment that he is explaining it to de Volder; it is much more

---

[52] Leibniz to de Volder, January 1705, G II 275.
[53] Leibniz to Des Bosses, 20 September 1712, LDB 274–6.

plausible to suppose that it is something that he has been contemplating for some time before. When did he come upon this new view? And, more importantly, why?

From Corporeal Substances to Simple Substances

The mid-1690s seems to have been crucial in the genesis of the concept of the monad and in the development of the view that I have been calling the monadology.[54] An important step in this process is the emergence of the notion of a simple substance.

As I noted earlier, though Leibniz had a reasonably well-developed view of the world by the mid-1680s, as we have seen in earlier chapters, very little of it had been revealed to the world. Leibniz gave some of his favored correspondents some substantial hints of what he was thinking. The fullest account, of course, is found in the letters he sent to Arnauld in 1686 and 1687. But there were other, more modest cases of Leibniz showing his hand. In an important letter to his old friend Simon Foucher in 1686, in response to Foucher's pleas for further knowledge of his views, Leibniz sent him a summary.[55] Jacques-Bénigne Bossuet, an influential French bishop and advisor to Louis XIV, also pressed Leibniz for his philosophical views in 1692, and received some clarifications.[56] But these and other friends and correspondents wanted more. And by 1694 Leibniz was of a mind to try to satisfy them.

The first public hint of this new initiative appeared in the March 1694 issue of the *Acta eruditorum*: "De primae philosophiae emendatione, et de notione substantiae." The focus of the essay is the notion of substance.

---

[54] The importance of these years is also underscored in Wilson (1989), ch. 5; Becco (1975b); Becco (1978), 137–41; and in Fichant (2004), 95ff. As I noted earlier, though, Fichant thinks that the real transition begins somewhat earlier, with the correspondence with Arnauld; see Fichant (2004), 81ff. As I have argued in earlier chapters, though, the view that Leibniz presents there is the corporeal substance picture that emerges out of doctrines developed in the late 1670s and early 1680s. While the correspondence with Arnauld is a central text, I take it to consolidate and develop earlier views rather than adding anything substantively new. Wilson, on the other hand, sees the monadology as emerging as dominant in 1695 or so. However, she sees it as part of the mix in his earlier writings. On her view of the 'Discours de métaphysique,' "the treatise reveals not a single system, but three separate schemes or semi-systems. ..." [Wilson (1989), 80]. In addition to a monadological semi-system, Wilson sees a second semi-system grounded in the logic of complete concepts, and a third grounded in corporeal substances, all three co-existing in tension with one another in the 1680s.

[55] G I 380–5 (WF 52–3).   [56] See WF 7–9 for references to the correspondence.

(The immediate occasion for these reflections was likely questions about the nature of substance that had been raised by Christian Thomasius in a disputation held in July 1693 in Halle.[57]) In the essay, Leibniz emphasizes one of the notions of substance that we have seen in earlier chapters, the conception of substance as grounded in force. He writes:

> the concept of *forces* or *powers*, which the Germans call *Kraft* and the French *la force*, and for whose explanation I have set up a distinct science of *dynamics*, brings the strongest light to bear upon our understanding of the true concept of *substance*.[58]

But it is clear that Leibniz wanted to use this question as the wedge by which he can introduce his new philosophical picture to the world at large. Before giving his conception of substance in terms of force, he writes:

> The importance of these matters will be particularly apparent from the concept of substance which I offer. This is so fruitful that there follow from it primary truths, even about God and minds and the nature of bodies—truths heretofore known in part though hardly demonstrated, and unknown in part, but of the greatest utility for the future in the other sciences.[59]

In this way the analysis of substance in terms of force seems to be fundamental to Leibniz's conception of his system at that moment.

Shortly after that essay came out in the *Acta eruditorum*, Leibniz announced his plans for a further exposition of his views. In a letter to Bossuet from 2/12 July 1694 he writes:

> With a view to submitting my ideas to the public judgment, I am working now to put down in writing what I think is the only intelligible explanation of the union of the soul with the body. . . . I have had this explanation for several years, and it is only a corollary of the notion that I have worked out of substance in general. If you think it appropriate, Monseigneur, the two enclosed pieces could be put into the *Journal des sçavans*, in order to give some indication of my plan. . . . I think I have at least made some progress with regard to the notion we should have of substance in general, and of corporeal substance in particular. Since I find nothing so intelligible as force, I believe that is what we must turn to in order to defend

---

[57] See Utermöhlen (1979). Utermöhlen gives a transcription of the original version of Leibniz's 1694 essay on p. 85–6, which was originally entitled "G. G. L. de Notione Substantiae ad quam edendam V. Cl. Christianus Thomasius Theologos et Philosophos nuper provacavit." For further details, see Rutherford (1995), 150.

[58] G IV 469 (L 433).   [59] Ibid.

the real presence, which I hold does not fit at all well with the view which takes the essence of body to be nothing but bare extension.[60]

The two texts that Leibniz joined to the letter consist of an essay, "Réflexions de Leibniz sur l'avancement de la métaphysique réelle, et particulièrement sur la nature de la substance expliquée par la force," and "Réponse du même aux objections faites contre l'explication de la nature du corps par la notion de la force."[61] The latter is a response to objections raised against Leibniz's view by Jacques Lenfant,[62] while the former is largely a French translation of the "De primae philosophiae...." But not entirely. At the end of the translation Leibniz adds the following remark about the relations between mind and body:

Finally, a most important point which will be clarified by these meditations is communication between substances, and the union of the soul with the body. I hope that this great problem will be thereby resolved in such a clear manner that that in itself will serve as a proof to show that we have found the key to part of these matters.[63]

But this is just a teaser, little more than the remark that he made in the letter to Bossuet that accompanied the essay. And in the essay that was supposed to accompany it, Leibniz gave little more than in the "De primae philosophiae..." itself. As in that other work, he emphasizes the importance of the notion of force for understanding the notion of substance. He writes that "force is constitutive of substance," and that "having put extension and its modifications or changes aside, there is nothing in nature more intelligible than force."[64] Here, as in the essay that he published, it is the notion of force that seems to ground Leibniz's conception of substance.

Bossuet didn't think it appropriate to publish these two essays in the *Journal*. In any case, they remained unpublished among his papers at his death. But Leibniz was already working on another fuller essay, what was to become the first exposition of his larger views on nature, the "Système nouveau pour expliquer la nature des substances et leur communication entre elles." In a letter dated 3 July 1694, Leibniz tells Bossuet that he is

---

[60] A1.10.143–4 (WF 30).

[61] The texts can be found in Bossuet (1909–1925), vol. 6, 523–8 and 528–30, translated in WF 31–5.

[62] On Lenfant and Leibniz, see Tognon (1982).   [63] Bossuet (1909–1925), vol. 6, 527 (WF 33).

[64] Bossuet (1909–1925), vol. 6, 528–9 (WF 34).

enclosing a new piece in which he treats not only the foundations of his dynamics, but also questions relating to minds and souls.[65] Leibniz never sent the letter or the enclosure, and it is impossible to say exactly what the text is to which Leibniz is referring, but it is likely one of the earlier surviving drafts of the "Système nouveau."[66]

A total of five drafts of the "Système nouveau" survive. The last is the version of the "Système nouveau" as published in 1695, with changes that are generally thought to be posterior to the publication, though it is difficult to say exactly when they were added. The second through the fourth are texts that lead directly up to the version finally published. But the first is rather different from the final text: except for the opening paragraph, it departs significantly from what Leibniz will later publish.[67]

In the first draft of the "Système nouveau," Leibniz begins where he did in his other expositions earlier in the year, with the centrality of the notion of force:

So I find that in nature it is necessary to employ not only the notion of extension but also that of force, which makes matter capable of acting and of resisting. . . . That is why I consider it to be what constitutes substance [*le constitutif de la substance*], since it is the principle of action, which is its characteristic feature. So I find that the efficient cause of physical actions lies in the province of metaphysics. In this I am very far from those who recognize in nature only what is material or extended. . . .[68]

But Leibniz moves very quickly from there to a different way of conceiving substance, in terms of its unity and individuality. He writes:

But to come to the account that we promised, I begin with the distinction that must be drawn between a substance and a collection, or an aggregate of several

---

[65] A1.10.134 (WF 35–6).

[66] For another perspective on the genesis of the "Système nouveau," see S. Brown (1996). Brown gives a good discussion of the background in the correspondences with Bossuet and Foucher. However, he reads the "Système nouveau" as an attempt to address Cartesian philosophers in a way that they will find comprehensible, and as a consequence, he sees the discussion of mind, body, and their interaction as a distortion of Leibniz's own views. My own focus will be more on the treatment of substance and how that changes over the course of the project. Perhaps because of my different focus I am less inclined to see the distortions that Brown does.

[67] For a description of the different drafts, see WF 9–10. Only the first and last are available in published editions at this time; see G IV 471–7 and 477–87. The version of the "Système nouveau" published in G IV 477–87 is actually the final ms. in this series, and not the version as published in the *Journal des sçavans*. For that reason, when quoting that text I shall not cite the text in G IV, but in Leibniz (1695).

[68] G IV 472 (WF 22).

substances. When I say 'me,' I speak of a single substance; but an army, a herd of animals, a pond full of fish (even if it is frozen solid with all its fish) will always be a collection of several substances. That is why, leaving aside souls or other such principles of unity, we will never find a corporeal mass or portion of matter which is a true substance. It will always be a collection, since matter is actually divided *ad infinitum*, in such a way that the least particle encloses a truly infinite world of created things, and perhaps of animals.[69]

Even though this is something of a departure from the other texts of 1694, which focus on the notion of force, this is not a real surprise; unity, after all, is the other horn of his earlier account of substance. There is nothing in this passage that we haven't seen in Leibniz's letters to Arnauld or in texts even earlier than that. But in what follows, there is something of an innovation, a new element subtly different from what we saw earlier. Leibniz writes:

However, since it must necessarily be that true unities can be found in corporeal nature, for otherwise there could be neither multiplicity nor collections, it is necessary that which makes a corporeal substance [*ce qui fait la substance corporelle*] is something which corresponds to what in us is called 'me,' which is indivisible and yet active: for being indivisible *and without parts*, it will not be a being by aggregation, but being active it will be something substantial. . . . [W]e must recognize in general that everything has to be full of . . . [things] which contain in themselves a principle of true unity which is analogous to the soul, and which is joined to some kind of organized body. Otherwise we would find nothing substantial in matter, and bodies would only be phenomena or like very orderly dreams. The ancients too, Plato above all, recognized perfectly well that by itself, that is to say without this indivisible principle that we have just described, matter would be nothing real or determinate, but there would be no corporeal substance.[70]

Again, this looks very much like the kind of view that Leibniz presented in earlier texts. But there is an interesting difference. Here he indicates that the soul or form that creates a single corporeal substance out of a multiplicity is one not only because it is indivisible, *but also because it lacks parts*. Unlike in earlier texts, true unity is connected with the lack of parts. In the correspondence with Arnauld, for example, what was important for unity was just indivisibility, and not the lack of parts; as we saw with

---

[69] G IV 473 (WF 23).   [70] G IV 473–4 (WF 23–4), emphasis added.

the example of the planarian, Leibniz is perfectly willing to say that the *corporeal substance* that is the planarian is indivisible even though a piece of the animal body might be separated from it and even become a corporeal substance itself. It is not clear how important Leibniz himself found this change, though; after all, even though souls are true unities insofar as they lack parts, he does go on to say that they can endow composite substances, corporeal substances, with unity by virtue of their own. Though they may be special, super-unities, one might say, they are not the only unities that Leibniz recognizes. Though they would seem to have parts, corporeal substances count as genuine unities as well.[71]

In the published version of the "Système nouveau" the view seems to evolve another step. Considerations linking substance to force are not altogether lacking in the published text. In the opening paragraphs, he makes the following remark, which echoes some of the things he had written in the texts of 1694:

[71] There are some passages from 1689 and 1690 that suggest that Leibniz at least toyed with the idea that even corporeal substance have no parts in the strict sense of the term. First of all, there is an interesting text that the Akademie editors date from 1689/90 where Leibniz offers an argument to the effect that because a corporeal substance can lose pieces of its body and still remain the same corporeal substance that it is, "corporeal matter" is not, strictly speaking, a part of the corporeal substance; see A6.4.1001–2. See also a similar passage in some notes the editors group with the Fardella Memo, A6.4.1672, which probably dates from March 1690. And secondly, in the Fardella Memo, Leibniz worries about whether (corporeal) substances should be considered as parts of matter insofar as they are not homogeneous with matter. (Substances, of course, are true unities, while matter is an aggregate of substances. Its parts would also have to be aggregates of substances, strictly speaking.) In the course of these speculations he remarks:

We must consider whether we can say that an animal is a part of matter, as a fish is part of a fish pond, or cattle are a part of a herd. And indeed, if the animal is conceived of as a thing having parts, that is, as a body divisible and destructible, endowed with a soul, then it must be conceded that the animal is part of matter, since every part of matter has parts. But it cannot then be conceded that it is a substance or an indestructible thing.   [A6.4.1671 (AG 105)]

The point seems to be that if the animal is considered as having parts, then we are not considering it *as* an indivisible substance, but as a body. This suggests, perhaps, that considered as a substance, we should not think of the constituents of an animal body as *parts* of the animal, in the strict sense. This latter text is echoed in a letter to Johann Bernoulli from August/September 1698: "even if the body of an animal, or my organic body is composed, in turn, of innumerable substances, they are not parts of the animal or of me" [GM III 537 (AG 167)]. But these texts seems somewhat isolated and tentative. On two occasions in the text connected with Fardella Leibniz introduces a question as something that he needs to think more about ("*considerandum*") (A6.4.1671, l. 12; A6.4.1674, l. 7). In any case, even if Leibniz may think that, strictly speaking, corporeal substances don't have parts, he doesn't infer from that that they are not extended, as he does in the text from 'Monadologie' §§ 1–3 that I have cited a number of times. In this way, even if they lack parts, corporeal substances remain quite different from monads.

I perceived that considering extended mass alone was not sufficient, and that it was necessary, in addition, to make use of the notion of force, which is very intelligible, despite the fact that it belongs in the domain of metaphysics.[72]

And referring to substantial forms, which he is arguing to revive, Leibniz notes that "their nature consists in force."[73] This also echoes the "Specimen dynamicum," published in the same year, which emphasizes the notion of force, as we saw in Chapter 4. But in the "Système nouveau" as it appeared in print, considerations relating to force are very clearly subordinated to arguments from unity. In this respect, one might see something of a rupture with the view presented in the essays of 1694, which emphasize the centrality of force for understanding substance. The argument proper of the "Système nouveau" begins with the following observations:

In the beginning, when I had freed myself from the yoke of Aristotle, I accepted the void and atoms, for they best satisfy the imagination. But on recovering from that, after much reflection, I perceived that it is impossible to find the principles of a true unity in matter alone, or in what is only passive, since everything in it is only a collection or aggregation of parts to infinity.[74]

While the argument for the rehabilitation of substantial forms that follows appears to be a reprise of the aggregate argument for corporeal substance that is found in earlier texts, such as the correspondence with Arnauld, at the end of part I of the "Système nouveau" there is a summary paragraph that seems to depart in interesting and perhaps significant ways from his earlier views.[75]

The paragraph in question summarizes the argument up until that point before starting in on his exposition of pre-established harmony. In the earlier part of the "Système nouveau" Leibniz had set out his views about unities, corporeal substances, and his theory of what he starts to call "natural machines" at that point, machines of infinite complexity all of

---

[72] Leibniz (1695), 295 (AG 139).   [73] Leibniz (1695), 296 (AG 139).

[74] Leibniz (1695), 295 (AG 139).

[75] The "Système nouveau" was published in two successive issues of the *Journal*; what I have called part I is the portion that appeared in the issue of 27 June 1695, and what I call part II is what appeared in the issue of 4 July. The breaking point is at pp. 300–1, the moment where Leibniz begins to take up the hypothesis of pre-established harmony.

whose constituents function in the behavior of the body.[76] The summary paragraph begins as follows:

In addition, by means of the soul or form there is a true unity corresponding to what is called the self [*moy*] in us. . . . [I]f there were no true substantial unities, there would be nothing substantial or real in the collection.[77]

Leibniz goes on to say that extended material atoms cannot constitute such unities. What seems to be wrong with material atoms is that they have parts:

Furthermore, they are still composed of parts, since the invincible attachment of one part to another (if we can reasonably conceive or assume this) does not eliminate diversity of those parts.[78]

So far, what Leibniz has written is quite consistent with the earlier view on which corporeal substances are the unities that ground the reality of the physical world. But Leibniz then writes the following remarkable passage:

There are only atoms of substance, that is, real unities *absolutely destitute of parts*, which are the source of actions, *the first absolute principles of the composition of things, and, as it were, the final elements in the analysis of substances* [*les premiers principes absolus de la composition des choses, & comme les derniers élemens de l'analise des substances*]. We could call them metaphysical points: they have something vital, a kind of perception, and mathematical points are the points of view from which they express the universe. But when corporeal substances are contracted, all their organs

---

[76] Leibniz seems to introduce the notion of a natural machine for the first time in the "Système nouveau." On this see Fichant (2003), who emphasizes the novelty of this idea at this moment. The importance of Leibniz's conception of a natural machine, and the centrality of his concept of life for his later metaphysics, is emphasized in Smith (forthcoming) and in the exciting essays collected in Smith and Nachtomy (forthcoming). But I suspect that the basic idea may actually go back somewhat earlier in Leibniz's thought. Leibniz certainly had the idea of the infinite complexity of corporeal substance from early on, something that is clearly present in the correspondence with Arnauld. And there is at least one passage from the 1685 notes on Cordemoy that suggests that he appreciated that this infinite complexity marks an important distinction between the natural and the artificial world. In response to the comparison in Cordemoy between a human being and a clock, Leibniz notes:

It seems to me that . . . no one can build a body perfectly similar to the human one, unless someone can conserve the Order by dividing to infinity. So it is not possible for an angel to fashion a man or any genuine animal, except from a seed, where it already preexists in some way. He could make a machine which would perhaps remind you of a man by its outward appearance if you did not examine it well enough, but it would not really be a man or an animal.   [A6.4.1801 (RA 283)]

[77] Leibniz (1695), 299–300 (AG 142).   [78] Leibniz (1695), 300 (AG 142).

together constitute only a physical point relative to us. Thus physical points are indivisible only in appearance; mathematical points are exact, but they are merely modalities. Only metaphysical points or points of substance (*constituted by the forms or souls* [*constituez par les formes ou ames*]) are exact and real, and without them there would be nothing real, since without true unities there would be no multitude.[79]

This is a difficult passage, though very suggestive. Here Leibniz seems to go beyond identifying a particular class of "super-unities," the souls or forms that transform the aggregates that are organic bodies into genuine corporeal substances. In this passage, Leibniz seems to suggest that for something to be a real unity, a genuine "atom of substance," it *must* lack parts. In this way, he seems to suggest that the unities that ground reality are not corporeal substances, which would seem to have parts, but the "metaphysical points or points of substance," forms and souls, which lack parts and, presumably, extension. This is certainly suggestive of the monads that will later appear in his thought. These real unities, Leibniz says, are "the final elements in the analysis of substances" and that the "metaphysical points" that ground reality are "constituted by forms or souls." This certainly suggests that the ultimate ground of reality is a realm of mind-like and non-extended substances, that which he will later call monads. Later I shall return to this passage and suggest other ways of reading it, and good reasons for considering such alternative readings seriously. But even so, this passage is certainly quite striking in connection with what Leibniz will later advance in a much more explicit and self-conscious way.

The claim that true substances as such lack parts arises in another interesting context in the same time period. I mentioned earlier the dispute in Halle by Christian Thomasius that seems to have given rise to Leibniz's 1694 publication, the "De primae philosophiae . . ." The exchange continued with another contribution from Thomasius, the "Dialogus de definitione substantiae," which appeared in the summer of 1694.[80] While Leibniz didn't publish a direct reply to this dialogue, among his manuscripts there are notes on Thomasius's text. While it is impossible to date Leibniz's text exactly, it is certainly before December 1696, and probably a bit earlier than that. In his dialogue, Thomasius gives some examples of things

---

[79] Leibniz (1695), 300 (AG 142), emphasis added.

[80] In Christian Thomasius, *Institutionum jurisprudentiae divinae libri III. Ed. secunda* (Halle, 1694), cited in Utermöhlen (1979), 86.

330 ENCHANTING THE WORLD

that are and are not substances. From this he derives the following definition of substance:

Thomasius:

From these things [follows] a definition: a substance is an entity [*Ens*] subsisting in itself. From what has preceded, I sum up the explication as follows: A substance is an entity *per se*, that is, an entity naturally united [*naturaliter unitum*], having boundaries all around it.

On the phrase "naturally united" Leibniz commented: "Substance seems to me not to have parts, that is, it is not united, but is one [*non est unitum, sed unum*]."[81] Also remarkable is another passage from this text. In addition to the remarks on individual claims in Thomasius's text, Leibniz adds a brief passage where he advances his own definition of substance:

Leibniz:

Substance is a complete entity of perfect unity [*Ens completum perfectae unitatis*]. Substance therefore has no parts, otherwise it would not be of perfect unity; it would not be a substance, but substances. It is a complete entity, which has a complete concept, from which, indeed, everything which can be attributed to the same subject can be deduced.

Concrete,[82] full, one.

Full, indeed, what involves all predicates of the same subject—through 'complete' it [i.e., a substance] is differentiated from accidents, through 'full' it is differentiated from incomplete things, and through 'one' from aggregates.

Maybe this [is the right definition of substance]: subject, ultimate, full, one.

This will do: *Substance* is an entity that is one and full. 'One' like a man, and not an army. 'Full' like a man, not a soul [*anima*], not a power [*virtus*]. Or, *Substance* is a simple complete entity.[83]

This seems quite radical: what Leibniz is advancing here is the idea that substance *as such* must lack parts; it must be *a genuinely unity, and not just an aggregate that is united*—an *ens unitum*—by virtue of having a substantial

---

[81] Both the Thomasius and the Leibniz texts are in Utermöhlen (1979), 88. On the dating, see ibid., pp. 89–91.

[82] Justin Smith has suggested that perhaps this should be read "compiete."

[83] The text is in Utermöhlen (1979), 88–9. The text is also signaled in Becco (1975b), 284. The last sentence is somewhat problematic. Utermöhlen reads it as: "Substantia est Ens simplum completum." Becco reads it as "Substantia est Ens simplex completum." "Simplus" is a very rare word in Latin. Though it can be used synonymously with "simplex," it would be an odd choice for Leibniz to make. I suspect that Becco has it right.

form.[84] This would *seem*, prima facie, to exclude corporeal substances from being genuine substances, and limit genuine substancehood to non-extended souls or minds.[85] Even more interesting is the last line of Leibniz's attempted definition of substance: "*Substance* is a simple complete entity." This text is among the earliest in which the idea of simplicity is used to characterize substance, and it is very significant that it enters in a context where Leibniz is keen to emphasize that true substances have no parts.

The term "simple substance" is, of course, closely associated with the monadology. Remember, again, the opening line of the 'Monadologie': "The monad, which we shall discuss here, is nothing but a simple substance that enters into composites—simple, that is, without parts." The term "simple substance" doesn't really enter Leibniz's philosophical vocabulary until surprisingly late as a genuine technical term. If we are to trust the Akademie editors, it appears in Leibniz's philosophical writings only a small handful of times before 1690. (I count only four occurrences.) And when it appears in those earlier texts, it is meant as a designation for the soul or substantial form of a corporeal substance, though in none of these passages does Leibniz claim that simple substances are the ultimate constituents of reality, as he will later say of the monads.[86] Indeed, it isn't

---

[84] Leibniz makes a similar claim in a letter to the Duchess of Orléans, March 1696: "Car les unités n'ont point de parties, autrement elles seraient multitudes, et ce qui n'a point de parties, ne peut pas se corrompre...." Quoted in Becco (1978), 139.

[85] It is curious, though, that calling substances "full," as he does in the previous sentence, is taken to indicate that "man" is the substance, and not "soul." Is the last sentence intended to replace what has gone before? Is there a sense of simplicity that makes it consistent with the claim that "man" counts as a substance?

[86] See A6.4.635, A6.4.1673, A6.4.1584. In the first two occurrences, the Akademie editors note that "simple" is a later addition. The last is in the heading to 'Discours de métaphysique' § 35. Becco (1975a), 67–8 and Becco (1975b), 280–1 claim on the basis of a close study of the ms. that it, too, is a later addition. There is also an occurrence of the term in one of the texts from March 1690 that the Akademie editors link to the Fardella memo:

There are infinite simple substances or created things in any particle of matter; and matter is composed from these, not as from parts, but as from constitutive principles or [*seu*] immediate requisites, just as points enter into the essence of a continuum and yet not as parts, for nothing is a part unless it is homogeneous with a whole, but substance is not homogeneous with matter or body any more than a point is with a line.   (A 6.4.1673)

But first of all, the critical apparatus of the Akademie edition indicates that the "simple" in the opening sentence was an addition, opening up the possibility of it having been a later emendation of an earlier text, something Leibniz often did. Furthermore, even if that word were from the original period, it is easy enough to read it in a way perfectly consistent with the corporeal substance view. If we read the "simple substances" as the souls or forms, and the "created things" as the corporeal substances, and the "or" as "or, perhaps better," then we have a restatement of the corporeal substance view.

even clear that the term has a consistent meaning for Leibniz in this period. It appears once in a letter to Arnauld, but only as a late addition to the letter as it was about to be sent. There he talks about wanting to distinguish "simple corporeal substances" from living things and animals, suggesting a distinction between simple and complex corporeal substances.[87] There is a another very interesting text, a letter to Sophie from 29 December/8 January 1692/3, the record of a conversation from 29 November 1692, where 'simple' is most naturally interpreted again as referring to a corporeal substance.[88] After 1700, though, it appears 130 times in the texts edited in the Gerhardt edition. This suggests that, after 1700, it became a technical term for Leibniz, understood, as in the 'Monadologie', as a substance that lacks parts.

In addition to the occurrence of simplicity in the connection with the definition of substance in the notes on Thomasius, the term "simple substance" appears in connection with the "Système nouveau." It is not in that text itself, as published in the *Journal des sçavans*,[89] but it does appear in another important text connected with it, the unpublished notes on

---

[87] Leibniz to Arnauld, 10 September 1687, Leibniz (1952), 89; Rodis-Lewis indicates that the word 'simple' was added to the copyist's text when it was sent to Arnauld. For the letter as preserved in Leibniz's draft in Hanover, which doesn't contain the term, see G II 121. The word 'simple' also appears in Leibniz's characterization of Cordemoy in his letter to Arnauld, 28 November/8 December 1686. There he talks about Cordemoy recognizing atoms "or extended indivisible bodies" so as to "find something fixed to make up a simple being [*un estre simple*]" (G II 78). But here we are dealing with a simple *being* and not a simple *substance*, as well as something that Leibniz explicitly thinks is extended.

[88] See A1.9.15–16. Leibniz there gives an exposition of the familiar view that inanimate bodies and the organic bodies that are constituents of corporeal substances are aggregates of genuine beings, "like an army or a flock or like a pool filled with fish." But, he asserts, " the soldiers are true beings, but the army is only a plurality of beings." He then writes:

And one can say as much about all these composite things, that they are only pluralities, or heaps of many entities. Only a simple is a true entity, strictly speaking, without the aid of the imagination. I speak of a simple which is a true unity. Now, it is obvious that composites cannot be without simples, nor pluralities without unities, nor finally beings of the imagination without true beings, strictly speaking. One cannot destroy unities, since destructions are only the dissipations of pluralities. A man or any other true substance is a unity, but the body of a man is a plurality. . . .

Here it seems plausible that a simple is just the same as a unity for Leibniz, and that he considers individual human beings to be simple in this sense. It is interesting and perhaps significant here that Leibniz talks about 'simples' and *not* 'simple substances.'

[89] It does appear in the later version of the text that Gerhardt chose to publish. See G IV 479 (AG 140). Becco (1975b), 283 argues that the addition of 'simple' to 'substance' in this passage dates from 1695, on the basis of the passage from Leibniz's notes on Foucher which we are about to examine. I am not convinced that it was that early. But whenever it was added, it was certainly not in the published version, nor did it appear the following year when the "Système nouveau" was reprinted for the Amsterdam edition of the *Journal*.

Foucher's objection to the "Système nouveau" that was discussed above in Chapter 4.

In this important text, Leibniz discusses the difference between mathematical extension and real bodies. Mathematical extension is not composed of parts, but is divisible into parts: in mathematics we don't have to worry about how extension can be grounded in something smaller or more basic. But the situation is different with actual things. Leibniz writes:

[I]n actual substantial things, the whole is a result or coming together of simple substances, or rather of a multitude of real unities. . . . Those who make up a line from points have looked for the first elements in ideal things or relations, something completely contrary to what they should have done; and those who found that relations like number or space . . . cannot be formed by the coming together of points were wrong, for the most part, to deny that substantial realities have first elements, as if the substantial realities had no primitive unities, or as if there were no simple substances. . . . [I]n realities in which only divisions actually made enter into consideration, the whole is only a result or coming together, like a flock of sheep. It is true that the number of simple substances which enter into a mass, however small, is infinite, since besides the soul, which brings about the real unity of the animal, the body of the sheep (for example) is actually subdivided—that is, it is, again, an assemblage of invisible animals or plants which are in the same way composites, outside of that which also brings about their real unity. Although this goes on to infinity, it is evident that, in the end, everything reduces [revenient à] to these unities, the rest or the results being nothing but well-founded phenomena.[90]

Interesting passage. Here Leibniz does seem to put something that he calls "simple substances" at the ground of everything. But even so, it isn't entirely clear what is going on here. While Leibniz doesn't say what it means for a substance to be simple, given his concern in the "Système nouveau" and in the notes on Thomasius with substances as lacking parts, it is quite plausible to suppose that simple substances are substances that lack parts. Nor is it entirely clear what he means when he says that simple substances are the "first elements" of things or that everything "reduces to" simple substances.

But suggestive as these passages are of the later monadology, they can also be interpreted in ways that make them perfectly consistent with his

---

[90] G IV 491–2 (AG 146–7).

earlier views. A simple substance would seem to be understood in contrast with a composite substance, a substance made up of parts, like a corporeal substance.[91] The examples he gives of simple substances include souls and forms, strongly suggesting that their simplicity implies that they are without extension. Leibniz does appear to argue that simple substances, substances without parts, are in some sense fundamental, and perhaps even the *only* entities that count as genuine substances. But in exactly *what* sense are they fundamental? In these texts, does Leibniz intend to establish them as the "true atoms of nature" or the "elements of things," as he will later characterize the monads?[92] One can read these passages in that way. But there are ways of reading them that allow us to understand them as advancing much the same view as he had earlier advanced in the correspondence with Arnauld. In the "Système nouveau" Leibniz refers to the unities "absolutely destitute of parts" as "the first absolute principles of the composition of things, and, as it were, the final elements in the analysis of substances." This can be read as an early statement of the monadology, but it can also be read simply as asserting that forms or souls are needed to transform complex organic bodies into genuine unities. Such forms or souls might be understood as the "final elements in the analysis of substances" insofar as, without them, organic bodies would be mere aggregates. One can also understand Leibniz in this way when he says that "metaphysical points or points of substance" are "constituted by forms or souls." They may be "constituted by the forms or souls" in the sense that these points of substance are to be *identified with* forms or souls. But the French here—"*constituez par les formes ou ames*"—can be understood in a more active way, that the forms or souls *transform* aggregates into metaphysical points or points of substance. One can read the notes on Foucher in a similar way. When Leibniz says that "in actual substantial things, the whole is a result or coming together of simple substances, or rather of a multitude of real unities," Leibniz can be read as asserting that in substantial things (i.e., bodies), the whole is an aggregate of simple substances. But in the last clause he seems to clarify that by asserting that, strictly speaking, what it contains is "real unities": these real unities might be corporeal substances. When he asserts that "substantial

---

[91] Remember, though, the qualification introduced above in n. 71.
[92] See 'Monadologie' § 3.

realities have first elements" that are "primitive unities" or "simple sub-stances," he can be read as asserting not that substantial realities are *made up* of simple substances, but that they are made up of corporeal substances that are transformed into unities by virtue of having souls or forms, as he will explicitly assert in the following sentences. And finally, when he argues that "everything reduces" to these unities, it is not implausible that the unities in question might be the corporeal substances he had been discuss-ing in the immediately preceding sentence, the "assemblage of invisible animals or plants" that "goes on to infinity" in the body of the corporeal substance. Now, the notes on Thomasius, where Leibniz offers a definition of substance on which substance *as such* must lack parts ("*Substance* is a simple complete entity"), would seem to be the strongest evidence that Leibniz had something like the later monadology picture in mind in these years. Maybe so, but even here there is room for doubt. In the penultimate phrase of that passage, the example Leibniz offers of a substance is that of a living thing: "like a man, not a soul."

Leibniz Discovers Monads

So far we have been talking about real unities, entities without parts, and simple substances, the latter terms which seem to have entered Leibniz's vocabulary in 1695 or so. But in these years, another new term enters Leibniz's philosophical vocabulary: the monad.

The term 'monad' or 'monas,' in its Greek form, has a long history before Leibniz. It appears in Goclenius, in both his Latin and Greek philosophical lexicons (1613 and 1615). The first definition he gives in the Greek lexicon is just "unitas," that is, unity. More specifically, he divides the monad into transcendent and inferior. The transcendent monad is the God of Pythagoras, the principle of things and the metaphysical unity. In its less exalted use, the monad is just the arithmetic unit or the simple term in logic.[93] In his commentary on the 'Monadologie' in his *Historia critica philosophiae* (1744), Jacob Brucker also relates the term 'monad' to Pythagoras as well as to other ancients, including Plato and his followers.[94]

---

[93] Goclenius (1613), 707; Goclenius (1615), 148–9.
[94] Brucker (1742–44), vol. 4B, 402–3.

More recently, Anne Becco has traced the use of the term among Leibniz's contemporaries and near-contemporaries, including F. M. van Helmont, Knorr van Rosenroth, Henry More, Ralph Cudworth, and Anne Conway. For her, the mystery is not why Leibniz came to use the term, but why he came to use it so late: "Devant une telle profusion de monadographies, pourquoi Leibniz en est-il venu *si tard* à la *Monadologie?*"[95]

The first occurrence of the word that we know of in Leibniz's texts is in a letter to L'Hospital dated 12/22 July 1695. The context is a brief discussion of the "Système nouveau," which had just come out in the *Journal des sçavans* in the June and July issues. Leibniz writes:

The key to my doctrine on this subject consists in the consideration of that which is genuinely a real unity, a monad [*une unité reelle, Monas*].[96]

The next documented occurrence occurs more than a year later, suggesting that in mid-1695 the term had not yet entered Leibniz's technical vocabulary. The context is a letter to his frequent correspondent Michelangelo Fardella from 3/13 September 1696. In that letter he is trying to get Fardella to help him develop and disseminate his metaphysical ideas in much the way L'Hospital and the Bernoullis helped him with his new calculus. In the course of that exhortation, he offers a brief summary of his views. He writes:

It seems to me that the nub of the matter consists in the true notion of substance, which is the same as the notion of a monad or real unity and, so to speak, a formal atom or essential point. For there are no atoms of matter, whence in vain do we seek unity in matter; and a mathematical point isn't essential but modal, whence the continuum is not made up out of points, and yet something substantial comes about from unities.[97]

The term 'monad' must have come up in the correspondence that follows, for in a letter to Fardella from 5/15 June 1697, Leibniz replies to a request for further clarification by noting that "what you ask about the nature

[95] Becco (1975b), 294.   [96] A3.6.451 (WF 57).

[97] Thanks to Herma Kliege-Biller of the Münster Leibniz-Forschungsstelle for an advanced preliminary version of the Fardella correspondence, and to Philip Beeley for transmitting it. The letter is also in Leibniz (1857), 325–8. Leibniz was hoping to sway Fardella into including discussions of his views in a book that Fardella was then in the process of writing, which was to appear in 1698 under the title *Animae humanae natura ab Augustino detecta*...(Venice: Sumptibus Hieronymi Albricci).

of monads and substances can easily be satisfied if you indicate what in particular you would like explained about the matter."[98]

But by mid-1697, the term 'monad' seems to have become established as a part of Leibniz's philosophical vocabulary. In a letter to Conrad Barthold Behrens from 24 December/3 January 1697/8, Leibniz writes about monads as unities in opposition to aggregates:

By the word 'substance' I here understand a substance, and not substances, that is, not some aggregate but a true one, which I call a monad, because it differs from an aggregate (such as every material mass is) just as a flock of sheep differs from a sheep, or a fish pond from a fish.

Leibniz continues:

Therefore in every substance endowed with a body is a dominant monad and an organic mass which it dominates.

He finishes by noting that "everything is full of souls, or, if you prefer, of monads analogous to souls, though not every soul is a mind, but only those which are endowed with an intellect."[99] And in a letter to Johann Gebhard Rabener from January (?) 1698, Leibniz wrote:

Furthermore, since matter is nothing but a real phenomenon of many aggregates, and, as they commonly say, an entity through aggregation, and, moreover, since an aggregate is constituted by simples, I later discovered that we must arrive at monads. Not, indeed, corporeal or spatial [monads], since the continuum is not composed of indivisibles, nor are there any material atoms, but, however, substantial [monads]. Therefore every true monad is a simple substance, and is in some sense analogous to a mind, and that hence it follows that [every monad] is coeval with the world, unless it was created by God in the course of time.[100] ⟶ Unextended/ immaterial

Later that year, in a letter to Johann Bernoulli from August/September 1698 Leibniz wrote:

By monad I understand a substance truly one, namely, one which is not an aggregate of substances.... [I]f there were no souls or something analogous to them, then there would be no I [*Ego*], no monads, no real unities, and therefore

---

[98] In the letters I have been able to consult I didn't find Fardella's request or any further discussion of monads after this remark, but that may just be either because the letters have been lost, or because they have not yet been transcribed. Cf., though, Leibniz to Fardella 6 April 1699, where there is a mention of "monadic force."

[99] A1.15.153.   [100] A1.15.260.

there would be no substantial multitudes; indeed, there would be nothing in bodies but phantasms. From this, one can easily judge that there is no part of matter in which monads do not exist.[101]

This letter comes at about the same time as the word 'monad' first appears in print in a Leibnizian text, the "De ipsa natura," published in the *Acta eruditorum* in the issue of September 1698.

The "De ipsa natura" is an important text. The full title reads, "On Nature Itself, or, on the Inherent Force and Actions of Created Things, Toward Confirming and Illustrating their Dynamics." In it Leibniz emphasizes the inherent activity of substance, and argues against both occasionalism, the view that only God is a genuinely active causal agent, and the Spinozism that Leibniz thinks follows directly from the denial of causal agency to created things.[102] Leibniz considered it one of his most important publications, and referred to it often in later writings and letters.

The term 'monad' appears five times in four passages in the "De ipsa natura." Two of the passages use the word only in passing, and aren't very informative. In one passage on mind–body interaction Leibniz talks about "the interaction between substances or monads" as arising "not from an influx," but through pre-established harmony.[103] In another passage he notes simply that real changes in things ultimately "derive from modifications of the monads existing in things."[104] But the other uses of the term are much more substantive, and give us a better idea of just what he has in mind by a monad at this moment. In one passage, Leibniz gives an argument that can be found many times in earlier writings, about why there must be something over and above the material in bodies, something like soul. He writes:

And this substantial principle itself [*ipsum substantiale principium*] is what is called the soul in living things and the substantial form in other things; insofar as, together with matter, it constitutes a substance that is truly one, or something one *per se,* it makes up what I call a monad [*id facit quod ego Monadem appello*], since, if these true and real unities were eliminated, only entities through aggregation, indeed (it follows from this), no true entities at all would be left in bodies. For, although there are atoms of substance, namely monads lacking parts [*monades partibus carentes*], there are no atoms of bulk [*moles*], that is, atoms of the least possible extension,

---

[101]   GM III 537 (AG 167).   [102]   On the intellectual background of the essay, see Nobis (1966).
[103]   "De ipsa natura" § 10, G IV 510 (AG 161).   [104]   "De ipsa natura" § 13, G IV 514 (AG 165).

nor are there any ultimate elements, since a continuum cannot be composed out of points.[105]

Monads come up again in a passage where he is talking about why we have to add soul or form to matter. He writes:

Spirit [*spiritus*] is to be understood, not as an intelligent being... but as a soul or as a form analogous to a soul, not as a simple modification, but as something constitutive, substantial, enduring, what I usually call a monad, in which there is something like perception and appetite.[106]

Here the monad seems to be identified with "a soul or ... a form analogous to a soul."

No doubt when Leibniz's philosophical papers and correspondence from these years are published the term "monad" will be found in many other texts; while Fardella and Bernoulli were important correspondents, and it is unsurprising that they would have been given Leibniz's inner thoughts, Behrens and Rabener seem not to have been on such close terms with Leibniz. If he told them about monads, who knows with whom else Leibniz may have shared his views? And who knows what currently unpublished notes from these years there may be in the archives that contain further clarifications of Leibniz's thought about monads in this period?

But though the term "monad" begins to appear in these years, it is somewhat obscure what exactly it means to Leibniz at this moment, or whether it should be read as an indication that he now has the doctrine that will later be associated with the term; as with the term "simple substance" or "substance without parts" that appears in Leibniz's vocabulary in the years just before, the term "monad" can almost always be interpreted in ways that are fully consistent with the corporeal substance view of the correspondence with Arnauld. In many of the passages that we have examined, "monad" seems simply to be a new word for "unity"; understood in that way, there is no reason why a corporeal substance couldn't be considered a monad. Some of the other passages do look as if they are using the term in a way that is more suggestive of the later uses. But maybe not. In a number of the passages he refers to souls or forms as monads. For example, in the letter to Behrens, he talks about a "dominant monad" that

---

[105] "De ipsa natura" § 11, G IV 511 (AG 162).   [106] "De ipsa natura" § 12, G IV 512 (AG 163).

brings about a corporeal substance. In the next sentence he acknowledges that the rational soul is a "true monad," and a few sentences later he seems to identify the souls with which everything is full with "monads analogous with souls." In the "De ipsa natura" he similarly talks about the souls everywhere in things as "what I usually call a monad," and refers to the "atoms of substance" as the "monads lacking parts." But while these passages all seem to assert that souls are monads, they don't assert that all monads are souls or soul-like. And when Leibniz refers to the atoms of substance as "monads lacking parts," it isn't obvious whether he is asserting that all monads as such lack parts, or that it is the particular kind of monads that lack parts, i.e. souls, that are the atoms of substance insofar as they bring about the unity of composite substances. Among the passages that we have been examining so far, only one seems decisively to support the view that Leibniz's monads at this moment are to be identified with the monads of the later writings. In the January 1698 letter to Rabener, Leibniz wrote that "every true monad is a simple substance, and is in some sense analogous to a mind." This, indeed, echoes the opening line of the 'Monadologie' where Leibniz identifies monads with simple substances, and immediately draws the conclusion that they are unextended. But this contrasts with another clear passage from Leibniz's correspondence with Johann Bernoulli from 20/30 September 1698:

What I call a complete monad or individual substance [*substantia singularis*] is not so much the soul, as it is the animal itself, or something analogous to it, endowed with a soul or form and an organic body.[107]

This, too, seems as clear as one would like, and as clearly in contradiction with the view that he expresses to Rabener and later in the 'Monadologie.'

Where does this leave us? Knowing where Leibniz will be going in his thought, we can see in these texts from 1694 to 1698 clear marks and traces of his future doctrines. But, again, I'm not sure that Leibniz himself could have seen this in those same texts, particularly in the earlier years in this period. Because we know where Leibniz will eventually end up, these words and phrases jump off the page at us. But it is not obvious how Leibniz himself understood them. It is not implausible to hold that in

---

[107] GM III 542 (AG 168).

1694 and the years immediately following, Leibniz had fleeting glimpses of where he was later to go, or even real moments of conviction in a world grounded in mind-like and non-extended simple substances without parts, monads as he later came to understand them: such a view was probably on his horizon. But I am not so sure that he could always distinguish this new world clearly from the world of corporeal substances that had occupied him for a decade and a half before. Our duck may have been his rabbit. And I am reasonably sure that insofar as he could distinguish it from what he had believed earlier, he was not yet willing to sign on to it in an explicit and whole-hearted way, at least in mid-decade. It would be nice to have all of the papers from the decade of the 1690s to examine, as we now have the philosophical papers that go up to 1690. But even these papers may not fully illuminate the situation. We may never be able to mark with certainty the moment at which the doctrine of the monadology emerges from the earlier corporeal substance view.

But even though we don't know when exactly it emerges and when exactly Leibniz first signs on to it, by 1700 it is definitely there, and Leibniz seems definitely committed to it.

The first clear and extended expression of the monadological metaphysics I can find in Leibniz's writings comes in June 1700, about a year and a half before Leibniz admitted his true thoughts to de Volder. The context is a series of letters with the Electress Sophie of Hanover, an intimate friend of Leibniz's and a long-time and frequent correspondent on intellectual matters. Sophie had sent Leibniz a text that had been given to her by another friend and correspondent of Leibniz's, the theologian Gerhard Wolter Molanus. In this text Molanus discussed the distinction between mind and body from a generally Cartesian orientation.[108] This gave Leibniz the opportunity to convey to Sophie some of his most recent thoughts. While he may well have talked with her in person after this, the last extended letter he had sent to Sophie before this one on matters philosophical was on 4 November 1696. In that letter, the views that he expressed to her were very much along the lines of the recently published "Système nouveau," to which he refers in the letter.[109] But the letter he sent

---

[108] The text is found in A1.18.92–6. The text was written on the occasion of a discussion between Molanus and Sophie's son, the Elector Georg-Ludwig. See A1.18.91. For Leibniz's very short but direct reply to Molanus, see A1.18.718.

[109] See A1.13.89–93.

her on 12 June 1700 seems different in interesting ways. There Leibniz wrote:

Everyone is agreed that *matter* has parts, and consequently it is a *multitude* of many substances, as a flock of sheep would be. But since every multitude presupposes *true unities*, it is obvious that these unities cannot be material, otherwise they would, again, be multitudes, and not true and pure unities, as are needed to make up a multitude. And thus the unities are substances apart [*substances à part*], which are not divisible, nor, as a consequence, perishable, since everything which is divisible has parts that one can distinguish there before separating them. However, since we are dealing with *unities of substance*, there must be force and perception in these very unities, since without that there would be no force or perception in all that which is made of them, which can only contain repetitions and relations of that which is already in these unities. And thus in bodies which have sensation there must be *unique substances*, or unities which have perception. It is this simple substance, this unity of substance, or this monad, which one calls *soul*. And consequently, souls, like all of the other unities of substance, are immaterial, indivisible, and imperishable, since all destruction of *substantial things* can only be through dissolution. And if these unities once have life, they must be immortal and always live. These unities truly constitute substances, and every unity makes up a unique single substance; everything else are only beings by aggregation or multitudes. Or better, they are accidents, that is attributes that endure or transient modes that belong to substances.[110]

Here it looks to me as if we have, in essence, the monadology that will occupy Leibniz for most of the rest of his philosophical career. As in many earlier texts, Leibniz argues here that matter is a multitude, but that multitudes presuppose "unities of substance." But the unities in question are definitely not the corporeal substances of the earlier view: "[T]hese unities cannot be material, otherwise they would, again, be multitudes." As such, it would seem that they must be non-extended. But most importantly, Leibniz writes, "these unities truly constitute substances, and every unity makes up a unique single substance." That is to say, these unities are all that there really exists; beside these true substances, all there are are aggregates or accidents. A bit later in the same text Leibniz introduces what will become a familiar trope in his later monadology:

It is true that the material that comes to us through sense enters into our interior organs, such as the brain and the spirits or subtle fluids which are contained in

[110] A1.18.113–14.

it. But the material cannot enter into a true unity, which has no pores or doors, otherwise it wouldn't be a unity but something composed. Thus that which is in a unity is not the material but the species or representation of the material, which represents that which is extended without having extension itself.[111]

As in later texts, the monads, the true substance, "has no pores or doors"; that is to say, it has no windows.

If there is any doubt about Leibniz's position here, Leibniz is clearer still in a text that he sent Sophie on 19 November 1701, at almost the same moment that he began to reveal his real views to de Volder:

[H]owever, every multitude must be formed and composed of an assemblage of true unities. . . . Now, that which has neither parts nor extension doesn't have any shape either, but it must have thought and force or effort, the source of which one also knows cannot come from extension or shapes. Consequently, we must seek this source in the unities, since there are only unities and multitudes in nature. Or rather, there is nothing real but the unities, since every assemblage is only the mode [façon] and appearance of a being, but in truth it only has being insofar as it contains true unities. . . . From this one can conclude that there are unities everywhere, or rather, that everything is unities.[112]

Here we have it, as explicitly as one could want: true unities lack all parts, all extension, and all shape. And all there are are such unities and multitudes made up of these unities. These non-extended and simple unities are in a clear sense foundational. Indeed, he seems to argue, stronger still, such unities are all that there really is in the world.

It is interesting that at first he seems to have been a bit shy of telling his correspondents about his real metaphysical views on the material world. In a letter to Thomas Burnett he sent on 2/12 February 1700, at about the same time he was opening his metaphysical soul to Sophie, he was still telling Burnett about a world of corporeal substance, giving him no hint that there was anything more to his thought.[113] And then there were the first letters to de Volder, where, again, there was no hint of the

---

[111] A1.18.115. The same formula appears in an earlier draft, A1.18.112.   [112] A1.20.74–75.

[113] "In bodies I distinguish corporeal substance from matter, and I distinguish primary from secondary matter. Secondary matter is an aggregate or composite of several corporeal substances, as a flock is composed of several animals. But each animal and each plant is also a corporeal substance, having in itself a principle of unity which makes it truly a substance and not an aggregate. And this principle of unity is that which one calls soul, or it is something analogous to soul. . . ." [A1.18.375–6 (AG 289–90)].

view that he later revealed to him, with disastrous consequences for their correspondence, that all true substances are simple. But by 1700 or 1701 or so, we can be pretty sure that Leibniz has signed on to the monadology picture that he seems to have been contemplating in one way or another since the mid-1690s.

Even though Leibniz had committed to the basic picture by then, there is every reason to believe that at the moment he first announced it to certain of his correspondents, he had not yet worked out all the details of the view. In the following chapter, we shall turn to that question and examine some aspects of how Leibniz develops his view in the first decade of the new century.

Why Monads?

By 1700 or so, Leibniz had clearly committed himself to the new metaphysics of simple substances, substances without parts, what he had come to call monads. But, one might ask, what led him to this apparently new view of the world? Leibniz came to the new world of corporeal substances in 1678/9 by way of two arguments, one from unity, and the other from force and activity. And it is through unity and activity that he was led to the new metaphysics as well, I would argue.

The path to the new monadological metaphysics through the notion of unity is fairly clear. As I have emphasized earlier, from 1678 or 1679 on, Leibniz was concerned with genuine unity as a criterion of substancehood. In the passages that we have been examining from the mid-1690s, Leibniz moves subtly from an emphasis on *individual* substance to an emphasis on *simple* substance. And, for the first time, Leibniz is beginning to worry about the way in which having parts may undermine genuine unity. He didn't worry about that in the correspondence with Arnauld. Remember Arnauld's planarian. The fact that you could cut the tail off, and that the tail would appear to retain vital motion, didn't in any way undermine the claim that it was a genuine unity. But in the later texts Leibniz seems to be taking genuine unity more seriously, as implying that a genuine substance has no parts. And if it has no parts, then it can only be a non-extended, mind-like being. And if all substances must be genuine unities in this stronger sense, if all substances must be *simple* substances, as Leibniz was later to write to de Volder, then we are in the monadology. In this way, pressing the unity criterion of substancehood does lead us directly to the monadology. I think that Leibniz certainly didn't see this in 1686 and 1687 when he was writing to Arnauld, and probably didn't see it in 1695 and 1696 when he was working through the issues connected with the "Système nouveau."

But by 1700 or 1701 he had certainly reached that conclusion. As we have seen, when he explains to de Volder, for example, that every substance is simple, he means it in exactly this sense: "When I say that every substance is simple, I understand by this that it lacks parts."[114] And simplicity in this precise sense has become for him a central part of what it is to be a genuine unity and thus a genuine substance:

> I regard substance itself…like the 'I' or something similar, as the indivisible or complete monad….And if there is nothing that is *truly one*, then every *true thing* will be eliminated….[S]ince simple things alone are true things, the rest are only beings through aggregation, and therefore phenomena, and, as Democritus used to say, exist by convention not by nature.[115]

In this way genuine unity leads Leibniz to simplicity, which eventually leads him to the view that such simple substances are genuinely foundational.[116]

But there is another path to the monadological metaphysics, through the notion of matter. Here, though, the path is a bit more complicated and something of a conjecture. What follows is a story, and it may be just a story. Unfortunately, we don't (yet) have the documents to be able to substantiate the conjectures that I am making about what is driving Leibniz. But it is an interesting way of seeing another factor that may have moved Leibniz in the direction of his later metaphysics.

I have attributed to Leibniz a metaphysical view in his middle period, the 1680s and 1690s, in which what is foundational are corporeal substances, unities of soul, and organic body. Leibniz takes this to be an update of the scholastic notions of form and matter, where the soul of the corporeal substance corresponds with the form, and the body with the matter. But,

---

[114] Leibniz to de Volder, April 1702, G II 239.

[115] Leibniz to de Volder, 20 June 1703, G II 251, 252.

[116] This, in essence, is the argument that Donald Rutherford suggests in Rutherford (1995), 272–3. Rutherford argues that pre-established harmony cannot provide Leibniz with the true unity he needs for something to be a substance, and so is driven to the view that only monads are true substances.

as I argued in Chapter 4, from early on, there is an ambiguity in Leibniz's conception of matter, one that is reflected in the distinction that he later drew between primary and secondary matter. On at least one of the principal formulations that he offers, secondary matter is an aggregate of substances, a collection of individuals, corporeal substances that are complete substances. Leibniz distinguishes this from primary matter, which he identifies with the primitive passive force of a substance. As such, primary matter is incomplete, something that, together with form, constitutes a complete substance. As I suggested in Chapter 4, secondary matter is the notion of matter that comes out of the "unity" argument for corporeal substance: it is the organic body of the corporeal substance, the collection of smaller corporeal substances that, united with a substantial form, results in the corporeal substance. Primary matter, on the other hand, derives from the arguments for corporeal substance that come from motion and its laws. Conceived of in this way, matter is that in the corporeal substance that gives rise to resistance and impenetrability, that from which extension derives. And as I argued earlier, there is every reason to think that just as Leibniz thought that the two kinds of arguments both led to the same conclusion, that is, the revival of substantial forms and the positing of corporeal substances, he believed that the two conceptions of matter associated with the two arguments are compatible with one another, that there is room for both in his world.

But that is not so clear. As understood in a standard scholastic text-book, Eustachius a Sancto Paulo's *Summa philosophica quadripartita* (1609), for example, primary matter is defined as "an incomplete substance in potentiality with respect to all forms," a formula that is very similar to the one that Leibniz uses in characterizing primary matter. But for Eustachius and his fellow Aristotelians, primary matter is also "the first subject of any-thing," that which remains constant in change, as a given substance loses one substantial form (say that which makes it water) and acquires another (say that which makes it earth).[117] It is a power or potentiality insofar as it is not actual unless united with a form, itself without form, that to which substantial form is attached at the bottom-most level. But where is there for Leibniz to put such primary matter? In his world in the middle period, there is an infinite chain of corporeal substances, animate creatures with

---

[117] Eustachius (1609), part III (Physica), vol. 2, 18ff.

souls (forms) and bodies (secondary matter, aggregates of animate creatures) that go to infinity. The form of a corporeal substance transforms complex organic bodies, natural machines, into genuine substances by contributing unity and activity. But these natural machines are aggregates of corporeal substances, infinitely complex, divided to infinity. But whither primary matter? In this Leibnizian world of bugs in bugs, there seems to be no room for primary matter, no place to put it.[118]

But it is interesting to note that one very prominent feature of the new view that he begins to outline to de Volder in 1702 is a place for primary matter.

> For the rest, in the monad, or complete simple substance, I do not unite anything with the entelechy except a primitive passive force, which is related to the whole mass of the organic body.... I therefore distinguish: (1) the primitive entelechy or soul; (2) matter, namely, primary matter or primitive passive power; (3) the monad completed by these two things; (4) the mass or secondary matter, or organic machine for which innumerable subordinate monads come together; and (5) the animal, or corporeal substance, which the monad dominating in the machine makes one.[119]

Secondary matter is now an aggregate of non-extended monads: it is the body of the corporeal substance, one of the notions of matter originally introduced to coordinate with the substantial form, introduced to bring unity to the world of material things.[120] But, as I argued earlier, with the new monadology comes a new sub-basement in his ontology, a genuine foundation. Leibniz can now say that there is a sense in which there is a foundation to everything, simple substances without parts, something below which one cannot go, the level of the monads. And with that he finally has a place to put primary matter, primitive passive force, the other notion of matter that he had originally posited in the revolution of the late 1670s. The primary matter, united with the entelechy, now constitutes the non-extended metaphysical atom that Leibniz wants to

[118] Rutherford (1995), 157 advances this as a reason for thinking that Leibniz held the monadological metaphysics even in the middle years. I see no reason to think that Leibniz was aware of the problem until much later in his career. While it may have driven him to the monadology in later years, I think that in the period of the correspondence with Arnauld, for example, Leibniz may never have asked himself this question.

[119] Leibniz to de Volder, 20 June 1703, G II 252.

[120] At least it is in this text. As we shall see below in Ch. 9, this view of bodies as aggregates of monads is only one of the views that he advances.

call a monad. In this way the duality of the notion of matter has been resolved, and the two different notions of matter now find their different places in Leibniz's metaphysics. It is, perhaps, unsurprising then that, once introduced in the mid-1690s, the distinction between primary and secondary matter becomes an established part of Leibniz's doctrine.[121] The duality remains something of a problem, though. Primitive passive force must now be understood in the context of the monadology not in terms of the impenetrability and resistance of extended bodies but more generally as the passive element of substance, understood in terms of the perceptions and appetitions of the non-extended substantial elements of things, the monads. But even so, one can imagine that Leibniz saw this as an advance over the earlier view.

With the benefit of hindsight, we may be able to see these later developments prefigured in Leibniz's earlier thought. Taken very seriously, the criterion of unity for substancehood can be seen to lead directly to the criterion of simplicity, the claim that substances lack parts. And from there it is a short step to the claim that genuine substances must be unextended and like souls. Similarly, if we look closely at the different ways that the notion of matter functions in Leibniz's thought in the early 1680s, it is clear that he has to draw a distinction between secondary matter (the organic body) and primary matter (the primitive passive force), and that finding a place for the primary matter drives him to posit a sub-basement of simple substances below the infinite series of corporeal substances, a place in which to put the primary matter.

In this sense one might say that Leibniz was implicitly already a monadological metaphysician in those earlier years, insofar as he already held doctrines that would lead him eventually to the position that he admitted to Sophie in 1700 and to de Volder in 1701. But that is to put the matter in a misleading way. If Leibniz was a monadologist in those earlier years,

---

[121] In addition to the passages cited, see also: Leibniz to Thomas Burnett, 2/12 February 1700, A1.18.375–6 (AG 289–90); *Nouv. Ess.* 2.23.23, 4.3.6; Response to Lami (1704(?)), G IV 572; Leibniz to Des Bosses, 11 March 1706, LDB 34; Leibniz to Des Bosses, 16 October 1706, LDB 78; Comments on Spinoza (1706), Leibniz (2002b), 6 (AG 274); Leibniz to Des Bosses, 30 April 1709, LDB 122–4; Leibniz to Rudolph Christian Wagner, 4 June 1710, G VII 529; Leibniz to Remond, 4 November 1715, G III 657; etc.

I suspect that he himself didn't really know it. Let me remind you of the letter he wrote Remond in 1714:

But when I looked for the ultimate reasons for mechanism, and even for the laws of motion, I was greatly surprised to see that they could not be found in mathematics but that I should have to return to metaphysics. This led me back to entelechies, and from the material to the formal, and at last brought me to understand after many corrections and forward steps in my thinking, that monads or simple substances are the only true substances and that material things are only phenomena, though well founded and well connected.[122]

Leibniz presents his monadological metaphysics as the necessary consequence of his starting place. But he acknowledges that it didn't all happen at once, but only "after many corrections and forward steps in my thinking...." We should not be surprised that we see in these earlier writings hints of the later monadology; it would be surprising if we didn't. But, at the same time, we shouldn't give them a significance that they may not have had for Leibniz himself. Though they may have led Leibniz to his mature view, he probably couldn't have seen it until years later.

[122] G III 606 (L 655).

9

Monads, Bodies, and Corporeal Substances: the Endgame

I began the story of Leibniz's development in Chapter 1 with a long quotation from a letter Leibniz wrote to Nicolas Remond on 10 January 1714, a letter to which we have returned a number of times in the course of our narrative. That letter was a response to a fawning letter that Remond had sent him shortly before. Remond began his letter as follows: "Since I read your *Theodicy*, I have not ceased thanking God for having allowed me to be born in a century enlightened by a mind such as yours."[1] It is unsurprising that Leibniz, not a modest man, couldn't resist such words. He replied by entering into a warm exchange with Remond.

Nicolas Remond was the head counselor to the Duc d'Orléans in Paris, a position of great influence, if not power. One might wonder if Leibniz saw in Remond (and in his patroness, the Duchesse d'Orléans, who knew Leibniz's patroness in Hanover) the possibility of an invitation to Paris, and who knows what further honors. But Leibniz was also interested in Remond as a person who might help him to publicize his philosophy in high places. Remond was clearly interested in Leibniz's philosophy; indeed, there was some loose talk of Remond sponsoring a poetic version of Leibniz's philosophy, to be written by his friend the abbé Fraguier, a kind of Leibnizian *De rerum natura*.[2] At the time that Leibniz received the first letter from Remond in late 1713, he was in Vienna, where he had been absent without leave since December 1712 or January 1713, much to the annoyance of his employers in Hanover. (He was to remain there until late August or early September 1714, much to the even greater annoyance of his employers, leaving only in the hopes of catching the last boat to England

---

[1] Remond to Leibniz, 2 June 1713, G III 603.
[2] See Remond to Leibniz, 5 May 1714, G III 616 and Leibniz to Remond, July 1714, G III 621.

when his employer Georg Ludwig in Hanover was made King George I in England.) In Vienna he was well received, made Privy Counselor to the Emperor Karl VI (with an extra salary, of course), and given access to the documents that he needed for his history of the House of Hanover. In Vienna, Leibniz served as the representative of the Elector of Hanover in some delicate diplomatic maneuvers in the Imperial Court, though I suspect that this did not fully make up for his unexcused absence from home. There Leibniz also made contact with Prince Eugène of Savoy, who commanded the Imperial armies.[3] Eugène was well placed, royal, and, most importantly for Leibniz, shared many of Leibniz's philosophical interests. Like Remond, he offered Leibniz the opportunity of making his philosophical ideas known in high circles.[4]

At the moment when Leibniz received his letter from Remond, it wasn't easy to learn the details of Leibniz's monadological metaphysics. Writing to Leibniz on 5 May 1714, Remond remarked that the abbé Fraguier "spoke rightly when he compared the knowledge we have of your system of monads to that which one would have of the sun by the single rays that escape the clouds that cover it."[5] Leibniz replied:

It is true that my *Theodicy* does not suffice to present my system as a whole. But if it is joined with what I have published in various journals . . . it will not fall far short of doing so, at least for the principles.[6]

The details of Leibniz's metaphysical system can indeed be found scattered through the journals, as well as touched upon in the *Theodicy* itself. But Leibniz also recognized that this isn't really enough. In the opening sentence of the letter, Leibniz told Remond that "I had hoped to add to this letter some further explanations about monads which you seemed to ask for, but it grew in my hands, and several distractions have prevented me from finishing it so soon."[7] Leibniz had drafted a response as an appendix to his letter, but, as he indicated to Remond, did not send it.[8]

---

[3] See Aiton (1985), 313.

[4] On Leibniz in Vienna, see Antognazza (2008), 488–95. On Leibniz's interactions with Remond and Eugène, and the genesis of the 'Monadologie' and the "Principes de la nature et de la grâce," see Antognazza (2008), 498–502.

[5] G III 616. Charles Hugony, a Frenchman known to Remond, also transmitted Remond's query about monads to Leibniz in a letter sent on 11 Feb. 1714; see Bodemann (1889), 98 and Leibniz's response, G III 682, to which he refers in his letter to Remond of 14 March 1714, G III 612.

[6] Leibniz to Remond, July 1714, G III 618 (L 656–7).

[7] Leibniz to Remond, July 1714, G III 618.   [8] The text can be found at G III 622–24.

This text was probably the common ancestor of what was to become two finished essays, the "Principes de la nature et de la grâce fondés en raison," and the 'Monadologie.'[9] The "Principes" was finished first, given to Eugène and sent to Remond by the end of August, before Leibniz left Vienna. The 'Monadologie' was finished soon after, and may possibly have been given to both as well, though the history of its final draft is rather murky. The former was intended to be a popular statement of Leibniz's system, and was intended to make his views more accessible to a wider audience. The latter is more technical and more precise, written in a style that would appeal more to the serious metaphysician. Although there are some interesting differences in doctrine, which I shall note later, they cover much the same material. Since there is reason to believe that the 'Monadologie' was written because he was not altogether satisfied with the treatment of the material in the "Principes" (the evidence is not overwhelming, but it is there),[10] let us concentrate for the moment on the more rigorous treatment Leibniz gives in the 'Monadologie.'

The 'Monadologie' is a systematic but brief treatment of some of the main themes from Leibniz's metaphysics that we have already seen, together with much more. It begins with a rather stark announcement of the basic ontology:

1. The monad, which we shall discuss here, is nothing but a simple substance that enters into composites—simple, that is, without parts. . . .

2. And there must be simple substances, since there are composites; for the composite is nothing more than a collection, or aggregate, of simples.

3. But where there are no parts, neither extension, nor shape, nor divisibility is possible. These monads are the true atoms of nature and, in brief, the elements of things.

At the center of the ontology is the simple substance, the true atom of nature, the ultimate element of things. There must be simple substances because there are composites. It is interesting here that Leibniz doesn't say "composite *substances*." While he talks freely about composite substances in the "Principes" and elsewhere in the period, in the 'Monadologie' he never

---

[9] For a lovely discussion of the history of these two texts, their relation to one another and the history of their composition, see Pasini (2005). See the references given there for alternative accounts of this history.

[10] See Boehm (1957), 247.

uses the locution once. This is no casual omission. When a copyist had written "composite substances" in a draft of §2 and crossed it out, Leibniz added his own barring, just to make sure that there was no mistake.[11] In the sections that follow, Leibniz goes on to develop the details of this picture. He first discusses the monads in some detail. Monads can arise and pass out of existence only through creation and annihilation (§§ 4–6); they have no windows, that is, they cannot exert genuine causal influence on one another (§ 7); they contain within themselves only perception and appetition (§§ 8–16); though not all monads are minds, insofar as they are non-extended and have perceptions and appetitions, all monads are mind-like (§§ 18–19), and so on.

After a presentation of his two great principles, the Principle of Contradiction and the Principle of Sufficient Reason (§§ 31ff), Leibniz turns in § 38 to God, "the primitive unity or the first [*originaire*] simple substance" [§ 47] and the relation between God and the created simple substances. This offers a kind of methodological interlude between the two main parts of the 'Monadologie.' Having started the text with an extended discussion of simples, in § 61 Leibniz turns to composites, not composite *substances*, but just composites.[12] The discussion begins in earnest with a discussion of the bodies that bear particular relations to a given monad: each monad has its own body (§ 62). He writes:

66. From this we see that there is a world of creatures, of living beings, of animals, of entelechies, of souls in the least part of matter.

67. Each portion of matter can be conceived as a garden full of plants, and as a pond full of fish. But each branch of a plant, each limb of an animal, each drop of its humors, is still another such garden or pond.

And as in the corporeal substance view, these living things are conceived of as souls that unite organic bodies which are, in turn, made up of smaller organic bodies, and so on to infinity:

70. Thus we see that each living body has a dominant entelechy, which in the animal is the soul; but the limbs of this living body are full of other living beings, plants, animals, each of which also has its entelechy, or its dominant soul.

---

[11] See Boehm (1957), 235.
[12] Embarrassingly enough, this was incorrectly translated in earlier printings of AG, though corrected in the later ones.

Leibniz continues with an extensive discussion of these souls and their organic bodies, and their relations with one another (§§ 71–81). The 'Monadologie' then ends with a sketch of the hypothesis of pre-established harmony and a discussion of the City of God, the community that we as human souls make up with God (§§ 82–90).

In a way this should look very familiar to the reader of the earlier writings, the correspondence with Arnauld, for example. There is the familiar world of bugs in bugs which Leibniz had outlined to Arnauld. And it should look familiar to the reader of the later part of the de Volder correspondence. The world is grounded in some way in simple, non-extended monads. But here is the problem. There is a conspicuous lacuna in the exposition, indeed a gaping hole. Leibniz passes deftly from the discussion of monads to the discussion of bodies. *But he never really tells the reader how the two are related.* When composites are introduced in § 61, the *implication* is that they are bodies. He writes:

In this respect, composites are analogous to simples. For everything is a plenum, which makes all matter interconnected. In a plenum, every motion has some effect on distant bodies, in proportion to their distance. For each body is affected, not only by those in contact with it, and in some way feels the effects of everything that happens to them, but also, through them, it feels the effects of those in contact with the bodies with which it is itself immediately in contact.   (§ 61)

But, interestingly enough, he never comes out and *says* that bodies are composites made up of simples. In the sections that follow, Leibniz goes on to talk about *bodies*, but never returns to the idea of a *composite*.[13] As a consequence, it is never clear in the 'Monadologie' how exactly the world of extended bodies is related to the world of simple substances, the world of non-extended and mind-like monads. At the basis are simple substances. And then there are bodies, perhaps composite *somethings*. But how are the simple substances related to the bodies? And what metaphysical status do composites, bodies, have in the metaphysics of the 'Monadologie'? The account of monads that Leibniz develops in this text is much richer and more detailed than in earlier texts; indeed, this text and its companion, the "Principes de la nature et de la grâce," may be the first in which Leibniz has

---

[13] This is a respect in which the 'Monadologie' is different from the "Principes." As I shall later note, in the "Principes," Leibniz talks explicitly about composite substances.

gathered all his thoughts about monads together and attempted a systematic exposition of the view. But there is something missing.

— ⟹ No explanation of connection between monads & bodies

Monads and Bodies

There are a number of strands in Leibniz's thought about the relation between monads and bodies. As Remond's comments suggest, this is not a discussion that takes place in a public forum, where monads themselves are hardly in view. However, the question is very much in evidence in two of Leibniz's most important sets of correspondence, the correspondence with de Volder and the later correspondence with Bartholomaeus Des Bosses.

On one strand of Leibniz's thought, bodies are to be understood as aggregates of monads.[14] This is strongly suggested in the opening of the 'Monadologie,' where as we saw earlier Leibniz writes:

1. The monad, which we shall discuss here, is nothing but a simple substance that enters into composites—simple, that is, without parts. . . .

2. And there must be simple substances, since there are composites; for the composite is nothing more than a collection, or aggregate, of simples.

3. But where there are no parts, neither extension, nor shape, nor divisibility is possible. These monads are the true atoms of nature and, in brief, the elements of things.

It is even clearer in the opening of the "Principes de la nature et de la grâce":

1. A substance is a being capable of action. It is simple or composite. A simple substance is that which has no parts. A composite substance is a collection of simple substances, or monads. Monas is a Greek word signifying unity, or what is one. Composites or bodies are multitudes; and simple substances—lives, souls, and minds—are unities. There must be simple substances everywhere, because, without simples, there would be no composites.[15]

---

[14] For an excellent discussion of this reading and some of the philosophical puzzles that emerge out of it, see Arthur (1989).

[15] See also the text that Leibniz had originally written for Remond in 1714 to explain his views: "I believe that the entire universe of creatures consists only in simple substances or monads, and in their aggregates. These simple substances are what we call mind in us and in spirits, and soul in animals. . . . Aggregates are what we call bodies" (G III 622).

But the view is also quite clearly found in earlier texts. In his letter to de Volder from winter 1703, sent again on 20 June 1703, he wrote that "simple things alone are true things, the rest are only beings through aggregation, and therefore phenomena, and, as Democritus used to say, exist by convention not in reality,"[16] a view that he repeated a number of times in that correspondence.[17]

Leibniz's correspondence with de Volder ended in January 1706, as I noted in the previous chapter. But almost immediately after Leibniz ended that exchange, he began another that was to be an important forum for him to develop his ideas. Bartholomaeus Des Bosses (1663–1738) was a Jesuit mathematician, more than seventeen years younger than Leibniz. Des Bosses also became the Latin translator of the *Theodicy*. In a way, these letters form a nice complement to the de Volder correspondence: de Volder was a Cartesian, while Des Bosses was a scholastic. The correspondence extended from 25 January 1706 until 29 May 1716, just a few months before his death. The exchange begins with a letter from Des Bosses to Leibniz. The two had met in Hanover earlier in January, and had spoken briefly. Des Bosses was a great admirer of Leibniz's philosophy. He was acquainted with Leibniz's philosophy, insofar as he could be through the published writings, and wanted to write a book that reconciled Aristotle, Leibniz's philosophy, and church doctrine.[18] Leibniz was obviously pleased by this, a project that fit well with his own irenic temperament, as well as promoting the diffusion of his own philosophy. Again, Leibniz was quite happy to enter into philosophical discussion with someone so enthusiastic about his thought.[19]

It isn't surprising, then, that the question of body in Leibniz's philosophy comes up early in the exchange, and becomes one of the central questions that the two discuss. And in one of Leibniz's first letters to Des Bosses, he presents the view of bodies as aggregates of monads:

from many monads there results [*resultare*] secondary matter, together with derivative forces, actions, and passions, which are only beings through aggregation,

---

[16] G II 252.

[17] See, e.g., Leibniz to de Volder, 21 January 1704 (G II 261–2); 30 June 1704 (G II 267); 19 January 1706 (G II 282). See also, e.g., Leibniz to Lady Masham, 10 July 1705 (G III 367).

[18] See LDB 6.

[19] On the relations between Leibniz and Des Bosses, see Antognazza (2008), 476–9 and the excellent introduction by Look and Rutherford to LDB.

and thus semi-mental things, like the rainbow and other well-founded phenomena.[20]

Later in the correspondence, Leibniz will introduce his difficult and much-discussed notion of the substantial bond, the *vinculum substantiale* that is supposed to transform aggregates of monads into genuine corporeal substances. We shall discuss this notion and the account of corporeal substances Leibniz offers in these texts later in this chapter. With the substantial bond there emerges a very different conception of what bodies are and how they are related to monads. But, as we shall see, it isn't always clear whether Leibniz meant to adopt the hypothesis. In numerous places, he contrasts what the world of bodies would be like with and without the hypothesis of substantial bonds. And, in at least some such texts, Leibniz suggests that without substantial bonds, bodies would be aggregates of monads:

If you deny that what is superadded to monads in order to make a union is substantial, then body cannot be said to be a substance, for in that case it will be a mere aggregate of monads, and I fear that you will fall back on the mere phenomena of bodies.[21]

And two years after this and related texts, we find the aggregate view of bodies expressed in the 'Monadologie,' the "Principes de la nature et de la grâce," and related texts.

This view has an obvious affinity with what I called "aggregate phenomenalism" above in Chapter 7, the earlier view that we saw in the 1680s that bodies, at least inanimate bodies that lack a soul that unifies them and transforms them into a genuine corporeal substance, are aggregates of corporeal substances and in that respect phenomenal. As with the earlier view, Leibniz often asserts that bodies conceived of as aggregates of monads are just phenomenal, "and, as Democritus used to say, exist by convention not in reality,"[22] as we saw in an earlier quotation. As with the earlier view, Leibniz would argue here that aggregates of monads are phenomenal in the sense that they have "a union supplied by the operation of the

---

[20] Leibniz to Des Bosses, 11 March 1706, LDB 34. See also Leibniz to Des Bosses, 31 July 1709, LDB 140.

[21] Leibniz to Des Bosses, 26 May 1712, LDB 240. See also the letters of 15 February 1612, LDB 224–6; 20 September 1712, LDB 276.

[22] Leibniz to de Volder, 20 June 1703, G II 252.

perceiving soul. . . ."²³ It is not surprising that in the context of the new monadology, Leibniz adapts tools that he had already fashioned to use in a somewhat different philosophical context.

But the new context does raise some novel problems for the view of bodies as aggregates, now of monads. On the earlier corporeal substance view, the extension of bodies derives from what he came to call their primary matter, the passive forces of resistance and impenetrability that are not themselves extended, but that give rise to extension. Insofar as such primary matter pertains to each corporeal substance, each corporeal substance is extended in a clear and intelligible sense. One can then understand the extension of inanimate bodies, aggregates of corporeal substances as arising from the extension of the corporeal substances that make them up. In one of his letters, for example, Des Bosses complains:

I do not yet understand from the things you have said so far—either because I have not sufficiently penetrated them or because you assume some principle that is unknown to me—how mass, which is real and has a real diffusion or extension, can result from monads alone, which lack diffusion and extension.²⁴

This would seem to be a real problem on the new monadological view.

The question may have been taken up for the first time in the letter Leibniz resent to de Volder on 20 June 1703.²⁵ The passage originally read:

For even if monads are not extended, they are nonetheless situated in extension in a certain way, i.e. they have an ordered relation of continuous existence to the others.

This was replaced by the following:

For even if monads are not extended, they nonetheless have a certain kind of situation in extension, i.e. they have a certain ordered relation of coexistence to other things, namely through the mass [massa] over which they preside.

The final version sent to de Volder reads as follows:

For even if monads are not extended, they nonetheless have a certain kind of situation in extension, i.e. they have a certain ordered relation of coexistence to

---

²³ Leibniz to Des Bosses, 15 February 1712, LDB 224. For a discussion of this sense of the phenomenal, see Ch. 7, particularly n. 77, where I discuss some of the problems that are raised by this claim.

²⁴ Des Bosses to Leibniz, 6 September 1709, LDB 146. See also Des Bosses to Leibniz, 25 June 1707, LDB 90; 22 April 1709, LDB 120; 30 July 1709, LDB 134–6; 20 May 1712, LDB 236–8; 12 December 1712, LDB 286. Cf. de Volder to Leibniz, 14 November 1704, G II 273.

²⁵ G II 253. The variants are due to Paul Lodge, as are the translations.

other things, namely through the machine [i.e., organic body] over which they preside.

Leibniz obviously worried over this passage quite a bit. In the end, he seems to have settled on the view that the position of a monad is linked with the position of its body. It is not clear how to understand this, and how the appeal to body helps here; this would seem just to push the question of understanding the extension of bodies as aggregates of monads back another mysterious step to bodies at another level.[26] When he comes back to this idea in a later text, the "machines" at issue in the letter to de Volder seem to have gone missing. In a letter to Des Bosses on 21 July 1707 Leibniz writes that "a simple substance, even though it does not have extension in itself, nonetheless has position, which is the foundation of extension."[27]

Now, it is difficult to say exactly how monads can have situation.[28] Nor was Leibniz completely comfortable with attributing position or situation to monads. In a later letter to Des Bosses, for example, he writes:

For monads in themselves do not even have situation with respect to each other—at least one that is real, which extends beyond the order of phenomena. Each is, as it were, a certain world apart, and they harmonize with each other through their phenomena, and not through any other intrinsic intercourse and connection.[29]

But if we have situation, then perhaps we can think of extension as, in a certain way, arising out of situation. In another letter to Des Bosses, Leibniz

---

[26] Despite Leibniz's hesitations on this issue, Adams (1994), 250–5 argues that we have to understand the position of monads in terms of the position of their associated bodies.

[27] LDB 98.

[28] An obvious suggestion is that the differential distribution of clear and confused perceptions within an individual monad and among different monads might help here. Adams (1994), 250–5 gives a convincing argument against this natural reading. More generally, see Cover and Hartz (1994) for a systematic discussion of the question of whether monads are in space. They argue that it was Leibniz's considered view that they do not. I'm not sure that Leibniz ever came to a considered view on this question, but even so, Cover and Hartz provide a very extensive and useful survey of the passages in which Leibniz discusses the issue.

[29] Leibniz to Des Bosses, 26 May 1712, LDB 240–2. This passage may not be inconsistent with the other passages where Leibniz attributes position to monads. One might hold, for example, that even though there is a sense in which they can be construed to have position with respect to one another, they don't *really* have a position insofar as there is no real Newtonian space out there for them to occupy. This might also be what Leibniz has in mind in another letter to Des Bosses, 16 June 1712: "Certainly monads will not for that reason properly be in an absolute place, since they are not actually ingredients but only requisites of matter" (LDB 254).

begins by alluding to the problem of aggregating monads into extended bodies that had worried his correspondent:

If you examine the issue more carefully, perhaps you will try to say that a definite point at least can be assigned to a soul. But a point is not a definite part of matter, and an infinity of points gathered into one would not make extension.[30]

After a brief and elementary proof that an infinity of non-extended points cannot produce extension, Leibniz continues:

Extension indeed arises from situation, but it adds continuity to situation. Points have situation, but they neither have nor compose continuity, and they cannot subsist by themselves.[31]

What does he mean here when he suggests that "extension . . . arises from situation" or that extension "adds continuity to situation"?

To flesh this out, let us return to an idea discussed above in Chapter 4. Remember there that, Leibniz argues, bodies of everyday experience are made up of an infinity of parts, and that as a result, their boundaries are infinitely complex and are not exact geometrical figures. On this view, though, the passive forces, the resistance and impenetrability of the infinite multitude of corporeal substances that make up the bodies of our everyday experience, are imperfect and inexact—but close—instantiations of the figures treated in geometry. The passive forces in corporeal substances give rise to structures that approximately instantiate Euclidean geometry. Geometrical extension is not in the world, but is imposed by us on the world. Insofar as it is our senses and imagination that impose extension on the world, as we discussed earlier in Chapter 4, one can hold that extension is phenomenal, and not real. This can be used to illuminate the account in the later writings and the way in which extension may be taken to arise now not from impenetrability and resistance, but from situation. The position or situation of an infinity of monads now replaces the impenetrability and resistance of the earlier corporeal substance view, and gives us the skeleton, as it were, the order on which we can hang full-fledged extension. In this way we can hold that extension arises from situation. But the infinity of monads situated with respect to one another is

---

[30] Leibniz to Des Bosses, 30 April 1709, LDB 122. I take this to be the beginning of a response to what Des Bosses had queried in his letter of 22 April 1709, LDB 120.

[31] LDB 124.

discrete, and not continuous, of course. In imposing a full-blown Euclidean geometrical structure on the world of situated monads, we are adding continuity. And again, as in the earlier view, insofar as it is we who impose geometry on the world in perceiving it as extended, one can hold that there is a clear sense in which the extension of these aggregates of monads that constitute bodies on this view is phenomenal.[32]

This gives us something of a handle on how we might begin to work out the details of Leibniz's view of extended bodies as aggregates of monads. But there is still a lot of work to be done here. Even if we can understand how extension might arise from the perception of an infinity of non-extended monads, it is still a bit puzzling as to how we can understand the claim that we perceive monads at all! Furthermore, Leibniz asserts again and again that not only is extension phenomenal, but so are forces, active and passive. In reinterpreting the world in terms of monads, the derivative

---

[32] The extremely interesting work of Vincenzo De Risi in De Risi (2007) is very relevant to these issues. De Risi wants to interpret Leibniz's later monadology through the developing science of the "*analysis situs*" or analysis of situation. The *analysis situs* concerned Leibniz from very early in his career, but, according to De Risi, wasn't really fully achieved until late in Leibniz's career, from 1712 onward. The basic notion in Leibniz's program is that of *situs* or situation. The objects A and B have the same situation as objects C and D iff they can be transformed so as to coincide with one another, for instance two line segments of equal length or the points on the vortices of two triangles with equal sides, etc. Cf. De Risi (2007), 132ff. In this way the notion of *situs* is connected with relational structures, and not with the properties of individual objects. While De Risi notes that Leibniz's ambitions for an *analysis situs* are quite broad, a central goal for the project is the definition of space in terms of the notion of situation [De Risi (2007), 165–7]. In particular, the central achievement of Leibniz's last years was a successful definition of space as the locus of all points, where points were understood as "absolute situation." In this way, space is constituted by points, that is to say, generated by points, though it isn't composed of points [De Risi (2007), 173–4]. This has obvious significance for the problem of body in Leibniz's later monadological metaphysics. If monads can be construed as having situation in some sense, then they can be construed as being in space, in some sense; nor is it surprising that Leibniz would turn to situation to define extension in his later thought as the *analysis situs* matures.

But De Risi's own reading of Leibniz goes considerably beyond this minimal application of the *analysis situs* to metaphysics. De Risi wants to insist that monads themselves definitely lack situation for Leibniz (De Risi (2007), 303, 313, 572), something about which Leibniz was more ambiguous, it seems to me. At the same time, he wants to argue that the perceptions of monads, whose content represents the relations among other monads, ground situation as a necessary feature of monadic perception [De Risi (2007), 320ff]. In this way, De Risi argues that the monad necessarily perceives an extended world of bodies in space. The comparison with Kant is not accidental: things in themselves are not in space, but space and extension [indeed, Euclidean space—see De Risi (2007), 566–9] are necessary features of our representation of the world. Furthermore, De Risi also holds that extended bodies are purely phenomenal in a sense that we shall discuss below, the common content of the representations of an infinity of monadic perceivers. This is a strong and challenging reading, which quite explicitly attempts to make Leibniz out to be both a phenomenologist of sorts and a transcendental philosopher. But interesting as it is as a speculative reading of what Leibniz might have thought, or how some of his later eighteenth-century German readers might have read him, I find the reading too distant from the texts. For a fuller discussion of De Risi's rich and important book, see Garber (forthcoming).

active and passive forces that had earlier been real parts of a real physical world—modes of corporeal substances—are now taken to be phenomenal: "I relegate derivative forces to the phenomena."[33] But what exactly does Leibniz mean by calling derivative forces phenomenal?

In addition to the view of bodies as aggregates, one can find at least one other conception of the relation between monads and bodies that features prominently in Leibniz's writings in this period. This view is suggested in some passages from a letter that Leibniz wrote to de Volder on 30 June 1704:

Indeed, considering the matter carefully it should be said that there is nothing in things except simple substances and in them perception and appetite. Moreover, matter and motion are not so much substances or things as the phenomena of perceivers, the reality of which is located in the harmony of perceivers with themselves (at difference times) and with other perceivers.[34]

Understood in this way, it would appear that bodies are to be understood as the contents of the perceptions of individual monads, which are coherent within individual monads, and coherent from one monad to another. It is somewhat problematic to attribute this view to Leibniz here. Earlier in the same letter he does advance a view that looks much more like the aggregate view that we have been examining:

Anything that can be divided into many things (which already actually exist) is aggregated from many things, and a thing that is aggregated from many is not one except from a mind, and has no reality except that which is borrowed from what it contains. Then I inferred from this that, therefore, there are indivisible unities in things, because otherwise there will be no true unity in things and no reality that is not borrowed, which is absurd. . . . I think that . . . we must return to indivisible unities as *primary constituents* in corporeal bulk, i.e. in the corporeal things to be constituted.[35]

But between the two passages quoted from this letter, Leibniz wrote the following:

But, accurately speaking, matter is not composed of constitutive unities, rather it results from them, since matter or extended mass is nothing but a phenomenon founded in things, like the rainbow or the perihelion. And there is no reality in anything except the reality of unities, and so phenomena can always be divided into lesser phenomena that could appear to other more subtle animals, and the

---

[33] Leibniz to de Volder, January 1705, G II 275.   [34] G II 270.   [35] G II 267.

smallest phenomena will never be reached. By contrast, substantial unities are not parts, but the foundations of the phenomena.[36]

This passage does suggest the kind of phenomenalism suggested in the first passage quoted, where the bodies are conceived of as the common dream of an infinity of monads. On this view, monads are no longer constituents of bodies in any real sense: they are what ground the existence of bodies, presumably through their perceptions of them. What is particularly striking here is the distance between the world of phenomena and the world of substances. Phenomena "can always be divided into lesser phenomena": there is no bottom level of phenomena. But existing on another plane, as it were, are the monads, whose perceptions ground the world of phenomena.

This strand is largely in the background of the exchange with de Volder. But in some of the later letters to Des Bosses, it becomes considerably more prominent, and emerges as an account of what the world would be like if there were no substantial bonds and thus no true corporeal substances. In the letter Leibniz wrote to Des Bosses on 15 February 1712, the letter that first introduces the notion of a substantial bond, Leibniz writes:

If that substantial bond of monads were absent, then all bodies with all their qualities would be only well-founded phenomena, like a rainbow or an image in a mirror, in a word, continuous dreams that agree perfectly with each other; and in this alone would consist the reality of those phenomena. For it should no more be said that monads are parts of bodies, that they touch each other, that they compose bodies, than it is right to say this of points and souls.[37]

The view is presented in a way that is even starker in a letter written a few months later:

It is true that the things that happen in the soul must agree with those which happen outside the soul; but for this it is sufficient that those things that happen in one soul correspond both among themselves and with those things that happen

---

[36] G II 268. It is in part because of the passage at G II 267 that Robert Adams argues that Leibniz thought that the more thoroughgoing phenomenalism suggested by the passage at G II 270 is fully consistent with the aggregate view of monads and bodies. See Adams (1994), 260–1. But the passage at G II 268, which Adams does not cite, provides a nice transition from the one to the other.

[37] LDB 226.

in any other soul; and there is no need to posit something outside of all souls or monads. According to this hypothesis, when we say that Socrates is sitting, nothing more is signified than that those things that we understand by 'Socrates' and 'sitting' are appearing to us and to others for whom it is a concern.[38]

Something very like this view can be found in the very last letter that Leibniz wrote to Des Bosses, just months before he died:

Moreover, if monads alone were substances, one of two things would be necessary: either bodies would be mere phenomena or a continuum would arise from points, which we agree is absurd. Real continuity can arise only from a substantial bond. If there existed nothing substantial besides monads, that is, if composites were mere phenomena, then extension itself would be nothing but a phenomenon resulting from coordinated simultaneous appearances, and by that fact, all the controversies concerning the composition of the continuum would cease.[39]

This passage is, admittedly, somewhat puzzling. But the "coordinated simultaneous appearances" to which Leibniz refers here might well be the "continuous dreams that agree perfectly with each other" which are at issue in the earlier letter.

Insofar as Leibniz is not entirely sure in much of this exchange whether to admit substantial bonds and thus corporeal substances, this dream-like view of body and the material world would seem to be a serious candidate for how the material world of bodies is related to the world of monads for Leibniz at this late stage of his philosophical development. But there is also an interesting variant of this view that appears in the correspondence with Des Bosses. Leibniz writes:

If bodies are phenomena, and are judged by our appearances, they will not be real, since they will appear differently to others. Thus, the reality of bodies, of space, motion and time seems to consist in this: that they are the phenomena of God, i.e., the object of his knowledge of vision. And the difference between the appearance of bodies with respect to us and their appearance with respect to God is in some way like the difference between a drawing in perspective and a ground plan. For whereas drawings in perspective differ according to the position of the viewer, a ground plan or geometrical representation is unique. God certainly sees things exactly such as they are according to geometrical truth, although likewise he also

---

[38] Leibniz to Des Bosses, 16 June 1712, LDB 256.
[39] Leibniz to Des Bosses, 16 May 1716, LDB 370.

knows how each thing appears to every other, and thus he contains in himself eminently all the other appearances.[40]

On what we might call the "common dream" view, the reality of bodies rests in the coherence of the phenomena of monads, both the coherence of their internal perceptions and the coherence of their perceptions across monads. But on this view it is the coherence of divine phenomena that is at issue here; the reality of body rests now on what we might call the Divine dream, on what God is supposed to perceive.

This view has some definite attractions over and above the view of bodies as aggregates of monads. For example, it is no longer a problem from where extension is supposed to derive. Extension is purely phenomenal, and appears *only* in the contents of monadic perceptions.[41] It is a feature of the common dreams monads have, but there is no pretense that it is anything more than that. Similarly, there is now a simple and coherent account of force, active and passive. All forces, at least bodily forces, now pertain directly to phenomena: they are the phenomenal properties of phenomenal bodies, and nothing more.[42] Exactly this question is at issue in a remark that Leibniz added to a letter to Bourguet, 22 March 1714:

The difficulty that one has about the communication of motion ceases when one considers that material things and their motions are only phenomena. Their reality is only in the agreement of the appearances of monads. And if the dreams of one single person were entirely coherent and if the dreams of all souls agreed with one another, one wouldn't need anything else in order to make of them body and matter.[43]

[40] Leibniz to Des Bosses, 15 February 1712, LDB 230–2. See also Leibniz to Des Bosses, 24 January 1713, LDB 296. For detailed discussions of this passage and its place in Leibniz's phenomenalism, see Brown (1987) and Rutherford (1994).

[41] Again, see the account of the spatiality of phenomenal representations in De Risi (2007), ch. 3, where he argues that phenomenal relations give rise to situation, which, in turn, grounds phenomenal space.

[42] De Risi (2007), ch. 4 attempts to derive Leibniz's notions of force from considerations relating to the mathematics of situation and the notion of a boundary. I think that he goes off the tracks here. One can get a great deal from situation in Leibniz's later thought, but here I think De Risi presses his theme too far.

[43] G III 567. I am following a suggestion of Graeme Hunter here and reading "n'auroit point besoin d'autre chose," "one wouldn't need anything else," for Gerhardt's "n'auroit point de soin d'autre chose," a strange phrase in French. This passage probably did not appear in the letter that Bourguet received.

The resolution of this problem comes at something of a cost, though: the world would have the same metaphysical status as a dream.

Here again it is interesting to note how what Leibniz is proposing is related to some of his earlier views. While the first conception of the relations between monads and bodies seems like a direct extension of his earlier aggregate phenomenalism, this is an even more direct extension of the kind of veil-of-perception phenomenalism with which Leibniz earlier experimented in response to skeptical worries about the existence of an external world, in particular, the kind I called extended-mind phenomenalism. In Chapter 7, I wondered if Leibniz had seriously considered such a view in the 1680s. Here, later in life, it is quite clear that he did. Again, in the face of new philosophical problems, it is interesting that Leibniz turns back to the tools that he built for other occasions and adapts them for use in the context of his new monadology.

Monads, Bodies, and Corporeal Substance

In the earlier portions of this chapter I have been trying to pin Leibniz down on the question of the nature of extended bodies within the context of the monadology. But there is another question, not altogether unrelated to this one. For Leibniz in this period, monads are true substances, the elements of things, in whatever sense he understands this locution. But are these the *only* substances that Leibniz recognizes? Are there no corporeal substances left in Leibniz's world? In particular, how do *bodies* fit into the world of *substances*?

Here, again, there seem to be a number of strands in Leibniz's thought. There are a number of striking passages in which Leibniz seems to hold that monads or simple substances alone are true substances, implying that he recognizes no other substances. Writing to Sophie on 19 November 1701, Leibniz discussed true unities, which have neither parts nor extension. In this context he claimed that "there is nothing real but the unities" and that "everything is unities."[44] These views are repeated a number of times

---

[44] A1.20.74–5.

in the letters to de Volder. In the letter from Winter 1703, sent again on 20 June 1703, he writes:

simple things alone are true things, the rest are only beings through aggregation, and therefore phenomena, and, as Democritus used to say, exist by convention not in reality.[45]

A year later he wrote in an often-quoted passage that, "considering the matter carefully it should be said that there is nothing in things except simple substances and in them perception and appetite."[46] Writing in January 1705, he is blunter still:

I do not really do away with body, but reduce it to what it is. For I show that corporeal mass, that is believed to have something besides simple substances, is not a substance, but a phenomenon resulting from simple substances, which alone have unity and absolute reality. . . . Anything more beyond this in things is posited in vain and added without argument. . . . Whoever adds anything to these things will accomplish nothing, and will both work in vain in giving explanations and be thrown into inextricable difficulties. . . . Indeed, I suppose nothing everywhere and throughout all things except that which we all admit in our own souls on many occasions, namely, internal spontaneous changes. And in this way I exhaust the totality of things with one act of the mind.[47]

In this way, Leibniz seems to hold, all there really is in the world are the monads.

While this view is clearest and presented most forcefully in the writings from the early part of the first decade of the eighteenth century, the view persists in a number of texts. For example, even after introducing the substantial bond to Des Bosses in February 1712, Leibniz expresses

---

[45] G II 252.   [46] Leibniz to de Volder, 30 June 1704, G II 270.
[47] Leibniz to de Volder, January 1705, G II 275–6. Paul Lodge has recently transcribed supplements to Leibniz's last letter to de Volder of 19 January 1706 that present a similar position:

I do not see what argument could prove that there is anything in extension, bulk, or motion beyond the phenomena, i.e. beyond the perceptions of simple substances.

Arguments, in my opinion, cannot prove the existence of anything besides perceivers and perceptions (if you subtract their common cause), and the things that should be admitted in them. In a perceiver, these are the transitions from perception to perception, with the same subject remaining; in perceptions, the harmony of perceivers. For the rest, we invent natures of things and wrestle with the chimeras of our minds as if with ghosts.

These will appear in his forthcoming edition of the Leibniz–de Volder letters.

to him a view very much like what he had expressed earlier to de Volder:

I regard the explanation of all phenomena solely through the perceptions of monads agreeing among themselves, with corporeal substance excluded, to be useful for a fundamental investigation of things. In this way of explaining things, space becomes the order of coexisting phenomena, as time is the order of successive phenomena, and there is no absolute or spatial nearness or distance between monads. To say that they are crowded together in a point or disseminated in space is to employ certain fictions of our mind when we willingly seek to imagine things that can only be understood. No extension or composition of the continuum is involved in this account either, and all the problems about points disappear.[48]

This view was repeated in a letter to another correspondent, Pierre Dangicourt, on 11 September 1716:

I am also of the opinion that, to speak exactly, there is no need of extended substance. . . . True substances are only simple substances or what I call 'monads.' And I believe that there are only monads in nature, the rest being only phenomena that result from them. Each monad is a mirror of the universe according to its point of view and is accompanied by a multitude of other monads which compose its organic body, of which it is the dominant monad.[49]

Here, a month before he died, Leibniz seems to deny that we need anything over and above monads.

But alongside these texts, there are others in which Leibniz seems to advance the view that beside monads or simple substances there are also compound or composite substances. There are a number of texts that are very suggestive of the view of corporeal substances found, for example, in the correspondence with Arnauld. For example, Leibniz wrote the following in a letter to Bierling, 12 August 1711:

Finally, you ask for definitions of matter, body, and spirit. Matter is that which consists in impenetrability [*Antitypia*], or that which resists penetration, and therefore bare matter is merely passive. Moreover, over and above matter, body also has active force. Furthermore, a body is either a corporeal substance or a mass composed of corporeal substances. I call a corporeal substance that which consists of a simple substance or monad (that is, a soul or something analogous to a soul)

---

[48] Leibniz to Des Bosses, 16 June 1712, LDB 255.   [49] Leibniz (1734), 1–2 (LDB 401 n. 105).

with an organic body united to it. But mass [*Massa*] is a aggregate of corporeal substances, as a cheese consists in a coming together of worms. Furthermore, a monad or simple substance in general contains perception and appetite.[50]

In this and a number of similar texts from the period,[51] it looks as if Leibniz is just reprising his earlier view of corporeal substances, souls that give unity to their organic bodies and transform them from mere aggregates whose unity is imposed on them by the perceiver into genuine substances.

But there are other texts that suggest somewhat different conceptions of composite substance. One such text is found in the letter of winter 1703, resent on 20 June 1704, where Leibniz gives an often-cited summary of his ontology:

I therefore distinguish: (1) the primitive entelechy or soul; (2) matter, namely, primary matter or primitive passive power; (3) the monad completed by these two things; (4) the mass or secondary matter, or organic machine for which innumerable subordinate monads come together; and (5) the animal, or corporeal substance, which the monad dominating in the machine makes one.[52]

This might be a simple restatement of the earlier corporeal substance view. But the remark in clause (4) suggests something else, that the organic machine is to be understood simply as an aggregate of monads (as opposed to an aggregate of corporeal substances).[53] This view is also suggested in the opening paragraphs of the "Principes de la nature et de la grâce." There Leibniz writes:

1. A substance is a being capable of action. It is simple or composite. A simple substance is that which has no parts. A composite substance is a collection of simple substances, or monads. Monas is a Greek word signifying unity, or what is one. Composites or bodies are multitudes; and simple substances—lives, souls, and minds—are unities. There must be simple substances everywhere, because, without simples, there would be no composites. As a result, all of nature is full of life.

---

[50] G VII 501–2.

[51] See, e.g., Leibniz to Jaquelot, 22 March 1703, G III 457; "Eclaircissements sur les natures plastiques..." (Appendix to "Considerations sur les natures plastiques...," May 1705), G VI 550; Leibniz to Des Maizeaux, 8 July 1711, G VII 535; Leibniz to Remond, 4 November 1715, G III 657; etc.

[52] G II 252.

[53] Of course, it is quite possible that Leibniz thought that the monads that make up the secondary matter are organized, with some dominating others. But even so, secondary matter would consist entirely of aggregates of non-extended entities, unlike in the middle years.

3. . . . There are simple substances everywhere, actually separated from one another by their own actions, which continually change their relations; and each distinct simple substance or monad, which makes up the center of a composite substance (an animal, for example) and is the principle of its unity, is surrounded by a mass composed of an infinity of other monads, which constitute the body belonging to this central monad. . . .

4. Each monad, together with a particular body, makes up a living substance.[54]

Here the view seems to be that the composite substance is just a collection of monads, united by a single monad "which makes up the center" and which is "the principle of unity" for that composite.[55]

This conception of composite substance is importantly different from the conception that he held earlier, in the correspondence with Arnauld, for example. On the earlier conception, there seemed to be a robust sense of body and matter at issue in the composite: the bodies that the form or soul was supposed to make into one was supposed to be the seat of passive force, where passive force was understood as involving resistance and impenetrability. While these bodies are not formally extended in the Cartesian sense, their resistance and impenetrability are what give rise to extension. However, on this later view, the bodies, now understood as composite substances, are themselves just aggregates of non-extended and mind-like simple substances. While each simple substance has primitive passive force in addition to matter, the primitive passive force here is understood not as the seat of resistance and impenetrability but as a feature of the internal states of the monads in question, their confused perception or imperfection.

But even if the composite substances in these texts are to be understood as aggregates of monads united by a dominant monad, there is at least one text from the period that seems to suggest that if these are composite substances, they are only substances by courtesy. The passage is in an essay generally thought to have been written around 1712, in which Leibniz draws out some of the consequences of the Principle of Sufficient Reason. The passage is very interesting and reveals of some of the pressures and

---

[54] Leibniz (2002a), 27–33 (AG 207–8).
[55] Interestingly enough, such a view is *not* found in the companion piece to the "Principes," the 'Monadologie,' where Leibniz seems to go out of his way to avoid using the term 'substance' for anything but monads, as I noted earlier.

tensions in Leibniz's thought. It begins with what appears to be a statement of the older view of corporeal substances:

Further, all creatures are either substantial or accidental. Those which are substantial are either substances or substantiated. I give the name 'substantiated' to aggregates of substances, such as an army of men, or a flock of sheep; and all bodies are such aggregates. A substance is either simple, such as a soul, which has no parts, or it is composite, such as an animal, which consists of a soul and an organic body. But an organic body, like every other body, is merely an aggregate of animals or other things which are living and therefore organic, or finally of small objects or masses; but these also are finally resolved into living things, from which it is evident that all bodies are finally resolved into living things. . . .

But then it takes a very strange turn:

and that what, in the analysis of substances, exist ultimately are simple sub-stances—namely, souls, or, if you prefer a more general term, *monads*, which are without parts. For even though every simple substance has an organic body which corresponds to it—otherwise it would not have any kind of orderly relation to other things in the universe, nor would it act or be acted upon in an orderly way—yet by itself it is without parts.

This suggests that on the ultimate analysis, composite substances are composed of monads. But then Leibniz takes the analysis yet a step further:

And because an organic body, or any other body whatsoever, can again be resolved into substances endowed with organic bodies, it is evident that in the end there are simple substances alone, and that in them are the sources of all things and of the modifications that come to things.[56]

And here we are in quite a different place from where we began: "in the end there are simple substances alone . . .," suggesting that what began as composite substances are not substances at all.

But there is another approach to composite substance in Leibniz's texts, one that goes beyond the older model of corporeal substance in the correspondence with Arnauld, and the monads-together model that appears to replace it in some later texts: the theory of the substantial bond that Leibniz developed in the correspondence with Des Bosses.[57]

---

[56] Leibniz (1903), 13–14 [Leibniz (1973b), 174–5].

[57] In my understanding of this view of Leibniz's I am deeply indebted to a monograph and a series of articles by Brandon Look, where he develops aspects of Leibniz's idea of a substantial bond. See

The earlier letters between the two wander over a wide variety of topics, from gossip to serious philosophical discussions. In the course of these conversational wanderings, Leibniz expresses much the same variety of views on body that he had earlier expressed to de Volder, suggesting that he hasn't really come to a stable view on the matter, as we saw earlier in the chapter. But early in 1712, there is an exchange of special significance. Des Bosses is then in the process of translating the *Theodicy* into Latin. In the letter of 28 January 1712, he proposes joining to the translation of the *Theodicy* "a certain brief *Specimen of a Peripatetic Dissertation on Corporeal Substance* that I conceived a little while ago with your encouragement...."[58] Leibniz picks up the thread immediately, as if this was an issue that had already been on his mind. He immediately responds in the very next letter, barely two weeks later, with some ideas about corporeal substance:

I shall read with great pleasure your dissertation on corporeal substance. If corporeal substance is something real over and above monads, as a line is taken to be something over and above points, we shall have to say that corporeal substance consists in a certain union, or rather in a real unifier superadded to monads by God....[59]

And from then to the end of their correspondence, the substantial bond is one of the central topics of their conversation. Indeed, it becomes almost Leibniz's obsession.

Though this letter is important and introduces the most focused discussion of this idea in Leibniz, it isn't the first time that he has mused about substantial bonds. Though it hadn't come up at all in the exchange with de Volder, it appears very early on in texts connected with his correspondence with Des Bosses. In a passage deleted from the draft of the letter to Des Bosses on 14 February 1706, Leibniz writes:

The union I find some difficulty explaining is that which joins the different simple substances or monads existing in our body with us, such that it makes one thing from them; nor is it sufficiently clear how, in addition to the existence of individual

the monograph, Look (1999), and the articles Look (1998a), (2000), (2002), and (2004). I am also deeply indebted to the excellent introduction to LDB by the editors and translators, Look and Donald Rutherford, as well as to their translations and editions, which they shared with me before the volume was published.

[58] LDB 216.   [59] Leibniz to Des Bosses, 15 February 1712, LDB 224.

monads, there may arise a new existing thing, unless they are joined by the bond of a continuous [thing] that the phenomena display to us.[60]

Leibniz had obviously been worrying about how to think about composite substances in the context of his monadology even before the exchange began. There is another hint of the doctrine, in another draft that doesn't seem to have made it all the way to Des Bosses, this time in 1710, and in connection with understanding how the Catholic account of transubstantiation could be understood on Leibniz's metaphysics:

Since bread, in fact, is not a substance, but a being by aggregation, or a substantiated being resulting from innumerable monads through some added union, its substantiality consists in this union. Accordingly, it is not necessary, on your view, that those monads be destroyed or changed by God, but only that through which they produce a new being be removed, namely, the union. In this way, the substantiality depending on it will cease, although there will remain the phenomenon, which now will arise not from those monads, but from some divinely substituted equivalent to the union of those monads. Thus no substantial subject will in fact participate.[61]

Here, again, there is some added union that will constitute the substantiality of the bread, something that pulls the monads that make up the body together to form a genuine substance. However, Leibniz the Lutheran concludes, "those of us who reject transubstantiation have no need of such things."

But then, in February 1712, Leibniz decides that it is time to reveal some of what he is thinking on this issue, and that Des Bosses is the person to whom he can reveal it. This is not the place for a full and detailed exposition of Leibniz's thought on the substantial bond. But it will be helpful to outline the progress of his thought on that question as he attempts to explain himself to Des Bosses in the last four and a half years of his life.

A reasonably full version of the substantial bond theory is outlined in the letter where it is introduced, and many of the details are filled out in letters written over the following year. Leibniz begins the relevant passage of his letter of 15 February 1712 as follows, in a text whose opening lines we have already seen:

I shall read with great pleasure your dissertation on corporeal substance. If corporeal substance is something real over and above monads, as a line is taken to be something

---

[60] LDB 22.   [61] Leibniz to Des Bosses, 2 May 1710 (draft), LDB 170.

over and above points, we shall have to say that corporeal substance consists in a certain union, or rather in a real unifier superadded to monads by God, and that from the union of the passive powers of monads there in fact arises primary matter, which is to say, that which is required for extension and antitypy, or for diffusion and resistance. From the union of monadic entelechies, on the other hand, there arises substantial form; but that which can be generated in this way, can be destroyed and will be destroyed with the cessation of the union, unless it is miraculously preserved by God. But such a form then will not be a soul, which is a simple and indivisible substance. And this form, just like matter, is in perpetual flux, since in fact no point can be designated in matter that preserves the same place for more than a moment and does not move away from neighboring points, however close. But a soul in its changes persists as the same thing, with the same subject remaining, which is not the case in a corporeal substance. Thus, one of two things must be said: either bodies are mere phenomena, and so extension also will be only a phenomenon, and monads alone will be real, but with a union supplied by the operation of the perceiving soul on the phenomenon; or, if faith drives us to corporeal substances, this substance consists in that unifying reality, which adds *something absolute* (and therefore substantial), albeit impermanent, to the things to be unified.[62]

What is at issue here seems to be the union of monads into a single substance; the substantial bond is "a real unifier superadded to monads by God." But not just any collection of monads can be united. In a related text that Look and Rutherford present as a supplement to the letter of 15 February 1712, Leibniz writes:

This addition to monads does not occur in just any way, otherwise any scattered things at all would be united in a new substance, and nothing determinate would arise in contiguous bodies. But it suffices that it unites those monads that are under the domination of one monad, that is, that make one organic body or one machine of nature.[63]

What is added is something that is not itself just another monad, but yet it is a something, something substantial rather than a mode of the monads, "*something absolute* (and therefore substantial), albeit impermanent, [added] to the things to be unified." In the same supplement to the letter of 15 February 1712 Leibniz writes:

Moreover, God not only considers single monads and the modifications of every monad whatsoever, but he also sees their relations, and the reality of relations and

[62] LDB 224–6.   [63] LDB 232.

truths consists in this. . . . But over and above these real relations, a more perfect relation can be conceived through which a single new substance arises from many substances. And this will not be a simple result, that is, it will not consist in true or real relations alone; but, moreover, it will add some new substantiality, or substantial bond, and this will be an effect not only of the divine intellect but also of the divine will.[64]

The act of divine will in question here is, one presumes, the creation of this something.

In unifying the monads that make up the new composite substance, the substantial bond produces a substance that itself has matter and form in much the sense in which the corporeal substances of the correspondence with Arnauld had matter and form. Most interestingly, the matter that arises out of the union grounds extension in exactly the way in which it did on his earlier view: "from the union of the passive powers of monads there in fact arises primary matter, which is to say, that which is required for extension and antitypy, or for diffusion and resistance." The primary matter that pertains to the composite substance at issue must be distinguished from the primary matter that pertains to monads, something that is understood entirely in terms of monadic perceptions. Leibniz writes in a letter of 20 September 1712:

if there are only monads with their perceptions, primary matter will be nothing other than the passive power of the monads, and an entelechy will be their active power; if you add composite substances, I would say that in these things a principle of resistance must be added to the active principle or motive force.[65]

Because of this, these composite substances seem to be genuinely extended in the same way that his older corporeal substances were, unlike the other conceptions of body with which Leibniz was consorting at that moment, the view of body as an aggregate of non-extended monads or the view of body as the common dream of a multitude of monads. On this new view, as on the old, extension will arise from the real diffusion of resistance and impenetrability. This is the contrast that Leibniz draws in another passage of the letter of 15 February 1712, which we have already seen in part:

The extension of body seems to be nothing but the continuation of matter through parts outside of parts, i.e., diffusion. Yet, if the 'outside of parts' ceases

---

[64] LDB 232.   [65] LDB 274–6.

supernaturally, the extension which is an accident of body will cease also. Then there will remain only extension as a phenomenon founded on monads, along with the other things which result from them, and which would alone exist, if there were no unifying substance. If that substantial bond of monads were absent, then all bodies with all their qualities would be only well-founded phenomena, like a rainbow or an image in a mirror, in a word, continuous dreams that agree perfectly with each other; and in this alone would consist the reality of those phenomena.[66]

But Leibniz's account of the form of the composite substance that emerges out of the union is somewhat different. Unlike the forms of Leibniz's earlier corporeal substances, which are eternal, these forms will be "in perpetual flux," as he put it in the letter of 15 February 1712. This is also true of the substantial bond itself, it would seem. In notes connected with Leibniz's letter to Des Bosses on 24 January 1713, he notes that "a being realizing phenomena is a temporal being, which arises and perishes, but a monad is a perpetual being."[67]

Leibniz is somewhat vague about the relations between the monads and the substantial bond that unites them. In some sense the substantial bond seems to reflect that perceptions and appetitions of the monads to which it is connected, while, in a certain sense, being independent of them. In his letter to Des Bosses from 24 January 1713 Leibniz wrote:

A substantial bond superadded to monads is, in my opinion, something absolute, which although it accurately corresponds in the course of nature to the affections of monads, namely their perceptions and appetitions, so that in a monad it can be read in which body its body is, nevertheless, supernaturally, the substantial bond can be independent of the monads and can be changed and accommodated to other monads, with the previous monads remaining.[68]

Trans-sub.

And similarly, in the letter of 20 September 1712 he wrote:

Furthermore, I should think that composite substance, or that thing that makes a bond of monads, since it is not a mere modification of monads or something existing in them as subjects (for the same modification could not be in many subjects at the same time), depends upon monads. This is not a logical dependence

---

[66] LDB 226.
[67] LDB 304. The "being realizing phenomena," that is the being that makes phenomena real here, is, of course, the substantial bond.
[68] LDB 296.

(that is, such that it cannot be supernaturally separated from them) but only a natural one, namely, so that it requires that they unite in a composite substance, unless God wills otherwise. For God can apply this same thing to unify other monads, so that it stops unifying the previous ones. He can also clearly remove it and substitute another thing that unifies other monads; and this can be done either in such a way that it ceases to unify other monads and is transferred from one group of monads to another, or in such a way that it retains its own monads, which it naturally unites, and now also unites new ones supernaturally.[69]

It is a little delicate to draw conclusions from this passage, written in the context of a discussion of the Eucharist, and involving both natural and supernatural elements. But it would appear from this that Leibniz's view was that the substantial bond, while it reflects the monads that it is attached to in a given corporeal substance, could be detached and reattached to another group of monads, and form a new corporeal substance, even if it requires God's omnipotence to do so. In this respect, the connection between the substantial bond and a particular group of monads is "natural" and not "logical."

The theory of the substantial bond remains a constant during the last years of Leibniz's correspondence with Des Bosses, which coincides with the last years of his life. But it undergoes a subtle evolution in the course of the discussion. The biggest change is announced in the letter of 23 August 1713:

having considered the matter, I change my opinion to this extent: I now think that nothing absurd arises, if indeed the substantial bond, or the substance itself of the composite is said to be ingenerable and incorruptible, because I think that no corporeal substance should really be admitted, except where there is an organic body with a dominant monad, or a living thing, that is, an animal, or something analogous to an animal. Everything else is, in fact, a mere aggregate, or an accidental unity, not a intrinsic unity. Since, therefore, as you know, I deny that not only the soul but also the animal dies, I shall therefore say not that the substantial bond, or the substance of the animated body arises and passes away naturally, but that, since it is something absolute, it only varies according to the changes of the animal. Hence corporeal substance, or the substantial bond of monads, although it requires monads naturally or physically, does not require them metaphysically, since it is nonetheless not in them as in a subject; and so it can

[69] LDB 268–70.

be destroyed or changed, while the monads are preserved, and accommodated to monads that do not naturally belong to it. Nor is any monad besides the dominant monad even naturally attached to the substantial bond, since the other monads are in a perpetual flux.[70]

This is interesting in a number of respects. Most importantly, it signals an interesting change of doctrine, that the substantial bond is now "ingenerable and incorruptible," just like the monads. And on this view, the substantial bond is now attached not to all of the monads in the aggregate that is made into a genuine substance, but only to the dominant monad of the aggregate. This, in a way, carries forward an idea that Leibniz first seems to articulate in notes connected with the letter of 24 January 1713, that the substantial bond *just is* the corporeal substance: "I do not know what a being realizing phenomena is except that very thing that I call a composite substance or substantial bond."[71] In the letter of 23 August 1713 Leibniz continues this thought, referring to "corporeal substance, or the substantial bond of monads." By the end of the series of letters, the corporeal substance and the substantial bond seem to be completely identified with one another. In the letter of 13 January 1716 Leibniz writes:

I do not see how it can be conceived that the thing realizing the phenomena is something apart from substance. For that realizing thing must bring it about that composite substance contains something substantial besides monads, otherwise there will be no composite substance, that is, composites will be mere phenomena. And in this I think that I am absolutely of the same opinion as the scholastics, and, in fact, I think that their primary matter and substantial form, namely the primitive active and passive powers of the composite, and the complete thing resulting from these, are really that substantial bond that I am urging.[72]

And then, in the final letter he wrote to Des Bosses on 29 May 1716, Leibniz remarks:

I do not say that there is a mediating bond between form and matter but, rather, that the substantial form itself of the composite and primary matter taken in the scholastic sense, that is, primitive active and passive power, belong to that bond, as the essence of the composite.[73]

---

[70] LDB 318–20.   [71] LDB 304.   [72] LDB 364.   [73] LDB 366.

Leibniz goes on to note the relation between this bond and the monads in the aggregate it is supposed to unite in terms that suggest earlier letters:

However, this substantial bond is naturally, and not essentially, a bond. For it requires monads but does not involve them essentially, since it can exist without monads and monads without it.[74]

But later in the letter he says something absolutely remarkable:

Composite substance does not consist formally in monads and their subordination, for then it would be a mere aggregate, that is, an accidental being; rather, it consists in primitive active and passive force, from which arise the qualities, actions and passions of the composite, which are perceived by the senses, if more than phenomena are assumed.[75]

The substantial bond now looks like the corporeal substance of the middle years resurrected, and beginning to shove the monads aside: one can legitimately wonder what work they are now really doing in the theory. The substantial bond, originally introduced to bind the monads together into a composite substance, has largely taken over.

How seriously did Leibniz take the theory of the substantial bond? It is often argued that the substantial bond was just a concession to the Catholic Des Bosses, an attempt to show him how a Catholic conception of the Eucharist could be accommodated within the context of a broadly Leibnizian metaphysic grounded in monads. Bertrand Russell, for example, dismissed it as "rather the concession of a diplomatist than the creed of a philosopher."[76] This judgment is taken to be confirmed by the fact that discussions of the substantial bond seem to be limited to the exchange between Leibniz and Des Bosses. But I don't find this argument entirely plausible. First of all, discussion of the substantial bond can be found outside of the correspondence with Des Bosses, and in contexts that are clearly non-theological.[77] Furthermore, Des Bosses himself doesn't see the Eucharist as an issue to worry about in the context of the monadology; as far as he is concerned, the straight monadology, perhaps supplemented by

---

[74] LDB 366.   [75] LDB 371.

[76] Russell (1937), 154. For similar judgments by more recent commentators, see Adams (1994). 299–303 and Rutherford (1995), 276–81. I should note that neither Adams nor Rutherford completely endorses Russell's view, though neither thinks that Leibniz fully endorsed the substantial bond.

[77] See Look (1998b) and Look (1999), 90ff, and Adams (1994), 301–2, n. 51.

what he thinks of as a *modal* bond is sufficient for Catholic theology.[78] It is Leibniz who is pressing the issue of composite substance as a problem for the monadology, quite independently of anything that Des Bosses is urging. And finally, while the Eucharist and transubstantiation are certainly at issue through much of the exchange, this is clearly not the only issue, or even the central issue. Any fair reading of the exchange would have to conclude that Leibniz was interested in it for its own sake. Now, in the beginning of the exchange, it is pretty clear that Leibniz wasn't committed to the view, and regarded the discussion from a somewhat detached point of view: "*if* corporeal substance is something real...,"[79] "*if* faith drives us to corporeal substances...,"[80] "This bond, *if it exists....*"[81] But, as the correspondence proceeds, it looks more and more as if he is seriously considering it. By the last letters, he is definitely taking it seriously, and taking ownership of the doctrine: "that substantial bond *that I am urging*...";[82] "*my* doctrine of composite substance...";[83] "*my* composite substance...."[84] Furthermore, as the discussion progresses, Leibniz comes to paint the world of a pure monadology, without a substantial bond in darker and darker terms: without a substantial bond to make extended bodies really real, the world around us would be only a dream, an illusion. It is as if Leibniz is trying to press Des Bosses toward taking the step with him of accepting what is needed to make composite substances real.

I think that it is very unlikely that Leibniz would have rested with the view that finally emerges at the end of the correspondence with Des Bosses: the question of the coherence of the view aside, it is implausible that he could at this stage have given up on monads. But at the same time, it seems clear to me that in these letters, Leibniz is genuinely worried about the reality of body and the physical world, and is experimenting around with a way of reviving his earlier and more robustly realistic view that will mesh with the new monadology. He seems willing to entertain giving up the radical monads-only metaphysics that he initially espoused in the letters with de Volder—and to introduce something new in nature over

---

78 See Des Bosses to Leibniz, 28 August 1712, LDB 262–64.
79 Leibniz to Des Bosses, 15 February 1712, LDB 224.
80 Leibniz to Des Bosses, 15 February 1712, LDB 226.
81 Leibniz to Des Bosses, 19 August 1715, LDB 348.
82 Leibniz to Des Bosses, 13 January 1716, LDB 364.   83 Ibid.
84 Leibniz to Des Bosses, 29 May 1716, LDB 372.

and above the monads—in order to save the reality of bodies. But I suspect that he had a hunch that he hadn't quite solved the problem yet.

What does it all Mean?

In this chapter we have been examining Leibniz's treatment of body in the context of a world grounded in monads. What, in the end, was Leibniz's view? Leibniz's account of body in these years doesn't make for a fully coherent picture. There are texts that suggest that bodies are aggregates of monads, and others that suggest that bodies are just the common coherent dreams of an infinity of monads. There are texts that suggest that all there are are monads in the world, and that everything else is just phenomena, while other texts suggest that there are, in addition, composite or corporeal substances. One can even find a variety of different conceptions of what these composite substances are supposed to be in these years. In some texts, they seem to be the familiar corporeal substance of his earlier years, souls or forms that transform organic machines into genuine unities, however those organic machines may be understood; in others the composite substances seem to be aggregates of monads united by virtue of a dominant monad; in yet others, the unity requires something that goes beyond the ontology of monads, a substantial bond, a strange entity that comes out looking more and more like an old-fashioned corporeal substance the more Leibniz looked at it. And while there are some temporal patterns that can be seen by the discerning eye—the career of the substantial bond, for example, which seems to enter only fairly late in the game—many of these positions seem to be mixed in no discernible order from 1700 or so, when Leibniz first seems to sign on to the monadological metaphysics to the time of his death in 1716. They seem to come and go, bob and weave through Leibniz's thought, as if Leibniz didn't even recognize that they are incompatible. What are we to make of this?

Here is an attempt to make at least some limited sense of the apparent chaos. One constant in Leibniz's thought from his early years to the end of his life is the world we experience, the world of bodies. But from 1700 or so to the end of his life another constant is the theory of monads: in one way or another, monads came to be understood as the ultimate elements of things, the bottom layer in our account of the way the world is, a supplement to the world of bodies rather than a replacement for it, strictly speaking. In this way the monadological metaphysics of Leibniz's later years should not be regarded as a simple alternative to the corporeal substance metaphysics of the middle years. It is too strong to say that the corporeal substance view persists unchanged until the end of Leibniz's career. Sometimes in his later writings, he does seem still to hang onto a domain of corporeal substances very much like the domain that he showed Arnauld in the late 1680s. But sometimes he offers other very different accounts of the make-up of bodies. Once monads are added to the mix, Leibniz is forced to rethink his conception of body, to query the substantiality of bodies and even consider phenomenalistic accounts of body of different sorts. But in a broader sense, the theory of monads is a kind of completion of his earlier accounts of body, adding another layer of depth and complexity to the level of body and corporeal substance, grounding it in something metaphysically more basic. It may sound strange to put it like this, but in some ways what Leibniz was doing is more like contemporary particle physics than it is like contemporary analytic metaphysics. It is not unfair to say that Leibniz uses metaphysical arguments to limn the ultimate nature of the physical world in the way in which a contemporary physicist might use mathematics or symmetry arguments for the same purpose. But putting it in that way distorts the project as well. What Leibniz is doing is a kind of enterprise that we don't do today, either in physics or in philosophy: it is (natural) philosophy as Leibniz and his contemporaries understood the enterprise.[85]

How does this help make sense of Leibniz's thought? A modern physicist may have good reason to believe that ultimate reality is quite different than what we experience around us: it may obey very different laws than macroscopic objects do, and violate constraints and regularities that we take for granted about the physical world in which we live. If something like string theory turns out to be true, the ultimate reality may be *very* different from anything that we experience. But yet, the physicist must try to figure out just how this fundamental physics can give rise to what we see around us. In adopting the world of microphysics we don't necessarily

---

[85] Donald Rutherford makes a similar remark in Rutherford (2008), 149, 153–4, though he takes it in a somewhat different direction than I do here. I think that we came upon this insight independently and at roughly the same time, in connection with a symposium on Leibniz and Idealism at the APA Central Division in April 2005.

give up the world of bodies we experience. This is the problem, familiar from the philosophy of science, of the relation between the scientific and manifest image, the world as it appears to the scientist, and the world as it appears to our everyday experience. Leibniz has a similar problem. One of Leibniz's commitments in his later years was to the world of non-extended and mind-like monads as the foundations of the real world. But he did not want simply to dismiss the world of bodies that we experience either. And this leads to a question: how is it that our everyday experience of bodies is related to what he takes to be the fundamental metaphysics, the world of monads? Certain metaphysical arguments convinced Leibniz that, at root, simple substances, monads, had to be at the bottom of everything. What he hadn't fully figured out, though, is how exactly bodies are to be grounded in the world of monads. This, I would claim, was the project of the letters with de Volder, the letters with Des Bosses, and other texts of this period. And, I would claim, there is no single doctrine that one can say is *the* Leibnizian solution to that problem. There are different strands that recur throughout the texts, but I don't think that he ever arrived at an answer that fully satisfied him.[86]

It is because of this that it is difficult to offer a neat and clean characterization of what exactly the monadological metaphysics comes to, or to offer a neat and clean comparison with the earlier corporeal substance view, as I tried to do in the last chapter. The earlier corporeal substance view is clear enough, but the monadological metaphysics is a kind of moving target, very difficult to pin down, since an essential piece of it, the relation between the metaphysically foundational world of monads and the experientially fundamental world of bodies, is constantly up for grabs. The best that you

---

[86] My proposal here may seem to resemble what Hartz and Wilson (2005) propose. They write:

We agree with Idealists that Leibniz loved the idea of Idealism. He saw it as beautiful, stunning, simple.... But Leibniz also wanted a real world, populated by articulated living creatures of infinite complexity.... He leaves two incompatible systems suspended in the mature writings without reconciliation. [Hartz and Wilson (2005), 19]

But Hartz and Wilson seem to leave Leibniz hanging. Wilson refers here to her earlier book, Wilson (1989), where she sees Leibniz's philosophy as consisting in incompatible and competing systems held simultaneously, though not in a fully conscious way; on this see also Wilson (1999b). I suspect that Hartz may see this differently, as the alternative Realist and Idealist views that, according to Hartz (2007), to be discussed below, coexist in Leibniz's thought in a fully self-conscious way, despite their evident inconsistency. On my view, Leibniz was fully conscious of both perspectives, but he didn't think that they were inconsistent, nor was he willing to leave the two positions "suspended...without reconciliation." Rather, I argue, he saw his project in his last years as trying to figure out how exactly they were to come together in a single consistent system.

can do is say that, on the new view, monads are the ultimate elements of things, as opposed to the corporeal substances of the earlier view. But not even this will do, since by the end, by the substantial bond view in the last letters with Des Bosses, even the monads seem to be called into question. Nor is it clear exactly what Leibniz thought it meant to say that monads are the ultimate elements of things.

It also makes it difficult to determine whether or not Leibniz was an idealist in his later years. For generations, historians of philosophy have assumed that Leibniz was an idealist. One can point to texts that, it would seem, could *only* be interpreted as idealist in a robust sense: "Indeed, considering the matter carefully it should be said that there is nothing in things except simple substances and in them perception and appetite."[87] Recent commentators have challenged this in various ways. In the earlier chapters of this book, as well as in related articles, I have tried to argue that Leibniz's theory of monads, non-extended and mind-like substances that ground everything, doesn't enter until fairly late in his career, and that many of the texts, such as the 'Discours de métaphysique' and the correspondence with Arnauld, are not to be understood in terms of a monadological metaphysics. If the monadological metaphysics is idealist, then these texts are not, nor was Leibniz an idealist in the period in which they were written. But some commentators have suggested that even after the introduction of monads in the late 1690s or early 1700s, Leibniz *still* wasn't an idealist. Here there are a number of different positions to choose from. In a recent article, Donald Rutherford has introduced a distinction between what he calls "substance idealism" and "matter idealism."[88] Substance idealism is the view that the ultimate constituents of the world are immaterial or mental, and he accepts the view that, at least in his later writings, Leibniz was a substance idealist. Matter idealism is the view that "material things exist only as appearances, ideas, or the contents of mental representations." Insofar as Leibniz believed that bodies are often construed as aggregates of monads, Rutherford argues that he should be regarded as a matter realist. In a recent book, Glenn Hartz has argued for a different thesis about the relation between idealism and realism in Leibniz's thought. For Hartz, realism and idealism are found in equal

[87] Leibniz to de Volder, 30 June 1704, G II 270.
[88] See Rutherford (2008). The distinction is introduced on pp. 141–2, at the very beginning of the essay, and developed throughout the rest.

measure in Leibniz's philosophy. He wants to argue for a view of realism and idealism "as theories of Reality, not absolute pronouncements about Reality."[89] His Leibniz doesn't feel that he has to make a choice between the two metaphysical views: he accepts both *as theories*. In this way, Hartz's Leibniz is what he calls a "theory pluralist":

On my interpretation, Leibniz is an Idealist facing Realist worries, and a Realist facing Idealist misgivings. A consistent Realist like Reid mocks Idealism and hopes the reader stays with "common sense"; a consistent Idealist like Berkeley makes similar maneuvers with respect to Realism and hopes the reader hangs on to phenomenalism. Leibniz is different from these "consistent" theorists in that he adopts Realism yet tries to address Idealist concerns, and also adopts Idealism while yet confronting the full fury of Realist concerns.[90]

In her recent book, Pauline Phemister sees Leibniz as being consistently on one side of the dichotomy. But unlike the traditional idealist inter-pretation, she sees Leibniz as being a realist about bodies and corporeal substances all the way through his career: "This book thus challenges the view that Leibnizian created substances are soul-like, replacing this with an image of the created world as a world of living corporeal sub-stances."[91] And on a note somewhat further still from standard readings, Peter Loptson has recently argued that there is an autonomous world of bodies that runs parallel to the world of monads. Loptson argues for what he calls an "epiphenomenalist" view on which there is "a fully replete, closed, fully deterministic physical causal order" coordin-ated with a world of monads, located at every body, that mirrors the world from the point of view of that body.[92] If I understand his view, Richard Arthur proposes a kind of dual-aspect theory, explicitly on the model of Spinoza's: "I propose, for Leibniz one and the same phenomenon can be taken now internally, as something existing in per-ception, and now externally, as the thing perceived."[93] Elsewhere he suggests that

while what is substantial, the principle of activity, is strictly immaterial, it is necessarily situated in a body and constitutes at any instant the form of that body.

---

[89] Hartz (2007), 2.   [90] Ibid., 7. See also Hartz and Wilson (2005).

[91] Phemister (2005), 3. The view is developed in detail throughout the book.

[92] Loptson and Arthur (2006), 15f. See also Loptson (1999), where Loptson presents and defends a similar alternative to idealism that he terms "pan-dualism."

[93] Loptson and Arthur (2006), 31.

so that referring to a dominant monad together with its organic body as a substance is defensible. . . ."[94]

This view he explicitly relates to what Phemister has proposed. And there are yet other complicated mergings of idealism and realism in the literature about Leibniz's mature philosophy.

But I wonder about the whole discussion. "Realist" and "idealist" are just not terms that Leibniz himself used to describe his position. Nor were they terms that were really available to him; as terms of art in philosophical discourse, they don't really enter the vocabulary until after Leibniz's death.[95] I wonder if this isn't just a bad question to be focusing on.[96] For this reason I have avoided the term in earlier discussions in this book. Leibniz, in the end, wants to maintain the importance of monads as a foundation for everything, at least in the monadological years after 1700 or so, and up until practically the end of the exchange with Des Bosses. And he never gives up the idea of a world of bodies ultimately grounded in living things, bugs in bugs to infinity. And he wants to figure out how to relate the two to one another. Here he is simply unsure how to go. Sometimes he gives more weight and heft to the bodies; when he does, we call him a realist. Sometimes he gives more reality to the monads, and when he does we call him an idealist. But at least in his later years, both monads and bodies are always there in one way or another. It is, perhaps, open to us to represent him as swinging from one pole to another on the metaphysical scheme of things. Or we can just see it for what it is, Leibniz in his metaphysical workshop, trying out different ways of connecting the two pieces of his world, both of which must find their places in his final story.

[94] Ibid., 34.

[95] Eisler (1910), vol. 1 516, lists Christian Wolff's *Psychologia rationalis* (1734) and Alexander Baumgarten's *Metaphysica* (1739) as the earliest appearances of the words "idealism" and "idealist" used in the modern sense. The *Trésor de la langue française* lists Diderot's *Lettre sur les aveugles* (1749) in this connection. It is interesting that in the Wolff, *Psychologia rationalis* § 36, where the term is introduced ("*Idealistae* dicuntur, qui nonnisi idealem corporum in animabus nostris existentiam concedunt . . ."). the sole example he gives of an idealist is not Leibniz, whose metaphysics he knew well, but Berkeley. Leibniz does use the word "idealist" once in his writings, in the "Reponse aux reflexions contenues dans la seconde Edition du Dictionnaire Critique de M. Bayle . . .," written in 1702, published in 1716. In discussing his pre-established harmony he notes: "what is of value in the theories of Epicurus and of Plato, of the greatest materialists and the greatest idealists, is united here" [G IV 560 (WF 114)]. However, here the term seems to point to Plato's doctrine of the forms, as contrasted with Epicurus's materialism, rather than the modern conception of idealism, as Wolff defines it.

[96] For reasons somewhat different than mine, Justin Smith has arrived at a similar conclusion. See Smith (2004), where he tries to place the question of Leibniz's supposed realism and idealism about body into the context of later Platonism.

Historians of philosophy want to find Leibniz's "considered view"; much of the debate in this area amounts to differences among commentators about where to come down on this question. But I'm not sure that there is a considered view to find. We tend to think of people's lives and thought in neat packages, with a beginning, a middle, and an end. Leibniz's life had an end, as do all mortal lives, but as often happens, he died *in medias res*, at a moment when he was still very much engaged in his life and in his intellectual projects. It is unsurprising then that he left behind many loose ends in his thought, questions he considered but did not resolve. In his later years, on my reading, Leibniz was struggling with the problems and struggling toward a considered view on these issues. But he died before he got there.

Epilogue

Leibniz died on 14 November 1716. Almost a year later to the day, on 13 November 1717, Fontenelle delivered his Éloge to the assembled academicians of the Académie Royale des Sciences in Paris. In the Introduction I noted the vast scope of Leibniz's erudition that Fontenelle chronicled. Fontenelle gave a fair amount of attention to certain aspects of Leibniz's view of the physical world. Fontenelle knew a fair bit about Leibniz's work in physics, some of which had been published. He knew the early letter to Thomasius as published in the introduction of the edition of Marius Nizolius in 1670, discussed above in Chapter 1, where Leibniz declares himself for the mechanical philosophy. He knew the *Hypothesis physica nova* and the *Theoria motus abstracti*, where Leibniz first began to set out his own system of physics in 1671.[1] He also knew about the critique of the Cartesian conservation law, the Cartesian conception of body and the revival of substantial forms in such writings as the "Brevis demonstratio," the "Système nouveau," and the "Specimen dynamicum."[2] But Fontenelle discusses very little about Leibniz's metaphysics. Leibniz's metaphysics is presented not as a central part of his intellectual personality, but as a kind of afterthought:

He was a metaphysician, and it was something almost impossible that he not be, since he had a mind too universal.[3]

While there are other ways of reading this statement, it can be read as a kind of dismissal of Leibniz's interest in metaphysics: the implication seems to be that Leibniz had to be interested in metaphysics simply because he was interested in everything! After a brief discussion of Leibniz's central philosophical principles, the Principle of Sufficient Reason, the

---

[1] Fontenelle (1740), 441–6.   [2] Ibid., 446–8.   [3] Ibid., 460.

Principle of Continuity, the Principle of the Best, Fontenelle turns to some aspects of what we now think of as Leibniz's philosophy. The central philosophical thesis that Fontenelle discusses, and, again, only briefly, is the hypothesis of pre-established harmony. As for Leibniz's monadology, Fontenelle's account of that is even briefer than his other discussions of Leibniz's metaphysics. The entire theory of monads gets hardly more than a page.[4] Fontenelle considers Leibniz's main metaphysical work not the 'Monadologie,' which he could not have known, but the Leibniz-Clarke correspondence, which Clarke published shortly after Leibniz's death.[5] This work, of course, barely mentions the monads. After the long familiarity modern readers have had with the 'Monadologie' and with other texts, mostly letters unpublished in Leibniz's lifetime where he discusses the theory of monads in great detail, it is somewhat difficult to imagine a time when Leibniz was *not* associated with the metaphysics of monads. But to the contemporaries who didn't have access to these texts, the Leibnizian world of monads was little more than a rumor.

The key text in the diffusion of Leibniz's monadological metaphysics was the 'Monadologie.' That text was not published during Leibniz's lifetime, and was not available to Fontenelle when he wrote his Éloge in 1717. However, it was available shortly thereafter. In 1720 it came out in a volume entitled *Lehr-Sätze über die* Monadologie..., published in Frankfurt and Leipzig. The following year, in 1721, it appeared in Latin in a supplementary volume of the *Acta eruditorum*, under the title "Principia philosophiae, autore G.G. Leibnitio."[6] It was a grand success. It is not surprising that the 'Monadologie' was quickly adopted, and quickly regarded as a central text in Leibniz's philosophy.[7] It is short, systematic,

---

[4] Fontenelle (1740), 462–3.   [5] Ibid., 463–4.

[6] On the history of the first publication of the 'Monadologie' in German and Latin, see Lamarra, Palaia, and Pimpinella (2001). The "Principes de la nature et de la grâce," the companion piece to the 'Monadologie,' was first published in November 1718 in the periodical *L'Europe savante*, though it didn't have the influence that the 'Monadologie' had.

[7] A nice illustration of the way in which later thinkers turned Leibniz's thought into a system is illustrated in Condillac (1749). Schwegman (2008), 188–90 notes that Condillac first systematizes Leibniz's monadology, before going on to criticize it exactly for being a system. He remarks that Samuel Formey criticizes Condillac exactly for turning Leibniz into a systematic philosopher. Formey writes as follows:

As for *Leibniz*, he would have been quite surprised, were he to return to the world, to find himself established as an Architect: he who possessed the most definite and peculiar character in this genre. ...Yet here is the System of Monads, you say, which exists nonetheless. And where does it exist, if not in the writings of those who have taken the care to develop the simple seed that Leibniz

and to the point, and gives the impression of being the true key to the master's deepest metaphysical thoughts. It is forceful and dogmatic, leaving little question about the author's philosophical convictions. It is fair to say that the 'Monadologie' shaped the later reading of Leibniz's thought, both for those like Wolff, Baumgarten, and Kant, who were interested in finding the truth about the world and saw Leibniz's texts as an important statement of important ideas, and for those like Brucker, who were interested in codifying the history of philosophical thought in a great historical sweep.[8] New Leibnizian texts continued to appear throughout the century and into the nineteenth and twentieth centuries.[9] But when new texts appeared, it is fair to say that they were read through the eyes of the 'Monadologie,' integrated into the picture of Leibniz's thought as understood through that text, a world exclusively constructed of monads with their perceptions and appetitions.

And in this way began the mythological Leibniz, the dogmatic idealist who from his early years to the end of his life lived in an austere and immaterial world of spiritual substances. But that's a story I leave to others to tell.

---

cast aside? This is so obviously the case, that before attempting to explain this system, the author warns *that he will speak for this philosopher*, but that he *will not make him say anything that he did not say, or WOULDN'T HAVE SAID, if he had himself undertaken to explain his system.* Leibniz is thus truly *the Doctor in Spite of Himself.* He will have a system, in spite of the fact that he did not. What a strange way to go about proving and refuting! [Samuel Formey, in the *Bibliothèque impartiale* (January–February 1750), 34–5, quoted in Schwegman (2008), 189]

Formey's remarks here are very insightful.

[8] There is a very considerable literature on the reception of Leibniz's philosophy in the eighteenth century. For a start, consult Beck (1969) and Wilson (1995), as discussed in Schwegman (2008), 188–90.

[9] For a comprehensive chronological bibliography of published editions of Leibniz's writings, see Ravier (1937), together with the corrections in Schrecker (1938).

Bibliography

Adams, Robert Merrihew (1983). "Phenomenalism and Corporeal Substance in Leibniz," *Midwest Studies in Philosophy* 8: 217–57.

—— (1994). *Leibniz: Determinist, Theist, Idealist* (New York: Oxford University Press).

Aiton, E. J. (1985). *Leibniz: a Biography* (Bristol and Boston: A. Hilger).

Angelelli, Ignacio (1994). "The Scholastic Background of Modern Philosophy: *Entitas* and Individuation in Leibniz," in J. J. E. Gracia (ed.), *Individuation in Scholasticism: The Later Middle Ages and the Counter-Reformation, 1150–1650* (Albany, NY: SUNY Press), 535–42.

Antognazza, Maria Rosa (2008). *Leibniz: An Intellectual Biography* (Cambridge: Cambridge University Press).

Ariew, Roger (1995). "G. W. Leibniz, Life and Works," in Nicholas Jolley (ed.), *The Cambridge Companion to Leibniz* (Cambridge: Cambridge University Press), 18–42.

—— (forthcoming). "Descartes and Leibniz on The Principle of Individuation," in Vlad Alexandrescu (ed.), *Branching Off: The Early Moderns in Quest of the Unity of Knowledge* (Bucharest: Zeta Books).

Arnauld, Antoine, and Pierre Nicole (1970). *La logique; ou, L'art de penser; contenant, outre les règles communes, plusieurs observations nouvelles, propres à former le jugement* (Paris: Flammarion).

Arthur, Richard (1989). "Russell's Conundrum: On the Relation of Leibniz's Monads to the Continuum," in James Brown and Jürgen Mittelstraß (eds.), *An Intimate Relation: Studies in the History and Philosophy of Science* (Dordrecht: Kluwer), 171–201.

—— (1998a). "Infinite Aggregates and Phenomenal Wholes: Leibniz's Theory of Substance as a Solution to the Continuum Problem," *Leibniz Review* 8: 25–45.

—— (1998b). "Cohesion, Division and Harmony: Physical Aspects of Leibniz's Continuum Problem (1671–1686)," *Perspectives on Science* 6: 110–35.

—— (2003). "The Enigma of Leibniz's Atomism," *Oxford Studies in Early Modern Philosophy* 1: 183–227.

—— (2006). "Animal Generation and Substance in Sennert and Leibniz," in Justin E. H. Smith (ed.), *The Problem of Animal Generation in Early Modern Philosophy* (Cambridge: Cambridge University Press), 147–74.

Bassler, O. Bradley (2002). "Motion and Mind in the Balance: The Transformation of Leibniz's Early Philosophy," *Studia Leibnitiana* 34: 221–31.

Baxter, Donald (1995). "Corporeal Substances and True Unities," *Studia Leibnitiana* 27: 154–84.

Becco, Anne (1975a). *Du simple selon Leibniz: Discours de métaphysique et Monadologie* (Paris: Vrin).

—— (1975b). "Aux sources de la monade: Paléographie et lexicographie leibniziennes," *Les Études Philosophiques* 3: 279–94.

—— (1978). "Leibniz et François-Mercure van Helmont: Bagatelle pour des monades," in *Magia naturalis und die Entstehung der modernen Naturwissenschaften: Symposion der Leibniz-Gesellschaft, Hannover, 14. u. 15. November 1975* (Wiesbaden: Steiner), 119–42.

Beck, Lewis White (1969). *Early German Philosophy: Kant and his Predecessors* (Cambridge, MA: Harvard University Press).

Beeley, Philip (1995). "Les sens dissimulants. Phénomènes et réalité dans l'*Hypothesis physica nova*," in Martine de Gaudemar (ed.), *La notion de nature chez Leibniz* (Stuttgart: Steiner), 17–30.

—— (1996a). *Kontinuität und Mechanismus: zur Philosophie des jungen Leibniz in ihren ideengeschichtlichen Kontext* (Stuttgart: Steiner).

—— (1996b). "Points, Extension, and the Mind–Body Problem. Remarks on the Development of Leibniz's Thought from the *Hypothesis Physica Nova* to the *Système Nouveau*," in Roger Woolhouse (ed.), *Leibniz's 'New System' (1695)* (Florence: Olschki), 15–35.

—— (1999). "Mathematics and Nature in Leibniz's Early Philosophy," in S. Brown (ed.), *The Young Leibniz and his Philosophy (1646–76)* (Dordrecht: Kluwer), 123–45.

Bennett, Jonathan (2001). *Learning from Six Philosophers: Descartes, Spinoza, Leibniz, Locke, Berkeley, Hume.* 2 vols. (Oxford: Oxford University Press).

—— (2005). "Leibniz's Two Realms," in Donald Rutherford and J. A. Cover (eds.), *Leibniz: Nature and Freedom* (Oxford: Oxford University Press), 135–55.

Bernstein, Howard R. (1980). "Conatus, Hobbes, and the Young Leibniz," *Studies in History and Philosophy of Science* 11: 25–37.

—— (1981). "Passivity and Inertia in Leibniz's *Dynamics*," *Studia Leibnitiana* 18: 97–113.

Bertoloni Meli, Domenico (1993). *Equivalence and Priority: Newton versus Leibniz* (Oxford: Oxford University Press).

—— (2006). "Inherent and Centrifugal Forces in Newton," *Archive for History of Exact Sciences* 60: 319–35.

Bodemann, Eduard (1889). *Der Briefwechsel des Gottfried Wilhelm Leibniz in der Königlichen öffentlichen Bibliothek zu Hannover* (Hanover: Hahn'sche Buchhandlung).

——(1895). *Die Leibniz-Handschriften der Königlichen öffentlichten Bibliothek zu Hannover* (Hanover and Leipzig: Hahn'sche Buchhandlung).

Bodéüs, Richard (1991). "Leibniz, Jean de Raey, et la physique reformée," *Studia Leibnitiana* 23: 103–10.

Boehm, Alfred (1938). *Le "vinculum substantiale" chez Leibniz: ses origines historiques* (Paris: Vrin).

Boehm, Rudolf (1957). "Notes sur l'histoire des 'Principes de la nature et de la grâce' et de la 'Monadologie' de Leibniz," *Revue philosophique de Louvain* 55: 232–351.

Bos, H. J. M. (1978). "The Influence of Huygens on the Formation of Leibniz' Ideas," *Studia Leibnitiana Supplementa* 17: 59–68.

Bossuet, Jacques-Bénigne (1909–25). *Correspondance de Bossuet.* Charles Urbain and Eugène Levesque (eds.). Nouv. éd. 15 vols. (Paris: Hachette).

Boyle, Robert (1688). *A Disquisition about the Final Causes of Natural Things* (London: John Taylor).

——(1999–2000). *The Works of Robert Boyle.* Michael Hunter and Edward Davis (eds.). 14 vols. (London and Brookfield, VT: Pickering and Chatto).

Breger, Herbert (1984). "Elastizität als Strukturprinzip der Materie bei Leibniz," in Albert Heinekamp (ed.), *Leibniz' Dynamica* (Stuttgart: Steiner), 112–21.

Broad, C.D. (1975). *Leibniz: An Introduction* (Cambridge: Cambridge University Press).

Brown, Gregory (1984). " 'Quod ostendendum susceperamus': What did Leibniz undertake to Show in the Brevis Demonstratio?" in Albert Heinekamp (ed.), *Leibniz' Dynamica* (Stuttgart: Steiner), 122–37.

——(1987). "God's Phenomena and the Pre-Established Harmony," *Studia Leibnitiana* 19: 200–14.

——(1992). "Is There a Pre-Established Harmony of Aggregates in the Leibnizian Dynamics, or Do Non-Substantial Bodies Interact?," *Journal of the History of Philosophy* 30: 53–75.

Brown, Stuart (1996). "Leibniz's *New System* Strategy," in Roger Woolhouse (ed.), *Leibniz's 'New System' (1695)* (Florence: Olschki), 37–61.

——(1999). "The Proto-Monadology of the *De Summa Rerum*," in S. Brown (ed.), *The Young Leibniz and his Philosophy (1646–76)* (Dordrecht: Kluwer), 263–87.

——(2004). "The Leibniz–Foucher Alliance and Its Philosophical Bases," in Paul Lodge (ed.), *Leibniz and His Correspondents* (Cambridge: Cambridge University Press), 74–96.

Brucker, Johann Jakob (1742–4). *Historia critica philosophiae a mundi incunabulis ad nostram usque aetatem deducta.* 5 vols. (Leipzig: Bernh. Christoph. Breitkopf).

Byrne, Alex, and David R. Hilbert (eds.) (1997). *Readings on Color.* 2 vols. (Cambridge, MA: MIT Press).

Carraud, Vincent (2002). *Causa sive ratio: La raison de la cause, de Suarez à Leibniz* (Paris: Presses Universitaires de France).

Cohen, I. Bernard (1999). "A Guide to Newton's *Principia,*" in Newton (1999), 1–370.

Condillac, Étienne Bunnot de (1749). *Traite des sistêmes, où l'on en demêle les inconvéniens et les avantages* (The Hague: Neaulme).

Conway, Anne (1996). *Principles of the Most Ancient and Modern Philosophy,* Sarah Hutton (ed.) (Cambridge: Cambridge University Press).

Cordemoy, Géraud de (1679). *Tractatus physici duo* (Geneva: Pictetus).

——(1968). *Œuvres philosophiques.* Pierre Clair and François Girbal (eds.) (Paris: Presses Universitaires de France).

Costabel, Pierre (1966). "Contribution à l'étude de l'offensive de Leibniz contre la philosophie cartésienne en 1691–1692," *Revue internationale de philosophie* 20: 264–87.

——(1973). *Leibniz and Dynamics* (Ithaca, NY: Cornell University Press).

Couturat, Louis (1972). "On Leibniz's Metaphysics," in Harry G. Frankfurt (ed.), *Leibniz: A Collection of Critical Essays* (Garden City, NY: Doubleday), 19–45.

Cover, Jan and Glenn Hartz (1994). "Are Leibnizian Monads Spatial?," *History of Philosophy Quarterly* 11: 295–316.

Cover, Jan and John O'Leary-Hawthorne (1999). *Substance and Individuation in Leibniz* (Cambridge: Cambridge University Press).

Curley, E. M. (1990). "Homo Audax: Leibniz, Oldenburg, and the TTP," in I. Marchlewitz and A. Heinekamp (eds.), *Leibniz' Auseinandersetzung mit Vorgängern und Zeitgenossen* (Stuttgart: Steiner), 277–312.

De Risi, Vincenzo (2007). *Geometry and Monadology: Leibniz's* Analysis Situs *and Philosophy of Space* (Basel, Boston and Berlin: Birkhäuser).

Dear, Peter R. (1995). *Discipline and Experience: The Mathematical Way in the Scientific Revolution* (Chicago: University of Chicago Press).

——(2001). *Revolutionizing the Sciences: European Knowledge and its Ambitions, 1500–1700* (Princeton: Princeton University Press).

——(2006). *The Intelligibility of Nature: How Science Makes Sense of the World* (Chicago: University of Chicago Press).

Descartes, René (1667). *Lettres de Mr Descartes,* Claude Clerselier (ed.). 2nd edn. 3 vols. (Paris: Chez Charles Angot).

—— (1984–91). *The Philosophical Writings of Descartes*, John Cottingham, Robert Stoothoff, Dugald Murdoch, and Anthony Kenny (eds. and trans.). 3 vols. (Cambridge: Cambridge University Press).

—— (1996). *Oeuvres de Descartes*, Ch. Adam and Paul Tannery (eds.), 11 vols. (Paris: Vrin).

Di Bella, Stephano (2002). "Leibniz on Causation: Efficiency, Explanation and Conceptual Dependence," *Quaestio* 2: 411–47.

—— (2005a). *The Science of the Individual: Leibniz's Ontology of Individual Substance* (Dordrecht: Springer).

—— (2005b). "Leibniz's Theory of Conditions: A Framework for Ontological Dependence," *Leibniz Review* 15: 67–93.

Digby, Sir Kenelm (1644). *Two Treatises in the One of Which the Nature of Bodies in the Other the Nature of Mans Soule is Looked Into in the Way of Discovery of the Immortality of Reasonable Soules* (Paris: G. Blaizot).

Dijksterhuis, E. J. (1961). *The Mechanization of the World Picture* (Oxford: Oxford University Press).

Diogenes Laertius (1925). *Lives of Eminent Philosophers*, Robert Drew Hicks (ed. and trans.) (London and New York: Heinemann and Putnam).

Dod, Bernard G. (1982). "Aristoteles Latinus," in N. Kretzmann, A. Kenny, and J. Pinborg (eds.), *The Cambridge History of Later Medieval Philosophy* (Cambridge: Cambridge University Press), 45–79.

Duchesneau, François (1993). *Leibniz et la méthode de la science* (Paris: Presses Universitaires de France).

—— (1994). *La dynamique de Leibniz* (Paris: Vrin).

—— (1998a). "Leibniz's Theoretical Shift in the *Phoranomus* and *Dynamica de Potentia*," *Perspectives on Science* 6: 77–109.

—— (1998b). *Les modèles du vivant de Descartes à Leibniz* (Paris: Vrin).

Dupleix, Scipion (1990). *La physique*, Roger Ariew (ed.) (Paris: Fayard).

Eisler, Rudolf (1910). *Wörterbuch der philosophischen Begriffe*, 3rd edn. 3 vols. (Berlin: Ernst Siegfried Mittler und Sohn).

Elster, Jon (1975). *Leibniz et la formation de l'esprit capitaliste* (Paris: Aubier-Montaigne).

Eustachius a Sancto Paulo (1609). *Summa philosophiae quadripartita, de rebus dialecticis, ethicis, physicis & metaphysicis* (Paris: C. Chastellain).

Fichant, Michel (1974). "La 'réforme' leibnizienne de la dynamique d'après des textes inédites," *Studia Leibnitiana Supplementa* 13: 195–214.

—— (1978). "Les concepts fondamentaux de la mécanique selon Leibniz, en 1676," in Gottfried-Wilhelm-Leibniz-Gesellschaft and Centre national de la recherche scientifique (France) (eds.), *Leibniz à Paris: 1672–1676: Symposion de* la G. W. Leibniz-Gesellschaft (Hannover) et du Centre National de la Recherche Scientifique (Paris) à Chantilly (France) de 14 au 18 novembre 1976 (Wiesbaden: Steiner), 219–32.

—— (1990). "Neue Einblicke in Leibniz' Reform seiner Dynamik (1678)," Studia Leibnitiana 22: 48–68.

—— (1993a). "Leibniz: Pensées sur l'instauration d'une physique nouvelle (1679) (Traduction et annotation de Michel Fichant)," Philosophie (39–40): 3–26.

—— (1993b). "Mécanisme et Métaphysique: le rétablissement des formes substantielles (1679)," Philosophie (39–40): 27–59.

—— (1994). G.W. Leibniz: La réforme de la dynamique: De corporum concursu (1678) et autres textes inédits (Paris: Vrin).

—— (2003). "Leibniz et les machines de la nature," Studia Leibnitiana 35: 1–28.

—— (2004). "Introduction: Invention métaphysique," in Leibniz (2004), 7–140.

—— (2005). "La constitution du concept de monade," in Enrico Pasini (ed.), La Monadologie de Leibniz: genèse et contexte (Milan: Mimesis), 31–54.

Fontenelle, Bernard Le Bouvier de (1740). "Eloge de Monsieur Leibnitz," in Eloges des academiciens avec l'histoire de l'academie royale des sciences en M. DC. XCIC . . . (The Hague: Isaac vander Kloot), 424–80.

Foucher, Simon (1675). Critique de la Recherche de la vérité (Paris: Chez Martin Coustelier).

—— (1676). Réponse pour la critique à la préface du second volume de la recherche de la verité (Paris: C. Agnot).

—— (1995). "Critique [of Nicolas Malebranche's] Of the Search for the Truth," Richard A. Watson (ed. and trans.), in Richard A. Watson and Marjorie Grene (eds. and trans.), Malebranche's First and Last Critics (Carbondale and Edwardsville, IL: Southern Illinois University Press).

Fouke, Daniel C. (1989). "Mechanical and 'Organical' Models in Seventeenth-Century Explanations of Biological Reproduction," Science in Context 3: 365–81.

—— (1991). "Leibniz's Opposition to Cartesian Bodies During the Paris Period (1672–1676)," Studia Leibnitiana 23: 195–206.

—— (1992). "Metaphysics and the Eucharist in the Early Leibniz," Studia Leibnitiana 24: 145–59.

Freudenthal, Gideon (1999). "Leibniz als Transzendentalphilosoph malgré lui. Der Status der Erhaltungssätze," in Hartmut Rudolph, Martin Fontius, and Gary Smith (eds.), Labora diligenter. Potsdamer Arbeitstagung zur Leibnizforschung vom 4. bis 6. Juli 1996 (Stuttgart: Steiner), 9–29.

—— (2002). "Perpetuum mobile: the Leibniz–Papin Controversy," Studies in History and Philosophy of Science 33: 573–637.

Friedmann, Georges (1962). Leibniz et Spinoza (Paris: Gallimard).

Futch, Michael J. (2005). "Leibnizian Causation," *British Journal for the Philosophy of Science* 56: 450–67.

Garber, Daniel (1982). "Motion and Metaphysics in the Young Leibniz," in Michael Hooker (ed.), *Leibniz: Critical and Interpretive Essays* (Minneapolis: University of Minnesota Press), 160–84.

—— (1985). "Leibniz and the Foundations of Physics: the Middle Years," in Kathleen Okruhlik and James Brown (eds.), *The Natural Philosophy of Leibniz* (Dordrecht: Reidel), 27–130.

—— (1992). *Descartes' Metaphysical Physics* (Chicago: University of Chicago Press).

—— (1995). "Leibniz: Physics and Philosophy," in Nicholas Jolley (ed.), *The Cambridge Companion to Leibniz* (Cambridge: Cambridge University Press), 270–352.

—— (2001a). "Mind, Body and the Laws of Nature in Descartes and Leibniz," in Daniel Garber, *Descartes Embodied: Reading Cartesian Philosophy through Cartesian Science* (Cambridge and New York: Cambridge University Press), 133–67.

—— (2001b). "Descartes and Occasionalism," in Daniel Garber, *Descartes Embodied: Reading Cartesian Philosophy through Cartesian Science* (Cambridge and New York: Cambridge University Press), 203–20.

—— (2001c). "How God Causes Motion: Descartes, Divine Sustenance, and Occasionalism," in Daniel Garber, *Descartes Embodied: Reading Cartesian Philosophy through Cartesian Science* (Cambridge and New York: Cambridge University Press), 189–202.

—— (2004). "Leibniz and Fardella: Body, Substance, and Idealism," in Paul Lodge (ed.), *Leibniz and his Correspondents* (Cambridge: Cambridge University Press), 123–40.

—— (2008). "Dead Force, Infinitesimals, and the Mathematicization of Nature," in Ursula Goldenbaum and Douglas Jesseph (eds.), *Infinitesimal Differences: Controversies between Leibniz and his Contemporaries* (Berlin and New York: Walter de Gruyter), 281–306.

—— (forthcoming). "Review of Vincenzo De Risi," *Geometry and Monadology: Leibniz's* Analysis Situs *and Philosophy of Space, Mind*.

Gassendi, Pierre (1658). *Opera omnia in sex tomos divisa*. 6 vols. (Lyon: Sumptibus Laurentii Anisson et Ioan. Bapt. Devenet).

Goclenius, Rudolph (1613). *Lexicon philosophicum, quo tanquam clave philosophiae fores aperiuntur* (Frankfurt: Typis viduae Matthiae Beckeri, impensis Petri Musculi et Ruperti Pistorii).

—— (1615). *Lexicon philosophicum graecvm . . .* (Marchioburgi: Typis Rudolphi Hutwelckeri, Impensis Petri Musculi).

Goldenbaum, Ursula (1994). "Qui ex conceptu extensionis secundum tuas meditationes varietas rerum a priori possit ostendi? Noch einmal zu Leibniz,
Spinoza und Tschirnhaus," in Albert Heinekamp and Herbert Breger (eds.),
VI. Internationaler Leibniz-Kongress: Leibniz und Europa (Hanover: Schlütersche),
266–75.

—— (1999a). "Transubstantiation, Physics and Philosophy at the Time of the
Catholic Demonstrations," in S. Brown (ed.), The Young Leibniz and his Philosophy
(1646–76) (Dordrecht: Kluwer), 79–102.

—— (1999b). "Die 'Commentatiuncula de judice' als Leibnizens erste philosophische Auseinandersetzung mit Spinoza nebst der Mitteilung über ein
neuaufgefundenes Leibnizstück," in Hartmut Rudolph, Martin Fontius, and
Gary Smith (eds.), Labora diligenter. Potsdamer Arbeitstagung zur Leibnizforschung
vom 4. bis 6. Juli 1996 (Stuttgart: Steiner), 61–127.

—— (2002). "Spinoza's Parrot, Socinian Syllogisms, and Leibniz's Metaphysics:
Leibniz's Three Strategies for Defending Christian Mysteries," American Catholic
Philosophical Quarterly 76: 551–74.

—— (2008). "Indivisibilia Vera—How Leibniz Came to Love Mathematics,"
in Ursula Goldenbaum and Douglas Jesseph (eds.), Infinitesimal Differences:
Controversies between Leibniz and his Contemporaries (Berlin and New York:
Walter de Gruyter), 53–94.

Grant, Edward (1971). Physical Science in the Middle Ages (New York: Wiley).

—— (1979). "The Condemnation of 1277, God's Absolute Power, and Physical
Thought in the Late Middle Ages," Viator 10: 211–44.

Gueroult, Martial (1967). Leibniz: dynamique et métaphysique (Paris: Aubier-
Montaigne).

Hall, A. Rupert (1980). Philosophers at War: the Quarrel Between Newton and Leibniz
(Cambridge: Cambridge University Press).

Hannequin, Arthur (1908). "La première philosophie de Leibnitz," in Arthur
Hannequin, Études d'histoire des sciences et d'histoire de la philosophie (Paris:
F. Alcan) 17–226.

Hartz, Glenn A. (1992). "Leibniz's Phenomenalisms," Philosophical Review 101:
511–49.

—— (1998). "Why Corporeal Substances Keep Popping Up in Leibniz's Later
Philosophy," British Journal for the History of Philosophy 6: 193–207.

—— (2007). Leibniz's Final System: Monads, Matter and Animals (London and New
York: Routledge).

Hartz, Glenn A., and Cover, J. A. (1988). "Space and Time in the Leibnizian
Metaphysic," Noûs 22: 493–519.

Hartz, Glenn A., and Catherine Wilson (2005). "Ideas and Animals: The Hard Problem of Leibnizian Metaphysics," *Studia Leibnitiana* 37: 1–19.

Hess, Hans-Jürgen (1978). "Die unveröffentlichten naturwissenschaftlichen und technischen Arbeiten von G. W. Leibniz aus der Zeit seines Parisaufenthaltes. Eine Kurzcharakteristik," in Gottfried-Wilhelm-Leibniz-Gesellschaft and Centre national de la recherche scientifique (France) (eds.), *Leibniz à Paris: 1672–1676* (Wiesbaden: Steiner), vol. 1, 183–217.

Hirschmann, David (1987–8). "The Kingdom of Wisdom and the Kingdom of Power in Leibniz," *Proceedings of the Aristotelian Society* 88: 147–59.

Hobbes, Thomas (1655). *Elementorum philosophiae sectio prima de corpore* (London: Andrew Crocke).

——(1656). *Elements of Philosophy the First Section Concerning Body* (London: Andrew Crocke).

——(1999). *De corpore: elementorum philosophiae sectio prima*, Karl Schuhmann (ed.) (Paris: Vrin).

Hoffman, Paul (1996). "The Being of Leibnizian Phenomena," *Studia Leibnitiana* 28: 108–18.

Hofmann, Joseph E. (1974). *Leibniz in Paris, 1672–1676: His Growth to Mathematical Maturity* (Cambridge: Cambridge University Press).

Hogan, Desmond (forthcoming). "Metaphysical Motives of Kant's Analytic–Synthetic Distinction."

Huygens, Christiaan (1888–1950). *Oeuvres complètes de Christiaan Huygens*, 22 vols. La Société hollandaise des sciences (eds.) (The Hague: M. Nijhoff).

Iltis, Carolyn (1971). "Leibniz and the Vis Viva Controversy," *Isis* 62: 21–35.

Ingenio, Alfonso (1988). "The New Philosophy of Nature," in C. Schmitt and Q. Skinner (eds.), *The Cambridge History of Renaissance Philosophy* (Cambridge: Cambridge University Press), 236–63.

Jolley, Nicholas (1986). "Leibniz and Phenomenalism," *Studia Leibnitiana* 18: 38–51.

——(2005a). *Leibniz* (London and New York: Routledge).

——(2005b). "Leibniz and Occasionalism," in Donald Rutherford and J. A. Cover (eds.), *Leibniz: Nature and Freedom* (Oxford: Oxford University Press), 121–34.

Kabitz, Willi (1909). *Die Philosophie des jungen Leibniz. Untersuchungen zur Entwicklungsgeschichte seines Systems* (Heidelberg: Winter).

Kant, Immanuel (1998). *Critique of Pure Reason*, Paul Guyer and Allen W. Wood (eds. and trans.) (Cambridge: Cambridge University Press).

Knobloch, Eberhard (1983). "Review of G. W. Leibniz, *Specimen Dynamicum*," *Annals of Science* 40: 501–4.

Kulstad, Mark (1977). "Leibniz's Concept of Expression," *Studia Leibnitiana* 11: 55–76.

—— (1993). "Causation and Preestablished Harmony in the Early Development of Leibniz's Philosophy," in Steven Nadler (ed.), *Causation in Early Modern Philosophy* (University Park, PA: Pennsylvania State University Press), 93–117.

—— (1999). "Leibniz's *De Summa Rerum*: The Origin of the Variety of Things, in Connection with the Spinoza–Tschirnhaus Correspondence," in F. Nef and D. Berlioz (eds.), *L'actualité de Leibniz: les deux labyrinthes* (*Studia Leibnitiana Supplementa* 34) (Stuttgart: Steiner), 69–86.

—— (2002). "Leibniz, Spinoza and Tschirnhaus: Metaphysics à Trois," in O. Koistinen and J. Biro (eds.), *Spinoza: Metaphysical Themes* (Oxford: Oxford University Press), 221–40.

—— (2006). "Leibniz on Expression: Reflections after Three Decades," in Jürgen Herbst, Herbert Breger, and Sven Erdner (eds.), *VIII. internationaler Leibniz-Kongress: Einheit in der Vielheit* (Hanover: Gottfried-Wilhelm-Leibniz-Gesellschaft), 413–19.

Laerke, Mogens (2008). *Leibniz lecteur de Spinoza: La genèse d'une opposition complexe* (Paris: Éditions Honoré Champion).

La Forge, Louis de (1974). *Œuvres philosophiques, avec une étude bio-bibliographique*, Pierre Clair (ed.) (Paris: Presses Universitaires de France).

Lamarra, Antonio, Roberto Palaia, and Pietro Pimpinella (2001). *Le prime traduzioni della Monadologie di Leibniz (1720–1721)* (Florence: Olschki).

Latour, Annick (2002). "Le concept leibnizien d'entéléchie et sa source aris-totélicienne," *Revue philosophique de Louvain* 100: 698–722.

Leibniz, Gottfried Wilhelm (1682). "Unicum opticae, catoptricae, et dioptricae principium," *Acta eruditorum*: 185–90.

—— (1695). "Sisteme nouveau de la nature et de la communication des substances, aussi bien que de l'union qu'il y a entre l'ame & le corps. Par M.D.L.," *Journal des sçavans*: 294–306.

—— (1734). *Recueil de diverses pieces sur la philosophie, les mathematiques, l'histoire &c. par M. de Leibniz*, Cretien Kortholt (ed.) (Hamburg: Abram Vandenhoeck).

—— (1849–63). *Leibnizens mathematische schriften*, C. I. Gerhardt (ed.). 7 vols. (Berlin: A. Asher).

—— (1854). *Réfutation inédite de Spinoza*, Louis Alexandre Foucher de Careil (ed.) (Paris: Typ. E. Brière).

—— (1857). *Nouvelles lettres et opuscules inédits*, Louis Alexandre Foucher de Careil (ed.) (Paris: A. Durand).

—— (1873). *Correspondenz von Leibniz mit der Prinzessin Sophie*. Otto Klopp (ed.), 3 vols. (Hanover: Klindworth's Verlag).

—— (1875–90). *Die philosophischen Schriften*, C. I. Gerhardt (ed.), 7 vols. (Berlin: Weidmann).

—— (1903) *Opuscules et fragments inédits de Leibniz*, Louis Couturat (ed.) (Paris: F. Alcan).

—— (1923 –). *Sämtliche Schriften und Briefe*, Deutsche Akademie der Wissenschaften zu Berlin (eds.) (Berlin: Akademie-Verlag).

—— (1952). *Lettres de Leibniz à Arnauld, d'après un manuscrit inédit*, Geneviève (Rodis-) Lewis (ed.) (Paris: Presses Universitaires de France).

—— (1966). *Logical papers*, G. H. R. Parkinson (ed. and trans.) (Oxford: Oxford University Press).

—— (1973a). *Marginalia in Newtoni "Principia mathematica": 1687*, Emil Alfred Fellmann (ed.) (Paris: Vrin).

—— (1973b). *Philosophical Writings*, G. H. R. Parkinson and Mary Morris (eds. and trans.). New edn. (London: Dent).

—— (1976). *Philosophical Papers and Letters*, Leroy E. Loemker (ed. and trans.). 2nd edn. (Dordrecht: D. Reidel).

—— (1982). *Specimen dynamicum*, Hans Günter Dosch, Glenn W. Most, Enno Rudolph, and Jörg Aichelin (eds. and trans.) (Hamburg: Meiner).

—— (1989). *Philosophical Essays*, Roger Ariew and Daniel Garber (eds. and trans.) (Indianapolis: Hackett).

—— (1991). "Phoranomus seu de potentia et legibus naturae," A. Robinet (ed.), *Physis* NS. 28: 429–541 and 797–885.

—— (1992). *De summa rerum: Metaphysical Papers, 1675–1676*, G. H. R. Parkinson (ed. and trans.) (New Haven: Yale University Press).

—— (1997). *Leibniz's 'New system' and Associated Contemporary Texts*, R. S. Woolhouse and Richard Francks (eds. and trans.) (Oxford: Oxford University Press).

—— (2001). *The Labyrinth of the Continuum: Writings on the Continuum Problem, 1672–1686*, Richard Arthur (ed. and trans.) (New Haven: Yale University Press).

—— (2002a). *Principes de la nature et de la grace fondés en raison; Principes de la philosophie, ou, Monadologie*, André Robinet (ed.), 5th edn. (Paris: Presses Universitaires de France).

—— (2002b). "Leibniz on Wachter's *Elucidarius cabalisticus*: A Critical Edition of the so-called 'Réfutation de Spinoza'," Phillip Beeley (ed.), *Leibniz Review* 12: 1–15.

—— (2004). *Discours de métaphysique suivi de Monadologie et autres textes*, Michel Fichant (ed. and trans.) (Paris: Gallimard).

—— (2005). *Confessio philosophi: Papers Concerning the Problem of Evil, 1671–1678*, R. C. Sleigh, Brandon Look, and James H. Stam (eds. and trans.) (New Haven: Yale University Press).

Leibniz, Gottfried Wilhelm and Antoine Arnauld (1846). *Briefwechsel zwischen Leibniz, Arnauld und dem Landgrafen Ernst von Hessen-Rheinfels*, C. L. Grotefend (ed.) (Hanover: Verlag der Hahnschen Hof-Buchhandlung).

——(1967). *The Leibniz–Arnauld Correspondence*, H. T. Mason (ed. and trans.) (Manchester: Manchester University Press).

——(1993). *Discours de métaphysique et correspondance avec Arnauld*, Georges Le Roy (ed.). 6th edn. (Paris: Vrin).

——(1997). *Der Briefwechsel mit Antoine Arnauld*. Reinhard Finster (ed. and trans.) (Hamburg: Meiner).

Leibniz, Gottfried Wilhelm, and Bartholomeus Des Bosses (2007). *The Leibniz–Des Bosses Correspondence*, Brandon Look and Donald Rutherford (eds. and trans.) (New Haven: Yale University Press).

Leibniz, Gottfried Wilhelm and Jacob Thomasius (1993). *Correspondance, 1663–1672*, Richard Bodéüs (ed. and trans.) (Paris: Vrin).

Lennon, Thomas (1974). "Occasionalism and the Cartesian Metaphysic of Motion," *Canadian Journal of Philosophy* 1 (suppl. pt 1): 29–40.

——(1993). *The Battle of the Gods and Giants: the Legacies of Descartes and Gassendi, 1655–1715* (Princeton: Princeton University Press).

Levey, Samuel (1998). "Leibniz on Mathematics and the Actually Infinite Division of Matter," *Philosophical Review* 107: 49–96.

——(1999). "Leibniz's Constructivism and Infinitely Folded Matter," in Rocco Gennaro and Charles Huenemann (eds.), *New Essays on the Rationalists* (Oxford: Oxford University Press), 134–62.

——(2003). "On Unity: Leibniz–Arnauld Revisited," *Philosophical Topics* 31: 245–75.

——(2005). "Leibniz on Precise Shapes and the Corporeal World," in Donald Rutherford and J. A. Cover (eds.), *Leibniz: Nature and Freedom* (Oxford: Oxford University Press), 69–94.

——(forthcoming). "*Dans les corps il n'y a point de figure parfaite*: Leibniz on Time, Change and Corporeal Substance," in *Oxford Studies in Early Modern Philosophy* 5.

Lindberg, David C. (ed.) (1978). *Science in the Middle Ages* (Chicago: University of Chicago Press).

Lodge, Paul (1997). "Force and the Nature of Body in Discourse on Metaphysics §§ 17–18," *Leibniz Review* 7: 116–24.

——(1998a). "Leibniz's Commitment to the Pre-established Harmony in the Late 1670s and Early 1680s," *Archiv für Geschichte der Philosophie* 80: 292–320.

—— (1998b). "Leibniz's Heterogeneity Argument Against the Cartesian Conception of Body," *Studia Leibnitiana* 30: 83–102.

—— (2001a). "Leibniz's Notion of an Aggregate," *British Journal for the History of Philosophy* 9: 467–86.

—— (2001b). "The Debate over Extended Substance in Leibniz's Correspondence with De Volder," *International Studies in the Philosophy of Science* 15: 155–65.

—— (2003). "Leibniz on Relativity and the Motion of Bodies," *Philosophical Topics* 31: 277–308.

—— (2004). "Leibniz's Close Encounter with Cartesianism in the Correspondence with De Volder," in Paul Lodge (ed.), *Leibniz and his Correspondents* (Cambridge: Cambridge University Press), 162–92.

—— (2005a). "Garber's Interpretation of Leibniz on Corporeal Substance in the 'Middle Years'" *Leibniz Review* 15: 1–26.

—— (2005b). "Burchard de Volder: Crypto-Spinozist or Disenchanted Cartesian?" in Tad Schmaltz (ed.), *Receptions of Descartes* (London and New York: Routledge), 128–46.

Loemker, Leroy E. (1955). "Boyle and Leibniz," *Journal of the History of Ideas* 16: 22–43.

Lohr, C.H. (1982). "The Medieval Interpretation of Aristotle," in N. Kretzmann, A. Kenny, and J. Pinborg (eds.), *The Cambridge History of Later Medieval Philosophy* (Cambridge: Cambridge University Press), 82–98.

Look, Brandon (1998a). "From the Metaphysical Union of Mind and Body to the Real Union of Monads: Leibniz on *Supposita* and *Vincula Substantialia*," *Southern Journal of Philosophy* 36: 505–29.

—— (1998b). "On an Unpublished Manuscript of Leibniz: New Light on the *Vinculum Substantiale* and the Correspondence with Des Bosses," *Leibniz Review* 8: 59–69.

—— (1999). *Leibniz and the "Vinculum Substantiale"* (*Studia Leibnitiana Sonderheft 30*) (Stuttgart: F. Steiner).

—— (2000). "Leibniz and the Substance of the *Vinculum Substantiale*," *Journal of the History of Philosophy* 38: 203–20.

—— (2002). "On Monadic Domination in Leibniz's Metaphysics," *British Journal for the History of Philosophy* 10: 379–99.

—— (2004). "On Substance and Relations in Leibniz's Correspondence with Des Bosses," in Paul Lodge (ed.), *Leibniz and his Correspondents* (Cambridge: Cambridge University Press), 238–61.

Loptson, Peter (1999). "Was Leibniz an Idealist?," *Philosophy* 74: 361–85.

Loptson, Peter, and Richard Arthur (2006). "Leibniz's Body Realism: Two Interpretations," *Leibniz Review* 16: 1–42.

McCullough, Laurence B. (1996). *Leibniz on Individuals and Individuation: the Persistence of Premodern Ideas in Modern Philosophy* (Dordrecht: Kluwer).

McDonough, Jeffrey (forthcoming-a). "Leibniz on Natural Teleology and the Laws of Optics," *Philosophy and Phenomenological Research*.

—— (forthcoming-b). "Leibniz's Two Realms Revisited," *Noûs*.

McGuire, J. E. (1985). "Phenomenalism, Relations, and Monadic Representation," in James Bogen and J. E. McGuire (eds.), *How Things Are* (Dordrecht: Reidel), 205–33.

Malcolm, Noel (2003). "Leibniz, Oldenburg, and Spinoza, in the Light of Leibniz's Letter to Oldenburg of 18/28 November 1676," *Studia Leibnitiana* 35: 225–43.

Malebranche, Nicolas (1958–84). *Oeuvres complètes*, André Robinet (ed.), 22 vols. (Paris: Vrin).

—— (1979–92). *Œuvres*, Geneviève Rodis-Lewis and Germain Malbreil (eds.), 2 vols. (Paris: Gallimard).

—— (1997a). *The Search After Truth and Elucidations of The Search After Truth*, Thomas M. Lennon and Paul J. Olscamp (eds. and trans.) (Cambridge: Cambridge University Press).

—— (1997b). *Dialogues on Metaphysics and on Religion*, Nicholas Jolley (ed.) and David Scott (trans.) (Cambridge: Cambridge University Press).

Mates, Benson (1986). *The Philosophy of Leibniz: Metaphysics and Language* (Oxford: Oxford University Press).

Mendelson, Michael (1995). "'Beyond the revolutions of matter': Mind, Body, and Pre-Established Harmony in the Earlier Leibniz," *Studia Leibnitiana* 27: 31–66.

Menn, Stephen (1998). "The Intellectual Setting of Seventeenth-Century Philosophy," in Daniel Garber and Michael Ayers (eds.), *The Cambridge History of Seventeenth-Century Philosophy* (Cambridge: Cambridge University Press), 33–86.

Mercer, Christia (1990). "The Seventeenth-Century Debate between the Moderns and the Aristotelians: Leibniz and Philosophia Reformata," *Studia Leibnitiana Supplementa* 27: 18–29.

—— (1993). "The Vitality and Importance of Early Modern Aristotelianism," in Tom Sorell (ed.), *The Rise of Modern Philosophy* (Oxford: Oxford University Press), 33–67.

—— (2001). *Leibniz's Metaphysics: Its Origins and Development* (Cambridge: Cambridge University Press).

Mercer, Christia, and Robert Sleigh (1995). "Metaphysics: The Early Period to the *Discourse on Metaphysics*," in Nicholas Jolley (ed.), *The Cambridge Companion to Leibniz* (Cambridge: Cambridge University Press), 67–123.

Miller, Richard B. (1988). "Leibniz on the Interaction of Bodies," *History of Philosophy Quarterly* 5: 245–55.

Molyneux, William (1692). *Dioptrica nova, A Treatise of Dioptricks* (London: Benj. Tooke).

Moreau, Denis (1999). *Deux Cartesiens: la polemique entre Antoine Arnauld et Nicolas Malebranche* (Paris: Vrin).

Most, Glenn W. (1984). "Zur Entwicklung von Leibniz' *Specimen Dynamicum*," in Albert Heinekamp (ed.), *Leibniz' Dynamica* (Stuttgart: Steiner), 148–63.

Mugnai, Massimo (2001). "Leibniz on Individuation: From the Early Years to the 'Discourse' and Beyond," *Studia Leibnitiana* 33: 36–54.

Müller, Kurt, and Gisela Krönert (1969). *Leben und Werk von Gottfried Wilhelm Leibniz. Eine Chronik* (Frankfurt a. M.: Klostermann).

Nachtomy, Ohad (2007). *Possibility, Agency, and Individuality in Leibniz's Metaphysics* (Dordrecht: Springer).

Nadler, Steven M. (1989). *Arnauld and the Cartesian Philosophy of Ideas (Studies in Intellectual History and the History of Philosophy)* (Princeton: Princeton University Press).

Newman, William Royall (2006). *Atoms and Alchemy: Chymistry and the Experimental Origins of the Scientific Revolution* (Chicago: University of Chicago Press).

Newton, Isaac, (1962). *Unpublished Scientific Papers of Isaac Newton: A Selection from the Portsmouth Collection in the University Library, Cambridge*, A. Rupert Hall and Marie Boas Hall (eds. and trans) (Cambridge: Cambridge University Press).

——(1999). *The Principia: Mathematical Principles of Natural Philosophy*, I. Bernard Cohen and Anne Miller Whitman (eds. and trans.) (Berkeley: University of California Press).

Nobis, H. M. (1966). "Die Bedeutung der Leibnizschrift 'De Ipsa Natura' im Lichte ihrer begriffsgeschichtlichen Voraussetzungen," *Zeitschrift für philosophische Forschung* 20: 525–38.

Oldenburg, Henry (1965–86). *The Correspondence of Henry Oldenburg*, A. Rupert Hall and Marie Boas Hall (eds.) (Madison, WI and London: University of Wisconsin Press, vols. 1–9; Mansell, vols. 10–11; Taylor and Francis, vols. 12–13).

O'Neill, Eileen (1993). "Influxus Physicus," in Steven Nadler (ed.), *Causation in Early Modern Philosophy* (University Park, PA: Pennsylvania State University Press), 27–55.

Osler, Margaret J. (1996). "From Immanent Natures to Nature as Artifice: the Reinterpretation of Final Causes in Seventeenth-Century Natural Philosophy," *Monist* 79: 388–407.

Papineau, David (1977). "The *Vis Viva* Controversy: Do Meanings Matter?," *Studies in History and Philosophy of Science* 8: 111–42.

Pasini, Enrico (2005). "La Monadologie: histoire de naissance," in Enrico Pasini (ed.), *La Monadologie de Leibniz: genèse et contexte* (Milan: Mimesis), 85–122.

Pellegrin, Marie-Frédérique (2006). *Le système de la loi de Nicolas Malebranche* (Paris: Vrin).

Phemister, Pauline (2001). "Corporeal Substances and the *Discourse on Metaphysics*," *Studia Leibnitiana* 33: 68–85.

—— (2005). *Leibniz and the Natural World: Activity, Passivity, and Corporeal Substances in Leibniz's Philosophy* (Dordrecht: Springer).

Poser, Hans (1984). "Apriorismus der Prinzipien und Kontingenz der Naturgesetze. Das Leibniz-Paradigma der Naturwissenschaft," in Albert Heinekamp (ed.), *Leibniz' Dynamica* (Stuttgart: Steiner), 164–79.

Ranea, Alberto Guillermo (1989). "The *a priori* Method and *actio* Principle Revised: Dynamics and Metaphysics in an Unpublished Controversy between Leibniz and Denis Papin," *Studia Leibnitiana* 21: 42–68.

Ravier, Emile (1937). *Bibliographie des œuvres de Leibniz* (Paris: F. Alcan).

Roberts, John T. (2003). "Leibniz on Force and Absolute Motion," *Philosophy of Science* 70: 553–73.

Robinet, André (1986). *Architectonique disjonctive, automates systémiques et idéalité transcendantale dans l'œuvre de G. W. Leibniz* (Paris: Vrin).

—— (1988). *G. W. Leibniz: Iter italicum (mars 1689–mars 1690): la dynamique de la république des letters* (Florence: Olschki).

Russell, Bertrand (1937). *A Critical Exposition of the Philosophy of Leibniz*, 2nd edn. (London: George Allen and Unwin).

—— (1972). *A History of Western Philosophy* (New York: Simon and Schuster).

Rutherford, Donald (1990). "Phenomenalism and the Reality of Body in Leibniz's Later Philosophy," *Studia Leibnitiana* 22: 11–28.

—— (1993). "Natures, Laws and Miracles: the Roots of Leibniz's Critique of Occasionalism," in Steven Nadler (ed.), *Causation in Early Modern Philosophy* (University Park, PA: Pennsylvania State University Press), 135–58.

—— (1994). "Leibniz and the Problem of Monadic Aggregation," *Archiv für Geschichte der Philosophie* 76: 65–90.

—— (1995). *Leibniz and the Rational Order of Nature* (Cambridge: Cambridge University Press).

——(2004). "Idealism Declined: Leibniz and Christian Wolff," in Paul Lodge (ed.), *Leibniz and his Correspondents* (Cambridge: Cambridge University Press), 214–37.

——(2008). "Leibniz as Idealist," *Oxford Studies in Early Modern Philosophy* 4: 141–90.

Scarrow, David S. (1973). "Reflections on the Idealist Interpretation of Leibniz's Philosophy," in *Acten des II. internationaler Leibniz-Kongress, Hannover 17.–22. Juli 1972* (Stuttgart: Steiner), 85–93.

Schmitt, Charles B. (1983). *Aristotle and the Renaissance* (Cambridge, MA: Harvard University Press).

Schrecker, Paul (1938). "Une bibliographie de Leibniz," *Revue philosophique de la France et de l'étranger* no. 126 (Ann. 63): 324–46.

Schwegman, Jeffrey (2008). "Étienne Bunnot de Condillac and the Practice of Enlightenment Philosophy" (Princeton University, Department of History, unpublished Ph.D. dissertation).

Shapin, Steven (1996). *The Scientific Revolution* (Chicago: University of Chicago Press).

Sleigh, R. C. (1990a). *Leibniz and Arnauld: a Commentary on their Correspondence* (New Haven: Yale University Press).

——(1990b). "Leibniz on Malebranche on Causality," in Jan Cover and Mark Kulstad (eds.), *Central Themes in Early Modern Philosophy: Essays Presented to Jonathan Bennett* (Indianapolis: Hackett), 161–93.

Slowik, Edward (2006). "The 'Dynamics' of Leibnizian Relationism: Reference Frames and Force in Leibniz's Plenum," *Studies in History and Philosophy of Modern Physics* 37: 617–34.

Smith, Justin E. H. (1998). "On the Fate of Composite Substances after 1704," *Studia Leibnitiana* 30: 204–10.

——(2002). "Leibniz's Hylomorphic Monad," *History of Philosophy Quarterly* 19: 21–42.

——(2004). "Christian Platonism and the Metaphysics of Body in Leibniz," *British Journal for the History of Philosophy* 12: 43–59.

——(forthcoming). *Divine Machines: Leibniz's Philosophy of Biology* (Princeton University Press).

Smith, Justin E. H. and Ohad Nachtomy (eds.) (forthcoming). *Machines of Nature and Corporeal Substances in Leibniz*.

Spinoza, Benedictus (1663). *Renati Des Cartes principiorum philosophiae pars I & II more geometrico demonstratae* (Amsterdam: Johannes Riewerts).

——(1925). *Opera*, Carl Gebhardt (ed.). 4 vols. (Heidelberg: C. Winter).

——(1985). *The Collected Works of Spinoza*, E. M. Curley (ed. and trans.) (Princeton: Princeton University Press).

Stammel, Hans (1984). "Der Status der Bewegungsgesetze in Leibniz' Philosophie und die apriorische Methode der Kraftmessung," in Albert Heinekamp (ed.), *Leibniz' Dynamica* (Stuttgart: Steiner), 180–8.

Swoyer, Chris (1995). "Leibnizian Expression," *Journal of the History of Philosophy* 33: 65–99.

Thomas Aquinas, St. (1965). *Selected Writings: The Principles of Nature, On Being and Essence, On the Virtues in General, On Free Choice*, Robert P. Goodwin (ed. and trans.) (Indianapolis: Bobbs-Merrill).

Tognon, Giuseppe (1982). "G.W. Leibniz: Dinamica e teologia. Il carteggio inedito con Jacques Lenfant [1693]," *Giornale critico della filosofia italiana* Ser. 5, Anno LXI (LXIII) (3): 278–329.

Tournemine, René-Joseph de (1703). "Conjecture sur l'union de l'ame et du corps," *Mémoires pour l'Histoire des Sciences et des Beaux Arts (Mémoires de Trévoux)*: 864–75 and 1063–85.

Utermöhlen, Gerda (1979). "Leibniz' antwort auf Christian Thomasius' frage: Quid sit substantia?," *Studia Leibnitiana* 11: 82–91.

Watson, Richard A. (1987). *The Breakdown of Cartesian Metaphysics* (Atlantic Highlands, NJ: Humanities Press).

Westfall, Richard S. (1971a). *The Construction of Modern Science: Mechanisms and Mechanics* (New York: Wiley).

—— (1971b). *Force in Newton's Physics: the Science of Dynamics in the Seventeenth Century* (London and New York: Macdonald and American Elsevier).

—— (1984). "The Problem of Force: Huygens, Newton, Leibniz," in *Leibniz' Dynamica* (Stuttgart: Steiner), 71–84.

Westphal, Jonathan (2001). "Leibniz and the Problem of Other Minds," *Studia Leibnitiana* 33: 206–15.

White, Thomas (1647). *Institutionum peripateticarum . . . pars theorica.* 2nd edn. (London: R. Whitaker).

Wilson, Catherine (1989). *Leibniz's Metaphysics: A Historical and Comparative Study* (Princeton: Princeton University Press).

—— (1997). "Motion, Sensation, and the Infinite: The Lasting Impression of Hobbes on Leibniz," *British Journal for the History of Philosophy* 5: 339–51.

—— (1999a). "Atoms, Minds and Vortices in *De Summa Rerum*," in Stuart Brown (ed.), *The Young Leibniz and his Philosophy (1646–76)* (Dordrecht: Kluwer), 223–43.

—— (1999b). "The Illusory Nature of Leibniz's System," in Rocco Gennaro and Charles Huenemann (eds.), *New Essays on the Rationalists* (Oxford: Oxford University Press), 372–88.

Woolhouse, Roger (1988). "Leibniz and Occasionalism," in Roger Woolhouse (ed.), *Metaphysics and the Philosophy of Science in the 17th and 18th Centuries: Essays in Honour of Gerd Buchdahl* (Dordrecht: Kluwer), 165–83.

Wundt, Max (1939). *Die deutsche Schulmetaphysik des 17. Jahrhunderts* (Tübingen: J. C. B. Mohr (Siebeck)).

Index

Note: Titles in "double quotes" are Leibniz's own, titles in 'single quotes' are those supplied by editors.

Académie Royale des Sciences, xv, 14, 132, 389
Adams, Robert Merrihew, xxn.7, 86n.115, 93–96, 157n.76–77, 160n.85, 167–70, 231n.21, 232n.28, 279n.40, 288n.61, 291n, 292n.70, 296n, 315n.39, 360n.26, 360n.28, 364n.36, 380n.76–77
"Addition a l'explication du système nouveau . . ." (Leibniz), 256n.88
aether, 18, 19, 38
aggregate phenomenalism, 293–96, 299–300, 358, 361–64
aggregates
    bodies and, 74–79, 296n, 356–63
    corporeal substances and, 74–79, 88, 129
    unity and, 74–79, 293–96, 299
Aiton, E. J., 11n.30, 71n.60–61, 131n.9, 352n.3
analysis situs, 362n
Anaxagoras, 6, 19n.58
Angelelli, Ignacio, 58n.13
"Animadversiones in partem generalem Principiorum Cartesianorum" (Leibniz), 50n.165, 164, 263
"Anima quomodo agat in corpus" (Leibniz), 196–97, 252n.81, 260–61
Antognazza, Maria Rosa, 2n.1, 5n.5, 6n.7, 10n.25–28, 11n.30, 14n.38, 24n.74, 68n.52, 72n.66, 100n.2, 230n.14–15, 273n.21, 307n.11, 352n.4, 357n.19
Ariew, Roger, 4n.2, 5n.5, 58, 59n.18
Aristotelian natural philosophy, 3–5
    the concrete theory of motion and, 19
    the final cause as central notion of, 226
    hylomorphic framework, scholastic version of, 127–28
    infinite divisibility in, 28
    Leibniz on, 6–9
    the mechanistic challenge to, 4–5
    substance in, 40–43, 51–52, 57

terminology of used in Fardella memo, 93–96
    and transubstantiation, 42–43
Aristotle, 5, 181, 226
Arnauld, Antoine, 71–77, 96, 141, 183, 199, 248n.69, 316. See also letters, to Arnauld
Arthur, Richard, 19n.58, 23n.72, 62n.31, 63n.35, 111n.36, 195n.37, 280n.45, 288n.61, 296n.77, 315n.41, 356n.14, 386
atomism
    from physical to substantial, 62–70
    substantial, 81–82, 90
Augustine of Hippo, Saint, 77

Bassler, O. Bradley, 25n.77
Baumgarten, Alexander, 387n.95, 391
Baxter, Donald, xxn.7
Bayle, Pierre, 305, 310–11n.25. See also letters, to Bayle
Becco, Anne, 321n.54, 330n.83, 331n.84, 331n.86, 332n.89, 336
Beck, Lewis White, 391n.8
Beeley, Philip, 6n.6, 10n.29, 15n.42–43, 19n.58, 20n.61, 22n.67, 23n.70, 27n.92, 28n.95–97, 29n.98–100, 45n.145, 103n.12, 170n.108, 201n.53, 336n.97
Behrens, Conrad Barthold, 339. See also letters, to Behrens
Bennett, Jonathan, 89n.126, 259n.101
Berkeley, George (bishop of Cloyne), 26, 272, 279
Bernoulli, Johann, 149n.57, 241n.50, 304, 339. See also letters, to Johann Bernoulli
Bernstein, Howard R., 15n.41, 16n.47, 177n.124
Bertet, Jean, 238

Bertoloni Meli, Domenico, 22n.67,
131n.9–10, 172n.114, 173n.115
Bodemann, Eduard, 352n.5
Bodéüs, Richard, 6n.9
bodies
activity and passivity of, 207–11
aggregates and, 74–79, 296n.77,
356–63
cohesion and hardness, 19, 23–24,
38–39
collision of, 15–21, 35, 105–6, 112–13,
115, 116–17, 200 (see also motion)
consistentia, 11–13
common dream view of, phenomena of
monads and the, 363–67
Cordemoy on, 68–69
definition of, 11–12, 52
elasticity of, 200–202
existence of external world (see external
world)
as extension (see extension)
force, grounded in, 115–25, 129–30,
175 (see also dynamics; force(s))
geometry and, 158–62
God and the existence of, 26
hardness and softness of, 19–20, 65
impenetrability of, 22–27, 45
infinity, division to, 27–29, 45, 62–63
(see also bugs in bugs)
minds and, 32–37, 196–97, 262–64 (see
also mind(s))
monads and, xxi, 354–67, ch. 9 passim
(see also monad(s))
motion and, 23–25, 45, 107 (see also
motion)
no-exact-shape argument, 158–60
noncommunication between mind
and, 196–97
organic, 69n.57
as phenomena (see phenomenalism)
physical and mathematical points,
distinction between, 28–29
resistance to motion (see also resistance)
early treatment of, 16–25, 46, 52,
99–102
the equality principle and, 102–6
as a kind of activity, 117–18
resurrection at the Second Coming,
problem of, 42–43
soul, form and, 49, 55, 87, 91–92,
150–55 (see also soul(s))

substance and, 40–43, 47, 120–22,
304–14 (see also substance(s))
substantial atomism and the
"division-to-dust" problem, 62–70
substantial bonds and, (see substantial
bond(s))
unities and (see unity)
See also corporeal substance(s), human
beings
Boehm, Alfred, 79n.95, 80n.96
Boehm, Rudolf, 353n.10, 354n.11
Boineburg, Baron Johann Christian
von, 10, 11n.30, 14, 41n.135, 44, 46
bond, substantial. See substantial bond(s)
Bos, H. J. M., 130n.7
Bossuet, Jacques Bénigne, 323. See also
letters, to Bossuet
Boyle, Robert, 227, 304
Breger, Herbert, 200n.52
"Brevis demonstratio erroris memorabilis
Cartesii et aliorum..." (Leibniz),
130–31, 146n.50, 148n.52,
148n.54, 304
Brown, Gregory, 148n.52, 199n.48,
366n.40
Brown, Stuart, xxn.7, 272n.18, 324n.66
Brucker, Johann Jakob, 335, 391
bugs in bugs, 83–84, 88–89, 158, 298,
316–17, 347, 355, 387
Byrne, Alex, 162n.90

"Calculus ratiocinator" (Leibniz), 288
Carraud, Vincent, 103n.11, 226n.3,
249n.74, 254n.83, 256n.88
Cartesianism
conservation of quantity of motion, law
of (see conservation principle,
Cartesian)
and divisibility of body, 69, 75, 90
extension as the essence of body (see
extension)
Leibniz's rejection of, 6–7, 52–53, 97,
127
occasionalism, doctrine of (see
occasionalism)
Cassirer, Ernst, 94n.133
"Causa Dei" (Leibniz), 256n.88
causality
activity and passivity and, 207–11
equality of cause and effect, principle of
(see equality principle)

evolution of Leibniz's thought
	on, 206–22
expression relation and, 212–22
"reasons" account of, 212–15, 220–21
CIC. See Complete Individual Concept
City of God, 355
Clarke, Samuel, 390
Clerselier, Claude, 27, 190, 192n.28
Cohen, I. Bernard, 176
cohesion, 19, 23–24, 38–39
color, 162–63
Complete Individual Concept
	(CIC), 182n.3, 185–89, 193–94,
	198–99, 202
composites and composite
	substances, 205–6, 310–11, 334,
	353–55, 369–81
conatus, 16–17, 31–33, 35, 200n.49
concomitance, doctrine of. See
	pre-established harmony, doctrine of
Condillac, Étienne Bunnot de, 390n.7
"Confessio naturae contra atheistas"
	(Leibniz)
	coherence of bodies, appeal to God to
		explain, 65n.42
	final causes and divine wisdom
		in, 227–28
	mechanical philosophy and theology,
		reconciliation of, 11–13, 22, 30,
		36n.121, 43n.144
"Confessio philosophi" (Leibniz), 32n.109,
	47n.153, 60n.22, 228–29
conservation of mv²
	the equality principle and, 148–50
	initial statement of, 45n.146, 105, 241
	and miracles, 241–42
	metaphysical implications of, 150–55
conservation principle, Cartesian, 18, 101,
	130–31, 144–55
"Considerations sur les principes de vie et
	sur les natures plastiques"
	(Leibniz), 264n.78
	"Eclaircissements sur les natures
		plastiques . . .", 370n.51
'Conspectus libelli' (Leibniz)
	corporeal substance, reasons for
		introducing, 143
	forms in bodies, necessity of, 99
	internal constitution of bodies, ways of
		knowing, 247

physics grounded in substantial
	forms, 49–52, 66–67, 266
on resistance, 118n.58
on unity, 55, 82n.101
'Contemplatio de historia literaria'
	(Leibniz), 50n.165
contingency
	the laws of nature and, 235–37, 245–50
	Spinoza's influence on Leibniz
		regarding, 230–32
continual recreation, doctrine of, 30–31
continuity, principle of, 247
contradiction, principle of, 354
'Contra philosophiam Cartesianam'
	(Leibniz)
	argument of "Specimen dynamicum,"
		repeated in, 132n.14, 133n.16
	primitive and derivative force,
		distinction between, 139
	primitive active and passive force,
		distinction between, 137, 181
	resistance, distinction between two sorts
		of, 136n.22
"Conversation du Marquis de Pianese . . .,
	et du Pere Emery Eremite . . ."
	(Leibniz), 233, 280n.44
Conway, Anne, 69n.57, 336
Cordemoy, Géraud de, 68–70, 81–82,
	190–91, 192n.28, 328n.76, 332n.87
corporeal substance(s)
	Adams' argument regarding, 93–96
	the aggregate argument and, ch. 2
		passim
	the Leibniz-Arnaud correspondence
		regarding, 76–90
	bodies and, 288–91, 359 (see also bodies)
	causality and, 210
	complexity of, 88–90
	force, constituted by, chs. 3–4 passim
	form and matter as constituting, chs. 2–5
		passim
	grounded in active and passive force,
		shift to and implications of, 127–29
	indivisibility and indestructibility
		of, 84–88
	the monadology and, 367–73, 378–80,
		382–83 (see also substantial bond(s))
	the non-communication thesis applied
		to, 204–5
	parts of matter and, 326n

corporeal substance(s) (cont.)
  shifting meaning in de Volder
    correspondence, 310–13
  souls and, relationship of, 91–92
  as unity, ch. 2 passim
"Corpus non est substantia"
  (Leibniz), 288–89
Costabel, Pierre, 70n.58, 120n.63, 131n.8,
  132n.13, 155n.70
Couturat, Louis, 259n.101
Cover, Jan A., 56n.4, 58n.13–14, 60n.22,
  89n.126, 159n.84, 360n.28
creation stories
  of Descartes, 18
  of Leibniz, 18–20
Cudworth, Ralph, 336
Curley, E. M., 60n.24, 227n.5, 232n.26,
  252n.81

"De aequipollentia causae et effectus"
  (Leibniz), 238, 242–44
Dear, Peter R., 5n.4, 20n.61
"De arcanis motus et mechanica ad puram
  geometriam reducenda"
  (Leibniz), 104, 106, 108n.28, 237–41,
  244
"De arcanis sublimium vel de summa
  rerum" (Leibniz), 252n.81
De arte combinatoria (Leibniz), 6
'De conatu et motu, sensu et cogitatione'
  (Leibniz), 26
"De corporum concursu" (Leibniz), 105,
  192–93, 237, 241–42
'Definitiones: aliquid, nihil'
  (Leibniz), 140n.38
'Definitiones cogitationesque metaphysicae'
  (Leibniz), 82n.101, 112n.43, 120–23,
  258, 262
"De ipsa natura" (Leibniz)
  activity of bodies, God's role in, 199
  Cartesian conception of extended body,
    argument against, 164–66
  the de Volder correspondence
    and, 304–5
  final causes, discovering laws of nature
    by consideration of, 257
  "monad" introduced in, 338–40
  on secondary matter, 142
  "substantial atom," use of the
    term, 81n.100

"De legibus naturae . . ."
  (Leibniz), 250n.74
'De libertate et gratia' (Leibniz), 197
"De lineis opticis" (Leibniz), 131n.10
Della Rocca, Michael, 206n
'De materia prima' (Leibniz), 140n.38
'De minimo et maximo. De corporibus et
  mentibus' (Leibniz), 26
Democritus, 357–58
"De modo distinguendi phaenomena realia
  ab imaginariis" (Leibniz)
  body as just extension, argument
    against, 155–56
  monadological reading of the middle
    period, used to support, 169–70,
    212n.77, 222–24
  phenomenalism in, 279–80, 282–86,
    297–98, 300
"Demonstrationes catholicae" project, 10,
  40, 47, 48, 225, 227, 250–51, 108
"Demonstrationum catholicarum
  conspectus" (Leibniz), 12n.35,
  30n.103
'Demonstratio substantiarum
  incorporearum' (Leibniz), 44n
'De mundo praesenti' (Leibniz), 124, 139,
  290n.65, 293
'De natura corporis' (Leibniz), 116–19,
  129, 193
'De natura veritatis, contingentiae et
  indifferentiae atque de libertate et
  praedeterminatione'
  (Leibniz), 253–54
"De primae philosophiae emendatione, et
  de notione substantiae" (Leibniz)
  on force, 155n.71
  force and substance, relationship of, 128,
    170–71, 318, 321–23
  grounding of mechanical
    philosophy, 51n.165
  publication of, 305
"De rerum originatione radicali"
  (Leibniz), 229, 259
"De resurrectióne corporum"
  (Leibniz), 42–43, 59
De Risi, Vincenzo, 362n.32, 366n.41–42
Des Bosses, Bartholomaeus, 357. See also
  letters, to Des Bosses
Descartes, René
  Arnauld and, 72

body, extension as essence of, 45, 49,
    52–53, 145, 163
conservation principle of, 18, 101,
    130–31, 145–49 (see also
    conservation principle, Cartesian)
creation story of, 18
and divisibility of body, 69, 75, 90
evil genius, hypothesis of, 276
external world, argument for the
    existence of, 275
final causes, rejection of, 226–27
God, conception of, 13
God in the physics of, 15, 190
Hobbes and, 16n.46, 17n.51
the indefinite in, 27
Leibniz as a heritor of, 179
Leibniz's critiques of, 6–7, 45, 52–53,
    97, 127
mind and body, direct interaction
    of, 262
on motion, 107n.24, 110n.33, 114n.47
optical phenomena explained through
    appeal to efficient causes, 257
on sensory perceptions, 162n.91–92
substancehood, de Volder's version of
    criterion of, 308
vortices, 20
De summa rerum (Leibniz), 59–60, 62
"De transsubstantione" (Leibniz), 8–9n.22,
    30n.102, 40–42, 59
"De usu et necessitate demonstrationum
    immortalitatis animae"
    (Leibniz), 35n.116
De veris principiis (Nizolius), Leibniz's
    introduction to, 31
Di Bella, Stephano, 182n.3, 198n.45,
    215n.82, 222n.99
Diderot, Denis, 387n.95
Digby, Sir Kenelm, 6, 9
Dijksterhuis, E. J., 14n.38
Diogenes Laertius, 62n.34
'Discours de métaphysique' (Leibniz)
    abandonment of argument in, 199
    on bodies, 156, 266n.110, 291
    on causal relations, 207–12,
        217n.89, 221–22
    complete concept
        argument, 61n.27, 182–89
    contingency, hypothetical necessity
        as, 246n.64

correspondence with Arnauld
    regarding, 71, 73
the equality principle as a subordinate
    maxim of nature, 255
the expression relation, 218
'force' and 'force mouvante,' indifferent
    usage of, 146n.50
force and quantity of motion, argument
    regarding, 145, 148n.52, 150–54
grounding of mechanical
    philosophy, 50n.165
kingdom of heaven, use of the notion
    of, 256n.88
miracles, the laws of nature and, 253n.82
the mirroring thesis, 222
monadological metaphysics not present
    in, 385
the non-communication thesis, 194–95
phenomenalism in, 281–82, 297
publication, preparation for, 305
substance, conception of, 182, 184–85,
    187n.11, 188–89, 193–94
substance, occasionalism and, 183–84
substantial forms, motion as an argument
    for rehabilitating, 119
unpublished despite care taken in
    writing, 183
Wilson's interpretation of, 321n.54
"Disputatio metaphysica de principio
    individui" (Leibniz), 55–59
"Distinctio mentis et corporis"
    (Leibniz), 279
divine justice, 228
divine wisdom
    the equality principle as a consequence
        of, 238–39, 244–45
    laws of nature grounded in, 236–37,
        246–48
    minor role in Leibniz's early
        works, 228–29
"division-to-dust" problem, 62–65
Dod, Bernard G., 4n.3
Duchesneau, François, 15n.42, 21n.63,
    131n.11, 149n.58, 150n.61, 206n.68,
    217n.88, 257n.90, 259n.96
Dupleix, Scipion, 4n.2
Dynamica de potentia et legibus naturae
    corporeae (Leibniz)
    conservation law, argument
        for, 148n.53, 149

Dynamica de potentia et legibus naturae corporeae (Leibniz) *(cont.)*
  equality principle as necessary to measure forces, 249
  non-communication of bodies, elasticity and, 201–2
  non-communication thesis, argument from Complete Individual Concept to, 199n.47
  publication intended but unfulfilled, 132–33, 305
  "Specimen praeliminare," 148n.55, 149n.58, 150n.60
  style of, 132–33
  substance, conception of, 198n.45
dynamics
  the Cartesian conservation law (*see* conservation principle, Cartesian)
  metaphysics of force and, 129–44
  occasionalism and, 193–94
  See also force(s); motion; physics; *Dynamica de potentia et legibus naturae corporeae*

Eckhardt, Johann Georg, xvii
Eisler, Rudolf, 387n.95
elasticity of bodies, 20–21, 116–17, 200–204
"Elementa rationis" (Leibniz), 50n.165
"Eloge de Monsieur Leibniz" (Fontenelle), xv–xvii, 389–90
Elster, Jon, 71n.60
entelechy, 2n.1. *See also* form(s)
Epicureans, 26–27, 233
Epicurus, 27, 62n.34, 387n.95
equality principle
  the Cartesian conservation principle and, 144, 147–48 (*see also* conservation principle, Cartesian)
  divine wisdom, as a consequence of, 238–39, 244–45
  emergence of, 102–6
  as geometrically necessary, 237–38
  inviolability of, 255
  place of in Leibniz's thought, 61n.27, 249–50
  proof of, efforts to produce a, 239–45
Ernst August, Duke of Hanover and Elector, 71
"Essay de dynamique" (Leibniz), 132, 146–47n.51

Estienne, Robert, 106n.21
Eucharist, the, 40–43, 47–48, 59, 157, 225–26, 374, 378, 380–81
Eugène of Savoy (François-Eugène, Prince of Savoy-Carignan), 352
Eustachius a Sancto Paulo, 4n.2, 96n.140, 346
"Expérience de Mons. l'Abbé Foucher, de Dijon, qu'il m'a dit l'an 1675, mois d'Avril" (Leibniz), 273
expression
  causality and, 207–22
  defined, 170, 216–18
  distinct and confused, distinction between, 219–20, 222–24
  and mirroring thesis, 222
extension
  body as, Leibniz's shift regarding, 52–53
  Cartesian notion of body as, Leibniz's critique of, 45, 155–66
  grounded in passive force, 156–58, 164, 359, 376
  grounded in situation, 359–62
  metaphysical status, 155–66
  and monads, 359–62
  de Volder on, 307–8
  See also body; matter
external world
  Foucher on knowledge of the existence of, 270–72
  Leibniz on knowledge of the existence of, 26, 273–79
  phenomenalisms addressing the problem of (*see* phenomenalism)
  sensation and, 271–72, 275–78

Fardella, Michelangelo, 90–92, 95–96, 336, 339. *See also* letters, to Fardella
Fardella memo, the (Leibniz), 90–96, 139, 326n.71, 331n.86
Fichant, Michel, xxn.7, 48n.158, 49n.162, 79n.94, 83n.106, 103n.12, 104n.15, 105n.20, 193n.30, 239n.44, 240n.46–47, 242n.51, 249n.74, 321n.54, 328n.76
Fifth Paper to Clarke (Leibniz), 61n.28, 248n.69
final causes
  in Aristotelian natural philosophy, 226
  efficient causes and, 255–60
  Leibniz's early attitudes toward, 227–29

rejection by Descartes and
    Spinoza, 226–27
Spinozism as catalyst for Leibniz's
    defense of, 232–35
Finster, Reinhardt, 71n.62
Fontenelle, Bernard Le Bouvier
    de, xv–xvii, 389–90
Fontialis, Jacobus
    as mentor to young Leibniz in Paris, 54,
        126
    and pataphysics, 302, 350
force(s)
    active and passive, forms and, 115–24
    conception of, the final change in
        metaphysics and, 317–20, 324–27
    dynamics and a metaphysics of, 129–44
    the four varieties of (active, passive,
        primitive, derivative), 133–40.
        178
    impressed, Newton's notion of, 173–76
    Leibniz-de Volder exchange
        regarding, 306–7
    Leibnizian and Newtonian, comparison
        of, 172–79
    living vs. dead, 135–36, 202
    motion and, 153–55
    substance and, 128–29, 171–72
    vis viva (living force)
        controversy, 130–31
Formey, Samuel, 390–91n.7
form(s)
    activity of bodies and, 99, chs. 3–4
        passim
    for the Aristotelian physicist, 4
    the Arnaud-Leibniz correspondence
        regarding, 73–81
    atomism and, 67
    the Complete Individual Concept and
        the revival of, 182–89
    force and, chs. 3–4 passim
    indivisibility and indestructibility
        of, 87–88
    Leibniz's interpretation of Aristotelian, 8
    and monads, 319–20, 333–35, 338–40,
        347–48, 375–6, 377, 379
    physics, in Leibniz's new, 47–52
    revival of, 48–50, 115–16, 128–9,
        181–82, 225–26, 289, 346
    theology and, 48–49, 225–26
    and unity, ch. 2 passim

Foucher, Leibniz's notes on, 117n.56, 139.
    161, 197n.43, 332–35
Foucher, Simon, 160–61, 268–77, 297.
    See also letters, to Foucher
Foucher de Careil,
    Louis-Alexander, 105n.19
Fouke, Daniel C., 10n.29, 40n.133,
    43n.144, 45n.146, 86n.116
Fraguier, Abbé Claude-François, 351–52
Freudenthal, Gideon, 131n.8, 148n.55.
    248n.70, 249–50n.73–74
Friedmann, Georges, 232n.28
Futch, Michael J., 198n.45, 211n.74

Galilei, Galileo, 147–49, 150n.60, 179
Garber, Daniel, 15n.43, 17n.51, 18n.53,
    31n.105–6, 33n.111, 74n.71, 76n.80.
    90n.127, 110n.33, 135n.19, 145n.46.
    146n.47–49, 146n.51, 157n.79.
    190n.19, 190n.21, 200n.52, 202n.59.
    254n.85, 362n.32
Gassendi, Pierre, 6, 10, 27, 47, 62n.31,
    227n.6
geometry, bodies and, 158–62
Georg Ludwig, Duke of Hanover and
    Elector, 341n.108, 352
George I (king of England), 352
Goclenius, Rudolphus, 335
God
    and activity in the world, 184, 189–94
        (see also occasionalism, continual
        recreation)
    bodies, the "Divine dream" view
        of, 365–67
    dependence of substances on, 194
    Descartes' physics, role in, 145–46
    divine wisdom, 228–29, 236–39.
        244–48
    and final causes (see final causes)
    grounds the existence of bodies, 26
    grounds the interconnections among
        perceptions, 283, 287
    in mechanical philosophy, 10–13.
        29–31, 233–35
    motion and, 11–12, 21–22, 30–31,
        101–2, 107–8
    See also theology
Goldenbaum, Ursula, 10, 13n.37, 14n.38.
    16n.47, 51n.166, 66n.45, 105n.19,
    251n.79

Gould, Stephen J., 43n.144
Grant, Edward, 4n.2–3
Griffin, Michael, 232n.28
Gueroult, Martial, 130n.7, 150n.61

haecceities, 57
Hall, A. Rupert, 39, 100n.2
Hall, Marie Boas, 39
Hamel, Jean Baptiste du, 9
Hannequin, Arthur, 6n.6, 15n.42,
    21n.63–64, 29n.100, 48n.160
Hartz, Glenn A., 89n.126, 159n.84,
    294n.73, 295n.76, 296n.77, 315n.41,
    360n.28, 384n.86, 385–86
Harz mountains, 70–71
Hess, Hans-Jürgen, 104n.15–17, 237n.39,
    238n.40
Hessen-Rheinfels, Landgrave Ernst
    von, 71, 72n.63, 73. See also letters, to
    Hessen-Rheinfels
Hilbert, David R., 162n.90
Hirschmann, David, 265n.109
Hobbes, Thomas
    causal axiom, as possible source
        for, 60n.24
    definitions as foundation of science, 241
    extension as essence of body, 24n.74
    immaterial substance, denial of, 233
    as influence on Leibniz, 3, 14–16,
        32–33, 127n
    memory and mind in, 33–35
    a point, definition of, 28n.95
    resistance in body, denial of, 17
    on sensation, 33–34, 123
    thought and motion, association of, 32
    See also letters, to Hobbes
Hoffman, Paul, 296n
Hofmann, Joseph E., 100n.2, 103n.10,
    103n.12
Hogan, Desmond, 148n.55, 248n.71,
    259n.101
Hooke, Robert, 19n.58
Hugony, Charles, 352n.5
human beings
    as model for corporeal substance, 78–79
    the soul and the body, relationship
        of, 78–81
    unity conferred by the soul in, 83
Hunter, Graeme, 204n.62, 312n.27,
    366n.43
Huygens, Christiaan, 14, 130

Huygens/Wren laws of impact, 13n.37, 21
Hypothesis physica nova, or Theoria motus
    concreti (Leibniz)
    argument of referred to in later
        works, 116–17
    bubbles, 36–37, 63
    collision in, 20–21
    divine wisdom, appeal to, 228
    division of body to infinity, 29
    elasticity, 20–21, 200
    geometric necessity, laws of motion
        grounded in, 21–22, 237
    no resistance in something at
        rest, 16–18, 46, 240

idealism, 33, 42, 315, 384–87
identity. See individuals, individuality, and
    individuation, and unity
Iltis, Carolyn, 131n.8, 148n.55
immaterialism, 272, 279
impenetrability (antitypy), 6, 8, 23–27, 45,
    124, 129, 136–37, 139, 142, 145n46,
    157, 162 167–69, 172, 319–20, 346,
    359, 361, 369, 371, 376
individuals, individuality, and
    individuation
    corporeal substances individuated by
        their form, 87
    metaphysical/substantial atomism
        and, 65–66, 70
    natural philosophy grounded on, 62
    scholastic problem of the principle
        of, 55–62
    in transubstantiation, 42–43
    See also identity, Complete Individual
        Concept
infinity, division to, 27–29, 45, 62–63. See
    also bugs in bugs
Ingenio, Alfonso, 4n.3

Jesseph, Douglas, 233n.29
Johann Friedrich, Duke of
    Hanover, 10n.28, 47, 59, 71–72. See
    also letters, to Johann Friedrich
John Duns Scotus, 57
Jolley, Nicholas, 193n.31, 253n.82, 296n
Jorgensen, Larry, 206n.68, 222n.99

Kabitz, Willi, 16n.47
Kant, Immanuel, 248–50, 362n.32, 391

Karl VI (emperor of Austria and Holy
    Roman Emperor), 352
Kingdoms, Two. *See* Two Kingdoms
    metaphor
Kircher, Athanasius, 19n.58
Kliege-Biller, Herma, 336n.97
Knobloch, Eberhard, 132n.14
Knorr von Rosenroth, Christian, 336
Krönert, Gisela, 22n.67, 151n
Kulstad, Mark, 105n.19, 197n.43, 216n.85

Laerke, Mogens, 105n.19, 230n.16
La Forge, Louis de, 190, 192n.28
Lamarra, Antonio, 390n.6
Larmor, Joseph, 20n.61
Latour, Annick, 2n.1
laws of nature
    centrality of, 249–50
    as contingent truths, 235–37, 245–50
    the equality principle (*see* equality
        principle)
    geometrically necessary *vs.* following
        from divine wisdom, 237–45
    Kantian synthetic a priori and, 248–50
    miracles as a violation of, 250–55
    a priori knowledge of, 15, 246–48
    will of God/divine wisdom, grounded
        in, 236–37
Leduc, Christian, 217n.88
Lenfant, Jacques, 323. *See also* letters, to
    Lenfant
Lennon, Thomas, 9n.24, 190n.19
letters
    to Alberti, 120n.64
    to Arnauld, 24–25, 32n.107, 41,
        50n.165, 69n.57, 70n.59, 73–90, 96,
        139–42, 156–57, 168, 184–86,
        213–14, 216–18, 219n.94, 246n.63,
        253n.82, 263, 267, 290–92, 294–95,
        305, 321, 325–26, 332, 334, 339,
        344–45
    to Basnage de Beauval, 305n.6
    to Bayle, 103n.13, 149n.58, 151, 154,
        255, 263n.108
    to Behrens, 337
    to Johann Bernoulli, 138, 142–43, 153,
        250, 256n.88, 326n.71, 337–38, 340
    from Johann Bernoulli to
        Leibniz, 149n.57, 304
    to Bertet, 238
    to Bierling, 369–70

    to Bossuet, 70n.58, 171, 318, 321–24
    to Bourguet, 366
    to Burnett, 2n.1, 70n.59, 343, 348n
    to Carcavey, 38
    to Clarke, 61n.28, 248n.69
    to Conring, 46, 238
    to Dangicourt, 369
    to Des Bosses, 89, 96n.140, 198n.45,
        320, 348n.121, 356–58, 360–61,
        364–66, 372–81
    from Des Bosses to Leibniz, 357, 359
    to Des Maizeaux, 370n.51
    to the Duchess of Orléans, 331n.84
    to Fabri, 44n
    to Fardella, 336–37
    to Foucher, 49n.163, 120n.64, 212, 214,
        217–18, 219n.94, 222, 273–77,
        280, 305n.6, 321
    to Hessen-Rheinfels, 182–83
    to Hobbes, 15, 34–35
    to Jaquelot, 370n.51
    to Johann Friedrich, 29, 31–32, 35–36,
        42, 48–49, 128, 225–26
    to La Chaise, 117n.56
    to Lenfant, 171, 318
    from Lenfant to Leibniz, 171, 318
    to L'Hospital, 132n.12, 146n.51, 153,
        195n.37, 336
    to Malebranche, 45n.145, 83n.104,
        120n.64, 192n.28, 196, 279
    to Mariotte, 200n.50
    to Masham, 357n.17
    from Newton to Leibniz, 103n.10
    to Oldenburg, 14n.38, 18n.53, 24n.74,
        33n.110, 38–39, 102–3
    to Pellisson-Fontanier, 128n.4, 154–55
    to Philipp, 239
    to Quesnel, 305n.6
    to Rabener, 337, 340
    to Remond, 1–2, 29, 37, 48, 51, 57n.12,
        70, 235–36, 245, 303, 348n.121,
        349, 351–52, 370n.51
    from Remond to Leibniz, 351–52
    to Sophie, 159, 161, 332, 341–43, 367
    from Spinoza to
        Oldenburg, 60n.24, 232, 251
    to Jakob Thomasius, 6–10, 12n.34, 23,
        27, 30, 140n.38, 191
    to Tschirnhaus, 297n.78
    to de Volder, 80n.96, 89, 120n.64,
        132n.14, 136–37n.23, 137n.24,

letters (cont.)
    149n.58, 150n.60, 164, 166–67,
    205, 304–14, 317, 319–20, 343–45,
    347, 356–63, 368–69, 385
  from de Volder to Leibniz, 306–11,
    313–14
  to Wagner, 348n.121
  to Weigel, 193n.32
"Lettre de M. L. sur un principe general
    utile à l'explication des loix de la
    nature par le consideration de la
    sagesse divine . . ." (Leibniz), 247
"Lettre de M. Leibnits à l'Auteur.
    contenant un Eclaircissement des
    difficultez que Monsieur Bayle a
    trouvées dans le système nouveau de
    l'Union de l'âme et du corps"
    (Leibniz), 305
Levey, Samuel, 45n.149, 74n.71, 158,
    160n.85, 297n.80, 298
L'Hospital, Marquis de Guillame François
    Antoine, 336. See also letters, to
    L'Hospital
Lindberg, David C., 4n.2
Lodge, Paul, 73n.68, 110n.35, 111n.39,
    136–37n.23, 150n.60, 153n.64,
    166n.96, 197n.43, 205n.67, 294n.73,
    296n.77, 304n.2–3, 306n.9, 307n.11,
    310n.24, 312n.27, 313n.32, 359n.25,
    368n.47
Loemker, Leroy E., 16n.47, 227n.7
Lohr, C. H., 4n.3
Look, Brandon, 144n.45, 357n.19,
    372–73n.57, 375, 380n.77
Loptson, Peter, 386
Lucretius, 27, 62n.34

machines, natural, 83n.106, 327–28. See
    also bugs in bugs
Magnenus, J. C., 6
Malcolm, Noel, 231n.21
Malebranche, Nicolas, 72, 190n.21, 191,
    195n.37, 247, 254n.83, 268–72. See
    also letters, to Malebranche
Mason, H. T., 71n.62, 72n.65
'Materiam et motum esse phaenomena
    tantum' (Leibniz), 297n.80
Mates, Benson, 58, 216n.87
matter
  Aristotelian conception of, 4
  Cordemoy on, 68–69

Leibniz's interpretation of Aristotelian, 8
  metaphysical status of, 166–72
  monads and, 166–68, 311–12, 318–20,
    374–76
  as passive force, 123–24, 156–57, 166
  as a path to the new monadological
    metaphysics, 345–48
  primary and secondary, distinction
    between, 140–44, 346–48
  as principle of divisibility, 156–57
  See also body, extension, substance(s)
Mauritius, Eric, 14
McCullough, Laurence B., 56n.4–7,
    57n.8–12, 58n.13–14, 58n.17,
    59n.20
McDonough, Jeffrey, 233n.29, 256n.88,
    256–57n.90, 259, 265n.109
McGuire, J. E., 296n
mechanical philosophy
  Aristotelianism, as challenge to, 4–5
  Aristotle and, Leibniz on, 7–9
  beginnings of Leibniz's interest in, 1–3,
    5–7
  Cartesianism (see Cartesianism)
  the concrete theory of motion and, 18
  and final causes, 226–35, 255–66
  God and, 10–13, 233–35
  secondary qualities and, 162–63
  substantial forms and, 43, 49–52 (See also
    Two Kingdoms metaphor)
"Meditatio de principio individui"
    (Leibniz), 60–61, 103, 108n.28, 242
"Meditationes de cognitione, veritate, et
    ideis" (Leibniz), 218–19, 248, 305
Mendelson, Michael, 195n.36, 197n.43
Menn, Stephen, 4n.3
Mercer, Christia, xxn.7, 5n.4, 6n.9, 9n.24,
    24n.75, 26n.84, 31n.106, 37–39,
    197n.43
Miller, Richard B., 199n.48
mind(s)
  body and, 35–37, 196–97, 262–64
  concurrent, substance and, 42
  individuation determined by, 60–61
  interconnection of, 284–86
  mathematical points and, 29
  momentary, body as, 32–35
  motion and, 30–33, 36–37, 107–8
  other minds, 284–85
  phenomenalism and (see
    phenomenalism)

the physical world and, early thought
    regarding, 29–39
theology and, 29–31
unity and, 65–67
and vortices, 36–37, 60–61
miracles, 250–55
"Mira de natura substantiae corporeae"
    (Leibniz), 112n.43, 294n.72,
    297n.80
mirroring thesis, 222, 284
Molanus, Gerhard Wolter, 341
Molyneux, William, 256n.89
monadological metaphysics
    diffusion of, 390–91
    in early works, supposed presence
        of, 29, 33, 37–40
    evolution of, 348–49
    initial expressions of, 341–44
    in Leibniz-Arnauld correspondence,
        absence of, 88–89
    in the middle period, supposed presence
        of, 93–96, 167–70, 222–24, 267,
        300–1, 333–35
    phenomenalism and, 300–301
    a preliminary overview of, 314–21
    unity and matter as pathways to, 344–48
    de Volder correspondence and the
        beginnings of a shift to, 303–14
'Monadologie' (Leibniz)
    aggregate view of bodies, 358
    monad(s)
        as the elements of things, 356
        as simple substances, 88, 316, 326n.71,
            331–32, 340
    overview of, 353–55
    pre-established harmony, doctrine
        of, 264n.78, 355
    publication and reception of, 390–91
    reason and contingent truth through
        divine choice, 244n.57
    "reasons" account of causality
        in, 220–21
    "substance," use of the term in, 371n.55
monad(s)
    bodies and, xxi, ch. 9 passim
    conception/definition of, 143n.43, 166,
        331–32, 339–40, 354
    corporeal substance and, 367–82
    early usage of the term, meaning
        associated with, 306n.8, 336–41
    and extension, 359–62

historical usage of the term, 335–36
substantial bond and, 372–82
in the de Volder
    correspondence, 311–12
See also simple substances
More, Henry, 27, 336
Moreau, Denis, 72n.64
Morris, Kathryn, 21n.63
Most, Glenn W., 132n.14, 133n.15
motion
    abstract laws in TMA, 14–18, 20–22
    body, as essence of, 23–26, 45
    Cartesian law of the conservation of
        quantity of (see conservation
        principle, Cartesian)
    conatus, 16–17, 31–33, 35, 200n.49
    concrete theory of in HPN, 15, 18–20
    force and, 106–115, 133–37, 153–55
    God in Descartes' explanation of, 15,
        190
    God in Leibniz's explanation of, 11–12,
        21–22, 30–31
    Huygens/Wren laws, 21
    mind and, 30–33, 36–37
    of planets, response to Newton's theory
        of, 131
    the reality of, 106–15
    relativity of, 106–15, 154
    and resistance (see resistance)
    sensation and, 33–34
    as source of hardness and resistance in
        bodies, 19–20, 36–37, 63–65
    See also dynamics
'Motum non esse absolutum quiddam'
    (Leibniz), 201n.54
Mugnai, Massimo, 56n.4, 60n.22, 61n.28
Müller, Kurt, 22n.67, 151n
multipresence, doctrine of, 47–49

Nachtomy, Ohad, 83n.106, 328n.76
Nadler, Steven M., 72n.64
natural laws. See laws of nature
necessitarianism, 73
    geometric (blind) vs. physical, 235–37
    of Leibniz, 230–32, 236
    of Spinoza, 199, 230–31, 246
Newman, William Royall, 5n.4
Newton, Isaac
    as catalyst for Leibniz's physics, 131
    de Volder and, 304
    First Letter to Leibniz, 102

Newton, Isaac (*cont.*)
    force, comparison with Leibniz
        regarding, 172–79
    gravitation, 254n.85
    as a heritor of the Galilean mathematical
        tradition, 179
    See also letters, from Newton to Leibniz
Nicole, Pierre, 248n.69
Nizolius, Marius, 6, 31, 389
Nobis, H. M., 338n.102
non-communication thesis
    bodies, as applied to, 199–204
    corporeal substances, as applied
        within, 204–6
    substances, as applied to, 194–99
"Notiones generales" (Leibniz), 162n.89,
    291n
notions, distinction between clear and
    confused, 218–19
Nouveaux essais sur l'entendement
    (Leibniz), 61n.28
*Nova methodus discendae docendaeque
    jurisprudentiae* (Leibniz), 15n.42

occasionalism
    activity of God in the world, question
        of, 183–84
    causal connections, Leibniz's agreement
        on, 195
    Descartes' and followers' embrace
        of, 189–91, 262–63
    flirtation with in early writings, 191–93
    rejection of, 115n.50, 118, 193–94
Oldenburg, Henry, 21, 39, 60n.24, 72, 102,
    232, 251. *See also* letters, to Oldenburg
O'Leary-Hawthorne, John, 56n.4,
    58n.13–14, 60n.22, 89n.126
O'Neill, Eileen, 198n.46
optics, 256–60
organism, organic, 69n.57
"Origo animarum et mentium"
    (Leibniz), 266n.111
Osler, Margaret J., 227n.7

"Pacidius Philalethi" (Leibniz), 45,
    114n.47, 192, 297n.80
Palaia, Roberto, 390n.6
Papin, Denis, 148n.55
Papineau, David, 131n.8
Pardies, Ignace Gaston, 22n.67

Paris, Leibniz's years in, 44–47, 48n.160
Parkinson, G. H. R., 277n.38
Pasini, Enrico, 353n.9
Pellegrin, Marie-Frédérique, 254n.83
perpetual motion machine, 148–49
Phemister, Pauline, 292n.69, 296n.77,
    314–15n.38, 315n.41, 386–87
phenomenalism
    aggregate, 293–96, 299–300, 358,
        361–64
    Berkeleyan, 26–27, 272, 279, 300
    extended-mind, 285–86, 299–300, 367
    human-mind, 277–85, 299–300
    the monadology and, 194n.33, 268,
        300–301
    primary-quality, 293, 296–300
    veil-of-perception, 286–92, 367
"Phoranomus seu de potentia et legibus
    naturae" (Leibniz), 119, 131, 149
physics
    Aristotelian, 3–5 (*see also* Aristotelian
        natural philosophy)
    bodies and (*see* bodies)
    conservation of mv² (*see* conservation of
        mv²)
    dynamics, theory of (*see* dynamics)
    the equality principle (*see* equality
        principle)
    final causes in, 234–35 (*see also* final
        causes)
    first approaches to, 5–22
    forces in (*see* force(s))
    motion (*see* motion)
    resistance and conservation, 99–106 (*see
        also* resistance)
    substantial forms and, chs. 3–4 *passim*
    See also mechanical philosophy
Pimpinella, Pietro, 390n.6
planetary theory, 131
Plato, 234, 325, 335, 387n.95
plenitude, principle of, 82–83
Poser, Hans, 248n.70
Predicate-In-Notion principle, 184–85,
    187–88, 199. *See also* Complete
    Individual Concept (CIC)
pre-established harmony, doctrine
    of, 79–81, 197n.43, 262–64, 283,
    345n.116
'Primae veritates' (Leibniz), 158–59, 186,
    198, 201n.54, 203
"Principes de la naturae et de la grâce

fondés en raison" (Leibniz), 69n.57,
    256n.88, 353, 355–56, 358, 370–71
'Principia mechanica'
    (Leibniz), 44n.145, 108–9
Principia Philosophiae (Descartes), Leibniz's
    1675 notes on, 45, 102n.7
"Principium mechanicae universae
    novum" (Leibniz), 240n.46
"Principium quoddam generale . . ."
    (Leibniz), 246n.63
'Propositiones quaedam physicae'
    (Leibniz), 36n.121, 44n
Pythagoras, 335

"Quid sit idea?" (Leibniz), 216

Rabener, Johann Gebhard, 339. *See also*
    letters, to Rabener
Raey, Johannes de, 9
rainbow, 290n.65
Ranea, Alberto Guillermo, 131n.8
Ravier, Emile, 391n.9
realism, 385–88
"Reflexions de Leibniz sur l'avancement de
    la métaphysique réelle, et
    particulièrement sur la nature de la
    substance expliquée par la force"
    (Leibniz), 323
'Regulae motus systematicae praestari
    mechanice' (Leibniz), 102n.8
Remond, Nicolas, 351–52. *See also* letters,
    to Remond
"Reponse aux reflexions . . ."
    (Leibniz), 257n.93
"Réponse du même aux objections faites
    contre l'explication de la nature du
    corps par la notion de la force"
    (Leibniz), 323
resistance
    body, as part of the definition
        of, 120–21
    the equality principle and, 102–6
    extension and, 371
    as a kind of activity, 117–18
    rejection of, 16–18, 46, 100–102, 240
resurrection of the body of Christ, 42–43,
    47, 59
Roberts, John T., 114n.48
Robinet, André, 48n.158, 131n.11,
    132n.12, 182n.2
Rodis-Lewis, Geneviève, 71n.62, 332n.87

Rohault, Jacques, 271
Royal Society of London, 14, 21
Russell, Bertrand, 77, 380
Rutherford, Donald, xxn.7, 80n.97,
    144n.45, 160n.85, 167n.99, 182n.3,
    193n.31, 199n.47, 206n.66, 296n.77,
    322n.57, 345n.116, 347n.118, 357n.19,
    366n.40, 373n.57, 375, 380n.76,
    383n.85, 385

Scaliger, J. C., 9
"Schediasma de resistentia medii et motu
    projectorum gravium in medio
    resistente" (Leibniz), 131
Schliesser, Eric, 172n.113
Schmitt, Charles B., 4n.3
Schrecker, Paul, 391n.9
Schwegman, Jeffrey, 390–91n.7–8
Schweitz, Lea, 43n.144
Sellars, Wilfrid, 159
Sennert, Daniel, 62n.31
Shapin, Steven, 5n.4
simple substances
    absence from earlier writings, 88–90
    emergence as a significant
        notion, 308–14, 321–25,
        330–35
    in monadological metaphysics, 317, 331,
        344–45, 353–54
    See also monad(s)
sin, 228–29
situation (*situs*), 312, 359–62
Sleigh, Robert C., xxn.7, 72n.63, 75n.77,
    151–52, 154, 159–60n.85, 193n.31,
    197n.43, 207, 231n.21, 291–92
Slowik, Edward, 114n.48
Smith, Justin E. H., 69n.57, 206n.66,
    217n.88, 315n.38, 315n.41, 328n.76,
    330n.82, 387n.96
Sophie, Duchess of Hanover and
    Electress, 341. *See also* letters, to
    Sophie
soul(s)
    bodies and, 87, 91–92
    the Complete Individual Concept
        and, 185–87, 189
    in monadological metaphysics, 354–55
    as substance of the body, 76–78
    unity in human beings produced
        by, 78–81, 83
    See also form(s); mind(s); unity

space
　body and, 23
　empty (vacua), existence of, 23,
　　44–45n.145
"Specimen demonstrationum
　　catholicarum" (Leibniz), 181n.1,
　　245n.61
"Specimen dynamicum" (Leibniz)
　conservation law, argument
　　for, 149n.56, 149n.58
　and final causes, 258
　force, treatment of, 133–40, 175–77,
　　327
　force and motion, respective reality
　　of, 155n.70
　intellectual autobiography
　　in, 52n.168, 119–20
　metaphysical foundations of the new
　　science of dynamics, 132–37
　non-communication thesis extended to
　　bodies, 202–3
　relation to the *Dynamica*, 132–33
　substantial forms, motion as an argument
　　for rehabilitating, 120
　the Two Kingdoms metaphor, 255–56
"Specimen inventorum" (Leibniz)
　on causal relations, 213–15
　the expression relation, 218
　on extension, 158
　the non-communication
　　thesis, 198n.45, 200–202, 204
　phenomenalism in, 298
　primitive active force and substantial
　　form, 139
Spinoza, Benedictus
　as a Cartesian, 7n.13
　Cartesian laws of motion discussed by
　　Leibniz and, 105
　final causes, rejection of, 227, 231–34
　Leibniz's familiarity with, 60n.24
　miracles, conception of, 251–52
　necessitarianism of, 199, 230–31,
　　246
Spitzel, Gottlieb, 11n.30
"Spongia exprobrationum"
　(Leibniz), 50n.165
Stammel, Hans, 150n.61
Steno, Nicholas, 229
Sturm, J. C., 164–65
Suarez, Francisco, 226n.3
substance(s)

Aristotelian conception of, 42–43,
　51–52, 57
body and, the Leibniz–de Volder
　correspondence regarding, 304–14
Complete Individual Concept (CIC) in
　every individual, 185–89, 193–94,
　198–99, 202
composite, 353–55, 205–6, 310–11,
　334, 369–81
corporeal (*see* corporeal substance(s))
from corporeal to simple, 321–35
the non-communication thesis, 194–206
one-substance, two-substance, and
　qualified monad interpretations
　of, 93–94
simple (*see* simple substance(s))
souls not substances, 92
theological issues and, 40–43, 47
See also form(s); matter; monad(s); unity
substantial atomism, 81–82, 90
substantial bond(s), 358, 364–65, 372–82
substantial forms. *See* form(s)
Sufficient Reason, Principle of, 16n.45,
　103n.11, 243–44, 254n.83, 274, 354,
　371–72
"Summa hypotheseos physicae novae"
　(Leibniz), 20n.61
Swoyer, Chris, 216n.86
"Système nouveau" (Leibniz)
　evolution of thought on substance
　　through drafts of, 323–29
　final causes, discovery of new laws of
　　nature and, 257n.93
　first extended philosophical essay in
　　print, 70n.59, 305
　Foucher's commentary on, 160
　grounding of mechanical
　　philosophy, 51n.165
　intellectual autobiography in, 52n.168
　"machines of nature," structure of
　　corporeal substances
　　as, 83n.106, 327–28
　mentioned to de Volder at the outset of
　　their correspondence, 304
　pre-established harmony, doctrine
　　of, 263
　primitive and derivative force,
　　distinction between, 138
　reference to in letter to Sophie, 341
　"substantial atom," use of the
　　term, 81n.100

substantial forms, intelligible restoration
of, 128
unities without parts as the final elements
in analysis of substances, 334

teleology. *See* final causes
"Tentamen anagogicum" (Leibniz), 234,
245n.61, 247n.67, 256n.90, 258–59
"Tentamen de motuum caelestium causis"
(Leibniz), 131, 172n.114, 304–5
Théodicée (Leibniz), 236–37, 245–46, 248,
256n.88
theology
creation and the laws of motion, 21–22
the Eucharist, 40–42, 59, 157, 225–26,
374, 380–81,
final causes in (*see* final causes)
mechanical philosophy and, Leibniz
on, 10–13
miracles, 250–55
multipresence, doctrine of, 47
physics and, separate domains of, 43
the resurrection, 42–43, 47
substantial forms and, 48–49, 225–26
See also "Demonstrationes Catholicae"
project; divine wisdom; God
Theoria motus abstracti (Leibniz)
argument of referred to in later
works, 116
body/mind distinction, 35
collision in, 17–18
"Fundamenta Praedemonstrabilia"
(Leibniz), 17n.52, 27–28, 38n.129
geometric necessity, laws of motion
grounded in, 237
infinity, division to, 27, 29
momentary minds, bodies as, 32–33
natural philosophy, statement of, 14–15,
17, 20, 22–23
no resistance in something at
rest, 16–18, 46, 240
Theoria motus concreti (Leibniz). *See*
Hypothesis physica nova, or *Theoria
motus concreti* (Leibniz)
Thomas Aquinas, Saint, 4n.2, 189, 226n.2
Thomasius, Christian, 169n.104, 322,
329–31
Thomasius, Jakob, 6–7, 55, 58. *See also*
letters, to Jakob Thomasius
Thomasius, notes on Christian, 142n.41,
169n.104, 329–31, 335

Thomson, William, 20n.61
Tognon, Giuseppe, 171n.110–11,
318n.47–48, 323n.62
Toletus, Franciscus, 157n.79
Tournemine, René-Joseph de, 80n.96
transubstantiation, 40–42, 59, 374,
381
Trew, Abdias, 9
Tschirnhaus, Ehrenfried, 60n.24, 105n.19,
156n.72. *See also* letters, to
Tschirnhaus
Two Kingdoms metaphor
optics and, 256–59
parallel explanations from efficient and
final causes, 255–60
parallel explanations from laws and
forms, 260–66

"Unicum opticae, catopricae et dioptricae
principium" (Leibniz), 256–57
unity
aggregates and, 74–79, 293–96,
299
in bodies, necessity of, ch. 2 *passim*
conception of, the final shift in
metaphysics and, 324–30
(corporeal) substance and, ch. 2
passim, 137–38, 181n
doctrine of pre-established harmony
and, 79–81
forms, metaphysical atomism and the
"division-to-dust" problem, 62–70
as a path to the new monadological
metaphysics, 344–45
physical *vs.* metaphysical, 65–66
Utermöhlen, Gerda, 142n.41, 169n.104,
322n.57, 329n.80, 330n.81,
330n.83

vacuum, existence of, 23, 44–45n.145
van Helmont, F. M., 336
vis viva (living force) controversy, 130–31
Volder, Burchard de, 303–14. *See also*
letters, to de Volder
vortices, as source of hardness in
bodies, 19–20, 36–37, 63–65

Wallis, John, 103, 201n.53
Watson, Richard A., 268n.2–3, 269n.4,
269n.6, 270n.12, 272n.17

Weigel, Erhard, 9. *See also* letters, to
    Weigel
Westfall, Richard S., 5n.4, 14n.38, 130n.7
Westphal, Jonathan, 284n.55
White, Thomas, 9, 27
whole is greater than its parts, proof
    of, 240–41
Wilkins, John, 25

Wilson, Catherine, 20n.60–61, 34n.115,
    37n.123, 63n.37, 86n.116, 182n.2,
    296n.77, 321n.54, 384n.86, 386n.89,
    391n.8
Wolff, Christian, 387n.95, 391
Woolhouse, Roger, 193n.31
Wren, Christopher, 14n.38
Wundt, Max, 6n.9